Modern Architecture

since 1900

Modern Architecture
since 1900

William J R Curtis

Prentice-Hall, Inc.
Englewood Cliffs,
New Jersey 07632

Library of Congress Cataloguing in Publication Data

Curtis, William J. R.
  Modern architecture since 1900.
  Includes index
  I. Architecture, Modern – 20th century. I. Title.
NA680.C87 1983   724.9'1   82–12289
ISBN 0–13–586694–4 (pbk.)

© 1987, 1982 by Phaidon Press Limited, Oxford
First published in the United States of America 1983
by Prentice-Hall, Inc., Englewood cliffs, New Jersey 07632
Second edition 1987

Design by Adrian Hodgkins
Printed and bound in Great Britain by
Butler and Tanner Limited, Frome
Colour plates printed by Midway Press, Bath

TITLE PAGE ILLUSTRATION: Le Corbusier, Parliament
Building, Chandigarh, India, 1953–62

10 9 8 7 6 5 4 3 2 1

Contents

Preface

Modern architecture was evolved less than a century ago to reconcile an idealized vision of society with the forces of the Industrial Revolution. While it made drastic breaks with the past it also allowed the basic principles of architecture to be rethought in new ways. The reverberations of this major change are only just being felt worldwide, and it may be that we are nearer the beginning of a tradition than the end of one. Even the recent reactions against modern architecture rely for the most part on their enemy for intellectual definition: as soon as forms are produced, they are seen to be extensions of the discoveries made earlier in this century. It seems a good moment to pause and to reflect on the shape of this new tradition. That is what this book sets out to do by examining the architecture of the past eighty years in detail.

I make no apologies for concentrating on buildings of high visual and intellectual quality: a tradition is formed from a sequence of such high points which hand on their discoveries to lesser followers. I have emphasized the problem of architectural language and have tried to show how a number of extraordinarily imaginative individuals expressed the deeper meanings of their times in symbolic forms. I thought it would be a good thing to strip away myths and to present the complex picture of modern architecture as simply and honestly as possible. As far as I know the views presented here do not belong to a particular 'school'. I have posed the same basic historical questions – 'what, why and how?' – that one would ask for any period.

While the book does not set out to substantiate a historical dogma or to persuade the reader that one style is better than another, it does reflect a point of view and does possess a strategy of its own. I have been concerned throughout with the ways in which ideas may be given form, and with the vital interplay between individual invention and the conventions provided by period style and tradition. At the core is a concern for authenticity within a personal vocabulary, in which form, function, structure and meaning are bound together with a certain conviction and character of inevitability. The reliance on 'movements' of the stock-in-trade survey, with its flat treatment of individual buildings and architects, has been avoided. Instead, the scale of approach has been deliberately varied from chapter to chapter, sometimes to give a close-up, sometimes to give a long or broad view. For a tradition is never an even, linear development of uniform impulse and intensity. It blends personal expressions of depth with lazy repetitions of formula and glib flashes of fashion: it draws together the cosmopolitan and the regional over certain embedded patterns of formal thinking; it links past principles and schemata with new solutions and intentions. To grasp the complex inner structure of a tradition, then, various approaches and intellectual tools will be necessary; and since a central obsession is the power of architectural abstraction to bind together levels of meaning. I have found it essential to concentrate on a few individual buildings in depth.

This book was conceived in the late 1970s and written between early 1980 and early 1981, a time during which I travelled a good deal. The last third of the manuscript was nearly lost at the bottom of the River Hawkesbury in Australia when a canoe tilted over, and Chapter 14 was in process when the author

Preface
to the Second
Edition

luckily escaped annihilation in Beirut. It is an odd turn of fate that Le Corbusier's Villa Savoye should be associated in my mind with the sound of gun-fire, and that Aalto's Villa Mairea will always recall the smell of Kentish blossoms. I mention these wanderings to emphasize that the book was written well outside the poky confines of the architectural fashion houses of our time. In it I have tried to convey the character of fine building, to look for lasting qualities, to keep the long historical view. I have attempted to show what modern architecture may mean in remote parts of a rapidly changing world.

History is a communal activity in the sense that one is bound to draw on past models, and the bibliographical notes at the end of this volume are reserved for specifically scholarly acknowledgements. But there are more immediate debts. I am grateful to Mark Ritchie of Phaidon for introducing me and my ideas to a firm it was a pleasure to work with; and to all the staff at the publisher's who have been involved in steering the scheme through. James Ackerman read the penultimate draft and made some good suggestions, while Karen Harder diligently transformed my scrawl into an elegant typescript. Finally I thank Catherine, my wife, for calmly and easily putting up with the odd states of mind that are bound to accompany the writing of a big book in a short time. I dedicate this book to her with a thought from Le Corbusier: to fix a plan is to have had ideas.

William Curtis
Boston, Massachusetts, 1981

The second edition of *Modern Architecture since 1900* contains no major changes except for a new chapter at the end entitled: 'The Search for Substance: Recent World Architecture (1987)'. This side-steps the worn critical postures of 'Modernism' and 'Post-Modernism' and singles out a few buildings that are liable to be seminal in the search for authenticity. In many parts of the world, primary lessons learned earlier in the century are being extended and transformed better to deal with the claims of context, region and tradition. The best recent work crystallizes the values of today but also manages to take architecture back to roots.

Ahmadabad, January 1987

Introduction

> We have long come to realize that art is not produced in an empty space, that no artist is independent of predecessors and models, and that he no less than the scientist and the philosopher is part of a specific tradition and works in a structured area of problems.
>
> E. Kris, 1952

The historian who sets out to write a history of modern architecture has necessarily to begin with a definition of his subject. Many past eras have referred to their own architectures as 'modern' so that the term on its own is scarcely discriminating. The 'modern architecture' which is the main topic of this book was an invention of the late nineteenth and early twentieth centuries and was conceived in reaction to the supposed chaos and eclecticism of the various earlier nineteenth-century revivals of historical forms. Basic to the ideal of a modern architecture was the notion that each age in the past had possessed its own authentic style, expressive of the true tenor of the epoch. According to the same outlook, a break was supposed to have occurred somewhere around the middle of the eighteenth century, when the Renaissance tradition had faltered, leaving a vacuum into which had flowed numerous 'inauthentic' adaptations and recombinations of past forms. The task, then, was to rediscover the true path of architecture, to unearth forms suited to the needs and aspirations of modern industrial societies, and to create images capable of embodying the ideals of a supposedly distinct 'modern age'.

Already by the mid-nineteenth century such French theorists as César Daly and Eugène Viollet-le-Duc were discussing the possibility of a genuine modern style, but they had little conception of its form. It was not until just before the turn of this century, with considerable stimulus from a variety of intervening structural inventions, that imaginative leaps were made in an attempt at visualizing the forms of a new architecture. This pioneer phase, which resulted in (among other things) Art Nouveau, was the property of the advanced industrial nations of Western Europe and the United States. Even then there was relatively little consensus concerning the appearance of a new architecture; there were, rather, broadly shared aspirations capable of visual translation in a variety of ways. 'Modern architecture', it was intimated, should be based directly on new means of construction and should be disciplined by the exigencies of function; its forms should be purged of the paraphernalia of historical reminiscence, its meanings attuned to specifically modern myths and experiences; its moralities should imply some vague vision of human betterment and its elements should be capable of broad application to certain unprecedented situations arising from the impact upon human life and culture of the machine. Modern architecture, in other words, should proffer a new set of symbolic forms more directly reflecting contemporary realities than had the rag-bag of 'historical styles'.

In actuality a number of styles emerged which claimed 'modernity' as a chief attribute between about 1890 and the 1920s, until in the latter decade it seemed as if a broad consensus had at last been achieved. At any rate, this is what some practitioners and propagandists wished their contemporaries to believe. They thus invested considerable effort in distinguishing the characteristics of 'the International Style' – that expressive language of simple, floating volumes and clear-cut geometries which seemed to be shared by such diverse architects as Le Corbusier, J. P. Oud, Gerrit Rietveld, Walter Gropius, Mies van der Rohe, and the rest. *This* they claimed was the one true architecture for the twentieth century. Other contemporary developments were conveniently overlooked, and everything was done to plaster over differences and preserve the façade of a unified front.

But history did not stand still, and the same creative individuals who had seemed to be pushing towards a common aim went their own separate ways; in turn, seminal ideas were transformed by followers. Thus the architecture which was supposed (wrongly, it turns out) to have expunged tradition founded a tradition of its own. In the years after the Second World War, many tributaries and transformations were developed around the world. Reactions, critiques, and crises – not to mention widely varied circumstances and intentions – compounded the variety. If a historian were to look back in a century's time at the period 1900–1975, he would not, therefore, be overwhelmed by some single, monolithic main line of development running from the 'pioneers of modern design' (to use Nikolaus Pevsner's phrase) up to the architecture of the last quarter of the twentieth century. But he would be struck by the emergence and domination of new traditions gradually overrunning the inheritance of attitudes and vocabularies bequeathed by the nineteenth century. Moreover, this insinuation of new ideas might be seen in global terms, working its way bit by bit into different national and regional traditions, transforming them and being transformed by them. This book takes such a long view.

Here it has to be admitted that there are particular difficulties of a sort which confront any interpreter of the recent past. The historian who sets out to write a history of modern architecture will be describing and interpreting traditions which have not yet come to an end. There is the danger that he may impose too exclusive a pattern on recent events, so making them point inevitably to whatever aspects of the architecture of his own time he happens to admire. History then degenerates into polemic. This is to be expected in the fashion-conscious literature which always seems to follow in the wake of contemporary movements, but similar faults are found to lie in the carefully pondered scholarly works which pass as the standard books on modern architecture. For all the force and clarity of their achievement, such early chroniclers as Sigfried Giedion, Henry-Russell Hitchcock, and Nikolaus Pevsner tended to share the progressivist fervour of their protagonists. Committed in advance to the idea of a unified 'spirit of the age', they felt they recognized its architectural expression in the works of the modern movement of the 1920s, and saw it as their job to write books of revelation, charting the unfolding world drama of the 'true architecture of the times'. (See bibliographical note, p. 389.)

It is obvious from my earlier remarks that I do not wish to add some glowing extra chapters to such a saga; nor, let it be said, do I wish to add to the ever-growing heap of those 'revisionist' histories intent on demonstrating that modern architecture was some temporary fall from architectural grace. The historian of the present perhaps has a unique and almost unprecedented opportunity to see his subject (or, at any rate the early stages of it) with a certain dispassionate distance, and this should not be thrown away by indulgence in propaganda. Each year more buildings are created and more quarries of evidence on developments earlier in the century are unearthed, and this alone necessitates a revision of the broad picture. But history involves constant reinterpretation as well as the presentation of new facts, and even buildings, personalities, and events that seemed once to have some immutable status must be rescrutinized and reconsidered. Between the ever-growing collection of specialist monographs of quality and the broader but somewhat biased surveys, there is little that can stand scrutiny as a balanced, readable overall view of the development of modern architecture from its beginnings until the recent past. This book is an attempt at bridging the gap.

The earliest historians of modern architecture (perhaps one should call them 'mythographers') tended to isolate their subject, to over-simplify it, to highlight its uniqueness in order to show how different the new creature was from its predecessors. Parallel developments, like Art Deco, National Romanticism, or the continuation of the Classical Beaux-Arts, were relegated to a sort of limbo, as if to say that a building in the 'wrong style' could not possibly be of value. This was both heinous and misleading. It seems to me that the various strands of modern architecture are best understood and evaluated by being set alongside other architectural developments parallel with them, for only then can one begin to explain what patrons and social groups used modern forms to express. Moreover, artistic quality, as always, transcends mere stylistic usage.

Another myth that the earliest writers on modern architecture tended to maintain – again to distinguish the new forms from their 'eclectic' predecessors – was the notion that these forms had emerged somehow 'untainted' by precedent. Again this married well with the progressivist bias in their history-writing, but it was scarcely a sensible way of explaining forms. In their eagerness to demonstrate their 'fresh new start', numerous architects between 1900 and 1930 certainly played down the influence of earlier architecture upon them, but this does not mean one should take their claims at face value. Indeed, the most profound architects of the past eighty years were steeped in tradition. What they rejected was not so much history *per se*, as the facile and superficial re-use of it. The past was not, therefore, rejected, but inherited and understood in new ways. Moreover, modern architecture itself eventually created the basis for a new tradition with its own themes, forms, and motifs.

Architecture is a complex art embracing form and function, symbol and social purpose, technique and belief. It would be as inadequate in this case simply to catalogue the ins and outs of style as it would be to reduce modern architecture to a piece in a chess game of class interests and competing social ideologies. It would be as mistaken to treat technical advances in isolation as it would be to overstress the role of social changes or the import of individual imagination. It may be that facts of biography are most appropriate (as in the case of Le Corbusier or Frank Lloyd Wright) or that analysis of structure or type is more in order (as with the American skyscraper between the wars); and while a book of this kind obviously cannot portray the entire cultural setting of twentieth-century architecture, it can avoid suggesting that buildings come about in a social vacuum by concentrating on patronage, political purpose, and ideological expression in some instances.

Here I must confess to a certain focused interest on questions of form and meaning. Most of the works to be discussed in this book are outstanding works of art which therefore defy simplistic pigeon-holing. They are neither billboards for political beliefs, nor mere stylized containers for functions, but rich compounds of ideas and forms, which achieve a highly articulate expression. I believe it should be a central aim of any history of architecture to explain why certain forms were felt appropriate to a particular task, and to probe into the underlying meanings. That simple and misleading word 'style' masks a multitude of sins, and when one investigates an artist of any depth one discovers a sort of mythical content which pervades the forms. Ultimately we have to do with the ways in which fantasies and ideas are translated into a vocabulary.

Next there is the tricky problem of where to begin: when does a specifically 'modern architecture' appear? Enough has been said already for it to be clear that there is no easy answer to this question. It is interesting to note the enormous variety of starting-points of earlier histories; these naturally reflected the writer's various notions of modern architecture. Thus, Nikolaus Pevsner, who wished to stress the social and moral basis of the new architecture, began his *Pioneers of Modern Design* (1936) with William Morris and the Arts and Crafts movement of the 1860s. Sigfried Giedion, who was obsessed with the spiritual fragmentation of his own time and saw modern architecture as a unifying agent, portrayed the nineteenth century, in his *Space, Time and Architecture* (1941), as a split era – on the one hand the 'decayed' forms of

eclecticism, on the other those 'emergent tendencies' (many of them in engineering) which pointed to a new synthesis of form, structure, and cultural probity. Henry-Russell Hitchcock, who was preoccupied with describing the visual features of the new style, suggested, in *The International Style* (1932, co-author Philip Johnson) that modern architecture synthesized Classical qualities of proportion with Gothic attitudes to structure. However, in his later writings Hitchcock became less adventurous, preferring to avoid sweeping theories of origins in favour of a meticulous, encyclopedic cataloguing of the sequence of styles.

Naturally the emphasis of history-writing was bound to change once the modern tradition itself grew longer and more varied. Historians of the post-Second World War years, like Colin Rowe and Reyner Banham (whose *Theory and Design in the First Machine Age* appeared in 1960), attempted to probe into the ideas behind the forms and to explain the complex iconography of modern architecture. They were not willing to accept the simplistic lineages set up by their predecessors, and revealed something of the indebtedness of modern architects to the nineteenth and earlier centuries. In this context one must also mention the exemplary intellectual range of Peter Collins's *Changing Ideals in Modern Architecture* (1965), which managed to trace so many of the ideological roots of modern architecture to the eighteenth century. Other writers like Leonardo Benevelo and Manfredo Tafuri built on these foundations to articulate their own versions of a pre-history; in these cases, though, there was a greater awareness than before of the political uses and meanings of architecture.

Here I must emphasize that the stress of this book is less on the roots of modern architecture than on its ensuing development. This is quite deliberate. For one thing, I wish to avoid covering well-known ground; for another, it is the later (rather than the earlier) phases of modern architecture which have been neglected. It is now over half a century since such seminal works as the Villa Savoye or the Barcelona Pavilion were created; but the past thirty years are still navigable only with the aid of a few treacherous maps filled with fashionable tags and 'isms'. A comprehensive treatment of the post-Second World War period is still impossible, but one can at least suggest a scheme which is not simply a one-way road towards some tendency or another of the very recent past.

Moreover, history does not work like a conveyor belt moving between one point and another, and each artist has his own complex links to different periods of the past. A personal language of architecture may blend lessons from ancient Greece with references to modern garages: the individual work of art is embedded in the texture of time on a variety of different levels. It only misleads to portray buildings as part of unified 'movements'. The more interesting the individual creation, the more difficult it will be to put it in a chronological slot.

Thus the problem of origins is handled in the first part of the book, not through some hapless search for the first truly modern building (or something of the kind), but through the more fruitful approach of tracing the way inherited strands of thought came together in various individual minds in the last decade of the nineteenth century and the first two of the twentieth, for it was in this period that *forms* were crystallized to express, simultaneously, a revulsion against superficial revivalism, and a confidence in the energies and significance of 'modern life'. It was the era of Art Nouveau, of Horta, Mackintosh, and Hoffmann; of Sullivan's and Wright's attempt at creating an 'organic' modern architecture in Chicago; of Perret's and Behrens's attempts at employing new methods and materials in the service of sober ideas which 'abstracted' basic Classical values; it was the era, too, of Cubist and Futurist experimentation in the arts. Pevsner justly described it as the 'pioneer phase' of modern design, and this seems a fair term so long as one is not then tempted to write off its creations as mere 'anticipations' of what came later.

One does not have to be an advocate of the notion of 'Classic moments' in art to single out the 1920s as a remarkable period of consolidation, especially in Holland, Germany, France, and Russia. This period has understandably been called the 'heroic age' of modern architecture; during it Le Corbusier, Mies van der Rohe, Walter Gropius, Gerrit Rietveld (to mention only a few) created a series of master-works which had the effect of dislodging the hold of previous traditions and setting new ground rules for the future.

The establishment of a tradition requires followers as well as leaders, and this has to be explained in a broader context than a mere internal stylistic 'evolution'. In the middle part of the book emphasis will therefore be placed on the range of personal approaches and ideological persuasions at work in the period between the wars. This will include discussion of the problematic relationship between modern architecture and revolutionary ideology in the Soviet Union in the twenties, and between modern architecture and totalitarian regimes in the thirties. We are concerned with something far deeper than a battle of styles: modern architecture was the expression of a variety of new social visions challenging the status quo and suggesting alternative possibilities for a way of life. The treatment of the inter-war years would certainly be incomplete without some consideration of developments in England and Scandinavia and of urbanistic experiments, especially the 'Radiant City' and 'Broadacre City' proposals of Le Corbusier and Wright.

Once a tradition has been founded, it is transformed as new possibilities of expression are sensed, as values change, or as new problems are encountered. Moreover, new individuals inherit the style and extend it in their own directions. The last part of the book will look at the dissemination of prototypes all over the world in the forties, fifties, sixties, and seventies. Here we come face to face with problems attached to the phenomena of transplantation (as modern architecture was grafted onto cultures quite different from those in which it began) and devaluation (as symbolic forms were gradually emptied of their original polemical content, and absorbed by commercial interests or state bureaucracies). Moreover, crises and criticisms occurred within the modern movement, suggesting a more overt reliance on the past.

As well as the late works of the aging 'masters' of modern architecture, this part of the book will consider such movements as the 'New Brutalism' and such groups as 'Team X' and the 'New York 5'; themes like regionalism and adaptation to local culture and climate in developing countries; building types like the high-rise apartment block and the glass-box skyscraper; and the emergence of individual architects like Louis Kahn, Kenzo Tange, James Stirling, Denys Lasdun, Jørn Utzon, Aldo Van Eyck, Robert Venturi, Michael Graves, and Aldo Rossi.

Perhaps it is inevitable that, as the book draws towards the present, the author will fall into some of the pitfalls of his predecessors in championing some aspects, and chastising others, of the contemporary situation. I can at least say that it has been my aim to present a balanced picture and that I have attempted to make the basis of any judgements clear. Modern architecture is at present in another critical phase, in which many of its underlying doctrines are being questioned and rejected. It remains to be seen whether this amounts to the collapse of a tradition or another crisis preceding a new phase of consolidation.

We live in a confused architectural present which views its own past through a veil of myths and half-truths (many of them manufactured by historians) with a mixture of romanticism, horror, and bewilderment. A freedom of choice for the future is best encouraged by a sensible, accurate, and discriminating understanding of one's place in tradition. This book was written partly with the idea that a historical bridge might be built across the stream of passing intellectual fashions from the distant to the more recent past, and partly with the hope that this might somehow help towards a new integration. But such aims have been secondary: the first thing a historian ought to do is to explain what happened and why, whatever people may now think of it.

OVERLEAF

Antoni Gaudí, Casa Milá, Barcelona, Spain, 1905–7, detail of roofscape.

Part 1: The Formative Strands of Modern Architecture

1. The Idea of a Modern Architecture in the Nineteenth Century

> Suppose that an architect of the twelfth or thirteenth century were to return among us, and that he were to be initiated into our modern ideas; if one put at his disposal the perfections of modern industry, he would not build an edifice of the time of Philip Augustus or St. Louis, because this would be to falsify the first law of art, which is to conform to the needs and customs of the times.
>
> E. Viollet-le-Duc, 1863

There is a tidy and misleading analogy between history and human life which proposes that architectural movements are born, have youth, mature, and eventually die. The historical process which led to the creation of the modern movement in architecture had none of this biological inevitability, and had no clear beginning which can be pinpointed with precision. There were a number of predisposing causes and strands of ideas each with its own pedigree. Although the critical synthesis began around the turn of this century, the idea of a *modern* architecture, in contrast to a revived style from some earlier period, had been in existence for nearly half a century.

But this notion of a 'modern' architecture was in turn rooted in developments of the late eighteenth century, in particular the emphasis on the idea of progress. For basic to the conception was a sense of history as something which moves forward through different 'epochs' each with a spiritual core manifesting itself directly in the facts of culture. From this intellectual standpoint it was possible to speak of the way a Greek temple or a Gothic cathedral had 'expressed their times' and to assume that modern buildings should do the same. It followed that revivals should be regarded as failures to establish a true expression. Destiny therefore required the creation of an authentic style 'of the times', unlike past ones, but as incontrovertible, as inevitable-seeming, as they. The question was: how could the forms of this 'contemporary' style be discovered?

Related to the birth of progressive ideals was another eighteenth-century development that left its legacy to the nineteenth: the loss of confidence in the Renaissance tradition and the theories which had supported it. This erosion was caused (in part) by the growth of an empiricist attitude which undermined the idealistic structure of Renaissance aesthetics, and by the development of history and archaeology as disciplines. These brought with them a greater discrimination of the past and a relativist view of tradition in which various periods could be seen as holding equal value. The notion of a single point of reference, 'Antiquity', thus became increasingly untenable. John Summerson has characterized this development as 'the loss of absolute authority' of Renaissance norms. A vacuum of sorts was created into which numerous temporary stylistic dictatorships would step, none of them with the force of conviction, or with the authority, of their predecessor. A point would eventually be reached in the nineteenth century when a revival of a Greek, a Renaissance, an Egyptian or a Gothic prototype might seem equally viable in the formulation of a style (fig. 1.1).

Another major force in the creation of the idea of modern architecture was the Industrial Revolution. This supplied new methods of construction (e.g., in iron), allowed new solutions, created new patrons and problems, and suggested new forms. A split of sorts was created between engineering and architecture, with the former often appearing the more inventive and responsive to contemporary needs. At a deeper level still, industrialization transformed the very patterns of life and led to the proliferation of new building problems – railway stations, suburban houses, sky-

1.1 Thomas Cole, *The Dream of the Architect*, 1840. Oil on canvas, 53 × 84 in. (134.7 × 213.4 cm.). Toledo Museum of Art, gift of Florence Scott Libbey: the nineteenth-century dilemma of style.

scrapers – for which there was no precedent. Thus the crisis concerning the use of tradition in invention was exacerbated by the creation of novel types with no certain pedigree. Moreover, mechanization disrupted the world of crafts and hastened the collapse of vernacular traditions. Machine-work and standardization engendered a split between hand, mind, and eye in the creation of utilitarian objects, with a consequent loss of vital touch and impulse. Mid-nineteenth-century moralists like John Ruskin and William Morris in England felt that mechanization was bound to cause degradation in all compartments of life, at the smallest and largest scales of design. They therefore advocated a

reintensification of the crafts and a reintegration of art and utility. Their aim was to stem the alienation they felt grew automatically from the disruptive effects of capitalist development. Those who were later to formulate the ideologies of modern architecture felt that this attitude was too nostalgic and sought instead to face up to the potentials of mechanization by co-opting them and infusing them with a new sense of form. This drama was to remain quite basic to the twentieth century: in essence the question was how to evolve a genuine culture in the face of the more brutish aspects of mass production.

Industrialization also created new economic

structures and centres of power. Where the patronage of architecture in eighteenth-century Europe had relied principally on the church, the state, and the aristocracy, it came increasingly to rely on the wealth, purposes, and aspirations of the new middle classes. As always, élites found in architecture a means for self-expression which could authenticate their position. In turn mechanization remoulded the lower orders of society and made inroads on the form of the city. Once again, architecture was affected. Indeed, a major theme of modern architecture would concern the reform of the industrial city and its replacement by a more harmonic and humane order. The roots of this attitude lay in the numerous critics of an inequable and chaotic social structure who wrote from the early nineteenth century onwards. Indeed, another aspect of the progressive mythos behind the conception of modern architecture was the belief in a just and rational society. One is not therefore surprised to discover the influence of Utopian Socialist tendencies stemming from Charles Fourier and Henri Saint-Simon on the moral outlook of later modern designers. The search for alternative social and urban structures would lie close to the heart of later modern architectural endeavour.

It can thus be seen that the notion of a modern architecture was inseparable from profound changes in the social and technological realms. The problem of architectural style did not exist in isolation, but was related to deeper currents of thought concerning the possibility of creating forms which were not pastiches of past styles but genuine expressions of the present. But then, what were the most important realities of the present? Underlying numerous nineteenth-century debates concerning the appropriateness of forms, there was a nagging uncertainty about what the true content of architecture should be. Thus there was a tendency to locate the ideal in some compartment or other of the past, or else to dream of some hazy, ill-defined future as an alternative to a grimy, unconsoling reality.

These, then, were some of the conditions and problems confronting the first theorists of a 'modern architecture'. Viollet-le-Duc, for example, writing in the 1860s and 1870s, felt that the nineteenth century must try to formulate its own style by finding forms 'appropriate' to the new social, economic, and technical conditions. This was fair enough in theory, but the question still remained: where should the forms of this new style be found? To this there were a number of possible answers. At one extreme were those who believed in great individual leaps of invention; at another were those who thought the matter would somehow look after itself if architects just got on with solving new problems logically and soundly. There was little admission that even a 'new' architecture was likely, ultimately, to be assembled out of old elements, albeit highly abstracted ones.

It could at least be said that the notion of a modern architecture implied a quite different attitude to the genesis of forms than those which had been operative in the previous few decades. One of these advocated revivalism of one or another particular period in the past, some historical styles being regarded as intrinsically superior to others. By imitating the chosen style it was lamely hoped that one might also reproduce its supposed excellences. But, there was the obvious danger that one might copy the externals without reproducing the core qualities, and so end up with tired academicism or pastiche. Moreover, the question naturally occurred: if a set of forms had been right for one context (be it Greek, Gothic, Egyptian, or Renaissance), could it possibly be right for another?

A more catholic view of the past implied that one should evolve a style by collecting the best features of a number of past styles and amalgamating them into a new synthesis. This position was known as 'eclecticism' and did at least have the strength of encouraging a broad understanding of tradition. However, eclecticism did not provide any rules for recombination and gave little idea of the essential differences between authentic synthesis and a merely bizarre concoction of past elements.

Indeed the problem of revival could not be considered apart from the problem of appropriateness in the present. Here it was hard to avoid arbitrariness because there were few guiding conventions relating forms, functions, and meanings. It was all very well for the English architect A. W. Pugin to have argued with such deep moral fervour in the 1830s that Gothic was the most spiritually uplifting and the most rational of styles; but counter-arguments of a similar kind in favour of Classical forms could just as easily be made. Intellectual gambits were thus often used to post-rationalize what were really intuitive preferences. The lure of determinist arguments was strong because they seemed to bring certainty to a situation of extreme flux. If one could claim (and possibly believe) that one's forms were ordained by the predestined course of history, the national spirit, the laws of nature, the dictates of science, or some other impressive entity, then one could temporarily assuage doubts concerning arbitrariness in the use of forms.

Within the confused pluralism of the 'battle of styles', it tended to be forgotten that lasting qualities of architectural excellence were liable to rely, as ever, on characteristics which transcended superficial issues of stylistic clothing. The nineteenth century had its share of master-works which were not categorizable by simplistic pigeon-holing. The outstanding archi-

1.2 Marc Antoine Laugier, the 'Primitive Hut', from *Essai sur l'architecture*, 1753: the quest for beginnings.

tectural quality of Henri Labrouste's Bibliothèque Ste-Geneviève in Paris of the 1840s, was not, after all, so much a function of its being a 'Classical revival', relying on certain acceptable and edifying prototypes, as it was a result of an extraordinarily deep synthesis of form and content. Similarly, the architectural feebleness of G. Scott's Foreign Office in London of a decade later was traceable not to the use of inferior sources, but to an inability on the part of the architect to transform his sanctioned prototypes into an authentic expression. The major talents of the nineteenth century – one thinks of Karl Friedrich Schinkel, of Henri Labrouste, of Henry Hobson Richardson – were able to probe the *principles* of past styles (not just to parrot their effects), then to translate these into authentic vocabularies of their own and achieve a prodigious imaginative unity in their results. One reason they were able to do this was that they possessed an intuitive vision of what was most appropriate to the social state of their time.

Another way of dealing with historical prototype was to indulge in myths of 'origins' and to suggest that one might achieve authentic results by returning to 'beginnings'. Known as 'primitivism', this position first received impetus in the mid-eighteenth century, especially in the writings of the Abbé Laugier. He conceived of the beginnings of architecture in an archetypical 'primitive hut' from which, it was held, the more ornate elements of the Classical system had evolved (fig. 1.2). It tended to be implied that simpler also meant better, and that the farther one went back the more authentic the form was bound to be. However, Laugier's 'primitive hut' had little basis in archaeology, and only a slight basis in texts which had speculated on the beginnings of architecture, and his version of the prototype reflected an essentially Classical bias. Thus primitivism could all too easily end up as a battle of the styles simply played out on a more abstract plane.

Although Laugier's ideas were more arbitrary than he pretended, ones like them had considerable appeal later on. He denied that there were absolute rules in architecture and spurned mere educated taste, arguing instead that the best forms were rooted in functional or structural demands. Notions of this sort gained extra momentum in the early nineteenth century in the writings of J. N. L. Durand and were further nourished by the disciplined (though by no means unintuitive) methods of engineers. At its most extreme this doctrine of so-called 'Rationalism' tended to lead to the dubious proposition that beautiful and appropriate forms would arise automatically if only problems were analysed 'on their own merits' instead of through the filter of precedent. There were a number of fallacies in this position, such as the notion that forms might arise from functional analysis alone without the intervention of some a priori image, but it was still a weapon with which to attack the whimsies of the most arbitrary revivalists.

One of the main inheritors of this 'Rationalist' viewpoint in the mid-nineteenth century was Eugène Viollet-le-Duc, a French theorist who gave great force to the idea of a 'modern' architecture. As was mentioned, he was disturbed by the inability of the nineteenth century to find its own style and felt that the answer must lie in the creation of forms 'true to the programme and true to the structure'. He remained a little vague on the nature of this truth and tended to assume (often erroneously) that the conspicuous excellence of great past works was due mainly to their capacity for expressing the programmatic and structural 'truths' of their own time. Thus while he was committed to an indistinct vision of some new architecture, he nonetheless believed that the past could have its uses in discovering this new style; he even imagined a situation in which one of the designers of the great Gothic cathedrals had been resuscitated and confronted with a modern building problem and modern means of construction. He argued that the result would not have been an imitation Gothic building, but an authentically modern one based on analogous intellectual procedures. The past must not be raided for its external effects, then, but for its underlying principles and processes.

Of course, most architects of note in earlier periods had always known that the past must be understood for its principles, but had still had the guidance of a prevalent style phase, a shared architectural language, in which to incorporate their findings. Viollet-le-Duc outlined a probing method for intellectual analysis but could still do little to supply the essential 'leap to form'. His imagination was not as strong as his intellect, and the handful of buildings and projects which he left behind him were clumsy assemblages of old images and modern constructional means, usually reflecting his underlying taste for medieval styles (fig. 1.3). There was little of that sense of 'inevitable unity' – of part linking with part in an ordered yet intuitive system – which distinguishes the true sense of style.

But if Viollet-le-Duc's *forms* did little to solve the problem of a modern architecture, his *ideas* lived on and were destined to have an enormous influence on the generation who became the 'pioneers' of modern architecture, especially when they sought to give architectural expression to new constructional means like concrete, or to new building types like skyscrapers; even the formal innovations of Art Nouveau were kindled in part by his ideals. He supplied a strong counter-tendency against the worst excesses of Beaux-

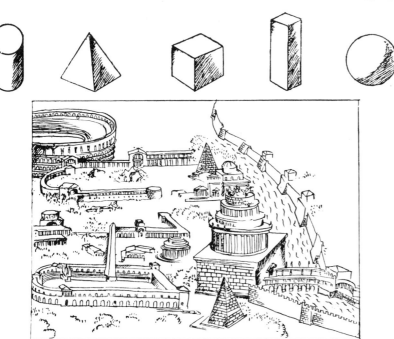

1.3 (*left*) Eugène Viollet-le-Duc, project for a concert hall in iron, *c.* 1864, from *Entretiens sur l'architecture*, 1872: the attempt to formulate a style on the basis of new materials.

1.4 (*above*) Le Corbusier, sketch of the primary geometrical solids alongside a view of ancient Rome, from *Vers une architecture*, 1923: the abstraction of fundamental lessons from the past.

Arts teaching, which frequently (though not always) erred in the direction of academicism, and gave currency to the idea that the great style of modern times would somehow emerge on the basis of new constructional techniques – not through some merely personal formal experiment – just as the great styles of the past had done. Thus Viollet-le-Duc's historical parallels supplied further scaffolding to the *idea* of a modern architecture.

But the question still remained: what should this modern architecture look like? From where should its forms be derived? Obviously tradition could not be jettisoned completely, otherwise there would be no forms at all; the idea of an *entirely new* architecture was simply illusory. Perhaps, then, it might be possible to abstract the essential lessons of earlier architecture in such a manner that a genuinely new combination would be achieved? Indeed, if one jumps forward to the 1920s and examines the seminal works of the modern movement, one finds that they relied on tradition in this more universal sense. One is struck by the confidence of men like Le Corbusier and Mies van der Rohe that they had, so to say, unearthed the central, abstract values of the medium of architecture itself; that they had created not so much a new style, but the quality of style in general – a quality central to all outstanding works of the past (fig. 1.4).

This abstract view of the history of architecture, this idea that the important features of past buildings lay in their proportions, their arrangement, their articulation of formal themes (and the like) rather than in their use of columns or pointed arches, may itself have had some basis in late eighteenth- and early nineteenth-century tendencies towards simplification. One thinks particularly of those drastically abstract modes of reformulating the past implicit in the stripped geometrical visions of Claude-Nicolas Ledoux and Étienne-Louis Boullée. The idea of universal formal values was given extra weight in the late nineteenth century by art historians like Heinrich Wölfflin and Adolf von Hildebrand, who rejected literary values in art in favour of underlying architectonic qualities, and who described past styles in terms of abstract, formal patterns. It is no accident that this way of perceiving the past should have coincided so closely with the emergence of abstract art: as we shall see, both this manner of viewing precedent, and the new language of space and form visualized by painters and sculptors, were to have an eventual influence on the creation of modern architecture.

But other ingredients would also come into play in the formulation of modern architecture – ingredients which had been intrinsic to numerous past buildings. One thinks particularly of analogies with other spheres of reality than architecture, with nature's forms and processes, or with the forms of mechanisms, paintings, and sculptures. Peter Collins has revealed the importance to the nineteenth century of 'mechanical' and 'biological' analogies in theory and design. At a certain level the forms of architecture may be thought of as mimetic: through a process of abstraction they may incorporate images and references. Time and again, if we dig beneath the surface of modern architects' personal styles, we will find a rich world of metaphor and allusion.

Thus, in finding forms to fit the pre-existing aspirations towards a modern architecture, the architects of the 1890s and the first decade of the twentieth century drew repeatedly on both tradition and nature in their formulation of a style. But they did so in ways that were at variance with their immediate predecessors, for their method involved a far greater degree of abstraction. In that respect their quests for novelty were not unconnected with avant-garde developments in the other arts: it can even be argued that some of the most drastic innovators (one thinks particularly of Wright and Perret in these two decades) were also, in some basic way, traditionalists. While they certainly hoped to create vocabularies entirely in tune with modern circumstances and means, they also wished to endow their results with a certain universality: they sought to create architectural languages with the depth, rigour, and range of application of the great styles of the past.

So it was not tradition that was jettisoned, but a slavish, superficial, and irrelevant adherence to it. The

1.5 Charles Garnier, the Opéra, Paris, 1861: Beaux-Arts Classicism in the grand manner of a sort that was rejected in the early twentieth century by the avant-garde.

1.6 'La Recherche du Style Nouveau'. *Rèvue des Arts Décoratifs*, 1895: the slow progress towards a new style.

rogue in all these respects was frequently (and sometimes unfairly) identified as the École des Beaux-Arts in Paris which was lampooned as the symbol of all that was tired and retardative (figs. 1.5, 1.6). This caricature of academe aside, it is essential to see the vital developments of the 1890s against a backdrop of confusion and caprice in which the problem of style was much discussed but rarely resolved. To the young architectural minds which were to pioneer Art Nouveau and the substantial new developments up to the First World War, writers like Viollet-le-Duc were an immensely powerful catalyst. They had little to stand on in the immediate past except facile revivalism and eclecticism, and therefore sought a new direction by going back to basics and forward to new inspirations simultaneously. In sources they were abundant; the question was how to forge these sources into a new synthesis appropriate to modern conditions.

2. The Search for New Forms and the Problem of Ornament

... the whole basis of the views of architecture prevailing today must be displaced by the recognition that the only possible point of departure for our artistic creation is modern life.

O. Wagner, 1895

While the beginnings of modern architecture cannot be traced to a single time, place, or personality, it is striking how many movements professing the value of the 'new' came into being in the 1890s. Evidently a reaction against tired social, philosophical, and aesthetic values was rumbling into life in centres as diverse as Paris, Berlin, Vienna, Brussels, and Chicago. However, novelty had differing significance in each milieu and, probably, in each architect's mind.

At the same time it would be foolish to ignore areas of overlap. Time and again we shall encounter the theme of renewal after a period of supposed corruption and decay; time and again we shall hear the rallying cry that a new, modern man is emerging, whose character an avant-garde is best able to intuit. Thus in assembling the fragments of the pre-First World War architectural world into a larger picture, it is essential to balance up the local contexts and individual intentions of architects with their piecemeal contributions to a new tradition. We have to deal here not with a simple evolutionary path, but with the tentative groundwork towards a later consensus.

Since the emphasis is on forms and not just ideas or techniques, it seems reasonable to begin with Art Nouveau, and therefore to concur with Hitchcock's assessments that 'it offered the first international programme for a basic renewal that the nineteenth century actually set out to realise' and that 'Art Nouveau was actually the first stage of modern architecture in Europe, if modern architecture be understood as implying primarily the total rejection of historicism.' But if Art Nouveau artists rejected historicism, they could not altogether reject tradition, for even the creator intent on producing new forms will rely, in some degree, on old ones. Indeed, what is often meant when the claim is made that such and such a movement was 'new', is that it switched its allegiances from recent and nearby traditions to ones more remote in space or time.

Even so it is possible to distinguish between innovations which extend the premisses of a pre-existing tradition, and more drastic breaks. Art Nouveau was of this second sort and embodied a strong reaction against the degraded Beaux-Arts Classicism widely practised in the 1870s and 1880s. As such it was a major step towards the intellectual and stylistic emancipation of modern architecture. However, the path from the curved abstractions of Art Nouveau to the stripped, white rectangular geometries of the 1920s was neither simple nor straightforward.

In architecture the most creative phase of Art Nouveau was from 1893 to about 1905 – a little more than a decade. The beginnings of the style have been variously dated. Arguably it first emerged in graphics and the decorative arts. Pevsner claimed a start in the early 1880s in England.

If the long, sensitive curve, reminiscent of the lily's stem, an insect's feeler, the filament of blossom, or occasionally a slender flame, the curve undulating, flowing and interplaying with the others, sprouting from the corners and covering asymmetrically all available surfaces, can be regarded as a *leitmotif* of Art Nouveau, then the first work of Art Nouveau which can be traced is Arthur H. Mackmurdo's cover of his book on Wren's city churches published in 1883.

Of course this is said with the knowledge of hindsight: Mackmurdo's design would be written off as a minor incident stemming from certain arabesques of the Pre-Raphaelites, the linear patterns of William Blake, and the fascination with natural forms of John Ruskin, if there had not subsequently been a broader indulgence in the formal qualities Pevsner outlines. There is little evidence that Mackmurdo's design was the start of a sequence. Rather it was an early manifestation of a broad shift in sensibility in the 1880s, also sensed in such diverse examples as the ornamental designs of Louis Sullivan, Antoni Gaudí, and William Burges, the melancholic and erotic drawings of Aubrey Beardsley (fig. 2.1), the symbolist paintings of Paul Gauguin and Maurice Denis. A consolidation did not occur until the early 1890s, particularly in Brussels, in the work of Fernand Khnopff, Jan Toorop, and a group of painters known as 'les Vingt', and in the architecture of Victor Horta which seemed a three-dimensional equivalent to the painters' two-dimensional linear inventiveness.

So revolutionary does Horta's breakthrough appear in retrospect that it is irritating that so little is known about his preceding development. He was born in 1861 in Ghent, studied art at the local academy, worked in the studio of an artist by the name of Jules Debuysson in Paris, entered the École des Beaux-Arts in Brussels, and then became a draughtsman for a minor neo-classical architect by the name of Alphonse Balat. In the mid-1880s he designed some uninteresting houses in Ghent. Next we have the Tassel House of 1892–3, a work of complete assurance, outstanding for its synthesis of architecture and the decorative arts and its declaration of new formal principles.

These were not evident in the somewhat bald façade with its bowing central volume, its restrained use of stonework, and its discreet introduction of an exposed iron beam, but in the ample space of the stairwell (fig. 2.3). The principal innovations lay in the frank expression of metal structure and in the tendril-like ornamentation which transformed gradually into the vegetal shapes of bannisters, wallpaper, and floor mosaics. The emphasis on the direct use of a modern material, and even the inspiration of natural forms for the metal ornament, recall Viollet-le-Duc's explorations in iron (fig. 2.2), while the expression of the effects of growth and tension call to mind the contemporary interests in 'empathy', and fascinations with organic analogies. Evidently Horta knew of Voysey's wallpaper designs and perhaps even of Owen Jones's *Grammar of Ornament* (1856); in either case he

2.1 Aubrey Beardsley, *Toilet of Salome II*, 1894, Drawing, $8\frac{3}{4} \times 6\frac{1}{4}$in. (22.2 × 16cm.). London, British Museum.

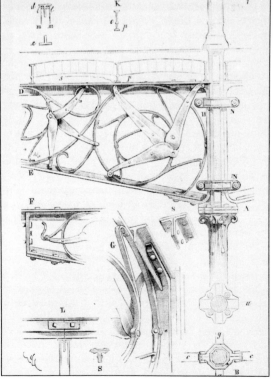

2.2 Eugène Viollet-le-Duc, proposal for a wrought iron bracket, from *Entretiens sur l'architecture*, 1872.

2.3 Victor Horta, Tassel House, Brussels, 1892–3, the stairwell.

will have sensed a feeling for natural forms combined with a deliberate freshness and exoticism. Thus the first mature statement in the new style was a synthesis of formal inspiration from the English Arts and Crafts, of the structural emphasis of French Rationalism, and of shapes and structures abstracted from nature.

Horta extended his style in a number of other town house designs in Brussels in the 1890s. These subtly evoked an inward-looking world by creating scenarios for a well-to-do, urbane *fin de siècle* clientele which could afford the indulgence of exotic tastes and delicate aestheticism. The props for the mood were the spacious stairwells, and long internal vistas through dining-rooms and over winter gardens; the rich contrasts of coloured glass, silk stuffs, gold, bronze, and exposed metal, and the vegetal forms of vaguely decadent character. Yet Horta's buildings never lapsed into mere theatricality; there was always a tense, underlying formal order; and the sequence of spaces from halls, up stairs, over galleries was tightly orchestrated. In the masterly Hôtel Solvay of 1895, his newly found style was successfully carried through in all aspects of the design, including the linking of interior volumes and the treatment of the façade, where an appropriately linear ornament was displayed.

While Horta clearly grasped the meaning of the way of life of his luxurious clients, his social concerns and range of expression were not restricted to this class. This is clear from his design for the Maison du Peuple of 1896–8, also in Brussels, built as the headquarters of the Belgian Socialist party. The site was a difficult one extending around a segment of a circular urban space and part of the way along two radial streets. The façade combined convex and concave curves, and the main entrance was placed on one of the shorter convex points. The visible expression of the iron skeleton was every bit as 'radical' as Sullivan's contemporary skyscraper designs in Chicago (where the structure was usually immersed in terracotta sheathing). In part this treatment was no doubt inspired by earlier nineteenth-century engineering structures like train-sheds and exhibition buildings, but the choice of materials and the emphasis on lighting the interiors through infill panes of glass seem to have had moral overtones related to the institution as well:

> ... it was an interesting commission as I saw straightaway – building a palace that wasn't to be a palace but a 'house' whose luxury feature would be the light and air that had been missing for so long from the working-class slums. ...

The integration of material, structure, and expressive intentions was even more successful on the interior, especially in the main auditorium at the top of the

building where the roof was formed from a sort of hammer-beam system in steel (fig. 2.4). The side walls and fenestration were reduced to thin infill screens, and the effect of the whole was an organic unity in which ornamentation and the visual accentuation of actual structure worked tightly together. The ceilings were ingeniously corrugated to control reverberation, and a double gallery was hung from the roof trusses and used to contain heating pipes. Thus despite its fantastic character, this 'attic' space was strongly conditioned by practical demands. As the architect himself exclaimed, paraphrasing an observer,

> 'What a fantasist this architect is – he must have his alternating lines and curves – but he really is a "master" at them.' ... but I am fuming: – 'You idiot, don't you see that everything is thought out in terms of architecture as construction, faithful to the brief to the point of sacrifice?'

Horta's experimentation with iron and steel was continued in another large-scale scheme, also for Brussels, the À L'Innovation Department Store of 1901, in which these materials were felt appropriate for their large internal spans and their capacity for wide openings. Practical considerations were again transcended in a façade composition in which delicate screens and large plates of glass provided a forward-looking image to a relatively new building type.

Horta continued to work in Brussels for another thirty years but rarely achieved the freshness of his earliest experiments. Another Belgian artist to continue the new-found mode well into the twentieth century was Henry van de Velde, who seems to have had a more theoretical turn of mind than Horta, and to have turned his hand to a broader range of activities. The son of a chemist in Antwerp, van de Velde became a painter and was much influenced by the Impressionists, the social realist imagery of Millet and eventually the paintings of Gauguin. In the 1890s his interest in the crafts grew, under the impact of William Morris's theoretical teachings, and he devoted himself to the applied arts. If Viollet-le-Duc was important to one branch of Art Nouveau for having encouraged the notion of a new style based on the direct expression of the constructional possibilities of new materials like iron, Morris was crucial as another forefather for having expressed the ideal of aesthetic and moral quality in all the objects of daily use. In due course one of the aims of Art Nouveau designers (one senses it already in Horta's houses) would be 'the total work of art' in which every light fixture would bear the same aesthetic character as the overall building.

In 1894–5, van de Velde designed a house for himself at Uccle, near Brussels, for which the furniture was specially created. His chair designs manifested an interest in expressive, organic structure: dynamic forces were intended to heighten the functions of the various members, giving the chairs a consciously lifelike or anthropomorphic character (fig. 2.5). Van de Velde made a distinction between ornamentation and ornament, the former being attached, the latter being a means for frankly revealing the inner structural forces or functional identity of a form. This interest in the frank expression of structure and function led him in his Haby's barber shop in Berlin (1901) to expose water pipes, gas conduits, and electrical ducts. Van de Velde admired what the machine might do in mass production, so long as a strong control over quality was maintained by the craftsman who designed the prototype; he felt that a subjective artistic element must always be present if banality was to be avoided. The French critic, Edmond de Goncourt, coined the phrase 'yachting style' in assessing van de Velde's designs when they were first made known in Paris; and the artist himself claimed that his means were:

> ... the same as those which were used in the very early stages of popular arts and crafts. It is only because I understand and marvel at how simply, coherently and beautifully a ship, weapon, car or wheelbarrow is built that my work is able to please the few remaining rationalists ... unconditionally and resolutely following the functional logic of an article and being unreservedly honest about the materials employed. ...

Van de Velde was a Socialist and hoped that industrial mass production of his objects might make visual quality available to the broad masses; yet his statements of architectural intent remained within a fairly aloof circle of patronage. In the Cologne Theatre of 1914, he attempted to create his version of a communal building celebrating widely held social values. But this *Gesamtkunstwerk* still remained the property of a cultivated élite.

Art Nouveau did not always remain the aloof creation of an avant-garde. Indeed, the style was quickly popularized in graphic and industrial design, in glassware, furniture, jewellery, and even clothing. The rapid spread of ideas was encouraged by the emergence of periodicals like the *Studio* which had a great impact on fashion; and by the pioneering commercial attitudes of men like Samuel Bing, who opened a shop for modern art called L'Art Nouveau on the Rue de Provence in Paris in 1895. Bing, and the German art critic Julius Meier-Graefe, had discovered van de Velde's house at Uccle and invited the artist to design some rooms for the shop. The fashion caught on quickly; and among those influenced were Émile Gallé

2.4 (*above*) Victor Horta, Maison du Peuple, Brussels, 1896–8, view of hall.

2.5 (*left*) Henry van de Velde, furniture designs for Bloemenwerf House, 1895. On the wall is an embroidery, *Angels Keep Watch*, 1893, by the artist (Zurich, Kunstgewerbemuseum).

the glass-maker, and Hector Guimard the architect. In New York, meanwhile, L. C. Tiffany was designing glass with delicate vegetal forms and rich stains of colour. In fact, he had come upon this manner independently, which tended to lend weight to the notion that here at last was a true expression of the underlying spirit of the age. The full triumph of the new style in the public taste was clearly evident at the Paris exhibition of 1900 and the Turin exhibition of 1902, in which 'Art Nouveau', 'Jugendstil', or the 'Style Liberty' (such were its various names), was dominant. By the turn of the century, then, Art Nouveau had taken on an international character. It was perceived to be a way out of the interminable jumbling of eclectic styles, and a valid reflection of exotic, somewhat escapist, somewhat progressivist, *fin de siècle* attitudes of mind. This is the way the Italian critic Silvius Paoletti responded to the Turin exhibition:

> To take the place of pitiless authoritarianism, rigid and regal magnificence, burdensome and undecorated display, we have delicate and intimate refinement, fresh freedom of thought, the subtle enthusiasm for new and continued sensations. All man's activities are more complex, rapid, intense and capture new pleasures, new horizons, new heights. And art has new aspirations, new voices and shines with a very new light.

While one ideal of Art Nouveau was the perfectly crafted and unified interior, the style also revealed its possibilities for much broader public applications. Most notable of these, perhaps, were Hector Guimard's designs for the Paris Métro of 1900 (fig. 2.6), in which naturally inspired forms were used to create arches and furnishings in iron which were then mass-produced from moulds. Like Horta, Guimard had passed through the academy, having been at the Paris École des Beaux-Arts from 1885 to the early 1890s. At the École des Arts Décoratifs from 1882 to 1885, he had already become acquainted with Viollet-le-Duc's Gothic rationalism, which he had then sought to reinterpret in a highly personal way. Another key influence was the British Arts and Crafts, which he studied while visiting England and Scotland in the 1890s. He also visited Horta, and this provided the essential catalyst.

Guimard began experimenting with the new style in his design for an exclusive block of flats in the recently developed 16ème arrondissement, known as the Castel-Béranger, in Rue la Fontaine. Here the entrance details and ornamental flourishes were somewhat isolated Art Nouveau incidents in an otherwise inconsistent design. Working a decade later at a much

smaller scale, in the nearby Villa Flore (fig. 2.7), Guimard was able to infuse the whole design with the bulbous and swelling character of a natural growth, and to model brick surfaces and iron details so that they seemed subservient to a single aesthetic impulse. The plan, with its suave links between oval forms and different diagonal axes, suggests that Guimard may have consulted the sophisticated solutions for tight urban sites of eighteenth-century Parisian hôtels; indeed, the playfulness and curvilinear tracery of the Rococo may be counted among the possible sources of Art Nouveau ornament.

However, in the hands of major talents, Art Nouveau was far more than a change in architectural dress, far more than a new system of decoration. In the best works of Horta, Guimard, and van de Velde, the very anatomy and spatial character of architecture were fundamentally transformed. Their forms were usually tightly constrained by functional discipline and by a Rationalist tendency to express structure and material. Furthermore, each artist in his own way attempted to embody a social vision and to enhance the institutions for which he built.

Similar points can be made about the Catalan architect Antoni Gaudí, whose extreme originality and idiosyncrasies show him to have been only a loose affiliate of Art Nouveau ideals. Indeed, one has to beware of pushing a historical abstraction too hard: a style phase in architecture is a sort of broad base of shared motifs, modes of expression and themes, from

2.6 (*left*) Hector Guimard, Métro station, Paris, 1900.

2.7 (*below*) Hector Guimard, Villa Flore, Paris, 1909.

2.8 (*right*) Antoni Gaudí, Expiatory Church of the Sagrada Familia, Barcelona, 1884–1926, transept façade.

which a great variety of personal styles may emerge.

Gaudí was born in 1852 and died in 1926. His earliest works date from the 1870s and indicate his reaction against the prevalent Second Empire mode towards the neo-Gothic. He was an avid reader of Ruskin's works and the inspiration of his early designs is clearly medieval, but there emerges early on that sense of the bizarre which was to characterize his highly personal style after the turn of the century. In the Palau Güell of 1885–9 the interiors were transformed into spaces of an almost ecclesiastical character, while the façades were elaborately ornamented with wave-like ironwork preceding Horta's experiments in Brussels by some years. Thus Gaudí's style, like Guimard's, was in part an abstraction of medieval forms. The imaginative transformation of these prototypes was motivated by Gaudí's private imagery and by his obsession with finding a truly Catalan 'regional' style.

In 1884, Gaudí was commissioned to continue Francisco del Villar's designs for the Expiatory Temple of the Holy Family (the 'Sagrada Familia') on the outskirts of Barcelona (fig. 2.8). The crypt followed Villar's design based on thirteenth- and fourteenth-century Gothic prototypes. The lowest visible levels were completed to Gaudí's design by 1893 in a transitional Gothic manner. To then move upwards through the various stages of the termination of the crossing is to be confronted bit by bit with the

2.10 (*left*) Antoni Gaudí, Casa Batlló, Barcelona, 1905–7.

2.11 (*right*) Antoni Gaudí, Casa Milá, Barcelona, 1905–7, chimneys.

2.12 (*below right*) Antoni Gaudí, Casa Milá, Barcelona, 1905–7, detail of façade at ground level.

2.9 (*far left*) Antoni Gaudí, wire model of the structure of the Chapel for the Colonia Güell, 1898–1900.

architect's flowering into one of the most curious and original architects of the past two hundred years. Elements which suggest a vague affinity with Art Nouveau give way finally to a language of utter fantasy, evocative of vegetable stems and dream-like anatomies. In fact, these surreal forms were not entirely without precedent, since it seems clear that Gaudí (who had worked briefly in North Africa) knew of the mud constructions of the Berbers, with their own inspiration in natural forms, their curious hermetic imagery, and their manifestation of animist beliefs.

The richness of Gaudí's art lies in the reconciliation of the fantastic and the practical, the subjective and the scientific, the spiritual and the material. His forms were never arbitrary, but rooted in structural principles and in an elaborate private world of social and emblematic meanings. The structure of the Sagrada Familia and designs like that for the crypt of the Santa Coloma de Cervelló (begun in 1898), were based on the optimization of structural forces which led the architect to variations on parabolic forms. Gaudí was thus much more of a 'Rationalist' than his work would lead one to believe on superficial inspection. But this appellation does not do him justice either, for he was deeply religious and believed that the material qualities of architecture must be the outer manifestation of a spiritual order. He intuited the presence of this order in the structures of nature which he felt to be a direct reflection of the Divine Mind. The 'laws' of structure, then, were not mere laws of materialist physics, but were evidence of the Creator. The parabola, in particular, with its beautiful economy, became an emblem for the sacral (fig. 2.9).

Thus Gaudí's vocabulary was infused with an elaborate symbolism for which the Gothic revival of his youth had provided a useful, conventional starting-point. His pantheism, like Ruskin's, extended to the smallest mineralogical wonders and to the grandest of natural forces. These features of nature were abstracted and expressed in a vocabulary loaded with metaphor and association. It is little wonder that the Surrealist generation of the twenties (particularly his fellow Catalan Salvador Dali) should have felt such an affinity for his work. For in Gaudí at his most bizarre there is the sensation of contact with deep psychic forces and irrational patterns of imaginative thought.

Gaudí's completely personal late style first emerged in the design for the Park Güell, carried out between 1900 and 1911. Beast-like benches embedded with fragments of coloured tile mark off the edges of the stepped terraces offering views over the city. There are nightmarish underground grottoes suggestive of dark clearings in some subterranean forest, and steps which flow like lava.

Gaudí's principal secular works were conceived in

parallel with the park, beginning with the Casa Batlló of 1905–7, a remodelling of a block of flats (fig. 2.10). Here a virtual sport of spotting analogies can be (and has been) played. Thus some critics have emphasized the maritime references of waves, corals, fishbones, and gaping jaws, while others have commented on the dragon-like roof and the possible religious significance of this as an allegory of good and evil. Whether such analogies strike close to Gaudí's intentions may never be known, but they suggest the powerful impact of the architect's forms on the imagination.

In the Casa Milá of 1905–7, the plastic conception of swirling curves was applied not just to the façade (fig. 2.12), but to the plan and interior spaces as well. The elevation is in constant motion with its deep-cut, overlapping ledges. Once again wave and cliff images come to mind (the building was known locally as 'La Pedrera' – the quarry), but it is a naturalism achieved by the most sophisticated ornamentation and stone-cutting. The contrived textures of the ledges give the impression that these forms have come about over the years through a process of gradual erosion.

Gaudí's buildings were so bizarre as to be inimitable (fig. 2.11), which naturally inhibited the propagation of his style in a local tradition. One of the complaints lodged against Art Nouveau in the first decade of this century was that its propositions relied too completely on a subjective approach, and that they were not geared sufficiently to the ideal of designing types for standardized mass production. This criticism has to be taken with some salt, for, as has been shown, both Guimard and van de Velde were able to mass-produce standardized profiles of some visual complexity. Moreover, Art Nouveau proved itself well suited to repeating print processes in such things as posters, and became a sort of popular style related to consumerism. By the turn of the century it had spread to many provincial centres which contributed their own regional accent. However, there was some resistance. In England, for example, Art Nouveau was regarded with suspicion as a wily and decadent departure from the sober aims of the Arts and Crafts. But in Scotland a style of enormous originality, related to Art Nouveau, was created by another uncategorizable individual, the Glasgow architect Charles Rennie Mackintosh.

Mackintosh is important at this juncture not only because of the imaginative force of his own designs, particularly the Glasgow School of Art, of 1897–1909, but because his development encapsulated the path beyond Art Nouveau towards a more sober form of expression in which broad dispositions of simple masses and sequences of dynamic spaces were stressed. His style emerged independently of Horta's but from loosely similar sources and concerns, and appeared first in his decoration of Miss Kate Cranston's various

'tea-rooms' in Glasgow of 1897–8. These designs were linear, abstract and heavily laden with Gaelic symbolism and Celtic references; it comes as no surprise to discover that the term 'Spook School' was invented to characterize Mackintosh and his circle (including his wife). In 1897 he won the competition to design the new School of Art in Glasgow. The building was to stand on an almost impossibly steep slope, which seemed to suggest that the main façade should be set at the highest part of the site (fig. 2.13), from which access could be had to the interiors. The programme was also demanding: the functions to be included were several studios, a lecture theatre, a library, a room and private studio for the director. Spaces to display work and to house a permanent collection of casts were also needed.

Mackintosh dealt with these constraints by laying

2.13 Charles Rennie Mackintosh, Glasgow School of Art, 1897–1909, façade.

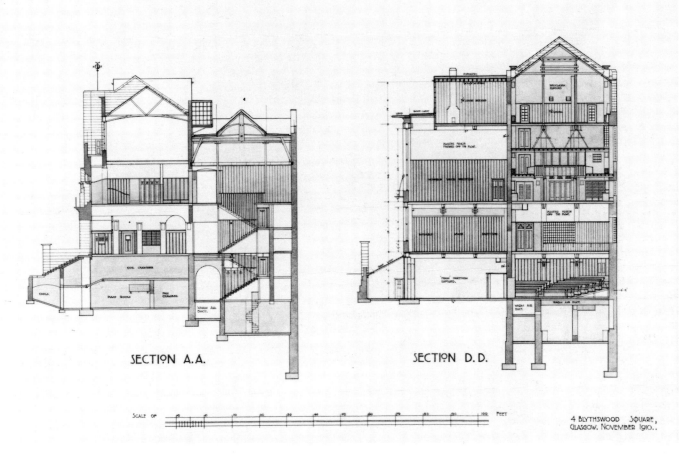

THE GLASGOW SCHOOL OF ART.

SECTION A.A.

SECTION D.D.

4 BLYTHSWOOD SQUARE,
GLASGOW. NOVEMBER 1910..

2.14 Charles Rennie Mackintosh, Glasgow School of Art, 1897–1909, sections.

out two tiers of studios along the north side facing Renfrew Street (the high end of the site) and further studios, the anatomy school, life modelling, the architecture school, the design and composition rooms, facing east and west. The director's room and studio were placed over the entrance, while the museum was set to the rear of the scheme at an upper level where it could be top lit. The richness of the scheme arose from the juxtaposition and sequence of rooms of different sizes, and the orchestration of different qualities of light; from the clever overlapping of the spaces in section (fig. 2.14); and from the way the stairs, corridors, and museums were modelled as if from a continuous volume of space. The interior movements and juxtapositions were partly expressed in the dynamics of the exterior forms. Thus the north elevation was a subtle fusion of symmetry and

asymmetry, in which the grand upper windows of the main studios were set into massive, grim masonry forms. The entrance way was emphasized by a cluster of motifs and an arch, over which the director's study was set in a recess. To the sides, the building's flanking walls fell away to the lower portion of the site as large expanses of subtly articulated stone surface, recalling (among other things) the architect's interest in regional farmhouse prototypes and Scottish baronial halls. The ironwork on the exterior, in the railings and in the cleaning brackets on the main windows, was loosely analogous to Art Nouveau, in its abstraction of natural motifs, but like the building as a whole, these details spoke less of effete curves and more of a taut, sculptural discipline (fig. 2.15).

These qualities were brought to the fore without distracting fussiness, in the library wing of the school,

2.15 (*left*) Charles
Rennie Mackintosh,
Glasgow School of Art,
1897–1909, detail of
ironwork.

2.16 (*right*) Otto
Wagner, Post Office
Savings Bank, Vienna,
1904–6, interior.

designed around 1908, in which chiselled abstract
shapes and groups of vertical windows on the outside
(Plate 1) were supplemented by rectangular wood
brackets in the reading-room interiors. The verticality
of the proportions recalls Art Nouveau, but the
stripped, pristine quality of the forms, and their
rectangular character, speak of a new direction. It is
understandable that Pevsner should have singled out
this interior as an early example of the sort of spatial
effects which were later to be central to the modern
movement.

It is therefore ironical that Mackintosh should have
been written off by English critics as dangerously
exotic, since it was precisely his geometrical control
and tendency to abstraction which appealed in
European artistic centres – partly as a support for their
own revulsion against the excesses of Art Nouveau.
Mackintosh was less appreciated in London than in
Vienna, where publications of his plans and drawings
made him known and influential, especially in
Secessionist circles around J. M. Olbrich. Olbrich and
the older Otto Wagner disliked both the pomposities of
Classical Academic design, *and* the 'new decadence' of
Art Nouveau. Indeed, Olbrich's Art Gallery designed
for the Friedrichstrasse in Vienna in 1898–9 was a
somewhat bizarre attempt at formulating an expressive language of pure geometries and massive
pylon forms. Wagner's Majolica House, a block of flats
built between 1898 and 1900, also implied a return to
fundamental architectonic values and to strict rectilinear proportions, despite the lingering feeling of
vegetal motifs in some of the detailing. In the late
1890s, in an article published in *Dekorative Kunst*
(Munich), the German architect August Endell wrote
of a 'non-historical' style of pure forms capable of
moving the spirit in a manner similar to the rhythms
of music.

> They teach us that there can be no new form, that
> all possibilities have been exhausted in the styles of
> the past, and that all art lies in an individually
> modified use of old forms. It even extends to selling
> the pitiful eclecticism of the last decades as the new
> style.
>
> To those with understanding, this despondency
> is simply laughable. For they can clearly see, that
> we are not only at the beginning of a new stylistic
> phase, but at the same time at the threshold of a
> completely new Art. An Art with forms which
> signify nothing, and remind us of nothing, which
> arouse our souls as deeply and as strongly as music
> has always been able to do . . .
>
> This is the power of form upon the mind, a direct,
> immediate influence without any intermediary
> stage . . . one of direct empathy.

In 1895, Otto Wagner published *Moderne Architektur*, in which he spoke of the need for architecture to
orientate itself to 'modern life', and recommended
qualities of simplicity and 'almost military uniformity'.
Moreover, he argued that the new style should be a
'realist' one, which seems to have implied a direct
expression of the means of construction and an
admiration for modern techniques and materials.
Finally, he seems to have felt that flat, slab-like cornices
and horizontal lines should be employed.

If we follow Wagner from his late nineteenth-
century designs to the Vienna Post Office Savings Bank
of 1904–6 (fig. 2.16), we enter an entirely different
world from that of Art Nouveau, a world in which a
nuts and bolts rationality and a stable and dignified
order have replaced the dynamic tendrils and
curvaceous effects. Indeed, Vienna, and a little later
Berlin and Paris, were to be among the strongholds of a
reaction against Art Nouveau which acquired increasing momentum in the first decade. This reaction was
fed in part by the Arts and Crafts ideals of simplicity and
integrity; by an abstract conception of Classicism as
something less to do with the use of the Orders, than
with a feeling for the 'essential' Classical values of
symmetry and clarity of proportion; and by a sense
that the architect must strive to give expression to the
values of the modern world through frank and
straightforward solutions to architectural problems in
which disciplines of function and structure must play

2.17 (*left*) Josef Hoffmann, Palais Stoclet, Brussels, 1905, detail of porch.

an increasing, and attached ornament a decreasing, role.

Apart from Wagner, who was already in his early sixties at the turn of the century, the two chief exponents of a new architecture in Vienna were Josef Hoffmann (1870–1954) and Adolf Loos (1870–1933). Hoffmann founded the Wiener Werkstätte in 1903 as a centre of activity in the field of decoration. In his design for the Purkersdorf convalescent home (1903), he reduced the walls to thin planar surfaces. His greatest opportunity came in 1905 with the commission of a luxurious mansion to be built outside Brussels for a Belgian financier who had lived in Vienna. The Palais Stoclet was to be a sort of suburban palace of the arts in which Adolphe and Suzanne Stoclet would assemble their treasures and entertain the artistic élite of Europe. It had thus to combine the moods of a museum, a luxury residence, and an exemplary setting of modern taste.

Hoffmann was able to respond to the 'aura' of the programme in a house of immense sophistication, combining devices of formality and informality, characteristics of an honorific and a more humble sort (figs. 2.17, 2.18). The rooms were linked *en suite* in a plan employing ingenious changes of direction and axes, in which such major spaces as the hall, the dining-room and the music-room (with its little stage) were expressed as protruding volumes in the façades. The overall composition was ingeniously balanced, but asymmetrical, the main points of emphasis being the fantastic stepped stair-tower with its attached statuary, the bow windows, and the *porte-cochère*. The forms were coated in thin stone-slab veneers detailed with linear mouldings to accentuate the planarity. On the interiors materials were stern, rectilinear, and precise, and included polished marbles and rich wood finishes. The influence of Mackintosh is felt in this house (a prototype for the design was clearly the Scot's 'House for an Art Lover' of 1902), but where he would have stressed the rustic and the humble, Hoffmann emphasized the grandiose and the cosmopolitan. The disciplined elegance of the Stoclet house is enhanced by the furnishings and by Klimt's splendid mural decorations. As well as echoes from Mackintosh, there are also memories of Olbrich, perhaps even of Schinkel. But the Palais Stoclet is one of those designs where there is little point in listing the sources and influences, as these have been digested and restated in a convincing personal style. In its imagery and mood it portrayed an exclusive way of life of a kind which was to be swept away by the devastation of the First World War – a sort of aristocratic bohemianism.

Adolf Loos's move towards a rectilinear and volumetric simplification was even more drastic than Hoffmann's. Loos was little affected by Art Nouveau, in part because he spent the mid-1890s in America (a country he praised highly for its plumbing and its bridges); in part because he seems to have sensed that that movement's reaction against the 'dead forms' of the academy was swinging too far towards the wilful, the personal and the decorative – all of which he felt to be inimical to lasting achievement in art. But Loos brought the perspective too of someone who had reflected on the form of many simple everyday objects, which he contrasted to the pretentious inventions of much self-conscious art. Some of his most penetrating essays are on such things as gentlemen's suits, sportswear, and Michael Thonet's mass-produced wooden chairs. He seems to have felt that these were the objects which gave evidence of, as it were, an unconscious style.

Up to 1910 much of Loos's design effort went into small-scale conversions. In his few house designs of that period he reduced the external vocabulary to rectangular stucco boxes punctured by simple openings, without even the reminiscence of a cornice or a

2.19 Adolf Loos, Steiner House, Vienna, 1910, rear view.

plinth. Usually his interiors were more elaborate, yet still distinguished by an overall rectangular control, and in the case of the Kärntner Bar of 1907, clearly influenced by a stripped Classical tendency. Perhaps the outstanding design of Loos's mature years was the Steiner House in Vienna of 1910 (fig. 2.19), where architectural effect relied on the adroit placement of large plate-glass windows in stripped and undecorated planar surfaces. However, it is still a long way (in meaning as well as form) from this villa, with its 'neo-classical' plan and its strict symmetry, to the inter-penetrating planes and dynamic asymmetries of the International Style of the 1920s. Even so, the achievement of such a drastic simplicity within a decade and a half of the beginnings of Art Nouveau, and a full decade before Le Corbusier's white, cubic villa designs of the 1920s, is worthy of comment.

In fact, it is by no means certain that Loos's pre-war designs had much influence on the emergence of the International Style after the First World War. His theories, especially on ornament, were far better known, perhaps because they put into words a number of concurrent, but not necessarily connected pre-judices, which the later generation was determined should be a unified doctrine. As a polemicist, Loos was brilliant; in an article entitled 'Ornament and Crime', he inveighed against 'ornament', on the grounds that it was evidence of a decadent culture.

Children are amoral, and – by our standards – so are Papuans. If a Papuan slaughters an enemy and eats him, that doesn't make him a criminal. But if a modern man kills someone and eats him, he must be either a criminal or a degenerate. The Papuans tattoo themselves, decorate their boats, their oars, everything they can get their hands on. But a modern man who tattoos himself is either a criminal or a degenerate. Why, there are prisons where eighty percent of the convicts are tattooed, and tattooed men who are not in prison are either latent criminals or degenerate aristocrats. When a tattooed man dies at liberty, it simply means that he hasn't had time to commit his crime. . . . What is natural to children and Papuan savages is a symptom of degeneration in modern man.

I have therefore evolved the following maxim, and pronounce it to the world: the evolution of culture marches with the elimination of ornament from useful objects.

Translated into the situation in which Loos found himself, this meant that Art Nouveau, for all its emancipation from the Academy, had to be seen as yet another of the superficial and transitory 'styles'. The discovery of a true style for the times would be found when ornament was done away with, and essential underlying qualities of form, proportion, clarity, and measure were allowed to emerge unadorned. At least, this is what Adolf Loos believed, and there was a generation of later architects ready to follow this lead in its search for the supposed 'universal style' for modern times.

3. Rationalism, the Engineering Tradition, and Reinforced Concrete

Living architecture is that which faithfully expresses its time. We shall seek it in all domains of construction. We shall choose works that, strictly subordinated to their use and realized by the judicious use of material, attain beauty by the disposition and harmonious proportions of the necessary elements of which they are made up.

A. Perret, 1923

While Art Nouveau appeared to break with the bonds of the past, to be a new style, it was soon perceived to be a subjective creation insufficiently rooted in lasting principles and incompletely attuned to the means and needs of an industrial society. In this view even men like Horta and Guimard, who had approached the heart of the matter of a new style, were lumped together with the most facile Art Nouveau decorators. In part the reaction was impelled by vaguely moral yearnings for the stern and unadorned, in part by Rationalist ideas which required a practical justification for formal effects. This was somewhat ironical because, as has been shown, Rationalism inspired some of the more disciplined creations of Art Nouveau.

By 1905, then, the style which had so quickly flowered was already beginning to wither; but after it, things could not be the same again. It opened up a language of abstraction and implied new ways in which nature's lessons could be incorporated into architecture. A fruitful tradition of expressive, organic form was founded, which would culminate in the free experimentation of Erich Mendelsohn, and the emotive creations of the so-called 'Amsterdam School' around the end of the First World War. More important still in the shorter term was the reaction *against* Art Nouveau. This took a number of different forms. In Vienna, Hoffmann and Loos suggested that the way forward to a true modern style lay in increasing formal simplification; in Berlin, Behrens resorted to Classical principles which he attempted to restate in a new form; in Paris, Perret sought a formal discipline in the constraints and creative potentials of new constructional systems,

especially reinforced concrete, in the belief that this would lead to genuine architectural forms of lasting quality.

This last notion, of course, stemmed from the ideas of Viollet-le-Duc, who had influenced some of the structural inventiveness of Art Nouveau. It has already been suggested that his theories were at times over-mechanical, but they still had an immense impact on those who felt, at the turn of the century, that a language based on 'truth to structure and truth to the programme' might be the best antidote to academic revivalism on the one hand and to personal whimsy on the other. Here one must mention the role of the nineteenth-century engineering tradition which had already demonstrated the possibility of new forms in new materials, and which Viollet-le-Duc had himself singled out in contrast to the 'dead languages' of the architects.

> ... naval architects and mechanical engineers do not, when building a steamship or a locomotive, seek to recall the forms of sailing ships or harnessed stage coaches of the Louis XIV period. They obey unquestioningly the new principles which are given them and produce their own character and proper style.

One effect of Viollet-le-Duc's opinions was to found a tradition of architectural history in which the role of practicality in great works of the past was overstressed. Thus Auguste Choisy, in his *Histoire de l'architecture* of 1899, spoke of Gothic architecture as 'the triumph of logic in art', whose form was 'governed not by traditional models, but by its function and by its function alone.' This view was reinforced by stunningly simple drawings in which buildings were portrayed as structural diagrams, as if structure and only structure had been the architect's concern (fig. 3.1). The implication of the Rationalist position seemed to be: if only modern architects would think as clearly as these predecessors and concentrate on function and structure, then their results would have the same authenticity.

In a sense both Viollet-le-Duc and Choisy were projecting backwards the values of nineteenth-century engineers. The stunning new effects of visual lightness and transparency of buildings like Paxton's Crystal Palace of 1851 (fig. 3.2) or Baltard's market sheds at Les Halles seemed indeed to be traceable to a judicious attention to the demands of programme and structure: but did these buildings in iron, and later utilitarian structures in steel, constitute a new *architecture?* Even those who could admire the structural feats (and the occasional formal elegance) of engineering realized that a certain poetic character of form might be missing. Thus, while the Rationalists and the engineers, each in their different ways, seemed able to emancipate themselves from revivalism, they faced another danger: the proliferation of a bland, materialistic functionalism lacking in the quality of a true expressive style.

One architect to feel such dilemmas acutely towards the end of the century was the American Louis Sullivan, who confronted the issue directly in trying to define a genuine form for the tall office building based on a steel-cage construction. Influenced by Viollet-le-Duc, he attempted to make the form 'follow' from the function, but discovered that a number of arrangements might be equally tenable and that the brute heap of matter which was the tall building could only acquire aesthetic value through an intuitive intervention on the part of the artist. Although Sullivan disclaimed the value of 'rules and other impedimenta',

3.1 (*below left*) Auguste Choisy, plate from *Histoire de l'architecture*, 1899, showing Hagia Sophia: architectural form as the 'rational' result of structure.

3.2 (*below*) Joseph Paxton, Crystal Palace, London, 1851.

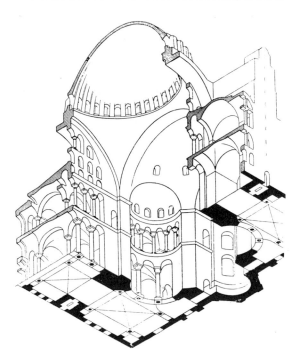

3.3 (*below*) Louis
Sullivan, Wainwright
Building, St. Louis,
Missouri, 1895

3.4 (*below
right*) François
Hennebique, trabeated
system for reinforced
concrete, 1892.

his solution for the skyscraper was guided by the
tripartite division of the Classical order (base, shaft,
and capital) and was reliant on analogies with natural
form (fig. 3.3). Sullivan had discovered that function
and structure could not on their own 'generate' an
adequate form, without the intervention of highly
abstracted historical or natural examples. Indeed,
Viollet-le-Duc's own clumsy attempts at evolving a
system 'true to iron' had been influenced by medieval
precedents, and perhaps even by the forms of bones.

So history had not dropped out of the picture

completely. Quite the contrary, for the question in a
sense became: which qualities abstracted from tradition might best serve the forms suggested inherently by
new construction techniques? At any rate, a query of
this sort underlay many of the experiments of the
early pioneers of a reinforced-concrete architecture.

Concrete had been employed by Roman and Early
Christian architects but had then dropped out of use
through most of the Middle Ages and Renaissance. It
was not until the second half of the nineteenth century
that the material was fully explored again, but usually
for mundane purposes where its cheapness, its wide
spans and its fireproof character all recommended it.
The invention of reinforcing, whereby steel rods were
inserted to increase the strength, belonged to the
1870s. Ernest Ransome in America and François
Hennebique in France, each evolved frame systems
employing this principle (fig. 3.4). These proved to be
well suited to the creation of open-plan work-spaces
with large windows where fire had previously been a
danger. Hennebique's system employed slender vertical posts, thin lateral beams on brackets, and floor
slabs. The result was somewhat like a timber frame,
which was scarcely surprising since the form-work
was generally made from wood. But concrete, of all
materials, was one of the most flexible, one of the least
determinant of form. It relied on the shape of the mould
and the shaping intelligence of the designer. Some
forms rather than others were certainly more logical in
certain situations: but the material in and of itself did
not generate a vocabulary.

This became all the more obvious when architects in
the last few years of the nineteenth century attempted
to discover a style based on the material. Where one
designer might argue that the malleable character
made it natural for Art Nouveau expression, another
might emphasize the role of a frame and panel system
and claim the value of Gothic antecedents – or even of
steel and glass ones. A similar range of positions might

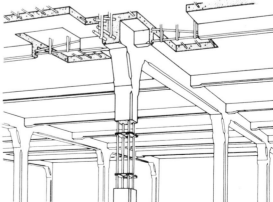

be taken with regard to the external expression of the material. Where one architect might regard it as commonplace and in need of covering with tiles or brick veneers, another might claim that it had its own inherent beauty and that it should be exposed.

Among the seminal experiments in France was the church of St.-Jean de Montmartre, begun in 1897, completed in 1905, and designed by Anatole de Baudot (fig. 3.5). In fact the church was formed from reinforced cement, rather than concrete, but the effects of lightness and the breadth of the spans with apparently slender supports were of a kind that either material would have been well suited to achieve. On the exterior relatively little attempt was made at expressing the skeleton, but inside a system was adopted which made clear the distinction between supports and infill panels. The flat pointed arches and the expression of the ribs suggested medieval proto-types, and it comes as no surprise to discover that Viollet-le-Duc had been de Baudot's mentor. But St.-Jean lacks formal resolution; it is an odd hybrid of

medieval and exotic sources, a loosely Art Nouveau accentuation, and entirely novel ideas related to the construction. The structure may be logical but the visual *expression* of the structure is indecisive. Nonetheless, the church suggested some ways in which the lessons of earlier styles could be applied to a modern situation.

In essence, this was the problem which would preoccupy Auguste Perret as well in the same years. Perret was forty years de Baudot's junior but was no less influenced by the ideas of Viollet-le-Duc. However, he had also undergone indoctrination in Classical principles at the École des Beaux-Arts in the 1890s under the tutelage of Julien Guadet, author of the book *Éléments et théories de l'architecture* (1904). The method that Gaudet attempted to instil in his students was the opposite of the slavish imitation of precedents that those hostile to the École liked to parody; his lectures were concerned with the Classical principles of composition and proportion, and with the analysis of building types; he tried to convey a feeling for essential qualities of Classicism, rather than a respect for superficial grammatical usages. A further element of Perret's formation needs to be stressed: both he and his brother Gustave were early trained in the basics of building construction in their father's firm. This blend of practicality, a Rationalist theoretical outlook and a firm, intuitive grasp of fundamentally Classical principles was to inform Perret's lifelong production.

The apartments designed by the architect at 25bis Rue Franklin in 1902 were based on the potentials of a trabeated, rectangular concrete-frame construction (fig. 3.8). The building stands in a row of vertical, rather gaunt grey stone neighbours, with splendid views down towards the Seine and the Eiffel Tower in the distance. Perret maximized these views by making the window openings as large as zoning laws allowed and by the effective device of placing the statutory lightcourt on the front of his building instead of at the back. The plan (fig. 3.7) conformed to the standard expectations of middle-class occupancy, and placed the salons at the centre of the façade, but the concrete-frame system allowed thin wall partitions, and some saving in space. This potential was most obvious at the ground level where the Perret firm moved its studio, and where the stanchions appeared in free space as premonitions of the *pilotis* so important to the architecture of the twenties. Perret exploited the set-backs on top of the building, and the flat roofs provided by his constructional system, to create a roof terrace.

What made the Rue Franklin flats architecture, instead of just construction, was the way these practical intentions were given a clear, tectonic form. The lowest storey was expressed as a separate unit, higher than those above it, while the next six storeys

3.5 (*left*) Anatole de Baudot, St.-Jean de Montmartre, Paris, 1897–1905, interior.

3.6 (*above*) Auguste Perret, apartments at 25 bis, Rue Franklin, Paris, 1902, detail of upper part of façade.

3.7 (*right*) Auguste Perret, apartments at 25 bis, Rue Franklin, Paris, 1902, plan.

3.8 (*far right*) Auguste Perret, apartments at 25 bis, Rue Franklin, Paris, 1902.

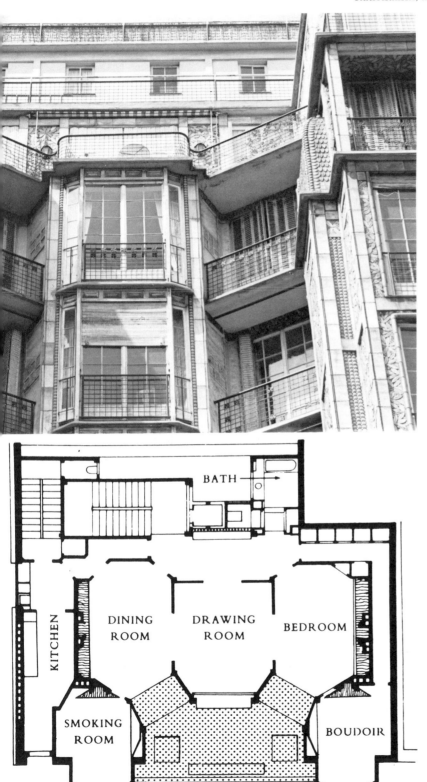

were expressed by slight overhangs and a variable placement of window depths within the U-shaped recess. The underlying rectangular frame was not exposed directly, but its presence was suggested by contrasting colours and textures in the tiles of the façade, while the theme of infill, non-weight-bearing panels was suggested by recessed, floral-designed ceramic surfaces. At the sixth storey, though, the frame broke free of the wall surfaces, giving some hint of the sort of airy and transparent effects to be pursued in modern architecture a generation later (fig. 3.6). The result of Perret's careful attention to proportion, detail and interval was a calculated work of great sobriety and repose. The whole was suffused with a serene Classicism, yet without the overt use of the Classical orders. The Rue Franklin flats, along with the later wing of the Glasgow School of Art by Mackintosh, the Stoclet house by Hoffmann, the Larkin building by Wright, the AEG Turbinenfabrik in Berlin by Behrens, and perhaps a handful of others, must certainly rank as one of the seminal works of the early modern movement. However, part of its strength lay, precisely, in the authoritative way in which it announced the potentials of a new material in a phraseology *rooted in tradition* (Plate 2).

In 1905, Perret made a further step by leaving the concrete completely exposed (though, admittedly, protected by white paint) in the garage design at 51 Rue de Ponthieu. It is possible that he felt freer to do this in a building whose function lay closer to the concrete 'warehouse aesthetic' of Hennebique, than did bourgeois apartments. And it may be that in his articulation of the garage façade (fig. 3.9), Perret was reacting to knowledge of Chicago frame buildings. In any case, the result transcends its influences in a clear statement infused with a true personal style. The concrete frame on the interior allowed considerable flexibility in planning to facilitate the circulation and parking of cars. In less sensitive hands this interior organization might well have led to a crude as-semblage of rectangular openings and stanchions in the façade. Perret brought order to the design by subtle placement of the window panes to give the right sense of depth, and by organizing the pattern of vertical and horizontal visual stresses – the apparent, not just the actual structure – in a simple rhythm of primary and secondary accents. The armature of the whole composition was defined by the stripped 'pilasters' rising from top to bottom supporting the abstracted 'cornice' at the top.

There can be little doubt that Perret had by this time decided that the 'correct' forms for concrete were rectangular ones, in part because of his aesthetic prejudices, in part because of the simplicity of making rectangular timber form-work from which the con-

3.9 Auguste Perret, Garage at 51 Rue de Ponthieu, Paris, 1905, façade.

3.10 Auguste Perret, Théâtre des Champs-Élysées, Paris, 1911, diagram of concrete frame.

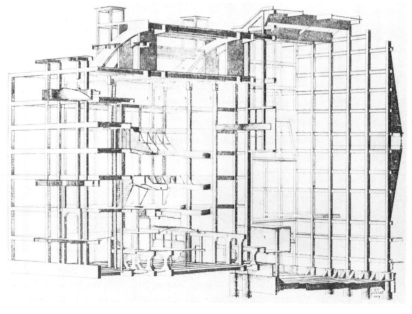

3.11 Albert Kahn,
automobile factory in
concrete, Detroit,
Michigan, c. 1909.

crete was cast in simple standard sections: thus his concrete vocabulary was reminiscent in some ways of wooden-frame buildings of the past. But his father had trained him in the intricacies of stone-cutting and stereotomy, and the mouldings and details of Perret's designs, which he could usually justify on extremely practical grounds (e.g., as drip mouldings), seem to be historical relatives of the flat wall and bracket elements observable in the French Classical tradition running back to the seventeenth century. It is intriguing to speculate how the Abbé Laugier (the mid-eighteenth century theorist mentioned in Chapter 1) might have reacted to Perret's work if he could have been brought back to life in 1902. One suspects that he would have recognized the intention of restating certain essentials of Classicism for new purposes and in new materials immediately. One guesses too that he might have respected the sentiments underlying Perret's dictum that 'one must never allow into a building any element destined solely for ornament, but rather turn to ornament all the parts necessary for the support.'

By 1911 the Perret brothers had become the undisputed leaders in concrete construction in France. They were approached by the impresario Gabriel Anstuc, who wished to erect a new theatre and hoped

that Perret might help to implement a design by Henry van de Velde. This collaboration was short-lived – as might have been expected – and the Champs-Élysées Theatre was carried out to Perret's design with façades based on van de Velde's elevations. Once again Perret demonstrated the depth of his Classical allegiances in the use of elements recalling stripped pilasters and cornices. On the interior, the spanning power of concrete was used to minimize interruptions of the view of the stage. The concrete frame of the building was almost a work of art in its own right (fig. 3.10), and was certainly to become a major inspiration to the generation which created the modern movement of the 1920s; the external treatment of the theatre they preferred to forget, as its traditionalism was not in tune with their aims.

In the United States, in parallel with Hennebique's pioneering experiments, the engineer Ernest Ransome and the architect Albert Kahn discovered many applications for the new material in factory, warehouse, and even grain silo design. Kahn devoted much of his life to the design of car factories, worked closely with Henry Ford, and, by 1908, was already producing his characteristic framed buildings in and around Detroit (fig. 3.11). He found concrete to be almost ideal

3.12 Robert Maillart, concrete bridge, Tavanasa, Switzerland, c. 1905.

in handling such fundamental requirements as cheapness, standardization, clear lighting, extensive ventilation, and unobstructed, flexible interiors through which the assembly line could be threaded. A characteristic morphology of grid plans, and simple rectangular elevations of pleasing proportion resulted. But Kahn never thought of his utilitarian designs as Architecture with a large 'A'; it was the European avant-garde, seeing them in photographs, who referred to them as icons of a new, universal language of architecture.

The one outstanding architect in the United States to grapple with the potentials of the new material was Frank Lloyd Wright. He was certainly attracted to it because of its cheapness and because it could create wide spans. Moreover, it could easily be moulded to his spatial ideas. With his 'Arts and Crafts' emphasis on the nature of materials, Wright also thought it best to leave the surfaces of concrete bare. One of his early masterpieces, the Unity Temple in Oak Park of 1906, was constructed in concrete. This building is best discussed in more detail in the context of Wright's philosophy and evolving vocabulary of abstract form; here it is enough to say that the building, like Perret's apartments, gave enhanced status to concrete, and

lent further weight to the impression that the 'correct' forms for the material were rectangular, stripped, and abstract, although Wright did not, like Perret, rely on the frame.

But rectangular forms were by no means the only ones suitable to concrete, as was well demonstrated by the engineering feats of Eugène Freyssinet in France and Robert Maillart the bridge builder in Switzerland, in the first two decades. Freyssinet's vast airship hangars at Orly (1916) were parabolic in section, while Maillart's bridges tended to rest on slender, attenuated curved supports (fig. 3.12). Max Berg's Jahrhunderthalle at Breslau, of 1911, also made much of the vast spanning potential of arcuated construction, and suggested an expressionist, dynamic tendency quite unlike Perret's. This great variation of possible forms for concrete only serves to emphasize that the tendency to think of the rectangular forms of the modern movement as somehow indelibly linked to concrete is an oversimplification. The generation which, for a variety of aesthetic and symbolic reasons, sought effects of thin planarity, overhanging horizontality, and geometrical simplicity, saw its forefathers as being Perret and Wright, while ignoring an equally viable curvilinear tradition.

Among the architects to provide a pedigree for the later rectangular aesthetic was the Frenchman Tony Garnier, who also linked the new material to another development to become crucial in the twenties: town planning for an industrial society. Garnier was born five years earlier than Perret, in 1869, and also attended Guadet's lectures at the École des Beaux-Arts in the 1890s. In 1899 he won the Prix de Rome with a design for a 'State Banking House' which was an exemplary demonstration of Beaux-Arts planning in the use of primary and secondary axes, absolute symmetry and the separation of circulation from areas served. Ostensibly Garnier was to have spent his time in Rome studying the monuments of antiquity, and doing reconstructions of Herculaneum; instead he turned his mind to the design of a modern ideal city known simply as the 'Cité Industrielle', which was not published until 1917, by which time the architect had managed to implement some of his ideas in the new town outside Lyons. The Cité Industrielle (fig. 3.13) was based on the notion of distinct zoning for residential, industrial, transport, and health areas, and drew together French urbanistic precedents in its use of grandiose axes, English Garden City ideals, and social ideas from the Utopian-Socialist tradition. But these houses were far from the Arts and Crafts in their use of flat roofs, their simple cubic geometries, and their use of concrete and standardization. If anything, the style

3.13 Tony Garnier, Cité Industrielle, city centre, residential district, *c.* 1904–17 (from the *Cité Industrielle*, 1917).

3.14 Tony Garnier, Cité Industrielle, city centre, railway station, *c.* 1904–17 (from the *Cité Industrielle*, 1917).

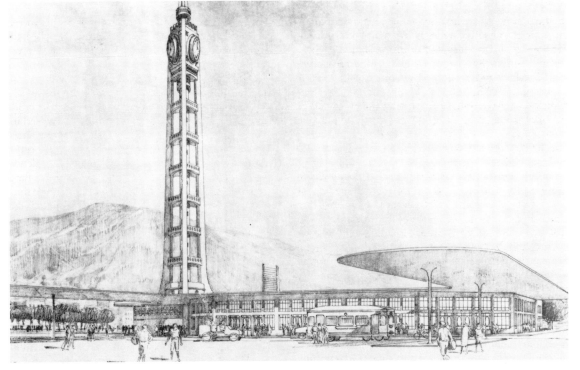

was a sort of stripped 'Grecian', but the minimum reference was made to Classical mouldings. The dwellings had simple rectangular windows punched through their surfaces, and in places concrete frames rose clear of the roofs and supported horizontal parasol slabs, lending an air of transparency to the imagery. The central railway station (fig. 3.14) was also constructed from concrete and made dramatic use of cantilevers and horizontal overhangs. Garnier's Cité gave a convincing imagery to the functions of a modern town and lent extra weight to the notion that rectangular cubic forms were the most suitable to reinforced-concrete construction and to standardization. Moreover, there was the further suggestion that sober values of clear geometrical repetition were the 'correct' ones for an emergent machine-age society.

Among those to be convinced of these patterns of thought, and to adhere to some of the principles behind Perret's vision of a reinforced-concrete architecture, was Charles Edouard Jeanneret, later to become Le Corbusier. So important is this figure to the history to be covered by this book, that it seems best to treat his formation individually in a later chapter. Here it is enough to say that Jeanneret was born in La Chaux-de-Fonds, Switzerland, in 1887; that his early designs reveal a mixture of Art Nouveau and Regionalist influences; that he spent part of his early twenties working in Perret's atelier where he learned the basic lessons of reinforced concrete, and imbibed Viollet-le-Duc's ideas; and that he worked two years later (1910) in the office of Peter Behrens in Berlin, where he absorbed the idea that a new architecture must rest on the idealization of types and norms designed to serve the needs of modern society, while being in harmony with the means of mass production. At least this is sufficient to supply a context to his seminal 'Dom-ino' concrete housing system of 1914–15.

This was designed as a housing kit to help in the rapid reconstruction of war-ravaged Flanders. Jeanneret optimistically expected that the war would end quickly and his ideal was to mass-produce a basic set of components, including the necessary moulds to make a simple, six-point support concrete skeleton with cantilevered slabs. The framework of the dwelling could then be assembled in less than three weeks, and rubble walls made from ruined buildings could be used as an infill. Windows and furnishings, all mass produced, were to be modelled on local precedents, and inserted into the skeleton. The very name 'Dom-ino' implied the Latin word for house (Domus) and the game 'dominoes' (the plan of a whole suburb did loosely resemble a row of number six dominoes). Intrinsic was the idea that simple, rectangular, mass-producible components be arranged to make modern dwellings and communities. From the very beginning

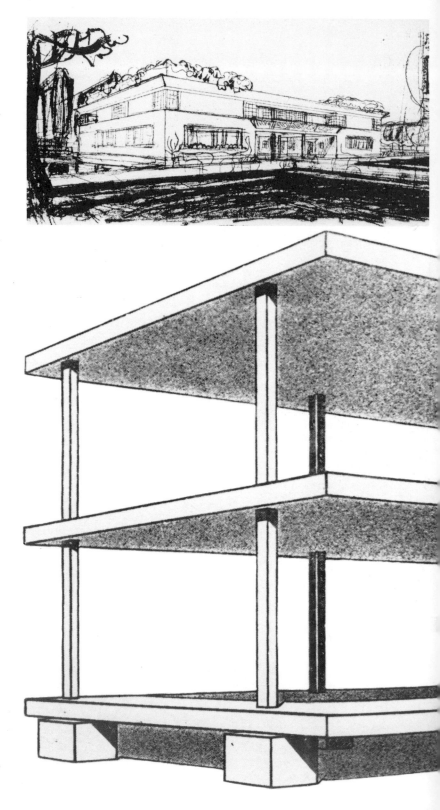

3.15 Charles Edouard Jeanneret (Le Corbusier), Dom-ino houses, 1914–15.

3.16 Charles Edouard Jeanneret (Le Corbusier), Dom-ino skeleton, 1914–15 (as drawn in *Oeuvre complète*, volume I, 1910–29).

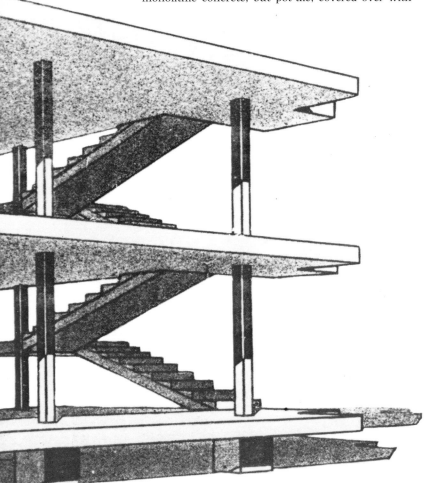

we can sense the future Le Corbusier's preoccupation with defining the elements of a new architectural and urbanistic language.

The central generator of the Dom-ino system and of both the architecture *and* the urbanism of the later Le Corbusier was the skeleton itself (designed with the help of Max Dubois). This was a structural unit consisting of three horizontal slabs, smooth below and above, each of the upper two supported on square sectional posts of concrete, the lower level lifted from the ground on squat concrete blocks (fig. 3.16). In the perspective of this skeleton (which was published only in the twenties) concrete stairs were shown connecting the levels. It was noticeable that the Dom-ino, by contrast with, say, the system of Hennebique, made no use of brackets or beams. Employing the principle of the cantilever, the slabs, moreover, extended well beyond the line of supports. In fact they were not to be monolithic concrete, but pot-tile, covered over with concrete and reinforced with interior beams of steel.

One advantage of Jeanneret's system would have been its rapid construction, but this was not put to the test. Another was intrinsic and indubitable: it did with concrete what Perret's system had not. It separated out the structural and the screening functions of the wall by removing the fill from the frame. Now the fill was attached to the end of the slabs, with the possibility of its existing as a planar surface hovering in space above a void. As the weight of the building was now held up by the skeleton, the external 'wall' (or other form of cladding) could be arranged without thought for the load on it and without the interruption of the frame. It could become effectively a sort of membrane to be punctured as functional necessities or compositional instincts required. In the Dom-ino houses glass was placed tantalizingly at the corners in some places, just where a traditional masonry structure would have been most solid structurally.

On the interior the Dom-ino system also allowed new freedoms. Partitions could be placed where one wished, in or out of line with the grid of supports. Space was saved and a new degree of functional flexibility achieved. Aesthetically the emphasis could now shift from the cutting out of spaces from masses, to the modulation of spaces with minimal supports.

However, this is to look at the Dom-ino skeleton with the help of hindsight, and with the knowledge of the transparent and lightweight effects of the later 'International Style'. It is therefore only fair to point out that the Dom-ino houses of 1915 were dumpy in visual effect for all their simplicity of volume, and that their interiors were confined and traditional for all the spatial potentials of the structural skeleton. They probably reflected Jeanneret's admiration for the unadorned dwellings of the Mediterranean, with their flat roofs and cubic shapes modelled by light. Indeed, the Dom-ino houses were the first of a number of attempts by the architect at founding a modern, industrialized equivalent to the vernaculars of the past (fig. 3.15).

But if the Dom-ino ideas anticipated some aspects of the architecture of the twenties, they also rested firmly in the Rationalist tradition. When Jeanneret had worked for Perret in 1908, he had used his first pay-packet to buy Viollet-le-Duc's *Dictionnaire de l'architecture*. In one of the margins he referred in a note to Perret's insistence on the 'structural skeleton'. In his own Dom-ino theorem the young man laid the basis for his future architectural system, but with help from his mentors, past and contemporary. In much the same way, Rationalism and reinforced concrete were two elements, but only two among many, which would eventually coalesce in the 'heroic' period of modern architecture, the 1920s.

4. Arts and Crafts Ideals in England and the USA

The arts and crafts are called upon to restore our awareness of honesty, integrity and simplicity in contemporary society. If this can be achieved, the whole of our cultural life will be profoundly affected. . . . The success of our movement will not only alter the appearance of houses and flats but will have direct repercussions on the character of an entire generation. . . . If the new trends are genuine, then an original, lasting style will emerge . . .

H. Muthesius, 1907

The search for values of simplicity and directness which motivated so many artistic developments in the first decade of the twentieth century had its roots in a variety of earlier intellectual positions. The last chapter traced one of these – Rationalism – and suggested how this aided the discovery of forms based on reinforced-concrete construction. There was another strand of ideas, however, which stemmed from Pugin, Ruskin, and Morris, according to which the 'corruption of nineteenth-century styles' would be counteracted by inspired craftsmanship, and which maintained that an authentic architecture would be achieved through the direct expression of pristine moral virtues. Each of these English thinkers was disgusted in his own way with the impact of the industrial revolution on the social organization, the methods of building, and the very moral basis of culture. Morris, in particular, had hoped to usher in a new period of integrated wholeness in which the highest aesthetic qualities would be ripped from the museum pedestal and linked again with the tools and artifacts of everyday use. The architect must therefore become a master of craft; and, to judge by Phillip Webb's and Morris's Red House of 1859 (fig. 4.1), this attitude tended to be translated formally into a medievalizing vocabulary in which the direct qualities of vernacular design were emulated to create a suitable emblem of the simple, good life.

Nikolaus Pevsner has traced the evolution of Arts and Crafts ideals through the last three decades of the nineteenth century and has demonstrated the impact of Morris's thinking on Walter Gropius and the Deutscher Werkbund in Germany in the first decade of

this century. It was only when Morris's ideals concerning the reintegration of art and life, craft and utility, were transformed to allow for mechanization that they became directly useful to the creation of the modern movement. But history does not work in straight lines, and the Arts and Crafts inheritance permeated a number of developments around the turn of the century which did not, it so happens, bear fruit in specifically 'modern' architecture.

It is natural to begin the story in England with the legacy of domestic architectural ideals handed down from Webb, Shaw, Godwin, and Mackmurdo, to a later generation including Voysey, Lutyens, Baillie-Scott, Mackintosh, Ashbee, and Lethaby. Charles Francis Voysey was born in 1857 and produced his own unique style just before the turn of the century in designs like that for a house in Bedford Park of 1891 or for a studio in St. Dunstan's Road, West Kensington, of the same year. In these, the aesthetic effect arose from the disposition of simple pebble-dashed and white-washed volumes punctured by rows of windows and enhanced by the geometrical play of chimneys and low-angled roofs. It is not hard to understand how formalist historians seeking a pedigree for the stripped white forms of later modern architecture should have turned to Voysey; however, the architect expressed embarrassment at having this role of 'pioneer of modern design' thrust upon him. His immersion in the simple joys of English vernacular design, his lack of fuss, his almost childlike obsession with the composition of rain barrels and gutters in façades, has very little in common with the ideas of a later generation for

4.1 Philip Webb, the 'Red House', Bexley Heath, Kent, 1859.

which simplicity had a very different universal and mechanistic significance.

Voysey's vision seems to have come to full maturity in his large houses in rural settings, such as Perrycroft, designed for a site in the Malvern hills in 1893 (fig. 4.2), or the Sturgess house of 1896, designed for the 'Hog's Back' in Surrey. The first of these made much use of sloping buttresses and deeply overhanging eaves, not only as structural, climatic, and compositional devices, but as ways of linking the building to the ground and suggesting continuity with local vernacular design. This was a central idea of Arts and Crafts architectural doctrine: indigenous materials and usages were to be translated to good use

by the modern practitioner.

Although Voysey was not a craftsman himself, he turned his mind to the design of wallpapers, furniture, fixtures, and fittings, for he felt that the same impulses should permeate all the interiors of a house as conditioned the overall form. Here again he pursued a rhetorical simplicity (fig. 4.3), which made a pointed contrast with the clutter and complexity of earlier Victorian design. Pevsner tended to associate this youthfulness with a wider reaction in values.

It is well known that everywhere in English cultural life a longing for fresh air and gaiety expressed itself at the end of Queen Victoria's reign.

4.2 Charles Francis Voysey, Perrycroft, Malvern, Worcestershire, 1893.

4.3 Charles Francis Voysey, The Orchard, Chorleywood, Hertfordshire, 1893, interior.

Another novel feature of Voysey's designs was the way they opened up interior volumes so that they tended to flow into one another. In Broadley's, a house overlooking Lake Windermere, the hall was carved out as a double space. In plan the main elements were subtly disposed within an order combining some degree of symmetry and formality with informal and asymmetrical qualities. In these ways Voysey succeeded in giving form to the patterns of social life of the English well-to-do at the turn of the century. It was a sort of procured rusticity; an emulation of the 'common speech' of the vernacular which was, of course, very self-conscious.

M. H. Baillie-Scott was nine years Voysey's junior and, unlike him, did much work on the continent. In his Blackwell house of 1900, also on Lake Windermere, he attempted to open up the interior space. Of course, this was not simply an aesthetic matter, but an attempt at expressing a way of life. Baillie-Scott has left evocative descriptions conjuring up the life of the middle-class home with the fire crackling in a central hall, the living-rooms opening out into one another, the inglenooks, the music gallery, the broad, winding stairs. Such arrangements were heavily loaded with deliberate manorial associations, with references to a romanticized national past. Both Voysey and Baillie-Scott managed to conjure up a powerful image of the Englishman's home which would eventually be disseminated through the building catalogues to provide many of the standard clichés of inter-war domestic suburban design.

Another central feature of much creative domestic design of the Edwardian period was the interest in fusing the building with the garden setting through the use of pergolas, pathways, sunken gardens, and the like. To be sure, the 'rusticity' of the Arts and Crafts house was not allowed to be too rude or too removed from the gentility and urbanity of the middle-class users. In Hill House at Helensburgh of 1903 (fig. 4.4), designed for Blackie the publisher, Charles Rennie Mackintosh designed not only the house and all its fixtures and fittings, but the outbuildings, the garden gates, the walls, the terraces, and the pergolas as well – all as part of a unified aesthetic conception. The result was a total work of art, an aesthetic enhancement of all the rituals of family life, from the 'public face' presented to arriving guests in the hall, to the relative formality of dining-room and living-room, to the more informal and private worlds of inglenooks, bedrooms, library, and garden seats.

4.4 Charles Rennie Mackintosh, Hill House, Helensburgh, Glasgow, perspective from the south-west, 1903. Pen and ink, $13\frac{1}{4} \times 22\frac{1}{2}$in. ($33.6 \times 57.2$cm.). Glasgow School of Art.

4.5 (*left*) Edwin Lutyens, Tigbourne Court, Surrey, 1898, view of entrance.

4.6 (*right*) Edwin Lutyens, the Plaisaunce. Overstrand, Norfolk, 1901, view of garden steps.

Some of the richest creations of this type in England were designed by Edwin Lutyens (1869–1944), who frequently worked closely with his cousin, the garden designer Gertrude Jekyll, for whom he built one of his earliest houses, at Munstead Wood near Godalming, Surrey. This was soon followed by a number of other outstanding houses in the area, including the Orchards at Godalming and Tigbourne Court (fig. 4.5), also in Surrey and also of 1898. Lutyens received direct inspiration from Shaw and Webb but exceeded both in the breadth of his sources, the range of his imagination, and his capacity for wittily turning a vernacular usage to his own advantage. He believed strongly in the use of local crafts and materials, both because this was practical and because it was liable to lead to a harmony between the house and its architectural or natural setting. Thus in his early designs one finds him employing Surrey tile fascias and wooden frames based on yeomen's houses, and varying the depth of his eaves according to local character and precedent. In Overstrand Hall, Norfolk (1901), typical indigenous combinations of flint and red-brick courses were employed, but adeptly transformed into a vocabulary suave in its accents and enhanced by clever collisions of Classical and medieval fragments.

It would be entirely inadequate, however, to reject Luytens as a mere eclectic who raided the rag-bag of history in order to satisfy the taste for exotic weekend scenarios of his extremely wealthy patrons. Underlying the play was a controlling sense of proportion and organizational principle; beneath the sparkle was a sober and probing mind, which was eventually to seek the certainties of Classical design. Moreover, the unity of Lutyens's designs was achieved by a judicious combination of axes and repeating geometrical motifs. Thus one finds 'themes' played out in plan, elevation, and volume, as when an arch turns into a semi-circular step, to be rediscovered as a wall niche, a dome, or a luxurious hemispherical Edwardian bath lined with mosaic. Geometrical play could extend to the elements of garden design as well. At the Plaisaunce (also in Norfolk, 1901) the convex spherical form of the baking-oven was restated in the concave hemisphere of the brick garden-seat canopy; the sunken gardens were in turn linked to the house by amphitheatre-like steps (fig. 4.6), circular ground patterns and curved levels.

Lutyens was also fascinated by the special character of each client and site, and always attempted to produce a unique response to these. At Lindisfarne he was requested to remodel a Scottish castle on a promontory overlooking the sea. He transformed the requirements into a bijou fortress, whose parapets harmonized with the surrounding rocks and whose imagery was entirely at one with the spirit of the place. At Heathcote, Ilkley (1906), the client required a more magnificent and prestigious imagery than was usual for Lutyens, and the site, being almost suburban and hemmed in by buildings on both sides, suggested the qualities of a formal villa. Thus the architect varied his manner to include something of the character of the English Baroque, with quotations from Vanbrugh and Hawksmoor. The body of the house was ingeniously linked to the setting by parterres, an apsidal 'great lawn' and subtle cross axes. The materials, meanwhile, were local ones: Guiseley stone with grey dressings from the Morley quarries. The result was a massive heap of a certain dour quality, perfectly suited to its region and placement. In the 'Salutation' at Sandwich, Kent, the gate lodge was made to harmonize with the character of a Kentish riverside town through the use of local tiles and white woodwork, which were handled with a sort of procured irregularity blending superbly with the aging character of the surroundings. Nowhere in Lutyens is there the disturbance of new social forces or of the industry whose very owners were frequently his clients. His designs evoked a safe and stable world of national continuity. They implied the conceit that the crafts had remained perpetually the same from region to region over the ages.

Voysey, Lutyens, Baillie-Scott, Prior, and the other English architects who might be loosely grouped as 'Arts and Crafts' in the first decade of the twentieth century were bold innovators in domestic design, but in most respects were traditionalists. The 'freedom' of their planning and the directness and 'honesty' of their use of materials were perhaps emblematic of a reaction against the clutter and pomposity of earlier English domestic architecture, but these architects were certainly far from attempting the creation of a brave new world. In a sense their designs were microcosms of deeply felt values concerning the meaning of the home: worlds in miniature in which details like door latches or dovecotes, as well as the overall mood, were infused with a sense of reverence for the ideal of a happy family life lived in a natural setting.

It was customary before the First World War to refer to the new style as 'the English Free Architecture', but by 1910 a strong reaction had set in, in favour of a direct neo-classical revival and a dependence on foreign and 'cosmopolitan' models rather than native, vernacular ones. At about the same time that the French Beaux-Arts was beginning to exert its influence in England, Arts and Crafts values were being, as it were, exported to Germany. A key personality here was Hermann Muthesius, who was posted at the German embassy in London precisely to study English domestic design. His book *Das englische Haus* of 1902 was a masterly survey of the national tradition of houses. Undoubtedly he was catering to a taste in Germany, stretching well back into the nineteenth century, for the English cottage and garden. But there were weightier ideals at work as well. Muthesius was working for a German élite who felt strongly the inferiority of their culture, and its disruption by industrialization. They sensed in the English movement an unruffled, sober character, as well as an intelligent application of formal quality to everyday design. Muthesius mythologized the Englishman and his home in this way:

... let me repeat once more that the Modern English artistic movement has no trace of those fanciful, superfluous and often affected ideas with which a part of the new continental movement is still engaged. Far from this, it tends more towards the primitive and the rustic; and here it fits perfectly well with the type of traditional rural house. Moreover this outcome is perfectly to the taste of the Englishman for whom there is nothing better than plain simplicity.... A minimum of 'forms', and a maximim of peaceful, comfortable and yet lively atmosphere, that is what he aims for.... Such accord seems to him to be a link with beloved mother Nature, to whom, despite all higher cultures, the English nation has remained more faithful than any other people. And today's house is proof of this ... The way in which it fits so admirably into surrounding Nature in the happiness of its colouring and the solidity of its form: in all these ways it stands there today as cultural proof of the healthy tendencies of a nation which amid all its wealth and advances in civilization has retained, to a remarkable degree, its appreciation of what is natural. Urban civilization, with its destructive influences, with its senseless haste and press, with its hothouse stimulation of those impulses towards vanity which are latent in man, with its elevation of the refined, the nervous, the abnormal to unnatural proportions, all this has had practically no harmful effect on the English nation.

German admiration of the English Arts and Crafts went further than this. It included an attempt at emulating the values of honesty of materials, etc., in the design of everyday objects, in the teaching programmes of schools of design, and eventually extended to a wholesale national obsession with the ideal of good formal quality in *industrial* design. Looking back in 1915, William Lethaby, who had been deeply involved with the English movement, could express his sadness at the 'timid reaction and the re-emergence of the catalogued styles' in England; and his admiration for 'advances in German industrial design founded on the English arts and crafts'. The manner in which a movement which had been conceived, in part, as a reaction against the crudities of mechanization became the basis of a national industrial design philosophy, must be explained in a later chapter; suffice it to say that Arts and Crafts values, once exported and transformed, were another major element in the jigsaw puzzle of the modern movement.

This was true not only in Europe, but also in America, where the catalyst of transformation was Frank Lloyd Wright. He was undoubtedly the most original architect to be influenced by Arts and Crafts ideals and, to that extent, can scarcely be considered typical. Nonetheless his formation occurred in a milieu of ideas derived from the earlier nineteenth century. There was no direct equivalent to William Morris in the American tradition, but his ideas were certainly well known. In the figure of Andrew Jackson Downing one has a mid-century thinker and designer who put a great store by the image of the individual, wooden-battened house – the rustic retreat – as somehow quintessentially American and democratic. Vincent Scully has traced the ensuing development of the so-called 'Stick' and 'Shingle' Styles in the last three decades of the nineteenth century, in which the direct expression of wooden construction, informal open-planning, verandas, and a romantic display of hipped roofs, chimneys, and gazebo elements all played a part. Arguably Shaw's influence on these developments was considerable; certainly local traditions of wooden construction played their part; but there was also something less definable – an ethos of freedom, and a concern for the relationship of the individual dwelling to its natural setting. As always, American architectural development was helped and hindered by the lack of a long, coherent national tradition: helped because this situation encouraged a degree of experimentation; hindered because there was relatively little guidance from earlier norms. It is in the figure of Henry Hobson Richardson – Beaux-Arts trained, with a deep appreciation of medieval sources and a rare instinct for what was most relevant to the emergent social order of the United States – that one finds a synthesis of the indigenous and the imported, of great force. The Ames Gate Lodge of 1882 at North Easton, Massachusetts (fig. 4.7), is linked to its site and its region by a strong sense of place and by an exaggerated use of indigenous stonework; yet the rusticity of the imagery is ennobled, formalized, enhanced by the architect's knowledge of far distant traditions including such exoticisms as early Christian arches from Syria and French medieval farm buildings.

Thus the search for a model domestic architecture in America was never very far from the larger question of defining an American architecture in general. There followed close behind a series of formulations and emotions unfolding around such ideas as: the search for a pastoral or middle-landscape ideal; the notion of an honest expression unfettered by European decadence; a conception of native functionalism; an aspiration towards a fitness and commodity mirroring nature's, which would lead by a short route to beauty and deeper meanings. Tinged with nostalgia for an earlier search for paradise in the 'New World', this sophisticated quest for a simplicity in touch with natural values crystallized in that most cultivated and artificial of 'natural' settings: the suburbia which began to proliferate around the mechanized American cities from the 1880s onwards.

As we shall see in Chapter 6, Wright grasped the full meaning of this situation and managed to take the suburban family house and weave a mythology around it. His earliest designs were drawn from the Shingle Style, from Japanese sources, from the Midwestern vernacular, and from the Queen Anne and Colonial revivals which briefly touched the Midwest of his youth in the 1880s and early 1890s (fig. 4.8). Arts and Crafts ideals imported from England, concerning the direct response to the nature of materials and the

4.7 Henry Hobson Richardson, Ames Gate Lodge, North Easton, Massachusetts, 1882.

total design of furnishings and building, including the setting, early permeated his outlook. However, unlike Morris and his English contemporaries, Voysey, Webb, and Lutyens, he grasped the positive importance of mechanization as well. In his essay 'The Art and Craft of the Machine', of 1901, he acknowledged that 'the machine is here to stay' and that this would influence not only the artist's techniques in building (e.g., straight lines of simple cut wood) but the entire fabric of the society for which he would build. A traditionalist in many senses, Wright remained; but his powerful feeling for abstract form and his vision of a new social order made him a link between the nineteenth-century craft ideal, and the propelling ideas of the later modern movement in Europe.

As well as the Prairie School extension of Wright's architecture, there were other developments in the United States, especially on the West Coast, which extended the Arts and Crafts movement. The West was still regarded as a last frontier and thus collected the detritus of over a century of pioneer mythology. From 1901 to 1916, Gustav Stickley spread the message of the 'Craftsman's Movement' in a magazine called *The Craftsman*. This recorded developments in bungalow and furniture design and illustrated ideal projects for individual homes (fig. 4.10). Among these suggestions were ones for single and double storey homes with deep overhanging eaves, verandas, climbing plants, and rusticated chimneys. The interiors were simple evocations of 'home' in which bare beams and wooden uprights, inglenooks and built-in benches, 'humble' materials and fireplaces in the hallway all contributed. The sources for this imagery were diverse, and seemed to include Swiss chalets, Japanese wooden houses, and a variety of American regional cabin and shack prototypes.

In California there was not only the sense of a new society, unbounded by conventions and (as yet) untainted by industry; there were also plentiful lots of land. Moreover, the climate encouraged an architecture opening to the outside. The masters of the genre of the luxurious, but still 'simple', California bungalow were the brothers Charles and Henry Greene (born in 1868 and 1870) who were educated in Calvin Woodward's Manual Training School in St. Louis in the late 1870s, where they were encouraged to handle natural materials (especially wood) and to give their conceptions visual form. In the late 1880s the brothers went East and studied at MIT (Massachusetts Institute of Technology) where they learned some of the axial devices and intellectual strategies of Beaux-Arts design. After graduating they spent some time working in the Boston area, where they no doubt examined the works of Richardson and a variety of local Stick and Shingle Style examples. Finally they

moved to the West. It was to take them a decade to work out a style based on their earlier influences: on the hybrid indigenous styles of California (especially those using simple wooden construction and deep overhanging balconies), and even on Japanese prototypes in which elegant proportions, finely handled joints, and a superb combination of the formal and the informal were achieved.

The masterpiece of their new regional style was the Gamble House in Pasadena of 1907–8 (fig. 4.9), built for one of the millionaire partners of the soap firm Procter and Gamble. The house represented the full aggrandizement and ennoblement of the California bungalow image, yet the building was still striking for its intimacy, intricacy, and scale. An effect of nobility was conferred on the whole by its placement on a sort of terrace plinth, lifted slightly above the level of the surrounding lawns and banks of ferns. The relative solidity of the main gabled portions was heightened by the delicate transparency of the sprawling Stick Style balconies containing sleeping porches, with their overlapping struts and deep reveals of shadow. The main materials on the exterior were the redwood of the beams and frame, and the olive-green 'shakes' (giant shingles) which blended well with the surrounding natural colours. On the interior these material qualities and textures were supplemented by glistening stained-glass panels, hand-polished maple, and the glow of Tiffany glass fixtures. The elegance of the overall proportions was continued into the smallest parts and details – the articulation of earthquake-proof sliding joints with pegs and thongs, and the visual subtlety of

4.8 (*above*) Frank Lloyd Wright's own house, Oak Park, Illinois (near Chicago), 1893.

4.9 (*right*) Charles and Henry Greene, Gamble House, Pasadena, California, 1907–8.

4.10 (*below right*) Gustav Stickley, bungalow design from *The Craftsman*, c. 1905. interior.

tapering beam ends in the balconies. One is not surprised to discover that the house was modified (as were most of the Greene brothers designs) in the course of construction, with the architects themselves frequently fashioning the wooden details on site to ensure a precise effect.

The Gamble House plan gives further clues to the architects' intentions. One arrives by way of an open terrace; the front door gives straight on to a wide open hall passing straight through the house to another terrace at the rear. The stairs, dining-room, and living-room (the latter two looking out over the pool and fernery) are all linked by this major space. The living-room, as in so many of Wright's contemporary designs, is symmetrical and on axis with the main fireplace, which is conceived as a major incident. The plan, and the spaces generated from it, admittedly lack the tension and control of Wright's prairie houses, but the combination of formal and informal qualities so appropriate to the social role and meaning of such a dwelling is a widely shared feature of much Arts and Crafts design of the period. So is the attempt at unifying the building with its setting, achieved in this case by the prevalent horizontality, the ambiguous situation of porches half inside, half outside, the sympathy for nature of the materials, the provision made for planting, and the irregularly edged plan blending with the garden. It is the theme of the 'natural house' taken to an extreme which the California climate and flora encouraged.

While 'craftsmen's' ideals were usually carried through in domestic contexts, this was not their only outlet, and both Mackintosh's School of Art and Wright's Unity Temple were notable examples of similar ideas being worked through in institutional settings. In Northern California, Bernard Maybeck produced an exemplary craftsman's building in his First Church of Christ, Scientist, in Berkeley of 1909–11 (fig. 4.11). Actually, the building defies simple categorization; it is both unique and eccentric. Maybeck had been trained as a furniture maker and had then revelled in his Beaux-Arts education in Paris. The church is steeped in tradition and relies strongly on the ceremonial axial compositional ideas basic to the Beaux-Arts outlook. But the architectural elements assembled above this hieratic plan have little to do with the grand Classical manner (although the same architect's designs at the Pacific Exhibition of 1915 were to show him a master of a personal style rooted in Classical prototypes); rather we are confronted by a jumble of styles – Gothic, Suburban California, Stick Style, and an almost fantastic variety of materials, including carved wood, industrial sash, asbestos, and wisteria. Yet the design has a convincing unity and far transcends its sources.

If Maybeck represents a rugged and obsessive extreme of the Craftsman's Movement in the western United States, then Irving Gill must be taken as the complement because of the sobriety and broad simplicity of his approach. Born in 1870, he was largely self-taught and much influenced by the fact that his father was a building contractor with a knack for finding short cuts in construction. Gill himself was an early advocate of reinforced concrete in domestic design, and like Perret thought that the material required a simple rectangular vocabulary. He was reinforced in this view by his personal reactions to the regional traditions of the south-western United States, especially the mud adobe constructions of the area and the white-walled Mission style dwellings with their planar, white surfaces, low roofs, and extending pergolas. But Gill's was no mere grass roots romantic-

ism; his work was motivated by a social vision of considerable breadth. He thought of California as the last frontier, and therefore a suitable place for the expression of a new way of life based on the best of old American democratic ideals. The significance of stripped simplicity in his work was therefore partly moral, but very far in its meanings from the machine idolization of the avant-garde in Europe who were to create the modern movement of the twenties. On the contrary, Gill sought to make the broad masses of his own designs an equivalent to the structures of nature.

> We should build our house simple, plain and substantial as a boulder, then leave the ornamentation of it to Nature, who will tone it with lichens, chisel it with storms, make it gracious and friendly with vines and flower shadows as she does the stone in the meadow. I believe also that houses should be built more substantially and should be made absolutely sanitary. If the cost of unimportant ornamentation were put into construction, then we would have a more lasting and a more dignified house.

Gill's interpretation of 'Nature' went deeper than an interest in sensitive siting and the effects of weathering on surfaces. Like Wright and Sullivan, he believed that the best geometries were those abstracted from nature's structures and processes; and that the forms of art should emulate the fitness to purpose of natural forms. In Gill's mind, the basic shapes of architectural grammar were analogous to natural features and capable of impressing the emotions of a spectator in precise ways (fig. 4.12).

4.11 Bernard Maybeck, First Church of Christ, Scientist, Berkeley, California, 1909–11.

4.12 Irving Gill, Dodge House, Los Angeles, California, 1914–16.

Every artist must sooner or later reckon directly, personally with these four principles – the mightiest of lines. The straight line borrowed from the horizon is a symbol of greatness, grandeur and nobility; the arch patterned from the dome of the sky represents exultation, reverence, aspiration; the circle is the sign of completeness, motion and progression, as may be seen when a stone touches water; the square is the symbol of power, justice, honesty and firmness. These are the bases, the units of architectural language, and without them there can be no direct or inspired architectural speech.

In the broad picture of the transition from the 'styles' of the nineteenth century to the creation of modern architecture, the continuation of the Arts and Crafts Movement into the twentieth century played a partial role, and inspired individual work of outstanding quality. Rather than a unified style, there were broadly shared concerns. It so happened that Gill anticipated some superficial aspects of the white, geometrical architecture of the 1920s, but his work was virtually unknown in Europe and his outlook quite different. Indeed much of the effort of the generation which was to create the modern movement in Europe was directed *against* handicraft aspirations. Nonetheless, Arts and Crafts ideals had an important purgative function by stressing values of simplicity, honesty, and necessity. Ideals such as these were to be fundamental to the Deutscher Werkbund in Germany, an organization which sought a more direct confrontation with mechanization.

5. Responses to Mechanization: the Deutscher Werkbund and Futurism

The problem of modern architecture is not a problem of rearranging its lines; not a question of finding new mouldings, new architraves for doors and windows; nor of replacing columns, pilasters and corbels with caryatids, hornets and frogs. . . . But to raise the new-built structure on a sane plan, gleaning every benefit of science and technology, settling nobly every demand of our habits and our spirits, rejecting all that is heavy, grotesque and unsympathetic to us (tradition, style, aesthetics, proportions), establishing new forms, new lines, new reasons for existence, solely out of the special conditions of Modern living, and its projection as aesthetic value in our sensibilities.

A. Sant' Elia, 1914

From the beginning the Arts and Crafts movement had been permeated with preservationist sentiments and a nostalgia for a supposed integrated society preceding the chaotic effects of industrialization. By contrast, in the decade before the First World War, especially in Germany and Italy, philosophical, poetic, and eventually formal attitudes emerged in which an adulatory view of mechanization was to be found. It has already been suggested that the very notion of 'modern' architecture presupposed a progressivist sense of history; it is only by examining the theories of the Deutscher Werkbund in Germany and of the Futurists in Italy (which contrasted considerably) and the parallel architectural ideas of men like Peter Behrens, Walter Gropius, and Antonio Sant' Elia, that one may grasp how mechanization came to be regarded as a sort of essential motor to the forward march of history, requiring an appropriate expression in architecture and design.

This is not to suggest for one minute that a consensus was reached on just how this should be done. In Germany, which industrialized later than England and France, and experienced some of the opportunities and traumas of the process deeply, there was much debate concerning the ideal relationship between the artist and industry. Broadly speaking there were four main strands of opinion. One of these was a direct continuation of Arts and Crafts values in the Kunstgewerbeschulen, where the belief was maintained that quality goods would be achieved only through a concentration on handicrafts. Closely related to this view was a highly individualistic idea of the role of artistic invention which held that authentic forms in architecture could arise only from the imprint of the expressive temperament; this position tended to extend the most subjective aspects of Art Nouveau and led to the 'Expressionist' outlook. A third position was materialist and down-to-earth by contrast, and tended to hold that the best forms would be those emerging from the logical and direct use of new materials to solve building problems; it was, in other words, a functionalist outlook. The fourth position (the one which will principally concern us) tended to regard the functionalist as an uncultivated brute, the expressionist as an irrelevant remnant of the cult of genius, and the craftsman as an extinct entity unless directed to the problems of designing objects for mass production. Thus it became the business of the artist/architect to design the 'type forms' – be they objects of industrial design, building elements, or pieces of urban structure – of a new, mechanized and, let it be said, German civilization. It was an ideology in which the artist had to function as a sort of mediator between formal invention and standardization, between personal style and the appropriate form for the *Zeitgeist* (or 'spirit of the times'), between a sense of the contemporary world, and reliance on age-old artistic principles.

One of the most vocal proponents of such an outlook was Hermann Muthesius, the founder of the Deutscher Werkbund in 1907. This organization was set up precisely to forge closer links between German industry and artists, in order to upgrade the quality of national product design in emulation of what Muthesius had seen in England. From the start this was

OVERLEAF

5.2 Peter Behrens, turbine factory for AEG, Berlin, 1908.

seen as being far more than a commercial matter, but one involving deep probings into the nature of 'the German spirit', the role of form in industry and the psychic life of the nation.

> Far higher than the material is the spiritual; far higher than function, material and technique, stands form. These three aspects might be impeccably handled but – if form were not – we would still be living in a merely brutish world. So there remains before us an aim, a much greater and more important task – to awaken once more an understanding of Form, and the renewal of architectonic sensibilities.

Muthesius put his faith in the cultivated industrial élite who, he hoped, could be educated to lead the German nation on its innate mission: the elevation of a general taste to a position of supremacy in world markets and affairs, and the efflorescence of an influential and genuine *Kultur*. The moral tenor of life was to be raised through the impact of well-designed objects in the market-place, in the home, and in the work-place – indeed, in the environment as a whole. Evidently he envisaged a sort of unified style to replace the confectionery of nineteenth-century eclecticism, which should be as clearly expressed in a lamp-post, a teacup, a monument, or even a factory building. Central to his outlook was a belief in the return to fundamental formal qualities which would express architectonically the dignity and the calm endeavour of a new, confident national German spirit. There are echoes in this outlook of the writings of Gottfried

Semper, who had forecast the necessity of a style appropriate to machine methods after his visit to the Crystal Palace and the Great Exhibition of 1851. And it comes as no surprise to find that Muthesius had a considerable sympathy for the grandeur of the Classical tradition – especially as manifested in the work of Karl Friedrich Schinkel – which seemed to sum up so well the combination of martial values and impersonal power, scholarship and formal abstraction, that Muthesius perhaps envisaged as essential to the necessary style for his own times.

> ... the re-establishment of an architectonic culture is a basic condition of all the arts. ... It is a question of bringing back into our way of life that order and discipline of which good Form is the outward manifestation.

From the English Arts and Crafts tradition Muthesius inherited a concern for the moral power of design to influence people's lives, a sense of integrity in the expression of the nature of materials, a feeling for the dignified embodiment of function, and an obsession with the 'dishonesty' of false revivalism. However, these notions were cross-bred, as it were, with the ideal of designing for the machine and with philosophical concepts derived from the German idealist tradition. Central to these was the notion that it was the destiny of Germany to realize some higher idea in the historical scheme of things, and a related notion that a sort of 'will-to-form' with a strong national taint would realize the forms of a genuine style. Such a style would not then be seen as a merely personal, conventional or wilful matter, but as an inevitable force of destiny: a universal necessity.

> It is evident that the ephemeral is incompatible with the true essence of architecture. The peculiar qualities of architecture, constancy, tranquillity and permanence and its thousand-year-old traditions of expression, have almost come to represent what is eternal in human history. ... Of all the arts, architecture is the one which tends most readily towards the typical and only thus can it really fulfil its aims. It is only by steadily striving for a single target that we shall be able to recover the quality and the unerring surety of touch that we admire in the achievements of the past, where singleness of purpose was inherent in the age.

It would be too simple, and too convenient, to see the architecture of Peter Behrens as a direct illustration of Muthesius's aspirations; but after about 1907 there was a considerable consonance in their positions, especially in the designs that Behrens executed for the

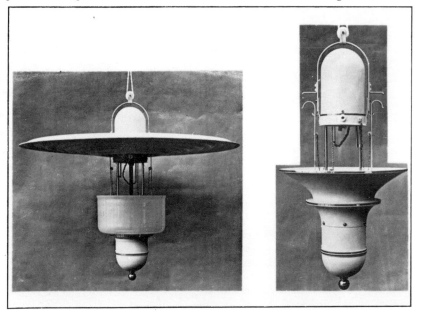

5.1 Peter Behrens, lamp designs for mass production, *c.* 1908.

giant electrical concern, AEG; these included objects for mass production, like lamps (fig. 5.1), posters, and furniture, as well as buildings. His artistic career to that date had been symptomatic of more general developments, starting with an immersion in Arts and Crafts ideals while present at the Darmstadt Artists' Colony, founded by the Grand Duke Ernst Ludwig von Hessen in 1899. Behrens, while one of the seven founding inmates of the colony (J.M. Olbrich was another), wrote of the 'physical pleasure existing in the useful and the suitable' and stressed the need for a new integration of the two. His own house of 1902 shows him to have passed through a dreamy Art Nouveau phase, with a rich fusion of curvilinear forms and melancholic emotions of the sort which appealed to an inward-looking frame of mind. Behrens's search for a genuine German art then seems to have taken him through a *rappel à l'ordre* which manifested itself in the stereometric and planar geometries of his Romanesque inspired buildings at the Oldenburg Exhibition of 1905. By the time he worked for the AEG, his outlook had matured considerably and his vocabulary began to exhibit overtly neo-classical characteristics. Like Muthesius, Behrens sensed in Schinkel a combination of nationalist and idealistic associations suitable to his own task of formulating an imagery for the industrial élite. Here it has to be said he was fortunate in the attention and interest of Emil Rathenau as his chief AEG patron, for here was a man who combined cultural and technical interests in a single outlook.

Both Rathenau and Behrens felt that industrial tasks must be seen as the essential cultural ones of the time. The factory thus took on a far greater significance than it had usually possessed. Behrens realized that his client required impressive and cultivated looking buildings in the grand manner. Many of the factories and warehouses he designed for the AEG between 1908 and 1914 were ingenious fusions of abstracted Classical vocabulary and straightforward structural skeletons. The Berlin Turbinenfabrik of 1908 (fig. 5.2), for example, had the character of a temple dedicated to some industrial cult. The colossal turbines had to be lifted and moved from one end of the hall to the other while work was done on them, a process requiring an uninterrupted central aisle and an overhead moving gantry. Behrens's solution was to make the whole building a series of elegant, parallel two-sided cranes meeting at the peak of the roof. There was a grand, even ennobling character to the whole, and effects of visual lightness and massiveness were cleverly orchestrated to emphasize the overall lines. Had Behrens been a mere functionalist he might simply have optimized the functions and clothed the resulting structure in cheap materials without concern for proportion, let alone the impact of forms on the spirit;

had he been an 'expressionist' (like his contemporary Hans Poelzig in Breslau) he might have sought to dramatize the process of movement with a highly sculptural formal arrangement. But Behrens steered a way between these approaches in a search for a sober and, indeed, 'typical' form in the 'Classical/German spirit'. The supports and profile were adjusted to give a dignified rhythm and impression of repose; the gantry shape was blended ingeniously with the image of a Classical pediment; and the repeated exposed steel supports along the side elevations were given the character of a *travée* of Classical supports. Meanwhile the vast areas of glass in the main façade were laid flush with the pediment plane, so as to give the sense of a thin screen hovering in front of the massive corner quoins in concrete, which provided a suitable sense of structural stability to the eye.

Behrens's intuition for primary geometrical volumes in the Classical tradition (perhaps enhanced by his reading of formalist art historians like Heinrich Wölfflin) allowed him to bring a sense of proportion to numerous other categories of industrial structure. His design for a gasworks at Frankfurt of 1911 (fig. 5.3), for example, was composed of simple cylinders in dramatic juxtaposition. Indeed engineering aesthetics was a topic of recurrent interest to the Deutscher Werkbund, and it was not unusual for debates to be held comparing the relative aesthetic value of one signal gantry over another. The Deutscher Werkbund *Jahrbuchs* of 1913–14 illustrated battleships and grain silos as examples of designs combining functional logic with impressive qualities of abstract form (fig. 5.4).

In the 1913 *Jahrbuch* there was an article entitled 'The Development of Modern Industrial Architecture' by a young architect called Walter Gropius who praised the AEG factories as 'monuments of sovereign strength, commanding their surroundings with truly Classical grandeur', and spoke too of:

> ... the compelling monumentality of the Canadian and American grain silos ... and the totally modern workshops of the North American firms which bear comparison with the buildings of Ancient Egypt ...

He further praised the 'natural feeling for large compact forms, fresh and intact' and suggested that modern European architects might:

> ... take this as a valuable hint and refuse to pay any more heed to fits of historical nostalgia or other intellectual considerations ... which stand in the way of true artistic naïveté.

But Gropius went further still and claimed that the spirit of modern times required its own expression in a new style characterized by 'exactly stamped form ... clear contrasts, the ordering of members ... unity of form and colour ...', which he argued was appropriate to 'the energy and economics of public life'. Among those 'to take this valuable hint' was the young Charles Edouard Jeanneret (later Le Corbusier), who worked in Behrens's office in 1910 and remained in touch with German developments after that date.

It is instructive to contrast Behrens's gas works design with Hans Poelzig's for a water tower in Breslau in 1908, or with the same architect's design for a chemical works at Luban in 1911 (fig. 5.5), as this gives some sense what is meant by the 'Expressionist Wing' of the Werkbund. 'Expressionism' is a blurred term at best, and has little validity as a stylistic label. In this context of industrial design it refers to an attitude

in which sobriety and stability were eschewed in favour of restless, dynamic, and highly emotive forms. In fact the functional rationale behind Poelzig's designs was every bit as tight as that governing Behrens's, but the emphasis of formal expression was different. The roots of Expressionist vocabulary lie in this case in Art Nouveau, and it was Art Nouveau with its emphasis on individualism which most disturbed Muthesius. Indeed, at the Werkbund Congress of 1914 there was a celebrated debate between Henry van de Velde and Muthesius which tended to be framed in terms of the individualist outlook versus the philosophy of 'the typical'. Ultimately, such a discussion was one over appropriateness: what should the 'true' modern style be like?

Behrens's office, with its stress on all aspects of industrial design, was the training ground of a number of artists who were to inherit the tensions and

5.3 (*left*) Peter Behrens, gasworks, Frankfurt, 1911.

5.4 (*below left*) American grain silos, from *Deutscher Werkbund Jahrbuch*, 1913.

5.5 (*below*) Hans Poelzig, chemical factory, Luban, 1911.

successes of the pre-1914 period and to contribute to the extremely creative phase of the 1920s. Chief among these were the future Le Corbusier, Mies van der Rohe and Walter Gropius himself; indeed, these three may have 'overlapped' briefly in 1910. Gropius was born in 1884 and trained at the Charlottenburg Hochschule and Munich; his earliest designs for housing show a marked concentration on simple volumes and shapes. In 1911, after a thorough training in Behrens's office, he received his own commission to redesign the Fagus shoe-last factory at Alfeld (fig. 5.6). This belonged to Karl Benscheidt, who had already overseen a design by one Eduard Werner, an industrial architect from Hanover. The plan and elevations had been fixed and had even passed the local building authorities when Gropius was brought in to provide improvements to the external treatment. He modified the interior suggestions of his predecessor only slightly. It is the visual treatment of the workshop block which is significant in the creation of an industrial style, indeed in the formation of a 'factory aesthetic' which would eventually influence the universal machine style of a decade later. The devices of the external wrapping of the building are intelligent adaptations of Behrens, but the effect is absolutely different, as here everything conspires to give a sense of weightlessness and transparency rather than of mass. The wall-piers have been recessed so that the glazing appears to float as a transparent skin. Window bars, brick mouldings and joints reinforce the main proportions, and the image successfully incorporates a symbolic reaction to mechanization as an idea. To be sure, Gropius seems to have grasped the essential mood of the programme of his client, which included the provision of the latest that modern American industrial planning could offer: good ventilation, a logical open plan for machine serial production, well-lit spaces for draughtsmen and managers to go about their business of helping improve the health of those with foot problems.

However, it is interesting to contrast the 'Fagus-werk' with Albert Kahn's contemporary Ford factory designs in Detroit (mentioned in Chapter 3 in connection with reinforced-concrete construction). These factories were built around naked commercial and functional considerations. Admittedly due attention was given to the relationship of solids and voids, but it does not seem to have occurred to either Kahn or Ford that their buildings might be the 'index to the spirit of the new times'! In Germany the attitude to factory design was quite different, and clothed in philosophical speculation. As Gropius was to put the matter after the war: his architecture was an attempt, not only at accommodating the functions of the modern world, but at symbolizing that world as well.

In 1914 Gropius and Adolf Meyer were given the important task of designing the Werkbund pavilion for the Cologne exhibition. This was to house objects of German industrial design in a framework which should itself be an exemplary demonstration of Werkbund ideals. The largest function was the Machine Hall, placed on the main axis and expressed as a simple, neo-classical railway shed. This was approached through a courtyard enclosed by a symmetrical entrance pavilion flanked by open glazed staircases. The symmetry of the scheme was broken by the 'Deutzer Gasmotoren' pavilion (fig. 5.8), attached to the rear end of the machine hall on the cross axis. The discipline of the plan (fig. 5.7) recalled Beaux-Arts' precedents, and the arrangement had a marked processional character.

The forms rising into space above this plan, however, had no obvious historical precedent. The stripped brick volumes of the entrance block with overhanging roofs and sharp horizontal parapets were perhaps an echo of Wright in a formal mood. But the glazed wrapping to the rear and the transparent, streamlined stair-towers (with the spiral stairs visible inside them) were stunning inventions which created, not only a sense of weightlessness and space, but also an aura of crisp and disciplined machinery, of elegant and dignified industrial control. Here there was another quasi-sacral building dedicated to the values of Germany's industrial élite, and it was typical of the mood and taste of the whole, that a reclining Classical

5.6 (*left*) Walter Gropius and Adolf Meyer, shoe-last factory. Alfeld, 1911, general view showing glass curtain wall.

5.7 (*right*) Walter Gropius, Werkbund Pavilion, Cologne, 1914, plan.

5.8 (*below*) Walter Gropius, Werkbund Pavilion, Cologne, 1914, view showing glass stairs and gas motor pavilion in far background.

OVERLEAF

5.9 Walter Gropius, Werkbund Pavilion, Cologne, 1914, rear view showing Deutzer Gasmotoren Pavilion, right, and Maschinen Halle, left.

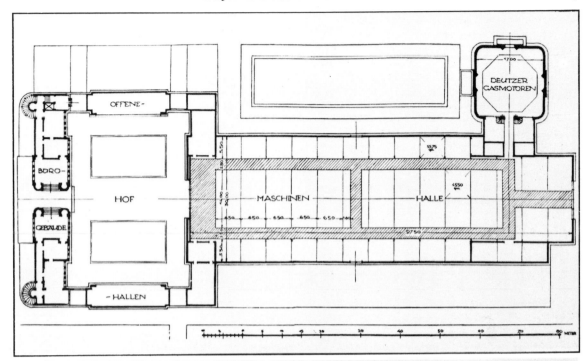

statue should have been placed at the end of a pool leading up to the Deutzer Pavilion preceding the 'sacral object': a gas turbine engine (fig. 5.9).

This transparent pavilion may well have been inspired by an even more fantastic evocation of industrialization, Bruno Taut's steel industry pavilion at the Leipzig fair of 1913 (fig. 5.10). This had been built in the form of a ziggurat surmounted by a sphere, the whole being constructed out of an elegant frame in the material the pavilion had been built to celebrate and advertise. Taut's work had more affinities with the 'Expressionist' wing of the Werkbund than with Gropius, and was pervaded by a mystical, if not Utopian, spirit somewhat at odds with the restraint and sobriety, the beliefs in standardization and normative solutions, of men like Behrens and Muthesius. Taut's design for the Glass Pavilion at Cologne (fig. 5.11) made the contrast even more clear. This was in the form of a sort of industrial mausoleum – a geodesic dome of different coloured glass standing on a high plinth reached by a grand flight of stairs. The interior was dappled with different coloured patches of light which reflected off glass brick stair-risers and slender steel surfaces, and were accentuated by moving lenses. There was all the craft here, and something of the atmosphere, of an elaborately chased, carefully made piece of Art Nouveau tableware. But the *fin de siècle* qualities were transcended by a Utopian, forward-looking aspiration: indeed the poet and fantastic novelist Paul Scheerbart, who saw glass as the material of the future, surely influenced Taut's imagery.

> We live for the most part in closed rooms. These form the environment from which our culture grows. Our culture is to a certain extent the product of our architecture. If we want our culture to rise to a higher level, we are obliged, for better or for worse, to change our architecture. And this only becomes possible if we take away the closed character from the rooms in which we live. We can only do that by introducing glass architecture, which lets in the light of the sun, the moon and the stars, not merely through a few windows, but through every possible wall, which will be made entirely of glass – of coloured glass. The new environment which we thus create must bring us a new culture.

It scarcely needs emphasizing that Gropius and Taut, each in his own way, was attempting to celebrate industrialization, to reveal its capacity for poetry, and to suggest its genuine, progressive cultural potential. It was to be the Gropius outlook and vocabulary, however, with the inherent suggestion that rectan-

5.10 (*left*) Bruno Taut, Steel Pavilion, Leipzig, 1913.

5.11 (*below left*) Bruno Taut, Glass Pavilion, Cologne, 1914.

gularity and transparency were appropriate visual features of a new industrial architectonic order, which would be more influential. However, before these fragmentary suggestions of Gropius's pre-war buildings could congeal as the mature style of the twenties, other catalysts would be necessary: particularly the spatial and formal devices of abstract art, and the poetic attitudes of Futurism, which would themselves be fused in the philosophy and form of De Stijl at the end of the 1910s.

Futurism was a poetic movement before it became a movement in painting and sculpture, and an architectural movement in the limited sense that there was a Futurist Manifesto of architecture of 1914, and an architect, Sant' Elia, whose drawings attempted to translate Futurist ideals into a new urban imagery – 'La Città Nuova' ('The New City'). The Foundation Manifesto of Futurism was published in *Le Figaro* of 20 February 1909, and was the creation of the poet Tommaso Filippo Marinetti. The Manifesto was a lively attack on traditionalism in culture, and championed an expression nourished by contemporary forces and the poetic sensations released by a new industrial environment. Anarchist in inspiration, the Futurist outlook had no particular political affiliation, but was in favour of revolutionary change, speed, dynamism of all sorts, and an aggressive adulation of the machine. Typically, the Foundation Manifesto suggested the destruction of museums and academies; the vitality of contemporary life was opposed to the tiredness of inherited art forms:

> We declare that the splendour of the world has been enriched by a new beauty – the beauty of speed. A racing car with its bonnet draped with exhaust pipes, like fire-breathing serpents – a roaring racing car, rattling along like a machine gun, is more beautiful than the winged Victory of Samothrace.

Of course Marinetti's writing did belong to an aesthetic tradition, one stretching back through French Symbolism to Baudelaire, the 'poet of modern life'. In a sense, then, the aim was to make the frontiers of art broader and more inclusive, rather than to do away with them altogether. The typical subject-matter of Futurism was the modern metropolis, seen as a sort of collective expression of the forces of society.

> We will sing of the stirring of great crowds – workers, pleasure seekers, rioters – and the confused sea of colour and sound as revolution sweeps through a modern metropolis. We will sing the midnight fervour of arsenals and shipyards blazing with electric moons; insatiable stations swallowing the smoking serpents of their trains; factories hung from the clouds by the twisted threads of their smoke; bridges flashing like knives in the sun, giant gymnasts that leap over rivers; adventurous steamers that scent the horizon; deep-chested locomotives that paw the ground with their wheels, like stallions harnessed with steel tubing; the easy flight of aeroplanes, their propellers beating the wind like banners, with a sound like the applause of a mighty crowd.

The Futurist Manifestos of Painting (1910) and Sculpture (1912) attempted to extend Futurist sensibility still further. Dynamism was the shared central conception, and the early painters in the movement, among them Boccioni and Severini, attempted to translate the Futurist ethos not only by choosing such subjects as trains leaving stations, building sites on the edge of industrial cities, and strikes, but by treating these themes in a vital play of complementary colours, divisionist lighting effects and unstable diagonal compositions. In 1911 the devices of analytical Cubism

5.12 Umberto Boccioni, *States of Mind. The Farewells*, 1911. Oil on canvas, $27\frac{3}{4} \times 37\frac{7}{8}$in. (70.5 × 96.2cm.). New York, Museum of Modern Art, gift of Nelson A. Rockefeller.

began to be absorbed by the Futurist painters, with the result that fragmentation, interpenetrations of space and form, abstraction and elements of reality were incorporated. The Cubist device of showing different viewpoints of an object was co-opted to express duration and the different states of objects unfolding in their environment (fig. 5.12). This was a key element of Futurist doctrine, related no doubt to the artists' adulation of Henri Bergson's philosophical ideas on time and flux. Bergson emphasized the primacy of change in all reality and the role of intuition in perceiving it. Futurist painters far transcended any banal 'realism of contemporary appearances' by attempting to create *symbolic equivalents* to their excited state of mind when faced by entirely new stimuli like speed, artificial light, steel and fast car rides.

Futurist sculpture likewise opened up new expressive territory in an attempt at expressing 'the universal dynamism' – the flux of modern life. The Sculpture Manifesto announced that the basis of this new form would be 'architectonic':

> ... not only as a construction of masses, but also because the sculptural block will contain within itself architectonic elements from the sculptural environment in which the object exists.

Boccioni's drawing *Bottiglia + Tavola + Casseggiata* of 1912 seems to demonstrate this 'field' conception of space, and suggests how important transparency and the intersection of planes were as principles of Futurist composition. When he came to translate these ideas into sculpture, the artist had to adopt different techniques, obviously, and his *Bottle Unfolding in Space* (fig. 5.13) attempted to evoke the shifting energies of an object, its palpitation and movement in its surroundings. *Forms of Continuity in Space* – a dynamic human figure striding forward with flailing planes of bronze rushing from its edges – used the evanescent lighting effects of polished surfaces to evoke dynamism. However, the Sculpture Manifesto was in theory opposed to traditional hierarchies of material value (bronze, marble, etc.) and suggested (again, no doubt, following the juxtaposition of humble and heroic values in Cubism) the incorporation of new synthetics:

> Destroy the purely literary and traditional nobility of bronze and marble. Deny that only one material should be used exclusively for the whole of a sculptural construction. Affirm that even twenty different materials can join in one work to increase the scope of its plastic emotion. We enumerate some: glass, wood, iron, cement, hair, leather, cloth, electric light, etc.

Although there was not, properly speaking, a 'Futurist Architecture', there was a sort of Futurist manifesto on the subject. This was perhaps composed by Antonio Sant' Elia, a young architect, with the help of Marinetti. In its first version – known as the 'Messaggio' – it functioned as the introduction to a show of Sant' Elia's drawings of the Città Nuova in 1914 (fig. 5.14). Not surprisingly, this theoretical architecture was conceived as a direct expression of contemporary forces, and a dynamic celebration of the uprooted, anti-natural tendencies of the modern city.

> Such an architecture cannot be subject to any law of historical continuity. It must be new as our state of mind is new. . . . In modern life the process of consequential stylistic development comes to a halt. Architecture, exhausted by tradition, begins again, forcibly from the beginning.

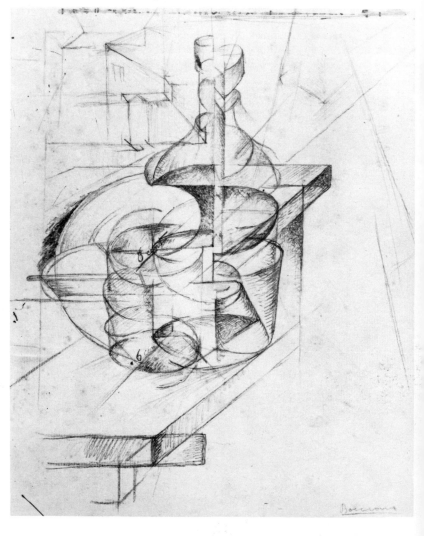

5.13 Umberto Boccioni, *Bottle Unfolding in Space*, 1912. Chalk drawing, $13\frac{1}{4} \times 9\frac{1}{2}$in. ($33.4 \times 23.9$cm.). Milan, Raccolta Bertarelli.

5.14 Antonio Sant' Elia, La Città Nuova, 1914, the central railway station and airport. Como, Museo Civico.

Thus the new architecture was to express 'new spiritual attitudes'; but it was also to find forms appropriate to new materials and means of construction:

> Calculations of the resistance of materials, the use of reinforced concrete and iron, exclude 'Architecture' as understood in the Classical and traditional sense. Modern structural materials and our scientific concepts absolutely do not lend themselves to the disciplines of historical styles, and are the chief cause of the grotesque aspect of modish constructions where we see the lightness and proud slenderness of girders, the slightness of reinforced concrete, bent to the heavy curve of the arch, aping the solidity of marble.

So far this was a negative definition which did not imply a precise form beyond saying that new buildings should be lighter and more open in expression, and no longer fettered by inappropriate inherited ideas. Later in the 'Messaggio', a clearer idea was given of the *style* of this new expression of the times:

> We must invent and rebuild *ex novo* our Modern City like an immense and tumultuous shipyard, active, mobile and everywhere dynamic, and the modern building like a gigantic machine. Lifts must no longer hide away like solitary worms in the stairwells, but the stairs – now useless – must be abolished; and the lifts must swarm up the façades like serpents of glass and iron. The house of cement, iron and glass, without curved or painted ornament, rich only in the inherent beauty of its lines and modelling, extraordinarily brutish in its mechanical simplicity . . . must rise from the brink of a tumultuous abyss; the street itself will no longer lie like a door-mat at the level of the thresholds, but plunge stories deep into the earth, gathering up the traffic of the metropolis connected for necessary transfers to metal cat-walks and high-speed conveyor belts.
>
> For these reasons I insist that we must abolish the monumental and the decorative; that we must resolve the problem of modern architecture without cribbing photographs of China, Persia or Japan, not stultifying ourselves with Vitruvian rules, but with strokes of genius, equipped only with a scientific and technological culture; that everything must be revolutionized; that we must exploit our roofs and put our basements to work; depreciate the importance of façades; transfer questions of taste out of the field of petty mouldings, fiddling capitals and insignificant porticoes, into the vaster field of the grouping of masses on the grandest scale. . . .

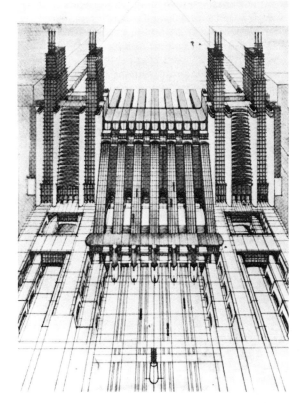

That the new architecture is the architecture of cold calculation, . . . boldness and simplicity; the architecture of reinforced concrete, iron, glass, textile fibres and all those replacements for wood, stone and brick that make for the attainment of maximum elasticity and lightness.

The 'Messaggio' then draws to a close with a plea for 'raw, naked and violently coloured materials'; with an affirmation that 'real architecture' transcends functionalism by being 'synthesis and expression'; with the suggestion that inspiration be found in 'the new mechanical world we have created, of which architecture must be the fairest expression, the fullest synthesis, the most effective artistic integration.'

It is probable that the 'Messaggio' was inspired by Sant' Elia's sketches rather than the other way round, but these were themselves intuitive responses to earlier Futurist attitudes. Although the theme of the exhibition was La Città Nuova, there was no overall plan, rather a collection of new building types and suggestions for such things as power stations (fig. 5.16), airports, airship hangars, multi-level stations, and stepped apartment buildings of a type called *Casa a Gradinate* (fig. 5.15). Although it was claimed that these buildings had no roots in tradition, the style of some of the sketches suggested a purification of Art Nouveau, and Sant' Elia had clearly been inspired – as Gropius, Behrens, and Muthesius had – by the bold and dramatic forms of nineteenth-century warehouses and bridges. It is possible too, that the theme of the multi-level city, like a colossal dynamic mechanism, may have been inspired by photographs or sections of New York City, showing multi-level elevated railways, and skyscrapers. Among Sant' Elia's jottings were some drawings which stripped buildings down to their most essential volumes of rectangles, cylinders, and cones. These were never as static in quality as Behrens's industrial designs of the same period, but they were a reminder that the Futurists, like the German architects, felt that pure forms and crisp straight lines were in some sense appropriate to mechanization. The Futurist Manifesto of sculpture had asserted that:

> The straight line will be alive and palpitating; will lend itself to all the expressive necessities of our material, and its basic severity will be a symbol of

the metallic severity of the lines of modern machinery.

Sant' Elia died in the war, but his ideas, and some of his images, lived on in avant-garde circles in Holland, Russia, Germany, and France. The importance of Futurism in the context of the history of modern architecture is clear: it pulled together a collection of progressivist attitudes, anti-traditional positions and tendencies towards abstract form, with the celebration of modern materials, and an indulgence in mechanical analogies. The contrast between the dynamic and anarchical values of Futurism and the more stolid, organized thought of the Deutscher Werkbund is obvious: but both movements rested on the central assumption that the spirit of the times was inevitably tied to the evolution of mechanization, and that an authentic modern architecture must take this into account in its functions, its methods of construction, its aesthetics, and its symbolic forms.

5.15 (*left*) Antonio Sant' Elia, *Casa a Gradinate*, 1914. Como, Museo Civico.

5.16 (*above*) Antonio Sant' Elia, power station, 1913. Como, Museo Civico.

6. The Architectural System of Frank Lloyd Wright

Radical though it may be, the work here illustrated is dedicated to a cause conservative in the best sense of the word. At no point does it involve denial of the elemental law and order inherent in all great architecture, rather it is a declaration of love for the spirit of that law and order, and a reverential recognition of the elements that made its ancient letter in its time vital and beautiful.

F. Lloyd Wright, 1908

Occasionally a single artist emerges who so profoundly reorganizes the basic assumptions of a period that he deserves to be considered in isolation. The creations of such individuals are marked by an extraordinary consistency and integrity traceable to both a mastery of means and a capacity to give an idealistic world view a deep expression. The solutions embodied in their work seem to solve problems that are relevant far beyond their particular circumstances. Whether they intend to or not, artists with such charisma become the founders of new traditions. In the formation of modern architecture two figures of this imaginative and intellectual calibre obviously stand out: Le Corbusier and Frank Lloyd Wright.

Frank Lloyd Wright's architecture has occupied a curious position in the histories of modern design. He has been portrayed as one of the first architects to break with eclecticism and to found a new style based on a spatial conception of interpenetrating planes and abstract masses, which (the story runs) then evolved, especially through its influence on Dutch developments, into the International Style. In this view, Wright's scattered remarks on the relevance of machine production to architecture are to be taken as evidence of his 'forward-looking' stance. But there is another version of Wright which emphasizes his roots in American social ideals and plays up his regionalist character and Arts and Crafts allegiances. In this scenario he emerges as a traditionalist intent on preserving the values of an individualist yet democratic frontier America against the onslaughts of mechanization. Both views contain some truth – and the very

fact that so much can be seen in the work and thought of a single artist should alert us to possible polarities in a single outlook. The emphasis of this chapter will be on the way this outlook was expressed in Wright's forms. It will be concerned with the way in which a mythical and ideal view of society was condensed in an architecture based on intuitive rules that was still capable of a varied and rich expression.

Wright was born in 1867. His father was a preacher and his mother held the fervent belief that her son would be a great architect. His parents eventually separated, and it is arguable that Wright's later obsession with the expression of idealized family relationships may have owed something, in a compensatory way, to the effect of an unhappy and uprooted home life on a sensitive nature. A strong early influence was the experience of working on his uncle's farm in Wisconsin: Wright later recalled how he would fix his attention on a tree, a hill, or a flower and wander off into reveries of abstract forms and shapes. Another crucial formative influence was some 'Froebel' blocks which his mother acquired for him at the Philadelphia exhibition of 1879 (fig. 6.9). Wright derived great delight from arranging these simple geometrical forms into formal patterns matching his intuitive compositional sense. It was part of the Froebel method that a configuration should be linked to a cosmic theme. The architect's later formal strategies in design, and his belief in the universality of fundamental geometrical forms may be traced in part to these early experiences.

Wright's architectural training was far from ortho-

dox. He began by studying engineering in 1885 at the University of Wisconsin but did not stay the course. Instead he moved to Chicago where he worked in the office of Joseph Lyman Silsbee, a designer of suburban houses. Here he learned much about the basic business of domestic design and immersed himself in the prevalent modes of suburban architecture. In 1887 Wright moved on to work for Louis Sullivan who, at the time, was occupied with evolving the principles and forms of an organic architecture, especially for the design of skyscrapers. As was suggested in an earlier chapter, Sullivan was an idealist who believed that the architect in the Midwest had a unique opportunity to form the images of a culture, uncluttered by imported and foreign forms, yet founded upon the ancient principles of architecture. His frequent use of organic analogies in his writings, building forms and ornamental designs was the outward expression of a belief

6.1 (*above*) Frank Lloyd
Wright, Winslow House,
River Forest, near
Chicago, Illinois, 1893;
the emergence of a clear
tripartite division in the
façade. (For plan see fig.
6.10.)

6.2 (*left*) Frank Lloyd
Wright, Winslow House,
River Forest, Illinois,
1893, rear view.

in the roots of architecture and society in a natural order. By a feat of visionary abstraction the artist was to dig below the surface of his society and see the inner meaning of human institutions, then give them an appropriate form. He was obsessed with the idea that the architect was specially endowed with the gift of prophesying the 'true' form of democracy.

Much of this Wright absorbed and eventually elaborated in his own way but in the realm of the individual family dwelling. He was quickly given much responsibility in the office but broke away after a period of about five years to set up his own practice in his studio alongside his home in Oak Park, a suburb of Chicago. His own house, designed when he was 22, gives some idea of his formative period. Shingle Style influences stemming from Silsbee were controlled by a strong formal discipline; elements like the porch and the overhanging roof were intrinsic to the Chicago suburban vernacular, being sensible ways of dealing with the extremes of climate and of linking house to garden; the focal position of the hearth was another traditional feature of the American home, which Wright was gradually to infuse with his own meanings. But the spaces of the lower floor flowed into one another more than was usual in a design of this kind, and the whole form was ingeniously controlled by axes in such a way that there was the feeling of rotation about the central core. With hindsight, one may begin to grasp here certain underlying tendencies which were to become clearer later on.

Wright's breakthrough building was the Winslow House of 1893, built in River Forest, a suburb of Chicago near Oak Park. Mr. Winslow was a business-man who had recently moved to Chicago and who wanted a house devoid of frills, but with a solid elegance. The formality of the building is evident in the first view. The main façade (fig. 6.1) is entirely symmetrical about the front door, which is set into a stone panel brought forward slightly from the wall plane. The second level is set back and textured in dark terracotta, and by contrast with the light-coloured bricks of the lower storey this zone appears to recede. The composition is capped by a third element, also strongly horizontal in emphasis, an overhanging roof with deep eaves. The detail is crisp, the lines are sharp, the joints are clearly expressed; the form is sober and dignified, but not lacking in vitality.

At the front the chimney is visible above the centre of the house, and when one passes to the interior one comes face to face with a fireplace set back behind a sort of rood-screen: an image suggesting that the hearth be seen in quasi-sacral terms as the emblem of the morally upright home. Formally the hearth stands at the core of the dwelling and forces the visitor into a rotational sequence through the reception spaces,

culminating in the dining-room on the main axis to the rear, and expressed externally as an apsidal volume. The rear elevation lacks the coherence of the front as it presents an asymmetrical, rather sprawling arrangement of forms (fig. 6.2). It was typical of Wright's planning approach that he should have placed the master bedroom over the most formal room below – the dining-room – and on the same axis. To the back end of the site, beyond the *porte-cochère*, is a little stable restating the vocabulary of the main house in miniature. It was here that Mr. Winslow and Wright together published a limited edition of exquisitely printed and illustrated volumes of William Channing Gannett's *House Beautiful*. The themes of this book have some bearing on Wright's own attitudes to the home, which he seems to have regarded as an almost sacred institution, requiring a noble and formal architectural treatment. The sense of the dwelling as a moral and religious influence was embedded in the culture in which Wright worked, but probably had an extra poignant and personal relevance to him. Norris Kelly Smith has even gone so far as to claim that the combination of formality and informality in Wright's house designs be read as an institutional metaphor expressing the artist's vision of the nature of freedom and dependence intrinsic to family life.

But themes on their own do not make an architecture without forms. What made the Winslow House so remarkable was the way it combined influences, yet transcended them, so implying the ingredients of Wright's own style. Silsbee was left far behind; the Classical tradition was raided for its axial control, the Shingle Style for its rotating plans; Sullivan's nature abstraction was reinterpreted, as was the master's intuition that buildings should have a base, a middle, and a head (also an idea with Classical overtones – the column with base, shaft, and capital). However, Wright's forms probed beyond inherited schemata to an instinctive sense of the order in nature, as one commentator well understood:

... it is the broadest, most satisfying thing that he has done. ... Upon the chosen site, nature has been at work for years, building the wonderful elm – and the character of the house was somewhat determined by the character of this tree. The sympathy that has been cultivated between them is felt by the cultivated and the uncultivated ... the impression conveyed by the exterior is the impression conveyed by the elm ... a certain simple power of an organic nature that seems to have as much right to its place and is as much part of the site as the tree. The analogy begins there and continues, for the details of the house are as much in their place and as constant in themselves and in relation to each other as the whole house is to its surroundings. . . . The architect shows his sympathy with nature.

This critic might have gone further in his suggestions of analogies with nature. The metaphor of the tree was to become a central one in Wright's thought, with implications of order and rootedness yet a capacity for growth and change. The tripartite scheme of roots, trunk, and branches was in turn to infiltrate his formal arrangements. At Winslow House the triple division of base, middle, and overhanging roof was spelled out with unprecedented clarity.

Without clients there would be no architecture and it is intriguing to speculate just what it was about Wright's buildings which brought him over a hundred commissions in the ensuing fifteen years. At the time Chicago was developing rapidly and so were its suburbs. These formed prosperous middle-class communities of new money, but, on the whole, conservative values. Many of Wright's clients were self-made men whom the architect himself described as having 'unspoiled instincts and untainted ideals'. Leonard K. Eaton more recently attempted to characterize them as 'outwardly conventional [but tending] to possess a streak of artistic or technological interest which predisposed them to accept new and radical solutions to the architectural problem of the dwelling house.' Moreover, Wright's clients wanted value for money and his was an architecture devoid of the elaborate trappings typical of much late nineteenth-century domestic design in the area. His plans were logical and well worked out to match each client's requirements, and were fitted to their sites so as to make the most of the small rectangular lots typically available. Considerable attention was devoted to the design of hot and cold water systems, and a crude form of air-conditioning was sometimes incorporated. In turn, this was an architect who liked to oversee building work closely and to supervise the very details of his designs.

However, one suspects that the appeal went deeper than just these pragmatic considerations. With their ample horizontal lines, their elegantly proportioned details, their built-in furniture and overhanging eaves, their ever-changing moods and qualities of space, Wright's designs possessed sobriety, fantasy, and a noble quality of scale. At the heart a broad fireplace finished with thin Roman bricks was usually set with logs on the very floor of the prairie, while in summer the stained-glass windows with their abstracted vegetal forms let the changing light dapple the interiors. The Wrightian prairie houses responded to the rituals and aspirations of a new suburban bourgeoisie (dinner parties and the like) but also evolved a traditional image of the American home. In a sense, the dwellings helped an emergent class to find its own identity.

The path from the Winslow House to the fully developed type of the 'Prairie House', nearly a decade later, was not straightforward. It was a process of endless experiment in which each new task allowed the extension and refinement of principles. Wright's domestic ideas were obviously stamped with Arts and Crafts values of the sort which encouraged restrained simplicity, the honest and direct use of materials, the integration of the building with nature, the unification of fixtures and fittings, and the expression of an elevated moral ideal. But he set out to reinterpret these premisses radically. He was more concerned with mechanization than most of his predecessors and contemporaries within the Arts and Crafts tradition. In 1901, in a paper entitled 'The Art and Craft of the Machine', Wright explained that simple geometrical forms could most easily be turned out by machine saws, and suggested that the architect must remain open to the tremors of a new mechanized age. By this he intended to imply not that the machine should be celebrated directly in mechanical analogies or images, but that industrialization be understood as a means to the larger end of providing a decent and uplifting environment for new patterns of life.

It was Japanese architecture which helped Wright achieve his synthesis. He did not visit the country until 1905, but long before that he had studied Oriental examples in books and in representations in Japanese prints (fig. 6.11). Evidently he admired the refined proportions, the exquisite carpentry, the use of humble materials, and the subtle placement in nature. Moreover, this was an architecture which modulated space and charged it with a spiritual character: the opposite, in his mind, of the Renaissance tendency to put up walls around box-like closed rooms and to decorate them with ornament. Wright was seeking an integral three-dimensional expression in which the exterior would convey interior volumes, and in which human scale would permeate all the parts. Moreover, Japanese prints – aside from their representation of architecture – suggested a language of shape and colour directly attuned to the feelings (rather as the Froebel blocks had done in earlier life). In other words, the prints provided further lessons in *abstraction*: they gave Wright deeper insight into the intuitive apprehension of 'higher' spiritual values.

More than that, the prints encouraged Wright to try and formulate a sort of ideal type for the dwelling above the particulars of any one case; Sullivan had tried something similar for the skyscraper, a formulation 'so broad as to admit no exception'. For Wright the key phase of crystallization seems to have been around

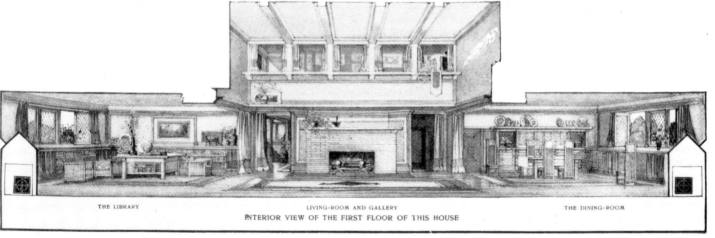

THE LIBRARY   LIVING-ROOM AND GALLERY   THE DINING-ROOM

INTERIOR VIEW OF THE FIRST FLOOR OF THIS HOUSE

6.3 Frank Lloyd Wright, project for 'A Home in a Prairie Town' (from *Ladies' Home Journal*, 1901). Exterior view and section.

1901 when he published his idea for 'A Home in a Prairie Town' in the *Ladies' Home Journal* (fig. 6.3). In retrospect, one may see this as a sort of 'theorem' summing up his discoveries to date, and laying the basis of a great period of creativity running from 1901 to 1910, and including such masterpieces as the Martin House, the Coonley House, the Robie House, the Larkin building, and the Unity Temple. The 'Home in a Prairie Town' was formed from long low horizontals stretching parallel to the flat land of the site. The sprawling roofs extended to the surroundings and drew the porches, the *porte-cochère* and the main volumes into a vital, asymmetrical unity. Windows were reduced to simple screens – there were few solid walls – and the spaces inside were linked together. Much of the furniture was built-in and the character of the interiors was commodious yet elegant. At the heart was the hearth and all the diverse spaces of the house were placed relative to this centripetal element. There

was still axial control and hierarchy, but the rotational and asymmetrical were combined with this in an architecture of sliding and overlapping planes enlivened by an intense rhythm.

The Ward Willitts House of 1902 (fig. 6.4), built in the North Chicago suburb of Highland Park, was one of the first in the mature phase of Wright's work. It stands back from the road, and the first impression is of low roofs extending behind the nearby trees and of hooded windows with dark chinks of glass set under eaves. The building is broken down into four main wings, so that the size is never overwhelming. One enters from a *porte-cochère* to the right of the building up some steps. Wright's houses usually had a 'path' running through them; in this case there is the instant choice of either turning back up the square spiral stairs to the bedroom level, or taking the most prominent route out of the vestibule by following the diagonal view into the living-room. This is on the main axis and is one and a

6.4 Frank Lloyd Wright,
Ward Willitts House,
Highland Park, near
Chicago, Illinois, 1902.

half storeys high. It has the chimney on its axis and vertical screen windows. The walls are plastered and smooth and there are slats of wood which bring down the scale and relate structure, furnishings and details to the main proportions. From this space one can see in turn along another diagonal into the dining-room, situated on a cross axis, with views on three sides into the garden; in the rear wing of the house is the kitchen.

Details such as grilles, brick textures in the fireplace, window mullions, even the leaded lines of the glass, bear the imprint of the same formal intelligence which conceived the whole, as if the smallest parts all had the generating idea implicit within them. Thus the abstract shapes of the plan, and the ornamentation of the windows, are sensed as variants on the same geometrical patterns. Indeed, the plan is almost a work of art in its own right and serves to illustrate Wright's compositional principles (fig. 6.5). There are primary and secondary axes which are reinforced by the centre lines of the roofs and the placement of the chimney, but many of the rooms are shifted on to subsidiary axes parallel to the main ones. The result is a sort of 'pin-wheel' rotation, experienced in three dimensions as a spatial tension which varies as one moves through the interior spaces. Parts and whole are held in a vital equilibrium. To Wright this dynamism was perhaps equivalent to the life force he sensed in nature: it gave his dwellings something of the quality of a spatial music in which rhythm, movement, repetition, and variation of similar elements achieved moods and emotions of different pitch and intensity.

The Willitts House was an early experiment with Wright's recently conceived theories. In it he tried out the various pieces of his 'Prairie House Type'. Over twenty years later he looked back on this period and attempted to put in writing the guiding principles of his domestic designs.

First. To reduce the number of necessary parts of the house and the separate rooms to a minimum, and make all come together as enclosed space – so divided that light, air and vista permeated the whole with a sense of unity.

Second. To associate the building as a whole with its site by extension and emphasis of all the planes parallel to the ground, but keeping the floors off the best part of the site, thus leaving that better part for use in connection with the life of the house. Extended level planes were found useful in this connection.

Third. To eliminate the room as a box and the house as another by making all walls enclosing screens – the ceilings and floors and enclosing screens to flow into each other as one large enclosure of space, with inner subdivisions only. Make all house proportions more liberally human, with less wasted space in structure, and structure more appropriate to material, so the whole more liveable. Liberal is the best word. Extended straight lines or streamlines were useful in this.

Fourth. To get the unwholesome basement up out of the ground, entirely above it, as a low pedestal for the living-position of the home, making the foundation itself visible as a low masonry platform on which the building should stand.

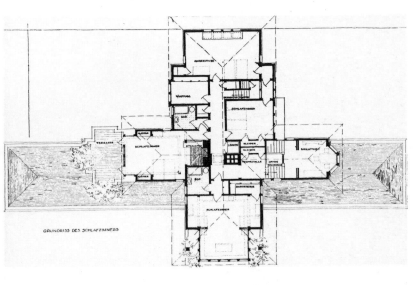

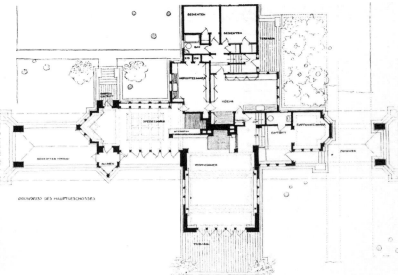

6.5 Frank Lloyd Wright, Ward Willitts House. Highland Park, Illinois, 1902, plans of ground level (*below*) and first floor (*above*). (From *Wasmuth* portfolio.)

materials in favour of mono materials so far as possible; to use no ornament that did not come out of the nature of the materials to make the whole building clearer and more expressive as a place to live in, and give the conception of the building appropriate revealing emphasis. Geometrical or straight lines were natural to the machinery at work in the building trades then, so the interiors took on this character naturally.

Seventh. To incorporate all heating, lighting, plumbing so that these systems became constituent parts of the building itself. These service features became architectural and in this attempt the ideal of an organic architecture was at work.

Eighth. To incorporate as organic architecture – as far as possible – furnishings, making them all one with the building and designing them in simple terms for machine work. Again all straight lines and rectangular forms.

Ninth. Eliminate the decorator. He was all curves and all efflorescence, if not all 'period.'

This is not to suggest that Wright's 'system' was rigid and prescribed. On the contrary it allowed him a firm base from which to experiment. Its flexibility was well demonstrated in his responses to different sizes of dwelling. Many of his early houses were modest, but as his reputation grew, so did the size of his commissions, to the point where he was soon building for the extremely wealthy. In the Martin House in Buffalo, New York (1904), he had to accommodate all the functions of a luxurious estate: stables, a guest-house, a large main dwelling, pergolas, gardens, a conservatory, etc. This is where Wright's method of organizing a plan with the help of a geometrical grid helped him to maintain uniform dimensions and to orchestrate axes and directions. The plan of the Martin House is a most sophisticated abstract pattern, not unlike a Mondrian painting, in which interior and exterior spaces, figure and ground, have equal value (fig. 7.3). In other words, the lawns, pergolas, and spaces between were organized by the same formal principles as those in the main buildings. The Coonley House of 1908 in Riverside (fig. 6.6) was another case where an entire wealthy precinct was unified but with full respect for different functional demands. These prairie house 'palaces' combined an aura of magnificence and dignity suitable to their patrons with subtle and refined control of detail and scale (fig. 6.7). In them Wright demonstrated that he could 'stretch' his vocabulary without loss of coherence.

Another major variant with which Wright had to cope was the site. Many of his early houses were situated on flat, rectangular lots of small to medium

Fifth. To harmonize all necessary openings to 'outside' or to 'inside' with good human proportions and make them occur naturally – singly or as a series in the scheme of the whole building. Usually they appeared as 'light-screens' instead of walls, because all the 'Architecture' of the house was chiefly the way these openings came in such walls as were grouped about the rooms as enclosing screens. The *room* as such was now the essential architectural expression, and there were to be no holes cut in walls as holes are cut in a box, because this was not in keeping with the ideal of 'plastic.' Cutting holes was violent.

Sixth. To eliminate combinations of different

size. But in 1904 he encountered an entirely new character of terrain when he was asked to design the small Glasner House in Glencoe on the North Shore of Chicago (fig. 6.8). The site was perched on the edge of a ravine which was heavily wooded. The habitual arrangement of a plinth-based, basementless house simply would not fit. Wright therefore planned the house so that the horizontal datum was supplied by the roofline; the forms of the building cascaded downwards from this line to meet the ravine at various levels. One entered on the upper level from the rear past the kitchen, to find the living/dining-room (combined) and master bedroom; the other rooms were placed downstairs. The volumes were anchored in place by three vertical elements, polygonal in plan: a library at one end, a tea-house over a bridge at the

other (not built), and a sewing room alongside the master bedroom (fig. 6.10).

As the living-room was at tree-top height and surrounded by bushes, flies and insects could be expected in the summer months. If all the windows had been made openable, they would have needed insect screens, which would have blocked the view. Wright solved the problem by cross-breeding his usual 'prairie house' fenestration with the well-tried 'Chicago window' (a central, fixed pane exclusively for light, and two small, side, vertical panes with screens exclusively for ventilation), which he stole from its usual commercial context; in this way it was possible to keep large areas free of insect meshes. The view through the long *travée* of windows with abstracted stained-glass tree motifs in them was quite magical. The interior was

6.6 Frank Lloyd Wright, Coonley House, Riverside, near Chicago, Illinois, 1908: the Prairie House on a palatial scale. (For plan see fig. 6.10.)

6.7 (*above right*) Frank Lloyd Wright, Coonley House, 1908, interior.

6.8 (*right*) Frank Lloyd Wright, Glasner House, Glencoe, Illinois, 1904, view through living-room windows. (For plan see fig. 6.10.)

rendered sensitive to every change of light and colour in the ravine (fig. 6.8). The resulting character was rustic rather than suburban, and was reinforced by the horizontal batten boarding of the lower portion, as well as the gazebo imagery of the polygonal volumes. The rich effect of a cantilevered roofline hovering above uneven terrain was one which Wright would employ again.

The artist's style may be thought of as a set of typical elements organized into wholes which themselves take on characteristic, generic patterns. A style based on principle will embody a sort of 'system' of building forms which combine and recombine according to grammatical and intuitive rules (figs. 6.9–11). Such a 'formula' is the opposite of a dry, repetitive 'cliché'; it is an abstraction which allows many creative possi-bilities around a few central themes. For such an artist – and Wright was such an artist – each new building task is a further opportunity to explore the ideal type (Plate 3). On occasion, an opportunity may arise which prompts the clarification of the artist's guiding vision.

Perhaps the Robie House of 1908 (fig. 6.12) was among the clearest of Wright's expressions of the Prairie House ideal; rather as the Villa Malcontenta was one of the most complete realizations of Palladio's dream of the villa. The client, Mr. Robie, was a bicycle manufacturer and only 27 years old when he employed Wright to design a home for him on an extremely tight corner site in South Chicago. He required a servants' wing and a billiard room, as well as the usual dining- and living-rooms, bedrooms, kitchen and bathrooms, and indicated that he wanted to 'see his neighbours on the side-walk without being seen' and that he would also like, if possible, views of a park situated a block away diagonally opposite. Wright interpreted these givens by translating them into form via his evolving vocabulary. In plan he arranged the building as two bands, sliding alongside one another, with some degree of overlap between (fig. 6.14). The smaller of these was to the rear of the site and contained the garage, boiler-room, laundry, and entrance on the ground floor, servants' rooms, the kitchen, and a guest-room on the first level. The other 'strip' was more prominent and arranged with chimney and stairs as a unit passing up through the centre. The billiard room and children's room were in the semi-basement, while the living- and dining-rooms were on the first level which became a sort of *piano nobile*. Indeed, it was not so much two rooms as one – a single space partially divided by the chimney-piece, detailed so as to give the effect that the ceiling lid hovered as a continuous plane from one end to the other (fig. 6.15). At the ends of this long space were window seats in prow-like protrusions, reinforcing the

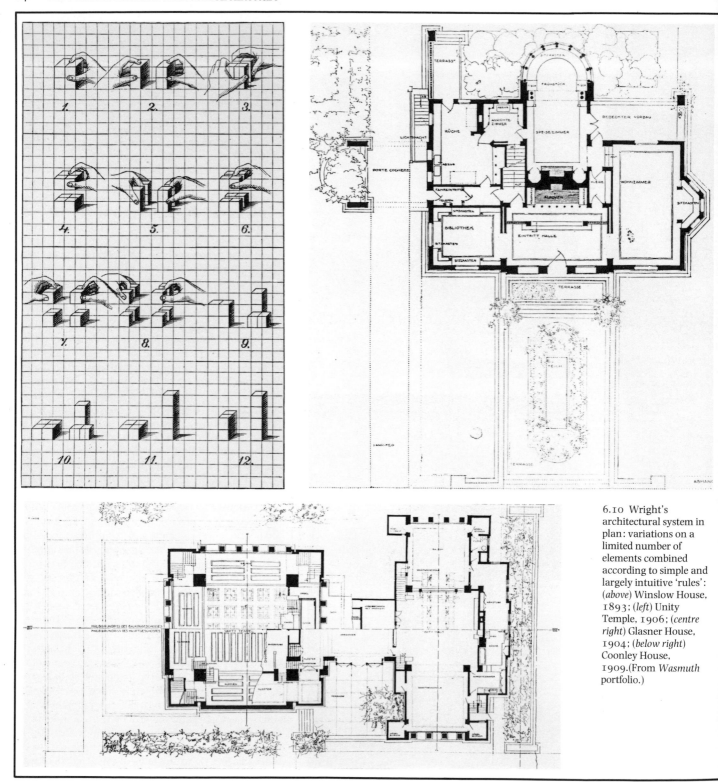

6.10 Wright's architectural system in plan: variations on a limited number of elements combined according to simple and largely intuitive 'rules': (*above*) Winslow House, 1893; (*left*) Unity Temple, 1906; (*centre right*) Glasner House, 1904; (*below right*) Coonley House, 1909. (From *Wasmuth* portfolio.)

6.9 (*far left*) The Froebel educational blocks.

6.11 (*above*) Japanese print of the kind which inspired Wright by their abstraction: Hukuju (fl. 1802–34), 'Monkey Bridge in Koshu Province', colour print, *c.* 1825. London, Victoria and Albert Museum.

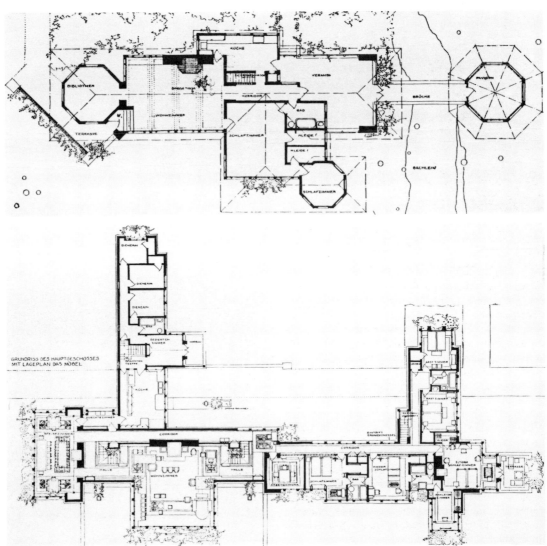

sense of the longitudinal axis, and echoing the triangular forms of the pitched roofs above. From this space, Mr. Robie could look down but not be seen, for the parapets and overhangs ensured visual protection.

The interior of the main space of the Robie House illustrates how ingeniously Wright could attune his customary solutions to a new individual case on formal, functional, structural, and symbolic levels simultaneously. Along each side of the main space was a rim set even lower than the rest of the ceiling. This reinforced the character of enclosure and accentuated the horizontality of the room. But it also served a number of functions because small 'Japanese' globe lights were attached to the rim, wires were set into it, and so were vents and spaces for moving air. The roof as a whole was an ingenious environmental device capable of being a heating cushion in winter or an extract flue in summer. The overhangs extended dramatically into the setting, supported by a steel beam from a shipyard in their broadest span. But again, this was not done for visual effect alone. The extending

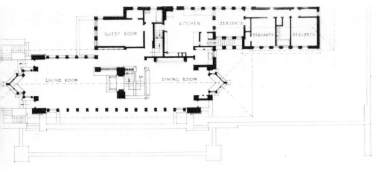

UPPER FLOOR

LOWER FLOOR

planes enhanced the feeling of shelter, protected the windows from rain, snow, and glare, released the edges of the building from any great structural load (permitting the extensive screen-windows) and mediated between inside and outside. The result of all these devices together was the antithesis of the closed box: it was as if the Winslow House of fifteen years before had been exploded outwards.

An architectural system requires a constant attitude in detailing as well as in the disposition of the main forms, and just as the overall 'formula' must adjust as each new unity is found, so typical details must be adjusted and transformed. In the Robie House Wright used elongated 'Roman' bricks laid with deep reveals of shadow in the joints so as to rhyme with the predominant horizontals (fig. 6.13). Another characteristic detail was the urn with a coping-stone top; in the Robie House these were made integral to the composition and adjusted to echo roof lines and parapets; yet another customary Wrightian element was the leaded, stained-glass window with motifs abstracted from natural forms; in the Robie House the patterns were attuned to the dominant horizontality, and to the triangular themes of the plan (fig. 6.16). Thus all the parts were drawn into a symphony – a master-work transcending merely period concerns.

6.12 (*above left*) Frank Lloyd Wright, Robie House, Chicago, 1908.

6.13 (*left*) Robie House, 1908, detail of urn.

6.14 (*above*) Robie House, Chicago, 1908, plans of main level and ground floor.

6.15 (*right*) Robie House, 1908, interior at main living/dining room level.

6.16 (*far right*) Robie House, 1908, detail of leaded glass window.

Alongside it, the designs of the so-called Prairie School – the followers of Wright – were mere shadows.

While most of Wright's works up to 1910 were houses, he also received commissions for other functions. His 'system' had then to stretch to accommodate new functional and expressive demands. In 1904, for example, the Larkin mail order company in Buffalo, New York, asked him to design an office building around their requirements. The site was by a railway and close to a gasworks. An inward-looking, hermetically sealed solution seemed advisable. From the Prairie House vocabulary Wright adopted the theme of trays slung from vertical piers, which he arranged around a high, top-lit atrium space. The stairs and ventilating equipment were set in tall towers to the corners from which the inner system was slung. These gave a massive and monumental character to the exterior and provided vertical emphases sufficient to unify the smaller parts and make the overall form coherent. With its severe, dominating silhouette, its strong axial character and its airy, nave-like interior space (fig. 7.4), it was perhaps understandable that the Larkin building should have been dubbed 'a cathedral of work' (it was inscribed with moralistic mottoes suggesting the religious value of labour), but the building also closely resembled Wright's designs for sideboards or other domestic furniture. Large or small, every design was handled according to consistent formal principles.

In 1906 Wright was commissioned to design a building with a truly sacral function. The Unitarians in Oak Park needed a new meeting-place. Evidently they thought of it in traditional terms involving a spire. But Wright insisted on redefining the programme and probing some of its fundamental meanings for a place of assembly. He decided to 'abolish in the art and craft of architecture, literature in any symbolic form whatsoever', and to provide a dignified space 'in which to study man himself for his God's sake'. He started with a *room* not unlike the most formal of his public reception or dining spaces in his houses – symmetrical, hieratic, focused by means of balconies on the pulpit:

> ... a noble room for worship in mind, and let that great room shape the whole edifice. Let the room inside be the architecture outside.

During the course of the design, Wright was intrigued by O. Kakuzo's *Book of Tea* in which the author referred to the rituals of the traditional Japanese tea ceremony, and described the space of the tea-house as 'the abode of vacancy'. For the main room of the Unity Temple Wright chose a square as a generator, perhaps because this was a centralized, focal and stable form with an inherent suggestion of wholeness and

6.17 Frank Lloyd Wright, Unity Temple, Oak Park, near Chicago, 1906, exterior view. The main space is to the left, the Sunday School to the right, the entrance zone between the two. (For plan see Fig. 6.10.)

unity. This he endowed with a numinous character through the subtle control of proportion and the filtering of light. The presence of this main volume was sensed directly on the exterior through the straightforward expression of the building's geometry and hierarchy of supports (fig. 6.17).

As well as a 'temple', the Unitarians required a space for children's Sunday School and a meeting-hall for get-togethers. These Wright placed in a lateral oblong, which he set with its short axis aligned to the square. The entrance hall to both spaces was placed as a 'neck' between them and was reached from the street up some steps on to a terrace. Over thirty-four studies were attempted before Wright was satisfied with the relationship between these main volumes. The power

element was flat and lifted free of the box beneath it, giving the impression of a sort of classical overhang at the top of the composition. The building had a clearly defined base as well, so that the tripartite 'grammar' of the elevation was once again employed. This fact was not lost on Wright's contemporaries, and one of his draughtsmen commented on the abstracted Classicism of the result, referring time and again to 'the temple'. It seems that Wright was fully aware of the Classical resonances in his design, and the suggestion has recently been made that he may have been influenced by the stripped Classical work of the early nineteenth-century German architect Schinkel, which was well known and liked in Chicago at the time. In Wright's mind, no doubt, Unity Temple was an exercise in 'first principles'.

Part of the richness of the Unity Temple form arose from the way the symmetrical spaces were in fact perceived on diagonals from the circuitous route passing through them; this was another consistent theme from the houses. The path to the interior passed through the hall, then down some steps into a half-level access cloister by which one negotiated the passage and the pulpit into the space under the side balconies. These were hung from four burly piers into which service ducts were run. The vitality of the interior space was created, in part, by the secondary rhythm of the half levels, and the character of the light filtering in through leaded screen-windows at cleres-tory level; these were detailed to give the impression that the slab was floating (fig. 6.18).

Thus the solution to the Unity Temple was found by the application of the principles Wright had been pursuing, and their reconsideration in the light of a sacred institution. He did not rely on a spurious symbolism, but on the direct impact of spaces, lit volumes, and forms suffused with a spiritual character. Whether Wright really regarded a 'church' as more sacred than a 'home' is, perhaps, open to question, but his response was to lend his domestic system an unusually hieratic, formal, and symmetrical grandeur. As in the Winslow House, Classical values were abstracted and transformed to the point where the architect's forms seemed to possess an almost natural character. This magnificent synthesis was a further reminder that Wright, for all his power of innovation, was a traditionalist interested in 'the elemental law and order inherent in all great architecture'.

In 1909 Wright left his wife to live with Mamah Borthwick Cheney, the wife of one of his clients. The following year he went with her to Europe for some months during which he assembled drawings of his past years of activity. These he published in the so-called *Wasmuth Volumes*. On his return to the United States, he withdrew from the framework of suburban

of the result lies in tense and elemental relationships and in the way the main themes are restated in all the smaller parts. Wright chose concrete as his building material because it was cheap and easy to use; but (as has been suggested) this was an extremely bold step for someone to take in 1906, especially for a religious building, the more so because he decided to leave the material bare on the exterior.

The main elements of vocabulary ingeniously controlled transitions in size between the overall volumes and the smaller parts, and recalled once again the typical elements of the Prairie House formula. They included corner piers (containing the stairs), walls, screen-windows, and thinner versions of the main piers to support the structure of the roof. This last

life and family responsibilities, to the Wisconsin countryside, where he built 'Taliesin', a house on the hill, in which the Prairie House system was further extended to meet the irregular levels of the land. This became his retreat, and his hymn to nature. He found himself increasingly divorced from the milieu in which he had first formed his architecture. In 1914, tragedy struck Taliesin when Wright's newly adopted family was massacred by a mad servant and the property was burned to the ground. The possible effects of the ensuing psychological disorientation on Wright's architecture are dealt with in a later chapter.

Thus by the outbreak of the First World War Wright had already created over a dozen masterpieces and had established an architectural language based on principles. Like his contemporaries in Europe, he had inherited the confusions of 'The Styles' and imbibed lessons from Viollet-le-Duc and the Arts and Crafts, as well as uniquely American influences, to formulate a grammar of design which far transcended the Chicago suburbs in its universal implications. His influence in America was already considerable, especially among those Midwestern followers of the so-called 'Prairie School'; some of these (one thinks particularly of Walter Burley Griffin) established worthwhile vocabularies of their own, which obviously bore the imprint of the master; but most produced pastiche. Wright's immediate influence was not restricted to America; the *Wasmuth Volumes*, and the occasional foreign visitor, ensured that the work also became known in Europe. This happened mainly through photographs and drawings. Thus a sort of 'mythological' version of Wright was created in various architects' minds, particularly in Holland, and was used to prop up a range of emergent theories and ideals in the general quest for a modern style.

6.18 Frank Lloyd Wright, Unity Temple, Oak Park, Illinois, 1906, interior.

7. Cubism and New Conceptions of Space

The new architecture is anti-cubic; that is, it does not seek to fix the various space cells together within a closed cube, but throws the functional space cells ... away from the centre ... towards the outside, whereby height, width, depth + time tend towards a wholly new plastic expression in open space. In this way architecture acquires a more or less floating aspect that, as it were, works against the gravitational forces of nature.

T. van Doesburg, 1924

If an architectural historian highly attuned to the significant traits of his own time had positioned himself in 1914 and looked back over the previous two decades in Western Europe and the United States, his main impression would have been of a rich and varied pluralism. In France, the United States, and England Beaux-Arts Classicism would have been seen extending its influence, alongside pockets of continued Medieval Revival; strands of National Romanticism linked to Arts and Crafts and Regionalist ideals would also have been prominent. Against this varied backdrop the innovations defined in earlier chapters – from Art Nouveau to Futurism, from Gaudí to Wright – would have stood out firmly. But even these 'modern' tendencies would have revealed a great diversity of approach.

Had the same historian positioned himself twenty years later and surveyed the scene of the preceding few decades, he might have been struck by the way the various pre-war strands of modern architecture tended to converge around 1920, culminating in the broadly shared qualities of the 'International Style'. Admittedly the historical landscape would have still contained major tributaries of revivalism, but these would have flowed with less force. Moreover, Art Deco and the various forms of Expressionism would have appeared as parallel movements of modern architecture, occasionally diverging from, occasionally overlapping with, the International Style.

Some of the elements which contributed to the synthesis of the post-war era have been singled out already: the very idea of a modern architecture;

Rationalist approaches to history and construction; visual and philosophical concerns with mechanization; attempts at distilling certain essentials of Classicism; moral yearnings towards honesty, integrity, and simplicity. However, without the influence of Cubism and Abstract art, the architecture of the twenties would probably have been very different. This was not a matter of architects lifting motifs from paintings and aping their forms, so much as it was a matter of infusing the entire three-dimensional anatomy of architecture with a geometrical and spatial character *analogous* to that first discovered in the illusionistic world behind the picture plane.

In fact the various paths from the discoveries of painters and sculptors to the vocabularies of architectural design were rarely straightforward. Aside from particular routes of influence from, say, Cubism to Russian geometrical abstraction to Constructivist design, or from Cubism to Purism to the architecture of Le Corbusier, it is possible to divine broad underlying areas of shared concern between the artists and architects of the avant-garde in the first part of this century. One finds the recurrent theme of purification of the means of expression through the device of abstraction. The emphasis on the underlying 'architectonic' order of the visual work of art is, in turn, often linked to a belief in 'higher', more spiritual meanings, transcending the mere reproduction of appearances. The rejection of traditional means of representation like perspective is in turn often linked to rediscoveries of 'primitive' and 'exotic' sources – African sculpture, Japanese prints, Oriental carpets. Considerable emotional investment is made in the idea of the creative individual preserving his authenticity in the face of the supposedly decaying forms of official, Academic and bourgeois culture.

Another feature of this intellectual scenario was the very idea of an avant-garde whose business was seen as the jettisoning of dead forms in a constant quest for innovation. Curiously though, the impetus towards permanent iconoclasm, accompanied by a contempt for the recent past, was often also linked to a generalized respect for far distant history. It was as though being 'modern' required that one should return to the fundamentals of one's art, and rethink it from the ground up. Moreover, the modern artist – as Kandinsky put the matter overtly in *Concerning the Spiritual in Art* (1912) – should function as a sort of high priest and prophet of a new culture. Once again one glimpses the progressivist notion of history, the pervasive belief in a *Zeitgeist* – the myth of the modern artist as someone who is supposed to make the inner meaning of his own times visible. Past styles were therefore, at least in theory, barriers against the deep mission of revealing abstract form in its universal character. It was as if the true modern style was to be the style to end all styles, as if it was supposed to be privy to some esperanto of expression, transcending countries and conventions, and rooted in central structures of the mind. The stripped white geometries of the modern movement, and the recurrent obsession with 'essentials' in surrounding polemics, can scarcely be understood apart from such trans-historical and pan-cultural aspirations.

It is ironical that rebellious avant-garde positions should have been influenced by scholars and historians of art. In the late nineteenth century, such writers as Heinrich Wölfflin and Konrad Fiedler had discussed style as if it could be defined in terms of dominant modes of spatial or formal patterning, and had gone so far as to suggest that such underlying visual structures were the key way in which past *Zeitgeists* had been expressed. The lesson for someone in the present who held a similar view of the relationship between culture and form was therefore obvious: he should seek the true sense of a modern style in some new spatial conception which (supposedly) gave direct expression to 'the spirit of modern times'.

Another strand contributing to the ideal of abstraction stemmed from late nineteenth-century Symbolist ideas and from the notion of 'empathy'. We have seen how August Endell in Munich could write of a 'new art' capable of expression without ancedote; at the turn of the century there were numerous other suggestions of a painting equivalent to music, and of a pure language of lines, shapes, volumes, colours, and

7.1 (*left*) Pablo Picasso, *L'Aficionado*, 1912. Oil on canvas, $52\frac{5}{8} \times 37\frac{7}{8}$ in. (134×81 cm.). Basle, Kunstmuseum.

7.2 (*right*) Piet Mondrian, *Composition in Blue, A.* Oil on canvas, $19\frac{3}{4} \times 17\frac{3}{8}$ in. (50×44 cm.). Otterlo, Rijksmuseum, Kröller-Müller.

7.3 (*below*) Frank Lloyd Wright, Martin Estate, Buffalo, New York, 1904, plan (from *Wasmuth* portfolio).

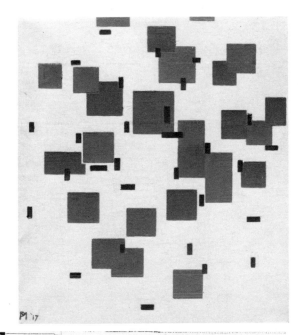

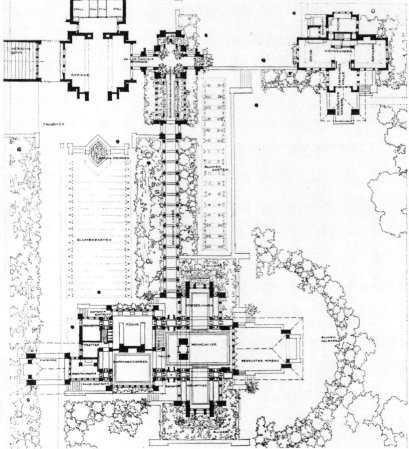

tones. This no doubt betokened a strong reaction against the moral and literary emphases of mid-nineteenth-century art. Even a champion of Classicism like Geoffrey Scott, in *The Architecture of Humanism* of 1914, could write of the direct impact on tactile sensibility of space, visual weight and tectonic pattern: 'Architecture directly and immediately perceived, is a combination of masses, of spaces and of lines.'

The influence of Cubism on architectural form was not direct, but through derivative artistic movements. In the crucial, formative stage between about 1907 and 1912, Pablo Picasso and Georges Braque, following certain hints in the late works of Cézanne and in Negro sculpture, developed a visual language blending abstraction with fragments of observed reality, allowing space and form to come to new terms, forcing heroic and humble subject-matter into new combinations (fig. 7.1). The effects of this visual revolution would be felt in sculpture, film, the graphic arts and, eventually, architecture. One crucial transition between Cubism and a more ordered vocabulary took place in France between 1912 and 1920 and culminated (as will be shown in the next chapter) in the doctrines and forms of Purism, then, eventually, in the architecture of Le Corbusier. This general development in which Cubist-derived forms were gradually simplified and infused with a machine-age content, would be repeated in Germany and Russia in the late 1910s and early 1920s (one thinks of the abstractions of Kasimir Malevich, Laszlo Moholy-Nagy and El Lissitzky and their eventual role as sources of architectural form), but only after the ground had been laid by the 'De Stijl' movement in Holland. This was founded in 1917 and brought together painters, sculptors, a furniture-maker, and architects in a loose affiliation of beliefs, and a broadly shared style of abstract and rectangular emphasis: chief among the painters were Theo van Doesburg and Piet Mondrian.

As early as 1907 Mondrian had already been tending towards abstraction in his paintings of trees and natural scenes. By 1914, with the help of Cubism, he had managed to simplify the language of painting to the point where he used combinations of vertical and horizontal lines; but these still referred, schematically, to observed phenomena. Increasingly, though, the elements of his paintings achieved their own autonomy, as Mondrian began to sense that a pure language of form, colour, and rhythm – a visual music in touch with the emotions – might be possible (fig. 7.2). His theosophical beliefs and his reading of Schoenmaekers's writings on 'spiritual mathematics' were certainly a stimulus here: the painter was in search of 'thought forms' to match his intuitions of a higher order transcending mere appearances. Indeed, the De Stijl movement as a whole – to which Mondrian would be loosely affiliated – would claim for abstract art a lofty role as a sort of tool of revelation.

It was Theo van Doesburg and Gerrit Rietveld who grasped most clearly the three-dimensional implications of such a geometrical abstraction. The general aim was not to decorate the modern building with painted murals, but to treat it as a sort of abstract sculpture, a 'total-work-of-art', an organism of colour, form, and intersecting planes. By 1918–20 Mondrian's and van Doesburg's paintings had become distillations of black, white, and primary colours and the simplest rectangular geometries, which made it all the easier to think of translating such qualities into the shapes of a functioning architecture, in which walls, floor planes, roofs, or windows might have analogous formal character to the flanges in the paintings. By 1923, van Doesburg was able to produce a remarkable set of models and diagrams for a house in which earlier De Stijl experiments were synthesized (fig. 7.12). The resulting order represented a complete break with the axial schemata of Beaux-Arts Classicism. Instead of simple symmetry, there was dynamic, asymmetrical balance; instead of voids set into solids, there were tense interactions of form and space; instead of closed forms, there were dynamic extensions of coloured planes into the surroundings.

The achievement of this novel 'spatial conception' was more than a three-dimensional projection of Mondrian's painting ideas, however; it reflected too the absorption of Frank Lloyd Wright's architectural ideas by the European avant-garde (fig. 7.3). These were known in Holland by 1910–11 through the superb plates of the *Wasmuth Volumes*, published in these years, and through the praise lavished on Wright by Hendrik Petrus Berlage, a sort of father-figure of modern architecture in Holland, whose bold and simple forms (e.g., the Amsterdam Stock Exchange of 1897–1904, fig. 7.5) bear some comparison with Mackintosh's or Richardson's. Berlage was deeply concerned with the problem of a genuine modern style, which he spoke of in terms of clear proportions, planar walls, and the primacy of space. It is not too surprising to discover how deeply he admired the architecture of Wright, which he had actually seen first-hand: this was his reaction to the Larkin building of 1904 (fig. 7.4):

> I came away with the conviction that I had seen a truly modern building, and filled with respect for a master who could create such a work, whose equal is yet to be found in Europe.

In other words, Berlage found in Wright qualities which corroborated his own ideals. Dutch 'Expressionists' – like Michel de Klerk and Piet Kramer – also found much to admire in his work that supported their own,

7.4 (*left*) Frank Lloyd
Wright, Larkin building,
Buffalo, New York,
1904, interior.

7.5 (*above
right*) Hendrik Petrus
Berlage, Stock
Exchange, Amsterdam,
1897–1904, view of
main hall.

7.6 (*right*) Michel de
Klerk, Zaanstraat
Housing, Amsterdam,
1917, the Post Office.

7.7 Rob van t'Hoff, villa at Huis ter Heide, 1916.

very different, aims. Even so idiosyncratic a building as de Klerk's Zaanstraat Post Office in Amsterdam of 1917, with its bizarre brick patterns, its humped roof profiles, and its textured tower, recalls the example of Wright in its horizontal dynamism, its layering of space, and its use of materials (fig. 7.6). In this case, it was, perhaps, the 'handicraft Wright', rather than the 'abstract Wright', who was being appreciated.

The generation of Gerrit Rietveld, Theo van Doesburg, and J. P. Oud, who were to contribute to 'De Stijl', and who rejected Expressionism as an outmoded manner from the era of individualism and handicraft, also claimed Wright as one of their guiding lights. They ignored his suburban and naturalistic imagery, and concentrated exclusively on the spatial character and the vocabulary of hovering and intersecting planes, which they perceived almost entirely divorced from the original social context. The fact that they knew Wright's work chiefly through drawings and photographs may have been important here, and it may be, as Banham has suggested, that this 'version' of Wright was partly created by the introduction to the second *Wasmuth* volume by C. R. Ashbee, who emphasized the architect's 'struggle for mastery over the machine'. The 'De Stijl version of Wright' was an oddly distorted but fruitful one, whose forms they believed symbolized the advance of machine civilization.

Holland had the benefit of peace between 1914 and 1918, and this allowed a gradual maturation of pre-war ideas such as was scarcely possible elsewhere in Europe. The fusion of Wrightian and Mondrianesque abstraction occurred in an atmosphere of continuous experimentation. Typical of this exploratory stage is the Villa at Huis ter Heide of 1916 by Rob van t'Hoff (fig. 7.7). This was flat-roofed, formed from simple rectangles and made from reinforced concrete; in some respects it was similar to Jeanneret's slightly earlier Dom-ino house projects. The influence of Wright was clear in the overhangs, the extending horizontals and the sliding volumes. In fact, van t'Hoff was one of the few European modern architects to have seen the American's work first-hand. There was little applied ornament: the main effects arose from the subtle division of masses and voids, the play of light and shade. Ideas which had permeated European and American avant-garde discussions just before the war were here able to find expression in an actual building.

J. P. Oud's project for seaside housing of 1917 (fig. 7.8) was also stripped to the most essential geometrical forms with flat roofs and a rhythm arising from repetition of similar parts. His scheme for a small factory of 1919 (fig. 7.9) attempted an inter-relationship of planes about the corner in an overlapping, asymmetrical fashion, but the effect was earth-bound and contrived in comparison to Wright's accomplished works of over a decade before. It would be some years before the full implications of an open-form, dynamic spatial conception would be sensed, then drawn together in three dimensions, in van Doesburg's aforementioned models, in the architectonic constructions of Malevich and Lissitzky, in the Schroeder House by Rietveld of 1924, in Friedrich Kiesler's extraordinary floating construction *Cité dans l'espace* of 1926, and eventually in Gropius's Bauhaus buildings at Dessau of the same year. Even Oud's remarkable housing at the Hook of Holland of 1924–28 relied on traditional planning devices of regular symmetry.

The period between the end of the war and the creation of these seminal works was characterized in Holland by an active exchange of ideas between the main artists of the De Stijl group, who were capable –

through their varied roots and experiences – of drawing on most strands of pre-war, avant-garde theory. De Stijl means simply The Style, or to be more precise *The* Style, for it was the common aim of all the participants to create a language of forms appropriate to contemporary realities, and free of the supposed bogus historical residues of nineteenth-century eclecticism. By 1917, it so happened, the influences of Wright and Mondrian had tended to foster a vocabulary in which simple geometrical forms, rectilinear grids, and intersecting planes were indeed part of a shared style; moreover, it was a style which seemed to have an almost universal application from painting to typography to sculpture to furniture design to architecture. Typically, the early polemics of De Stijl claimed for this coincidental and happy unity of aim an almost divine sanction, as if the *Zeitgeist* of the modern

7.8 J. P. Oud, 'Strand boulevard' or seaside housing project, 1917.

7.9 J. P. Oud, project for a factory, 1919.

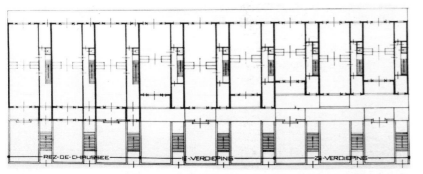

era had singled out a group of men in Holland for some epic intervention. Thus the emergent shared vocabulary was claimed as the most true one for the times and clothed in a moral rectitude and Utopian sentiment which contrasted it with the 'archaistic confusion' of 'modern baroque' (i.e., the sort of husky brick 'Expressionism' of Kramer and de Klerk). By 1920 De Stijl had succeeded in drawing together the devices of abstract art with a multi-layered content including Futurist ideals, the spiritualism of Mondrian, the drive towards simple and typical forms espoused by Gropius in the pre-war years, and a Utopian slant that took these forms to be appropriate to the social emancipation of the post-war era. There is here a loose parallel to the Parisian development of Purism in the same period, where a *rappel à l'ordre* also succeeded in drawing together the Cubist tradition with a language of symbolic forms felt to be appropriate to the 'machine age'; the difference, obviously, lay in the 'non-objective' character of De Stijl, and in the tendency of the Dutch movement to avoid using curves.

From the beginning, De Stijl proclamations emphasized the emergence of a new order in which 'materialism' was to be left behind and replaced by spiritualized, mechanized abstraction.

The machine is *par excellence* a phenomenon of spiritual discipline. Materialism as a way of life and art took handicraft as its direct psychological expression. The new spiritual artistic sensibility of the twentieth century has not only felt the beauty of the machine, but has also taken cognizance of its unlimited possibilities for the arts. Under the supremacy of materialism, handicraft reduced men to the level of machines; the proper tendency for the machine (in the sense of cultural development) is as the unique medium for the very opposite, social liberation.

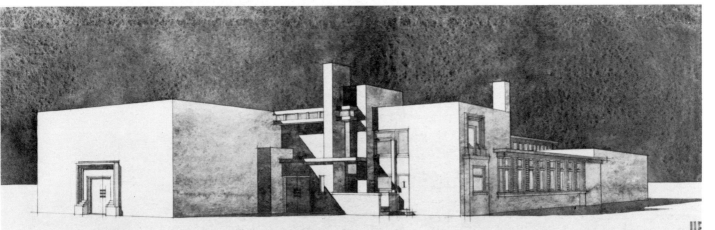

The appropriate symbolic visual expression of this outlook was felt to lie in what Oud later characterized as 'an unhistorical Classicism' – in other words a style which took simplification even further than it had gone in the pre-war generation. Here, indeed, was the value of Mondrian's paintings and Wright's architecture to De Stijl, for each seemed to imply a formal language of tensely related, simple forms and shapes resolved into compelling unities. Controlled asymmetry and the enlivened contrast of hovering planes seem to have taken on an almost sacral meaning to De Stijl artists as the correct mode for revealing the nature of the emergent epoch (fig. 7.11).

Spatial ideas that were later to be drawn into architecture were often first revealed at the smaller scale of painting or sculpture, or in mere drawings of buildings where technical problems of realization could be avoided. A pivotal work of early De Stijl was Rietveld's chair design of 1917–18 (fig. 7.10), because here an attempt was made to find a functioning equivalent in three dimensions to a rectilinear abstract painting. There can be no doubt that Rietveld received some stimulus from Wright's earlier furniture designs (with their own pedigree in Arts and Crafts ideals, machine-cut wood, and Japanese simplicity), but here the meaning was a little different. Despite the fact that the chair was clearly a one-off, handmade object, it was intended to have the symbolic significance of a prototype of machine art and the character of a standardized object, manifesting:

> The need for number and measure, for cleanliness and order, for standardization and repetition, for perfection and high finish . . .

The struts and rails of the chair were detailed to suggest that one element was floating independently of another, with the implication that all the parts were hovering in a tangible, continuous space. Probably this was conceived as a sort of three-dimensional equivalent to the space of Mondrian's paintings with their lines 'extending to infinity'. But the significance of this spatial conception in the minds of De Stijl artists was nothing less than epochal. It was seen as the true one for the twentieth century – an 'optically immaterial, almost hovering appearance'. Such an ideal was to blend particularly well with the possibilities of cantilevered concrete construction, and the shimmering, transparent effects of industrial glazing in architecture.

Van Doesburg's remarkable spatial diagrams (fig. 7.12) and models of 1923 have been mentioned already, but these were never realized directly as architecture; probably the first actual building to embody the full range of De Stijl formal, spatial, and

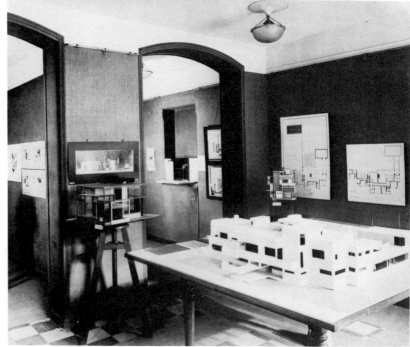

iconographic intentions was therefore the Schroeder House of 1923–4 (fig. 7.13), designed by Rietveld as a family dwelling for a site at the end of a suburban row in Utrecht. With its rectangular, smooth shapes and the bright primary colours of its struts, the Schroeder House stands out dramatically from its dark brick neighbours. The building is formed from intersecting planar walls detailed in such a way that some of them appear to hover in space, while others extend horizontally, and still others join to define thin volumes. There is no single axis or simple symmetry: rather one part is held in tenuous, dynamic and asymmetrical relationship to the other, as had been suggested in Mondrian's paintings seven years earlier. The planes are in turn articulated by the thin lines of window mullions, balcony railings and upstanding struts, which are coloured black, blue, red, and yellow, and stand out cleanly against the grey and white wall surfaces. Again De Stijl painting comes to mind, but the manner in which one element is expressed independently, and made to stand discretely in space, also recalls the 'Elementarism' of Rietveld's chair. Some of the thin metal supports are in fact attached girders – quotations

7.10 (*above left*) Gerrit Thomas Rietveld, Red-Blue Chair, 1917–18.

7.11 (*below left*) De Stijl group exhibition at Léonce Rosenberg, Paris, 1925.

7.12 (*above right*) Theo van Doesburg, spatial diagram for a house, 1923: the centrifugal conception of space, with planes extending into the surroundings. Gouache on paper, $22\frac{1}{8} \times 22$ in. (56.3×56 cm.). Amsterdam, Stedelijk Museum.

7.13 (*right*) Gerrit Thomas Rietveld, Schroeder House, Utrecht, 1923–4.

from the world of industrial standardization – detailed to give the sense that all the parts of the building are weightless. Voids and volumes of space are integrated in the composition as active constituents.

The interiors of the Schroeder House continue the same aesthetic themes. Details like the light fixtures or the glass stair-casing are integrated with the building's overall style and proportions. The downstairs contains two bedrooms and a studio, with the kitchen/living area to the south-east corner, where it originally afforded views over the neighbouring flat landscape (a motorway now blocks the view). Upstairs there are working/sleeping areas giving on to balconies, and a living-room, but partitions may be removed altogether to give an entirely free plan (fig. 7.14). The client, Mrs. Schroeder, was herself a pioneer and wanted an unconventional environment for her three children which would also give her a place to work at her own art. It seems probable that she inspired some of the more 'revolutionary' aspects of the building, like the openness of the upstairs 'free plan' and some of the ingenious built-in furniture.

Rietveld worked closely with his client in the course of design by using demountable cardboard and wooden models. The earliest scheme was more cubic and closed in character than the final one, and it was only gradually that the three-dimensional vitality was achieved. One advantage of this method of work was that it allowed a consistency of approach from small to large. The scale of the building is in fact quite petite and intricate, and considerable attention has been given to small touches like ledges, stairs, shelves, window ledges and mullions. Details inside and out are themselves like small 'models' of the whole and have been fashioned to reveal the life of the underlying form (fig. 7.15). One is reminded constantly of Rietveld's artistry as a cabinet-maker; it is as if the whole was some oversized intricate piece of De Stijl furniture. The Schroeder House is thus a 'total-work-of-art' in which fixtures and overall form are consistent expressions of the same idea, and in which painting, sculpture, architecture, and the practical arts are all fused.

While the Schroeder House, like Rietveld's earlier furniture designs, was built through the most careful handicraft, carpentry, and intuitive trial and error, its symbolic message concerned a new way of life created by the supposed spiritual liberation of mechanization. If these crisp, superbly proportioned shapes and rooms had been merely pleasing forms, they would probably have had no lasting power; as it is, they are the outward manifestation of a polemical content, of a transcending social ideal. They embody a version of the 'good life', and this adds extra force to the formal arrangement. Architecture is, after all, an art, an

7.14 Gerrit Thomas Rietveld, Schroeder House, Utrecht, 1923–4, interior of upper level with screens removed.

expressive language for the articulation of ideas and feelings as well as for the service of utilitarian functions. Part of the richness of the Schroeder House lies precisely in the way function and structure, and such 'straightforward facts' as the girders or the simple slabs, have been rarefied, given a deeper significance (Plate 4). As Oud had written some years earlier, anticipating such an architecture:

7.15 Gerrit Thomas Rietveld, Schroeder House, Utrecht, 1923–4, detail of light fixture.

Without falling into barren rationalism, it would remain above all objective, but within this objectivity would experience higher things . . .

He had gone on to say that:

. . . an architecture rationally based on the circumstances of life today would be in every sense opposed to the sort of architecture that has existed until now. . . . its ordained task would be, in perfect devotion to an almost impersonal method of technical creation, to shape organisms of clear form and pure proportions. In place of the natural attractions of uncultivated materials . . . it would unfold the stimulating qualities of sophisticated materials, the limpidity of glass, the shine and roundness of finishes, lustrous and shining colour, the glitter of steel and so forth. Thus the develop-ment of the art of building goes towards an architecture more bound to matter than ever before in essence, but in appearance rising clear of material considerations; free from all impressionist creation of atmosphere, in the fullness of light. brought to purity of proportion and colour, organic clarity of form; an architecture that, in its freedom from inessentialism, could surpass even Classical purity.

There is much in this passage which could be translated without much distortion and applied to the seminal works of Walter Gropius, Le Corbusier and Mies van der Rohe in the early twenties. Each of these architects was seeking in his own way to give form to his poetic reactions to the technological and social realities of his time; each had grown up in the dusk of Art Nouveau and had been exposed to the ideas of Rationalism and the Deutscher Werkbund; each too had imbibed spiritual conceptions of the typical and of abstraction. Moreover, each had learned crucial lessons from the stripped Classicism of the first decade, and from the syntax of Cubism, before achieving his own version of an architecture that 'in its freedom from inessentialism could surpass even Classical purity'. In turn each architect had experienced the traumas of the First World War, and optimistically hoped to en-courage a new world to rise out of the ashes. It is scarcely surprising therefore – given the community of formative ideas – that there should have emerged a certain consonance of expression in the latter half of the twenties. However, it is insufficient simply to lump the whole matter together as 'the New Objectivity' or 'the International Style'. As was suggested in the introduction: shared themes are best understood in the light of individual intentions and unique conditions.

Part 2: The Crystallization of Modern Architecture between the Wars

8. Le Corbusier's Quest for Ideal Form

Architecture is the masterly, correct and magnificent play of volumes brought together in light.

Le Corbusier, 1923

The 1920s in Europe, Russia and, to some degree, the United States was one of those rare periods in the history of architecture when new forms were created which seemed to overthrow previous styles and set a new, common basis for individual invention. Known as the 'International Style', this shared language of expression was more than a mere style; it was also more than a revolution in building technique, though its characteristic effects of hovering volumes and interpenetrating planes admittedly relied on the machine-age materials of concrete, steel, and glass. Like most major shifts in the history of forms, the modern movement gave body to new ideas. It expressed polemical attitudes and Utopian sentiments; and whatever qualities individual buildings may have shared, they were still the products of artists with personal styles and private preoccupations. It is only by probing into the fantasies behind the forms that one may understand their meaning. This applies particularly to Le Corbusier, whose vast imaginative world included a vision of the ideal city, a philosophy of nature, and a strong feeling for the Classical tradition. He was one of those rare individuals who succeed in investing their creations with a universal tone.

Le Corbusier (whose real name was Charles Edouard Jeanneret) was born in the Swiss watch-making town of La Chaux-de-Fonds in 1887 and was therefore twenty years younger than Frank Lloyd Wright, a generation younger than Hoffmann and Perret, and almost the same age as Walter Gropius and Mies van der Rohe. He trained as an engraver, and a watch-case he made at the age of 15 won a prize at the Turin

exhibition of 1902. It shows clearly the impact of Art Nouveau, as do the decorations of a number of chalet-like structures he designed in his late teens and early twenties around his native town. A major early influence on his formation was L'Eplattenier, his teacher at the local art school. It was he who encouraged Jeanneret's habit of the close study and observation of nature. He prompted his student to look beyond appearances to the underlying structures of plants and fossils and stressed the beauty of simple geometrical forms. Jeanneret's design for an art school of 1910 (fig. 8.1) is a useful gauge of his early thinking,

8.1 Charles Edouard Jeanneret (Le Corbusier), project for an art school, 1910.

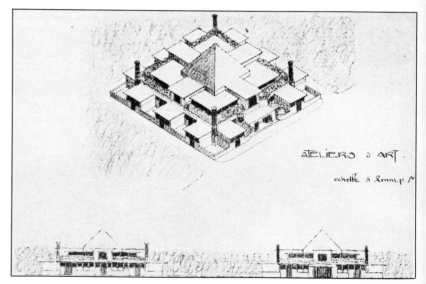

with its emphasis on simple cubes and a pyramid, and its unadorned surfaces. It perhaps shows debts to Egyptian architecture or even to the stripped Classicism of the eighteenth-century architect Ledoux. But one should beware of reading too clear a development into Jeanneret's early years: he tried many different styles and forms of expression before he found his true way.

The young Jeanneret was deeply introspective. He oscillated between periods of great uncertainty and periods of exaggerated confidence when he sensed he must have some Olympian destiny. He read Nietzsche and absorbed a messianic view of the artist as someone in touch with a higher order who produces redemptive forms for the world below. Jeanneret was suspicious of the conventional system of Beaux-Arts education and avoided it (though some of its lessons later crept into his work). He preferred to learn by doing and his erratic self-education included much reading, extensive travel, and experience in a variety of architectural ateliers. He seems to have had an uncanny talent for turning up in what history has since proved to be the 'right' places. By the time he was 24, he had managed to work in the offices of two of Pevsner's 'Pioneers' of modern architecture: Auguste Perret and Peter Behrens.

As was shown in Chapter 3, Perret taught Jeanneret the business of reinforced-concrete construction and introduced him to the tradition of French Rationalist theory stemming from Auguste Choisy and Eugène Viollet-le-Duc. Jeanneret was only 20 when he worked for a few months in the master's office, but it was enough to convince him that this material should, in a sense, become his own. By 1914, with the aid of Max Dubois, he had invented the Dom-ino system which

went far beyond Perret in its exploitation of the cantilever principle and its inherent possibility of an architecture of hovering, horizontal volumes. Moreover, the Dom-ino skeleton would become a central instrument of Le Corbusier's urbanism, as well as of his architecture.

Jeanneret's curious blend of practicality and idealism was next enriched by working in Germany in 1910 for Peter Behrens, who was then designing his factories for the AEG. As we have seen in an earlier chapter, Behrens had connections with Hermann Muthesius and the Deutscher Werkbund and tended to see mechanization as a central, positive force in the creation of a new culture, so long as the artist could inject the higher values of form into the industrial process. In Germany Jeanneret encountered the forces of big business and the idea that an architect should oversee the smallest and largest articles of design. It may have been there that he came to believe in the necessity for 'types' — standard elements of design amenable to mass production on the one hand and to the uses of society on the other. He saw and admired the Fagus factory and Werkbund Pavilion by Gropius, with their exciting use of glass envelopes, and began to grasp the necessity for an alliance between art and the machine.

But in considering the early influences on the artist one cannot be restricted to developments which were contemporary with his formation. From his early days, Jeanneret had been in the habit of sketching buildings of all periods in order to understand their organization and underlying principles. In 1911, he set out on a long journey through Italy, Greece, and Asia Minor. This was very much in the tradition of the Northern Romantic who goes to the Mediterranean in search of Western cultural roots and he later called it his 'Voyage d' Orient'. It was a quest for the perennial values of architecture, and his sketchbooks are filled with drawings of mosques in Istanbul, the white cubic dwellings of the Greek coast and the Roman houses at Pompeii. But the greatest impression was made by the Acropolis at Athens. He visited the Parthenon every day, sometimes for hours, sketching it from many angles (fig. 8.2). He was impressed by the strength of the underlying idea, by the sculptural energy, by the precision of the forms (even then he compared the Parthenon to a 'machine'), and by the relationship to the site and far distant views of mountain and sea. There was something too about the ceremonial procession over rising strata of rock which Jeanneret never forgot. The Parthenon gave him a glimpse of an elusive absolute which continued to haunt him.

Jeanneret's attitude to tradition was far from that of the superficial copyist. He drew incisive thumbnail sketches to help him pick out salient features and to

8.2 Charles Edouard Jeanneret (Le Corbusier), sketch of the Acropolis in Athens done during the 'Voyage d'Orient', 1911.

lock images in his memory. He attempted to cut through to the *anatomy* of past architecture, to reveal principles of organization, and to relate plan shape to the dynamic and sensuous experience of volumes in sequence and in relation to setting. One minute it might be a Turkish wooden interior which captured his attention, the next it might be the symphonic character of the volumes of the Suleimanyie mosque (which, revealingly, he drew in an axonometric, perhaps following the schematic guidance of Choisy's drawings). All these impressions then blended together to become part of a rich stock of forms – the stuff of the later Le Corbusier's imagination.

In Italy he was repelled by the encrustations of the decadent phase of the Baroque and by various nineteenth-century horrors; he was repelled too by the *intellectual* 'encrustations' formed by Academic opinion which he felt distorted Classical antiquity by serving it up as a series of 'tasteful' and 'correct' recipes. Jeanneret took his intellectual revenge on this position by pursuing the underlying formal vitality of Classical antiquity. If it is true, as one notable historian of Renaissance architecture has claimed, that 'every great artist finds his own antiquity', then Jeanneret's 'version' lay in the giant brick volumes of the Baths, in the cylinder of the Pantheon, in the spatial dramas of Hadrian's Villa at Tivoli, and in the systematic and ordered standardization of the Classical devices of construction and support. In 1911, he wrote revealingly of the Italian phase of his great journey:

Italy is a graveyard where the dogma of my religion now lies rotting. All the bric-a-brac that was my delight now fills me with horror. I gabble elementary geometry; I am possessed with the colour white, the cube, the sphere, the cylinder and the pyramid. Prisms rise and balance each other, setting up rhythms . . . in the midday sun the cubes open out into a surface, at nightfall a rainbow seems to rise from the forms, in the morning they are real, casting light and shadow and sharply outlined as a drawing. . . . We should no longer be *artists*, but rather penetrate the age, fuse with it until we are indistinguishable . . . We too are distinguished, great and worthy of past ages. We shall even do better still, *that* is my belief . . .

Jeanneret spent the first two years of the war in Switzerland, working towards the foundation of a Jura Regionalist movement drawing together a supposed 'Mediterranean' synthesis of Germanic and French ideas, but this did not come to much. Even so, the ambition is of some use in understanding the Villa Schwob, a private house which he was asked to design for a site on the edge of La Chaux-de-Fonds (fig. 8.3). This was made from reinforced concrete, had a double-height central space with overhanging galleries, a flat roof and double glazing in its windows. Perret's, and perhaps Tessenow's, influences can be seen in the elevations and the use of concrete; Wright's in the spacious interiors (Jeanneret probably knew illustrations of the American's work in the *Wasmuth Volumes*); and it is possible to discern, in the cornice,

8.3 Charles Edouard Jeanneret (Le Corbusier), Villa Schwob, La Chaux-de-fonds, Switzerland, 1916.

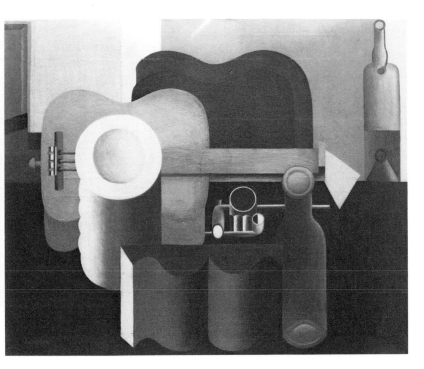

8.4 Charles Edouard Jeanneret (Le Corbusier), *Still Life*, 1920. Oil on canvas, $31\frac{7}{8} \times 34\frac{1}{4}$ in. (80.9 × 99.7 cm.). New York. Museum of Modern Art. Van Gogh Purchase Fund.

symmetry and proportions, a pervading Classical sense. Among the architect's sketches some indicate that the cornice was partly inspired by Turkish wooden houses. But this building was more than the sum of its sources; its powerful combinations of curved and rectangular forms pointed to a strong organizing talent. However, it was a talent still trying to find its true mode of expression.

By 1917 Jeanneret had settled in Paris. There had been legal wrangles over the Villa Schwob, and in any case he may have found provincial life too stifling. Soon he met Amédée Ozenfant, who introduced him to the post-Cubist avant-garde, including such artists as Fernand Léger and the poet Guillaume Apollinaire. Ozenfant, the eventual author of *Foundations of Modern Art*, had many interests: painting, photography, psychology, anthropology, and pamphleteering. Like Jeanneret he was intrigued by the beauty of machines. He tended to see them as the Futurists had done a little earlier, as purveyors of Romantic sensations. However, in this intellectual milieu, which was much pre-occupied with the Golden Section and the supposed constant laws of perception, Futurist attitudes were given a geometrically disciplined visual form. The synthesis of industrial subject-matter and a hieratic manner shows clearly in such paintings as *The City* by Fernand Léger of 1917.

Ozenfant encouraged Jeanneret to paint and intro-duced him to the ideas of modern art which had been evolving in Paris since the days of Cézanne; evidently

Jeanneret had known little about these developments during his 1908 stay in the city when he had worked with Perret and had spent lonely hours wandering around the museums or looking at the recent steel and glass structures. Jeanneret felt at home with the new medium immediately and by 1918 he and Ozenfant had collected enough work together to exhibit. They called themselves 'Purists' and their catalogue was a sort of manifesto entitled *Après le Cubisme* (After Cubism). While their paintings took over from Cubism such devices as the combination of abstract forms with representational fragments, and the handling of space in tight, ambiguous layers, their new direction was a critique of the bizarre and fragmented world of Picasso and Braque in favour of mathematical order and precision. This *rappel à l'ordre* perhaps expressed a feeling of consolidation after the chaos of the war. The Purists, moreover, established their pedigree in the Classical tradition: they revered Poussin, Seurat and Piero della Francesca, and praised the dignity and calm intellectual control of their works.

Ozenfant and Jeanneret were aware of the ab-straction of De Stijl but rejected a non-objective art. Their subject-matter followed Cubism in being drawn from the banal objects of the café table, the studio and the machine shop: guitars, bottles, and pipes were presented in their most typical forms. A strain of Platonism in the Purist outlook led the artists to pursue essential underlying ideas and to be preoccupied with the classification of ideal types in design. Jeanneret's still life of 1920 (fig. 8.4) is a good example of his work in this period. The outlines of bottle and guitar have been reduced to simple geometrical shapes laid out parallel to the picture surface; outlines and colours are crisp and distinct; visual tension is introduced by overlaps and spatial ambiguities; the Cubist principle of fusing different views of an object has been regularized – the bottle top, for example, is a pure circle. An attempt is made to reveal the heroic qualities of simple, everyday, mass-produced things.

Jeanneret's activity as a painter was to be most important to him when he became Le Corbusier the architect, because it provided him with a laboratory of forms. Dissatisfied with the eclecticism of the nineteenth century, with Art Nouveau and the various 'styles', he required a vocabulary which conformed to his private ideas and his taste for simple geometry, but which also seemed to have relevance to the mechan-ized world in which he lived. As much as possible too, he required forms with a universal character which addressed, over time, the basic aesthetic values he had sensed in tradition. Now Purist paintings provided all these things, and henceforth he was to believe that pure, precise geometrical forms were the appropriate ones for the machine age.

Jeanneret's first years in Paris brought him no commissions and much anxiety, but by 1920 he was at last beginning to sense his true direction as an architect. It was then that he took the name 'Le Corbusier' and founded the magazine *L' Esprit Nouveau* with Ozenfant. This opened on a positive note which, again, suggested a consolidation after the upheaval of the war years:

> There is a new spirit: it is a spirit of construction and synthesis guided by a clear conception.

Some of the articles which Le Corbusier had published in the magazine were later gathered together as a book which appeared in 1923 with the title *Vers une architecture – Towards an Architecture* (frequently mistranslated, 'Towards a New Architecture'). This has been one of the most influential architectural books of the century, combining deep wisdom, poetic observation, rich illustration of ideas, and a confident appeal in favour of an architectural language in tune with the machine era that Le Corbusier sensed rising around him. But as well as putting the case for a new architecture, and providing some hints (for himself as well as others) concerning its eventual appearance, Le Corbusier also stressed the role of tradition in providing great examples whose lessons might be transformed to contemporary purposes. *Vers une architecture* was certainly far from being a defence of 'functionalism' (as some commentators have complained); indeed, it was permeated with a lofty view of the role of art and emphasized the poetic value of sculptural form.

> The Architect, by his arrangement of forms, realizes an order which is a pure creation of his spirit; by forms and shapes he affects our senses to an acute degree and provokes plastic emotions; by the relationships which he creates, he wakes profound echoes in us. . . .

Extending some of the ideas of Purist painting to architecture, Le Corbusier argued that there were basic and absolutely beautiful forms transcending the mere conventions of period and style. Like his contemporaries in Holland, the artists of De Stijl, he believed in a sort of universal visual language of the spirit.

> Architecture is the masterly, correct and magnificent play of volumes brought together in light. Our eyes are made to see forms in light; light and shade reveal these forms; cubes, cones, spheres and cylinders or pyramids are the great primary forms which light reveals to advantage. The image of these is distinct and tangible within us and

THE "EMPRESS OF ASIA" (CANADIAN PACIFIC)
" Architecture is the masterly, correct and magnificent play of masses brought together in light."

without ambiguity. It is for this reason that these are *beautiful forms, the most beautiful* forms. Everybody is agreed to that, the child, the savage and the metaphysician. It is of the very nature of the plastic arts.

While Le Corbusier found evidence of the underlying primary forms in the pyramids, the Parthenon, the Roman baths, the Pantheon, the Pont du Gard, Michelangelo, Mansart, etc., he felt the architecture of the recent past to be impoverished and lacking in lasting value. It was in certain *engineering* objects that he sensed the presence of the harmony he desired – grain silos, factories, ships, aeroplanes and cars – and these were illustrated extensively in the book. Silos and factories, for example, were praised for their clear and distinct articulation of volumes and surfaces; ships and aeroplanes for their rigorous expression of function (fig. 8.5). It was obvious that all the objects he chose to illustrate conformed with his Purist prejudices, but he also believed them to be symptoms of the emerging spirit of the age; in this, of course, he was certainly reflecting knowledge of Deutscher Werkbund speculations on engineering aesthetics. The solution to the problem of defining the architecture of 'the new era' seemed, then, to lie in the *transformation* of such images into the symbolic forms of art. Purism pointed the way here, and it was clear too that the resultant vocabulary should also exhibit the Classical values the architect had intuited in the past.

8.5 Illustration of an ocean liner from *Vers une architecture*, 1923.

what then? Well it remains to use the car as a challenge to our houses and our greatest buildings. It is here that we come to a stop.

What then would the modern equivalents be to the standard elements of the Classical system of the past? Le Corbusier was to find this out, precisely, by using the car as a challenge to the house, and the resulting prototype, the Maison Citrohan of 1922 (fig. 8.7), was to be a sort of Paestum or Humber to the later villas, which were much more refined versions of the same system. 'Citrohan' was a deliberate pun on 'Citroën', and it is clear that Le Corbusier, like Gropius and Oud in the same period, was intent on using mass-production processes, like those which Ford had used for cars, to solve the housing crisis of the post-war years. His prototype was a white box on stilts with a flat roof, planar, rectangular windows of an industrial kind, and a double-height living-room behind a huge

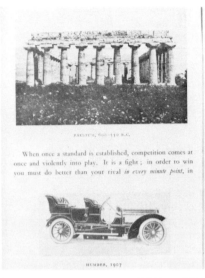

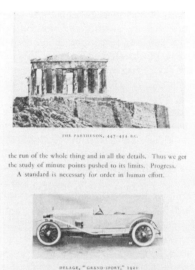

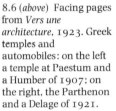

8.6 (*above*) Facing pages from *Vers une architecture*, 1923. Greek temples and automobiles: on the left a temple at Paestum and a Humber of 1907; on the right, the Parthenon and a Delage of 1921.

8.7 (*right*) Le Corbusier, the Maison Citrohan, 1922.

The equation of machine art and Classicism came to a head towards the centre of the book where pictures of one of the temples at Paestum (dated by Le Corbusier as 600–500 BC) and the later Parthenon were placed on opposing pages; with a Humber automobile of 1907 confronting a Delage car of 1921 in a similar fashion underneath (fig. 8.6). This brilliant use of the photograph was supposed to reinforce the idea of 'standards' – such basic elements as columns, triglyphs, etc., in the temples; and wheels, light chassis, etc., in the cars – 'type forms' which, once defined and related as a system, might then evolve towards perfection.

Let us display, then, the Parthenon and the motor car so that it may be clear that it is a question of two products of selection in different fields, one which has reached its climax and the other which is evolving. That enriches the automobile. And

studio window. The back parts of the house contained the kitchen, bathroom and bedrooms in smaller compartments and at the lowest level was a heating plant; cars meanwhile could tuck into the space created by the reinforced-concrete piles or *pilotis*. Halfway up and on top were terraces. The building as a whole was made of concrete – hence the large uninterrupted spans of the interior – and much of it would, in fact, have to have been constructed on site. But the *idea* of the mass-production dwelling was as important as the fact, and the Citrohan envisaged a way of life freed of the unnecessary clutter of the customary bourgeois dwelling of the time. In *Vers une architecture* Le Corbusier had spoken of the new dwelling as a 'machine for living in' and by this he meant a house whose functions had been examined from the ground up and stripped to the essentials. Healthy in mind and body, the ideal inhabitant would no doubt have been suffused with 'L'Esprit Nouveau' as he looked out past pure white walls to the 'essential joys' of light, space, and greenery. Of course, for all its claims at universal relevance, the way of life symbolized by the Citrohan was a projection of the rather odd values of a monastic and reclusive artist of the Parisian avant-garde.

The Citrohan was a conflation of earlier Le Corbusier concerns: the mass-producible Dom-ino houses; the Mediterranean cubic dwellings with whitewashed surfaces he had seen on his travels; the ocean liners he so admired for their 'tenacity and discipline'. There were lingering debts as well to the unornamented forms of Adolf Loos and the flat-roofed concrete houses illustrated in Garnier's 'Cité Industrielle'. Le Corbusier had also been impressed by the studio houses built in Paris in the early part of the century, with their large areas of glazing; and the double-height room with a balcony at the back was inspired by a similar arrangement in a Paris café.

It was only in 1925 that Le Corbusier managed to find someone willing to carry out his ideas for mass-production houses on a large scale, for it was then that he persuaded an eccentric Bordeaux industrialist, Henri Frugés, to build housing for his workers at Pessac along the guidelines of the Citrohan. Meanwhile the architect had to be content with transforming his prototype as circumstances allowed. Since his clients tended to come from that sector of Parisian society which Wyndham Lewis aptly called 'upper-middle-class bohemia', Le Corbusier had to forgo his ambition of effecting a major transformation of the modern environment and be content with designing elegant demonstrations of his general principles on small suburban lots around Paris. Thus between 1920 and 1924 we find him building houses or studios for his friend Ozenfant, for the sculptor Lipchitz, and for the Swiss banker and collector of paintings, Raoul La Roche.

Maison La Roche/Jeanneret was designed in 1923 just as Le Corbusier's architectural ideas were beginning to crystallize. It stands at the end of a cul-de-sac in the 16ème arrondissement and its L-shaped plan fits into two sides of the oblong site. In fact two houses are combined – one for La Roche, the other for Le Corbusier's sister-in-law – and one of the major problems of the commission was to unify the divergent demands of Le Corbusier's relative, who was newly married and wanted a compact house, with those of a collector who wanted to use his dwelling to display his superb Purist and Cubist works of art. The main volumes of the house are the long oblong which contains Jeanneret's dwelling and the private areas of La Roche, and a curved element lifted free of the ground on slender supports which contains a studio (fig. 8.8); between the two is La Roche's entrance hall

and exhibition space. This is three storeys high and is penetrated by overhanging balconies and a sort of bridge running just inside the glass which provides a variety of elevated viewpoints and calls to mind a liner's deck illustrated in *Vers une architecture* with the caption:

> Architects note: The value of a long gallery or promenade – satisfying and interesting volume; unity in materials; a fine grouping of the constructional elements, sanely exhibited and rationally assembled.

Windows are set flush with the façade plane so that the effect is of a thin skin wrapped tautly around the sequence of interior spaces. These have sparse surfaces and uncluttered walls painted white, green or brown. The overlapping of planes, and transparent areas of glazing recall the analogous qualities of interpenetration in Purist pictures. But there is also a connection with the subject-matter of Purism, for the fixtures of the house – radiators, naked light bulbs, simple Thonet chairs, door latches, metal windows – are obviously of industrial extraction. Like the bottles and machine parts in the pictures they are *objet-types* – objects which 'tend toward a type which is determined by the evolution of forms between the ideal of maximum utility, and the necessities of economic manufacture.' Some rhetoric was involved here, as the main window frame had to be specially made to look like a mass-produced factory one.

The spaces of Maison La Roche have been ingeniously linked in sequence to allow the gradual exploration of the interior. Le Corbusier christened such a route the *promenade architecturale* and criticized the star shapes and axes of the plans of the École des Beaux-Arts because they were mere patterns on paper; a good plan would 'contain a great quantity of ideas' and would project volumes into space in an ordered hierarchy of a more subtle kind, taking into account the site, the play of light, and the gradual revelation of a building's form and idea over time. As one passes through the triple volume of Maison La Roche one begins to grasp Le Corbusier's intentions. The elements slide by into new relationships, and interior and exterior are temporarily fused: one glimpses the outer white wall of the curved studio dappled with shadows, juxtaposed to interior walls of analogous character. The promenade then continues around into this curved volume and up to the highest level of the house by means of a curved ramp fitted into the profile of the wall (fig. 8.9). One doubles back, sees the intersecting balconies down below, and emerges on the roof terrace, which recalls immediately the deck of a ship: a small garden set about with evergreens is created at the

8.8 Le Corbusier, Maison La Roche/Jeanneret Auteuil, Paris, 1923, view towards the studio wing.

level of the surrounding roof-tops.

Much play is also made with the idea of a building as an object poised in space, especially in the studio wing. The curved surfaces in light contrast strongly with the recess of shadow beneath and a single, cylindrical *piloti* stands at the centre, set back under the slab. This is on the axis of the long access road and is seen against the background of an ivy-covered wall terminating the site. The hovering quality of this volume recalls Rietveld's Schroeder House of the same date, analysed

in the last chapter; the illusion of weightlessness was to be one of the central formal characteristics of the 'International Style'.

It was typical of Le Corbusier's intellectual approach that at the same time that he conceived the Citrohan, he should have outlined plans for an entire modern city, 'The Contemporary City for Three Million Inhabitants'. This was exhibited at the Salon d'Automne in 1922. The political and philosophical ideas behind Le Corbusier's urbanism are examined in

8.9 Le Corbusier, Maison La Roche, Paris, 1923, view of interior of curved studio wing; note ramp to left.

more detail in Chapter 12. Here it is enough to point out that architecture and urbanism were overlapping concerns for him, propelled by a single vision of technology as a progressive force which, if guided by the right ideals, might reinstate a natural and harmonic order. This Utopian vision, with its roots in such nineteenth-century thinkers as Charles Fourier, Henri Saint-Simon and Ebenezer Howard, was given a body in the 'Contemporary City', a city of skyscrapers in a park, where techniques of modern construction, automobiles and aeroplanes were brought together in an ordered diagram, with nature and the machine reconciled and harmonized. A later vision of the same kind, the 'Ville Voisin', in which Le Corbusier's pro-capitalist stance was dramatically revealed in a scheme for inserting huge glass skyscrapers in the centre of Paris, was exhibited at the Exposition des Arts Décoratifs in 1925 in the Pavillon de L'Esprit Nouveau. The pavilion was in the form of an apartment from the ideal city (which was in effect a rephrased Citrohan) furnished with modern machine-age objects and Purist works of art. It was as if the Utopian wished to carry his vision of the millennium – his poem to modern life – into the smallest details of the private interior and the largest setting of public life, simultaneously. As we shall see, the dictatorial implications of

Le Corbusier's paradise on earth only emerged later on.

The period between about 1918 and 1923 was extraordinarily turbulent and creative for Le Corbusier, for it was then that he laid down the basic themes of his life's work. By 1925, when he received his next domestic commission in Paris, he was in far greater control of his means of expression. The site was once again cramped, being part of a row of houses, but it did offer views towards the Bois de Boulogne nearby. Only the main façade would be seen and much effort would obviously have to go into this single view. The client was an American painter called Cook, who was willing to let Le Corbusier experiment.

The façade as it stands today is almost square (fig. 8.10); so is the plan. Thus the form is almost a cube, one of those ideal forms singled out in the aesthetic speculations of the magazine *L'Esprit Nouveau*. The symmetry of this overall shape is reinforced by the strip windows which run from one side to the other, and by a single cylindrical *piloti* on the central axis. Within this stable outline are a variety of asymmetrical rhythms. The porter's curved cabin contrasts with the rectangular surfaces, and the balcony at the top left pulls away from the façade. The main relationships and tensions of the design are enlivened by areas of shadow and light, taut rectangles of glazing alongside stucco, and the thin lines of railings, edges and joints. Pushes and pulls, laterally and in depth, are seen to resolve around the pivotal element of the central *piloti*.

But this is to discuss maison Cook in mainly formal terms. As one passes into the interior or examines a section or plan, one becomes aware of the way the functions of the house have been ingeniously slotted, like the pieces of some three-dimensional jigsaw puzzle, into the overall cubic shape. The traditional arrangement is turned upside-down, as the bedrooms and maid's room are on the first floor, and the living-room, kitchen and dining-room are on the second. The living-room is double-height and at its back is a stairway up to the little library on top, adjacent to the roof terrace, with long views towards the Bois de Boulogne. As one passes up the stairs, which stand at the rear of the building alongside the central axis, one is fed into a variety of rooms at each level. The architect has employed the concrete skeleton to sculpt a sequence of compressed and expanding spaces of variable character, proportion, lighting and view. The curved partitions dramatize the 'free plan', catch the light, and stand like objects in the lucid space; inevitably they call to mind the bottles and guitars of Purist pictures. Unity and control are maintained by the rule of geometry and proportion, and by the consistent dimensioning of such elements as the strip windows.

But there is the clarity too of an artist who has gained full control of his vocabulary. 'Sources' (such as the Farman Goliath aeroplane cockpit echoed in the porter's little cabin underneath), have been totally integrated and the style is now assured. Le Corbusier seems to have recognized this as he later wrote:

> Here are applied with great clarity the certainties from discoveries to date: the *pilotis*, the roof garden, the free plan, the free façade, the ribbon window sliding sideways. Regulating lines are automatically generated by simple architectural elements at a *human scale*, which also controls the floor heights, the window dimensions, doors and railings. The classic plan is turned upside down: the underneath of the house is free. The main reception room is right on top of the house. You step directly on to the roof garden from which you have a commanding view of the Bois de Boulogne. One is in Paris no longer; it is as if one were in the countryside.

The 'certainties to date' of *pilotis*, roof garden, free plan, free façade, and ribbon windows had been

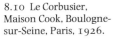

8.10 Le Corbusier, Maison Cook, Boulogne-sur-Seine, Paris, 1926.

christened the 'Five Points of a New Architecture' by the architect in 1926 (fig. 8.11). They were an extension of the Dom-ino principles and were to remain one of Le Corbusier's major devices for the rest of his life. It was typical of him that he should have endeavoured to create a generic solution, one which transcended particular cases. Perhaps the choice of *five* points is significant – as if he were trying to canonize a modern equivalent to the Five Classical orders. Certainly his system was a solution to the problem he had set himself many years before: the creation of a vocabulary based on reinforced concrete construction and applicable to all the tasks of modern industrial civilization.

It is worth examining the 'five points' in the abstract. The *piloti* was the central element from which the others evolved: it lifted buildings off the ground allowing landscape or traffic to pass underneath, and was the basic device in both city planning and architecture. The roof terrace also had such a double identity, being one of the essential means by which the architect intended to reintroduce nature into the city; planting also supplied ways of insulating the flat concrete roof. With *pilotis* supporting the weight of a building, its interior and exterior walls could pass anywhere according to functional demand or aesthetic intention, and the free plan allowed rooms of different sizes to be slotted into the skeleton and spaces to be orchestrated in sequence. The free façade, meanwhile, could be a total void running from slab to slab, a thin membrane, or a window of any size. Theoretically any sort of opening could be left, depending on the demands of view, climate, privacy and composition. In fact, through most of the twenties, Le Corbusier preferred a horizontal strip window running the full length of his buildings. Ostensibly this was because the *fenêtre en longueur* or 'strip window' let in most light; but it had as much to do with the feeling of repose of horizontal bands in a façade, and the effects of transparency and planarity that the strip window allowed. Most of these ideas had existed discretely in earlier architecture: Le Corbusier's innovation was to put them all together in a single system with a broad range of application – a system which worked on formal, symbolic, and structural levels.

If one returns to Maison Cook it is evident that Le Corbusier has not only employed the 'five points', but has also emphasized them rhetorically as a sort of demonstration. The *piloti* is the centre of attention and is set back from the façade plane, dramatizing the separation of structure from external cladding. The passage under the house is also emphasized by the pedestrian path on one side and the car tracks on the other, as if to imply a new form for the city as well as for the building; moreover, a little planter is set under-

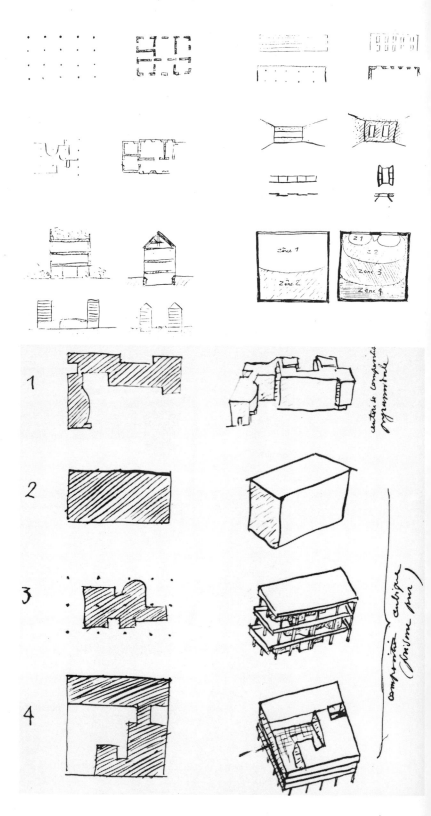

8.11 (*left*) Le Corbusier, the 'Five Points of a New Architecure', 1926: diagrams comparing the potentials of reinforced concrete and traditional masonry systems of construction.

8.12 (*below left*) Le Corbusier, four studies of the potentials of the 'Five Points of a New Architecture', (from top to bottom): Maison La Roche/Jeanneret 1923, Villa Stein 1927, Villa at Carthage 1927, Villa Savoye 1929. Like Wright, Le Corbusier possessed a consistent architectural system which allowed great variation with a few standard elements.

8.13 (*right*) Le Corbusier, Villa Stein at Garches, near Paris, 1926–7, front façade.

neath the overhang suggesting that nature too might pass underneath. The roof garden is rendered visible on top by means of penetrations, and the free façade is accentuated by the windows running from one end to the other. It is even possible to sense the character of the free plan inside, through the curved shapes which imply concave and convex objects within the 'box'.

Having assured himself of the 'five points' in the design of Maison Cook, Le Corbusier was on firm ground to explore further possibilities of his system. In a scheme for a house near Carthage in Tunisia in 1926, he let the skeleton predominate so that the overhanging slabs created deeply shaded terraces open to the sea breeze and the view; the interior functions being enclosed in curved partitions which could be seen from the outside (fig. 8.12). In the following year, in a design for the League of Nations Competition, he showed how the system could be orchestrated at a monumental scale to handle a variety of different programme elements and express them separately. And in another scheme for a villa in 1926 (the Villa Meyer), he created a fantasy of roof-terrace spaces linked as outdoor rooms through stairs and subtly placed openings. In short, he accentuated first one aspect, then another, of a vocabulary that was by now mature.

Le Corbusier's next major opportunity to build came

in 1926 when he was asked by a relative of Gertrude Stein to design a large villa at Garches, a few miles to the west of Paris (fig. 8.13). The site was a long and narrow stretch of land approached from one end, with room for a garden front and back. Here, at last, was the chance to make a building as a full, free-standing volume.

The first view of 'Les Terrasses' (as the Villa Stein was eventually called) is from the porter's lodge at the gateway. Compared to Maison Cook it is extremely grand in character. One approaches along a driveway and is able to grasp, bit by bit, the complexities of the façade articulation. Two strip windows run from one side to the other surmounted by an almost top-heavy area of wall punctured at its centre by an opening which hints at the presence of a roof terrace, but which also has the character of a benediction loggia. The lowest level has a variety of openings cut into it: a garage far to the left; a small entrance to the servants' quarters under a tiny balcony (but shifted slightly off the balcony's axis); a large area of industrial glazing suggesting the presence of a hall; the main entrance surmounted by a canopy; and, finally, at the right-hand extremity, some more glazing with thin horizontal bars. As at Maison Cook, various axes and sub-axes are discernible. Rectangles of different sizes set up rhythms across the façade which are held in tense equilibrium within the simple geometrical outline. There is no *piloti* in sight, but the way the windows extend to the edges is enough to suggest that the façade is a non-weight-bearing skin.

If one enters by the main door one passes into a foyer with a stair up immediately to the right. This brings one to a sort of *piano nobile* which is set aside for the most public and ceremonial functions. The grand salon is situated here, and after the constricted hallway beneath, and the narrow gangway at the top of the stairs, the space expands dramatically. So does the view: from the moment one enters, one sees the garden and terrace. The Steins were collectors of works of art and these have been placed strategically, like household gods, along the processional route through the house. The character of the Villa Stein is honorific. Its interior space is regularized and controlled by the grid of the *pilotis*: they give the rooms 'a constant scale, a rhythm, a cadence of repose', to use the architect's own words.

The lower level of Villa Stein is given over to the servants' quarters, which are entered through the smaller door seen in the first view. The kitchen, dining-room and library, though, are clustered around the salon on the *piano nobile*. The second floor, meanwhile, contains bedrooms, boudoirs and bathrooms, and its plan is arranged quite differently from the floor below it. Two of the rooms give on to an open-air deck suspended above the main platform of the rear terrace (the part of *Vers une architecture* entitled 'The Manual of the Dwelling' had made much of the idea of fresh air and view for individual rooms), while the master bedroom is entered along the main axis of the house. The small hallway in front of it is formed by two equal-sized curves making a kind of vestibule. The way that curved partitions have been arranged within the overall format is like a Purist composition, where curves and rectangles slide, overlap, and harmonize into a felt unity within a rectangular frame (fig. 8.14).

At the top of the house are more bedrooms and two roof terraces – one at the front, one at the back. A storage space is set into a curved volume which recalls immediately the funnel of a liner. Other nautical allusions are found in the railings, the spiral stairs, and the overall crispness of the forms. The caption under one of the ship illustrations in the chapter 'Eyes Which Do Not See' in *Vers une architecture* reads: 'An architecture pure, neat, clear, clean and healthy.' It might well be used to describe the Villa Stein.

The garden façade of 'Les Terrasses' (fig. 8.16) is more broken up than the main one, and more horizontal in emphasis. The terrace breaks into the closed box and sets the theme of stratified horizontal planes sliding, receding or stepping back towards the heart of the building. Here there is no doubt at all about

8.14 Le Corbusier, Villa Stein at Garches, near Paris, 1926–7, axonometric drawing.

8.15 Le Corbusier, early sketches of Villa Stein, 1926.

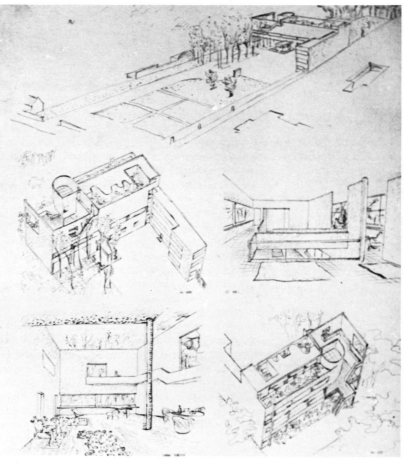

8.16 Le Corbusier, Villa Stein at Garches, near Paris, 1926–7, rear garden façade.

the presence of a frame within – for the overhangs, spatial penetrations and illusions of transparency rely on the cantilevered slabs. The movement of these hovering elements is contained between the flanking side walls which are now perceived as thin planes (they were seen as volumes in the front view). As in Maison Cook, curved forms introduce a counterpoint across space: the 'funnel' on top rhymes with the cylinder underneath the terrace stairs. In the same period that the house was designed, Le Corbusier's paintings were becoming more complex and ambiguous. The rigid forms of early Purism were being replaced by a more fluid and fluent visual language. The Villa Stein confirms that the artist was capable of orchestrating complex spatial ideas into a harmonious whole by 1927 in his architecture as well.

But the house at Garches also indicates Le Corbusier's ability to transform tradition. While it fulfils his vision of a *machine à habiter*, its *piano nobile*, its processional entrance and sequences, its proportions and its noble mood echo the character of a Renaissance villa. One historian has even pointed out that the 2:1:2:1:2 proportional system which regulates the façade bays and the grid is the same as the one used by Palladio at the Villa Malcontenta. There is no direct evidence that the prototype was in Le

Corbusier's mind, but he certainly succeeded in creating a modern villa with something of the harmony and order of his Renaissance predecessor. One wonders if the Steins, who spent some of their summers in a villa near Florence, appreciated that their new acquisition was in the Classical spirit as well as in 'L'Esprit Nouveau'.

By 1927, at the age of 40, Le Corbusier had thus succeeded in producing a number of master-works in a new style, but a style based on fundamental principles abstracted from tradition, as well as on imaginative responses to contemporary life. More than that, he had, like Wright, established an architectural system blending logical, structural, and intuitive rules in which type elements were capable of apparently endless combinations. Moreover, he had established a number of modern prototypes applicable from the scale of the window to the scale of the entire city. This system of forms and beliefs would continue to nourish his architecture but would undergo considerable changes later in his life. However, his discoveries between 1914 and 1927 transcended his personal situation, for they were solutions as well to the larger problem of an authentic modern architectural language. It is necessary now to place his breakthrough in the broader context of Europe and the United States.

9. Walter Gropius, German Expressionism, and the Bauhaus

> The new times demand their own expression. Exactly stamped form devoid of all accident, clear contrasts, the ordering of members, the arrangement of like parts in series, unity of form and colour. . . .
>
> W. Gropius, 1913

While some of the crucial foundations for modern architecture had been laid in Germany before the war, the preparatory work had to wait until the mid-1920s to come to fruition. With the defeat of the German armies in 1918, and the collapse of the old imperial order, Muthesius's dream of a unified, national *Kultur* guided by an élite of artist technocrats was shattered. Instead of competing in the market-place, the frightful technical ingenuities of the great industrial nations had ended up competing on the field of battle. The war may have been 'won' by the allied side, but the bulwarks of an already sagging liberal Christian civilization had been further eroded in the process. In Germany the reaction to economic chaos was revolution, and this brought with it a polarization of the political extremes of left and right. In the arts, groups of visionaries modelled their manifestos on those of the radical workers' groups and hoped that political revolution might be accompanied by a cultural one. Gropius caught the ambivalent mood of the period – oscillating between despair at an internal collapse and hope in some radiant, new social edifice – when he wrote in 1919:

> Today's artist lives in an era of dissolution without guidance. He stands alone. The old forms are in ruins, the benumbed world is shaken up, the old human spirit is invalidated and in flux towards a new form. We float in space and cannot perceive the new order.

This was the perfect ground for the growth of Utopianism tinged with an underlying *angst*. Severe economic inflation contributed to the mood by minimizing the likelihood of actual construction. Thus architects in Germany reverted to the creation of paper projects in which they foresaw the image of a new society. Bruno Taut, in the bizarre watercolours of his *Alpine Architektur*, portrayed collective buildings of glass facets, rising like crystals from glaciers and mountain peaks (fig. 9.1). These were meant to embody an 'apolitical socialism', an ideal realm for the brotherhood of man, in which national boundaries and individual greed would dissolve away, and in which a 'natural' society undisturbed by inherited class divisions would emerge. In *Die Stadtkrone* the architect even tried to embody the new collective religion in a town plan with a symbolic centre in the form of a cosmic world mountain or a stepped pyramid. This 'centre' was clearly supposed to make up for the loss of centre of modern, alienated man, and to root him to 'deeper' meanings in an integrated society. Following such pre-war visionaries as Paul Scheerbart and Wassily Kandinsky, Taut thought it was the business of the *artist* to reveal the form of this new polity which was to rise from the ruins of European civilization.

This tendency to believe that architectural forms might themselves have redemptive potential recalls the moralism of Pugin, who had imagined that good Christian forms (i.e., Gothic ones) would accelerate a moral regeneration. The appeal of a similar idea in circumstances where the creative individual felt cut off from his surroundings, and without bearings, is

Der Kristallberg

9.1 (*above*) Bruno Taut, 'Crystal Mountain', *Alpine Architektur*, 1919.

9.2 (*right*) Lyonel Feininger, 'Cathedral of Socialism', from the cover of the first Bauhaus proclamation, 1919.

every artist.

Let us create a new guild of craftsmen, without the class snobbery that tries to erect a haughty barrier between artist and craftsman. Let us conceive, consider and create together the new building of the future that will bring all into one single integrated creation: architecture, painting and sculpture rising to heaven out of the hands of a million craftsmen, the crystal symbol of the new faith of the future.

Permeating Gropius's thinking at this stage was adulation for the way in which Gothic cathedrals had supposedly represented the deepest collective aspirations of the medieval *Volk*. This myth was joined to another one in Gropius's mind: that the cathedrals had been produced by bands of inspired craftsmen without the interference of 'self-conscious designers'. Turning such beliefs around, he assumed that if a band of craftsmen could somehow be initiated into the needs and means of the modern era, then they might combine to produce the authentic collective imagery of the times. Correspondingly, the proclamation had on its cover a woodcut by Lyonel Feininger representing the 'Cathedral of Socialism' (fig. 9.2) – a jagged,

understandable. Even so, it comes as a shock to find Walter Gropius indulging in fantasies of a similar tone in the period around the founding of the Bauhaus, that is, in 1919. After all, he had been one of the champions of Muthesius's ideal of standardization; his position had seemed to stress the notion of a broad co-operation between the architect, the industrial process and the values of a technocratic clientele.

The Bauhaus was formed by the fusion of two existing institutions in Weimar: the old Academy of Fine Arts and a Kunstgewerbeschule founded under van de Velde in 1906. This odd marriage had more support from the state government than from the local Weimar establishment, and was the first step towards Gropius's eventual aim of a regeneration of German visual culture through a fusion of Arts and Crafts. The first Bauhaus proclamation was permeated with the ideal of a new social and spiritual integration in which artists and craftsmen would unite to create a sort of collective symbolic building of the future:

The complete building is the ultimate aim of the visual arts. . . . Architects, painters and sculptors must recognize once more the nature of buildings as composite entities. Only then will their works be permeated with that architectonic feeling which has become lost in the art of the salons.

A groundwork of craft discipline is essential to

expressionist image, soaked in visionary sentiments, clearly intended to be evocative rather than buildable, and in its crystal-like shapes resembling Taut's fantasies. Indeed, both Gropius and Taut were fully aware of Scheerbart's pre-war praise of glass, and of Adolf Behne's more recent proclamations in the same vein:

> It is not the crazy caprice of a poet that glass architecture will bring a new culture. It is a fact.

Gropius's expressed beliefs in the necessity for reuniting aesthetic sensibility and utilitarian design were in line with his experiences within the Werkbund; but there was no mention in his proclamation of the design of types for mass production. It seemed as if he had returned to the roots of the Arts and Crafts movement, to William Morris, and to the belief in handicraft as the sole viable guarantee of design quality. The earliest curriculum at the Bauhaus mirrored this position: the student was regarded as a sort of apprentice to an updated version of the medieval

9.3 (*left*) Student work produced in the *Vorkurs* under the tutelage of Johannes Itten at the Bauhaus, 1923.

9.4 (*below*) Walter Gropius, Sommerfeld House, Berlin, 1921.

guild and was expected to learn weaving and other crafts which might eventually be useful in the decoration or articulation of living spaces and buildings. Parallel with these courses was the *Form-lehre* – instruction in the basis of formal arrangement, including composition and the study of colour, texture, and expression; eventually this course would, in fact, be taught best by painters of easel pictures, men like Paul Klee, Wassily Kandinsky and Oskar Schlemmer. However, preceding these middle levels of the Bauhaus education, every student would have to pass through the *Vorkurs* in which, under the direction of Johannes Itten (and, later, Josef Albers and Laszlo Moholy-Nagy), he would be encouraged to 'unlearn' the habits and clichés of European 'academic' traditions, and to make a new beginning through experimentation with natural materials and abstract forms. Thus it was hoped that each student would tap his deepest instinctive expression in the definition of forms which would not have been 'imposed' by conventions. The ideology here was primitivism of a pure type: the interior world of the psyche was to reveal itself in all its naturalness; and working together with the nature of materials was supposed to generate authentic forms mirroring the deepest collective beliefs.

Johannes Itten, the first teacher of the *Vorkurs*, was a Swiss painter who had imbibed the pre-war educational ideas of Adolf Hölzel and Franz Cižek in Vienna, and believed in the central role of form/feeling training in education. Moreover, extending Symbolist ideas of the pre-war generation (especially some of Kandinsky's theories set forth in *Concerning the Spiritual in Art*), he held that there was an inner connection between certain visual configurations and certain states of mind. It is clear that Itten believed he was conducting his students into a form of religious initiation. He actually encouraged meditation, deep-breathing exercises and physical training as aids to mental relaxation and self-discovery in his classes. Many students joined the Mazdaznan cult, which involved fasting, a vegetarian diet, and various spiritual disciplines. One pauses for a moment, to guess how Muthesius, the Werkbund theorist, or Rathenau, the pre-war client, might have reacted to this idea of an education for the designers of the future!

The work produced under Itten in the earliest sessions of the *Vorkurs* had a notably primitive flavour, which perhaps mirrored a prevalent state of gloom at the decline of the West, and a tendency to clutch on to tribal and magical artifacts for guidance (fig. 9.3). While Itten insisted that these productions should not be regarded as 'finished works of art', they were influenced by productions of the Zurich Dada avant-garde, including Schwitters's rubbish constructions and the fantastic disassembled machine-collages of Max Ernst. The mood here was one of cultivated despair underlined by a sense of absurdity at the impact of a fully mechanized war. Moreover, like the Dadaists, Itten's students were evidently interested in African masks and fetishes. Altogether 'Primitivism' seems to have been a major strand in 'Expressionist' attitudes of both the pre- and post-war periods.

While the Bauhaus potters could at least sell their wares, the majority of Bauhaus students had little chance to contribute their designs to the 'new cathedral of the future' in a Germany rent by inflation and poverty. However, in 1920, Gropius received a commission to design a house for Adolf Sommerfeld, a timber merchant who had managed to acquire the entire teak lining of a ship at a time when building materials were extremely scarce. Gropius drew up his design in 1920 and used the services of some of his students in the ornamentation of the interiors and the designs of some of the fixtures. The Sommerfeld House (fig. 9.4) is a sophisticated essay in procured *naïveté*; it combines aspects of Gropius's pre-war formal and compositional approaches, with a medievalizing mood, a vernacular image and elements which may well have been influenced by Wright's ornamentation of Midway Gardens. In retrospect, the building seems very far from the machine-age architecture Gropius was to create only a few years later, but the peculiarities of the commission must be taken into account to balance too exaggerated a claim for Gropius's so-called 'Expressionism' in the immediate post-war years.

'Expressionism' is, in any case, an imprecise term; it is commonly used to group together a number of diverse artists working in Holland and Germany between roughly 1910 and 1925, and to describe a so-called 'anti-Rational' tendency in art which – so the argument goes – manifests itself in works of complex, jagged, or free-flowing form. The premiss here tends to be an over-simple one whereby 'rational' tendencies are taken to manifest themselves in 'opposite' stylistic qualities like simplicity, rectangularity, and stasis. The difficulty comes in assuming that the frenzied, the emotive, and the bizarre must manifest themselves in a particular style, and in ignoring the fact that most works of art of any depth are characterized by tensions between emotional expressiveness and formal control. 'Expressionism' then is a term which is all the more slippery for the way it is sometimes employed to describe attitudes of mind, sometimes forms. It is used here in a spirit of caution and as a reluctant continuation of a well-worn convention according to which architecture by men like de Klerk and Kramer in Holland, and Poelzig, Taut, Bartning, Mendelsohn, and Gropius in Germany (in a particular phase of their lives) are customarily called 'Expressionists'.

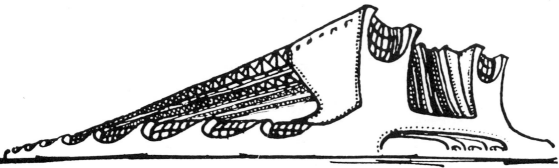

9.5 (*left*) Erich Mendelsohn, sketch of factories, *c.* 1915.

9.6 (*below*) Erich Mendelsohn, Einstein Tower, Potsdam, 1919–22.

The simplistic nature of such characterizations is revealed all the more when one confronts the major talent. This is particularly true of Erich Mendelsohn, whose formation took place before the war under the impact of Art Nouveau. Mendelsohn was Jewish, and recent attempts at linking his forms to the geometrical symbolism of ancient Jewish mystical texts should not be dismissed out of hand. Certainly he felt that it was one of the functions of art to make a spiritual order visible and to reveal the inner processes and rhythms of nature. He absorbed the theory of empathy, according to which the essential character of forms was perceived through a translation, mimetically, of the tactile sense into the forms of architecture. Some of these concerns are already clear in a series of remarkable sketches Mendelsohn drew while in the trenches during the First World War (fig. 9.5). These are of building types like film studios, a car-body factory, and a crematorium. The forms are sensed in a state of extreme tension ('dynamism' was the word the artist preferred) and the structural stresses are dramatized and accentuated so that parts and whole merge together. Mendelsohn criticized Behrens's architecture for its additive 'cardboard' quality and sought instead the integration of all details into the rhythms of a controlling image; at the same time he rejected the more extreme creations of the 'Wendingen' expressionists (a Dutch group which delighted in sprawling and eccentric plans) on the ground that they lacked control. For Mendelsohn the tension of a work was increased and enriched by a fusion of the organic with a strong geometrical armature employing axes.

In 1919 Mendelsohn had a chance to build one of his fantastic, biomorphic essays when he was asked to design an observatory at Potsdam. The 'Einstein Tower' (fig. 9.6) was a free-form, curved sculpture, into which windows and other details were carved so as to accentuate the overall dynamism. In fact, the plan was a masterly example of axial arrangement and functional hierarchy and the material was not at all the single 'plastic' sculptural one it appeared, but brick cosmetically coated in plaster and cement. Evidently the *idea* of the tower was related to Einsteinian themes

theory of dead material, and given themselves to the dutiful service of Nature.

By the time he designed the Luckenwalde hat factory of 1923, Mendelsohn's style had become more stereometrical and disciplined in its use of regular geometries; and by the second half of the twenties, in the numerous department stores, cinemas, and villas he built in and around Berlin, his vocabulary had resorted to many of the mechanistic analogies and characteristic elements (e.g., strip windows and cantilevered curved stairs) of the International Style. Nonetheless, the quality of an inner energy and tension in his forms remained unmistakable.

Ludwig Mies van der Rohe was another German architect to pass through an 'Expressionist' phase between the end of the war and the rectilinear abstract style of his seminal works from 1923 onwards. As we have seen, he was trained in the office of Peter Behrens before the war, but this apprenticeship came after experience in his father's stonemason's office, and some time in the furniture business of Bruno Paul. He early identified the characteristics he wished to emulate in the neo-classical severity and geometrical precision of Schinkel, and in the planarity and directness in the use of materials of Berlage. By the outbreak of the war, Mies had set up his own practice and designed a number of buildings, including the Kröller-Müller Villa of 1913, in a rectilinear, stripped Classical style which laid considerable stress on values of order, repose, symmetry, and discipline.

After the war Mies van der Rohe directed the architectural section of one of the radical groups (in his case the 'Novembergruppe') which seemed to share the visionary attitudes of Taut, Behne, and Gropius. His entry to the Friedrichstrasse Skyscraper Competition of 1921 might almost be read in Rationalist terms as an attempt at stripping a tall framed building down to its essential structure, which was then wrapped with a glass curtain-wall as a 'minimalist' solution – a sort of ultimate destination of the tall steel-framed building. However, this would be to miss half of the point. The sharp forms, romantic silhouettes, and rich play of reflecting and transparent surfaces seem to suggest a crystal cathedral as well as an office building. The glass tower reveals Utopian sentiments not unlike those of Taut's glass visions, or Le Corbusier's Cartesian towers floating above the parks of the Ville Contemporaine. The suggestion is almost made that the tall building is an index of progressivist fervour, an image to be central to some vaguely defined new state. It is a sad irony of ensuing history that the pure glass prism should have started off as the symbol of a new faith and ended up as the banal formula for the housing of big business and bureaucracy.

9.7 Ludwig Mies van der Rohe, glass skyscraper project.

of matter and energy:

Since the recognition that the two conceptions hitherto kept separable by science – Matter and Energy – are only different conditions of the same basic stuff, that nothing in the Universe is without Relativity to the Cosmos, without concern with the whole – since then, engineers have abandoned the

In a further development of this scheme, Mies modified the plan to curved forms radiating from a circulation core and described his experiments with glass and transparency (fig. 9.7):

> At first glance the curved perimeter of the plan seems arbitrary. But these curves were determined by three factors: sufficient illumination of the interior; the massing of the building from the street; and lastly, the play of reflections.

Indeed, the fascination with *glass* recalls once again Scheerbart's poetic dreams, if not the adulation of lustrous, artificial, and floating materials in the proclamations of De Stijl. Mies seems to have been concerned with a redemption of sorts, through technological means. The forms of his architecture achieved the character of transcendental symbols. Le Corbusier explained the nature of this 'idealization' succinctly:

> Architectural abstraction has this about it which is magnificently peculiar to itself, that while it is rooted in hard fact it spiritualizes it . . .

Mies Van der Rohe's project for a concrete office block in 1922 (fig. 9.8) indicates a slight change of mood and form. Emphasis has now shifted to the horizontal layering of space and the expression of hovering planes, the building as a whole being formed from cantilevered trays on piers with brackets. The plan was a grid of structural posts with partitions inserted between them, but the arrangement still contained vestiges of his Classical approach in its symmetry, stress of the central axis, and articulation of a sort of 'floating' cornice plane at the top (perhaps influenced by Sullivan's similar treatment in the Carson Pirie Scott Store of 1905). Visual 'corrections' and tensions were also introduced by the way each floor was made to step out a little further than the one below it as one moved up the building; these might be related to the architect's 'expressionist' tendencies; equally they might be seen as intelligent reinterpretations of effects of Classical entasis. The concrete office block was more geared to the actual technical potentials of the time than the sublime glass skyscrapers had been. In 1923 Mies became a founding member of the 'G' group in Berlin, which declared its opposition to 'formalism' and its theoretical support for forms closely related to practicality and construction. He wrote of his building in these terms:

> . . . a house of work . . . of organization, of clarity, of economy. Bright, wide workrooms, easy to oversee, undivided except as the undertaking is divided. The maximum effect with the minimum expenditure of

means. The materials are concrete, iron, glass.

Evidently the dreamer was coming back to earth. It should be mentioned that by 1923 the German economy was showing marked signs of improvement and that this made the adjustment of the avant-garde to reality both desirable and tenable.

An artist's vocabulary takes time to mature and there may be a pivotal work in which an underlying concept is first revealed, but which may take years to congeal with the artist's other discoveries. Mies van der Rohe's brick villa design of 1923 (fig. 9.9) seems to have had this role in his evolution. The plan was formed from walls laid out as planes, some of which extended into the surroundings. The spaces between were defined by a principle of overlapping, and without recourse to a dominant axis. It was as if Mies had drawn together certain qualities of the pre-war Kröller-Müller project, with the formal concepts of modern art, for his idea seemed to be a fusion of stripped Classical values, of the pin-wheel qualities of Wright, and of the abstract paintings of Mondrian, van Doesburg, or perhaps Lissitzky. Once again one finds the fruitful translation of painting abstraction into architecture. However, the volumes in this case were entirely earthbound, and it was to take Mies some years to find a way of expressing such spatial ideas in a way that animated the whole fabric in three dimensions. Throughout his later career, he would oscillate continually between symmetrical, axial, and crypto-Classical plans and ones based on dynamic rotation and the centrifugal splay of planes.

The period from 1922 to 1923 seems to have been a crucial one in Germany (as in France) for the growth of modern architecture and the emergence of the International Style. For it was then too that a new orientation began to emerge at the Bauhaus and in Gropius's thinking and designing. In 1922 van Doesburg visited Weimar and had a great impact on

9.8 (*above*) Ludwig Mies van der Rohe, concrete office building project, 1922.

9.9 (*above right*) Ludwig Mies van der Rohe, brick villa project, 1923, view and plan.

9.10 (*right*) Walter Gropius, director's office at the Weimar Bauhaus, 1923: the design clearly reflects the impact of Elementarist abstract art.

9.11 (*far right*) Laszlo Moholy-Nagy, *Light-Space Modulator*, 1923–30. Steel, plastic and wood, height $59\frac{1}{2}$ in. (151 cm.). Cambridge, Mass., Busch – Reisinger Museum, Harvard University, gift of Mrs. Sibyl Moholy-Nagy.

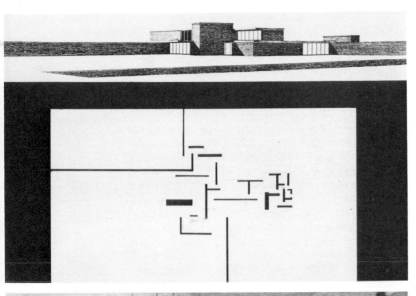

the school. From then on De Stijl-influenced forms became the basis of a general language of design, and a greater emphasis was again placed on reintegrating form and industry. Itten realized his time had come and resigned. The *Vorkurs* was handed over to Laszlo Moholy-Nagy, whose sophisticated 'Elementarist' vocabulary of rectilinear machine abstraction was in line with van Doesburg and with artistic educational experiments in post-Revolutionary Russia (e.g., the Vkhutemas School) (fig. 9.11). Gropius's own office design of 1923 (fig. 9.10) was blatantly a three-dimensional translation of some of these ideas, as was his *Chicago Tribune* skyscraper design of 1922 (to be analysed in more detail in a later chapter). Gropius's 'style for the times', with which he sought to fulfil his dream of a new communal art, seemed increasingly to be reverting to the basic forms of circles, spheres, rectangles, cubes, triangles and pyramids. While the Bauhaus teachers may have denied strongly the existence of a 'Bauhaus style', the shared body of forms and ideas derived from geometrical abstract art epidemic within the *Vorkurs* from 1923 onwards, insured that artists and craftsmen who later designed ceramics, fabrics, furniture (fig. 9.12), even buildings, did so on the basis of a sort of shared visual grammar.

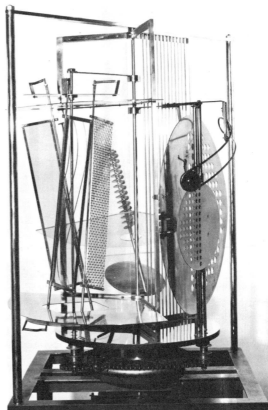

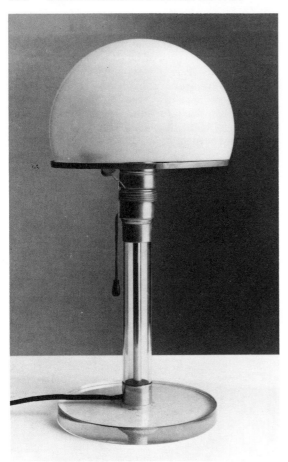

This was clearly a shift in emphasis from the 1919 attitudes, and it appears that 'coming to terms' with the machine included for Gropius a two-level response: on the one hand students should learn about the design of types for mass production, on the other they should seek to design forms which crystallized the values of a mechanized epoch. Gropius's answer of how this might be done involved a curriculum divided between *Formlehre* and *Werklehre*. The apprentice would pass through a *Vorkurs* lasting six months, and instruction in a particular craft lasting three years, before being exposed to the master's programme in which he would receive instruction in architecture and the technology of mass production. For it was central to Gropius's thesis – as it had been before the war – that the brutality of mere utilitarian design and the kitsch of consumerism might both be avoided if the most sensitive spirits could upgrade the basic formal character of all the objects of their period by the injection of feeling and sensitivity into utilitarian objects. As before, the highest aim was held to be the unity and synthesis of all the arts in the total work of art: a building. This would not merely have other works of art attached to it, but would synthesize the basic values of painting, sculpture, and architecture into an emotive structure which would symbolize the culture of the times.

By now Gropius was increasingly clear what form this architectural synthesis might take:

> Architecture in the last few generations has become weakly sentimental, aesthetic and decorative . . . this kind of architecture we disown. We aim to create a clear, organic architecture whose inner logic will be radiant and naked, unencumbered by lying facings and trickery; we want an architecture adapted to our world of machines, radios and fast cars, . . . with the increasing strength of the new materials – steel, concrete, glass – and with the new audacity of engineering, the ponderousness of the old methods of building is giving way to a new lightness and airiness.

In some ways, of course, this was a hotchpotch of ideas derived from Futurism, the Deutscher Werkbund, and De Stijl. What is interesting in this context is the way the traumas of the war and the ensuing few years caused Gropius to infuse a more mystical approach than in his pre-war years and to reject the framework of Beaux-Arts axiality in his planning. Instead, he adopted a spatial conception which clearly derived from van Doesburg, Rietveld, Lissitzky, and Moholy-Nagy:

> . . . the symmetrical relationships of the parts of the

9.12 Bauhaus lamp design, *c.* 1923.

In the year 1923 Gropius also published *Idee und Aufbau*, a proclamation of Bauhaus philosophy, as the leading article accompanying the Bauhaus exhibition of that year. This was more sober and optimistic than the Foundation Manifesto had been. Once again we find Hegelian ideas concerning 'the spirit of the age' and the creation of forms appropriate to that spirit:

> The dominant spirit of our epoch is already recognizable although its form is not yet clearly defined. The old dualistic world concept which envisaged the ego in opposition to the universe is rapidly losing ground. In its place is rising the idea of a universality in which all opposing forces exist in a state of absolute balance.

The book went on to outline the new orientation of the Bauhaus:

> The Bauhaus believes the machine to be our modern medium of design and seeks to come to terms with it.

building and their orientation towards a central axis is being replaced by a new conception of equilibrium which transmutes this dead symmetry of similar parts into an asymmetrical but rhythmical balance.

Until 1925, Gropius had little chance to carry out his new architectural ideas, apart from Bauhaus-sponsored house prototype experiments. But in that year right-wing criticism of the Bauhaus reached such a pitch that he decided to move the school. The accusations included 'cultural degeneracy', 'Bolshevism', and a general foreignness, which some of the good citizens of Weimar may have felt to be irreconcilable with their genteel sense of a national cultural tradition ornamented by Goethe and Classicism. However, some of the charges were an eerie premonition of savage criticisms which would return with new force in the thirties, when they were backed by the rising Nazi tide:

> ... what the Bauhaus offered in these first public displays stands so far beyond the pale of any kind of art that it can only be considered in pathological terms ... The clearly recognizable philosophical attitude which is entirely devoted to negating everything that exists causes the Bauhaus people to lose all social connection, in the widest sense, with the rest of the world. ... The work of the Bauhaus carries signs of the deepest spiritual isolation and disintegration. The public therefore rightly objects to the notion that in this manner young artists and craftsmen in Thuringia who still have honest and sober aspirations are simply going to be banned from a thorough education if the Staatliche Bauhaus continues to exist in its present form. A small band of interested persons, who for the most part are foreigners, should not be allowed to suffocate the healthy mass of youthful German art students like a layer of oil on clear water. Moreover, this undertaking was only ostensibly based on artistic endeavours. It was, in reality, intended to be politically partisan from the beginning, for it proclaimed itself the rallying point of the sky-storming socialists who believed in the future and who wanted to build a cathedral of socialism. Well, the reality around us shows what this cathedral looks like.
>
> The Bauhaus in Weimar too, contributes a fitting note with its 'works of art' that are put together with the ingredients of a junk pile ...

The mayor of Dessau, by contrast, showed considerable sympathy for the ideals of the school. Within a year a site had been chosen on flat land outside the town on which Gropius was to design a new building for his institution. This was an opportunity for him to create an exemplary modern building in which all the arts would be synthesized, and the philosophy of the school would be expressed.

The site was unconstricted and open; the programme was large; so the solution would have to break down the main volumes in such a way that they could be experienced from any angle, but without loss of overall coherence. Gropius expressed the separate elements as rectangular volumes of varying size, which were then linked by intermediary oblongs containing corridors or smaller rooms. Thus the art studios and the craft workshops were linked by a bridge which crossed over a road traversing the site. The next level of articulation involved the accentuation of volumes and planes, verticals and horizontals, through the composition of window surfaces: a set-piece Bauhaus exercise in the heightened expression of three-dimensional tensions in space, but one which still had to take practicalities into account. Gropius varied his fenestration to accentuate the largeness or smallness of the spaces within, and to admit various qualities of light according to function (figs. 9.13, 9.14).

Evidently, Gropius was given a large amount of plate glass at the time he commenced design, but the 'duty' of including this clearly did not violate his general aesthetic aims. The glazing far transcended its merely formal or functional characteristics, becoming an emblem of the machine age. At times the glass was laid flush with the façade, reinforcing the overall volumetric character of a space enclosed by a skin; at times it was recessed, accentuating the hovering white horizontal floor planes: and all of these choices of detail were to articulate the larger movements and themes of the design. What is so striking about the Bauhaus buildings in retrospect is the precision of the formal thinking, and the fusion of Gropius's earlier ideas and vocabulary. The experiences of the pre-war Faguswerk and Deutscher Werkbund years; the spiritual idealism and Utopianism of the post-war period; the search for a language blending abstraction and mechanization – all are here, but synthesized into a statement which was paralleled in its assurance by perhaps only the Schroeder House or Maison Cook at this stage in the unfolding history of the modern movement.

Indeed, the Bauhaus solution was more than a personal statement of assurance: it marked a major step in the maturing system of forms many other architects were beginning to adopt. And just as in, say, the early phases of Gothic or Renaissance architecture there was a gradual coalescence of sources into a new, coherent system of expression, so, at the Bauhaus, the International Style came of age. There were lessons

9.13 Walter Gropius, Bauhaus building, Dessau, 1926.

9.14 Walter Gropius, Bauhaus building, Dessau, 1926, aerial view.

9.15 Marcel Breuer, tubular steel armchair, *c.* 1926. New York, Museum of Modern Art, gift of Herbert Bayer.

here for all who were trying to forge their own vocabulary within the shared values of the period, and soon after its completion, the building was published worldwide. Among the photos were aerial ones which gave it the appearance of a giant Elementarist sculpture.

Gropius designed residences for the masters and for himself close to the school, so that by the end of 1926 a new colony had grown up around Dessau which seems, initially, to have been more tolerated than it had been in Weimar. This was the Golden Age of the Bauhaus, with Wassily Kandinsky and Paul Klee teaching in the *Formlehre*, Laszlo Moholy-Nagy and Marcel Breuer instructing in design, Oskar Schlemmer producing his ballets, and the first apprentices beginning to make their mark in the outside world. The German public took a great interest in the school,

which was constantly under fire for its supposed 'decadent' and 'subversive' tendencies. This interest stemmed, in part, from the flood of articles and books published by the Bauhaus staff, particularly the *Bauhausbücher*, which presented the ideas of Klee, Kandinsky, Moholy-Nagy, Gropius, and others in their respective fields.

It is instructive to examine some of the artistic and intellectual products of the later phase of the Bauhaus as a means of gauging its change of direction since the early Weimar years. In the factory workshops, for example, Marcel Breuer and Mart Stam evolved tubular steel chair designs (fig. 9.15) as models for standardized mass production; these had cantilevered overhangs and an airy and lightweight appearance in tune with Gropius's general ideal of finding forms which 'symbolized the modern world'. The contrast

was considerable with Breuer's 1921 designs for chairs made of wood, with their exaggerated handicraft character and their far dumpier form. Similar contrasts can be made over the six years between 1920 and 1926 with light fixtures, ashtrays, tapestries, and other objects; indeed, it is also instructive to compare the *Bauhutte* of the Sommerfeld House with 'the machine for teaching' of the Bauhaus buildings, for this reveals a similar shift in emphasis and meaning.

Now that the Bauhaus was at last settled in its new home, Gropius turned his attention increasingly to the problems of standardization in architecture. This was manifest in housing studies he instituted in the school, which culminated in the rationalization of collective apartment blocks, open to space, light, air, and view. In 1928 he was employed by Siemens to build company workers' housing outside Berlin (fig. 9.17). After 1925, with the stabilization of the mark, cities like Frankfurt and Stuttgart had already employed such modern architects as Bruno Taut (who had sobered since his Expressionist days) and Ernst May to design large-scale, low-cost housing, and a variety of standard models had been evolved. In principle, the layouts frequently drew on English Garden City ideals. but in form the houses were simple and cubic. This led

critics to perceive in them an anti-German sense, and Gropius too was criticized for the supposed 'unnatural', 'anti-human', and 'mechanistic' character of his architecture. Thus as the new architecture extended beyond the scope of paper projects and private and specialized commissions, it was increasingly likely to be misunderstood, particularly when the 'factory aesthetic' invaded the precinct of the home. Especially in the hands of the hardest-headed 'Neue Sachlichkeit' ('new objectivity') planners in Berlin, who eschewed 'formalism' and the pursuit of 'higher spiritual meanings', there was the constant danger that the intended aesthetic effects of sobriety and controlled repetition might be misread as blandness and lifelessness. The collision between architects' norms and the public's was often drastic.

Moreover, debates over the form of housing revealed a variety of positions within German modern architecture, from the hard-headed attitudes of some of the adherents of the 'G' group in Berlin, who continued to proclaim functionalist and rationalist ideals, to the more 'spiritual' aspirations of men like Gropius and Mendelsohn, for whom formal poetics were essential to architecture. Even Mies van der Rohe (who was in reality closer to the latter camp than the former) could

9.16 (*left*) Weissen-hofsiedlung, Stuttgart, 1927, general view.

9.17 (*above*) Walter Gropius, Siemensstadt housing, Berlin, 1928.

be found parroting the attitudes of strict objectivity:

> We reject all aesthetic speculation, all doctrine, all formalism. We refuse to recognize problems of form; we recognize only problems of building. Form is not the aim of our work; only the result. Form by itself does not exist. Form as an aim is formalism, and that we reject.

In 1925, Mies had been asked by the Deutscher Werkbund to oversee the design of the first major exhibition of the organization since 1914. This was to be devoted to housing models, which were to be co-ordinated in a single *Siedlung* design (fig. 9.16) on a brow overlooking Stuttgart (see Chapter 13). The majority of the contributors were German, indeed were from Berlin (e.g., Mies himself, Gropius, Hilbersheimer, Taut, Scharoun), but J. P. Oud and Mart Stam were invited from Holland, V. Bourgeois from Belgium, and Le Corbusier from France. Mies's overall site plan was like an abstract sculpture of different sized blocks laid out to echo the form of the terrain, with his own design for a block of twenty-four apartments at the crown. This was a simple geometrical volume with fixed bathroom cores and ingenious interior planning. Le Corbusier ended up designing two schemes – a much accentuated 'Citrohan' dwelling, and a larger version on dramatically advertised *pilotis*. Meanwhile, Scharoun's design at the other end of the site, with its curved balcony forms and completely different spatial character, was a reminder of the variety of individual inflections within the modern movement. Even so, the overwhelming impression was of a general conformity of expression, in which simple cubic volumes, stripped planar shapes, open plans, and machine-age details were the hallmarks. The extreme right in Germany were quick to denounce the whole thing as further evidence of an international communist plot, and there were even caricatures of the *Siedlung* in which camels and Arabs were shown wandering around a sup-posedly degenerate 'kasbah'. But to the proponents and supporters of International Modern architecture, the exhibition transcended its fascinating lessons in housing by exhibiting directly the character of what was later (by Alfred Barr in 1932) to be called 'the International Style'. In retrospect, 1927 appears to have been a crucial year of self-realization on an international front for the new architecture.

In 1928, Gropius left the Bauhaus and handed over the reins to Hannes Meyer. Meyer's philosophy differed considerably from his predecessor's: he despised the formalist camp for their bogus 'humanism' and defined architecture laconically as the result of the equation 'function × economics'. It might be thought that this was a proclamation of the purest capitalist in-strumentalism; in fact, it betokened a Socialist puritanism which (despite Meyer's protests to the contrary) was expressed in an architectural style made eloquent by its lack of pretensions and its direct expression of functional volumes and the supposed 'ordinariness' of machine-produced components. Meyer was far less squeamish about the radicalization of the Bauhaus than Gropius had been; he encouraged the design of cheap plywood furniture, and even pointedly changed the name of the 'architecture' department to 'building'. This lent extra support to the notion that the Bauhaus was indeed some sort of Trojan horse of Bolshevism, and criticisms against the school became vitriolic in the late twenties and early thirties, especially when the Nazi party understood how much political capital was to be made from supporting aesthetic dogmas of a regionalist and nationalist bent. Finally, Mies van der Rohe oversaw the school in its last years up to its closure in 1933.

But the Bauhaus idea did not die. When Gropius, Mies van der Rohe, Moholy-Nagy, Breuer, and Albers emigrated to the United States in the late thirties, they took their ideas with them. However, this is already to speak of a later stage of dissemination in the history of the modern movement.

10. Architecture and Revolution in Russia

> We are convinced that the new forms of Soviet architecture will be found not by way of the imitation of the architectural forms of the past but on a basis of critical thinking ... by way of a profound understanding of living processes and their translation into architectural form.
>
> A. and V. Vesnin, 1926

While the forms of modern architecture created during the 1920s cannot be understood apart from the social ideals which gave rise to them, simplistic equations between ideology and formal usage should be regarded with suspicion. The German examples cited in the last chapter serve to show, among other things, a spectrum of political attitudes within the modern movement from the spiritualized 'apolitical socialism' of Gropius to the far more hard-headed, left-wing stance of Hannes Meyer. Likewise, whatever Utopian yearnings they may have shared, the versions of an ideal life entertained by such artists as Le Corbusier, Gerrit Rietveld, and Erich Mendelsohn varied considerably. One should be cautious then of imputing to the whole of modern architecture some monolithic ideology; and even once it has become clear what a rich variety of values was operative, there is no direct step from a set of ideas to a set of forms.

These cautionary remarks seem pertinent to the Soviet architecture of the twenties, since this emerged in a post-Revolutionary atmosphere which encouraged dogmatic assertions about the supposed 'truth' of modern architecture to the new social order. In fact the matter was by no means straightforward. Creative individuals were faced with the awesome task of formulating an architecture which was supposed to 'express' not so much the values of an existent order, but one it was felt *ought* to emerge from the progressive attitudes of the revolution. Here there were many problems. To begin with, it was clear that earlier national traditions could play little part as these were 'tainted' with the values of the old regime or with a narrow nationalism inappropriate to the clarion call of a world revolution. Then it was uncertain what functions should be catered for to help in the general process of emancipation, and what images should be employed in the definition of a supposedly 'proletariat' culture. Perhaps even more basic: it was not entirely agreed whether architecture should follow or lead in the definition of a new order. Reviewing the various positions of the 1920s, one finds a multiplicity of reactions to these problems, all the way from those who considered architecture a minor element in social reform to those who felt, on the contrary, that artistic endeavours should stand at the vanguard of change.

The turbulent artistic debates of the 1920s can scarcely be understood without some sense of the nineteenth-century background in Russia. Here the general rule was an eclecticism emulating European trends in support of the somewhat effete tastes of the aristocracy. Despite the attempts of Count Anatoly Nikolaevich Demidov at launching a Slavic Revival, the aping of monumental, Western European Classical prototypes continued well beyond the turn of the century; indeed, we shall see that this tradition was later co-opted to state purposes under the dictatorship of Stalin. The short burst of activity of the avant-garde in the 1920s was thus an interlude of a sort. However, it was anticipated, in part, by the 'Populist' movement of the late nineteenth century, with its close attention to the realities of the masses; by the activities of the 'Ropetskaia' group (who took folklore as their guide); and, most important, by the 'Prolecult' movement founded in 1906, which achieved an uneasy alliance between workers' unions and the aspirations of the avant-garde.

Thus an avant-garde culture of sorts had existed within the old order, drawing heavily on influences from Western Europe, particularly in painting and sculpture. However, these are art forms which may be created in private; in architecture there was little vital deviation from the reactionary modes of the nineteenth-century revivalists. It was not difficult for the later generation to see this tired aestheticism as a direct portrait of what they thought of as a defunct social system. Whatever the requirements of patronage, no major talent seems have emerged, in any case, during the few decades preceding the Revolution. But the overthrow of the old order did not guarantee a vital wave in the arts, though it may have encouraged it. The period after 1917 was one of frenzied visual experimentation in which ideas tended to exist more on paper than anywhere else. This was natural given the confused economic circumstances of the years up until about 1924, in which construction was all but impossible. It was an atmosphere which, as in the same period in Germany, encouraged a heady and impractical Utopianism.

The need to destroy all links with the reactionary past brought problems for the architect seeking a visual language of expression appropriate to new ideals. He could not create *ex nihilo* even if he did have 'a profound understanding of living processes' (to

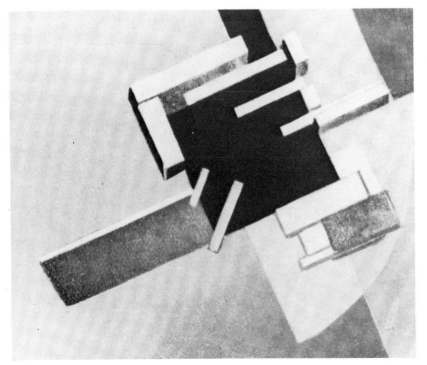

10.1 El Lissitzky, 'Proun' (city), 1920.

paraphrase the Vesnin brothers). A vocabulary which fitted the situation had to be created. But where could the creator now turn for his forms? Could contemporary realities 'generate' a vocabulary on their own, or should the individual admit that he had to lay a personal interpretation on events? Should the individual building be treated as a neutral solution to a carefully analysed programme with the stress on practicality? Or should the artist seek metaphors and images which distilled his excitement at the post-revolutionary possibilities? Perhaps he should attempt to create provocative emblems which gave a hint of the future state; or perhaps he should concentrate on the design of non-unique prototypes for later mass production in the service of the greater number. Such questions and dilemmas as these underlay the debates and formal explorations of the late 1910s and the early 1920s. Such 'bibles' as the writings of Marx and Engels supplied little guidance as these could be pulled in to support a wide divergence of approaches: neither writer had had more than a confused idea of the way 'art' had functioned in the cultures of the past.

The first crucial discussions which would have a direct impact on architecture and town planning were held in February 1918 when the Pan-Russian executive committee abolished private property and proclaimed the socialization of the soil. Artists found an immediate outlet in the design of propaganda trains and posters, and the daubing of walls with strident visual statements. Art schools newly set up in Moscow and the provinces overthrew the vestiges of Beaux-Arts education, and introduced ideas of basic design (derived from abstract art), and theories based on a belief in a universal aesthetic language (already present in Malevich's 'Suprematism'). Constructivist artists like Naum Gabo and Antoine Pevsner attempted to create a scientific-technological sculpture from steel, glass, and plastic, in which Cubist and Futurist conceptions of sculpture were extended to basic rhythms of space and form supposed to mimic the structures of physics. Furious debates ensued concerning the legacy of bourgeois 'spiritual' aesthetics: should the artist reintegrate with social functions by concentrating on the design of utilitarian objects? The idealistic and the pragmatic were bridged by Lissitzky, whose abstract 'Prouns' were conceived as ideograms with a Utopian content, but also as a basic form language applicable to sculpture, furniture, typography, or buildings (fig. 10.1). N. A. Ladovsky's psycho-technical laboratory at the Vkhutemas school encouraged free experimentation with basic geometrical shapes to discover the rules of a new language of composition which might, when economic reconstruction allowed it, eventually pervade architectural thinking and even the form of the city.

A partial solution to the problem of originating a contemporary architectural vocabulary without reference to the institutions or images of Tsarist Russia lay in the groundwork already done in Western Europe towards the definition of modern architecture. Futurist ideas were co-opted, shaved of their proto-Fascist character, and mated with Marxist ideals in the quest for suitable metaphors to express the supposed inner dynamism of the revolutionary process. Machine worship became a tenet of faith, as if mechanization could be thought of as identical with the social and historical path of progress. This was not, perhaps, a curious choice of emphasis given the 'backwardness' of the Soviet Union in industrial terms, but for this same reason it meant that an imagery was elaborated which was quite foreign to the large majority who were peasants. Besides, the activities of the avant-garde were largely restricted to the cities, and had little to give to evolving vernacular traditions.

Thus the avant-garde – a curious minority class of its own – took on the task of formulating a visual language supposed to be instinct with the aspirations of Soviet society as a whole. Intrinsic to this position was the belief that the artist must have some special intuition of the deeper processes of society, which would transcend mere populist expression. In the Soviet Union an iconography was evolved which blended the floating planes of abstract art with direct quotations from the factory floor and the production line (fig. 10.3). A rhetorical and highly demonstrative machine fetishism seems often to have been the result, in which the factory aesthetic, ships' hooters, and elaborate splays of wires might be assembled into dramatic architectural collages posing as theatrical stage sets (e.g., Meyerhold's stage designs of around 1920) or as entire buildings. For the time being, the question of the possible irrelevance of all this fantasy world to a country whose technology lagged far behind Western Europe's, and whose intelligentsia, however well intentioned, was divorced from the values of the majority, was conveniently left aside.

Some sense of the new orientation in Russia is to be gleaned from Tatlin's paper project for a Monument to the Third International of 1920 (fig. 10.2). Inside two interlacing spirals of open structural lattice-work were suspended three volumes – a cube, a pyramid, and a cylinder – containing the various congress halls of the state. Each of these chambers was designed to revolve at a different speed – once a year, once a month, and once a day – in accordance with the supposed cosmic importance of the enclosed institutions. Tatlin intended that the monument should be over 300 metres tall (even taller than the Eiffel Tower) and painted red, the colour symbolizing the Revolution. The inspiration for this romantic display of engineering seems to have

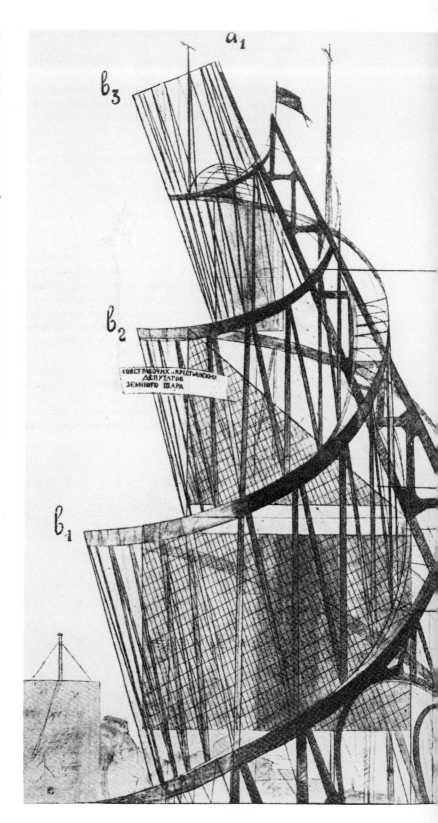

10.2 (*left*) Vladimir Tatlin, Monument to the Third International, project, 1920.

10.3 (*below right*) El Lissitzky, design for Lenin's Tribune, early 1920s.

come from such diverse sources as oil derricks, fairground constructions, and Futurist images like Boccioni's spiralling *Bottle Unfolding in Space*. However, the transparent lattices and abstract sculptural forms were more than a display of private virtuosity; the spirals were intended as suitable expressions of the new order. Nikolai Punin wrote of the inherently vital and dynamic characteristics of the spiral:

> The spiral is a line of liberation for humanity: with one extremity resting on the ground, it flees the earth with the other; and thereby becomes a symbol of disinterestedness, and of the converse of earthly pettiness.

In this case, though, the tilt of the main volumes was contained within a *double* helix drawing gradually to a resolution at the top. It may be that this was intended to have the extra significance of an image of the dialectical historical process, between thesis and antithesis, with the eventual harmony of a synthesis. If so, Tatlin's tower must be read as an emblem of Marxist ideology, in which the actual movements of the parts,

and the sculptural dynamism of the armature, symbolized the very idea of a revolutionary society aspiring to the 'highest state' of an egalitarian, proletarian Utopia.

Much like Boullée's grandiose visions of the late eighteenth century, Tatlin's tower was scarcely buildable at the time it was conceived; the model itself was assembled from old cigar-box wood and tin cans. But the power of the idea was still considerable. Had it been built, it would have dwarfed all nearby buildings, effectively challenging and overbearing the monumental churches and palaces of the *ancien régime*. Thus, in iconographic terms, it might be right to speak of Tatlin's design as another attempt at realizing a 'Cathedral of Socialism', dedicated in this case to nothing less than a new religion. The historian eager to find parallels in other media may recognize similarities of theme in Serge Eisenstein's slightly later film *Battleship Potemkin*, in which the notion of salvation through revolution was also played out with the help of mechanistic images (e.g., the battleship), and through a scheme of alternating contrasts using montage. What is so striking about each of these works of art is the way in which revolutionary values were sublimated in a manner far transcending banal realist portrayal.

Although much of the small amount of building done in the early 1920s in Russia was conservative in nature, there were gradual incursions of the avant-garde, especially in the world of architectural competitions. The competition for the Palace of Labour of 1923–24 drew forth a rich variety of solutions. The programme envisaged a colossal 8,000-seat auditorium, another one for 2,500, a meteorological observatory, an astro-physical laboratory, a social science museum, a museum of labour, a library, a restaurant for 6,000 diners, and a myriad of offices. The institution was a novel one and little help could be found in consulting traditional types. The solution produced by the Vesnin brothers (fig. 10.4) made much of the separate articulation of the different functions in simple contrasting forms linked by dramatic circulation bridges. The theatres and main social spaces were contained in an oval zone, the administrative areas in a rectangular tower. Reinforced-concrete construction was not simply employed but sculpturally heightened through the latticework expression of the vertical and horizontal members of the frame. A crude attempt was made to express the dynamic interpenetration of volumes, as well as a degree of axial formality appropriate to the institutional character. The main forms were then liberally dressed with the paraphernalia of radio masts, taut wires, and ships' hooters; once again a communal building was expressed, essentially, as a social engine.

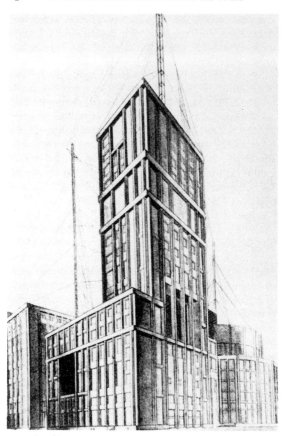

But like so many other projects of the period, this one was not built.

The Vesnin brothers also designed a scheme for the Pravda building in 1924 (fig. 10.7). This exhibited a new degree of formal control – a more successful fusion of the devices of abstract art with the articulation of function and mechanistic moving parts. The building was envisaged as a sort of skyscraper kiosk and succeeded in embodying the architects' excitement at the notion of a modern communications centre. The attached searchlight, the revolving billboards and the moving lifts visible within glass cages all recalled the Futurist notion of a building as a sort of machine, if not precisely Sant' Elian images of a new architecture made of light materials, with lifts snaking up and down. But the rhetorical imagery was here submitted to a rigorous geometrical and functional control, with the floor slabs expressed as thin planes, and the roof slab expressed as a thicker 'cornice'. It is ironical that such a celebration of modern technology should have been conceived in a country where, well into the 1920s, even reinforced-concrete buildings had to be created by the crudest mass labour and handicraft methods. The irony is doubled when one considers that

was a masterly propaganda instrument. The plan was traversed by a diagonal ascending way allowing views on to the exhibits on either side, and effecting the penetration of inner and outer spaces. The volumes of the main pavilion were rhomboidal in form, rather than simply rectangular, and the illusions of perspective that this produced added to the visual tension of the design. The main building was demountable and made of wood, but its *imagery* was a flagrant celebration of the factory aesthetic. For those untutored in the associational meanings of modern architectural forms (presumably the majority of the visitors) the identity and meaning of the building were reinforced by a sort of pergola straddling the walkway, made of interlacing girders and hammers and sickles. The contrast between this deliberately humble, cut-to-the-bone treatment and the chintzy, consumerist kitsch of most of the other national pavilions can only have added to the force of the messages. Only Le Corbusier's 'Pavillon de L'Esprit Nouveau', tucked to one side of the exhibition site, was equal to this display of probity. Nonetheless, both artists' designs were curious microcosms of larger world views striving for an actual social outlet; they stood like Utopian fragments alongside the sophisticated but shallow expressions of middle-class commercialized taste, exotically drenched in the new possibilities of expression revealed by Art Deco.

Thus the period up to 1925 was one of tentative paper experimentation, or of small-scale building hypotheses, for the Soviet avant-garde. The second half of the 1920s – as in Germany – was a period of realization. The modern architects took it upon themselves to imagine new functions as well as new forms. Indeed, Melnikov himself was among the first architects to conceive 'social condensers' – clubs or public buildings containing theatres, communal libraries, and lounges for the dissemination of ideas, the celebration of public life, and a controlled form of 'leisure'. Again Melnikov could not conceive of such functions in neutral formal terms: he sought to translate the programmes into jagged sculptural volumes. In his design for the Rusakov Workers' Club in Moscow of 1927–8 (fig. 10.8), the auditorium was made to converge on the stage, and its rear extension was made to overhang the back of the building. The sharp intersections and contrasts of shape were articulated in details. Melnikov, like other members of the ASNOVA school, tended to believe there was an underlying language of forms which could be relied upon to elicit specific emotions in the spectator. He saw it as the task of architecture to co-opt this universal language of form in the service of the vital themes of revolution.

This position was heavily attacked on the grounds

10.4 (*above far left*) The Vesnin brothers, Palace of Labour, competition project, 1923.

10.5 (*above left*) Konstantin Melnikov, USSR pavilion, Exposition des Arts Décoratifs, Paris, 1925.

10.6 (*far left*) El Lissitzky, 'Cloud-hanger' project, 1926.

10.7 (*left*) The Vesnin brothers, Pravda building, project, 1924.

10.8 (*above*) Konstantin Melnikov, Rusakov Workers' Club, Moscow, 1927–8.

in the United States, where the appropriate technology was in existence, little attempt was made to celebrate it. Thus the architect of the Soviet avant-garde found himself trapped in a Utopian hall of mirrors, dreaming up unbuildable schemes for a society of uncertain form. One senses something of the same difficulty with Lissitzky's extraordinary schemes for 'cloud-hanger' skyscrapers, cantilevered on giant piers over key Moscow intersections (fig. 10.6.).

The Exposition des Arts Décoratifs in Paris in 1925 gave the Soviet Union the opportunity to design a show-case of industrial goods; clearly the building would also have to be a banner of Soviet ideology. The architect chosen for the task was Konstantin Melnikov, a member of the Association of New Architects (ASNOVA), a former teacher at the Vkhutemas school, and an artist dedicated to the notion that a dynamic sculptural expression, stirring the masses, was the right style for the new order. His pavilion (fig. 10.5)

that it was rooted in bogus, bourgeois, 'idealistic' aesthetics. A typical critique emerged in the theories of the Association of Contemporary Architects (OSA) – including men like M. Ginzburg, M. Barshch, V. Vladimirov, A. and V. Vesnin – which pilloried ASNOVA for its self-indulgence and lack of attention to practicality. In a well-documented debate which took place in 1929, F. Yalovkin of the OSA criticized the descendants of the 'formalist camp':

> The principal difference between the present associations consists in their very aim, i.e. for the constructivists (the OSA), the social role of architecture is essentially as one of the instruments for the building of socialism by means of the collectivization of life, by means of the rationalization of labour, by means of the utilization of scientific data and so on, whereas for [the formalists] the social role 'acquires a special significance' and the essence of this 'special significance' is that you make architecture an art, not contemplative but 'active', which 'must become a means' for the liberation of the masses, a powerful lever in the building of socialism and a new collectivist way of life, organizing the psyche and actively educating the will and feeling of the masses towards the struggle for communism. . . . Their pathetic ejaculations about art are reminiscent of antediluvian searchings for a god; for we believe that what is needed is not the invention of an art . . . but work on the organization of architecture, proceeding from the data of economics, science, and technology. It is to this great work that we call all the architects of the Soviet Union.

At the opposite end of the spectrum from formalist tendencies were functionalist ones, according to which sociology and technique would on their own dictate the new forms. In this case the criticism could be produced that the functionalist was imitating the debasement of life implicit in Western industrialization. The OSA group managed in their ideology and their architecture to steer carefully between these extremes, despite their tendency to veer towards a severe puritanism of expression. Such architects of the group as Moisei Ginzburg turned their attention to housing and to the creation of collectivist dwellings. Inherent in his plans and in the various theoretical researches of the OSA was the belief that the clear logic of planning and the sanity of orderly forms could have some limited moral effect on the gradually evolving forms of society. A typical product of the group was the Narkomfin apartment building built in Moscow in 1928 (fig. 10.9). The concept marked a transition between the traditional apartment house containing

10.9 (*left*) Moisei Ginzburg and I. Milinis, Narkomfin apartments, Moscow, 1928.

10.10 (*top right*) OSA group, study of an 'F type' apartment, section, 1928.

10.11 (*centre right*) I. Nikolayev, student dormitory, Moscow, 1929, model.

10.12 (*bottom right*) I. Nikolayev, student dormitory, Moscow, 1929, residential slab.

entirely private flats and a new type of communal housing in which some areas were shared, and in which a judicious balance was sought between the individual, the family, and the larger social group. The impact of Le Corbusier's formal vocabulary was indisputable: the housing was contained in a long low box lifted from the ground on stilts, and the *fenêtre en longueur* (strip window) was here used as a primary device for articulating the whole. The OSA devoted much time to housing studies, considering such questions as the functional family cell, the minimum standards commensurate with mass production, and the meaning of different access spaces. The Narkomfin building was a laboratory of their social researches. It incorporated a variety of 'F type', the minimum, one-family units (fig. 10.10), with larger 'K type' units with three rooms on two levels. The section of the building as a whole was an ingenious invention using a three-over-two arrangement. Thus living-rooms on one side of the building could be ample in height and well lit, while bedrooms and bathrooms could be smaller, more economic in their use of space and contained on the other side of the building. But this functional arrangement had further properties: the 3/2 system allowed access decks to be threaded along the entire

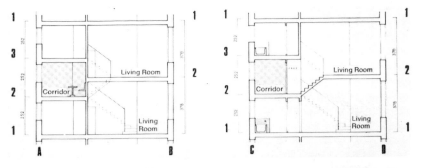

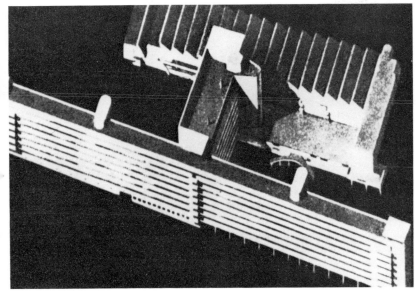

length of the building at every third level, and apartments to be jigsawed together so that views and light on both sides could be enjoyed. These 'street-decks' were more than mere functional access corridors, however: they could be seen as symbolic elements expressing communal aspirations; in the Narkomfin building they were actually heated to encourage interaction all through the year. The other communal parts of the building, such as the canteen, kitchen, gymnasium, library, and day nursery, were contained in an earth-bound rectangular element linked to the main oblong by a bridge. Le Corbusier's idea of the roof terrace was here employed as a further communal space for use in the summer months. It would be preposterous to claim that Ginzburg and his associates were not concerned with aesthetic matters in such a crisp and well-proportioned formal statement. But the contrast with the sculptural acrobatics of ASNOVA architects is still obvious: the OSA sought to generate the overall volumes of a building from a stringent rationale taking into account living patterns, circulation, cost, building procedure, etc. This 'diagram' was then translated into a restrained aesthetic terminology which suggested social values of co-operation and moral stability.

The *parti* employing a slab for private living with attached communal elements in separate volumes was much used for student hostels in Russia in the late 1920s (figs. 10.11, 10.12) and may have had a direct influence on Le Corbusier's Pavillon Suisse in the Cité Universitaire, Paris, of 1930–31. Indeed, by 1927 Soviet architecture was well known in European publications, and there was a regular traffic of ideas to and fro. The role of Russian abstract art at the Bauhaus has already been mentioned, and was no doubt aided by the impact of an exhibition of Soviet art (including Lissitzky's 'Proun room'), in Berlin in 1922; but influences clearly worked the other way too, and it is scarcely an exaggeration to claim that without Le Corbusier, Soviet architects of the late 1920s would have had far less idea than they did how to translate their visions into forms and then into three-dimensional realities. In 1927 Le Corbusier was invited to design a major project in Moscow: the headquarters of the central co-operatives known as the 'Centrosoyus'. The programme called for the combination of office spaces with lecture halls, conference rooms and large public forums. The challenge this problem posed to Le Corbusier's vocabulary was in some ways analogous to the one posed by the League of Nations competition of the same period. The architect had to 'stretch' an architectural system which had been applied initially to the design of villas, and in the process was forced to discover means for articulating hierarchies of varied functions, and for breaking down

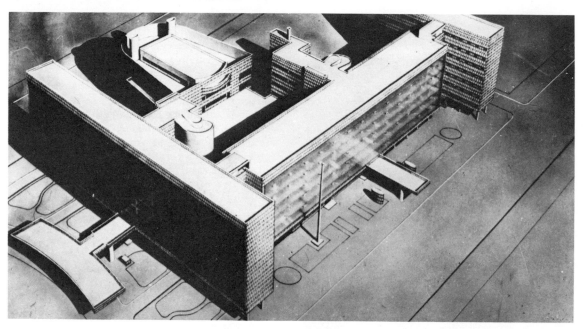

10.13 Le Corbusier, Centrosoyus building, Moscow, second project model, 1928.

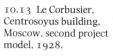

the overall form into discrete parts which still had, somehow, to be integrated harmoniously. In both schemes it was also necessary to respond to different site conditions on each side. The design process of the Centrosoyus shows the architect grappling with these problems and evolving a scheme in which circulation was a strong organizing principle, and primary and secondary axes were used to define major routes and emphases (fig. 10.13). The result relies strongly on the increased spatial complexity manifest in his paintings in the previous two or three years. The Purist language was being forced to become more ambiguous and multivalent. But the Centrosoyus seems to indicate too that Le Corbusier wished to outdo the Constructivists on their own ground by taking over from them devices like the sculptural expression of circulation zones, and the dynamic equilibrium of asymmetrical volumes across space; indeed, he attempted to handle these elements with greater control and conviction than in the originals. The Centrosoyus also marked one of the architect's first attempts at handling a fully glazed façade with the help of a crude mechanical heating and ventilating system, which was scarcely equal to the climatic extremes of Moscow's summers and winters. The bulbous forms of the auditoria and circulation ramps were quickly absorbed into the general vocabulary of modern architecture and devalued to the level of official cliché in numerous ensuing state projects.

The dream of a sort of secular equivalent to a cathedral – a collectivist emblem signifying an integrated culture – seems to have lain close to the surface of Soviet architectural imagination through-

out the twenties. But there were few individual artists equal to the imaginative challenge. One architect whose work far transcends the bickering division between formal expression and functional necessity expressed in the OSA/ASNOVA debates was Ivan Leonidov. Like Le Corbusier, whom he much admired, he seems to have been able to forge a synthesis of poetry and fact, of form and function, which at the same time dug to deeper levels of aspiration than the pantomime technocrats. This is clear in his proposal for a Lenin Institute of 1927 (fig. 10.14). The reading-room is expressed as a glass sphere, a form which perhaps conveys a universalizing intention and a metaphor of enlightenment simultaneously. But this world image is not earth-bound: it has almost the character of a balloon which wishes to pull free of its cables and rise into the air. The twin themes of visual lightness and spatial hovering seem intimately connected with a content of a metaphysical sort, as if the architect was attempting to extract an almost sacral meaning from the pantheon of Soviet heroes and Marxist ideas. The other main element is the stack tower, expressed as a slender skyscraper to which delicate power lines and radial antennae are attached in tension. The space between and around these two forms is activated by the slender planes of horizontal offices which intersect the round podium on which the main sculptural objects are placed. Elements slide past one another in the manner of a Lissitzky abstraction, or even a 'pin-wheel' Wrightian plan, and extend towards the corners of the world. Leonidov's scheme incorporates a full range of Constructivist com-

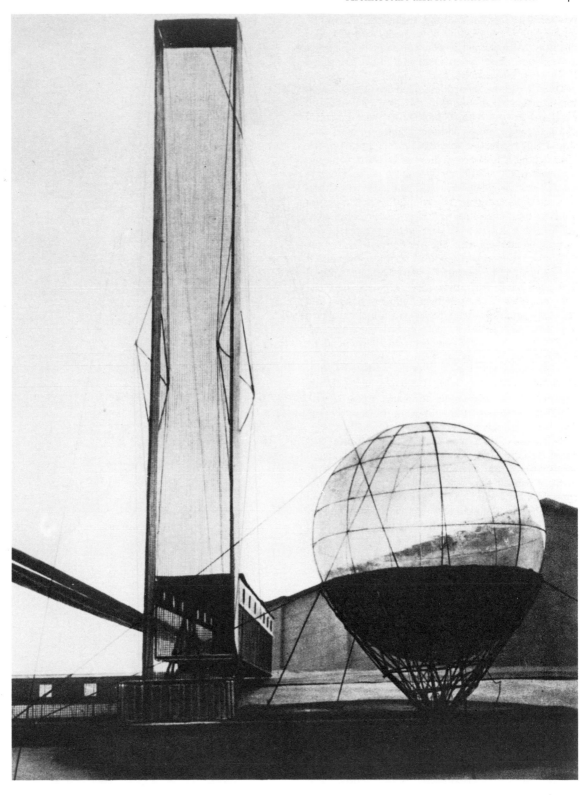

10.14 Ivan Leonidov,
Lenin Institute, project,
1927.

positional devices and indicates the maturity of a style phase, but a mere listing of elements scarcely does credit to the power of the idea. Once again, one is left guessing as to how the architect might have translated this fantasy into material form.

Thus it can be seen that architects in the Soviet Union applied their minds to the full range of social functions in the 1920s, including housing, social clubs, theatres, offices, libraries, dams, factories, and state institutions. But they also gave thought to the ideal relationships between them all, to town planning, and even to the spatial reorganization of the country-side. Artistic imagination here attempted to work hand in hand with economic reorganization at the largest scale in the generation of a new visual and spatial culture (fig. 10.15). Of the various garden city paradigms adopted from the West and transformed, the linear city was perhaps most pertinent, because it fused together the means of production (agricultural and industrial) with networks of power and circulation, allowed the interpenetration of nature and the city, and encouraged the integration of rural and industrial proletariats in spatially ordered surroundings. Social condensers and family dwellings could be distributed evenly in parallel bands to the main routes, and the linear, non-hierarchical character of such a city form was felt to be particularly appropriate to the egalitarian aspirations of the inhabitants (fig. 10.16). Thus the linear form was adopted in the design of the new city of Magnitogorsk in the late 1920s.

By the end of the 1920s, though, the various avant-garde groups came under the increasingly close scrutiny of central state control. The Politburo seems to have sensed that traditional images of national consolidation, including the readaptation of Classical and eclectic monumentality in architecture, might serve its purposes better than the imagery of modern architecture. Meanwhile, the divergence between avant-garde values and popular ones was becoming increasingly clear. It is ironical that the products of the Soviet modern movement should have been accused of bourgeois formalism almost exactly at the same time that the products of the German modern movement were pilloried as 'Bolshevist' and un-German. Totalitarian manipulation of visual culture took different forms, but the triple pressures of State control, emphasis on regional values, and need for centralized traditional images of State power have eerie similarities in both Stalin's Russia and Hitler's Germany.

The drama in which the modern movement played out its final act was the Palace of the Soviets competition of 1931. The programme called for a colossal building incorporating two auditoria, press galleries, meeting rooms, libraries, and a monumental image equal to the progressivist technical and social

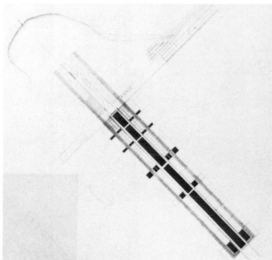

10.15 (*above*) T. Varentsov, urban project for regional centre, 1927.

10.16 (*left*) B. Lavrov, linear city proposal, mid-1920s.

10.17 (*below*) Le Corbusier, Palace of the Soviets, Moscow, competition project model, 1931.

10.18 B. M. Iofan,
Palace of the Soviets,
competition winner
(second version, 1934).

structivism. The roof of the main hall was suspended on wires from a parabolic arch which would have dominated the skyline of Moscow. The lower auditorium had a scarcely less dramatic structural treatment: cantilevered flanges were splayed in plan to create a focal concentration towards the space between the two main volumes. Here there was an open-air space – a sort of modern *agora* – linked to the surrounding public space of the city by ramps and walkways. Within were vast hypostyle halls of *pilotis* where, presumably, the business of debate and discussion would have continued between the main sessions. Once again Le Corbusier demonstrated his ability to probe the underlying meaning of a social programme and to translate this into aesthetic forms.

But his palace was not to be. The model went back to Paris, as Gropius's did to Berlin. Official taste intervened and gave the prize to a Soviet entry by B. M. Iofan and I. V. Zholtovsky (fig. 10.18). This was an ostentatious and banal wedding cake building in the form of a stepped mausoleum surmounted by a colossal statue of Lenin, even larger than Manhattan's Statue of Liberty (on which, curiously enough, it may have been partly modelled). The supporting steel frame was encased in massive, ill-proportioned cladding of stone, and the imagery bordered on kitsch for all its 'acceptable' Realism. Evidently the dreamers of modern visions had outstripped the aspirations of their potential clientele and, in the process, had pointed to severe problems of communication between the perceptions of an avant-garde steeped in the devices of abstraction, and the values of a mass culture as envisioned by a centralized state. Indeed, in 1932, the remaining architects of the avant-garde were marshalled under State control and either left architecture, or else immersed themselves in the official but apparently uninspiring doctrines of Realism. Melnikov's project for a Ministry of Heavy Industry of 1934 is a representative work of this phase of compromise, with its grotesque statuary and heavy-handed machine ornaments.

But as well as being representative of the problems of state interference, this design may perhaps also be seen as an epitaph to the avant-garde's premature attempt at dreaming up the forms of a culture without sufficient communal support. Despite their constant protestations to the contrary, the Soviet modern architects – in their rise and fall – had acknowledged schisms typical of Western industrialized culture, between history and modernity, the artist and 'the people'. All too often they had resorted to a secularized version of Kandinsky's conception of the artist as a prophet of new forms. 'The Volk is not with us', Klee had written in his diaries; the same was to prove true in a variety of area of modern culture in the twenties.

aspirations of the Soviet State. Entries poured in from all over the world and included major ideas from Gropius, Mendelsohn, Perret, and Le Corbusier. Some of the architects chose to pack the functions into a single dynamic sculptural form, while others separated the volumes of the two main auditoria out and arranged colossal machine-age sculptures against the existing Moscow skyline. In principle, this was the approach of Le Corbusier, whose entry must be ranked as one of his masterpieces (fig. 10.17). The two auditoria were arranged on the same axis and were direct sculptural expressions of the acoustically optimized forms of the interior profiles. It was an idea the architect had employed in his League of Nations proposal three years earlier. Instead of resorting to domes or other defunct iconography, Le Corbusier invented a new symbolism with, clearly, some prompting from Tatlin and earlier fantasies of Con-

11. Skyscraper and Suburb: America between the Wars

The architects of this land and generation are now brought face to face with something new under the sun – namely that evolution and integration of social conditions, that special grouping of them, that results in a demand for the erection of tall office buildings. . . .

Problem: How shall we impart to this sterile pile, this crude, harsh, brutal agglomeration, this stark, staring exclamation of eternal strife, the graciousness of those higher forms of sensibility and culture that rest on the lower and fiercer passions? How shall we proclaim from the dizzy height of this strange, weird modern housetop the peaceful evangel of sentiment, of beauty, the cult of a higher life?

L. Sullivan, 1896

The decade between the end of the First World War and the Wall Street crash of 1929 was a boom period for building investment in the United States. This was mirrored directly in the profile of the large cities, in the mushrooming of skyscrapers, the rapid growth of highways, and the creation of suburban sprawl. The resultant pressures on urban services were overwhelming, but perceptions of this crisis of mechanization were far from most architects' minds. Intellectual forces were co-opted in an effort of *laissez-faire* expansion whose motives and values went largely unexplored. The anxiety-laden probings and apocalyptic Utopianism of the European avant-garde had few equivalents in the United States. Reformist yearnings were reserved, on the whole, for anti-urban dreams, or for the microcosm of the individual dwelling usually in a context isolated from the city, where time-honoured American themes concerning the individual's contemplation of the sublimities of nature could be played out once again.

The search for alternative social and urbanistic structures, which played such a central role in European modern architecture, was foreign indeed to a country in a conservative mood which could draw upon the cosy mythology that any necessary revolutionary steps in the polity had occurred over a century before. Moreover, in the visual arts there was scarcely an equivalent to the avant-gardes of the main metropolitan centres of France and Germany. The Armory Show of 1913 had made Cubism and Abstraction widely known in America, but these movements had been regarded as suspect, foreign imports by the majority. Even the activities of Stieglitz's '291', which cut through academic and sentimental clichés to the imaginative potentials of the New World, had little impact on architecture. Despite the Futurist overtones and urban romanticism instinct in some of Stieglitz's and Steichen's photographs, and in the work of such painters as Charles Sheeler, Joseph Stella, and Marsden Hartley, architects remained unmoved by the technological wonders of their country. Engineering continued to be seen as merely the material means for supporting historically sanctioned combinations of styles which were, so to say, stuck on. Hartley put the matter succinctly:

I often wonder why it is that America . . . has not the European courage as well as capacity for fresh developments in cultural matters. . . . There is . . . an obvious lethargy in the appreciation of creative taste and a still lingering yet old fashioned faith in the continual necessity for importation. America has a great body of assimilators and out of this gift for uncreative assimilation has come the type of art we are supposed to accept as our own.

Cultural critics such as Lewis Mumford (e.g., *The Brown Decades*, 1931) would write of a dreadful regression from the probity and integrity they had sensed in the architecture of Henry Hobson Richardson, John Wellborn Root, William Le Baron Jenney, Louis Sullivan, and Frank Lloyd Wright three decades earlier. It was customary in this connection to stress the symbolic importance of the Columbia World

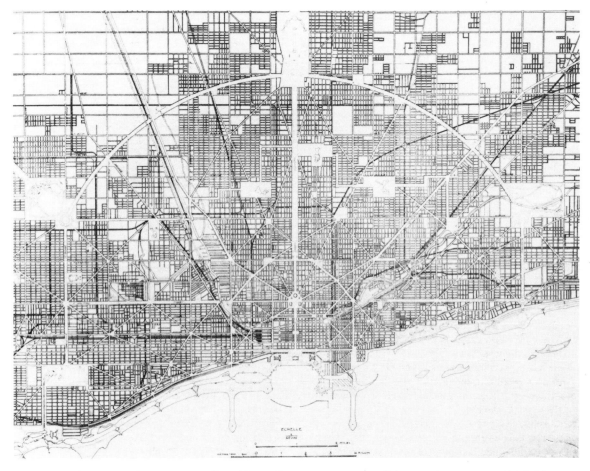

Exposition of 1893 as the event signalling 'the Fall from Grace', for it was the giant Beaux-Arts Classical 'White City' which had set in motion a fashion for pompous revival which Sullivan later bemoaned (in bitter old age) as having set back the course of American architecture by fifty years. Actually, this was gross over-simplification: not only was Sullivan's and Wright's best work produced after that date, but the American Renaissance was not always superficial. It is more to the point to recall that a variety of viable parallel tendencies were operative up until about 1914 (including the extension of the Prairie School after Wright), and to explain what needs of expression the Classical Beaux-Arts fulfilled.

Here one necessarily oversimplifies: the American Beaux-Arts supplied a set of recipes for civic institutions such as museums, metropolitan libraries, opera houses, clubs, and university monuments. It implied links with Classical civilization and made available traditional imperial symbols to the institutions of the state in an era when the United States was first sensing its role as a world power. In the

private sector of plutocratic patronage (Frick, Morgan, Rockefeller, etc.) instant Classicism was a useful prop, an embellishment for 'the age of elegance'. In the 'City Beautiful' movement images drawn from Imperial Rome or Haussmann's Paris were brought in to ennoble and tame the gridded, utilitarian, money-making machine of the American metropolis. The movement was well represented by Burnham's vast plans for Chicago of 1909 (Fig. 11.1), in which not a skyscraper was to be seen (despite the fact that this architect had done well from designing them). A domed civic centre towered above the heart of the city. The radial boulevards and parks were supposed to supply open space and to free the traffic, but they were also conceived in theatrical terms. Burnham's plan was suffused with nostalgia for a pre-industrial culture.

Something of this cult of instant beautification lingered on into the twenties, but with less moral concern for urban improvement. Educated taste still stood between American imaginations and the raw possibilities of indigenous technology. It was a curious situation: on the one side American architects and clients clambering for the instant sanction of European culture; on the other a European avant-garde looking romantically to America as the promised land of all things modern. The matter was summed up by a caption in Le Corbusier's *Vers une architecture*, which appeared under an illustration of a San Francisco skyscraper encrusted with feebly executed Renaissance ornament: 'Let us listen to the counsels of American engineers. But let us beware of American architects.'

Economic expansion in the boom years relied heavily on mass production, advertising, the deliberate fostering of consumerist imagery, and such communications devices as the radio, telephone, and automobile. New corporations of unprecedented size brought increasing specialization to labour and required giant head offices in the city centres. They needed tall buildings which could also project images of themselves and their products. Many of the basic structural and fireproofing problems of the skyscraper had been solved by the previous two generations. Emphasis now switched to stylistic clothing, to the symbolic function of the building in the cityscape as institutional and corporate image.

The skyscraper had emerged in the 1870s in New York and Chicago as a response to the storage, merchandising, and managerial needs of railway and steampower trade. Exploitation of land prices as well as functional necessity had forced the building upwards; steel wire, the elevator, and the steel frame had allowed this to occur. The typical structural anatomy combined a grid plan, partitioned spaces, and open façades, and this could lead to various possible vocabularies. Here was the core of an American dilemma which also stood near the heart of the problem of a modern architecture: should the creature be left alone as function and finance suggested, a scarcely articulated object of engineering? Or should the native invention be clothed in cultural dress imported from elsewhere and given the veneer of civilization? Louis Sullivan attempted to find an answer by steering his way between the utilitarian and the decorative, and (as was shown in Chapter 3) relied on Rationalist procedures in analysing the task. In an essay entitled 'The Tall Office Building Artistically Considered' (1896), he claimed that the skyscraper had an inherent shape resulting from social demand, functional layout, and constructional means, arguing that it was intrinsically tripartite, with lower levels for entrance, showrooms, and mezzanine offices, with middle levels to accommodate the office space and with a top to contain the machine rooms and the turn-around for the elevators. In turn, he proposed that the 'essence' of the type lay in its aspiring verticality; one notes the conceit

by which an artificial form was handled as if it had an 'intrinsic', organic nature striving for expression.

Few architects had the depth of synthesis of Sullivan, and the general rule of skyscraper design in the late 1890s and the first two decades of the twentieth century was eclectic experimentation which departed from the ideal of an authentic modern style. History was treated like a used-clothes store and raided for its garments with little thought for their original purpose and still less for the new body they were to clothe. Between 1900 and 1920, Manhattan was transformed into an ersatz historical dreamscape where Mayan temples stood only feet away from Gothic spires and Classical mausolea. The New York zoning law of 1916, requiring set-backs to admit light and air to the buildings and streets below, went further to encourage a stepped pyramid form, often surmounting a shaft-like tower standing on a broader pedestal: ziggurats and Meso-American extravaganza wedded well with shapes of this kind.

Such, then, was the history of the skyscraper in outline, leading up to the *Chicago Tribune* competition of 1922. The newspaper wanted 'one of the most beautiful buildings in the world'; the site stood just north of the Chicago loop beyond the river, where Michigan Avenue was cranked, allowing more breathing space than was usual in the gridded city, and an uncustomary long, diagonal view; the programme required mainly office space. But these requirements did little to determine a form beyond suggesting some variation on a tower, probably with elevators towards the centre and with a slender shaft rising high enough to provide a striking image in contrast to the surroundings. The notes sent to competition applicants made much of the visual quality of the design: here was a chance to concentrate on matters of form and to provide a prototype for the 'beautification' of American cities.

Competitions are a useful gauge of the true outlook of a period because they give evidence of a wide variety of different responses to the same constraints. In all there were nearly three hundred entries to the *Chicago Tribune* competition: they make it quite clear that in 1922 there was no American – or worldwide – consensus on style. A survey of the entries reads like a lexicon of eclecticism and half-understood prototypes with little evidence of subtle transformation from precedent. Typical was a design modelled on Giotto's campanile in Florence (fig. 11.2); in order to preserve the recognizable proportions of the prototype yet still fulfil the volumetric demands of the programme, the architect found it necessary to tack a bulky appendage to the rear. There were also many quasi-Classical solutions employing a jumble of columns, pediments, temple motifs, and domes. These ran up against the

11.2 (*left*) Entry to the *Chicago Tribune* competition, 1922, modelled on Giotto's campanile in Florence – (figs. 11.2–11.6 are from *Chicago Tribune Competition*, 1922).

11.3 (*centre*) Entry to the *Chicago Tribune* competition, 1922, modelled on Renaissance prototypes.

11.4 (*right*) Adolf Loos, *Chicago Tribune* competition entry, 1922.

basic incompatibility of a skyscraper's dimensions with the Classical orders; columns were either attached like matchsticks with no genuine tectonic value in relation to the underlying mass, or else blown up to a colossal size to clothe some major portion of the tower, in which case their girth tended to interfere with the clarity of the overall form (fig. 11.3); whatever their incongruities of form, these solutions never gave adequate visual expression to the facts of steel frame construction within. Perhaps with tongue in cheek, Adolf Loos proposed to solve the problem of incompatible dimensions by making the *entire shaft* of the skyscraper into a Doric column (fig. 11.4). This took Sullivan's suggestion of a tripartite form for the building type all too literally. Other architects descended into pantomime by pursuing the imagery of a trumped-up, populist Americanism. One entry had its top fashioned as an Indian with his tomahawk raised above his head.

The European entries were restrained, humourless, and sincere by comparison, and provided an intriguing cross-section through emergent modern architectural tendencies. Bruno Taut's design, tapering gradually towards the top, was an Expressionist hybrid combining the images of his pre-war Steel and Glass pavilions. It issued from an utterly different ideological world from the American designs, and was frank and enthusiastic in its attitude to steel technology. Its true cousins were Mies van der Rohe's glass tower 'cathedrals', rather than the eclectic piles which were its local competitors. Ludwig Hilbersheimer's design was composed of stark, rectangular volumes, articulated solely by the checkerboard pattern of the frame; it embodied a strict, Rationalist outlook. A Dutch entry (by Bijvoet and Duiker) was compositionally extravagant by contrast, with its extending horizontal flanges and overlapping planes. Walter Gropius's scheme (fig. 11.5) also employed a vocabulary based on the rectangular frame. The entrance was indicated by a sort of portico, and the main divisions in the design were articulated by slight changes in rhythm and bay spacing, by recesses and balcony planes of varying depth. The overall impression was of a tense interrelationship of asymmetrical parts, well suited to the three-quarter view by which the building would be most easily seen. Inside, the plan was open, uncluttered, and well lit from all sides, while to the rear his building's elevation aligned with the frame of the pre-existing printing office. If the design showed sensitivity to the earlier Chicago school (it used the indigenous tripartite Chicago window), it also incorporated devices which were just then emerging at the Bauhaus through the impact of van Doesburg, Moholy-Nagy, and Constructivism. Gropius's scheme was conceived as a mechanistic abstraction, celebrating the idea of a modern communications building; its effects of lightness and transparency were as hallmarks of the new architecture; in it, technological facts were infused with idealistic sentiments.

Evidently the jury did not think so: to their eyes, it probably looked more like engineering than archi-

tecture. They awarded first prize to a neo-Gothic design by Raymond Hood and John Mead Howells (Fig. 11.6). This succeeded, as adeptly as had Gropius, in solving many of the basic problems of the site and the building type. The primary emphasis was vertical, the shafts were set back at the top to become a spikey crown in which the machine rooms and a small museum were placed. Secondary piers emphasized the tall middle portion or shaft, while the lowest part, where the entrance was situated, acted as a base and responded in height to the pre-existing printing office to the rear. While the frame holding Hood's design up was disguised under stonework, the sense of a vertical thrust was successfully articulated by the Gothic piers in the façades: these did not confront the architect with the same modular difficulties as Classical orders, for piers could be stretched almost indefinitely. But Hood's choice of Gothic may have had moral associations as

11.5 (*far left*) Walter Gropius, *Chicago Tribune* competition entry, 1922.

11.6 (*left*) Raymond Hood and John Mead Howells, winning entry to the *Chicago Tribune* competition, 1922.

well. One of the presentation renderings showed the *Tribune* building in perspective, riding high above the smoke and smuts of the Chicago environment – a white cathedral of enlightenment towering above base concerns. Such evocations appealed to the newspaper proprietors' sense of their own moral purpose. Hood's and Howell's design brilliantly caught the right nostalgic and slightly romantic mood. Sigfried Giedion later had his revenge on behalf of Gropius by publishing his compatriot's scheme alongside Burnham and Root's Reliance Building of 1893 (as if to say that the former was the next logical step from the latter in the evolution of the 'true' modern prism) and by leaving Hood's design out of account altogether. From the point of view of the European avant-garde, of course, the jury's decision was merely evidence of reactionary tendencies.

The scheme which came in second was more

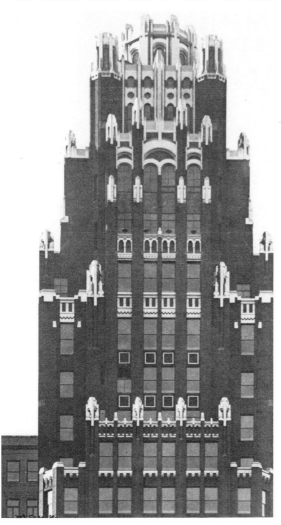

11.7 (*right*) Raymond Hood, American Radiator building, New York, 1924, detail of top.

influential than any of the others in the inter-war years. This was designed by the Finnish architect Eliel Saarinen and was in no easily categorizable style with its telescoping forms, slight set-backs, and vertical linear articulations. Interestingly, Sullivan praised this design, perhaps because he sensed in it an abstraction of nature akin to his own earlier theories. The following year Saarinen elaborated a proposal for the urban redevelopment of the area close to the Chicago Loop and the lakeshore, thus indicating his urbanistic understanding of the tall building and a certain *naïveté* with regard to the speculator's mentality, which was scarcely likely to allow open space for leisure when the same land could be exploited for profit. The forces which brought tall buildings into being ignored the character of civic space and tended to destroy not only the street as a social realm, but the complex grain of pre-existing historical and social relationships. To this process of disruption, most architectural suggestions were merely an affirmative veneer.

Two years after his success with the *Chicago Tribune* building, Raymond Hood designed the American Radiator building in New York (Fig. 11.7). This followed the pattern of his earlier building, but the vocabulary was now less obviously revived, being more abstract and relying upon (among other things) the appearance of the company's radiator products. With its black brick facing, gold finials, and elegant proportions, the building crystallized an American machine-age fantasy more whimsical and ornate than the glass and steel evocations of mechanization produced in Europe. There was little sense in Hood's one-off designs of a quest for type forms; quite the contrary, the architect took a certain delight in posing as a dilettante, for whom consistency of style and a search for the authentic were tedious and grim burdens for those unlucky enough not to have the exuberant capitalist city as their playground. Even the images of the modern movement could be reduced to mere motifs, as is clear from Hood's design for the McGraw-Hill building of 1928–9 with its 'appliqué' of strip windows and its plain volumetric forms (fig. 11.8). The silhouette as a whole resulted from a judicious visual composition within the rules of the set-back laws. The top was a streamlined invention, with the dynamism and populist character of Raymond Loewy's 'Moderne' industrial designs, or of Fritz Lang's Expressionist city in the film *Metropolis*. In the slightly later *Daily News* building, Hood adopted yet another dress – one perhaps derived from Saarinen's *Tribune* design – by stressing verticality to an extreme. The lobby (along with the crown of the skyscraper, the area most likely to attract public attention) was turned into a middle-brow scenario on the theme of the *Daily News* as a network of information spreading across the world. A giant, gloomily lit globe was sunk in a central pit, while the gadgetry of thermometers, wind-speed indicators, and clocks provided the precise hour in the main cities of the world and gave the whole thing a vaguely science fiction air. However one characterizes this phase of American design – 'Moderne', 'Art Deco', or 'Jazz Modern' – it flew in the face of European modern movement puritanism in its obsession with ornament, axial composition, gaudy polychromy, and a sort of consumerist theatricality.

The swansong of the twenties in New York was the Chrysler building, designed by William Van Alen between 1928 and 1930 (fig. 11.9). In its celebration of financial success, this captured perfectly the heady atmosphere of pre-crash capitalism. It rose to 850 feet and so was the tallest building in the world for a short time (being outstripped by the Empire State building in the early thirties). Light silver-grey in colour, it stood on a base twenty storeys high. Above this was a middle section shaft rising another 560 feet. Then this too began to step inwards, tapering finally to a stainless steel sunburst motif with scalloped windows sur-

11.8 (*below left*) Raymond Hood, McGraw-Hill building, New York, 1928–9.

11.9 (*left*) William Van Alen, Chrysler building, New York, 1928–30.

mounted by a spire. The lobby was conceived as a dream world of revealed lighting effects, expensive russet-coloured marbles and lustrous metals, and had something of the feeling of a Hollywood stage set. Each of the lifts was lined in a different wooden intarsia design with ornamental motifs recalling the heraldry of the main body of the building. The skin of the tower was patterned with dark grey bricks against the silvery surfaces, and the corners gave the impression of quoins of increased mass. In the centre of each façade, the windows were detailed to give a sense of vertical forces rising the whole height of the shaft, and terminating at a curved centrepiece; these mimicked the actual movements of the elevators running up and down at the core. The plan of the Chrysler building was based on primary and secondary axes (Van Alen had been Beaux-Arts trained), and the elaborate design of the skin reflected his interest in a sort of new 'wall' architecture as an appropriate treatment for the steel frame. It seems that his ideas may have been modelled in part on weaving, fabric, or basket-work designs (Plate 5).

However one categorizes the Chrysler building stylistically ('Art Deco' or perhaps even 'Expressionist'), its forms were among the most elegant in the field of skyscraper design to that date. But these appearances were also manifestations of a fantasy about the client which in turn touched on broader social meanings. At the corners on the fortieth floor, just below the base of the main shaft, were four giant metal Chrysler radiator caps with wings. Next to them a frieze of abstracted car wheels with huge silver studs for hub-caps encircled the building. The chevron logo of Chrysler occurred in the brickwork at various levels; on top, within the sunburst motif and beneath the spire, there originally stood a glass case containing Walter Chrysler's first set of tools (reportedly closed on the day the Empire State surpassed the Chrysler building in height). Around the base of the sunburst, projecting like gargoyles towards the horizons, were colossal American eagles. The compound message was clear: it was a celebration of self-advancement within the American economic system. Here was a 'Cathedral of Capitalism' in response to the various quasi-socialist

11.10 Hugh Ferris, idealized skyscraper from *The Metropolis of Tomorrow*, 1929.

paper project skyscrapers conceived in Europe earlier in the decade.

While the American skyscraper designers of the twenties succeeded in the limited task of dressing up big business in attractive costume, they rarely produced work of depth. Those 'higher forms of sensibility and culture' which Sullivan had attempted to express (perhaps Quixotically) in his skyscraper designs of the 1890s were notably lacking. Shortly before his death, Sullivan had despaired of the possibility of an authentic American architecture in the capitalist city, as he had watched the eclectic heaps rise around him.

> These buildings, as they increase in number, make the city poorer morally and spiritually: They drag it down and down into the mire. This is not American civilization; it is the rottenness of Gomorrah. This is not Democracy – it is savagery. . . . So truly does this architecture reflect the causes that have brought it into being.

Sullivan's cry reflected a basic dilemma of the artist architect designing in the commercial world: how could the brute 'causes' of finance be translated into the lasting stuff of a profound aesthetic symbolism? A question of this kind lay near the heart of European fascination with the tall building too. Le Corbusier was also appalled by the facile treatment of Manhattan's skyscrapers, and by their urban irresponsibility, but he was nonetheless magnetized by the romanticism of the resulting skyline and by the manifestation of financial force, managerial organization, and technological know-how which brought such buildings into being: he described Manhattan as 'the workhouse of the new era'. By contrast with the American skyscrapers of the twenties, his idealized images of the tall building in the Ville Contemporaine (1922) (and in the later Ville Voisin of 1925) were entirely glazed, regular in form, and conceived not only as emblems of technological power (they were to contain the Saint-Simonian élite of his city), but also as urbanistic tools for releasing the floor of the city for nature and circulation:

> The skyscraper is a tool. A magnificent tool for the concentration of population and for the decongestion of the soil; a tool of classification, and for interior efficiency; a prodigious force for the improvement of working conditions and a creator of economies; for these reasons it is also a dispenser of richness.

Thus artists of the European avant-garde employed images of Manhattan as triggers in the search for Utopian alternatives to the European industrial city.

11.11 (*left*) Raymond Hood and team, Rockefeller Center, New York, 1931–40.

11.12 (*above right*) Frank Lloyd Wright, National Life Insurance building project, 1924, section.

11.13 (*right*) Frank Lloyd Wright, Barnsdall House, Los Angeles, California, 1920.

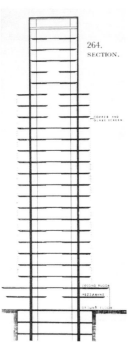

264.
SECTION.

America was not without its dreamers, the most notable being Hugh Ferris, who published a book called *The Metropolis of Tomorrow* in 1929. This was liberally illustrated with his superb conté crayon sketches of tall buildings (fig. 11.10). Some of the drawings were theoretical studies of possible set-back variations within the constraints of the 1916 zoning laws; others were renderings of other architects' proposals for skyscrapers; but towards the end of the book was a sequence of extraordinary views in which Manhattan emerged in a biblical, almost Babylonian guise. Some of the buildings were even made to look like crystals or magical geological fragments. This other-worldly urban landscape was divided into three main sectors – the scientific, the cultural, and the commercial – each with its own symbolic skyscraper. Each of these functions was in turn related to basic divisions in the mind with mystical triangular diagrams. Ferris tried to imply that his image of the metropolis was infused with a divine aura. Again we find the artist hoping for transcendent values beyond the crude materialism of the modern city.

After the financial crash of 1929, fewer tall buildings were constructed, but two major skyscraper projects emerged in mid-Manhattan. The Empire State building by Shreve, Lamb and Harmon became the tallest building in the world in 1931 and enclosed an entire vertical city of functions, but the visual solution lacked the subtlety and elegance of the Chrysler building. The other major scheme of the period was the Rockefeller Center – a group of buildings incorporating rental office space, the RCA building, a popular music hall and movie palace (Radio City), and a square with a sunken floor with a perimeter of shops (which later

became an ice rink). A vast team of architects was involved in the design – Reinhard, Hofmeister; Corbert, Harrison, Macmurray; Fouilhoux and Hood – the last named being the overseeing designer. Here at last was an attempt at sensitizing the spaces around the base of the skyscraper; Hood's design even included roof terraces on the lowest buildings (fig. 11.11).

Perhaps the most exploratory skyscraper designs of the 1920s in the United States were never built. These were by Frank Lloyd Wright, who had a notorious distaste for the modern city, but who still admitted the role of tall buildings in his ideal scheme of things. His National Life Insurance project of 1924 (fig. 11.12) extended some of the propositions and elements of his pre-war architecture, including the idea of overhanging trays held up by piers, and the conception of a stratified interior space. In the St. Mark's Tower project of 1929, the box-frame vision of the tall building was rejected in favour of a central core with radiating platforms, split levels, mixed working and living functions, and triangular geometries. Here an old Wrightian metaphor was given a new emphasis: the tree with its central trunk and extending branches.

The twenties was a troubled decade for Wright in which he lived an uprooted existence plagued by personal, legal, and financial difficulties. After the disastrous burning of Taliesin in 1914, he spent much of his time in Japan overseeing the design and construction of the Imperial Hotel in Tokyo with its ingenious tap-root foundations which successfully withstood the earthquake of 1922. In the late 1910s and the early 1920s it was once again the individual home which most preoccupied him. He received a number of commissions for luxurious houses in

southern California, chief among them the Barnsdall residence in Los Angeles (fig. 11.13), for a client almost as eccentric as himself. On first inspection the massive, fortress-like forms with their sloping concrete walls, inward-looking courts, ponds and flat roofs would seem to suggest a strong break with the Prairie Houses. However, if one consults the plan arrangement one finds the usual organizational principles combining axes and cross axes, effects of formality and in-formality, and a unity of conception between interiors and exteriors (see pp. 102–3).

Even so, it would be foolish to underrate the significance of the obvious changes. Wright's emphasis on the enclosing wall, instead of the screen-window with horizontal overhang of the Prairie House period, must be seen in the context of a new mood, if not a new ideological direction. The Californian buildings expres-sed a remoteness from the outside world which may well have been in tune with the outlook of his rather aloof new patrons and the architect's own feelings of isolation. Wright was now estranged from the tight-knit suburban community of Oak Park which had sustained him before the war, and it was in the twenties that the version of the architect as an erratic, aristocratic genius at odds with 'mobocracy' gained currency.

On its own, a psychological explanation for Wright's change in style would be inadequate. Surely one reason for the thick walls and inward-turning courts was the climate of the south-west. Wright's regional sensitivities required a new response, and he followed some of the cues supplied by traditional adobe struc-tures with their thick sloping walls and flat roofs. In transforming this vernacular tradition he had the useful intermediary of Irving Gill, who had already evolved an ingenious concrete architecture for the local conditions. However, one guesses that more was at stake in Wright's broad vision, and that he may have been dreaming in Pan-American terms: the battered forms and fussy geometrical concrete block patterns (with their abstractions of natural motifs) reflected his fascination with Mayan prototypes. In *A Testament*, he wrote:

> I remember how, as a boy, primitive American architecture – Toltec, Aztec, Mayan, Inca – stirred my wonder, excited my wishful admiration. . . .
> Those great American abstractions were all earth-architectures; gigantic masses of masonry raised up on one great stone paved terrain . . .

The Millard House in Pasadena (Fig. 11.15) was treated as if it were a procured ruin, its textured ornamental effects being incomplete without clamber-ing foliage and weathering. The Ennis House, which stood on a prominent site with long views, was

11.14 (*left*) Rudolf Schindler, Schindler/Chase House, Los Angeles, California, 1921, view from house to garden.

11.15 (*below*) Frank Lloyd Wright, Millard House, Pasadena, California, 1921.

surrounded by almost ceremonial terraces; its domestic scale was transcended with a grandiose, monumental statement. Once again Wright indulged in the idea of the beginnings of architecture in nature.

During the 1910s and 1920s two Austrian-born architects who passed through Wright's atelier imbibed his principles while still preserving their own artistic identities (a rare combination). The first was Rudolf Schindler, who came from Vienna in 1914, after grappling with the influence of Otto Wagner and the Secession. Schindler had a strong intuitive grasp of the tendencies towards abstract form already manifest in pre-war Viennese architecture, and after a period supervising Wright's California houses, set out on his own. The Schindler House of 1921 (fig. 11.14) shows how he reacted to the California setting, which it was then still just possible to celebrate as a virgin land. He responded to the landscape, the earth colours, the trees, and the vast spaces, and attempted to translate his grasp of these characteristics into an inward looking shelter of low-ceilinged spaces with the access to densely overgrown inner courts. The house was designed for himself and his wife, and another newly married couple, the Chases. Ingenious planning

allowed the creation of separate private spaces for each individual. At the upper level low protruding sleeping porches were added, used mostly in the summer months. Schindler adopted Irving Gill's tilt concrete technology and built the house from thin slabs, slightly inward-sloping, with small window chinks left between them. The aesthetics of the interior were clearly indebted to Japanese architecture, especially the contrived incompleteness of the tea-house. The garden areas were reached principally through movable canvas screens – features which were inspired by a temporary camp in which Schindler and his wife stayed while the house was being designed. The sense of a primeval shelter – a curious blend between cave and tent – seems to have been deliberate, for Schindler (like Wright) was much concerned with the basic psychological need for protection and with a tactile sense of space.

In 1922 Schindler was employed by Dr. Phillip Lovell to design a weekend house at Newport Beach (fig. 11.16). This was to contain sleeping lofts, a lounge, a temporary kitchen, and an area for the storage of boat equipment and surfboards. Realizing that beach clobber could be stored underneath and

11.16 Rudolf Schindler, Lovell Beach House, Newport Beach, California, 1923–4.

wishing to exploit the views to the ocean, Schindler took his cue from the local seaside pier architecture and raised the building on solid, flange-shaped stilts. He chose concrete for its cheapness, its durability, and its space-creating capacity (through the use of cantilevers) to execute his idea. The upper portions of the Lovell beach house were formed from interlocking trays which gave a bold, horizontal overhang to the main elevation and provided a lofty double-height living space with a correspondingly large window to the seaside. The sleeping lofts were placed on the upper tray at the outer extremity; the same tray then extended inwards to create a gallery looking down into the living-room. The solution was unpretentious and simple. There were obviously lingering debts to Wright, but the house was still stamped with a uniquely Schindlerian character. Moreover, the spatial ideas behind the scheme and the reduction to simple stripped volumes and hovering horizontals bore some obvious similarities with European progressive work. There is no evidence that Schindler knew of such recent experiments; he seems rather to have come to similar conclusions by his own route. His outlook lay

closer to Wright's organic philosophy than to the mechanistic abstractions of the European avant-garde. When he eventually saw pictures of the stark architecture of the twenties created 6,000 miles away, he spoke of the emptiness of spirit and lack of warmth of buildings produced by men who had suffered through the trenches. Schindler combined a sophisticated ideal of the simple life with reverence for the order of nature. In a sense, Dr. Lovell was the ideal client for him, for he ran a 'Physical Culture Center' and saw himself as an intellectual progressive.

The other Viennese architect to come to California via Wright's office was Richard Neutra, who worked with Schindler until he secured some of his own commissions. They made a joint entry to the League of Nations competition in 1927, and then Neutra embarked on the design of another house for Lovell, this time to stand on the side of a spur looking over a lush valley in Los Angeles (Fig. 11.17). The building grew away from the hillside so that one entered at an upper level and passed along a landing into the airy upper part of a triple-volume stair well before coming to the more private areas of the dwelling

11.17 (*above left*) Richard Neutra, Lovell House, Los Angeles, California, 1927.

aries of exterior terraces, the overhangs of sun shades, or the partial shelter of a swimming pool. The details had a more precise and mechanistic character than Schindler's: Neutra was well aware of recent work in Europe, so was able to draw lessons from a broader range of experiments (Plate 6). Neutra had himself contributed to transatlantic mythologies in a book entitled *Wie Baut Amerika?* (*How does America Build?*, 1927). Thus the Lovell House was an intriguing hybrid of International Modern architecture, the organicism of Wright, and Neutra's own vision of the healthy and natural way of life. In the ensuing designs of both Schindler (e.g., the Sachs Apartments 1929, the Wolfe House 1928, the Oliver House 1933) and Neutra (the Kaufmann Desert House 1946–7), one may tentatively speak of a regionalist emphasis within modern architecture.

A review of experimental tendencies in the United States during the twenties would be incomplete without the Philadelphia Savings Fund Society (PSFS) skyscraper designed by George Howe and William Lescaze between 1926 and 1931 (Fig. 11.18). Here inherited typological thinking about the American skyscraper and the emergent vocabulary of the International Style came together in a way which modified each. Howe had been trained in the Beaux-Arts system while Lescaze had first-hand experience of designing with the new forms in Europe. To trace the sketches of the PSFS project from the earliest in 1926 (when Lescaze had not yet come into the picture) to the latest in 1930, is to gauge not only the vicissitudes of an individual design process in which formal and functional conflicts were gradually resolved, but also the transition from one architectural style phase to another. An axial, encrusted, eclectic skyscraper of the kind all too familiar from the *Chicago Tribune* competition gave way bit by bit to an asymmetrical, machine-age design, in which structure, volume, and differentiations of function were articulated in a disciplined yet subtle way. Even within the strict confines of the International Style, there were many possible variations of treatment. For example, the architects spent much time studying alternative ways for reconciling the structural verticals (which they wished to 'express honestly') with a horizontal planar expression (which they felt to be associatively right for a building of modern and efficient image). The relationship of the large vertical volumes of the main slab with the attached elevator zone to the rear, and with the 'pedestal' of the banking area, also took a long time to resolve.

The finished PSFS building (1932) was one of the first skyscrapers actually to be built in the new style. The design of the lower portion of the building combined subway access, shops, and a raised level

11.18 George Howe and William Lescaze, Philadelphia Savings Fund Society building, Philadelphia, 1926–31.

perched over the landscape with superb views into the valley. The different functions were expressed in varying window sizes unified by floating white horizontals in concrete set off against the steel supports, window-frames and dark areas of shadow, and detailed to give the maximum effects of lightness and planarity. In places these bands ceased to have any enclosing function, becoming instead the loose bound-

banking floor reached by escalator. These, the honorific zones of the structure, were amplified in scale and treated in dignified materials such as marble veneers and chrome. The upper floors were well-lit open plush offices which were also air-conditioned (the mechanical services floor made a clear caesura in the façade composition). The overall image conveyed efficiency and crispness. This was not a question of 'stylism', of packaging into pre-conceived forms, as it had been with Raymond Hood's designs; nor was it mere 'functionalism'. The PSFS form was backed by a rigorous architectural philosophy which, at its most high-flown, embraced abstruse notions of 'space/time' appropriate to modern life, but on a more down-to-earth level manifested a deep concern for the touch-stones of functional design. Howe wrote revealingly of the PSFS:

> Sound architecture must be able to bear the closest analytical examination externally, internally, structurally and mechanically, and the solution of each problem which presents itself in the development of a design must be not only possible, but possible in a concise and orderly form as a consequence of the organic foundation of the original conception . . .
>
> Modern architecture originated not in a search for a purely practical solution of modern problems but in a dissatisfaction with the superficial, inorganic beauty of superimposed traditional architectural elements and ornament. As would naturally be the case, the search for an organic beauty led back to the very conception of design and it was found that the beauty sought could be found . . . only in an expression of the human, structural and mechanical functions of architecture. Our purpose as artists, as opposed to mere builders, in moulding these functions . . . has been to achieve beauty. . . .

The experimental works of modern architecture in the United States were backed by a variety of ideologies and, at their most successful, they were genuine attempts at coming to terms with the problem of a serious architectural culture. Curiously though, the Museum of Modern Art show on modern architecture of 1932 organized by Alfred Barr, Henry-Russell Hitchcock, and Philip Johnson, which gave popular currency to the term 'International Style', was silent on the social content of the new architecture. Hitchcock and Johnson's catalogue, *The International Style: Architecture Since 1922*, attempted instead to illustrate and define the basic visual motifs and modes of expression irrespective of differences in function, meaning, and belief. Perhaps influenced by historians of Renaissance art like Heinrich Wölfflin, who had tried to define the most characteristic general forms of an earlier epoch, the authors outlined what they took to be the main visual principles of the new style.

> There is first of all a new conception of architecture as volume, rather than as mass. Secondly, regularity rather than axial symmetry serves as the chief means of ordering design. These two principles with a third proscribing arbitrary applied decoration mark the productions of the International Style.

It is ironical that this formalist emphasis should have been made in the Depression years and just before the launching of Roosevelt's New Deal, an atmosphere in which stylistic niceties scarcely seemed relevant, but a situation to which the ideological probings of the modern movement might well have been appropriate. In a sense, Hitchcock and Johnson did modern architecture a severe disservice by dishing it up in the way they did. Wright denounced the abstract box architecture for its lack of an integrated view of man, and its superficial formalism; Regionalists bemoaned the importation of yet another cosmopolitan gloss; Buckminster Fuller inveighed against the lack of a real functionality, the superficial flirtation with technology; and in the field of civic design various branches of Revivalism went virtually untouched. Apart from some curious experiments by Kocher, Frey and Keck in the mid-thirties, and the continuing (but little-known) works of Schindler and Neutra on the West Coast, that is about where the matter of 'the International Modern Movement' in the United States was left until the end of the thirties. Meanwhile, of course, Wright proceeded to produce some of his most idiosyncratic and vital creations in the same years.

Taking the period 1920–35 in the United States as a whole, it is clear that there were many parallel trends in architecture, but that the innovators, as usual, were atypical. The Beaux-Arts system of education continued virtually unchallenged in America; it was the arrival of Mies van der Rohe, Walter Gropius, and Marcel Breuer towards the end of the thirties which set the scene for the growth of a modern architectural establishment after the Second World War. Paradoxically – as we shall see – the eventual 'victory' of the modern movement was to be rather hollow, as it was soon debased into a commercialized fashion. The glass towers envisaged on paper by the Utopian fantasists of the twenties were destined to become the symbols of the corporate status quo, while the idealism of the early modern movement would be absorbed into the mainstream of mass consumerist values.

12. The Ideal Community: Alternatives to the Industrial City

Men who try to create a new architecture, a free architecture for a free
people, anticipate the creation of a new social order....

K. Teige, 1928

The search for new ways of life basic to so much modern architecture of the twenties was also manifest in idealistic blueprints for the replanning of the industrial city. But whereas individual commissions for villas, schools, factories, and university dormitories allowed socially committed artists to realize fragments of larger dreams in microcosm, the power to build urban totalities was rarely granted. Avant-garde visions of the city therefore usually remained on paper. Even so, they were able gradually to infiltrate the imaginations of later generations and hence to alter the very concept and image of the modern town.

The numerous ideal city plans of the 1920s suggest an ambition to build the world anew, to start afresh, to rid culture once and for all of the detritus of 'dead forms'. However, just as the new architecture often had roots in history, so the new cities were usually concoctions of existing urban elements reassembled in new ways. The fact is that Utopias are historically bound; they have ideological roots and formal precedents; and if one scratches beneath the rhetoric of the 'brave new world', one often finds a vein of nostalgia running through the futurism.

The core problems that were addressed by such urbanists as Garnier, Berlage, Le Corbusier, Gropius, May and Milyutin had a history inextricably linked to the evolution of the industrial city in the nineteenth century. Mechanization, new means of production and transportation had then transformed the pre-existing morphology of the city into an unrecognizable and incoherent morass of institutions and infrastructures of circulation catering to capitalist development.

Moreover, cities in industrialized regions of England and France had grown with uncontrolled speed as the peasantry had flocked to the urban areas for employment and had been housed in the most squalid conditions. In the same period populations increased drastically. The resulting slum landscapes of factories, tenements, and grimy streets were without decent communal or private amenities. They were described by Engels in 1845 after a visit to Manchester: 'a filth and a disgusting grime the equal of which is not to be found'.

But the disruptions of industrialization extended well beyond the working-class slums into other areas of the city. The combined forces of land speculation and railway transport cut into the old fabric and destroyed the existing hierarchy. The new middle classes required homes remote from the dirt created by the sources of their own wealth. Thus the fringes of the city extended outwards, enveloping the countryside with suburban lots and new patterns of roads. A recurrent theme of reformers throughout the nineteenth century and in the early twentieth was that a supposed harmony between the social order and nature had been lost and should be reclaimed.

There were many ways in which critiques of the industrial city were framed. Marx and Engels argued that the true roots of the evil lay in the rottenness of the social order engendered by capitalism; they therefore advocated revolution as the prerequisite for a decent political *and* architectural environment. Earlier in the century, Utopian Socialists such as Henri Saint-Simon and Charles Fourier had argued in favour of alternative social structures based on new forms of rule and co-operation. Saint-Simon had advocated the overthrow of the ruling classes and their replacement by technocrats who would propel society along the inevitable path of human progress. Fourier had entertained a theory of passional attractions in human nature whereby opposites would be resolved in a sort of perfect balance of forces between individual desires and social expectations. This dream of a natural co-operation untrammelled by the irrelevancies of previous social contracts was carried through in the fantasy of an ideal collective palace: a 'phalanstère' (fig. 12.1). This was supposed to stand in a rural setting and to contain all the functions necessary to support a community of about 1,800 people, who would avoid the dangers of the 'division of labour' by spending their days developing their talents and nurturing the growth of whole, uncramped personalities. The 'phalanstère' had an uncanny resemblance to a Baroque palace, as if Fourier were making available to the populace as a whole the enrichments and potentials of the pre-revolutionary aristocracy. The various quarters (including rooms, ballrooms, a hostelry, a library and an observatory) were to be linked by a long interior street to encourage chance contacts and to embody the idea of an egalitarian society.

There were other urban proposals for countering the pressures of industrialism, which were less drastic than either the revolutionary or the Utopian models and relied more on the forces of the status quo. One thinks in this connection of the numerous attempts at designing decent workers' towns – from Bournville to Pullman City – in which the philanthropic side of capitalist ownership emerged. Or again, there were Haussmann's remarkable plans for Paris involving the cutting of new boulevards and the planting of parks; these undoubtedly reflected mixed motives, as they created more hygienic spaces while opening up routes for commerce, military control, and vast axes linking one part of the city's historical symbols of power theatrically to another. In the United States soon after mid-century, Frederick Law Olmsted outlined his proposals for Central Park in New York, in which nature was brought to the heart of the industrial metropolis in an attempt at humanizing it. The park in Olmsted's eyes was an ideal public realm celebrating the inevitable drift of history towards an increasingly democratic state.

In Europe a number of other paradigms were created in the second half of the nineteenth century, which were destined to influence twentieth-century ideas. One of these emerged in the writings of Camillo Sitte, a Viennese, who was opposed to the planning of grand vistas and axes, and sought a closer relationship

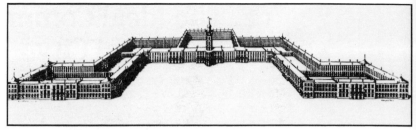

between irregularities of earlier city forms and the layout of spaces and squares; he thus unknowingly became the father-figure for many later movements intent on maintaining the close-knit scale of the pre-industrial city against the onslaughts of grand *tabula rasa* plans of every stripe. Another tradition stemmed from the ideas of the Spaniard, Arturo Soria y Mata, who advocated an invention called the 'linear city' for ameliorating the crush of population on large centres, for linking living and working areas to circulation, and for making a more ordered relationship between country and city. His town was to be laid out in parallel bands along circulation routes, which might link up pre-existing cities as far apart as Barcelona and Moscow; we have already seen later transformations of this idea in the Soviet Union.

Another model for dealing with over-population and decentralization emerged just before the turn of the century in the writings of the Englishman Ebenezer Howard, particularly in a book entitled *Tomorrow: A Peaceful Path to Real Reform* (1898). Howard was disturbed by the disruption and waste he saw in London and other industrial cities and argued in

12.1 Charles Fourier, the 'Phalanstère'; engraving *c.* 1834.

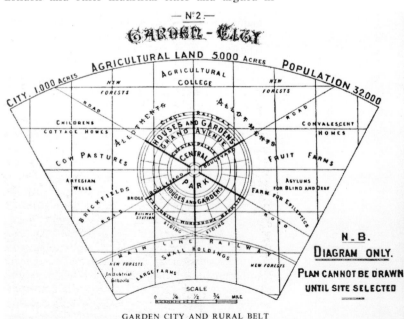

GARDEN CITY AND RURAL BELT

favour of new communities of manageable size, in which rural and urban worlds would be brought together in a happy synthesis (fig. 12.2). Essentially his vision of focal communities was a variant on the English village, but with additional amenities like railways and small-scale industry. The unit was the family in its individual home; these houses were to be laid out along well-planted streets, converging gradually upon the broader communal green and civic buildings towards the centre. Howard was much influenced by that moral strain of socialist criticism which descended from William Morris and John Ruskin. He would have agreed with the latter when he wrote in favour of: 'clean streets with free countryside all around; a belt of fine gardens and orchards, so that from every point in the city one can reach the pure air, the grass and the distant horizon.' However, Howard's thinking also stemmed from a more drastically Utopian tradition of 'alternative communities' like the one envisaged earlier in the century by Robert Owen. Permeating the dream was a nostalgia for a pre-industrial world, and when a version of the Garden City idea was eventually carried out in reality at Letchworth, it was appropriately complemented by the Arts and Crafts imagery and ideals of Raymond Unwin's architecture.

Garden City principles were taken over and transformed by Tony Garnier in his proposals for a Cité Industrielle, conceived between about 1901 and 1917 when his ideas were published (fig. 12.3). This scheme was mentioned earlier in connection with reinforced concrete, the material most widely employed in the plan's design. It was Garnier's intention to lay out all the problems and solutions of the 'most general case' of the industrial city. He proposed a medium-sized case of about 35,000 inhabitants for which he attempted to co-ordinate all the social, productive, and transport functions. Zoning was employed to separate industry from the home, and railways were used to link the two with trade centres. The ideal site conveniently foresaw terraces in the landscape which helped to articulate the different zones, but the hierarchy of parts was ordered and heightened by the use of axes (recalling his Beaux-Arts training and his interest in ancient Classical towns). There was a large civic area towards the centre, but Garnier made no provision for religious buildings. This no doubt mirrored his socialist conviction that the new society would render such 'palliatives' unnecessary. As in Howard's Utopia, small family villas were laid out along side streets lined with trees, protected from overcrowding, the noise and smell of traffic, and industry. There were also some apartment buildings on a larger scale, also flat-roofed and rectangular. Walkways were provided alongside each building, so allowing pedestrians to filter across the city at any point and permitting a dense planting of trees. Garnier claimed that 'the land of the city, taken overall, is like a big park, without any fences to delimit the various sections.' Hygienic factors also played a major part in his plan.

12.2 (*left*) Ebenezer Howard, diagram of the Garden City principle showing the main elements and their relationship (from *Garden Cities of Tomorrow*, 1902).

12.3 (*right*) Tony Garnier, Cité Industrielle, 1901–17, residential quarter (from the *Cité Industrielle*, 1917).

Thus the Garden City was here rethought in ways which faced up to the techniques, potentials, and values of an industrial society. Garnier's imagery was pervaded by a sober yet romantic aura of the progressive potential of industrial technique to further a programme of social emancipation. Class struggles and oppositions of interest seemed to have no place in this Arcadian dream of Grecian villas, places of co-operation, and tree-lined avenues. The Arts and Crafts imagery of Unwin's sound English working-men living a healthy and moral life in a rural setting gave way to a flat-topped architecture evocative of the larger organizations of the industrial state. But for all its progressive mood, there was still a touch of nostalgia, as Manfredo Tafuri has suggested by referring to the Cité Industrielle as 'a New Hellas':

> For him the future was anchored in a past fondly pictured as a Golden Age, as an ideal equilibrium to be won again.

Owing to his connections with the Socialist Mayor of Lyons, Edouard Herriot, Garnier was able to translate part of this ideal city into reality; but something of the dream-like character of the drawn version was lost.

Another major work of urbanism which linked nineteenth-century notions with the progressive planners of the twenties was that undertaken by Berlage for the extension of South Amsterdam between 1902 and about 1920 (fig. 12.4). Outside the perimeter fortification walls, the growth of Amsterdam throughout the nineteenth century had continued in a pell-mell fashion. The influx of industry required a vast provision of decent housing conceived on the scale of neighbourhoods. Berlage brought order to the chaos with the help of grand avenues defining major pieces of massive and substantial character; these were in turn penetrated by secondary systems of roads and quiet squares containing shops, schools, and public institutions. The main unit of collective dwelling was the perimeter block around large internal courts containing gardens. Many of these were laid out on symmetrical plans with massive central elements. The buildings were finely detailed in dark brick, and arches, windows, corners, etc. conspired to give the whole area a unity of theme and sobriety of effect, offset by the looser order of trees and pathways.

A similar basic pattern was adopted by the 'Expressionist' architects Piet Kramer and Michel de Klerk in their various collective block designs in

12.4 (*above left*) Hendrik Petrus Berlage, aerial view of the 'New South' area of Amsterdam showing perimeter blocks, 1902–20.

12.5 Michel de Klerk, Eigen Haard housing, Amsterdam, 1915–19.

Amsterdam. De Klerk's Eigen Haard housing of 1919 (fig. 12.5) was also beyond the edge of the coherent historical centre, and the architect attempted to solidify the urban fabric by virtually monumentalizing the housing problem and treating the perimeter as a single sculptural unit. However, this was brilliantly articulated by changes in rhythm, texture, scale, and colour to hint at changes of interior function and disposition, and to respond to the varying pressures of a triangular site. To one end, on the centre of the baseline of the triangle, a gateway was cut through the outer edge and a steeple used to mark its presence.

Once again, the mood was a sober and solid one, as if the architecture was seeking deliberately to counter the uprootedness and flux of modern urban existence with something reassuring and evocative of some earlier guild co-operation. Speaking of his plans for Amsterdam, Berlage had claimed he was instituting 'a sort of town-planning revival'; de Klerk too, seems to have sought a balance between an innovative solution to new demands, and a feeling of continuity.

A polarity between promise in some hazy ideal future and reminiscence of a more integrated past seems to have been intrinsic to the urbanistic thought processes of Le Corbusier. The 'Contemporary City for Three Million Inhabitants' of 1922 was mentioned earlier in the context of the architect's pervasive conception of the 'machine age', and his search for a harmony in modern culture. Like Garnier, Le Corbusier was content with nothing less than a total theorem for all the processes of industrial society. It has to be said that he over-simplified these drastically in his plans.

The Contemporary City is known from a series of drawings which Le Corbusier exhibited at the Salon D'Automne in Paris in 1922. The plan was based on a regular geometry and was cut across by a main axis of road circulation coming to a transportation centre laid out on a number of levels, the topmost of which was an airport. Around this centre, and conforming to the grid of the city, were 24 glass skyscrapers 600 feet high. These were supposed to contain 'the brains' of the

12.6 Le Corbusier, Contemporary City for Three Million Inhabitants, 1922, view of skyscrapers and transport intersection at the core.

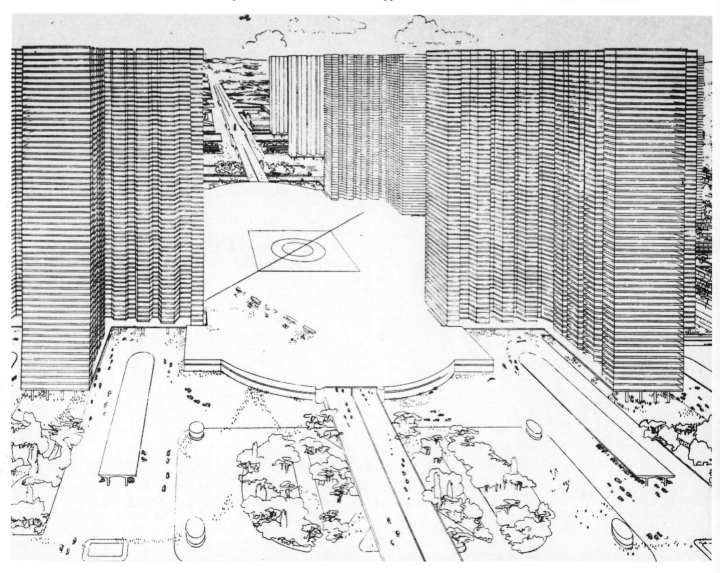

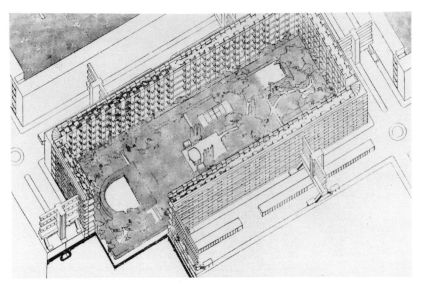

12.7 Le Corbusier, Contemporary City, 1922, the *immeubles villas*.

society – the technocrats, the managers, and the bankers. Most of the rest of the city was taken up with high-density apartment buildings laid out regularly in a park-like setting. The workers' suburbs and the main industrial zone were placed some distance away, so reinforcing the distinction between a managerial élite and the lower orders. The whole was pervaded by a spirit of almost obsessive rationality and discipline: scarcely a curved line was to be seen.

The rationale for the plan was straightforward. High-density living was to be combined with the maximum of open space and fresh air through the use of new techniques like steel and concrete construction and with the help of the motor car. Mechanized traffic was to be separated from the pedestrian by the use of *pilotis*; indeed the entire green floor of the city was to be kept free as the buildings too were lifted up. The traditional street was demolished; Le Corbusier associated it with the choking fumes and diseased areas of nineteenth-century slums. Instead of the grimy industrial city, a brave new world of light, greenery, air, cleanliness, and efficiency was to arise. Country and city were to be reintegrated so that the city became a vast park. Le Corbusier saw technology as a double-headed creature capable of good or ill; his city plan was an attempt at co-opting and harmonizing the forces and possibilities of industry in the service of human betterment and emancipation.

There were a number of ideological components: it seems clear that Le Corbusier had absorbed the ideas of Saint-Simon, especially the conception of a benevolent élite of technocrats who would act as the agents of a progress for all. This vision of the state was embodied in the skyscrapers at the city's core (fig. 12.6) and in the romanticization of technology implicit in both the

grand treatment of the roads and the machine-age tenor of the other buildings. Of course, the architect could not locate a strict equivalent to a Saint-Simonian élite in his own time, and his later Ville Voisin of 1925 (in which he suggested the construction of a business district of skyscrapers in the centre of Paris) was a heavy-handed attempt at exciting the interest of big business in his schemes. It was later in the twenties that Le Corbusier began to realize some of the severe problems of a capitalist economy, and began to shift his political ground. Until then he maintained a romantic conception of technocracy as a progressive force in its own right. Once again we find an element of determinism in this artist's outlook.

The actual images of Le Corbusier's Ville Contemporaine also had a complex lineage. It was as if he had assembled fragments of cities he liked over a single regular plan. The technological aura of Manhattan (known from photographs) was spliced together with the roads and glass buildings of Sant'Elia's Città Nuova. The boulevards, grand avenues, and parks of Paris were mated with a geometrical order reminiscent of ideal city plans from the Renaissance. Howard's Garden City and Garnier's Cité Industrielle were rephrased on a far larger scale. The sensibility of Purism was blended with memories of grand Classical cities of the past. The whole was infused with that love of the typical and the abstract that we have sensed in Le Corbusier's architecture. It was as if he was not content with merely defining the 'standards' of a new architecture, but also had to take on the question of the typical elements of the town – indeed the society – of the future. Was this simply a theoretical exercise or did he seriously hope to build the whole thing? Neither point is certain, but clearly Le Corbusier was not squeamish about projecting his own vision of Utopia in the belief that it was good for all. One guesses that if it had been built, the Ville Contemporaine would have possessed a crushing uniformity.

The residential buildings for Le Corbusier's élite were of two types – set-backs (to re-emerge in the thirties as the *à redent* apartment houses of the Radiant City) and perimeter blocks laid out around courtyards and called *immeubles villas* (fig. 12.7). The latter were made up from double-height units, each with a large garden terrace, stacked up to a height equivalent to twelve single storeys. The interior of each double-height maisonette was similar to that envisaged in the Maison Citrohan. Evidently it was Le Corbusier's intention to turn the powers of mass production to the solution of the housing question at the widest scale. Communal facilities such as restaurants, tennis courts, roof terraces, and lawns were included. The atmosphere was quite luxurious, like a middle-class hotel rather than the communist collective condensers envisaged

in the Soviet Union later in the decade.

Like the city as a whole, the *immeubles villas* drew upon diverse sources which had captured Le Corbusier's imagination during his travels. Most notable was the monastery at Ema in Tuscany which he had visited as a young man. This too was formed around a courtyard and had individual cells of double height with views over private gardens. It was an organization which was to recur in many of Le Corbusier's architectural essays on collective living in later life. The monastery was a type which fascinated him because it seemed to embody an ideal balance between public and private existence, and between the built and the natural worlds.

Although Le Corbusier was never to build a total version of any of his ideal cities, their spirit still informed much of his later production. This was true of many other architects in the twenties as well, who employed individual opportunities as experiments towards the larger whole. In a sense, the housing exhibition at the Weissenhofsiedlung in Stuttgart in

1927 played this role for the participants. But in the Weimar Republic there were agencies which allowed the construction of modern housing on a broad front. Indeed the constitution of the new German republic of 1919 stressed State control over the use of land, one intention being the provision of homes for all. In fact, housing reforms could only become effective after about 1923 with the temporary stabilization of the economy. The results were seen most dramatically in such cities as Breslau, Hamburg, Celle, Berlin, and Frankfurt.

Frankfurt was a special case because there the aims of the trade unions and the social democratic co-operatives were most effective in influencing policy. The mayor of the city, Ludwig Landmann, had a special interest in housing which he had expressed in a book entitled *Das Siedlungsamt der Grosstadt* in 1919. In 1925 he invited the architect Ernst May to Frankfurt, invested him with the powers of city architect and supported him with official machinery to appropriate land for modernization. May had already realized a series of small agricultural communities in Silesia in the early twenties which had reflected the obvious influence of Howard's ideas; but his new task was on a colossal scale by comparison. The numerous *Siedlungen* which he and his associates designed for Frankfurt in the next five years were only loosely based on Garden City principles, though much attention was devoted to the natural setting, the creation of hygienic living spaces, and proximity to the place of work. Equally important was the commitment to industrial mass production of rationally based housing prototypes. May undertook the most detailed researches into the logistics of use and production on all scales, from the outside spaces to the individual dwellings and the tiniest fixtures. From this emerged, for example, the famous 'Frankfurt kitchen', supposedly a compact and exceptionally functional design. This spirit of analysis seems to have thrilled committed modern architects elsewhere in Europe, who felt that it was evidence of the divergence of technology away from the rapacious purposes of *laissez-faire* economics towards a socially responsible aim. On the other hand, opponents were quick to parody the 'inhuman' and 'scientific' invasion of the home.

In layout and appearance the *Siedlungen* were also far removed from the free-standing family houses of the Garden City with their pitched roofs and rustic overtones. A characteristic layout was a long, low block between three and five storeys high, with access ways and stairs between paired flats which were placed on each floor. This led to an almost monotonous repetition of standardized modules and constructional elements, which the architects attempted to humanize by judicious attention to proportion, scale, light, shade, and detail. The tight budgets allowed no frills, but the resulting asceticism was turned to good use as an expression of co-operative discipline and moral rigour. The planar white or coloured surfaces were enlivened in any case by the play of shadows from trees and the juxtaposition of lawns and planting.

Thus Garden City ideas and the abstract forms of the new architecture came together in a compelling imagery which was intended to display the values of enlightened socialism. It seemed briefly as if the Utopian aspirations of the avant-garde and the social realities of the time were in step; the Römerstadt (fig. 12.8), the Bruchfeldstrasse, and the Praunheim housing schemes were widely published and eagerly upheld by left-wing champions as examples of what could be achieved when modern architecture was allowed its 'true' destination: not the aggrandizement of chic middle-class bohemia, but the emancipation of

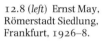

12.8 (*left*) Ernst May, Römerstadt Siedlung, Frankfurt, 1926–8.

12.9 (*right*) Bruno Taut, Britz-Siedlung, Berlin, 1928, aerial view of 'horseshoe' housing.

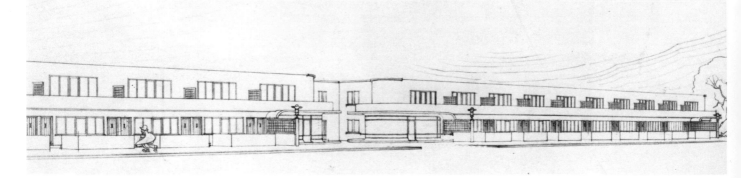

12.10 (*left*) J. P. Oud, housing at the Hook of Holland, 1924.

12.11 (*below left*) J. P. Oud, housing at the Hook of Holland, 1924, drawing.

12.12 (*right*) J. P. Oud, Kiefhoek housing, Rotterdam, 1925.

12.13 (*below right*) J. P. Oud, Kiefhoek housing, Rotterdam, 1925, aerial view drawing.

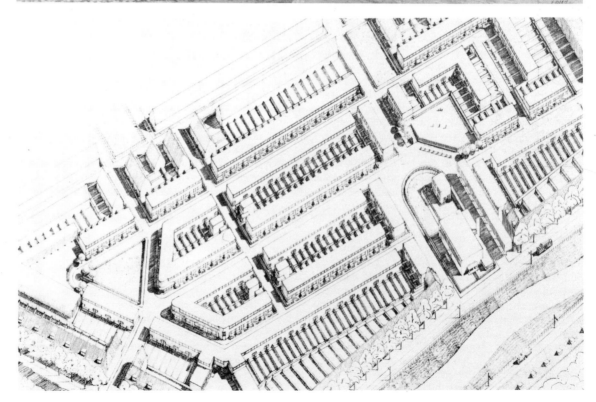

the working class from bondage, the amelioration of environmental conditions on a wide front, the harmonization of mechanization and nature. However, the bubble soon burst at the end of the decade when increases in the cost of materials led to a rapid decrease in quality, when it became clear (as was the case in Russia) that the imagery was by no means necessarily shared or understood by the populace, and when the forces of reaction turned violently on the new architecture for its supposed communist inspiration.

Although patronage in Berlin worked otherwise than in Frankfurt, it too had its share of remarkable housing schemes. Among the most notable, perhaps, were those by Gropius for the Siemensstadt, and those by Bruno Taut and Martin Wagner at the Britz-Siedlung. Taut had by this time long abandoned the Expressionist and quasi-sacral yearnings of the late 1910s. Instead he had adopted the manner of the 'New Objectivity' which he probably thought most appropriate to the stringent social programme implicit in the new housing schemes. However, he was far from being a mere 'functionalist' in intention, and sought to imbue the standardized and repetitive forms of his designs with an aura of dignity and with a communal spirit. The Britz plan was centred on a horseshoe-like open space embraced by a strip of housing (fig. 12.9). From this focus, parallel oblongs were disposed with layers of green space between. The image of the freestanding 'bourgeois' villa was deliberately rejected, just as the unsanitary working-class tenements of the nineteenth century were corrected. Thus the form language was intended to convey a sort of purgative intention. However, there was the perpetual danger that repetition simply might degenerate into mere banality when the probity of the socialist vision was absent. This tended to happen in the many weak derivatives of the classic *Siedlungen*.

It is possible that May, Wagner, Taut, and the rest were influenced by the remarkable and slightly earlier housing designs of J. P. Oud in Holland. As early as 1918, at the age of 28, Oud had been appointed the chief architect of Rotterdam. His earliest designs in this role were clearly modelled on Berlage's prototypes. Only gradually did he manage to break away from hackneyed plan arrangements and to synthesize De Stijl discoveries with an architectural language that had still to handle the requirements of workers' habitation. The moment of crystallization seems to have occurred in his designs for housing at the Hook of Holland of 1924 (figs. 12.10 and 11). Here sanitary intentions were transcended by a remarkably expressive formal design. The two identical blocks contained two rows of superimposed dwellings, and the extremities were rounded. The walls were plastered and whitewashed, while the low base was made of yellow brick, the doorsteps of red brick, and the doorposts of grey concrete. Doors, lamps, pillars, and other details were painted in blue, red, black, and yellow, inevitably recalling the character of Mondrian's paintings or some touches in the Schroeder House by Rietveld. The asymmetrical dynamism of De Stijl was not so easily translatable to the larger scale, but in the Kiefhoek housing in Rotterdam of 1925 Oud managed to slide the surrounding spaces one into another (figs. 12.12, 12.13). Again the houses were kept down to two storeys. The thin, whitewashed boxes with their tight and exquisite details stood out strongly against the red brick surroundings, and were a dramatic departure from the texture and weight of earlier Dutch housing experiments in the 'Expressionist' mode. The possible problems of a clash with the immediate context were scarcely noted at the time. However, it was a matter of fact that these stark abstract prototypes, so emblematic of the new order, did not blend in. Moreover, Oud had the advantage of regularized street patterns and flat terrains which wedded well with his style and approach; there was no guarantee that the supposed universal qualities of the designs would be transferable to other conditions.

The dilemmas of social interpretation faced by European avant-garde architects were not so far removed from those faced by their counterparts in Soviet Russia at the same time. The avant-garde was in constant danger of projecting its own values on reality and indulging in over-simple environmental determinism of the kind which claimed that good architecture must be good for all morally and socially. As was shown in Chapter 10, groups like the OSA researched into living patterns and constructional techniques in order to seek out prototypes for workers' housing and to discover forms 'expressive' of the new state of things. This was only part of a larger vision of renewal, which was more ambitiously registered in town plans. In his book *Russia: An Architecture for World Revolution* of 1930, El Lissitzky presented a synopsis of avant-garde tendencies over the previous decade, building type by building type, and tended to imply that the clubs, housing schemes, factories, etc., were all basic elements of some new urban order. In a section entitled 'The New City', he wrote:

Social evolution leads to the elimination of the old dichotomy between city and country. The city endeavours to draw nature right into its centre and by means of industrialization to introduce a higher level of culture into the country.

This was in the spirit of Marx's and Engels's original

12.14 Moisei Ginzburg, 'Green Moscow' project, 1929–30.

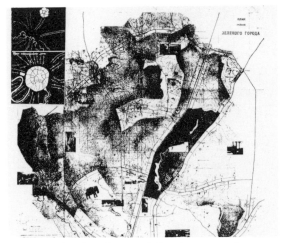

pleas for the demolition of the distinction between urban and rural proletariats, and also seemed to echo Lenin's plea for 'the fusion of industry and agriculture', but even once the article of faith had been accepted, there were a number of possible ways to translate the idea into an urban plan.

There thus ensued a series of city-planning debates. In the late twenties Zelenko and Sabsovich contrived the theory of communal houses to be placed in new residential and industrial centres every twenty-five miles or so away from existing cities; these were supposed to become nuclei of ideologically transformed peasantries, and were vaguely reminiscent of Fourier's 'phalanstères'. This theorem was attacked by the 'disurbanists' (particularly Ginzburg and Barshch) who caricatured the communal houses as rural barracks and argued that industry and agriculture should be dispersed throughout entire territories, so dissolving the old boundaries of city and country altogether. The project for a 'Green Moscow' proposed in 1929–30 (fig. 12.14) suggested that the heart of the historical city should be preserved, for leisure and cultural activities, while linear cities were created on a radial pattern from the centre. These were to be made up of movable wooden houses on stilts linked by railways which would be free of charge. An even more extreme and anarchical faction in the 'disurbanist' school argued for complete fragmentation and for the avoidance of coherent formal structure altogether.

The case for the linear city was pursued most avidly by N. A. Milyutin in a book entitled *The Problem of Building Socialist Cities*, in which he argued that industry should be built in a linear manner with a parallel residential strip separated from it by a green belt a few hundred yards wide. The railways were to be located away from the green belt on the far side of the industry, while a main road gave access to the residential zones. The linear form was recommended

for its supposed flexibility and because it avoided centric images of power.

A review of collective housing proposals in the twenties would be incomplete without some discussion of Vienna. A census taken in 1917 revealed that nearly three-quarters of Viennese lodgings were unhygienic and overcrowded. Under the Social Democrat Otto Bauer, rents were controlled, private properties were bought, and a programme for building 5,000 apartments a year was set in progress. Architects like Josef Frank and Adolf Loos responded to the crisis by suggesting low-population-density, single-home suburbs. However, the commune followed the lead of Peter Behrens in favour of colossal super-blocks with their own collective facilities. The model selected became known as the 'Hof' – a closed or semi-closed block of extremely high density, to be built according to traditional methods. The resulting enormous structures became known as 'workers' fortresses'; indeed, the Karl Marx Hof was the scene of a pitched battle in 1934 between the forces of the left and the extreme right.

This latter building was designed by Karl Ehn in 1927 and stretched for more than half a mile (Fig. 12.15). It contained 1,382 apartments plus offices, laundries, green spaces, a library, an out-patients clinic, and green areas; it covered an area of more than quarter of a square mile. The vast problems of scale posed by handling a building of this size were somewhat clumsily resolved by adopting a linear block arrangement which was then articulated by broad entrance arches with massive surmounting towers. The whole had something of the character of a viaduct or rampart wall; in fact, each of these historical prototypes would recommend itself to later planners who attempted to design *Unités* on this scale. The style of the Karl Marx Hof was an ungainly descendant of the Wagner School. One historian purported to see in the building an example of 'the populist epical idiom'.

In 1928 the first meeting of the Congrès Internationaux de L'Architecture Moderne took place at the castle of Mme de Mandrot at La Sarraz near Lausanne, and discussions among some of Europe's leading modern architects turned to the interrelationships of architecture and town planning. The final statement of the meeting (at which Gropius and Le Corbusier were among the protagonists) argued that architecture should be put 'back in its true sphere which is economic, sociological, and altogether at the service of humanity.' It also stated that:

Town planning is the design of the different settings for the development of material, emotional and spiritual life in all its manifestations, individual and collective, and it includes both town and country.

OVERLEAF

12.15 Karl Ehn, Karl Marx Hof, Vienna, 1927

The ensuing CIAM meeting took place at Frankfurt in 1929 and discussion centred on the problem of the 'Existenzminimum' (the 'minimum habitation'). In 1930, in Brussels, housing emerged once again when debates on the relative value of middle or high-rise planning occurred. Gropius presented his studies of lighting angles and plot ratios, while others raised once again the difficult problem of political implementation. The fourth congress took place in 1933 on board ship between Marseilles and Athens, and on this occasion the general announcement (later called the Charter of Athens) returned to the problem of the modern city and to general town-planning principles:

> Today, most cities are in a state of total chaos. These cities do not come anywhere near achieving their aim, which is to satisfy the biological and psychological needs of their inhabitants.
> From the beginnings of the machine age this situation bespeaks the proliferation of private interests. . . .
> On a spiritual and material level, the city should ensure individual freedom and the benefits of collective action.
> Reorganization within the urban pattern must be regulated on the human scale only.
> The key points in town planning lie in the four functions: living, working, recreation (in free time), circulation. . . .
> The basic nucleus of town planning is the living cell (a dwelling) and its introduction into a group constitutes a unit of habitation of suitable size.
> Starting from this unit, the relations between living place, place of work and place of recreation can be worked out.
> To solve this serious problem it is vital to utilize the resources of modern technological progress.

Once again the avant-garde had to resort to a theoretical blueprint in the description of the ideal urban totality. This was bound to be the case in the absence of state authorities sympathetic to the cause, as the German architects knew only too well. Elsewhere in the same document it was admitted that 'private interest' should be subordinated to 'public interest', but it was by no means clear how this should happen. In the event the modern urbanist/architect was forced into the position of making piecemeal demonstrations where unique aesthetic qualities might well obscure the prototypical nature of the experiment. The ideal city was bound to remain on paper without a society and without a consensus in favour of the values it represented.

13. The International Style, the Individual Talent, and the Myth of Functionalism

Styles, like languages, differ in the sequence of articulation and in the number of questions they allow the artist to ask. . . .

E. H. Gombrich, 1960

By the beginning of the 1930s, it was possible for the discerning and selective eye to survey the productions of the previous decade and to single out a new style. From Moscow to Milan, from La Jolla to Japan, buildings of different function, size, material, meaning, and expressive power could be found which still had obvious features in common. One could speak of the shared characteristics in terms of recurrent motifs like strip windows, flat roofs, grids of supports, cantilevered horizontal planes, metal railings and curved partitions; or, one could define the general qualities of the style by more abstract features like the recurrent tendency to use simple rectangular volumes articulated by crisply cut openings, or to emphasize hovering planes and interpenetrating spaces. Hitchcock and Johnson (as was shown in Chapter 11) went still further by attempting to outline the main visual principles of the new style (the stress on volume rather than mass, regularity, the avoidance of ornament, etc.). Moreover, they claimed for this new 'International Style' a major historical significance.

Now that it is possible to emulate the great styles of the past in their essence without imitating their surface, the problem of establishing one dominant style, which the nineteenth century set itself in terms of alternative revivals, is coming to a solution . . . There is now a single body of discipline fixed enough to integrate contemporary style as a reality and yet elastic enough to permit individual interpretation and to encourage general growth.

The authors supported their case with a selection of black-and-white photographs of buildings in places as far apart as California and Czechoslovakia. This method of presentation played down differences in size, colour, and material. But the intellectual filters were just as crucial as the photographic ones in establishing a historical picture. Hitchcock and Johnson were evidently determined to honour a genuine modern style and therefore were bound to ignore such oddities as Wright or Expressionism which did not fit. Their approach was strong on the general, the shared, and the typical, but weak on the personal, the practical, and the particular.

To grasp what is meant by divergences of personal style, one has only to think of two seminal buildings of the 1920s analysed earlier in this book: Le Corbusier's Maison Cook of 1925–6 and Rietveld's Schroeder House of 1924. These have more in common with one another than either of them has with, say, an Art Nouveau or an Expressionist dwelling, so it is just to group them together; but one is still struck by the difference in spatial emphasis between Le Corbusier's planar box with its jigsaw intrusions of *pilotis* and partitions, and Rietveld's exploding planes which overlap and extend into the surroundings (a contrast which embodies some of the crucial differences between Purism and De Stijl). Many finer visual distinctions could no doubt be drawn between Rietveld's and Le Corbusier's other works, in order to characterize their personal styles. By degrees, one might even dig into each artist's world of meaning: on

13.1 (*above*) Hans Scharoun, house at Weissenhofsiedlung, Stuttgart, 1927.

13.2 (*above right*) Ludwig Mies van der Rohe, apartment building, Weissenhofsiedlung, Stuttgart, 1927.

13.3 (*right*) Le Corbusier, exhibition dwelling, Weissenhofsiedlung, Stuttgart, 1927.

some levels it would be possible to discern shared themes to do with the spiritualization of the machine, but if one pursued the matter further one would find contrasting private metaphors, sources of form, and ideological positions. The preceding few chapters have shown what a variety of social ideals was expressed through analogous forms during the 1920s.

Perhaps 1927 was the first year of maturity of the new style, in which forms could be assumed, and problems worked out on the basis of discoveries which were then assured. It was the year of the Villa Stein at Garches, of the Bauhaus, of Golosov's Workers' Club in Russia, of the League of Nations competition and the Weissenhofsiedlung at Stuttgart. The former event acted as a sharp reminder that the new forms had a long way to go before they received official acceptance; the latter, ostensibly an exhibition of housing ideas sponsored by the Deutscher Werkbund, was an affirmation that a shared language had at last been achieved. Even so the individual items in this contemporary museum of international architecture exhibited considerable divergences of approach. Scharoun's house (fig. 13.1) was composed of overlapping curves and was quite 'Expressionist' in character compared with the stereometric discipline of the other designs. Le Corbusier's larger building, with its *pilotis*, its taut, hovering box, its expanses of glazing, its nautical imagery, and its almost obsessive demonstration of the 'five points' (fig. 13.3), differed from Mies van der Rohe's far more contained, closed, earthbound and planimetric block of flats (fig. 13.2),

13.4 (*above*) Johannes A. Brinckmann, Leendert C. van der Vlugt, Mart Stam, Van Nelle Factory, near Rotterdam, 1927–9.

13.5 (*left*) Bernard Bijvoet and Johannes Duiker, Zonnestraal Sanatorium, Hilversum, 1926–8.

in which the windows were holes punched through walls (rather than openings partially filled by cladding) and the interiors were cellular in character, rather than being based on the free plan.

In part such distinctions had to do with differences of function, and from 1925 onwards the style which had so often been pioneered in small villas had increasingly to prove its worth in handling much larger and more complex programmes. The Bauhaus buildings at Dessau were one case where the architecture employed variations in the system, to orchestrate a variety of functions. Another case, on an even larger scale, was the Van Nelle Factory outside Rotterdam by Johannes Brinckmann, Leendert van der Vlugt and Mart Stam (fig. 13.4). The main production functions – tobacco, coffee, and tea factories – were placed in free-plan spaces entirely open to the edges to admit the maximum of light and air, and placed end to end in a stepping form, so that the separation was expressed, while the form as a whole was unified by hovering horizontal metallic bands floating a full 300 yards without apparent support. This glazed fantasy was linked laterally by dramatic conveyors and criss-cross transparent bridges to the storage and transport buildings along the parallel canal. The highest volume was joined longitudinally by another glazed bridge to the main office wing, curved to fit the profile of the arrival street, and to provide a suitable accentuation of its honorific meaning. The composition was topped by a small semicircular glazed room, like some much expanded precision piece from a glass machine; in this a canteen was placed so that workers could come together while the humming mechanical processes of their joint endeavour continued below them. The horizontal accent was relieved by verticals containing lifts and vertical pipes, but detailed to give the sense of the thinnest possible paper-like surfaces, rather than any traditional sense of mass.

Despite the fact that these forms had the clearest basis in functional decisions concerning the process of manufacture, and despite the fact that they could be related to the naked facts of concrete and steel construction, the pragmatic was transcended, idealized, given a poetic, expressive presence. We have to deal with matters far deeper than style, matters of which style is only an outward manifestation. These hovering glazed strips and evocative details resulted from a search for deeper symbolic meanings in the mechanical process. One recalls Lissitzky's panegyric to the Vesnin brothers' project for the Pravda building of 1924, 'the building is characteristic of an age that thirsts after glass, steel and concrete', and Le Corbusier's reaction to the evocative transparency of the Van Nelle Factory in which he sensed a social vision of emancipation:

The sheer façades of the building, bright glass and grey metal, rise up ... against the sky ...
Everything is open to the outside. And this is of enormous significance to all those who are working, on all eight floors *inside* ... The Van Nelle tobacco factory in Rotterdam, a creation of the modern age, has removed all the former connotations of despair from the word 'proletarian'. And this deflection of the egoistic property instinct towards a feeling for collective action leads to a most happy result: the phenomenon of personal participation in every stage of the human enterprise.

The programme of the Van Nelle virtually implied a linear arrangement of oblong blocks; the Zonnestraal Sanatorium at Hilversum (1926–8) by Johannes Duiker and Bernard Bijvoet required a more dispersed plan as its main functions were a medical complex, an administrative block, and individual linear wards requiring direct access to the outside (fig. 13.5). The principal purpose of the sanatorium was to cure eye diseases contracted by members of the diamond workers union, and the clinical forms of modern architecture seemed well suited to the ethos and the social programme. The main volumes were disposed on a sort of butterfly plan with the administration and communal facilities at the head and the sprawling wards in the wings. The individual functions were differentiated by variations in form and fenestration.

Both the Van Nelle Factory and the Zonnestraal Sanatorium were influenced in part by Elementarist and Constructivist attitudes emanating ultimately from the Soviet Union, yet in order to grasp how different these buildings were from Russian work of the same period, one has only to compare them to Golosov's Workers' Club in Moscow of 1927–8 (fig. 13.6). Here the machine rhetoric of the great glass cylinder containing the stairs was more overt and less controlled than in the Van Nelle. Compared to the thin, planar surfaces, the intersecting horizontal bands were chunky, even massive in appearance. The architect attempted to exploit violent contrasts of space and form, and to clash together, almost brutally, the different materials of his building, so as to dramatize functional differences and to create emotive mechanistic symbols.

Compared to any of the aforementioned three examples, Mendelsohn's Schocken department store at Chemnitz of 1928–30 (fig. 13.8) presents a suave, unified and smooth appearance. The site was triangular, and the interiors were opened up by a grid of thin supports; stairs and lifts were shifted to the apices of the triangle. The façade was a single broad curve, with an almost uninterrupted shop window at the

13.6 (*left*) I. Golosov, Zuyev Workers' Club, Moscow, 1927–8.

13.7 (*right*) Le Corbusier, League of Nations, Geneva, competition project, 1927.

13.8 (*below*) Erich Mendelsohn, Schocken store, Chemnitz, 1928–30.

13.9 (*below right*) Hannes Meyer, League of Nations, Geneva, competition projects, 1927.

base, and continuous strip windows at the upper levels. No attempt was made to articulate the stairways or the circulation, or to dramatize changes of volume or material: rather there was a dynamic *gestalt*, a simple yet living form subsuming all parts and details. One is reminded, of course, of Mendelsohn's earlier development, of the fusion of all the parts of his so-called 'Expressionist phase', of his method of conceiving buildings as totalities in small, dynamic sketches. By contrast, the Van Nelle Factory belonged to a different world – the world of Elementarist, rectangular, abstract art; nonetheless the *superficialities* of style were the same.

The hovering volumes and weightless illusions of the International Style were related to the horizontal layering of space suggested by concrete cantilever construction; a building like the Van Nelle Factory did at least require a predominantly horizontal treatment. But the elements of the new style had sometimes to cope with buildings of which the function implied a primarily vertical emphasis. Such was the case with the skyscraper, and the problem of maintaining unity was severe. In the *Chicago Tribune* competition, Gropius's entry employed a sophisticated combination of rectangular frame, vertical panels, and cantilevered horizontal planes to unify the form; Mies van der Rohe's slightly earlier glass towers tended to adopt the solution of total glazing (hardly realizable at the time), while Le Corbusier's glass towers in the Ville Contemporaine expressed the floor slabs as thin lines (again, the glazing solution was scarcely practical); Howe and Lescaze's design for the PSFS skyscraper in Philadelphia (1926–32) skilfully blended vertical and horizontal articulations which were rooted in functional differences.

Factories, skyscrapers, blocks of flats, department stores, and workers' clubs were, at least, specifically 'modern' functions; on occasion though, the new architecture had to handle more traditional tasks like civic monuments and parliament buildings, where questions of size, hierarchy, and symbolism were crucial. The League of Nations competition of 1927 offers an intriguing insight into the way a variety of modern architects and 'traditionalists' approached the same 'monumental' programme and site. The building was to be a sort of world parliament, and to contain a giant assembly, lobbies, a secretariat, and a multiplicity of supporting bureaucratic functions; it was to

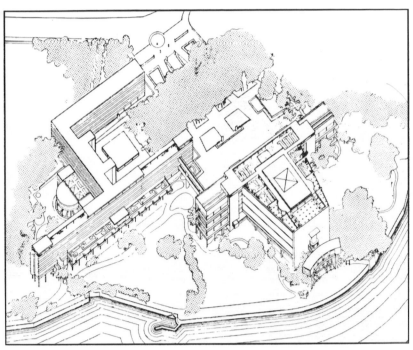

stand near Geneva on the lake side. The symbolic and rhetorical aspects of the problem were pivotal, and among the many entries were a number of half-baked attempts at a global and holistic imagery in the form of circular buildings, mandalas, and the like. Eventually, a rather clumsy Beaux-Arts scheme was chosen (designed by P.-H. Nénot), but only after a scandalous interlude in which Le Corbusier, who had appeared to be the winner, was disqualified on the grounds he had used the wrong sort of ink.

Le Corbusier's design (fig. 13.7) was a masterly composition in which a hierarchy was suggested between the most important room, the assembly, placed on a dominant axis, and the supporting functions of the secretariat, disposed as uniform lateral blocks looking over strips of landscape and the nearby lake. The volume of the assembly was derived primarily from acoustic considerations and was curved in profile; it would have been reached gradually through a grand entrance facing the lake, via a sequence of spaces of strongly ceremonial character linked on axis. Le Corbusier solved the problem of a monumental entrance by using grandiose *pilotis* and an attached sculptural group to suggest the character

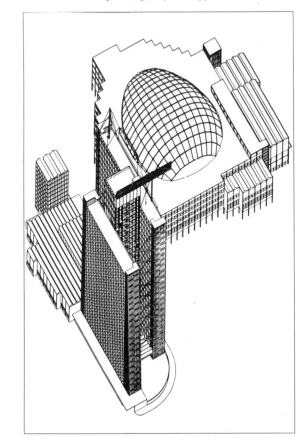

of a portico. The secretariat was treated in a more neutral way, with long windows, balconies, and *pilotis*, allowing the passage of circulation beneath. This was to be a communal machine for enlightened, well-meaning functionaries whose life would be daily nourished through contact with nature; evocative classical overtones were implied in the dignified and hieratic mood of the assembly chamber. It was a modern palace for the world élite.

It is intriguing to compare Le Corbusier's design with Hannes Meyer's entry in the same competition (fig. 13.9). Kenneth Frampton has characterized the contrast as one between 'the humanist and the utilitarian' ideals. Meyer was suspicious of the poetic Utopianism of men like Le Corbusier, and of the élitist values implicit in the programme. In his scheme, the secretariat was the dominant element and was contained in an open-frame tower, a celebration of engineering recalling the architect's admiration for Russian Constructivism. The deliberate accentuation of the factory aesthetic and 'found industrial' objects was no doubt intended as a sort of proletarian imagery, again following the 'code' of the Russian avant-garde. There was no hankering after what the architect might have regarded as a specious traditionalism to bolster the honorific character of the institution. Meyer even played down the possible hierarchical characteristics of his scheme by designing the whole on a standardized and repetitive module. Even so, these images were loaded with a social content of a kind that the 'New Objectivity' architects in Germany had striven to express by an 'honest' assessment of function and technique: Meyer's scheme was a palace for the people. The architect wrote revealingly of it:

> If the intentions of the League of Nations are sincere, then it cannot possibly cram such a novel social organization into the strait-jacket of traditional architecture. No pillared reception rooms for weary monarchs but hygienic workrooms for the busy representatives of their people. No back corridors for backstairs diplomacy but open glazed rooms for public negotiation of honest men.

The contrast between Le Corbusier's and Meyer's designs, and the ideologies they articulated, calls to mind some of the debates between so-called 'formalists' and 'functionalists' in Russia and Germany about the same time. Le Corbusier was later castigated for his dangerous 'Utopianism' and replied that he saw man's deepest aspirations as transcending the mere categories of left and right. His design for the League of Nations was a celebration of his belief in a rational, enlightened humanity, possessing abstract principles of justice and law. In his eyes an over-emphasis on the utilitarian aspects of the problem would have been inappropriate. He sought instead to embody some of the higher ideals of the enclosed institution. The comparison of the two schemes is so valuable because it demonstrates different personal and ideological emphases in buildings which it might still be possible to group together under the same broad stylistic label.

The International Style had some adherents who only partly understood the underlying principles, and who adopted the forms as a new external dress. In such cases, modern forms became a sort of packaging, a cosmetic application, rather than the expression of deeper meanings, or the disciplined result of attention to the functional discipline suggested by a task. This was one of the dangers of speaking of the new architecture as a 'style' at all: it suggested that a set of visual formulae could be picked up and then applied. Perhaps the work of the Dutch architect Willem Dudok supplies an example of this competent 'stylism' (fig. 13.10); or in France, that of Robert Mallet-Stevens. Each was capable of making of modern reductivism a sort of pleasing simplicity, which was nonetheless lacking in the transcending visionary content of the authentic modern movement.

Of course, to the die-hard functionalist, distinctions like these were not relevant; so far as he was concerned, all style was false imposition. In the late 1920s the engineer-philosopher R. Buckminster Fuller designed an aluminium house around a central mast of mechanical services. He claimed that this 'Dymaxion House' (fig. 13.11) was far more tightly related to functional and technological optimization than the cosmetic productions of the modern movement, which he rejected out of hand:

> The 'International Style' . . . demonstrated fashion-inoculation without necessary knowledge of the scientific fundamentals of structural mechanics and chemistry.
>
> The International Style 'simplification' then was but superficial. It peeled off yesterday's exterior embellishment and put on instead formalized novelties of quasi-simplicity, permitted by the same hidden structural elements of modern alloys that had permitted the discarded Beaux-Arts garmentation . . . The new International Stylist hung 'stark motif walls' of vast super-meticulous brick assemblage, which had no tensile cohesiveness within its own bonds, but was, in fact, locked within hidden steel frames supported by steel *without visible means of support*. In many such illusory ways did the 'International Style' gain dramatic sensory impingement on society as does a trick man gain the attention of children . . .

13.10 (*above*) William M. Dudok, Hilversum Town Hall, 1926–8.

13.11 (*right*) Richard Buckminster Fuller, Dymaxion House, 1929.

Running through this assessment was a belief in the 'honest' use and assemblage of technique and function, without the 'imposition' of symbolic or aesthetic filters; and as a critique of the plumbing and structural veracity of modern architecture, Fuller's criticisms may have had a point. But as architectural criticism, his remarks were frankly beside the point. They remind one that, for all the rhetoric used in the twenties concerning the honest expression of function, structure, and technology, the game had to go on once removed, as it were, in the field of symbolic forms, if the pragmatic was to be translated into art. One can go further, and say that it was in the tension between such apprehended facts as, say, an industrial window, or a standardized reinforced-concrete support, and the symbolic associations they evoked, that part of the expressive power of the new architecture lay. Whether or not the wash-basin in the Villa Savoye entrance was good plumbing, it was a standard fixture whose meaning was transformed by juxtaposition with surrounding *objet-types* – the *pilotis*, the industrial windows, etc. – whose external form mirrored a higher ideal: modern architects sought a kind of poetry of everyday facts transcended by ideas. In the end, to claim that structure was handled 'dishonestly', or that the latest fixtures were not included or designed by the architects, would be a little like complaining of a Renaissance architect that his avowed revival of a particular ancient prototype was 'inexact'. The architects of the machine age transformed the stuff of industrial production into new forms and meanings, but in such a way that the original 'reality' of, say, a glass brick or a nautical detail would be among the layers of reference of the final form. William Jordy described this 'symbolic objectivity' rather well:

> The goal of symbolic objectivity was to align architecture with the pervasive factuality of modern existence, with that 'ineloquence' (to call up Bernard Berenson's tag) which characterizes the modern imagination. The aims of simplification and purification at the core of the movement, providing it with a morality of Calvinist austerity, actually stemmed from a diffuse convention on the part of many progressive designers and theorists during the nineteenth century to the effect that architecture should be 'honest', 'truthful', and 'real', especially with respect to the revelation of functional programme and of materials and structure. During the twenties this moralistic heritage acquired an antiseptic cleanliness, and irreducible bareness, which symbolically, if not quite literally, accords with the morality of objectivity . . .

But the objection against taking 'functionalist' slogans at face value is even more fundamental. For even those few architects of the 1920s who saw themselves as pursuing a purely functional architecture were still stuck with the fact that functions do not, on their own, generate forms. Even the most tightly defined set of requirements may be answered in a variety of ways, and *a priori* images concerning the eventual appearance of the building will enter the design process at some point. Thus functions could only be translated into the forms and spaces of architecture through the screen of a style, and in this case it was a style of symbolic forms which referred, among other things, to the notion of functionality.

The typical formal aspects of the International Style were stretched in new directions when atypical materials were employed. An example of this was Bernard Bijvoet's and Pierre Chareau's Maison de Verre of 1928–32 (fig. 13.12), a building combining the functions of a medical clinic and a private house in a quiet enclave off a Paris street. Here the pervasive materials were glass brick and thin steel struts, elegantly composed into a linear aesthetic recalling the

slender wooden frames and screens of traditional Japanese construction. The interior plan was complex, but the most impressive space was the three-storey living-room/library with its slung galleries, its adjustable louvers, and its exposed bolts. It is possible that the imagery was here inspired by such things as the stacks at the Bibliothèque Nationale by Henri Labrouste, or the companion ladders and engineering rooms of ships. Whatever the precise sources, they were here transformed into an iconography of mechanization suitable to the theme of an elegant *machine à habiter*.

Materials and their associations must be considered part of the matrix of a style. The plaster walls and planar surfaces so often employed in the 1920s were perhaps intended to convey a non-material quality, to suggest the opposite of handicraft: the abstraction of the machine. The sheen of glass, and thinness of aluminium, were likewise evocative of aeroplanes or mass-produced objects. A style may be considered a complex of formal relationships in which certain moods and meanings are most at home; it provides a set of conventions, which, in the compelling and profound work of art, come together in such a way that the conventionality is forgotten. The pedant may insist that abstract art and mechanism, that ocean liners and Classical values, have no necessary connection, but when he has experienced the Villa Stein at Garches, these doubts are dispelled by a poetic sense of inevitability.

13.12 (*above*) Pierre Chareau and Bernard Bijvoet, Maison de Verre, Paris, 1928–32.

13.13 (*above right*) Ludwig Mies van der Rohe, Barcelona Pavilion, 1929, plan.

13.14 (*right*) Ludwig Mies van der Rohe, Barcelona Pavilion, 1929.

OVERLEAF

13.15 Ludwig Mies van der Rohe, Barcelona Pavilion, 1929.

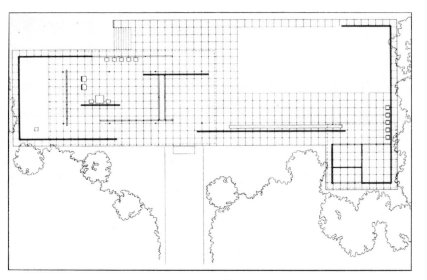

It is a paradox of great works of art that they should announce with unparalleled force the values of a new outlook while simultaneously invoking at a deep level, the values which informed classic moments in the past. This is another reason why it is never adequate to characterize a work merely in terms of a style phase linked to other works of art contemporary with it. Focillon has suggested that 'the time that gives support to a work of art does not give definition either to its principle or to its specific form.' This shrewd observation seems specially pertinent to two masterworks of the International Style: the Villa Savoye at Poissy by Le Corbusier, and the Barcelona Pavilion by Mies van der Rohe, both of 1929.

The latter was built as a temporary structure at the Barcelona exhibition of that year, and had the honorific function of representing the cultural values of modern Germany (figs. 13.13, 13.14, 13.15). Mies wrote revealingly of the task:

The era of monumental expositions that make money is past. Today we judge an exposition by what it accomplishes in the cultural field.

Economic, technical and cultural conditions have changed radically. It is very important for our culture and our society, as well as for technology and industry, to find good solutions. German industry, and indeed, European industry as a whole must understand and solve these specific tasks. The path must lead from quantity towards quality, from the extensive to the intensive.

Along this path industry and technology will join with the forces of thought and culture.

Evidently the pavilion was supposed to have an ambassadorial function and to reflect values not unlike those which had informed the Deutscher Werkbund before the First World War. One is not surprised to discover that Mies van der Rohe's design embodied a deliberate synthesis of form and technique, of modern and Classical values. As a demonstration of the power of modern structural invention to create unprecedented spatial effects, the building was a *tour de force*. The thin roof slab was poised delicately on eight cruciform steel supports coated in chrome: a conception recalling the Dom-ino skeleton, but only a single storey in height. In this context the structural frame was far from being a low-cost instrument of standardization; it was clad in expensive materials – marble and onyx veneers, semi-reflecting glass, sharp-edged stainless steel. This simple trabeated and symmetrical structure was placed to one end of a raised podium and carefully composed to relate to two rectangular pools, which added further to the sense of luxury and the feeling of dematerialization through reflections. A counterpoint was set in motion by shifting the axis of the main pool off that of the rectangular pavilion, and this visual movement was carried through in the way vertical planar partitions were set down, some within the covered space, others extending into the surroundings, all of them independent of the grid of supports. Thus, while some of them actually bore weight, the *idea* expressed was of the independence of wall planes from traditional supporting roles. Joints and details in the fabric were carefully controlled so as not to disturb a taut, weightless character in most of the surfaces.

The visual pushes and pulls engendered by the irregular placement of the partitions corresponded with the meandering path that the visitor took through the interior. This was furnished with heavy leather chairs supported by criss-cross stainless steel flanges coated in chrome ('Barcelona chairs'). Otherwise the space was completely uncluttered, a demonstration, perhaps, of a new way of life, supposed to have a special appeal to the cultivated industrial élite. Recalling the Deutscher Werkbund Pavilion of 1914, there was a Classical contemporary female statue by one of the Pavilion pools: it made an odd touch alongside the rectangular rigours of Mies's machine-age fantasy, but it was a further reminder that the building as a whole was guided by a Classical sense.

In terms of Mies van der Rohe's evolving vocabulary, the form of the Pavilion was a synthesis of the sort of pivotal plan he had experimented with in the brick villa of 1923, with the hovering horizontal slabs and grid structures he had envisaged in his office block project of 1922. In the intervening seven years he had had the opportunity to test variations of his ideas – in the Rosa Luxemburg monument of 1924, in the Weissenhof designs of 1925–7, and in the superbly proportioned Krefeld house of 1927–8. The Barcelona Pavilion accumulated all these discoveries into a single statement, which did not, however, suffer from the overburdening of ideas. In the mind of its creator, perhaps, the Pavilion may have been the purest embodiment of the *Zeitgeist*. For Mies van der Rohe the most significant spiritual artifacts were those which translated 'the will of the epoch into space'.

But the Pavilion, like the Schroeder House, the Bauhaus buildings or Le Corbusier's villas, was also an elegant solution to broader, shared problems of expression of the period. Historians have rightly drawn attention to the similarity of the plan to Mondrian's paintings; to the 'factuality' of the materials employed (relating Mies to the 'New Objectivity'); to the simplicity of the wall surfaces recalling Berlage's pleas for well-proportioned surfaces unadorned from top to bottom; to the novelty and richness of the space conception with its floating planes and painterly illusions and ambiguities. It is entirely understandable, then, that Hitchcock and Johnson should have singled out the building as an exemplar of the International Style.

Yet the roots of Mies van der Rohe's master-work seem to lie deeper than this in history. Attention has already been drawn to the architect's early admiration for Schinkel, manifest particularly in his neo-classical designs of the pre-First World War years. It was the reduction of form to the most expressive simple geometries which most excited him about his great Prussian predecessor. Surely one recognizes a similar concentration on essentials of Classicism in the Barcelona Pavilion, especially in its impeccable proportions, its sense of repose, and its restatement in abstract form of the elemental column and entablature. In this way the simplifications of the International Style were capable of blending an imagery of contemporary concerns with a reminiscence of architecture's most enduring values.

14. The Image and Idea of Le Corbusier's Villa Savoye at Poissy

To make a plan is to determine and fix ideas.
It is to have had ideas.
It is to so order these ideas that they become intelligible, capable of execution and communicable.
... A plan is to some extent like an analytical contents table. In a form so condensed that it seems as clear as a crystal and like a geometrical figure, it contains an enormous quantity of ideas and the impulse of an intention.

Le Corbusier, 1923

The last chapter examined the validity of the notion of the 'International Style' and found it strong in some respects, weak in others. It seems that the early apologists of modern architecture were over-preoccupied with defining a supra-historical identity for the style and were not sufficiently attentive to individual and personal intentions. There *was* a broadly shared language of expression in the 1920s in certain countries of Western Europe and part of the United States, but this was only one of a number, and the most interesting works conceived within it were so individual as to remain uncategorizable.

Beyond even the individual architectural language of the artist there is another level which has to be grasped if the inner meaning of a new tradition is to be understood. This lies in the special intellectual chemistry of the classic work. Here one is interested in the way the problems of a particular context have been solved, and in the manner in which an individual work of art extends both the personal themes of an artist and the broader preoccupations of a period. In this case the Villa Savoye at Poissy of 1928–9 by Le Corbusier has been singled out for monographic scrutiny. For, like the Barcelona Pavilion, the Villa 'contains an enormous quantity of ideas' and splices together concerns of its own time and perennial values of the architectural art. To probe into its underlying meanings is necessarily to enter still further Le Corbusier's patterns of thinking in his early maturity.

Architecture embraces not just three dimensions, but four. It is by its nature involved with time and change. We grasp the form of a building gradually as

we move towards it and through it, comparing scenographic incidents one with another, and incorporating them into a growing sense of the whole. The same building seems ever different under changing conditions of weather and light, as values of silhouette, shape, and depth are played down or accentuated. These qualities of movement and change lie near the heart of the Villa Savoye's conception. Thus a description of the building is best conducted as a sort of promenade.

The Villa Savoye (also known evocatively as 'Les Heures Claires') stands about twenty miles north-west of Paris on the outskirts of the small town of Poissy, on a site bordered by trees on three sides, yet with a long view beyond the fourth towards the softly rolling fields and valleys of the Île de France. Perhaps one arrives by car, in which case one leaves the road and passes by a small white cubic gate lodge which guards the entrance to the drive. The gravel way turns slowly into the trees, its destination mysterious. Then one catches the first view of the villa standing fifty yards away towards the centre of a field.

The first impression is of a horizontal white box, poised on *pilotis*, set off against the rustic surroundings, the far panorama and the sky. The driveway passes through the undercroft, circles the building beneath the overhang, and re-emerges to return to the road on the left-hand side. The main first-level box is surmounted by curved volumes just visible to the rear. Bit by bit one gathers that the villa is not as detached as it first appeared. It is sculpted and hollowed to allow the surroundings to enter it, and its formal energies

14.1 Le Corbusier, 'Les Heures Claires', the Villa Savoye at Poissy, 1928–9, axonometric sketch showing relationship of roof terrace to sun and the processional character of automobile approach.

14.2 Le Corbusier, Villa Savoye, 1928–9, exterior view.

emanate to the borders of the site (figs. 14.1, 14.2).

The main 'façade' is somewhat blank and forbidding and gives the impression (later to be disproved) of a completely symmetrical building, rooted to the ground in its middle part. The strong horizontal emphasis is supplied by the overall shape, the single strip window running from one end to the other of the (main) upper level (fig. 14.3), and the repeated horizontals of the factory glazing at the lower level (hiding the mundane functions of servants' and chauffeur's quarters). The predominant verticals at this stage are the ranks of cylindrical *pilotis* receding on each side behind the suggested façade plane: they supply an airy sense of lightness.

The approach to the building has a curious quality of ritual, as if one were being drawn without choice into some Corbusian machine-age ceremony. The car passes beneath the overhang as a forceful reminder of a guiding point of the artist's doctrine. The entrance is

14.3 Le Corbusier, Villa Savoye, 1928–9. view towards entrance.

14.4 Le Corbusier, Villa Savoye, 1928–9, interior view towards entrance with wash basin in hall in foreground and ramp to left.

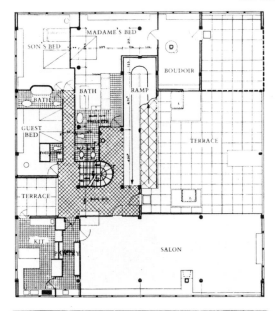

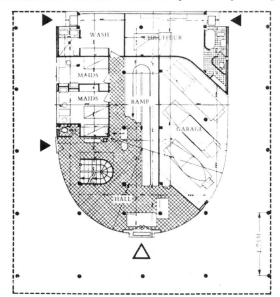

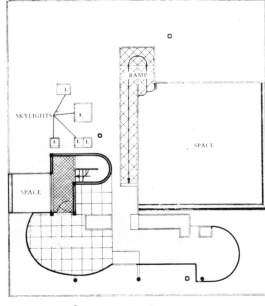

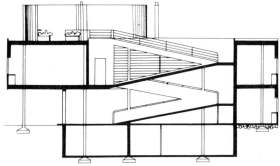

14.5 Le Corbusier, Villa Savoye, 1928–9, plans and longitudinal section of final scheme, 1929: (*top right*) ground floor plan; (*top*) first floor plan; (*centre*) roof level plan; (*bottom*) longitudinal section.

found at the apex of a curve formed by the glazed lower level. A chauffeur is assumed, and as one is put down on the main axis, the car continues to follow the curve, then to slide in diagonally beneath the rectangular superstructure.

One passes through the main doors into the vestibule, a space defined by curved glass surfaces to either side. The main choices are clear. Straight ahead a ramp passes along the main axis of the building to the upper levels. To the left is a spiral stair linking the servants' zone to the world above. Ahead and slightly to the left is the hall leading to the chauffeur's quarters, a wash-basin standing mysteriously in it (fig. 14.4). The surfaces are brittle and smooth, the atmosphere clinical. The space is set about with the pure forms of cylindrical *pilotis*. Those near the door are grouped to form a sort of portico and – a subtle touch – one of them is made square in plan to correspond to the corner of an interior wall flanking the other side of the base of the ramp. Another refined detail catches the eye: the small white tiles in the floor are laid out on the diagonal, and effect a subtle link between the various curved and rectangular geometries.

The ramp is the very spine of the idea: in plan it stands on the axis and passes between the grid of *pilotis* (not so regularly spaced as one might at first imagine); in section it suggests a dynamic passage through the horizontal floor slabs, bringing with it a gradual expansion of space the higher one goes. The plan of the building is square, one of the ideal shapes which the architect so admired, and part of the richness of the Villa Savoye comes from the dynamics of curved forms within a stable perimeter (fig. 14.5). The ramp guides the 'promenade architecturale' and links the various

14.6 (*left*) Le Corbusier, Villa Savoye, 1928–9, view from salon on main, first-floor level, towards the roof terrace and the ramp.

14.7 (*right*) Le Corbusier, Villa Savoye, 1928–9, view up last leg of ramp towards solarium.

events: in turn it supplies an ennobling, almost ceremonial character of ascent.

After turning back on its original direction, the ramp emerges on the first floor, the main living level of the house (as at Garches, a *piano nobile*) where the most formal and most public spaces are situated. They stand around the roof terrace, a sort of outdoor room concealed from the exterior by a uniform strip window without glass. This catches the sun at all times of the day (it faces in a southerly direction) and helps to fill the house with light. The biggest room is the salon (fig. 14.6) with large glazing giving straight on to the terrace with a strip window facing the best view, that of the distant hills, to the north-west. To the other two sides of the roof terrace are the more 'private' areas: the kitchen (in the corner) with its own tiny terrace; the guest bedroom; Madame Savoye's bedroom, boudoir, and bathroom; and her son's bedroom and bathroom. The Villa Savoye was not an all-the-year home, but a sort of country retreat or summer weekend residence – a villa in the ancient tradition, where the well-to-do might retire and enjoy the greenery and fresh air of the countryside. Among other curiosities on the main level are the fireplace in the salon expressed as a free-standing stack, and a blue-tiled reclining seat next to the main bathroom, suggesting something of both Madame Savoye's and Le Corbusier's obsessive interest in cleanliness and athleticism.

The related themes of health, fresh air, sunlight, and intellectual clarity are reinforced as one continues up the ramp to the topmost level, again making a return at a middle level landing. The floor of the ramp is finished in paving laid on a diagonal to reinforce the sense of movement, in contrast to the orthogonal details of analogous flagstones on the main terrace. It is in these upper regions that the artist's nautical fantasies are felt most vividly, especially in the delicate tubular 'ship's' railings, and the curious stack containing the top of spiral stair. This is a relative of other cylinders in the composition; the spiral stair can be seen 'peeling' away below it behind liquidly dark and semi-transparent areas of glazing. As at Garches, and in Le Corbusier's paintings, the richness of the effect comes from the harmony and similarity of basic geometrical forms, from the control of proportion and ratio, and from effects of illusion whereby objects are glimpsed through layers of glass or through windows cut clean through the plainest of white surfaces. Ambiguity constantly reinforces visual tension (Plate 7).

The final slope of the ramp ascends towards the solarium (fig. 14.7) – seen first from the outside as a hovering curved volume, but from this position, a thin strip-like plane – with a small window cut clean into it. It is this which now holds the attention, a rectangle of blue sky and passing clouds, seen in an entirely monochrome surround. As one draws level with it, one

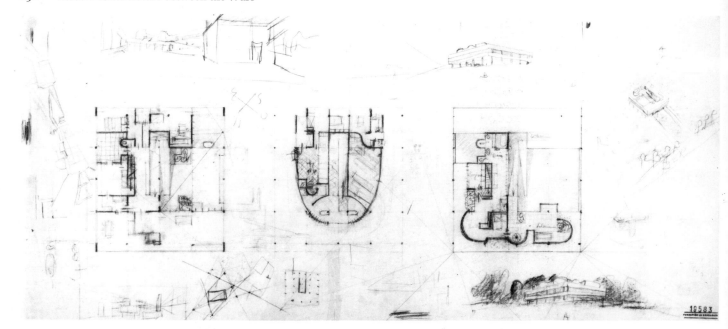

has the breathtaking view of the distant valleys which captured the attention in the very first approach. Then the building was seen surrounded by the setting; now the setting is framed by the building. The adequate provision of greenery was a central part of Le Corbusier's machine-age mythology. At the Villa Savoye nature is celebrated as dramatically as the idea of the house as a *machine à habiter* or the processional theme of the car, by means of carefully orchestrated views of trees and grass. The vignettes of the exterior have an almost super-real intensity, as if the artist has clipped bits of the outside world and spliced them together in a collage.

If the Villa Savoye draws together a number of earlier Le Corbusier themes, it also reveals the continuation of earlier formal experiments. In *Vers une architecture* he had referred to the idea of setting down 'standards' and then, through a gradual process of experiment and refinement, 'perfecting' them by paring them down to their most essential character-istics. He claimed that this had occurred between Paestum and the Parthenon. In a sense one may see the Villa Savoye as a culmination of a similar path of refinement but telescoped into the single decade of the 1920s. The propositions of the Maison Citrohan, the principles of the 'five points of a new architecture', the proposals of *Vers une architecture*, the suggestions of the various intermediary schemes (e.g., Maison Cook, the unrealized Maison Meyer, Villa Stein) were ennobled, dignified, and simplified to an extreme degree. One is bound to say that the Villa Savoye, like the Robie House, like certain of Palladio's mature villas,

represents a high point of expression within a vocabulary of type forms.

When the architect was first approached with the commission in 1928, Le Corbusier had at last achieved his synthesis: he was a mature architect of the highest order. It is intriguing to speculate on his possible initial responses to Madame Savoye's suggestions for a country house and to a site which was not, for once, hemmed in by other buildings. It is tempting to speculate that he was intrigued by the possibility of weaving his own fantasy of modern life around a sort of ritualistic celebration of his client's high bourgeois habits – the arrival by car, the 'ablutions' in the chauffeur's hall, the companion stair for the servants, the ramp for the initiated or the well-to-do. One guesses, too, that Le Corbusier must have immediately realized that this site gave him the possibility of making a sculpture in the round – rather than a building with a single façade like Maison Cook, or a front and back like the Villa Stein at Garches.

Unfortunately, the evidence of Le Corbusier's sketches for the Villa Savoye is incomplete, patchy, and not firmly dated. It seems that there were about three different schemes between October 1928 and April 1929. As was often the case in his design processes, some ideas which emerged early were later discarded, only to be picked up again and reincorporated into the final project: for the earliest sketches are in fact quite close to the finished building. Among the intermediary explorations was one of an almost neo-classical formality with a symmetrical box protruding behind the screens of the façade (fig. 14.9); and another

14.8 Le Corbusier, Villa Savoye, development sketches on a single sheet, late 1928 (Fondation Le Corbusier no. 19583). Note that part of the curved upper level is given to Madame Savoye's quarters.

(alluded to a moment ago) in which the top level was made curved and habitable (fig. 14.8). To follow these drawings is to see a style in action. It is also to gauge the conflicts between function and form, client and architect. There were many programmatic problems along the way, among them the difficulty of accommodating the cars and their turning circle at the lowest level, especially when, for a short phase, the entire scheme was reduced in size. A synthesis had to be sought which accommodated the 'external' constraints of practicality and the architect's own ideal intentions.

Although the villa must be understood as a relative of Le Corbusier's earlier designs, it was not as if he simply took pieces from old designs and stuck them together. Rather, a vital new image was unearthed, which articulated new possibilities of form and meaning in an unprecedented synthesis. This is why it is only of limited value to point out that the idea of the automobile passing under the building was first made clear – with all its urbanistic and architectural implications – at Maison Cook; or that the ramp first occurred as a principal feature in the studio wing of Maison La Roche, for in the Villa Savoye these devices were employed in a vital new combination. A similar observation can be made about the accent given the 'five points of a new architecture': the strip window had never been used so potently to unify all four sides of a design, and the *pilotis* – employed as a major device on the *interior* of Garches, was here used as a dominant feature of both interior and exterior design. At the end of the 1920s, Le Corbusier published a series of sketches of his principal villa designs of the decade, including La Roche, Garches, the Villa Baizeau for Carthage, and finally, Villa Savoye. In each case he attached notes describing salient features such as the pure formal character at Garches, or the internal and

external interpenetrations of the Carthage dwelling. The Villa Savoye managed to synthesize qualities of all the other three (fig. 8.12).

But every time Le Corbusier re-used a form it had many levels of practical and mythical significance in its new context. An example of this at the Villa Savoye is the curved solarium on top of the building. In this particular design the curve began its life as the shelter for a small terrace and as the curved wall to the boudoir of Madame Savoye (placed suggestively at the culmination of the ramp procession in the earliest scheme). Formally it defined a counterpoint with the rectangular volumes beneath it; volumetrically it had a shifting identity, at times appearing as a funnel floating above the glazed zones below, at times an uncurled screen. Within Le Corbusier's overall syntax it was clearly a relative of numerous other curved 'free-plan' partitions which served to sculpt different functions independently of perimeter walls or grids of supports; here, though, the screen had a double identity as a 'partition' and a curved 'exterior wall'. As a plan shape the solarium curves had strong affinities with the guitar outlines in Le Corbusier's earlier Purist pictures, but it was not as if he traced out the discoveries of his paintings on to his building plans: rather, the same formal intelligence working in different media achieved analogous results. The long distant view of the Villa Savoye has, understandably, been compared with a Purist still life on a table top (the solarium was originally rose in colour and would have stood out strongly against the white rectangles beneath), and the associations with ships' funnels or machine parts are not hard to make. Yet all such 'references' are held in check by a prodigious force of intellectual abstraction, as if the curve were *all* of these things at once.

Like any masterpiece, the Villa Savoye evades facile categorization. It is simple and complex, cerebral and sensuous. Laden with ideas, it still expresses these directly through shapes, volumes, and spaces 'in a certain relationship'. A 'classic' moment of modern architecture, it also has affinities with the great architecture of the past. It was a central concern of Le Corbusier's philosophy that a vision of contemporary life be given expression in architectural forms of enduring value, and in the Villa Savoye one recognizes echoes of old Classical themes: repose, proportion, clarity, a simple language of trabeation. Perhaps one may even go so far as to suggest a reminiscence of the Parthenon which had so obsessed Le Corbusier twenty years before. Surely the mechanized procession culminating in an entrance point at the opposite end of the building suggests affinities with the ceremonial route the artist had noted in the Acropolis. In its tense mathematical relationships and tight contours, in its

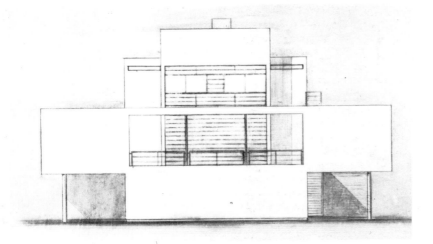

14.9 Le Corbusier, Villa Savoye, development sketch: elevation of *c.* November 1928 (Fondation Le Corbusier no. 19691 1).

radiating power to the setting, the Villa Savoye also invoked qualities Le Corbusier had admired in the great Classical prototype. A caption from the chapter in *Vers une architecture* called 'Architecture Pure Creation of the Mind' might apply to the ancient or the modern building equally well (figs. 14.10, 14.11):

From what is emotion born? From a certain relationship between definite elements: cylinders, an even floor, even walls. From a certain harmony with the things that make up the site. From a plastic system that spreads its effects over every part of the composition. From a unity of idea that reaches from the unity of materials used to the unity of the general contour.

It is tempting to regard the *piloti*, that central element of Le Corbusier's architectural language, so resonant with meanings related to Purism, standardization, the definition of concrete, and the creation of a new urbanism, as being a reinterpreted Classical column as well. The cylinder was one of those 'absolutely beautiful' Platonic forms singled out for special attention in *Vers une architecture*: it was a primary form capable of touching the mind at the deepest levels. At the same time the *piloti* was

14.10 Le Corbusier, Villa Savoye, Poissy, 1928–9: certain essentials of Classicism re-thought in a modern vocabulary.

14.11 Ictinus and Callicrates (and, according to Le Corbusier, Phidias), the Parthenon, Acropolis, Athens, 448–432 BC.

conceived as the correct expression for concrete and an *objet-type* in the class of supports: it embodied the essential idea of the column, stripped of all accidental or ornamental effects. Once again Idealism and Rationalism were united in Le Corbusier's thought.

Thus the Villa Savoye embodied a world view and synthesized a number of strands of its creator's philosophy. Its language was based on a modern structural technique as Viollet-le-Duc had required, and its imagery referred to modern engineering objects which were regarded as symbols of contemporary reality. Its idealization of a way of life addressed the needs of machine-age society, positing a Utopian social

order, while its forms were intensified with the help of proportional expertise and Purist painting. Its individual elements – the *piloti*, the strip window, etc. – were elevated, like the columns and triglyphs of a Greek temple, to the level of timeless solutions; the abstraction of its forms implied a lofty and spiritual role for architecture. Above all, though, the architectural language of the Villa Savoye was the result of a radical quest, a returning to roots, a rethinking of the fundamentals of the art. That is why it is reasonable to compare the building to that paradigm of simple trabeation, Laugier's primitive hut, an architecture supposedly reflecting natural law.

15. Wright and Le Corbusier in the 1930s

> The creative artist is by nature and by office the qualified leader in any
> society, natural, native interpreter of the visible form of any social order in or
> under which we choose to live.
>
> F. Lloyd Wright, 1935

By about 1930 modern architecture had become a major force and public presence in the culture of the West and its lessons were being adapted by countless new followers. The creative pressure could not be kept up indefinitely and in the early 1930s the onus shifted from the continuing revolution of forms to the extension of recently discovered prototypes. This tentative construction of a 'tradition of the new' was soon hampered by external circumstances such as the repressive attitudes of totalitarian regimes; but there were also internal difficulties related to the problem of symbolic devaluation.

The prodigious authenticity of buildings like the Villa Savoye was extremely hard to follow. The ideas brought together in such a synthesis had been filtered through the poetic intelligence of a single artist and represented an irreducible pattern of myth. Repetition of the same forms without sufficient transformation into a new content could only result in pastiche. One is bound to say that a valid extension of the principles of modern design of the sort achieved by Aalto, Lubetkin and Terragni in the 1930s was more the exception than the rule. It is striking how quickly there emerged a sort of modern academicism, in which clichéd usages of *pilotis* or whitewashed walls became the signs that one was 'up to date'.

Further complications were caused by the foundation of numerous subsidiary branches of the modern movement around the world. Czechoslovakia was already involved during the 1920s (one thinks of Ludvik Kysela's elegant shop for Bata of 1929) and so was Japan (Antonin Raymond's house in Tokyo already fused modern abstraction and local tradition in 1924). In Spain there were also hints of a modern movement in the late 1920s, and these were consolidated by José Luis Sert (a co-worker of Le Corbusier who was destined to become president of CIAM) until the Civil War intervened. In South Africa Rex Martienssen and the Transvaal group made an elegant translation of Purism in the early thirties, and in Brazil the activities of Lucio Costa ensured the foundation for a future *entente cordiale* with European modernism. Finally, of course, one must mention England, Italy and Finland, all countries with isolated germs of modern ideas in the 1920s destined to come to fruition in the 1930s. To understand these patterns of dissemination properly it will be necessary to examine some cases in detail (see Chapters 16 and 17); for the moment one may say that the reception of modern forms was rarely smooth and usually accompanied by debates concerning their appropriateness (or lack of it) to national cultural traditions.

However, a distinction must be drawn between countries which received modern architecture ready-made from the outside, and countries which, while they obviously relied on foreign stimulus, evolved modern movements of their own in parallel with the major developments of Western Europe. South Africa offers an example of the first situation, Czechoslovakia of the second. The Czech Devetsil group, founded in 1920, contained a number of architects of originality, such as Karel Teige, Jaromir Krejcar and Josef Chochol, who tentatively formulated the need for a new architecture. They eventually publicized their radical ideas in magazines like *Stavba* and *Stavitel*. These served as a forum for debates concerning the social role of modern architecture and as sources of information on developments east and west of Czechoslovakia. One is not surprised to discover a rich blend of ideas from both European and Soviet avant-garde sources. For example, Teige's 1929 attack on Le Corbusier's monumental scheme for the 'Mondaneum' (to have stood near Geneva but never built) smacks of the sort of anti-formalist bias of a Russian group like the OSA.

The variety of theoretical positions was matched by a certain pluralism of vocabulary. The industrial school at Mlada Boleslav by J. Kroha of 1923–5 shows that the Czech modern movement was in stride with the exploratory phase of modern architecture in France, Germany and Holland. Otto Eisler's 'Double House' at Brno in 1926 employed some of the constituent elements of the International Style on the exterior (e.g., a flat roof, planar wall surfaces, rectangular volumes) but its interior planning was closed and compartmental by comparison with the free-plan experiments of Le Corbusier. The Exhibition of Contemporary Culture held in Brno in 1928 brought together most advanced tendencies in Czech design. To counter Teige's restrained puritanism there was the somewhat extravagant Pavilion of The City of Brno by B. Fuchs with its dramatic cantilevered spiral stair on the exterior, its orange tiles and glass bricks, its obvious celebration of material differences and structural elements. Kroha's Fine Arts Pavilion was partly based on Constructivist prototypes while Kysela's afore-mentioned Bata Shop in Prague of the following year made much play with transparent effects of full glazing in the hovering overhangs of its street façade.

It is a measure of the enlightened and adventurous character of patronage in Brno that Mies Van der Rohe should have designed one of his finest works close to the town. This was the Tugendhat House of 1930. The site stood above a slope and offered good views over the landscape. The architect gave the building a closed character to the street side, where the most private and the smallest rooms were placed. But on the garden side he opened the building up as a series of free-flowing spaces articulated by slender stainless steel supports. He also supplied a long window from floor to ceiling running the entire length of the rear façade. Thus something of the honorific character of the Barcelona Pavilion was brought into a domestic context.

The situation in South Africa in the twenties was altogether different and was obviously influenced by the considerable geographical distance from in-novatory centres and by cultural dependence on England, which was without a modern movement until the thirties. In reaction against a rather glib High Victorianism which had infected South African design in the late nineteenth century, Herbert Baker had evolved a viable synthesis of the Cape tradition, the English Arts and Crafts and the Mediterranean vernacular in the years prior to the First World War. But by the mid-1920s South African architecture was tired and in need of new life. In 1925 Stanley Furner began teaching at the University of Witwatersrand and publishing avant-garde developments from Europe. His most gifted student, Rex Martienssen, travelled to Holland and to France, where he visited Le Corbusier. Martienssen, who early developed an enthusiasm for Greek architecture and culture, understood the Classical underpinnings of Purism, and in the early 1930s in partnership with John Fassler and Bernard Cooke designed a number of buildings of high quality, among them the Peterhouse flats and funeral home in Johannesburg (1934–5). This reflected a variety of influences from Europe, most notably Gropius and Le Corbusier, but the building had a logic and a power of its own arising from the ingenious combination of varying functional demands on a urban site and from the tight control of proportions. The composition was crowned by a large curved solarium recalling the Villa Savoye, while the strong South African sunlight ensured dramatic contracts of light and shade in the apertures cut through taut and planar wall surfaces. In the same year the partnership designed a number of luxury suburban residences – most notably the Stern House – in which they took maximum advantage of the South African climate in the provision of a roof terrace and patios shaded by overhangs. In this case the composition maximized the interplay between voids and solids, planes and volumes, in an evocation of the healthy open-air life which had definite Mediterranean overtones. Another partnership to play a major role in the foundation of a South African modern movement was that of Hanson, Tomkin and Finkelstein. But their work rarely achieved the same pitch as Martienssen's, whose unusual intellectual gifts ensured a firm basis of principle in his activities as a creator and an educator. Martienssen was one of the few inheritors of the seminal works of the modern movement to realize that good modern architecture could embody a continuity of artistic fundamentals as well as a revolution in technology, social attitudes and forms.

If the modern movement was passing into foreign hands, the originators still had the problem of deciding what to do next. The careers of German and Soviet architects were severely disrupted by political events, while the activities of Wright and Le Corbusier were frustrated by economic depression. Nonetheless the 1930s was an inventive period for both men, characterized by a disparity between their grand societal visions and their limited opportunities to build.

15.1 (*left*) Frank Lloyd Wright, 'Falling Water', the Bear Run, Pennsylvania, 1936.

15.2 (*right*) Frank Lloyd Wright, 'Falling Water', 1936, detail showing flow of space between interior and exterior and steps down to water.

15.3 (*below*) Frank Lloyd Wright, 'Falling Water', 1936, elevation.

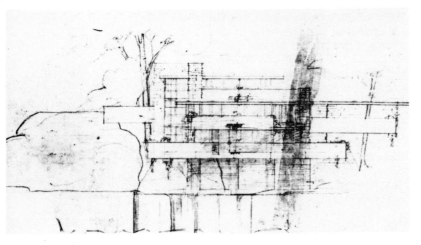

Olgivanna (his third wife), and as he solved his financial problems with the help of the Taliesin foundation – a sort of rural retreat and architectural school in which young men helped about the farm and the estate while learning the basics of Wright's 'organic' philosophy. It is arguable too that the intellectual atmosphere of the New Deal provided a richer soil than had the boom period of the twenties for Wright's reformist tendencies. In the thirties he devoted much attention to the design of cheap, single family dwellings (e.g., the Usonian houses) and to the projection of a sort of decentralized Utopia – 'Broadacre City' – in order to give American life a coherent social form in a period of crisis. But it was in two individual masterpieces of marginal social relevance that he revealed to the world at large that he was far from spent as a formal inventor of the highest order.

The first of these was a country retreat known as 'Falling Water' for the Pittsburgh millionaire Edgar J. Kaufmann. This was placed above a waterfall in a deep ravine in Pennsylvania known as 'the Bear Run' (fig. 15.1). The building was formed from cantilevered concrete trays rooted to a core embedded in the boulders. Its horizontal layers soared free of apparent support over the cascades and pools of the stream. Walls were avoided almost entirely, the sense of shelter being provided by the overhangs and by screen-like windows detailed to enhance the vertical and horizontal rhythms. The chimney core was made from local stone laid rough, in contrast to the smooth finish of the concrete balconies. A major part of the interior space was given over to a large living-room, suitable to the function of a weekend house. The effects of dappled light, surrounding foliage and tumbling water, and the feeling of horizontal expansion in all directions from the interiors, gave an exact image of Wright's well-known maxims concerning integration of architecture and nature (fig. 15.2). This conception was carried through the entire formal ensemble which was controlled, but never rigid. There was the sense of a vital, ever-changing order as elements and context shifted into new relationships. The spaces around the waterfall and the screens of the trees were all drawn into the composition: nature and art were made to complement one another. This is how Kaufmann's son (who was responsible for introducing his father to Wright's work) assessed the house years later:

When Wright came to the site he appreciated the powerful sound of the falls, the vitality of the young forest, the dramatic rock ledges and boulders; these were elements to be interwoven with the serenely soaring spaces of his structure. But Wright's insight penetrated more deeply. He understood that people were creatures of nature, hence an architecture

Neither artist compromised his idealistic stance in the face of difficulties, but the moral determinism of each was partially undermined. By the end of the 1930s it was obvious that their sweeping statements of social and urbanistic doctrine were capable of only piecemeal demonstration.

As was shown earlier (see Chapter 11), the twenties was a difficult time for Wright, who was by then already in his late fifties. Dogged by personal and financial problems and a general indifference to his architectural ideals, he adopted the quirks of the misunderstood eccentric. In the thirties much of this changed as his life achieved a new stability with

which conformed to nature would conform to what was basic in people. For example, although all of Falling Water is opened by broad bands of windows, people inside are sheltered as in a deep cave, secure in the sense of the hill behind them. Their attention is directed toward the outside by low ceilings; no lordly hall sets the tone but, instead, the luminous textures of the woodland rhythmically enframed. The materials of the structure blend with the colorings of the rocks and trees, while occasional accents are provided by bright furnishings, like the wildflowers or birds outside. The paths within the house, stairs and passages, meander without formality or urgency. . . . Sociability and privacy are both available, as are the comforts of home and the adventures of the seasons. So people are cossetted into relaxing, into exploring the enjoyment of life refreshed in nature. Visitors too, in due measure experience Wright's architecture as an expansion of living.

A superficial reading of Wright's achievement at Falling Water might point to the white horizontals and claim that he was here being influenced by the simplifications of the 'International Style'. This would be to fall into the sort of facile stylistic categorization warned against earlier in this book. For not only were the forms of the house rooted in Wright's earlier principles and discoveries (e.g., the stratified landscape terraces of Taliesin, the formal arrangements and trays of the prairie houses, the pervasive fascination with natural forms); they were also infused with meanings and associations which put him at odds with the philosophical and compositional tendencies of the European modern movement (fig. 15.3). Once again we have to deal with a contrast between an American romanticism – a democratic ideal concerning the primacy of the free life lived in nature – and the very different values implied by the various philosophies of the European avant-garde. Wright attempted to distance himself from the modern movement in a display of scorn:

Human houses should not be like boxes blazing in the sun, nor should we outrage the Machine by trying to make dwelling places too complementary to machinery. Any building for humane purposes should be an elemental, sympathetic feature of the ground, complementary to its nature environment . . . But most 'modernistic' houses manage to look as though cut from cardboard with scissors . . . glued together in box-like forms – in a childish attempt to make buildings resemble steamships, flying machines or locomotives . . . So far I see in most of the cardboard houses of the 'modernistic'

movement small evidence that their designers have mastered either the machinery or the mechanical processes which build the house. . . . Of late they are the superficial, New 'Surface-and-Mass' Aesthetic falsely claiming French Painting as a Parent.

Opposed to this box architecture, Wright placed his own organic ideal with its emphasis on the inner vitality of expression, on the fusion of structure, function, and idea, and on the inspiration of natural forms. At Falling Water he may even have adopted the subtle position of a *corrective* to the 'box architecture' of the International Style and a demonstration of the way simple forms might create a vital, life-enhancing space. In a talk to the Taliesin Fellowship Wright claimed:

. . . now you are released by way of glass and the cantilever and the sense of space which becomes operative. Now you are related to the landscape. . . . You are as much part of it as the trees, the flowers, the ground. . . . You are now free to become a natural feature of your environment and that, I believe, was intended by your maker.

To this outlook, the various organic analogies in Wright's forms were the formal equivalent. At Falling Water two natural elements seem to be interwoven in a fabric of imaginative abstraction: the rock strata bordering the site, and the trees with their hierarchy of supports, circulation, and texture. A few years before designing the house Wright had eulogized 'the rock ledges of a stone-quarry':

There is suggestion in the strata and character in the formations. . . . For in the stony bone-work of the Earth, the principles that shaped stone as it lies, or as it rises and remains to be sculptured by winds and tide – there sleep forms and styles enough for all the ages of man.

The tree on the other hand was a pervasive metaphor in Wright's thinking from his earliest years. The stunning synthesis of Falling Water is tribute to the depth of his earlier reflections as much as it is a a sign of his continuing vitality as an inventor. Like the Villa Savoye, the building 'contains a great quantity of ideas', but compressed into a simple guiding image; it too relied on years of experimentation with an architectural system based on principles, and on a philosophy of life (Plate 8).

The other major *tour de force* also designed by Wright in 1936 was the Administration Center of Johnson Wax in Racine, Wisconsin (fig. 15.4). The site and programme could scarcely have been more different: the building had to stand on a flat lot in a somewhat

15.4 (*right*) Frank Lloyd Wright, Johnson Wax Adminstration Center, Racine, Wisconsin, 1936.

15.5 (*below*) Frank Lloyd Wright, Johnson Wax, Racine, Wisconsin, 1936, interior view of mushroom supports.

ugly urban setting; it was to contain offices and work spaces. However, unlike the managers of the giant, impersonal corporations then beginning to dominate American life, the Johnsons wished their organization to maintain the character of a sort of extended family under a beneficent patriarchy. Wright grasped this character and mood at once in the course of design. He attempted to form an inward-looking community which would foster togetherness while mirroring the hierarchy of the firm. The administration building was therefore designed as a large window-less rectangle covered in brick, lit from above, with trays suspended inwards from its edges looking into a hypostyle hall two storeys high to the core. This grand but well-scaled space was articulated by a grid of slender mushroom supports in concrete (fig. 15.5); it was intended to contain the main working-places of the secretaries. The management was to be situated in the upper levels of the rectangle off the trays. Wright called the two wings on top of the building a 'penthouse' because the executive offices and the private office of the President were to be situated there; again, Wright interpreted, 'idealized' and gave form to an institutional framework.

The exteriors of the Johnson Wax building had curved corners and a streamlined character not unlike certain 'Moderne' designs by Raymond Loewy in the early thirties. Perhaps these touches reflected a deliberate attempt on Wright's part at designing in a 'populist' mode. The streamlined quality was continued on the interior in the horizontal attenuation of trays and parapets, and in the extraordinary glass tube details Wright designed for the integrated lighting system. But the mood of the interior space far transcended such glossy surface effects: it communicated stability and formality, yet without being overbearing. After the closed character of the exterior, the glazed ceilings and tubes of the interiors glowed with warmth and light. The grid of the supports in no way summoned up the bleak repetitiveness of the banal grids pervasive in much commercial office space design: each support was elegant and delicate; together the rows of tapering shapes, their circular tops floating like lily-pads on a translucent surface, created a sort of underwater world. Wright despised the values represented by most commercial architecture – profiteering, brashness, the uniformity of the hive; he sought instead to mould rich spaces in which life, work, and art would enhance one another. The proof of the building's success lay in the way employees chose to linger in it after work, as if it were an oasis against the chaos and economic depression in the world outside. The polished glass and metal surfaces, deliberately chosen with Johnson's wax products in mind, were lavishly cared for and kept continually spick.

Like Falling Water, the Johnson Wax building was superficially different from Wright's earlier architecture. On a deeper level, though, its organization was also rooted in his earlier experiments. The pedigree of the Johnson Wax included the Larkin Building of 1904 (also an inward-looking, symmetrical 'Cathedral of Work'); the Unity Temple (where two major volumes on axis with one another were also entered through the slot between them, and in which Wright also used slung balconies and filtered overhead lighting); The Tokyo Imperial Hotel (in which he first extensively experimented with mushroom supports in the earthquake-proof foundations); and a project for the *Capital Journal* building in Salem, Oregon, of 1931, where a hypostyle of similar supports was envisaged. Perhaps Wright's image of the columnated hall owed something to ancient Egyptian hypostyles, just as his naturally inspired columns may have been indebted to papyrus or lotus supports in the same prototypes. The architect had to prove to his nervous clients that his slender columns could support the anticipated loads by building a mock-up and piling heavy weights on to it. This experiment only went to confirm the integration of Wright's practical engineering knowledge with his

15.6 Frank Lloyd Wright, Johnson Wax, 1936, the mushroom supports under construction.

intuitive structural sense (fig. 15.6).

In the 1940s the Johnson Wax organization chose to expand and build a laboratory tower which Wright was also commissioned to design. He adapted and fused the mushroom support idea with the needs of the programme, by placing the services in the core and the laboratories on cantilevered trays with intervening overhangs of lesser width. The result was an elegant, round-cornered vertical box wrapped in deflecting glass (to handle the sun's rays) in which the main floor slabs registered on the exterior as horizontal bands. The alternate floors were smaller in extent, and set back from the façade, so that the laboratories on the interior had all-round views and were split-levelled, allowing a division between messy laboratory work and study. Once again Wright exhibited an attitude quite at odds with the grid/box formula for the tall building.

Another major achievement of Wright's resurgence in the thirties was the design of a low-cost house prototype called the 'Usonian' home. This word was drawn from Samuel Butler's term for the United States in his Utopian novel *Erewhon* of 1872. Wright designed a kit of parts including a concrete-slab foundation floated on a drained bed of cinders and sand, into which radiating hot-water pipes were inserted. The roof was a simple insulated slab containing a ventilation system and was made to overhang the edges of the dwelling to throw water clear, to give a sense of shelter, to protect from glare and to provide a

15.7 Frank Lloyd Wright visiting the Johnson Wax Building in his late years.

horizontal related to the earth plane. The walls were prefabricated from three layers of board and two of tar-paper. But there was more to the Usonian idea than a clever labour- and money-saving assembly. The drawing room was abolished in favour of an alcove with a table in it, a space blending kitchen and living areas together. This was a response, clearly, to the servantless clients who would be expected to buy Usonian houses, and a reflection of the rejection of pre-First World War formalities in American life generally. It was no accident that Wright's formula should have been adopted so rapidly by building contractors and cheap home catalogues. For its free-plan interiors and exterior patios captured precisely the ethos of an emergent middle-class suburban existence. In Wright's hands, of course, the Usonian houses were judiciously proportioned and detailed, the standard plans being varied to blend with unique sites; the insensitive imitators were all too often clumsy 'ranch-style' shoe-boxes, laid out in jerry-built monotony on the boom tracts of the 1950s.

In 1930 Wright was 63 and in difficulties; at the same time, Le Corbusier was 43 and on the crest of a wave of success. The 1920s had witnessed his rapid emergence from obscurity to a position at the vanguard of the European modern movement. By the time he received the commission for the Villa Savoye he had become an international figure, invited to design buildings as far afield as Moscow and North Africa. One gathers from stray remarks in his writings

that he thought of himself as some kind of messiah destined to supply the forms of a new machine-age civilization. Although the thirties was far sparer in actual commissions than the twenties had been, this did nothing to diminish the architect's sense of a world mission. On the contrary, the scope of his thinking continued to broaden, particularly with regard to the design of cities. In this period he delivered plans for places as varied as Algiers, Rio de Janeiro, and New York, and formulated the universal principles of the *cité-type* for modern regeneration: the 'Ville Radieuse' ('Radiant City').

The Villa Savoye had been a masterpiece, but it left its creator with the problem of avoiding self-imitation; he had to decide which aspects of his architectural system to extend and which to leave behind. Naturally this process of retrospection and selection was not entirely rational and did not occur independently of the tasks and opportunities the early thirties offered. It so happened that many of his commissions in this period were for large and complex buildings to which the typology of the villas was inadequate. Le Corbusier had therefore to stretch his system and to turn instead to the lessons of his earlier grand schemes – the Centrosoyus, the League of Nations, and, of course, his ideal urban projects. Thus in the Palace of the Soviets competition entry of 1931 (analysed in Chapter 10) he gave discrete expression to different functional volumes which were then linked in hierarchy by axes and flanges of circulation. In the Maison de Refuge of 1930–31 – a hostel for the down-and-outs of Paris – a similar strategy of separation was employed. The entrance zone, containing the porter's lodge, the reception, etc., was expressed as a sequence of free-standing volumes including a white cylinder, which stood out dramatically against the dark and sleek backdrop of the fully glazed main façade. The strip window was no longer employed; nor was its essential complement in his earlier vocabulary, the white-washed planar wall. Instead Le Corbusier resorted to glass brick or the full floor-to-ceiling 'pan de verre' ('pane of glass'). There were probably a number of interrelated reasons for this change. Perhaps he was discovering that layers of strip windows did not harmonize well with the larger façade surfaces he was forced to articulate; perhaps he regarded full glazing as a more honest expression of the free façade; perhaps this treatment had associations appropriate to the image of a collective *machine à habiter*. Whatever the motivations, the new solution brought its own problems: lack of privacy, leaks, heat loss, and heat gain.

In the late twenties there were gradual shifts in the emphasis of Le Corbusier's painting vocabulary. The human figure began to replace still lifes and machine parts. Biomorphic abstractions, influenced no doubt by the contemporary paintings of Picasso and Miró, became more frequent. The handling was looser, less controlled and precise than in the earlier Purist works. In architecture these changes perhaps had an equivalent in a greater sense of texture and a more direct use of materials. Formal analogies with pebbles and shells began to replace the machine abstractions of the twenties. In the Maison Errazuris, designed for Chile in 1933, *pilotis* and slabs were redone using logs and rustic details. The Petite Maison de Weekend (built in 1935 as a hide-away for a wealthy client in the outskirts of Paris) was a sort of neolithic cave, with low vaults, turf on the roof and a deliberate juxtaposition of glass bricks with husky natural materials (fig. 15.11). This building laid the basis for the sophisticated peasantism of Le Corbusier's architecture of the 1950s.

A transitional work standing between the villas of the twenties and this later primitivism was the Pavillon

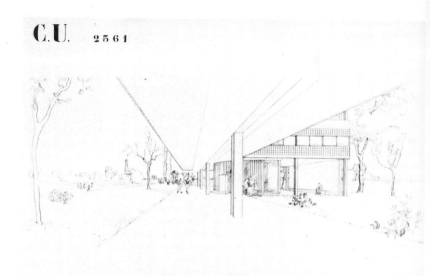

15.8 (*left*) Le Corbusier, Pavillon Suisse, 1930–31, early project, showing view under steel *pilotis*, later replaced by robust concrete supports. (Fondation Le Corbusier, no. 15, 804).

15.9 (*below left*) Le Corbusier, Pavillon Suisse, Cité Universitaire, Paris, 1930–31, view of north façade showing curved approach driveway and rubble wall at ground level.

15.10 (*right*) Le Corbusier, Pavillon Suisse, Paris, 1930–31, view of glazed south façade containing student rooms.

15.11 (*below*) Le Corbusier, Petite Maison de Weekend, near Paris, 1935, axonometric drawing.

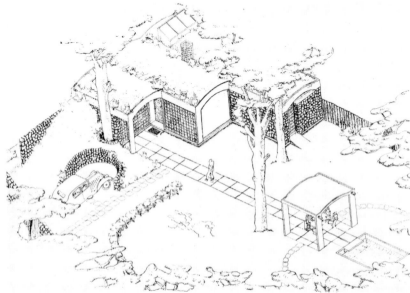

Suisse of 1930–31. This was a dormitory for Swiss students at the Cité Universitaire in Paris, and the problem involved combining single rooms for the students with communal facilities like a sitting-room, a hall, a breakfast-room and a small library; a porter's lodge and a director's apartment also had to be incorporated. The site was an ambiguous one in that it stood at the perimeter of the Cité Universitaire with good views to the south over open green spaces (destined to become sports fields) and with an access road approaching it from the main part of the campus. There was, in other words, no obvious 'front' or 'back': the solution adopted would have to address both sides simultaneously.

Le Corbusier's response to these constraints emerged gradually through a series of four schemes between early 1930 and 1931. In all cases, he placed the student rooms in a steel-frame box lifted off the ground on stanchions. Initially these supports were in the form of slender 'I' beams in steel (fig. 15.8), but later they were fashioned as robust concrete *pilotis* of subtle curvilinear shape resembling, in plan, dumb-bells or dogbones. The space underneath the box was given over to relaxation and also created a transitional portico for the entrance through which the greenery of the surroundings could be glimpsed. The individual rooms of the students were expressed as cells in the rectangular façade and were made to face south (fig. 15.10). Access was from the rear by corridors which were then linked to ancillary volumes containing the stairs, a lift, and the communal zones. In the earliest schemes these attached forms were rectangular and also poised on stilts; later, they were brought down to the ground and curved to respond to the turning circle at the end of the roadway, and to differentiate their function. Once again Le Corbusier articulated differences between public and private areas in a design.

The range of materials was much wider than hitherto in Le Corbusier's work. Not only were the *pilotis* organic in shape, in contrast to the Purist cylinders of the villas; they were also left in bare concrete, without paint or covering of any kind. Stone veneers, steel, and glass were adeptly handled in the main box, while glass bricks were situated in the stair-tower, and rubble-facing was used on the lower curved wall (fig. 15.9). Amber tiles, different grades of concrete floor, and various interior paint-finishes enhanced the main divisions in the design. Perhaps Le Corbusier had sensed the problems of upkeep in his earlier stucco façades. Certainly the Pavillon Suisse finishes were better suited to weathering than those of the villas. Again, though, the texture corresponded with shifts of emphasis in the artist's formal ideas.

It is important to recognize the continuities in the Pavillon Suisse as well as the changes. The structural principle of the building was still based on the 'five points', even if the strip window was now blended with the fully glazed façade. There was a roof terrace on top and a free plan in the communal areas, while the main *pilotis*, despite their change in shape, were still celebrated as the prominent elements of support. Had smaller, more stick-like *pilotis* been employed, they might have given an insubstantial feeling to the structure. Just as Michelangelo had discovered, in his largest schemes, that the Classical orders needed major modification, so Le Corbusier was discovering that a change in size required more than a change in dimension in the central element of his architectural system. The *pilotis* were therefore given a subtly modelled form which supplied simultaneously a stocky support for actual and visual stability, and a suitably attenuated and elegant profile to be seen close to. In fact it is by no means clear that *pilotis* were the best solution in this case, as the site stood over a disused quarry, thus necessitating piles sixty feet deep. It seems that Le Corbusier adhered to points of principle at the expense of common sense. A partial clue to his motivation in sticking so rigorously to his 'solution-type' for structure is to be found in the pictures in the *Oeuvre complète*, where much was made of the way the undercrofts could be employed for circulation and for social activity. In one of the captions Le Corbusier referred to a certain 'M. Maurin', a physicist 'used to working in the laboratory', and quoted from a letter that this estimable gentleman of science was supposed to have written to him:

> 'I have seen the Pavillon Suisse. Don't you think that the pilotis you have used could serve to bring the definitive solution to the passage of circulation of a large town.' M. Maurin, physicist, used to working in a laboratory, discovered spontaneously the rudiments of an urbanistic and architectural doctrine that Le Corbusier had expressed for ten years, without exhausting, in all his works and writings.

In other words, the local problem of the student dormitory was exploited to make a more general point of urbanistic and collectivist doctrine. The true cousins of the Pavillon Suisse were the social condensers which Le Corbusier saw and admired in the Soviet Union, in the late twenties, and the housing schemes from his own ideal city, the 'Ville Radieuse', which the architect was elaborating at the same time. These collective habitations were laid out in long strips *à redent* (i.e., stepping back and forth in indentations) and had roof terraces with running tracks (fig. 15.12). Like the Pavillon Suisse, they were glazed to the southward side and looked out over playing-fields and parks;

moreover, they were lifted up on *pilotis*, so allowing uninterrupted parklands to pass beneath. The 'essential joys' of space, light and greenery were made available to all as an antidote to the choked, airless slums created by nineteenth-century industrialization. The Pavillon Suisse was a fragment of this larger Utopia, both a demonstration and an experiment. Le Corbusier himself hinted at this dual role when he wrote in 1934:

> So what have we done in these years 1929–34? First of all a few buildings, then many large-scale urbanistic studies. These buildings have played the role of laboratories. We wanted each element of construction during that period to be the experimental proof which would allow us to take the necessary urbanistic initiatives.

Le Corbusier embodied his vision of an ideal society in his city plans. Underpinning all his urban initiatives was a naïve faith in the power of a well-ordered environment to reunite man, nature, and the machine in an unalienated harmony. Mechanization was seen

15.12 Le Corbusier, the *à redent* collective dwellings of the Ville Radieuse, *c.* 1930.

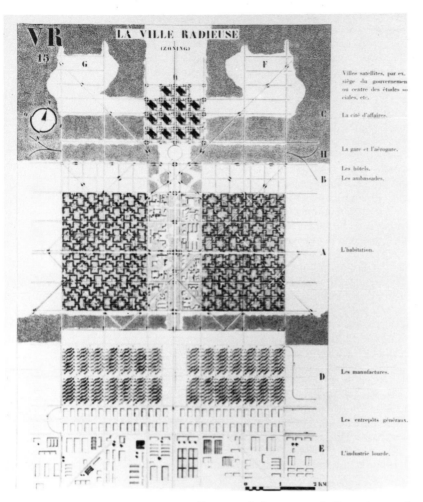

In the image labels on the right side:
- VR 15 G F
- LA VILLE RADIEUSE (ZONING)
- Villes satellites, par ex. siège du gouvernement ou centre des études sociales, etc.
- La cité d'affaires.
- La gare et l'aérogare.
- Les hôtels. Les ambassades.
- L'habitation.
- Les manufactures.
- Les entrepôts généraux.
- L'industrie lourde.

15.13 Le Corbusier, the Ville Radieuse, c. 1930, overall plan.

proposed a 'pyramid of natural hierarchies' from a base on the shop floor, through a middle level of elected managers to an apex in a regional council. A hierarchy of representative administrators was thus used to replace the old state. Le Corbusier hoped (naïvely) that this would be a more effective and a more representative method of government than that provided within democracies with their perennial oscillation between right and left. Naturally the system he envisaged gave a special place to planners and architects who were effectively situated near the top of the pyramid: it was their business to give form to the new society.

Such ideas as these were ripe when Le Corbusier put together a new version of his ideal city, the Ville Radieuse, in the late twenties and early thirties. As in the Ville Contemporaine the main building types were skyscrapers and apartment houses, but the former were now grouped at the head of the city while the latter (the ones resembling the Pavillon Suisse) were laid out in long strips à redent, thus creating semi-courts and harbours along their length (fig. 15.12). There was no longer a division between the élite and the working class as there had been in the Ville Contemporaine: everyone lived in the Unités, which combined individual rationalized apartments and communal functions like gymnasia and child-care centres. Typically the à redent apartment houses were a conflation of a great variety of earlier collectivist images. There were echoes of Eugène Hénard's 'Boulevards à redans' of 1903 and memories of Charles Fourier's early nineteenth-century Utopian community idea, the 'phalanstère'; this latter scheme shared with Le Corbusier's the common prototype of the Baroque palace (e.g., Versailles) with its stepped plan and linear form. The concept of the continuous roof terrace for leisure activities may in turn have been stimulated by the public decks of ocean liners: in the book La Ville radieuse (1933) Le Corbusier wrote tellingly of the good life lived in the open air and sunlight surveying 'a sea of verdure'.

The Ville Radieuse as a whole was highly centralized and densely populated, yet most of its surface was given over to zones of leisure – parks, playing-fields, etc. (fig. 5.13). Following his earlier principles, Le Corbusier also created broad roads to facilitate the rapid passage of traffic to and from the countryside and from place to place within the city; pedestrians were able to circulate on separate levels; and the traditional 'corridor-street' was completely destroyed. Once again this 'ideal' order was expressed, as in Renaissance Utopian plans, through symmetry, clear geometry, and symbolic analogies. For the form of the Ville Radieuse had a spine, a heart, and a head, and thus incorporated a sort of ideal twentieth-century man –

as essentially two-sided: it caused disruption and decay, it undermined society and brought it to the edge of revolution; but it also provided the means for realizing a new order whose constitution the Utopian artist imagined he could himself form.

After his failure to sell the concepts of the Ville Contemporaine in the rehashed version of the Ville Voisin of 1925, Le Corbusier began to lose his earlier confidence in the powers of big business and centralized technocracy to bring his ideal to the plane of reality. His experiences in Moscow in the late twenties did little to encourage a swing towards the left either, although he appears to have admired the housing experiments of the OSA group and the linear city theories of Milyutin (see Chapter 12). At the same time Le Corbusier's confidence in the power of democracy to counter chaos continued to dwindle. It was in the late twenties, then, that he was attracted to the ideas of 'Syndicalism', which grew out of the trade union movement of the late nineteenth century and which

perfectly functioning and in a harmonious balance with nature. This hierarchical order was spliced together with some of the ideas for zoning and extendability which the architect had seen in Russian linear city proposals.

Le Corbusier was never given the opportunity to build his ideal city *in toto*, but throughout the thirties he worked hard at spreading his urban gospel and at persuading various authorities to follow his way. In 1933 the Congrès Internationaux de L'Architecture Moderne met off Athens on the SS Patras to discuss the state of the modern city. Against the superb landscape background of the Peloponnese, the modern architects of Europe drew up the blueprints for what they hoped would be an enlightened new civilization coming to terms with mechanization. Le Corbusier, of course, was adopted as the unofficial pope, and the 'Charter of Athens' was really a restatement of the Ville Radieuse philosophy but without the poetry. At this point the guiding principles of Le Corbusier's urbanism were dangerously separated from a particular personal vision and rendered as a sort of catechism. Reyner Banham has summed up the situation succinctly:

> The Mediterranean cruise was clearly a welcome relief from the worsening situation of Europe and in this brief respite from reality the delegates produced the most Olympian, rhetorical and ultimately destructive document to come out of CIAM. . . . The hundred and eleven propositions that comprise the charter consist in part of statements about the conditions of towns, and in part of proposals for the rectification of those conditions, grouped under five main headings: Dwellings, Recreation, Work, Transportation, and Historic Buildings. . . . this persuasive generality which gives the Athens Charter its air of universal applicability conceals a very narrow conception of both architecture and town planning and committed CIAM unequivocally to: (a) rigid functional zoning of city plans, with green belts between the areas reserved to different functions, and (b) a single type of urban housing, expressed in the words of the Charter as 'high, widely-spaced apartment blocks wherever the necessity of housing high density of population exists.' At a distance of thirty years we recognize this as merely the expression of an aesthetic preference, but at the time it had the power of a Mosaic commandment and effectively paralyzed research into other forms of housing.

While Le Corbusier's followers seemed bent on calcifying his urban doctrines, he was, in fact, reacting with considerable flexibility in his proposals for particular sites. Among the most spectacular of his many unrealized schemes was the sequence of plans for Algiers between 1931 and 1940. The core idea was for a sort of curved concrete-skeleton viaduct with a motorway running along the top of it (fig. 15.14), various different kinds of housing plugged into it, and a pedestrian street passing at the middle level. To one end was a zone of curved apartment buildings of high density, set in such a way that they did not threaten the integrity of the old Arab *medina*; in turn these created a sculpted enclave on the scale of the nearby mountains and sea. The principal building of the scheme was a tall skyscraper close to the port to head the entire administration of the colony. This went through a series of metamorphoses from a glazed box to a highly monumental, textured object furnished with *brise-soleil* (sun breakers) in the form of extending slabs, balconies, and overhangs. Of course, this was a complete turn about from the Maison de Refuge and the Pavillon Suisse. Despite the provision of mechanical heating and ventilation in the former, the south-facing glass façade had functioned as a greenhouse in the summer and the architect had been forced to invent a new functional element, an attached crate or sunshade. Partly inspired by North African precedents, partly out of a desire to integrate the *brise-soleil* with the body of a building structure, Le Corbusier succeeded in the latest of his Algiers skyscrapers in using his new element as a major means of formal articulation. The combined *brise-soleil*/balcony was to prove particularly useful to him in his monumental designs after the war.

The Algiers plan as a whole resulted from a cross-breeding of general principles and local traditions. Le Corbusier was deeply impressed by the waterside viaducts of Algiers with houses built into their arches, and this may have triggered his megastructural image. Moreover, he studied the unity of architecture, urbanism, and landscape in the kasbah and in the mud-built fortified villages of the Mzab in the central area of Algeria. His sketchbooks from this period are also full of women whose curves transform gradually into the contours of landscapes: perhaps partly with tongue in cheek, Le Corbusier later claimed that he discovered the beauty of the female form 'for the first time' during his stay in North Africa. Within his own typology, the viaduct/housing was, of course, a variant on the *à redent* houses and the motorways of the Ville Radieuse, but the image of cars racing along the top was perhaps brought to fruition by knowledge of G. Matté Trucco's famous test track on the roof of the Fiat factory in Turin. Thus there was a deliberate blending of general and particular, of preconceived notions and unique geographical responses. One guesses that the adolescent Jeanneret's dream of a renaissance of Mediterranean culture may have

15.14 Le Corbusier,
Plan 'Obus' for Algiers,
c. 1932, view of curved
viaduct.

surfaced in the Algiers scheme. For all its blatant colonialism, the project was far less destructive of the Arab quarter than had been the disastrous nineteenth-century incursions.

The thirties was thus a period of epic thinking for Le Corbusier when he acted as 'a historical world individual'. In 1935 he visited the United States and criticized Manhattan, saying that the skyscrapers were too small and too close together; of course, his essential purpose was to preach the Ville Radieuse in the hope that the American authorities might turn the most powerful technology in the world over to his plans. Again he was disappointed, pouring his dreams and regrets into the book *When the Cathedrals were White* (1937), in which he condemned the wastefulness of American suburbs and the irrationality of skyscraper forms. These he intended to replace with a new

variant, 'the Cartesian skyscraper', a vast vertical building for living and for working, which ensured that the city with a park at its centre (Manhattan) would become a park with a city in it (the Ville Radieuse). Le Corbusier even went so far as to hope that Mussolini might build his ideal dream and as late as 1941 was evidently attempting to persuade the Vichy government to listen to his ideas (without success). Certainly this was a case of opportunism; equally it must be pointed out that Le Corbusier believed the good his city plans would do would more than justify any double-dealing necessary to bring them into being.

Frank Lloyd Wright's Broadacre City (1936) was also the fruit of many years' reflection on the meaning of life and the problems of reconciling an ideal state with individual liberty in a mechanized society. On first inspection it might seem odd that his scheme should be called a 'city' at all since it was the opposite of Le Corbusier's ideal: it was the epitome of a decentralized community in which the individual family home and holding were to be the basic units, and in which the only tall buildings were miles apart, separated by vast tracts of countryside. Wright argued that the telephone and the automobile were making the centralized city obsolete, and that mechanization, paradoxically, was allowing the return of Americans to their true destiny: a society of free individuals living in a rural democracy. As in most of Wright's ideas, there was about this a curious blend of the progressive and the conservative. Broadacre City was supposed to release people from the tyranny of centralized capitalism – of 'rent' (a word Wright used to describe all forms of alienation and exploitation) – to deliver them from the evil ways of the city and to return them to a purer and more natural state, where they would be self-reliant rural proprietors on the Jeffersonian model. In this way individual dignity would, he hoped, be restored; like Le Corbusier, Wright thought of himself as a prophet, able (in his case) to intuit 'the plastic form of a genuine democracy'.

Broadacre City was laid out to conform with the Midwestern grid (fig. 15.15), and divided up into sites of an acre or more in which individual 'Usonian' houses were sited. Once again great emphasis was placed on the single family as the central bond of the community. However, there were also co-operative markets, theatres and 'community centers' dotted about among the fields. The tall towers standing here and there were complex in texture and shape; they broke with the countryside grid and acted as beacons across the landscape; they were similar in appearance to his St. Marks Tower project of 1929. To one side of the model which Wright and his Taliesin associates put together in 1935–6, there was even a cathedral of no fixed denomination. However, like Le Corbusier, Wright tended to think that the realization of his Utopia would make traditional religion obsolete. There were also schools and places he called 'Design Centers'. These were no doubt modelled on his earliest Froebel experiences and on Taliesin, as they were supposed to provide an initiation into the spiritual values in nature through a training in the perception of form. The aim was to produce the well-rounded citizens of the future.

Eye and hand, body and what we call mind thus becoming more and more senstive to nature . . .

The thirties was therefore a decade in which both Le Corbusier and Wright succeeded in transforming earlier themes, enriching them and extending them, and in producing buildings of high quality. Both men were also preoccupied with the entire range of building types from habitation to places of work to places of leisure, contemplation, and creation. Both tended to see the artist as a philosopher king who might intuit the forms of an ideal society; and, despite the obvious contrasts in their urban models and their sources, both planners were preoccupied with similar questions: how to overcome the schisms within the division of labour, how to reintegrate man and nature, how to employ the machine yet maintain a sense of wholeness socially and visually. Each had as little success as the other in persuading any influential authority to adopt his larger ideas; each had to be content with realizing his Utopia in fragmentary experiments; and as the decade wore on, it became clear that the disjunctions within modern European and American society were far too deep to be healed by soothing architectural palliatives. The era of justice and harmony seemed less and less likely to dawn. The dusty model of Broadacre City and the splendid drawings of the Ville Radieuse remained the property of their creators: two individualist artist thinkers who optimistically, but mistakenly, imagined that architectural form could fashion a new, integrated civilization.

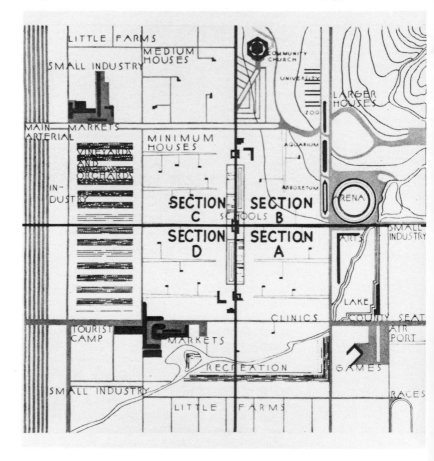

15.15 Frank Lloyd Wright, Broadacre City, 1936, plan of part of the city showing typical grid of circulation (from *When Democracy Builds*, 1945).

16. Totalitarian Critiques of the Modern Movement

> I am convinced that art, since it forms the most uncorrupted, the most immediate reflection of the people's soul, exercises unconsciously by far the greatest direct influence upon the masses of the people.
>
> A. Hitler, 1935

Throughout history monumental architecture has been employed to embody the values of dominant ideologies and groups, and as an instrument of state propaganda. The totalitarian regimes that came to power between the wars (first in Italy, a little later in Russia and Germany), each devoted considerable attention to the ways in which buildings and urban plans might be used to legitimize their position at home and abroad, and to convey their beliefs through symbolism and association. A persistent theme in all three countries was the reinforcement of nationalist sentiments by appeal to earlier national architectural traditions. Allied to this was a nostalgia for supposedly indigenous virtues which were to be reclaimed from the onslaughts of modern fragmentation. It was necessary for totalitarian regimes to foster the impression that their right to rule was embedded in the deepest aspirations of the people. State patronage had therefore to steer a careful way between evocations of past imperial power and suggestions of populist support. The pretence had to be maintained that official taste was a conduit, so to speak, for broader communal impulses.

In these circumstances modern architecture seemed at best irrelevant, at worst a dangerous threat in need of extinction. It could, after all, be portrayed as an internationalist novelty created by a fringe avant-garde working independently of dominant values; it could be claimed too that it lacked rhetorical devices capable of conveying simple messages to the majority. Modern architecture was also open to the charge that it was 'foreign', that it had not grown from national cultural roots and craft traditions: in Germany it was frequently portrayed as an oriental import or (still worse!) as the thin edge of a Bolshevist plot originating in the East. In Russia, simultaneously, one might well find it being treated as a commodity from the West, as a last fragment of decaying European civilization. In these sweeping condemnations one has, of course, to bear in mind the distinction between intended and received meanings. The true symbolic and ideological texture of modern architecture was far more refined than blunt and imperceptive criticisms of this kind allowed. Moreover, it was not always rejected out of hand: the Nazis (for example) were quite happy to claim the structural economy and technological imagery of modern architecture when it suited them (e.g., in certain utilitarian buildings for the Luftwaffe), while in Italy, the 'progressive' character of modern design – if expressed with suitably Latin emphasis – could be acceptable to the regime. Again one has to guard against over-simple polarities: there was no clear-cut totalitarian critical position, nor a single accepted style.

In Germany political debates over the new architecture had continued throughout the twenties. Socialist support of large housing schemes had tended to give the flat-roofed *Siedlungen*, and the architects who had designed them, the automatic stigma of Communism. It makes little difference that only some modern architects were adherents of Marxism, or that a great variety of expression for socialist ideals was possible: right-wing critics were suspicious of the new architecture and determined to tar it all with the same

212 · Modern Architecture between the Wars

brush. The tone of one brand of criticism already prevalent in the late twenties is well caught by the following:

According to the leaders of the Bauhaus – rooms must look like studios, like operating theatres; all warmth is banned from them. Therefore no wood; rugs and upholstery are sins against the holy ghost of 'Sachlichkeit'. Glass instead, all kinds of metal or artificial stone – these are the stylish materials! The new man is no longer a man, he is a 'geometrical animal'. He needs no dwelling, no home, only a 'dwelling machine'. This man is not an individual, not a personality, but a collective entity, a piece of mass man. And therefore they build 'housing developments', apartment blocks of desolate uniformity, in which everything is standardized. These are tenements, built not as a necessity, as in the rapidly growing cities during the second half of the nineteenth century, but as a matter of principle. They want to kill personality in men, they want collectivism, for the highest goal of these architects is Marxism, Communism.

In this version we find modern architecture portrayed as something rootless, materialistic, uncomfortable, inhuman, Communist, and anti-German. Another style of criticism concentrated on the supposed impracticality of modern buildings, their leaking flat roofs, the peeling of their white plaster surfaces, the rusting of their windows, the ignorance manifest in them of time-worn methods for handling extremes of climate. Then again there were the racist arguments. These emphasized the way the new architecture was lifted free of the soil and its lack of nourishment from local and regional vernacular sources. The most extreme slurs were reserved for the distortions of modern painting, which were compared to deformed and 'inferior' races; with architecture this distasteful haranguing had a less easy target, nonetheless the flat roof was singled out as flagrant evidence of 'un-German-ness'. In one hysterical outburst this constituent feature of the new architecture was branded as 'oriental, Jewish and Bolshevik' simultaneously. The soap-box oratory could often become extremely confused: while one criticism might try to link modern architecture to an international Socialist conspiracy, another might latch on to the industrial imagery and interpret it as an expression of:

... the unclean collaboration of certain branches of great industry, dominated by Jews, with the Marxist parties.

Finally modern architecture could be rejected on the grounds that it was simply ugly and therefore not ennobling of German culture.

The trigger springs were thus already set when the Nazis came to power in 1933. It has to be emphasized that there was no single monolithic Nazi doctrine concerning either the criticism or the creation of architecture, that even official opinions often diverged, and that these odd mixtures of opinions had been lying around for some time. One does note, however, a preponderance of the racist style of argument combined with a fairly sound general assessment that modern architectural imagery would not be suitable to grand civic monumentality or to regionalist, volkisch expression. Moreover, there was another feature of the modern movement which made it unsuitable. The Reich needed to assert the hierarchy of building types as visual evidence of the hierarchy of power: an architectural system that tended to blur distinctions between building types was not ideally suited to this sort of symbolic differentiation.

It is interesting therefore to see how modern architects fared in Germany in the thirties. The fact is that most of them were outlawed, unpopular, or simply decided to leave. The Bauhaus was eventually closed in 1933, and its staff scattered in all directions, many of them to seek refuge in England and the United States. Mies van der Rohe was an outstanding exception, as he did not leave Germany until 1937; he was even a joint winner in the competition for the new Reichsbank for Berlin in 1933. His scheme was distinguished by its severe monumentality, achieved through the simplest means of clear proportions, symmetry, and a sort of grim elegance. Here was a case where technology and the monumental sense came together in a formula which appealed to conservative elements. But the project was not built, and the monumentality generally favoured later in the thirties made more obvious use of the past.

It is central to the story that Hitler was himself a frustrated architect and perhaps saw statecraft itself as a kind of monumental design. As an adolescent he had dreamed of redesigning Linz. Towards the end of his life it became his ambition to leave behind a new imperial Berlin, testifying to the world domination of the Reich. Just as he sensed that the great buildings of the past bore witness to a coherence of belief, so he hoped that the new bonds of German unity might, almost automatically, find expression in great communal projects and a healthy vernacular rooted in native blood and soil. On this point it might be said that his thinking partially paralleled Gropius's, Wright's, and Le Corbusier's, since he too expected the individual artist to grasp the whole inner feeling of an epoch and then to give it form. He played down the actual pluralism of modern life, in a monomaniacal belief that

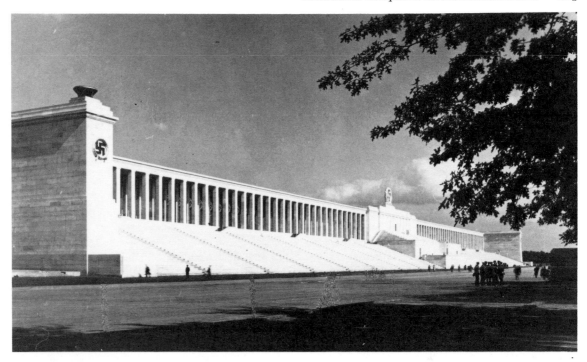

16.1 (*above*) Albert
Speer, Zeppelinfeld,
Nuremberg, 1936.

16.2 (*below*) Gerdy
Troost, House of
German Art,
Prinzregentenstrasse,
Munich, 1934–6.

he had risen to power by some inherent force of the whole *Volk*. His National Socialist beliefs led him to distrust previous German élites – including, let it be said – that élite of perception, the avant-garde. His patronage was ideally suited for the production of a bathetic, banal, instant culture of little lasting depth: and that is what most Nazi architecture usually became.

There was the further problem of representation – a problem that the other dictatorial regimes shared: What should their architecture *look* like? What appearance should a specifically *Nazi* building have? Half-baked art history was dragged in to suggest that Gothic architecture one minute, Classical architecture the next, lay closest to the reconsolidated national genius of the German people. Even modern architecture could be made acceptable on occasion, so long as it was restricted to 'lower' buildings in the hierarchy: factories, office buildings, and the like. It is never very precise, then, to speak of one essential 'Nazi architecture' in the 1930s.

As soon as he came to power, Hitler chose Gerdy Troost as his main architectural adviser. Troost had been a member of the Nazi party since 1924 and his love for simplified but traditional Classicism made him the ideal man to express the Führer's aspirations towards a monumental 'community' architecture, extolling the discipline, order, and strength of the new state. Both patron and architect shared a love of Schinkel and an intuition for a supposed link between Greek and Teutonic culture. It was no anomaly, then, that the House of German Art in the Prinzregentenstrasse (1934–6) should have had a stripped Doric order, a low horizontal attic, and sharp but clean lines (fig. 16.2).

In 1934 Troost died and his place was taken by a young man named Albert Speer. Speer became the stage designer, as it were, for Nazi pageantry, by providing an instant monumentality of quick effect and mainly rhetorical emphasis. He drew on whatever sources seemed most suitable for evoking an overwhelming scale – Egyptian, Babylonian, Classical, neo-classical – and pared down inherited forms into a vocabulary of stripped surfaces, stone veneers, and regimental repetition. His design for the 'Zeppelinfeld' arena at Nuremburg of 1936 is a good example of this species of monumentality (fig. 16.1). It was one of the settings for the colossal Nazi rallies and so was a collective *Volk* building in the full sense. In the same year Speer had the stunning idea (perhaps suggested by certain festivalia used in the French Revolution) of pointing a thousand searchlights into the air during a night event. Slender shafts of light rose miles into the sky and the idea was christened 'the Cathedral of ice'. A similar bombast and militarism inspired the vast

16.5 Karl Vesser, Nazi Youth hostel, Urfeld, c. 1935.

16.3 (*above left*) Albert Speer and Adolf Hitler, plan for Berlin, 1937–40.

16.4 (*left*) Albert Speer, New Chancellery, Berlin, 1938, view of long hall.

Olympic Stadium and attached buildings outside Berlin in 1936. These had the extra propaganda function of impressing the world with refound German might. Nazi monuments were a little like Hitler's oratory: forceful, repetitive but ultimately banal. They tended to deaden opposition with statements of overwhelming conformity and force.

Speer pandered to Hitler's fantasies and became, in a sense, the Führer's own architectural interpreter. In 1937, the inner circle of the Reich decided that the Chancellery building in Berlin must be rebuilt on a scale commensurate with the increasingly imperial stature of the leader. Speer produced a suitable scenario at top speed. Hitler's personal salon and office were placed off an overbearing marble corridor (fig. 16.4) almost as long as the Galerie des Glaces at Versailles. It was reached through a sequence of formal spaces – a courtyard of honour, a vestibule, a mosaic room, a round hall – while at the other end of the building was the Cabinet conference room. Admittedly the plan was a quite elegant and ornamental composition pulling together various antique models; but when built, the stripped Classical forms had a dull and drab quality. Stone was imported from all parts of Germany for this project and the buildings were erected in less than eighteen months. Nazi insignia and emblems were embossed on walls and furniture, to give added impact to the heavy-handed and obvious messages of the architecture with its overwhelming scale, its polished, rich materials, its pompous axial regimentation, and its disciplined repetition. The psychological game was clear: the visiting statesman or ambassador was to see that the New Reich had become a patron of the monumental arts, and was to be placed at an instant disadvantage by a two hundred

yard walk over polished floors, past swastika flags and impeccably designed uniforms, before he wheeled on to the cross-axis, presumably to see the Führer waiting behind his desk in a room of grandiose proportions. It was in the bunker next to this building that Hitler came to his end in 1945 while Russian shells demolished all this Nazi handiwork.

Speer's and Hitler's megalomania did not stop there. In 1937 they launched plans for the reordering of Berlin, employing long avenues, axes, and a stage scenery drawn from Paris, Ancient Rome and Washington (fig. 16.3). The focal point was to be a centralized domical monument larger than any dome yet built and known simply as the 'Great Hall'. This was to be a pantheon of sorts containing images and inscriptions dedicated to the heroes and heroic aims of Nazism. It was to stand facing a boulevard, at the other end of which would be a triumphal arch in honour of Hitler. Had it been built, the Hall could have contained St. Peter's in Rome in its vaulted interior space. This sublime scale recalls those fantasy schemes for pure geometrical cenotaphs and cathedrals painted by E. L. Boullée towards the end of the eighteenth century. Indeed, neo-classical images of funeral pyres influenced the extraordinary war memorials envisaged by Wilhelm Kreis to stand as grim beacons of Nazi superiority on the conquered lands of 'inferior races'. But such Nazi emblems had about them a quality of empty gesture for all their vastness: they were a classic case of what Giedion called 'the devaluation of symbols'.

In parallel with civic monuments, domestic and rural projects were also sponsored by the Nazis in the thirties. The recurrent themes of athletic prowess and rustic purity were nurtured in numerous deliberately 'regionalist' buildings. The long standing suspicion of urban centres as infamous breeding grounds of 'uprootedness', 'cosmopolitanism', and other anti-nationalist sins, could here find an outlet. It was noted earlier that the flat roof particularly excited the hostility of certain right-wing critics as evidence of alien influence; as a corollary, the type, shape, and materials of hip roofs were regarded as primary signals of a building's allegiance to the vernacular traditions of a particular region. Karl Vesser's design for a Nazi youth hostel at Urfeld (fig. 16.5) employed the overhanging eaves and balconies of the local Bavarian village houses and stood on a stone base of a vaguely martial character; Göring's hunting lodge was a theatrical evocation of Teutonic memories quite at odds with the 'brave new world' and machine imagery of the new architecture. Nazi regionalism was not a genuine vernacular but a sophisticated and procured Arts and Crafts rusticity catering to the overflow towns and suburbs. The imagery was supposed to suggest the conservation of the homeland and the local community as opposed to the 'disturbances' of the modern metropolis and festering discontents brought on by rapid industrialization and (of course) by 'dangerous' foreign ideas. This *Heimatstil* was to foster open, healthy social relationships and conformity to the prevalent state doctrines. Even telephone buildings and utilitarian structures could be fitted up with an appropriate thatched overhang to preserve the sense of regional continuity.

Although Nazi power was based in a large degree on rapid mechanization, on the creation of efficient factories, autobahns, and munitions industries, the 'factory aesthetic' had no place in the domestic sphere. Its intrusion into housing was seen not only as a break with decorum, but also as a sinister dislocation of family integrity by hostile and materialistic forces. It is instructive in this connection that Hitler made much of the fact that only handicrafts were employed in the construction of one of his residences. This is all the more ironical given the stress that the majority of modern movement architects had placed on the supposed 'spirituality' of their simple abstract forms. They too had sought to transcend materialism.

However, modern doctrines did have their uses in the design of buildings of more humble and utilitarian function where qualities of discipline, clarity of structure, and clear lighting could also have moral overtones. Here it has to be admitted that the nationalist streak in previous Deutscher Werkbund theorizing permitted some cross-breeding of ideas. H. Rimpl's design for a Heinkel factory of 1936 is a good example of this clear-cut rationalism. In fact, Rimpl had been a student of Mies van der Rohe, and the design anticipated something of the character of Mies's later buildings for the campus at Illinois Institute of Technology in Chicago. German engineers took an interest in aesthetic and even ideological matters. A supreme emblem of National Socialist industrial design was, of course, the famous 'Volkswagen' automobile; during the war the concrete fortresses and bunkers of the 'Atlantic Wall' had a stunning aesthetic clarity despite their grim function.

At the Paris International exhibition of 1937 the German pavilion stood opposite the Russian one (figs. 16.6, 16.7). To the unpractised eye it might have been difficult to tell the difference since both states employed a combination of gross realism and stark monumentality as their official ambassadorial style. Speer's design stressed the vertical and was modelled on a stripped neo-classical tribune of some kind. It was surmounted by a stern eagle. Iofan's Soviet design opposite was assembled from stepped masses of vaguely streamlined character (not unlike some of New York's skyscrapers of the late twenties) and was topped by the enormous

lunging figures of a man and a woman supposed, no doubt, to reflect the energy and populism of the Soviet state. Both nations' design policies had clearly altered since Mies van der Rohe's Barcelona Pavilion of 1929 or since the Paris Exposition des Arts Décoratifs of 1925, when Melnikov had been allowed by his sponsors to create his daring evocation of the factory aesthetic, proclaiming the values of a forward-looking, supposedly egalitarian society.

As has been shown in Chapter 10, the intervening event of the Palace of the Soviets competition of 1931 had already offered clear signals of changing official taste in the Soviet Union, and implied too, in its outcome, that the messages of modern architecture were suspected of being too arcane for the general public. In the early thirties 'Realism' in the arts became

16.6 Albert Speer, German Pavilion, Paris Exhibition, 1937.

aggrandizement of the central state and its official folk heroes seems to have accounted for Iofan's victory in the Palace of the Soviets competition with its statue of Lenin on top and (in the later version) its wedding cake mausoleum mawkishly clad in Classical elements. The aerodynamic forms of the 1937 Soviet Pavilion in Paris clearly issued from the same family; so did the kitsch decorations of the Moscow subways; so, eventually, did the plans for the university on the Lenin hills, approached from the centre of the city by way of an axial road starting in Red Square and running for twenty miles. In 1941 the Marx-Engels Institute in Tiflis was designed by A. V. Schoussev with giant Corinthian columns in its façade. The grand manner of the Tsar had returned with a vengeance, but without its earlier tasteful sense of ornament. Parallels between Marxist and Greek democratic ideals of statehood were subsumed by the slogan 'columns for the people', but imperialist overtones were obvious. Indeed there was some convergence between Nazi and Soviet positions: in each case the avant-garde was regarded with suspicion, while continuity was sought with pre-revolutionary modes. Older members of the architectural profession who had seemed outmoded even came back into action; a thin traditionalism triumphed.

There were also some points of similarity in the attitudes towards housing and city-planning. As in Germany, the pitched roof was recommended for climatic reasons and because it was supposed to be closer to 'popular' aspirations. Those avant-garde planners who had left Germany for Russia in the late twenties to build the architecture of the world revolution for the new society (e.g., Ernst May) were stranded, by the mid-thirties, between two tides of reaction. But the writing had been on the wall for some time, as this official Soviet pronouncement of 1930 makes clear:

It is impossible suddenly to overcome obstacles that are centuries old, the fruit of the cultural and economic backwardness of society. Yet this is the system implicit in these unrealizable and Utopian plans for the reconstruction, at State expense, of new cities based on the total collectivization of living, including collective provisioning, collective care of children, the prohibition of private kitchens. The hasty realization of such schemes, Utopian and doctrinaire, which take no account of the material resources of our country and of the limits within which the people, with their set habits and preferences, can be prepared for them, could easily result in considerable losses and could also discredit the basic principles of the Socialist reconstruction of society.

16.7 B. M. Iofan, Soviet Pavilion, Paris Exhibition, 1937.

the official line. In painting this tended to mean that abstraction should be avoided on the grounds that it might become a self-indulgent filter between the artist, 'reality', and the public; the worst term of censure was 'formalism'. The 'reality' upon which artists were supposed to concentrate was largely preselected, and involved proletarian subjects of daily life or heroic deeds in the service of the state. The 'appropriate' style in painting was a descendant of nineteenth-century 'realists' such as Courbet.

How could such arguments be transposed to architecture? One way was through the decoration of buildings with suitable sculptures, paintings, and reliefs. Another was through the use of an easily legible monumentality employing devices of allusion, axiality, and grandiose scale. A shift in emphasis towards the

The situation in Italy in the same decade was every bit as complex. Mussolini felt no constitutional restraint on his imperial ambitions and had the convenience of ancient Rome as his stage-set and plaything. Like Hitler, he took a direct interest in planning affairs. By 1925 a new plan for the renovation of Rome had been set in motion. Straight streets were to be cut through the patchwork urban fabric to link up key monuments of the distant past with ones which Mussolini himself intended to build with Piacentini as his architectural aide. The blend of theatricality, functionalism, and propaganda of this scheme recalled Haussmann's plans for Paris or the Baroque planning projects of the popes. Major historical monuments like the Colosseum were to be shorn of their encumberments (dislodged people being forcibly rehoused), so facilitating the flow of traffic and the perception of Rome's great past. The urban scene of the 'New Rome' – centre of the 'Mediterranean Dream' – would glisten with automobiles alongside the ruins and combine the efficiency and speed of a modern metropolis with ancient imperial memories (Marinetti the Futurist was a friend of the Duce).

Mussolini himself soon realized the power of traditional cultural images in his projection of a new nationalist spirit. He affected a pedigree in Roman history and staged elaborate political events in the Campidoglio and the Palazzo Venezia. He identified with Augustus (although he ended up hanging from a lamppost before he could leave the 'Third Rome' a city of marble). In line with this search for parallels in antiquity, a design was drawn up in the thirties for the Piazza Augusteo by V. Ballio-Morpugo next to the Tiber (fig. 16.10). The Ara Pacis was enclosed in a glazed building opposite the Mausoleum of Augustus and juxtaposed with new stripped Classical buildings of indescribable dullness bearing an iconography concerning the fruits of a peaceful existence brought by Fascism. The imagery suggested the basis in Roman tradition of a synthesis of peasant and soldierly virtues. It was a trumped-up mythology which suffered all the more from the lack of aesthetic conviction with which it was expressed.

Modern architecture took hold later in Italy than in Germany, Holland, and France, and encountered less hostility from State taste than it did in Nazi Germany. In part this was due to the fact that Fascism was already well established when the Italian modern movement got under way, and so there was no automatic identification with a previous, suspect Socialist ideology as was the case in Germany. Then it is one of the intriguing features of the modern movement in Italy that it minimized 'functionalist' and 'machine-age' polemics, playing up instead an abstract aestheticism deliberately evocative of Classical preced-

ents. This was constantly in danger of degenerating into a suave formalism (fig. 16.8), or, still worse, a stripped monumentality in which vast areas of travertine, with the consistency of linoleum, conjured up an instant skin-deep traditionalism. At its best, the consciousness of history opened up new dimensions of meaning for the modern tradition in which the concrete frame (the *piloti*, the stripped support, the plain opening) and elemental characteristics of the Classical system were mutually reinforcing at a deeper, more abstract level. It may not have been mere diplomacy, then, when the 'Gruppo 7' (a group with modern leanings who launched themselves in 1926) claimed that they did not advocate a break with tradition:

16.8 (*top*) M. Piacentini and associates, University of Rome, Senate building, 1935.

16.9 G. Matté Trucco, Fiat factory, Turin, 1923.

16.10 V. Ballio-Morpugo, clearance around the Mausoleum of Augustus, Rome, 1937.

In Italy there is such a pronounced Classical substratum, and the spirit of tradition – not the forms it takes, which is something quite different – is so deep that, obviously and almost mechanically, the new architecture could not fail to retain a typical national character.

The members of the group were L. Figini, G. Frette, S. Larco, G. Pollini, C. E. Rava, G. Terragni, and U. Castagnola (the last being later replaced by A. Libera); they declared their intention of founding an 'Architettura Razionale'.

The new architecture ... must be the result of a close adherence to logic and rationality ... We do not claim to create *a style*, but from the constant application of rationality, the perfect correspondence of the building to its aims ... *style* must inevitably result.

At an exhibition in 1928 the Group nonetheless showed their adherence to aspects of pre-existing modern forms from abroad. Figini and Pollini's scheme for a 'Casa di Dopolavoro' (a workers' club) had notable Constructivist affinities, while Terragni's 'Officino produzione di Gaz' ('Gas Company Headquar-

ters') was an elegant fusion of Purism and industrial forms. Even though Sant' Elia's 'Città Nuova' sketches of 1912–14 and such remarkable industrial buildings as G. Matté Trucco's Fiat Factory of 1923 with its test track on the roof preceded the 1928 exhibition, it was not until after this date that it was possible to speak of anything like a consolidated modern movement in Italy (fig. 16.9). Not surprisingly it was in the northern cities – Milan and Turin in particular – that modern architecture took root, for here a technocratic patronage sensed some reflection of its own aspirations in the new forms. Figini and Pollini's 'Casa di Elettricità' of 1930 at Monza is an excellent example of the tasteful, almost over-elegant modernism of this period; meanwhile Figini's own house of 1934 was a taut adaptation of Le Corbusier's vocabulary. Michelucci's design for Florence railway station (1934–6) was evidence of the intrusion of modern architecture into the field of major public commissions, while between 1934 and 1937 the enlightened patronage of Adriano Olivetti (director of the business machines company) allowed the creation of an entire centre at Ivrea in which industrial buildings, products and housing were conceived as an integrated form.

In retrospect the outstanding architectural figure of the thirties in Italy was Giuseppe Terragni. Born in

1904, he soon outstripped the academicism of his education and by the mid-twenties was aware of the modern movement then crystallizing in Northern Europe. Terragni admired Le Corbusier in particular. His understanding of the French/Swiss architect, who was a generation older than himself, went far deeper than that of most Italian modernists who imbibed the technological imagery and the purity of form, but did not always grasp the deeper principles of organization and the links with tradition. Terragni was a traditionalist in about the same way Le Corbusier was: he believed that 'essential' architectural values could be rethought, and successfully incorporated into a modern mode of expression. More precisely than that, Terragni was at heart a Classicist and was able to perceive in Le Corbusier's buildings and writings qualities of proportion, abstraction, and urbane reference that the cruder Italian modernists missed.

This combination of aptitudes and circumstances made Terragni uniquely endowed to forge a bond between the progressivist and traditionalist aspects of Fascist mythology, and·to give to these patterns of

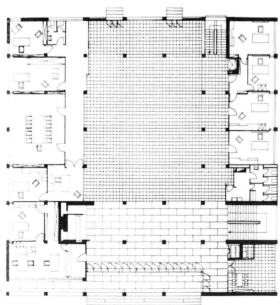

16.11 (*above*) Giuseppe Terragni, Casa del Fascio, Como, 1934.

16.12 (*left*) Giuseppe Terragni, Casa del Fascio, Como, 1934, plan.

16.13 Giuseppe Terragni, Casa del Fascio, Como, 1934, detail of frame at top of building.

thought and feeling a form. This is already evident in the Casa del Fascio (the local headquarters of the Fascist party) of 1934 in Como (fig. 16.11) which stands across from the traditional urban institutions facing on to a piazza. The façade is a taut linear design, in which architectural effect is created by crisp contrasts of thin planes and voids. Frame and walls are juxtaposed in a manner which suggests that the architect has rigorously redefined the fundamental meanings of such perennial elements as 'support', 'opening' or 'enclosure'. However, the iconography of this frame façade, with its subtle net of layered space, has less to do with the technological 'objectivity' of much architecture of the twenties, than it has to do with a sort of abstracted, Latin mode (fig. 16.13). This is a Classical façade with a portico rethought to give a suitably open image to a modern institution in an urban setting. Terragni wrote of his own building:

> Here is the Mussolinian concept that Fascism is a glass house into which everyone can peer giving rise to the architectural interpretation that is the complement of that metaphor; no encumbrance, no barrier, no obstacle, between the political hierarchy and the people. .

The vital and creative tension between the modern and the Classical extends from the overall arrangement of the plan (fig. 16.12) to the image of the façade, to the choice of materials and to the character of proportions (square in plan with the façade height equal to half one side). The inner atrium, a space for public assembly linked easily with the piazza outside, is disposed in a manner which loosely recalls the *cortile* of a cinquecento *palazzo*, while the building is clothed in a finely cut marble which avoids mechanistic reference and suggests an honorific character, yet is detailed in

such a way that the banal massiveness of so much Fascist neo-classicism is avoided. The Casa del Fascio, the contemporary High Point I flats in London by Lubetkin, and Aalto's near contemporary Sanatorium at Paimio were clear evidence of the way an authentic modern tradition was forming up in the early thirties, in which seminal ideas of the modern movement were being blended with new impulses and metaphors. The same period, of course, witnessed the rapid devaluation of white forms and flat roofs into mannered clichés and banal formulae. Terragni's own creative endeavours were nourished increasingly by intellectual ruminations on history and on the beginnings of architecture in archetypical institutions. The ever more complex levels of his imagery found an outlet eventually in a curious scheme, never built, for a monument to Dante, to stand in the Roman Forum, and to be an emblem of the continuity of Italianate culture, the unity of the new empire, and its parallels with earlier ones.

The 'Danteum' (as it was to be called) was to include a Dante study centre and was to stand on a site next to the Basilica of Maxentius (fig. 16.15). The scheme was commissioned in 1938 by Rino Valdameri, Director of the Brera in Milan, and an early version was approved by Mussolini, but both the patron and the architect were killed in the war. In essence the scheme was a sort of analogue to Dante's *Divine Comedy* and was arranged around an ascending processional route which linked rectangular compartments of different mood and articulation, representing the inferno, purgatory, and paradise (fig. 16.14), the last being a space open to the sky with a grid of glass columns in it. The basic formal elements were walls and cylindrical columns disposed in proportional relationships keyed into both the Golden Section, the dimensions of the nearby Basilica of Maxentius, and an abstruse numerological symbolism of Terragni's own, which he believed to be consonant with Dante's thought. But the grids and hypostyles of columns were allied to the architect's notions of the beginnings of architecture as well, and incorporated what he felt to be archetypical forms (e.g., cylinders, rectangles), archetypical relationships (e.g., rows, grids), basic types (e.g., freestanding columns, porticoes, hypostyles), and fundamental institutional types (e.g., temple, palace). Indeed, the building blended together, subtly and beautifully, sources derived from Egyptian temple design with the vocabulary of modern architecture, with the abstraction of modern painting, with the basic elements of the neighbouring Roman buildings. The Danteum was intended as a sort of microcosm of the Duce's empire, its triumph, its cultural achievement, and its divine sanction, which supposedly linked the era of Fascism with other great eras in Italy's history.

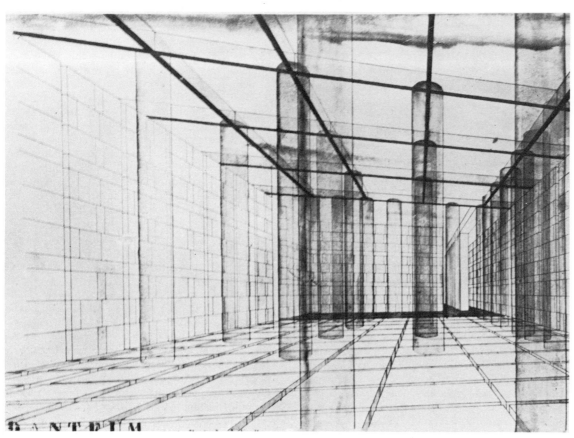

16.14 (*left*) Giuseppe Terragni, Danteum, 1938, perspective of 'Paradiso'.

16.15 (*below*) Giuseppe Terragni, Danteum project, for Roman Forum, 1938.

This was a case, clearly, where modern devices of abstraction were employed not to escape the past, but to enter it more fully on a number of levels simultaneously.

Thus, despite the fact that it was never built, the Danteum project must rank as one of the most subtle and complex ideas to be conceived within the tradition of the modern movement. Moreover, its intellectual strategy was a demonstration of one possible way of fusing the ancient and the modern without ending in a betrayal of both. After inspecting Terragni's work, especially his extraordinary scheme for the Palazzo della Civiltà Italiana, in which frame and screen became beautiful surrogates for Classical rhetorical elements, one is left guessing whether this architect, had he been a German, would have surmounted the strictures of ideological prejudice and created a similar rich mix of meanings under Nazi patronage. By contrast, Speer's architecture was banal and obvious: but was this due to its trumped-up content or to the artist's lesser talents? One thing is clear: the totalitarian critiques of modern architecture bit deep and revealed problems and rifts between avant-garde culture and some of the traditional, preservationist,

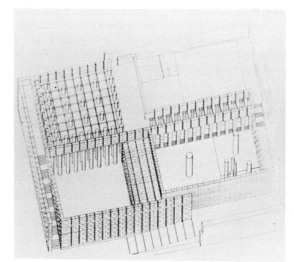

and institutional functions of architecture. In turn, the repression of the modern movement at such an early stage of its development in Germany forced some of the protagonists to emigrate and take their forms with them to foreign soils.

17. The Spread of Modern Architecture to England and Scandinavia

... one might see the history of architecture in our century as a flowing stream, at first slow moving, broad and free, and varied by many eddies and side currents before 1920, but then confined in the twenties to a narrower channel, so that for a while it rushed forward at almost revolutionary speed. By the early thirties the stream was certainly beginning to widen and meander again.

H. R. Hitchcock, 1965

It is perhaps in the nature of major creative revolutions that the period of peak creation be followed by a phase in which the implications of recent innovations are gradually absorbed and explored. This had already begun to happen to the modern movement in the thirties, when a 'second generation' of modern architects – men like Terragni, Aalto, and Lubetkin – began to make their impact. They were all born close to the turn of the century and so were old enough to have been brought up in the twilight of *fin-de-siècle* tendencies, yet young enough to have experienced the promise of the new architecture with full force. Like any immediate inheritors of a new faith they had the problem of absorbing and transforming novel ideas without resorting to slavish imitation or skin-deep dogmatism. Problems of transmission were complicated in the thirties by the political climate and the emigration of forms to foreign soils. Moreover, the 'masters' were not standing idle and a young architect might be on the point of mastering certain lessons of the Villa Savoye only to be confronted by the Petite Maison de Weekend or the invention of the *brise-soleil*. With this tendency towards a slight time-lag, it is scarcely surprising that many of the key breakthroughs in the works of Wright, Aalto, and Le Corbusier of the thirties should have waited for the post-war years to exert their broader influence.

While modern architecture was reaching its peak in the late twenties in France, Germany, Holland, and Russia, it was exerting only the slightest influence in Scandinavia and England. But by the mid-thirties the situation had almost reversed, and these were among the most active centres of modern experimentation left. In part this phenomenon was traceable to the influx of immigrants from countries where modern architecture had been repressed; equally it was due to happy coincidences of talent, and to national cultural situations which virtually demanded a rejection of tired forms and an inoculation of new creative energy. However, the predisposing causes in England and Scandinavia contrasted sharply.

England, of course, had played a major role in fostering Arts and Crafts values at the turn of the century. W. R. Lethaby and his faction might almost have brought a vital English architecture to full flower had their views not gone out of fashion to be replaced by a scholarly Beaux-Arts revival supported, on the whole, by architectural mediocrities. Even Mackintosh had been better understood in Vienna than in London. In England a cluster of predisposing factors, which seem in retrospect to have been crucial in channelling the direction of the new architecture on the continent, was missing. Apart from the short-lived impact of Wyndham Lewis's Vorticism, there was no Cubist revolution in the arts. The activities of the Design and Industries Association were scarcely the equivalent of the idealistic obsession with injecting 'good form' into industrial products of the Deutscher Werkbund. There was a lack of progressive clientele and talent; and a general complacency after wartime victory made fantasies of a 'brave new world' or a mechanized social Utopia seem neither relevant nor necessary. The intellectual radicals of the time had an almost pathological distaste for mechanization; English

17.1 (*left*) Berthold Lubetkin and Tecton, High Point I, Highgate, London, 1933–5, view from the garden.

17.2 (*above*) Berthold Lubetkin and Tecton, Penguin Pool, London Zoo, 1933.

17.3 Berthold Lubetkin and Tecton, High Point I, Highgate, London, 1933–5, plan of ground floor.

reformers were either pragmatic, or medievalizing, or concerned with more fundamental ills than bad architecture – if they were not of the precious 'art for art's sake' variety. Nothing could have been further from the English situation and temper than the abstract social ideology of De Stijl or the Bauhaus, the machine fetishism of Futurism, or the total solutions of Le Corbusier's Ville Contemporaine.

The period between 1910 and 1930 in England has been characterized variously as the 'Regency revival', 'the playboy era', or the phase of 'ancestor worship' in design. Standing clear of the prevalent mediocrity was of course Lutyens, but he, for all his unique and uncategorizable quality, stood at the end of a tradition rather than at the beginning of a new one. There were a few 'modern' experiments in the late twenties, like Behrens's design for a house for J. Basset-Lowke of 1926 at Northampton and Tait's designs for the Crittall window manufacturers' workers' housing at Silver End, Essex, of 1927; but it was typical of the situation as a whole that it should have been the 'watered-down' versions of modern architecture – e.g.,

those of Dudok and Mallet-Stevens – which received attention in England. It was not until 1929 with the Crawfords Advertising building in London by Etchells (translator into English of *Vers une architecture*) and the white cubic concrete forms of Amyas Connell's house for Ashmole, at Amersham (1930) that a more rigorous modernism was made manifest. Joseph Emberton's Royal Corinthian Yacht Club of 1931, meanwhile, was clear evidence that the new architecture was at least being understood for its structural principles. This building was even included in Hitchcock and Johnson's *International Style* of the following year.

The outstanding architect of the thirties in England was undoubtedly Berthold Lubetkin. Born in 1901 in the Caucasus in Russia, he had experienced the architectural debates following the Soviet Revolution first-hand, had studied in Paris at the Atelier Perret, where he had been initiated into the secrets of reinforced-concrete construction, and had absorbed the principles of Le Corbusier's 'five points of a new architecture'. The flats designed by Lubetkin and R. Ginsberg at 25 Avenue de Versailles in 1927 were a suave reinterpretation of Maison Cook, mated to certain ideas derived from the Soviet context. Lubetkin maintained contacts with Russia in this period, designed the Soviet Pavilion for Strasbourg in 1929, and kept a firm grasp on the ideological issues then being hammered out in his homeland.

In 1930 Lubetkin went to England and gathered about him six young Englishmen: the group was christened 'Tecton'. Among their earliest commissions were two for London Zoo, the Gorilla House and the Penguin Pool (fig. 17.2). The latter was designed with the aid of Ove Arup the engineer, as a shallow oval pool in reinforced concrete with two curved ramps interlacing at its centre on which the birds could parade or from which they could dive into the water. The ramps were packed with steel reinforcing and were a structural *tour de force* for the time, but it was the imagery and the taut abstraction which were so new in the English context. The penguin pool recalls some of Meyerhold's constructivist stage-sets or Gabo's scientific sculptures from the twenties, and was further evidence of Lubetkin's indebtedness to the formal inventions of the previous decade in Russia.

Lubetkin and Tecton's next major work was High Point I flats, Highgate (1933–5), designed for a site surrounded by greenery with long views south over the whole of London. The flats were packed into a cross of Lorraine plan so as to maximize views, cross-ventilation, and contact with the outside (fig. 17.1). The main eight-storey body of the building was lifted up on *pilotis* and surmounted by a public roof terrace. The lower storey was also communal, containing

0 5 10 15 20 25 30 35 40 45 50

lobby, winter garden, main hall, access to the lifts, a tea-room, and a fantastic curved ramp descending to the garden at the rear – a vaguely Baroque flourish. This lower zone of the building was expressed as curved free-plan elements swinging out and back from the prevalent rectangular order of the grid of supports and the axial discipline of the main forms (fig. 17.3). The vocabulary was, once again, an intelligent adaptation of Le Corbusier's white forms of the twenties and of the system of the 'five points of a new architecture'. In this case, though, the walls were weight-bearing, and the rooms cellular and compact. More than that, High Point I was among the earliest demonstrations of the synthesis of architecture and urbanistic doctrine, derived from both Le Corbusier and Soviet collective housing of the twenties. Le Corbusier himself visited the building and (uncharacteristically) praised it as one of the first 'vertical garden cities of the future'. A tower standing in a green park, its white wings spread out, its details tight and clear, High Point I became a rallying point of the emergent English modern movement, and a demonstration of what could be done when rigorous functional analysis, formal lyricism, and a social vision were synthesized. Of course the collectivist polemic of the building was a little uneasy in its upper-middle-class context, but the rhetoric was nonetheless clear; these were principles which might later be applied to collective housing on a broader scale.

It is when one probes the abstraction of High Point I further that one appreciates the complexity of its sources. The conception owes much to those 'social condensers' designed in Russia only five years before; the radio mast at High Point was even detailed as a sort of Constructivist, high-tension sculpture. Perhaps the aeroplane imagery of the plan incorporates something of the notion of a social engine of the future. But along with those references from the machine-age imagery of the twenties, there was a Classical quality as well. The distinction of 'areas served' and 'circulation' by means of different geometries recalls the principles of Beaux-Arts planning. Indeed the plan as a whole is a masterly exercise in the articulation of movement through a sequence of ceremonial spaces and of the control of primary and secondary axes that will stand comparison with the plan of Charles Garnier's Paris Opéra (1861–74). Once again, we have to do with a fusion of lessons learned from various earlier periods in history.

By 1935, when High Point I was completed, a number of other modern buildings had also been erected in England. Lawn Road flats Hampstead (1934) by Wells Coates – a Canadian born in Tokyo – was another collective statement (fig. 17.4). The individual flats were packed like the cabins on a ship

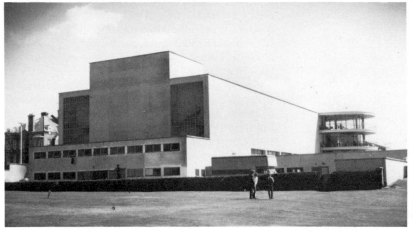

17.4 (*top*) Wells Coates, 'Isokon' flats at Lawn Road, Hampstead, London, 1934.

17.5 (*centre*) Erich Mendelsohn and Serge Chermayeff, Bexhill Pavilion, Sussex, 1934.

17.6 (*below*) Amyas Connell, Colin Lucas, Basil Ward, house at Frognal, Hampstead, London, 1938.

into a simple oblong form served by cantilevered balconies. The memories of Le Corbusier and perhaps Mendelsohn are evident (especially in the sketches with their *tracées regulateurs* and their looming, dynamic perspectives), yet the building has an authenticity of its own. In the English context Lawn Road was an emblem of a new way of life. Significantly, many of its first inmates were cosmopolitan English intellectuals of leftist opinion or such immigrants from the continent as Mondrian, Gropius and Breuer. Gropius set up a partnership with Maxwell Fry, Breuer with F. R. S. Yorke, but it would be wrong to see their influence as anything other than an encouragement for a movement which had its own momentum.

Erich Mendelsohn also arrived in England in 1934 to escape Nazi persecution, and, in partnership with Serge Chermayeff, immediately won the competition for the De La Warr seaside pavilion at Bexhill in Sussex (fig. 17.5). This was to be a place for public entertainment of the usual south coast resort type, with a theatre/cinema, bars, a cafeteria, some offices, a bandstand, and a swimming pool (later abandoned). The site was on the edge of the English Channel with south exposure and long views. The scheme was close, programmatically, to some of the buildings Mendelsohn had designed in Berlin in the twenties, such as cinemas, bars and canteens; he therefore felt free to experiment formally, and his early sketches show a sort of looming dynamic structure, fully fenestrated to give views over the sea. Even the rectilinear final building has the quality of dynamism of the First World War sketches (fig. 9.5), a quality which upset 'functionalist' prigs who detected what they called 'formalism'.

Although the overall conception came about in organic, freely expressive sketches, the layout of the plan shows careful logic. The theatre/cinema was treated as a major entity and allowed to take up the whole west end of the building; its axial symmetry, and the fact that it scarcely needed daylight made its exterior treatment as a closed, rectangular box appropriate. The bar, restaurant and cafeteria functions were grouped to the other end of the building on a long strip and given wide horizontal windows by means of concrete cantilevered terraces and a 'free façade'. These two main zones were linked by a hallway running between them, which also served to link the town and the sea. This element was demonstrated on the exterior by means of curved glass projections at each end. The one on the sea side was a *tour de force* in concrete, with stairs spiralling up inside a glazed semi-cylinder linking the whole height of the building, and the main light-fixture treated as an abstract sculpture suspended at the centre.

Public commissions on this scale were rare for

modern architects in England during the thirties, and many of them had to be content with designing small houses which took on the significance of experiments for some hoped-for future collective programme. The partnership of Lucas, Connell and Ward (an Englishman and two New Zealanders) developed a style of their own on the basis of Dutch, French, and Russian precedents, in which solids and voids were juxtaposed in strong contrasts, and reinforced-concrete construction was adapted to the unique demands of clients and sites. Thus 'New Farm' at Grayswood (1932) was splayed in plan, in an attempt to maximize views and to link it to the landscape, while the house in Frognal of 1938 (fig. 17.6) was more sedate, and combined the formality of an urban façade with informality to the rear, where a terrace and full-length glazing allowed a link with the garden. The model for this building was probably Le Corbusier's Villa Stein at Garches, and it is interesting to compare the force of a major prototype with a much softened, but creditable adaptation. The house at Frognal included brick because a local planning authority had insisted on some reference to typical local materials.

Indeed, 'modern' buildings were often regarded with suspicion in England. In their design for a small house in the Sussex countryside of 1935, Lucas, Connell and Ward were presented by the local council with the option of either using a pitched roof and retaining their intended white walls, or a flat roof, but employing wooden cladding. They chose the second option. To compare Lubetkin's design for a bungalow at Whipsnade, with its curved aerofoil forms and its tight discipline, to the house at Frognal and, say, Breuer's and Yorke's house at Angmering of 1936, is to be impressed by the great variety of expression being worked out within the inherited forms of the International Style. At the same time it is to be made aware how far the imported foreign ideas were from prevalent English notions of 'the home'.

Two of the most remarkable buildings of the modern movement in England served commercial purposes: Boots Warehouse at Beeston by Owen Williams of 1930–32 (fig. 17.7) and Peter Jones's Store in Sloane Square, London, by Slater, Moberly, Reilly and Crabtree of 1936. Both were clad in glass curtain walls, and both used a concrete-skeleton construction to open up wide spaces on the interior, and to create unobstructed voids where outside and inside met at ground level. These were used as loading bays for packing and unpacking drugs in the Boots case; and as uninterrupted shop windows for the display of merchandise in Peter Jones. There the similarities ended, for the Boots building had an assertive, even brutal character, quite in contrast to the elegantly proportioned mullions and urbanity of Peter Jones.

17.7 Owen Williams, Boots Warehouse, Beeston, Nottinghamshire, 1930–2.

Owen Williams was an engineer with a remarkable tectonic sensibility: his building had mushroom columns holding it up, which were perfectly suited to their purpose, as they created wider spans and allowed movement of goods around them. The central space of the Boots warehouse was a sort of nave interrupted by cross-galleries and top-lit by a thin glass brick and concrete membrane roof. The effect was tough but ennobling, a quality which understandably endeared it to the so-called 'New Brutalists' of the 1950s.

By the end of the thirties, some of the avant-garde were beginning to labour and stretch inside the strait-jacket of the International Style; they were perhaps sensing its limitations visually and perhaps intuiting its foreignness, ideologically, to the English scene. The most outstanding case of the pursuit of more overtly formal values was Lubetkin's High Point II of 1936–8, designed to go alongside High Point I (fig. 17.8). Admittedly there were unusual constraints on the design (including a hostile local planning authority), but these do not account for the almost neo-Palladian façade composition; a plastic expressiveness in the overall form which reminds one of Lubetkin's admiration for the Baroque; the rich textural effect of a variety of materials; and the use of Classical caryatids on the canopy. Here there was obvious, and indeed rather decorative, wilful aesthetic experimentation – what the critic J. M. Richards might have called 'celebrity architecture' in contrast to a hoped for 'anonymous' modern vernacular. Lubetkin was

expressing yearnings for the Grand Architectural tradition, and reacting, perhaps, to the greater complexity of texture and material in Le Corbusier's works of the early thirties. The *Architectural Review* assessed High Point II as 'an important move forward from functionalism'; but the Puritan left-wing element who espoused the utilitarian and moral qualities of modern architecture, and played down its aesthetic aspects, were outraged. This is how Anthony Cox, a young socialist architect, criticized High Point II:

Standing in the garden and looking up at the two blocks, 1935 and 1938, it is clear that something has changed, and that the change is not merely due to the higher level of building technique, or to the use of a smooth, clean tile facing to the concrete. . . . It is as if during the three years that separate the buildings, rigid conclusions have been reached as to what is formally necessary in architecture. This tendency towards certain formal conclusions, that are very near clichés, is noticeable in the work of many modern English architects, but in Tecton's later work it is more than a tendency. It is considerably marked and mature. . . . The change in aim must be due to personal reasons, to a turning inwards towards private formal meanings which have no general recognizable social basis . . . Is it really an 'important move forward from functionalism' from which development is possible; or is it a symptom of decline, an end in itself?

17.8 Berthold Lubetkin and Tecton, High Point II flats seen alongside High Point I from the garden, 1936–8.

It is ironical that the criteria by which Lubetkin was here being judged were ones that he may himself have introduced into the English architectural world. However, there is some truth in Cox's assessment. High Point II has a flaccid elegance in contrast to the taut, sharp-edged polemic of the earlier building. Perhaps Lubetkin was beginning to sense the divergence between his own socialist aims, and the values of the only clientele who would or indeed could put up his buildings. Or perhaps a tendency to formalism is inevitable at a certain stage in working out the implications of a style. However one sees it, the 'formalism' of High Point II was symptomatic of a much broader problem: given that mere imitations of the prototypes of the twenties would be inadequate, what direction should the modern movement now take? Given that a sort of modern academicism was to be avoided, where would sources of a new vitality lie?

The work of Alvar Aalto during the thirties provides one example of these problems being solved with full conviction, and with due response to regional climate and traditions. Aalto was born in 1898 in Finland, studied in Helsinki, and grew up in an atmosphere fraught with questions of national identity for the Finns seeking autonomy from the Russian sphere of influence. Broadly speaking there were two main strands in the 'high' architectural culture of the late nineteenth century which influenced Aalto: a stripped Classical style stemming from certain late eighteenth-century sources and coming to a refined twentieth-

century resolution in the works of Gunnar Asplund; and a National Romantic tendency which drew on the Gothic revival and on the nineteenth-century American architect, H. H. Richardson, while seeking inspiration in national myths and local vernaculars. Aalto would eventually succeed, with the help of modern architectural abstraction, in forging a synthesis between these inherited tendencies. And in that respect the true vernacular (rather than romantic interpretations of it) was a crucial trigger, as it gave evidence of type forms adapted to the stringencies of the Finnish climate, to the character of the landscape, and to the outlook of the people. At the same time, of course, it bore witness to a direct and elegant use of local materials, particularly timber.

The modern movement began to seep into Scandinavia only gradually in the twenties. By 1931 the Stockholm Exhibition buildings, designed by Asplund, were in the new style. However, Aalto and his compatriot Erik Bryggman encountered the new ideas a little earlier than this, especially through Dutch and German examples. Aalto's Turku Sanomat newspaper building (for which design began in 1928) was conceived in the terminology of the new architecture, was based on the 'five points of a new architecture', and in its plastic accentuation of structure (fig. 17.9), its variation of space, and the disciplined articulation of the façade even suggested the imprint of a vital new talent on received canons. Aalto's gradual growth from his neo-classical beginnings to the clarity of his 'functional' style, can be seen clearly in the evolution of three main projects for the Viipuri library between 1927 and 1935. But while he rejected overt usage of the Classical orders, he still retained abstract schemata from the Classical tradition (e.g., the frequent use of a *piano nobile*, a processional character in circulation, a refined sense of proportion in the placement of voids and solids). The library plan employs ingenious shifting symmetries, and its internal volumes flow into one another under a ceiling formed of gradually stepping planes perforated by skylights. Such rich modulations of space and light are enhanced, in the meeting room, by the curved and textured wooden roof (fig. 17.10), which gives some hint of the naturalism of Aalto's later development. The character of the building was such as to suggest already the rejection of mechanistic qualities in earlier modern architecture; moreover, the functional discipline of the work was bound up with a poetic reaction to human needs rather than with arid calculation.

In the design of the Paimio Sanatorium (1929–32), Aalto gave body to his 'humanist' aspirations in a work which must be counted one of the masterpieces of the modern movement (fig. 17.11). The building stands on high ground twenty miles from Helsinki, overlooking forests and lakes. At the time it was built, the best cure for tuberculosis (the Sanatorium was to specialize in the cure of this disease) was felt to be exposure to sun, fresh air, and greenery. This was one of these cases where the aims of the client and the 'sanitary' philosophical and visual aspects of the new style were in accord from the beginning. The patients' rooms were placed in a long six-storey slab facing south, served by corridors running along the north side, and with an open roof terrace, part covered by a canopy, on the top floor; the beds could be wheeled here on particularly warm days. The structure of this part of the building was a tapered concrete 'trunk' from which the floors were cantilevered, thus allowing the openness of façades and freedom of circulation. The mono-material character of this wing was accentuated by curved details and a sculptural sense of volume, which belied the more cardboard qualities of certain other buildings in the International Style.

Behind the slab were grouped the 'serving' elements of the hallway, the doctors' wing and lounge, and the nurses' wing. Each function was expressed in a slightly different form, and angled to the topography of the site (fig. 17.12). The effect on approaching the building was that the slab and the lounge block funnelled one towards the entrance. Variations in fenestration and detail ensured that the main divisions in the form were articulated throughout. Rising like a well-proportioned ship above the Finnish landscape, the Sanatorium announced its healing function through

clean forms, tidy proportions, and well-lit volumes. At the same time, its horizontal balconies and garden terracing supplied links to the surrounding landmasses.

It has been convincingly argued that the Paimio Sanatorium was modelled, in part, on Duiker's Zonnestraal Sanatorium of 1927, outside Hilversum (fig. 13.5), a building in which the various functions were also splayed in different directions on a wooded site. Moreover, there are particular details, like the extractor stack of the Zonnestraal, which have been reworked by Aalto. Equally, it might be argued that he was drawing on the formula for collective dwellings

17.9 (*top*) Alvar Aalto, Turku Sanomat Newspaper Office, Turku, Finland, 1928–30.

17.10 Alvar Aalto, Viipuri Library, Finland, 1927–35, interior view of meeting room showing sinuous wooden ceiling.

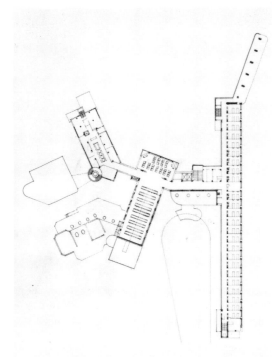

17.11 (*above right*) Alvar Aalto, Paimio Sanatorium, Finland, 1929–32.

17.12 (*right*) Alvar Aalto, Paimio Sanatorium, Finland, 1929–32, plan of ensemble.

evolved a couple of years earlier in the Soviet Union; in those buildings individual rooms were placed in a slab, and collective functions were grouped in ancillary volumes of different geometry or form. It has been suggested already that such a formulation may have influenced Le Corbusier's Pavillon Suisse as well: in both the student hostel and the tuberculosis sanatorium, forms were found which extended the vocabulary of earlier modern architecture into new, and more complex, formal territory.

In 1933 Aalto went to the CIAM meeting on the SS Patras. Here, against the setting of the Greek islands, the Parthenon, and the sea, he met Le Corbusier, Mies van der Rohe, Walter Gropius – indeed the protagonists of modern architecture; and they in turn were impressed by a newly emergent talent. At home it had been possible by degrees to convert patrons to an understanding of the new architecture, a process which had not been easy. However, between 1934 and the outbreak of the war, Aalto was kept busy with the large commission for the Sunila pulp mills (including worker's housing) and with entries to a variety of competitions, including one for the Finnish embassy in Moscow. In 1936 he designed a house for himself and his wife outside Helsinki which made use of local materials like brick and wood, contrasting textures and subtle curves; plants and natural materials were integrated in a statement that was more humanly tactile than the white concrete forms of five years earlier. The transition has been called the shift to 'Romantic Modernism'; but whatever one calls it, it was a style which was increasingly personal, and in which a more accommodating relationship to both the Finnish vernacular tradition and the regional demands of climate and landscape were worked out. Aalto was later to write:

> Architecture cannot disengage itself from natural and human factors, on the contrary, it must never do so. . . . Its function rather is to bring nature ever closer to us.

Perhaps the masterpiece of this phase in Aalto's development was the Villa Mairea of 1938, built for Maire and Harry Gullichsen as a sort of villa, guest-house, and rural retreat (fig. 17.13). His clients were immensely wealthy and told their architect that 'he should regard it as an experimental house'. Aalto seems to have treated this as an opportunity to pull together many of the themes which had been preoccupying him in the preceding years, but which he had not always been able to introduce in actual buildings; in much the same way, Le Corbusier had taken the opportunity offered him by a well-to-do client to condense his driving preoccupations in the Villa Savoye.

The plan of the Villa Mairea is a modified L-shape of the kind Aalto had used frequently before, and would use often again (fig. 17.14). It was a layout which automatically created a semi-private enclosure to one side, and a more exclusive, formal edge to confront the public world on the other. It is possible that the architect's fascination with these 'semi-courtyards' may have been partially inspired by typical Finnish farm layouts, where a similar form was used to protect livestock from the rigours of winter, and to define an inward-looking community. In the Villa Mairea the lawn and the swimming pool were situated in the enclosure, alongside a variety of rooms looking over them; indeed, these outdoor features were integrated into the composition by careful placement, and through the use of horizontals and overhangs in the main composition. The pool was kidney-shaped, and wedded with the nearby semi-wooded topography as well. In contrast to these softening characteristics, the main façade had a more rigid, formal mood, and even possessed a sort of Classical *porte-cochère* restated in a garden pergola vocabulary.

The interiors of the Villa were richly furnished in natural woods and stonework and brick, and varied in spatial quality from the grand to the cabin-like.

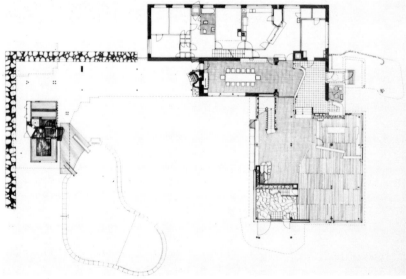

Sequences were orchestrated to make the most of different views and lighting effects, and there was a hierarchy to the rooms, which culminated in the master bedroom, standing at the pinnacle of the house overlooking the little enclosure below. The spaces below this – the library, dining-room, sitting-room,

studio (for Maire's painting) and art gallery – varied in height and were even overlapping in section, recalling spatial devices discovered in the Viipuri library, for example. To one end the house descended to a sort of 'rustic' wing, which wrapped around two sides of the swimming pool and contained the sauna. This wing alone was emblematic of Aalto's increasingly 'naturalistic' concerns: it was a wooden palisade with an overhanging flat roof surmounted by a ragged band of turf (fig. 17.15). The spirit of this primitivist, Nordic garden temple brooding next to a dark pool of water surrounded by boulders could not be further from the pristine solarium of the Villa Savoye, with its Mediterranean evocations and its crisp, machine-age imagery. But in details like these, each architect managed to condense an entire world outlook, and to indicate his ability to transform the rituals of upper-middle-class existence into the stuff of a lasting architectural dream.

Indeed, the Villa Mairea is the condensation of so many ideas that it is tempting to see it as the pivotal building for Aalto in which, so to say, he sloughed off the last inherited skin, and revealed his true nature. The formal disciplines of Classicism, the philosophy

and form of the International Modern movement, and the perennial lessons of a regional vernacular all contributed to the synthesis, but it was a fusion which utterly transformed its sources. After the Villa Mairea, the style was assured at a deep level: variation seemed to occur on the basis of a few fundamental themes and forms, capable of apparently endless combinations and meanings. The result was a style deeply related to ideas about the human condition, in which weathered materials, lyrical spaces, and magical effects of light produced a lasting primal poetry far beyond merely 'modern' concerns.

Aalto's Villa Mairea is a fitting place to begin to close the second part of this book because it is a building which rests on the discoveries of the early modern movement, yet transcends them. This was, indeed, 'an important move forward from functionalism' and not simply a relapse into decorative formalism. It was to examples like this that a post-war generation could turn, in their own attempt to break with the increasingly restrictive bondage of modern formulae and in their own quest for an authentic architecture blending internationalist and regionalist, modern and ancient concerns.

18. The Continuity of Older Traditions

... after all, architecture is an art and from time immemorial it has been regarded as one of the greatest. Beautiful buildings, the Parthenon for instance, the Pantheon, Chartres or St. Paul's have moved men more profoundly than any but the very greatest masterpieces of painting and sculpture; but who is going to be moved, except to resentment, by buildings such as Herr Mendelsohn produces in Germany or M. Le Corbusier in France, or by buildings of steel and brick that purport to be made of concrete, buildings cased in steel and glass, buildings that appear to follow no principle but that of contradicting everything that has ever been done before? I suggest that our modernists are wrong in principle.

R. Blomfield, 1932

The early historians and propagandists of modern architecture tended to portray it as the single true style of the times and to relegate deviants to a historical dustbin. While this historiographical exercise undoubtedly had a useful purgative function, it conveyed an extremely lopsided historical picture and encouraged a partisan view of architectural quality. In its early days the modern movement, like any other young movement, was in a minority. The majority of buildings constructed in, say, the year 1930 were continuations of earlier traditions and vernaculars. It is useful to be reminded of this pluralist background in considering the very significance of avant-garde production. Furthermore, the determinist slant of the aforementioned writers tended to leave the impression that a building which failed to ally itself to new tendencies must be inferior. But the fact that a building might be a transformation of Gothic forms (e.g., the Hood design for the *Chicago Tribune*) did not guarantee its inferiority any more than the use of the new style guaranteed quality. It has to be said, at this juncture, that writers who were opposed to modern architecture sometimes adapted counterpart tactics by automatically opposing anything new.

While modern architects as diverse as Wright, Le Corbusier, Mies van der Rohe and Aalto sought to express contemporary life and new spatial ideas, and threw off the garments of the nineteenth-century 'styles' in order to crystallize their version of the fundamentals of 'style' in general, they were deeply rooted in tradition. The distinction between 'modernists' and 'traditionalists' can therefore be overstressed.

I do not believe that it is being over-sophisticated to suggest that the outstanding works of modern architecture transcended period concerns, and became close relatives of other outstanding buildings of the past which had, likewise, cut far deeper than the changing trends of their own times.

Be this as it may, the obvious still has to be stated: the Villa Savoye and the Bauhaus buildings did not employ Classical orders, arches, or rib vaults! They were part of the same general grouping in ways that the Chrysler building by Van Alen or Edwin Lutyens's designs for New Delhi were not. At the time the modern movement first emerged, its differences from other architecture were far more easily identified than its similarities. It was clear that this was something new and that its anatomy was in profound ways different from that of predecessors; it was not simply a change of clothes. Moreover, 'the moderns' eventually won in the sense that their schemata were the ones generally adopted around the world. It was no divine law of progress that brought this about; rather (as we have begun to see) the reasons for adopting the new forms over pre-existing traditions varied considerably from place to place. Whatever the lasting qualities of some buildings within these pre-existing traditions, their formulations seemed less and less relevant to the next few generations. Such perhaps is the picture after any major revolution in sensibility, which the modern movement certainly was.

Another effect of treating the history of modern architecture as a sort of conveyor belt (as the early mythographers tended to), was that 'survivals' from

18.1 Auguste Perret, Church of Notre Dame du Raincy, 1924, view of nave.

earlier 'pioneer' phases also tended to be relegated. Art Nouveau, for example, was a temporary phase for such individuals as Behrens and Le Corbusier, but its effects lingered on well into the twenties in places as varied as Majorca and Buenos Aires. A major artist like Gaudí was still extending his personal manner up to the time of his death in 1926. It is wrong then to pin a style to a particular 'historical moment'. Rather, a variety of options of expression remained open and were often continued with conviction. After all, Auguste Perret continued his pre-war manner with little impact from, and in parallel with, the seminal works of the 'white architecture of the twenties'. The church of Notre Dame du Raincy of 1924 (fig. 18.1) was even the logical culmination of all that Perret had been pursuing for reinforced concrete for the previous three decades.

Another major omission in the early historiography of the modern movement was 'Expressionism', because the extreme bizarreness and emotionalism underlying some works labelled by this term were at odds with the personal taste of men like Pevsner, Giedion, and Hitchcock, and because the inherent belief of these writers in a unifying *Zeitgeist* at the core of modern culture left them looking for a single 'true' modern style. The Einstein tower by Mendelsohn was something of an embarrassment in this scheme of things, while a curious creation like the theosophically inspired Goetheanum at Dornach of 1925–8 (fig. 18.2) simply had to be left out of the account altogether. This was despite the fact that both buildings were inspired by revolutionary conceptions and were certainly capable of standing alongside much that was within the safer, supposedly more 'rational' pale of the 'International Style'. Here again historians showed how easily they could be influenced by the prejudices of artists, for many of the architects who were 'safe' had passed through Expressionism and rejected it as a sort of juvenile phase before their mature flowering.

There can be little doubt in retrospect that Expressionism was an extension of certain basic qualities of Art Nouveau. However, there were other strands which stemmed from the same source, in particular the manner of design called 'Art Deco' after its appearance at the Exposition des Arts Décoratifs in 1925. This loose affiliation of exotic and highly decorative tendencies was quite at odds with the fundamentalism and rigorous moral tenor of the New Architecture, but it nonetheless reached its full (and brief) efflorescence at about the same time. In the decorative arts one thinks of the glass-work of Lalique, or of evocative, spangled interiors in which neo-Egyptian motifs, chevron geometries, and luxuriant indulgence in lustrous materials played a part. 'Art Deco' scarcely presents a coherent stylistic entity, and

18.2 Rudolf Steiner, Goetheanum II, Dornach, 1925–8.

it has to be admitted that there was little of lasting architectural value in it; nonetheless, buildings of considerable richness like the Richfield building in Los Angeles of 1928 or the Hoover factory in London of 1935 (fig. 18.3) (not to mention the Chrysler building in New York) were all related to Art Deco trends. In each of these cases, an inherited armature of Beaux-Arts axial planning was cloaked in modern materials and elaborately decorated and coloured wall surfaces. The attitude behind such forms was far indeed from the ideals of dematerialization, 'honesty' and puritanism, which were inherent in the smooth white planes and stark surfaces of the International Style. Ornament was embraced and elaborated in gaudy stripes and violent contrasts of texture; and the style was frequently and blatantly employed in the service of commercial advertising – to attract, to delight, and to persuade. There was a notable lack of that cultural high-mindedness with regard to industrialism which had propelled the more profound thinkers of the modern movement. Art Deco served as a middle-brow bridge between modernism and consumerism. This was also true of the 'Streamlined Moderne' style prevalent in industrial design in the United States in the late twenties and early thirties (fig. 18.4). The market laws of obsolescence and fashion were here met with less anguish than in the moral positions of the modern mainstream.

This leads to a further point about the modern movement which, possibly, applies to many novel systems of forms: for a time it remained beyond the grasp of public understanding and sympathy. Although it had been a central underlying doctrine that the architect was somehow specially endowed

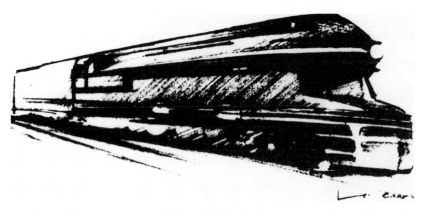

18.3 (*top*) Wallis, Gilbert and Partners, Hoover factory, Perivale, Middlesex, 1932–5.

18.4 Raymond Loewy, sketch for streamlined train, 1930.

with the ability to intuit communal aspirations, the majority taste remained allied to more traditional modes, and more customary associations. Perhaps this problem of communication was further exacerbated by the very position of avant-garde culture with its haughty disdain for the clichéd and the conventional. It is perhaps understandable that the juries of the *Chicago Tribune*, the League of Nations, and even the Palace of the Soviets competitions voted the way they did. Part of the problem was a lack of understanding about how the new forms could possibly convey generally held beliefs.

The point is made in another less grandiose field of design: the family home. The new domestic architecture tended to become the cultural property of either isolated pockets of upper-middle-class bohemia, or else of large-scale planning bureaucracies of a progressivist outlook. The taste of 'everyman' in the twenties tended to be more at home with images derived from the Arts and Crafts movement, which had itself been based on time-worn notions of the dwelling. The extreme Nazi criticisms of the factory appearance and lack of psychological warmth in modern architecture were not so very far away from complaints which might have been delivered by many decent home owners in the West at the same time. Far from being perceived as elements of a new universal language of design, the creations stemming from the Bauhaus or from Purism were as likely to be seen as emblems of a highbrow clique. It was to take over two decades for the imagery of 'the modern' to become popularized and, so to say, vernacularized; and, of course, once this had happened much of the original meaning and polemical impulse had been lost. Perhaps a confusion of this sort was inevitable, given avant-garde premisses: obsessed with the idea that a major decay was in process, the avant-garde thought it was its business to rescue the values of higher forms and to instate new prototypes. Divorce from conventions was intrinsic to this process.

In the majority of Western European countries, the United States and the Soviet Union, the 'official tastes' against which the avant-garde launched some of its battles tended to derive from nineteenth-century eclecticism. As we have seen in the case of skyscraper design in the United States, the hotchpotch of styles was actually capable of supporting a broad range of associations and meanings. It is intriguing to reflect that in 1929, the year the Villa Savoye was designed in Paris, major collegiate construction in the United States was still fully committed to neo-Georgian (fig. 18.5) and neo-Gothic modes. To the avant-garde, of course, this seemed like further evidence of retrogressive sentimentalism; however, in a situation

the broad resurgence of neo-classicism which occurred in the West during the 1930s. Presumably, too, a representative coverage would concern itself with the many exported eclectic 'colonial' styles which proliferated in countries whose official culture was imported or imposed. However, the aims of this book are a little different, so it is necessary to single out a few key examples of 'traditions other than the modern', in an attempt to explain why 'historical' forms were employed, and to what effect.

One context in which traditional attitudes lived on was the design of state monuments and memorials. A case in point was the Lincoln Memorial in Washington, D.C., designed in 1911 by Henry Bacon, and completed in 1922 (fig. 18.6). The forms of Bacon's solution were inconceivable without the pre-existing tradition of Beaux-Arts Classicism within the United States, stemming from R. M. Hunt and R. F. McKim. However, the pre-existing neo-classical context of Washington – not to mention various moral associations attached to Classical forms within the American tradition – also have to be taken into account. The idea for a memorial to Lincoln had first been formulated soon after his death, but it was only in the twentieth century that debates were set in motion over a site and an architect. The former was chosen

18.5 (*left*) Shepley, Bulfinch, Coolidge and Abbott. Memorial Church, Harvard University, Cambridge, Mass., 1929–33.

18.6 (*below*) Henry Bacon, Lincoln Memorial, Washington D.C., 1911–22. The Washington Memorial obelisk and Capitol dome are in the background.

where modern forms were not even known, this was scarcely fair criticism. Even if modern architecture had been known, it is doubtful that it would have been employed in a context where associations with past learning and with tradition were sought. The same was often true of major civic monuments and of churches, tasks which virtually demanded continuity of symbolism, rather than a radical break. In domestic architecture in the United States between the wars, some of the same regionalist currents we have sensed in Europe as counterforces to internationalism also ran strong; it was highly misleading of the early apostles of modernism to have condemned traditional tendencies across the board. It would have been more sensible to have considered the unique symbolic purposes required in a particular context and to have enquired what forms were most likely to fulfil these functions. The fact was that 'modern' forms were better able to handle some contexts, and 'traditional' forms to handle others.

Were this a book on the architecture of the entire twentieth century, instead of a study of the traditions of modern architecture in their cultural setting, it would be necessary to devote a number of chapters to such phenomena as the continuation of the Gothic revival well into the thirties in the United States, and

18.7 Edwin Lutyens, Viceroy's House, New Delhi, 1915–24.

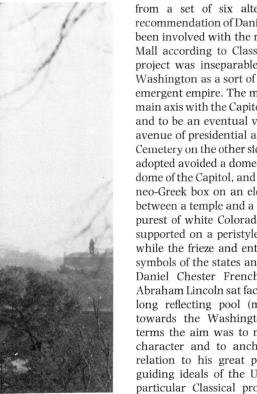

from a set of six alternatives, the latter on the recommendation of Daniel Burnham, who had already been involved with the replanning of the Washington Mall according to Classical planning principles. The project was inseparable in this era from a sense of Washington as a sort of new Rome at the centre of an emergent empire. The monument had to stand on the main axis with the Capitol and the Washington Obelisk and to be an eventual visual link between this grand avenue of presidential associations and the Arlington Cemetery on the other side of the Potomac. The scheme adopted avoided a dome, so as not to distract from the dome of the Capitol, and was a low, horizontal, elegant neo-Greek box on an elevated mound. It was a cross between a temple and a tomb, and was made from the purest of white Colorado marbles. The low attic was supported on a peristyle of sharp-cut Doric columns, while the frieze and entablature were engraved with symbols of the states and their unity. On the interior, Daniel Chester French's sculpture of the seated Abraham Lincoln sat facing down the main axis over a long reflecting pool (modelled on the Taj Mahal) towards the Washington Monument. In symbolic terms the aim was to mirror the purity of Lincoln's character and to anchor his historical position in relation to his great predecessors and *vis-à-vis* the guiding ideals of the Union. The synthesis of these particular Classical prototypes fitted no simple or-

thodox procedure; but the fusion had architectural value nonetheless. It is intriguing to speculate how this building could have handled this range of evocations and emotions without the references to Classical antiquity and to American re-uses of Classicism of the previous century and a half. As will be shown in the final section of this book, the modern movement had eventually to solve analogous rhetorical problems by turning back to ancient precedents, but without such obvious re-use of historical vocabulary.

Another example of the intelligent abstraction of precedent is provided by Edwin Lutyens's designs for the Viceroy's House at New Delhi of 1915–24 (fig. 18.7). The pejorative associations attached to the term 'eclectic' would simply be insulting in this instance. Once again, the issue unfolds around the ability of the inventor to fuse a new order out of inherited forms, and to imply a new range of meanings for a new context. The symbolic task in this case was nothing less than the authentication of the authority of the British Raj. Lutyens drew upon a range of imperial associations and symbols within both European and Classical traditions to achieve the right tone. The Viceroy's House was placed at the end of a three-mile axis in a manner resonating with evocations of such Baroque prototypes as Versailles, Blenheim, and Greenwich Hospital. The dome over the main axis was a curious hybrid of Classical and Mogul emblems of authority

18.8 (*left*) P. V. Jensen-Klint, Grundtvig Church, Copenhagen, 1922.

18.9 (*right*) Erick Gunnar Asplund, Stockholm Public Library, 1920–28.

which also seemed to return to the (perhaps proto-typical) image of a 'head'. The roofscapes with their inverted basins and deep-cut overhangs were also derived from such sources as the 'Chattris' of Fathepur Sikri (late sixteenth century). The articulation with bases and horizontal mouldings was itself a fusion of Classical proportions and climatic and structural devices nearer at hand. What stopped the whole from being a mere assemblage of quotations was the way that Lutyens was able to grasp the principles of earlier styles and to blend them with his own imaginative intentions and private metaphors. The fusion of old and new relied upon a feat of abstraction and a capacity to generate expressive forms in a new context: the critical issue at stake was less the distinction between 'modernist' and 'traditionalist' positions than between authentic form and pastiche.

Another example of the successful synthesis of past prototypes and new meanings is provided by the Grundtvig Church outside Copenhagen, by P. V. Jensen-Klint (fig. 18.8). This was originally designed just before the First World War, but it was brought to completion in the early twenties. Here the sources were medieval. The design was based on a generic form of ecclesiastical architecture prevalent in Zeeland using stepped gable ends and vertical brick-beading. Such indigenous motifs were transformed into a language of sharp geometries, over a plan that was also a variant on a traditional type. Jensen-Klint's solution was clearly influenced by so-called 'National Roman-tic' attitudes, which required that one draw upon national traditions and define images essentially linked to a particular culture and landscape. According to the standard critical views of modernism, this procedure should have been destined to reproduce a 'dead' formula; but Jensen-Klint was able to breathe new life into forms which were nonetheless heavily influenced by earlier definitions of religious types.

A similar point can be made about another Scandinavian example: the Stockholm Public Library by Gunnar Asplund of 1920–28 (fig. 18.9). Here the solution was clearly modelled on a cluster of themes derived from neo-classicism and the nineteenth-century tradition of library design. The reading-room was set upon a round plan and expressed as a centralized cylinder poking up through a rectangular box. It was a formula with numerous antecedents including, ultimately, the stripped geometrical vocabu-lary of the French eighteenth-century architect Claude Nicolas Ledoux. Had Asplund been a lesser architect, he might have produced a mere pastiche. As it was, he was able to reinvigorate earlier forms with his own expressive intentions and metaphors. The suggestion has even been made that Asplund's vocabulary rested on a sort of substructure of physiological imagery. In

the case of the library the original section emerged from a sort of reconstituted cranium – presumably an idea the architect felt appropriate to the function. He rejected the clothing of neo-classicism only a year or two after completing the library, when he adopted the usages of the International Style at the Stockholm exhibition, but his underlying metaphors and formal strategies did not change drastically. In the Stockholm Crematorium (1939) Asplund drove together his earlier neo-classicism and the stripped forms and spatial ideas he had worked out from the International Modern movement (fig. 18.10). The main portico was a superbly disciplined abstraction of load and support, while the plan was a rich combination of open, flowing spaces and closed compartments. Again, it is arguable that the design contained hermetic imagery linked, in this instance, to themes of life and death.

France and England were generally less fortunate than this in their 'traditionalist' architects in the period from around 1910 to 1940. P.-H. Nénot, for example (mentioned in Chapter 13 in connection with the League of Nations), was fully endowed with all the scholarly trappings of Beaux-Arts respectibility, but lacked a gift for original synthesis. The same may be said of the English architect Reginald Blomfield, who was one of a number of exponents of the stylish importation of Beaux-Arts Classicism from France around 1910. His extensive façades on Regent Street of 1922 (fig. 18.11), for instance, were uninspired reworkings of motifs derived from Palladio and Sansovino. One can understand, on inspection, why a younger generation felt the need for change; it is even arguable that Perret, Behrens and Wright (in one generation), Le Corbusier, Mies van der Rohe and Aalto (in another), had a deeper insight into the essentials of Classicism than their learned counterparts who made a more overt reference to the past. The Unity Temple, for example, reflected a far more profound rethinking of architectural basics than anything produced at the same time by a revivalist.

Even so, Blomfield became one of the leading spokesmen of the 'traditionalist' position. In a debate which took place in 1932 between himself and Amyas Connell, Blomfield claimed that the new architecture was bound to end up in barbarism because of its stress on function and its lack of concern with the great lessons of the past.

I part company with the modernists, not for their dismissal of Gothic tracery and Classical orders or meaningless ornament, or for their use of steel and reinforced concrete or any other material suitable for building, but because they insist on our regarding architecture, no longer as an art, but only as a branch of engineering.

18.10 Erik Gunnar Asplund, crematorium at Enskede, Stockholm, 1939.

Against this Blomfield set the position of the 'traditionalist' (which he was better able to convey in words
than in his own architecture):

> ... civilisation is far too old and complicated for a
> clean sweep. It runs back for thousands of years,
> and in all those years man has been building up
> certain instinctive preferences or prejudices, if you
> like, which lie at the back of consciousness. They
> may be stamped out for a time, but they will
> inevitably play their part again ...

One suspects that if Blomfield had spent less time
taking the slogans of 'functionalism' literally, and
more time examining actual works of modern architecture, he might have understood that his position
was not so drastically opposed to 'modern' architects
as he imagined. After all, one of the main messages of
Vers une architecture had been that one should return to
the great signposts of the Classical past in order to
resolve the problem of a modern architecture. The
difference between Le Corbusier and Blomfield lay, of
course, not only in the divergence of their respective
talents, but also in their attitude to the contemporary
world. Le Corbusier might have argued that the *only*
way to use the lessons of the past fruitfully was to
rethink them in terms of the present; Blomfield, on the

other hand, put forth the Academic position, which
was liable to lead to sterility, as there was insufficient
transformation of precedent.

The Connell/Blomfield debate was by no means an
isolated instance of a sort of caricaturing of both
'modernist' and 'traditionalist' outlooks; numerous
versions of the same discussion occurred in the 1920s
and 1930s. Unfortunately this polemical atmosphere
did little to clarify the true relationship between
modern architecture and the past. The matter was
scarcely helped by the early mythographers of the
modern movement, Hitchcock, Pevsner and Giedion
(whose seminal works appeared in 1932, 1936 and
1941 respectively), as these lent extra weight to the
notion that the new architecture was indeed altogether new. This attitude was entirely understandable given the historical context and, in a sense, it
became the official line; it was bequeathed to the
generation who came to the fore after the Second
World War. Their upbringing occurred under the
mantle of a new tradition whose slogans of modernity
they understood, but whose subtleties with respect to
tradition they failed to grasp. The way to the more
distant past was therefore temporarily barred by
lopsided dogma. Thus historians, who had played such
a crucial role in the very invention of the idea of a
modern architecture, continued to influence its
development by the promulgation of their myths.

1 (*left*) Charles Rennie
Mackintosh, Glasgow
School of Art, library
wing, 1908.
2 (*right*) Auguste Perret,
apartments at 25bis,
Rue Franklin, Paris,
1902, top portion of
façade.

3 (*left*) Frank Lloyd
Wright, Fricke House,
Oak Park, Illinois, 1902.
4 (*below*) Gerrit Thomas
Rietveld, Schroeder
House, Utrecht, 1923–4.
5 (*right*) William Van
Alen, Chrysler Building,
New York, 1928–30.

6 (*above*) Richard
Neutra, Lovell House,
Los Angeles, California,
1927.
7 (*left*) Le Corbusier, 'Les
Heures Claires', the Villa
Savoye, Poissy, 1928–9,
view towards ramp and
stack containing spiral
stair, at the main, first-
floor level.
8 (*right*) Frank Lloyd
Wright, Falling Water,
the Bear Run,
Pennsylvania, 1936.

9 (*left*) Ludwig Mies van der Rohe, Lake Shore Drive apartments, Chicago, 1950, view up towers showing attached 'I' beams.
10 (*above*) Le Corbusier, Parliament Building, Chandigarh, India, 1953–62.
11 (*right*) Alvar Aalto, Town Hall and civic centre, Säynätsalo, Finland, 1949–52.

12 (*left*) James Stirling, Engineering Building, Leicester University, England, 1965–7.
13 (*above*) Denys Lasdun, Royal College of Physicians, Regents Park, London, 1960.
14 (*right*) Luis Barragán, own house in Mexico City, 1948.

15 (*left*) Rafael Moneo,
Museo de Arte Romano,
Merida, Spain, 1981–5.
16 (*right*) Raj Rewal,
National Institute of
Immunology, New
Delhi, 1983–.

Part 3: Transformation and Dissemination after 1940

19. Modern Architecture in America: Immigration and Consolidation

> In the 1920s one was forced to do away with nineteenth-century tendencies, when one had to begin again from scratch. Today the situation is completely different. We stand at the beginning of a new tradition. One need no longer destroy what the preceding generation accomplished, but one has to expand it. . . .
>
> S. Giedion, 1955

Even now it is difficult to assess the full impact of the Second World War on architecture. Like the earlier world war, it destroyed a previous social and economic order, and to that extent eroded some of the impulses which had brought modern architecture into existence. It discredited technology with the avant-garde and so disrupted a key element in an earlier Utopia, and brought with it a severe physical and cultural destruction, especially in Europe, the Soviet Union, and Japan. Rebuilding was necessary, but optimism in architectural innovation had been severely undermined. The intellectual climate varied considerably from country to country, but there was nothing to compare with the creative quest for a brave new world which had filled a certain vacuum after the First World War in Europe.

Despite radically altered circumstances, the 'new tradition' was not so easily defeated, though: all the masters of modern architecture were still alive, and so were many of their guiding ideas. There was no going back and pretending that the architectural revolution of the twenties had not occurred, no use pretending that another revolution of parallel depth was likely to happen. The architect seeking forms in the late 1940s found himself in the position of an extender of tradition. Whatever new meanings might be sought, whatever functions might need handling, whatever regional traditions might need respecting, transformation could occur only on the basis of, or in reaction to, the earlier modern movement.

It has to be stressed that creative transformation was a necessity: simply to have repeated the solutions of the inter-war period would have been to court the worst form of academicism; unfortunately, this often happened, offering a classic case of 'symbolic devaluation' and of the misapplication of prototypes. One of the striking features of the years between the end of the war and about 1960 was a battle between factions intent on a tired international formula, and factions seeking a revitalization on the basis of a new post-war state of mind. Even the 'masters' themselves were faced with the dual problem of extending their earlier discoveries and of seeking new solutions simultaneously.

Another feature of the broad picture after the war was the international 'victory' of modern architecture. From Rio de Janeiro to Sydney, from Tokyo to Beirut, the inheritance of pre-war architecture began to pop up. In part the spread of images (many of them bastardized and stereotyped) was encouraged by the internationalization of trade, with the United States supplying many of the standard emblems of 'modernization'. In part it was a matter of indigenous élites seeking a break with either earlier nineteenth-century colonial traditions, or else with earlier national or regional tendencies which they found too restrictive. In some countries – for example, England and Brazil – it was a matter of extending tentative pre-war beginnings, though the contrast between countries which had industrialized gradually and those which had done so in a single generation was dramatic. In other countries – for example, India or Australia – modern architecture had to begin from scratch. When examining the international picture it is crucial to

PREVIOUS PAGE

Louis I. Kahn, Jonas Salk Institute for Biological Studies, La Jolla, California, 1959–65, view towards sea between study rooms.

19.1 Walter Gropius, Gropius House, Lincoln, Massachusetts, 1938.

understand at what stage of maturity, and with what depth of content, modern forms first entered a local scene; then to try and gauge how the foreign body was received, rejected, or made amenable to pre-existing cultural matter.

Some of the dramas of transmigration were already being played out in the thirties. We have seen how architects as diverse as Aalto and Schindler were concerned with finding forms well attuned to local climates and patterns of life. The emigration of some of the modern masters added another dimension to the process of change. Mies van der Rohe and Walter Gropius, for example, both arrived in the United States in 1937. They brought with them mature philosophies and vocabularies, and their arrival gave immense prestige to the International Modern movement in America. However, they still entered a culture quite foreign to their original aims. They changed it, but it also changed them. Arguably, Mies van der Rohe survived the transatlantic crossing more satisfactorily than did Gropius.

Gropius left Germany in 1934, realizing that Nazism and modern architecture were irreconcilable, and spent three years in England before being invited by

Dean Hudnut of the Harvard Graduate School of Design to teach there. Soon after his arrival in Massachusetts, he built a house for himself and his wife in Lincoln (fig. 19.1), just beyond the Boston suburbs. The crisp white forms, wide openings, and free plan marked this out as a foreign, internationalist intrusion; however, there were some respectful regionalist touches, such as indigenous wooden framing and white-painted New England siding. It seems that Gropius may have sensed, in the stripped forms of the early Massachusetts vernacular, a concentration on essentials akin to his own. Marcel Breuer, Gropius's colleague from the Bauhaus, soon followed to Boston, and he too built himself a house combining ideas derived from the collective housing experiments of the twenties, with curious rustic intrusions like a rubble wall of local stone. Compared with the taut machine-age designs of a decade earlier, there was a considerable mellowness, which perhaps betokened a loss of polemical edge. Jordy has described this character well with the phrase 'the domestication of modern'. Both Breuer and Gropius had experienced the upheaval of the diaspora; some loss of intensity was probably inevitable; forms which had been created to deal with the social conditions of Weimar were bound to mean something different in the vicinity of Walden Pond.

As important as their individual buildings was their influence as teachers. At Harvard (always a school with a national and international influence) an era of Beaux-Arts inspired instruction came to an end. The past, once the source of all wisdom, came to be regarded with suspicion. Suave manipulation of inherited elements of tradition was replaced by a nuts and bolts rationality, allied to more nebulous notions of a 'new architecture' supposedly in tune with the dictates of contemporary social and technological reality. An appealing progressivist sentiment was also implied (though the original ideological imperatives were never spelt out), and when the apologist and historian of modern architecture, Sigfried Giedion, presented the work of his European friends as the only true tradition of the modern epoch in his Charles Eliot Norton lectures at Harvard of 1938 (later published as the monumental *Space, Time and Architecture*), it seemed as if manifest destiny must have singled out

Massachusetts.

Of course, there had been 'modern' developments in the USA before this date, as we have seen: the buildings of Howe and Lescaze, Neutra and Schindler, the uncategorizable middle works of Wright, the experiments of Buckminster Fuller; and Hitchcock and Johnson's book *The International Style* of 1932 had done much to change taste. But Gropius brought with him the full authority of one of the founding fathers. With the dousing of the modern movement in Europe in the thirties, it seemed as if the liberal generosity of America was allowing a flame to keep burning which might otherwise have gone out. A new generation of young Americans, sickened by the weak eclecticism rife in America, flocked to Cambridge to hear the new gospel. Paul Rudolph, Edward L. Barnes, Ieoh Ming Pei, Philip Johnson, and Benjamin Thompson were among the first disciples.

Modern architecture in its American beginnings was primarily a suburban matter. But after the war came more general acceptance and larger commissions. In 1948, Gropius and his firm TAC (The

19.2 Walter Gropius and The Architects Collaborative, Harkness Commons dormitories, Harvard University, 1948.

19.3 Ludwig Mies van der Rohe, Illinois Institute of Technology, Chicago, 1940, model of ensemble.

brought with it the onus of representing the establishment: and once the devalued International Style became a tired orthodoxy, a new rejection and re-evaluation became absolutely necessary.

In America the process was already under way by the late fifties, with divergent results. On the one hand there were those 'Expressionists' who, like Eero Saarinen, sought 'to extend the ABC' of modern architecture into curvaceous, occasionally powerful, sometimes delicious, but all-too-often mannered realms of expression. Then again, there were reversions to historicism: the Beaux-Arts was never far beneath the surface, and a bland neo-classicism was pursued by Philip Johnson, Edward Durell Stone, Wallace Harrison and Max Abramovitz, perhaps because the monumental tasks handed to these architects seemed to require a greater degree of rhetoric and reference than the spindly forms of Gropian modernism allowed. Or again, there were forceful new integrations, like that of Louis I. Kahn, who achieved a synthesis of modern and ancient values.

The picture of dissemination in the 1950s in America cannot be understood at all without the late works of Mies van der Rohe and Frank Lloyd Wright. Mies van der Rohe appears to have had fewer problems of adjustment in the diaspora than Gropius. Indeed, his arrival in Chicago, the home of the steel frame, seems to have been engineered by fate. Like Gropius, he owed one of his earliest commissions to university patronage: from 1940 to 1952 he redesigned the Illinois Institute of Technology campus. The idea shows most clearly in the model (fig. 19.3). The main functions were grouped in rectangular steel-framed boxes on a podium, in a composition combining neo-classical axiality with the asymmetrical planning ideas of the twenties. It was as if a sort of industrialized abstraction had strayed from some foreign land into the grid of the surrounding south side of Chicago. The lower buildings in the hierarchy were like elegant factories, and may well have been partially inspired by Albert Kahn's steel-frame factory designs. With their brick panel infills, their tight steel detailing, their sober proportions, and their air of straightforward 'factuality', they were a unique blend of Mies van der Rohe's stern intellectual quest for impersonality and the potentials of high-quality American steel craftsmanship. The local fire laws required that steel be coated in a layer of fireproofing, so that in order to express the structure 'honestly', the architect had to adopt the artifice of an extra veneer of steel around the fireproof casing. At the corners of the buildings this led to a curious detail in which the recessed core of steel structure was hinted at in a cut-away involving a steel veneer over concrete fireproofing over the actual structure within the wall. This was variously praised for its 'structural clarity'

Architects Collaborative) designed a new Graduate Center complex for Harvard University, comprising low dormitory blocks (fig. 19.2) and a commons building of amplified scale. In the local context, the intrusion of the 'factory aesthetic', the flat roofs, strip windows and asymmetrical forms, was a symbolic event of some importance, since the same university had favoured neo-Georgian sentimentality in its dormitory designs two decades earlier. In the same period Breuer designed Ferry House dormitory at Vassar, in a softer, less demanding modern mode, while Aalto's Baker House at MIT already pointed the way beyond the rigidities of the International Style.

Gropius stressed teamwork and the necessity to seek a sort of anonymity arising, supposedly, from the logic of programme and structure, and from a sense of 'objectivity' about modern conditions. In the wrong hands this quest for simplicity could very easily become mere banality: the rationality could all too easily degenerate into the wilderness of real estate values and management science. To trace Gropius's American development from the hopeful beginnings (which certainly lacked the force and conviction of his earlier works), to such designs of the mid-sixties as the Pan Am skyscraper in New York or the J. F. Kennedy building in Boston is to see a loss of expressive power and to be made aware of a decline. Can this be accounted for in merely biographical terms, or is it perhaps symptomatic of a larger situation in the post-war period when the 'alternative' vision of modern architecture was gradually absorbed by the institutions of consumer capitalism? The 'victory' of modern forms certainly

and its supposed Mondrianesque, metaphysical implications – as if such a corner implied 'lines running on to infinity'.

At the head of the campus was Crown Hall, destined to become the architecture building (fig. 19.4). Once again the image of the factory was dominant – the idea for this vast, uninterrupted 'universal' space seems traceable directly to Kahn's Bomber Assembly Plant of 1939, which also employed a dramatic truss system. However, the neo-classical qualities of Mies van der Rohe's design are just as crucial: these were schematic and relied on an interpretation of such essentials as symmetry, proportion, the clear expression of load and support, and a certain honorific mood. Crown Hall is approached up a grand flight of steps and is detailed with all the care and clarity that Schinkel might have mustered in similar circumstances. In reducing the building to the essence, Mies believed it possible to transform naked construction into the most basic underlying form. This is surely what was implied by his well-known statement 'less is more'. Such a simplicity was the result of a prodigious abstraction, and indeed a highly idealistic view of architecture's spiritual mission. One is, once again, only too aware how easily less could become *less* rather than more, in the hands of Mies's followers. In much the same way Mondrian's followers managed to reduce his sublime abstractions to mere checkerboard or tablecloth patterns.

The glass box implied a generalized view of human function: a space good for everything, in which little attempt was made to respond to individual incident or a sense of place. In the Farnsworth House of 1946, Mies van der Rohe indicated how a similar idea could be applied to the domestic pavilion, with a supremely anti-natural attitude: the obverse of Wright's landscape Romanticism. This design, for all its idiosyncrasy and impracticalities, fathered a host of imitations around the world, the most notable being, probably, Philip Johnson's erudite and elegant Glass House at New Canaan of 1951 (fig. 19.5). The 'machine in the garden' had been an image of some insistent meaning in American culture, and here it was restated. Johnson claimed a multiplicity of 'sources' for his design, from Mies van der Rohe, to Schinkel, to Palladio, to the brick-stack/wooden-frame constructions of the earliest settlers. However one assesses the references, the fact

19.4 Ludwig Mies van der Rohe, Illinois Institute of Technology, Crown Hall, 1952–6.

remains that a Miesian aesthetic was here being transformed into a chic evocation of high living different in tone from the originals. Colin Rowe caught the atmosphere of such a shift in meaning in American modern architecture when he later wrote:

> The revolutionary theme was never a very prominent component of American speculation about building. European modern architecture, even when it operated within the cracks and crannies of the capitalist system, existed within an ultimately socialist ambience: American modern architecture did not. And it was thus, and either by inadvertence or design, that when in the 1930s, European architecture came to infiltrate the United States, it was introduced simply as a new approach to building – and not much more. That is: it was introduced, largely purged of its ideological or societal content; and it became available not, as an evident manifestation (or cause) of Socialism in some form or other, but rather as a 'décor de la vie' for Greenwich, Connecticut, or as a suitable veneer for the corporate activities of 'enlightened capitalism.'

However, the steel box could have other domestic applications than Johnson's quasi-Classical one, especially when broken open, irregularized, or cross-bred with more sprawling domestic plan types. Charles Eames's own house in California of 1949 (fig. 19.6) was, in a sense, the obverse of Mies van der Rohe's Platonism – the building was assembled from standard parts and composed in a sensitive irregularity which reflected an interest in Japanese wooden-frame traditions and a refined sense of the 'ordinary'. The siting of the Eames 'shed' was subtle, alongside a row of eucalyptus trees which filtered the light into an interior where judiciously selected objects were as much part of the architecture as the building itself. The aesthetic effect arose from the careful juxtaposition of 'ready-made' elements, but without the claims on a higher abstract order implied by Mies. In the same period in California, the case-study houses by Ellwood and others showed how ideas of standardization could be employed to create extremely specific landscape responses, and open patio plans: the very opposite of Mies van der Rohe's pristine boxes.

Thus the steel frame with glass infill seems to have had the status of a 'leitmotif' in the first decade after the war in America, but it was a leitmotif capable of supporting a wide range of philosophies and ideas. Probably the most typical usage was in the design of

19.5 Philip Johnson, Glass House, New Canaan, Connecticut, 1951.

tall office buildings and, less frequently, apartment blocks; in both cases Mies van der Rohe may be said to have made a major impression with seminal buildings. 860, Lake Shore Drive apartments, Chicago, was designed by him in 1948 and stands in two towers on a triangular lot with views across Lake Michigan (fig. 19.8). Here the theme of the elegant, steel-framed glass rectangular slab on stilts is stated with unparalleled purity. The two towers rise to twenty-six storeys and are the same in plan and size, but are disposed on adjacent sites so that the oblong-plan forms face different ways and are perceived in constant tension (fig. 19.7). They are linked at the lower levels by hovering steel overhangs. The lobby spaces of the towers are situated in glazed, transparent undercrofts beneath the rows of stilts and are furnished with polished steel and marble. Elevators stand to the core, and rise through the centre of each block, giving access to luxury apartments situated around the edges. The uniformity of interior plans is expressed as a repeated bay system on the façades. However, on closer inspection, it becomes apparent that there are minute variations in the dimensions of the window bays at the end of each horizontal row of four, where the vertical structural posts pass up the façade. This results in an increase of vertical stress visually, and in an illusionistic sense of depth and movement. Further visual subtleties are introduced by the slender 'I' beams attached to the façade at regular intervals. These have no practical structural function, but what might be called a 'visual structural' role: they emphasize the verticality of the building and preserve a uniform rhythm and texture over what are in fact a variety of interior structural realities. The main structural posts are once again wrapped in concrete fireproofing which is then wrapped in steel; and where the façades come together at the corner, adjacent 'I' beams conspire to produce a sharp visual emphasis to the theme of two attached planes linked to an underlying armature. The 'Rationalist puritan' may be upset by the extent of these 'artificialities', but they are employed precisely to heighten one's awareness of the inner nature of the frame. One calls to mind Geoffrey Scott's dictum that architecture studies 'not structure in itself but the effect of structure on the human spirit' (Plate 9).

But the 'I' beams, and the purity of Mies van der Rohe's trabeated rectangular skeleton seem to have further meaning than that. These exquisitely rolled industrial elements, smooth blue-black against the glint of glass and the silver chrome, are themselves celebrated as objects of machine production. At the same time they recall Classical pilasters and imply a harmonic, geometrical order. And yet they remain simply what they are: commonplace steel beams. They call to mind once again Oud's suggestion made thirty

years earlier that the new architecture should lead to the experience of 'higher things' through a ruthless objectivity. Mies himself tried to express a similar thought when he stated:

> I believe that architecture has little or nothing to do with the invention of interesting forms or with personal inclinations.
>
> True architecture is always objective and is the expression of the inner structure of our time from which it springs.

There can be little doubt that Mies van der Rohe was stimulated in his search for simplicity by the frame buildings of the early Chicago School (particularly Burnham and Root's Reliance Building of 1893) and by the romanticization of American garage and factory structures which had been so prevalent among the European avant-garde in the twenties. It was a position in which the 'true' products of American

19.6 Charles Eames, Eames House, Santa Monica, California, 1949.

19.7 (*inset*) Ludwig Mies van der Rohe, Lake Shore Drive apartments, Chicago, 1950, plan.

19.8 Ludwig Mies van der Rohe, Lake Shore Drive apartments, 1950.

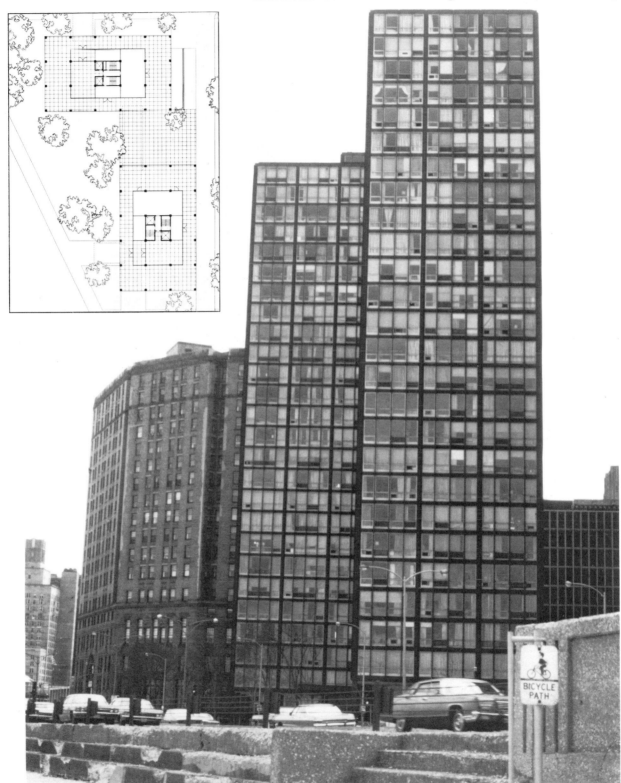

culture were seen to be the anonymous vernacular creations, while the self-conscious, and usually eclectic, qualities of 'artistic architecture' were rejected as an aberration. As we have seen in an earlier chapter, such transatlantic myths played a central role in determining the appearance of some of the European entries to the *Chicago Tribune* competition. Mies van der Rohe's arrival in Chicago in the late thirties, his later commissions in the city, and his enormous influence, ensured that the images of the European avant-garde of the twenties became realities in the America of the fifties (admittedly with a change in meaning). Indeed, his glass slab prototypes became parents of a world-wide progeny: a tribute, no doubt, to his intellectual clarity. However, his imagery also conjured up associations of efficiency, cleanliness, organization, and standardization which fitted the bill for what one might call the heraldry of big-business America. Thus it was the (often) crudely handled glass-box imitations of Mies van der Rohe which proliferated around the world as a species of corporate imagery. None of the excellence and most of the faults of the prototype were reproduced: the brash results are to be seen today in most major cities.

The Seagram building on Park Avenue in New York, designed by Mies and Johnson between 1954 and 1958 (fig. 19.9), must be counted a seminal building in this development. The skyscraper here achieved a grand and honorific character, sober and symmetrical, clothed in elegant materials such as bronze-tinted auburn glass. Seagram stands opposite McKim, Mead and White's palace-like Racquets Club of 1918, but an affinity is sensed between old and new in terms of nobility and Classical restraint. One approaches along a main axis between symmetrical rectangular pools flanked by ledges of marble. A portico is implied by the overhanging slab and this then guides one to the main lobby, a space of little consequence. Every detail of the interior design has been carefully considered in relation to the whole; and, as at Lake Shore, attached vertical mullions have a variety of visual and symbolic attributes.

In a sense, then, Seagram stands in the line of ideas stemming from the Deutscher Werkbund – form upgrading and idealizing industrial technique. But it has to be admitted that the filters of aesthetic excellence rarely intervened in this way between the mass production of building components and the construction of architecture. Mies van der Rohe was able to make of the repetitive and abstract qualities of modern urban existence a sort of sublime order. But the imitators portrayed the uniformity neat, ending up with the aspects of (to paraphrase Muthesius) 'a merely brutish world'. The muteness of Mies van der Rohe became magnified as the dumbness and sensual

19.9 Ludwig Mies van der Rohe, Seagram building, New York, 1957.

redundancy of glass-box city centres of the 1960s and 1970s around the world – the slick, alienated environment of 'Alphaville'.

Between the sublimities of Mies van der Rohe and the emptiness of the mere glass box there were gradations of quality. In particular one thinks of the school of architects stemming from the German master and best represented by firms like Skidmore, Owings and Merrill. This firm's Lever House of 1951 (for which Gordon Bunshaft was chief designer) stands almost opposite the Seagram building on Park Avenue in Manhattan (fig. 19.10). By contrast it was weightless, almost planar, in appearance. Perhaps following some of the hints of the PSFS building twenty years earlier, the Lever building employed a podium for its mezzanine offices, which created a courtyard at ground level, and a roof terrace on top. The main slab then rose clear as a hovering volume clad in a network of chrome lines and blue-and-green tinted glass. The machine rooms

19.10 (*above*) Skidmore, Owings and Merrill, Lever House, New York, 1951.

19.11 (*above right*) Le Corbusier (main idea), Wallace Harrison and Max Abramovitz, United Nations Headquarters, New York, 1947–50.

containing the air-conditioning plant were expressed at the top in a variation in pattern, while the presence of the individual floor slabs was hinted at through the horizontal banding. An effect of weightlessness and dematerialization was achieved by recessing the main vertical supports within the skin, by reducing mullions to the thinnest of lines, and through the use of polished, shimmering surfaces and semi-reflecting glass. Of course, such a sealed-box solution relied totally on air-conditioning and mechanical ventilation for its environmental quality. Modifications of the slab using sunshades, balconies, and other natural climatic devices would emerge later on the American skyline. For the moment, Lever, Seagram, and such buildings as Belluschi's Equitable Life Assurance building in Portland (1944–7) and Eero Saarinen's 'horizontal skyscrapers' for the General Motors Technical Center at Warren, Michigan (1955), set the pattern for forward-looking commercial architecture.

But the glass box could also be employed in non-commercial contexts, as is clear from the UN complex by Wallace Harrison and Max Abramovitz of 1947–50 (fig. 19.11). Here the Secretariat was the dominant image and was housed in a slab overlooking the East River. The Assembly was contained in a symmetrical curved volume alongside, expressing something of the interior function. Members' lounges, press galleries, etc., were situated in a third volume, between the other two and the river. The effect of the scheme arose from the way the main elements were disposed as sculptural objects on a platform, with walkways, a small park and other public facilities weaving between. Lewis Mumford, reviewing the scheme, doubted the appropriateness of a slab to the symbolic aspirations of the new post-war congress of nations, until he reflected that perhaps the bureaucracy would be the most notable feature of the organization.

Perhaps if the UN had been carried out as originally intended, a poetry and power appropriate to the idealism of the enclosed institution would have been achieved. For there can be little doubt that Harrison and Abramovitz adapted their building from an original idea by Le Corbusier known as project '23A' (fig. 19.12) and enshrined in a wooden model and some notebook sketches. It was not the first time this architect had set his mind to the design of a world parliament, as we have seen, and it is notable that a similar articulation was employed to distinguish the honorific assembly, a curved, sculptural mass, from the less intense, standardized containers of the Secretariat, as had been used in the League of Nations scheme twenty years earlier. But in the UN, the Secretariat was given greater importance by being made vertical. It is even possible that Le Corbusier was here influenced by Meyer's League of Nations entry which had employed a tower. Probably, too, he was seeking to demonstrate to Americans the 'true morphology' of the skyscraper, and seeking to display a sort of fragment of the 'Ville Radieuse', liberating Manhattan from congestion, introducing light, space, and greenery into the life of the metropolis. Evidently he intended to follow the lead of his Algiers tower of 1941 and to integrate *brise-soleil* with the UN façades. These gave a weighty and monumental character to a building (as at Marseilles or Chandigarh) and amounted to a major transformation of the glass-box formula. In this instance Le Corbusier proposed to regulate the proportions of his building with yet another recent invention, his proportional system – the 'Modulor'. This drew together the Golden Section, the six-foot human figure, and harmonic proportions in an elaborate proportioning device loaded with Corbusian ideology, and concerned with the harmonization of machine-age design. When one bears in mind that Le Corbusier also envisaged a Museum of World Culture in the form of a spiral ziggurat, to stand alongside the UN, one becomes aware of the extent to which the project excited his universal aspirations.

But this is to discuss a project which was never built or of which only a shadow was constructed. Le Corbusier's advice was accepted freely, but he did not receive the commission and returned to Europe empty-handed and embittered. The present building is a diluted concept in search of appropriate articulation and details: the lobbies with their curvaceous cantilevers, and their abstract art adornments, speak more of the clichés of the 'international hotel style' of the 1950s than they do of dignified places of assembly. To grasp how Le Corbusier would handle a programme on this scale, we have to turn to his Indian buildings, in which primitivist yearnings and rough concrete come together in a fusion of enormous power.

It remains to consider Wright in the immediate postwar years. By the end of the war he was nearly 70 and involved with the design of the Guggenheim Museum, which was not to be constructed for over a decade. This was to stand on a site opposite Central Park in Manhattan and to house an extensive collection of non-objective art. Wright's initial reaction to the programme was to suggest a sort of 'center for the arts', including attached studios: he perhaps saw it as an antidote to the visual squalor of city centres. But by degrees he reverted to a more conventional

19.12 Le Corbusier, project '23A' for the United Nations Headquarters, 1947.

programme, though by no means to a conventional solution. The building as it stands is organized around an expanding spiral ramp which rises around a central volume in ever wider bands (figs. 19.13, 19.14). Ancillary volumes containing offices and the director's apartment are fashioned in the same smooth, curved layers, and from the outside the building is a complete antidote to the grid of the city and the prevalent box-and-frame architecture. One passes through a low zone of transition (which loosely recalls the Johnson Wax entry) and comes into a stunning space with light coming in from the top. However, the material – concrete – is curiously smooth and without texture; it is as if an idea had failed to find quite the right skin. Wright himself declared something of his intention in designing the museum in this form.

Here for the first time architecture appears plastic, one floor flowing into another (more like sculpture) instead of the usual superimposition of stratified layers cutting and butting into each other by way of post and beam construction.

The whole building, cast in concrete, is more like an egg shell – in form a great simplicity. . . . The light concrete flesh is rendered strong enough everywhere to do its work by embedded filaments of steel either separate or in mesh. The structural calculations are thus those of the cantilever and continuity rather than the post and beam. The net result of such construction is a greater repose, the atmosphere of the quiet unbroken wave: no meeting of the eye with abrupt changes of form.

The Guggenheim Museum appears to draw together

19.13 (*above*) Frank Lloyd Wright, Guggenheim Museum, New York, 1944–57, exterior.

19.14 Frank Lloyd Wright, Guggenheim Museum, New York, 1944–57, interior.

a number of themes with roots deep in Wright's earlier experiences. The idea of an inward-looking communal space with overhanging galleries was surely a centralized variant on the interiors of the Unity Temple, the Larkin building, or the Johnson Wax building. The search for spatial continuity between interpenetrating horizontal layers of cantilevered trays seems to run through Wright's work from the early prairie houses – indeed it is instructive to compare the Robie House elevation to the Guggenheim to see how basic devices of massing recur within a much-changed idiom. Curved forms had also occurred early in Wright's career – initially perhaps stemming from the pantheistic geometries of the Froebel blocks – and were reinforced by the organic shapes occurring in nature. In designs like the mural for the Coonley House play-room, they were composed in mysterious floating coloured blobs, not unlike Kandinsky's nearly contemporary pioneering abstract paintings. But curves only emerged gradually in his actual buildings, a notable case being the Sugar Loaf Mountain project of 1925 in which a spiral traffic ramp was envisaged encircling a domical Planetarium and rising to the summit. In the thirties, curves recurred more frequently, in such buildings as the Johnson Wax, and seemed to mirror an intention of achieving a greater fluidity of form, light, space, structure, and material. In parallel with the Guggenheim, Wright designed a petite and exquisite show-room for jewellery and elegant home-wares in San Francisco which used the theme of an interior spiralling ramp. The Guggenheim thus assembled a number of earlier motifs in the architect's work, drawing them together in a new way.

But a building is more than the assembly of inherited elements of language: it must bear the imprint of new intentions and result in a new synthesis. Part of Wright's specific intention in the Guggenheim was to create a museum in harmony with non-objective art.

> The building was intended by Solomon R. Guggenheim to make a suitable place for the exhibition of an advanced form of painting wherein line, color and form are a language in themselves … independent of reproduction of objects animate or inanimate, thus placing painting in a realm hitherto enjoyed by music alone.
>
> This advanced painting has seldom been presented in other than the incongruous rooms of old static architecture. Here in the harmonious fluid quiet created by this building interior the new painting will be seen for itself under favorable conditions.

It has to be said that there was much wishful thinking in the architect's own assessment, as the outward sloping walls, the 'lobster bisque' colours, and the lighting system of Wright's design were found to be at variance with some of the fundamental requirements for viewing works of art. Wright, after all, saw architecture as the mother art, and conceived of furniture, paintings, and sculptures as almost a form of integral ornament.

On another level, the Guggenheim surely had the status of a demonstration of Wright's ideal of an 'organic' architecture, in which form and space were fused. Space had of course been central to his vision from the beginning: as a tactile medium of varying intensity and psychological character, and as the means for ennobling human action. Many years before, Wright had written of the Unity Temple in a way which could equally describe the Guggenheim:

> You will find the sense of the great room coming through – space not walled in now but more or less free to appear … the new reality, that is *space* instead of matter.

Thus the Guggenheim was a sort of apotheosis of Wright's organic philosophy in which plan, section, and elevation ideas of his earlier experimentation were brought together in a cogent, three-dimensional weave of form, space, and abstraction. Perhaps only a spiral in concrete could have embodied his intentions, for this form combined centrality and procession, equilibrium and movement, and an inherent sense of growth and aspiration. Even so, it has to be said that the Guggenheim lacks the force of many of Wright's earlier works. The mannered fussiness of certain of the joints and ornaments anticipates the 'space-ship' kitsch of the later Marin County Court House, completed just after Wright's death. Since then his work has had little appreciable impact on American architecture. The followers – the Taliesin fellows – tended to reproduce the surface effects of his style with little grasp of the underlying order.

Thus it can be seen that the masters of the pre-war period attempted, in the decade after 1945, to bring to fruition ideas which had been with them for some time. This is surely not surprising, as the late works of any artist of calibre are liable to involve some balance of retrospection and innovation. Gropius's post-war works were the least satisfactory, while Wright's remained idiosyncratic monuments to his individuality and isolation from prevalent values. Mies van der Rohe's architecture seemed to fit a certain bill as a provider of commercial prototypes. It remains to consider certain other masters to see how they fared outside the United States – particularly Aalto, and, of course, Le Corbusier, who managed the difficult transition after 1945 most resplendently.

20. Form and Meaning in the Late Works of Le Corbusier

> The principle which gives support to a work of art is not necessarily contemporary with it. It is quite capable of slipping back into the past or forward into the future. . . . The artist inhabits a time which is by no means necessarily the history of his own time.
>
> H. Focillon, 1939

Between 1945 and 1965, when he died, Le Corbusier produced a series of elusive masterpieces, each of them characterized by a complex interweaving of old themes and new means of expression, by an increasing sense of primitivism, and by a deliberate cultivation of ancient associations. There was none of the loss of nerve manifest in the late works of Gropius, nor the regression into feeble mannerism which seemed to afflict Wright, nor the technological perfectionism of Mies van der Rohe. Like the aging Michelangelo, Le Corbusier entered an increasingly private and mystical world of poetry in his last years. But any tendency to expressionistic wilfulness was held in check by a strong intellectual discipline and a refinement of earlier type forms and themes. The introduction of new devices like *béton brut* (bare concrete), the *brise-soleil* (the sun breaker), or complex curved geometries, should not blind one to the elaboration of earlier principles, such as the 'five points of a new architecture'. Part of the richness of Le Corbusier's late works lies, precisely, in the tension between well-worn formulations and new patterns of form and meaning.

There were already hints of Le Corbusier's later direction in some of his designs of the thirties, such as the Petite Maison de Weekend. In these the brittle and pristine world of Purism had been broken open to reveal something more archaic, deliberately crude, and rooted in the organic. The mechanical slaughter of the Second World War may have gone further to disrupt Le Corbusier's confidence in the machine and its 'progressive' potential. The poet of the machine age spent the early forties in rustic seclusion in the Pyrenees, emerging from his retreat in fitful and unsuccessful attempts at persuading the Vichy authorities to build his Algiers plan. At the same time he painted a series of biomorphic monsters known simply as 'Ubus' after Alfred Jarry's well-known and preposterous character 'Ubu Roi'. These seemed to sum up the artist's mixed feelings of futility and irony, and to correspond to a mental state of withdrawal. In these years Surrealism also held out an appeal in the search for primal subject-matter and subconscious imagery; one notes a loose parallel between Le Corbusier's biological sculptures and developments in avant-garde painting and sculpture in the USA (e.g., early Jackson Pollock or David Smith), in which totemic and primitivist features also came to the fore. By the end of the war, when he returned to Paris, Le Corbusier was in his late fifties; he had not built for over a decade. It is scarcely surprising, then, that each of his post-war commissions should have been treated as an opportunity to cram together many levels of ideas. He became increasingly obsessed with leaving behind him autobiographical mementoes and lexicons of principle.

The late forties in France was not the most propitious time for an architect of Le Corbusier's formal calibre. Of course, there were vast programmes of rehousing, but he failed in his ambition of becoming France's 'chief architect/urbanist of reconstruction'. Instead of seeing his grand models adopted, he had to be content, once again, with piecemeal demonstrations. Thus the Unité d'Habitation at Marseilles (and the handful of other Unités he was called upon to design during the fifties) were fragmentary realizations

20.1 (*left*) Le Corbusier, Notre-Dame-du-Haut, Ronchamp, 1950–54; the open-air chapel is in the east wall to the right.

20.2 (*below*) Le Corbusier, Notre-Dame-du-Haut, Ronchamp, 1950–54, site plan.

compared with his expectations. Even so (as will be shown in the next chapter), these buildings did effectively serve the function of prototypes. The allure of the Marseilles Unité was as powerful as the hold over the post-war imagination of Mies van der Rohe's glass towers; these were among the seminal images of the fifties. At the same time the 'theorems' of the UN skyscraper and the Modulor proportional system failed to have the grand societal impact which their creator had craved.

It was almost as if the post-war world conspired to stop the Le Corbusier of 'standards' and industrialized prototypes from having an effect, leaving, presumably, the idiosyncratic poet of form to dig ever deeper into private worlds of metaphor. The society at which the artist had directed his pre-war Utopias had undoubtedly changed. He seemed now to seek inspiration less in the 'miracles of contemporary life' than in a fraternity with nature and with the great works of the past. A nostalgia for the giant ruins of antiquity began to creep in. Of course, the search for perennial and unchanging values had always been a primary motivation; now it went on less disturbed by a quest for 'modernity'.

Such preliminary remarks seem appropriate to the

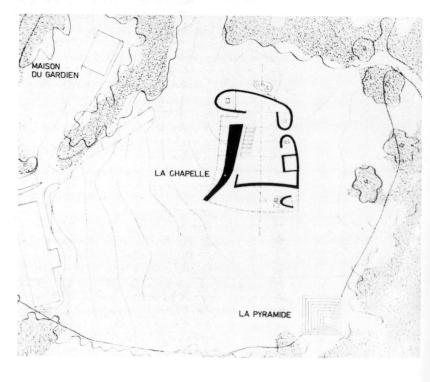

MAISON DU GARDIEN

LA CHAPELLE

LA PYRAMIDE

Chapel of Notre-Dame-du-Haut at Ronchamp of 1950–4 (figs. 20.1, 20.2). This stands brooding on a hilltop in the Vosges mountains with views across valleys of evergreens towards the far horizons. A dark roof with pointed angle and complex curvature rests uneasily on convex and concave battered rubble walls punctured by irregular openings and sprayed in whitewashed gunnite concrete. The fluidity of the resulting composition is held in check by three hooded towers facing in varying directions. These and the undulating surfaces echo the pressures of the surrounding landscape. The interior is hollowed out like a cave and has a sloping floor which focuses attention towards the altar. The smaller chapels are top-lit within the towers while the perforated side wall streams the light into an otherwise sober interior. The junction between roof and walls is deftly handled with a slight gap so that a crack of daylight gleams through: what seemed solid outside becomes planar and thin when inside. Such ambiguities of mass and space, support and supported, are basic to the formal character of the chapel, and the readings vary as one changes position. Ronchamp is a sculpture to be seen in the round: exterior and interior movements of the spectator become involved with the dynamics of the composition and are central to the concept of the work.

Typical of this sense of unfolding ambiguity is the space *outside* the east wall, where an open-air altar sits under the boat-like roof (fig. 20.1). This outdoor sanctuary is replete with pulpit and an image of the Madonna in a glazed box embedded in the wall (so that it can be seen from the inside too). The 'nave' of the church now becomes the grass platform stretching to the edge of the hill. There is the stunning backdrop of woods and hills, while, to one side, a ziggurat of old stones marks the spot where a previous church was destroyed in the final years of the war. The site had traditionally been a place for pilgrimages (even in pre-Christian times), and Le Corbusier managed to capture the spirit of the place. The gradual ascent up the hill has a ritualistic character, which the architect turned to good effect by organizing the building as a sequence of *événements plastiques* ('sculptural events') incorporating the setting and the surrounding horizons. The culmination of the procession might vary: it might be a Mass in the open air or a private prayer in the interior with its numinous space and filtered light.

At the time of its completion in 1955, the Chapel at Ronchamp shocked the critics who flocked to see it. Pevsner complained of a retreat into 'irrationality' (thus betraying his prejudice that Le Corbusier's earlier works had been somehow 'rational'), while James Stirling was dismayed by 'conscious imperfectionism' and 'mannerism', and questioned whether the building 'should influence the course of modern archi-

tecture'. One thing seemed to be clear amidst these confused reactions: the master of European modern architecture had changed direction profoundly. The commentators seemed to forget that these changes had been in the making for some time; that the architect's style had been in gradual transition for two decades, since his works of the twenties, which they seemed to regard as 'normative'. The forms of Ronchamp were not without precedent in Le Corbusier's rugged wooden sculptures, in his sketches of shells and boats (the roof structure was, in fact, directly inspired by a crab shell), in the landscape sculptures of the buildings in his Algiers schemes and in the curved rubble wall of Pavillon Suisse.

Le Corbusier was not a member of any particular faith, yet his outlook was fundamentally idealistic. He later wrote that he was interested in 'the effect of architectural forms and the spirit of architecture in the construction of a vessel of intense concentration and meditation' and in what he called 'an acoustic component in the domain of form'. In other words, he sought to evoke religious emotions through the play of form, space, and light, and without recourse to any obvious church typology. The patronage conditions were well suited to this kind of free interpretation, as Father Couturier (with whom Le Corbusier liaised throughout the design) believed that a vital, existential expression of religious consciousness was best achieved, not by forcing an artist into a traditional ecclesiastical straitjacket, but by allowing the free play of imagination. Le Corbusier seemed to mirror this intention of the client when he wrote:

I have not experienced the miracle of faith but I have often known the miracle of inexpressible space, the apotheosis of plastic emotion.

In fact some of Le Corbusier's inspirations at Ronchamp were heathen in tone. The attitude to landscape and to natural forms provided the key to his sacral interpretation. As a young man he had soaked himself in nature worship, in the writings of Ruskin, in the symbolic allegories of Art Nouveau, and had even had the vision of a sort of temple to nature to stand on a Jura mountain top. The forms of Ronchamp speak of a similar pantheism; this was an artist for whom natural forms were capable of a divine and magical character. Immediately before he received the commission, Le Corbusier had been giving thought to the design of a shrine at St.-Baume (never built), which he had envisaged as a sort of top-lit cave embedded among boulders. Ronchamp was pervaded by a similar primitive animism.

Other connections can be found with a great variety of 'sources'. It seems that the top lighting of the

20.3 Le Corbusier,
Monastery of La
Tourette, Eveux, near
Lyons, 1955.

'Canopus' at Hadrian's Villa (sketched in 1911) may have inspired the lighting system of the towers; certain mud buildings from the Mzab, seen in Algeria in the mid-thirties, may have influenced the main perforated wall; a fascination with sluices may have registered in the water scoop of the Ronchamp roof. Dolmens and Cycladic vernacular structures have even been adduced as other clues, and it is possible that the procession to the Parthenon was once again inspirational. But, whatever the sources and other memories, the important point is that they were here brought together in a coherent work of art: they became inseparable elements of a synthesis.

It was soon after Ronchamp was completed that Le Corbusier was asked to design another religious structure, the Dominican monastery of La Tourette at Eveux, not far from Lyons (fig. 20.3). Monasteries had, of course, had a strong hold over Le Corbusier's imagination as collective paradigms since his visit to the Charterhouse at Ema in Tuscany in 1907, when he had been deeply impressed by the ordered rule of the architecture, the balance between public and private realms, and the emphasis on contemplation of nature from the cells. In designing La Tourette he was therefore able to draw on years of researches in his reinterpretation of an ancient type. It is striking that he employed vestiges of the traditional cloister arrangement in his plan and that his use of bare concrete and stark forms was intended as an equivalent to the stern

stonework of old Dominican buildings. However, the site – a slope overlooking meadows – required considerable modification of the inherited device of the cloistered court. The resulting monastery did not ape the prototypes but transformed them, restating them in a new structural terminology in concrete, and in a social vocabulary related to Le Corbusier's admiration of the well-regulated community living towards a common, ideal purpose.

The form of La Tourette expressed some of these institutional concerns. The individual cells were placed around the crowning overhang, wrapped around three of the outside edges and expressed as deep-cut rectangular embrasures. Each monk had his individual balcony framing a private view over trees or far distant hills to the west. The communal portions of the monastery were set in the recessed lower levels, the most public (e.g., classrooms and library) being placed close to the entrance. The refectory was situated at one level down from the entrance floor, but since the site sloped so steeply, it provided a splendid vantage-point over the meadows. The chapel was entered from this lower level too, but was entirely inward-looking and was a full triple volume in height. It made a solid block along one side of the building, an anchor on the slope, and its interior (to paraphrase Le Corbusier) was 'd'une pauvreté totale' ('of a total poverty'). In other words, it possessed a stern moral beauty arising from the interplay of stark concrete surfaces, colour and

20.4 Le Corbusier, Maisons Jaoul, Neuilly-sur-Seine, 1956.

light. All these major spaces of the plan were linked by corridors and platforms, some of them entirely glazed to offer views to the interior of the court or over the landscape.

What gave these variously articulated functions the power of architecture was the way they were linked and orchestrated within a clear overall form. There was precision in the relationship of plane and volume, of the dense and the transparent, the heavy and the light. Much of the necessary experimentation for the use of bare concrete had gone on at Marseilles – half a decade before – but La Tourette still succeeded in extending the vocabulary. One may recognize the old Le Corbusier theme of the box on stilts, but dismembered and rearranged in a sort of collage composition in which 'found objects' – a triangular skylight, a stack, a protruding balcony – introduced staccato incidents. Moreover, La Tourette was still based on the principles of the 'five points of a new architecture', but the number and type of architectural elements had increased. Instead of just cylindrical supports, there were now directional piers as well; instead of the thin planes of stucco of the earlier works, there were robust walls; instead of the plane glass or strip windows, there were now *brise-soleil*, *ondulatoires* (the rhythmically positioned concrete struts laid out according to the Modulor), and *aerateurs* – the last being vertical wooden ventilating panels inserted into the fenestration membrane. Le Corbusier's *recherche patiente*

('patient research') proceeded in this way: each new project became a testing ground for new ideas, as well as an extension of old. La Tourette demonstrated how the increase in the number of elements allowed a greater variety of articulation both functionally and formally. Aside from the obvious features – like rough concrete, inverted overhangs, and slab-like piers – it was this conceptual richness which endeared La Tourette to followers seeking a way out of the limitations of the inherited 'International Style'.

Two little houses designed at approximately the same time as La Tourette – the Maisons Jaoul in Neuilly-sur-Seine – were also widely imitated (fig. 20.4). Here the contrast with Le Corbusier's early works was even more dramatic, for these deliberately crude brick dwellings, with their rough concrete frames, their curved 'Catalan' vaults and their turf roofs, stood less than two miles from the Maison Cook and the Villa Stein at Garches, and could not be explained away as rustic religious sprees. Peter Smithson, the English architect, characterized the combination of sophistication and primitivism nicely when he spoke of the Jaoul Houses as being 'on the knife edge of peasantism'. Stirling once again registered nervousness in a well-known comparison of Jaoul with Garches, in which he suggested that the polemical drive of early modern architecture, the expression of a new way of life in built forms, was giving way to a more comfortable, less challenging view of social progress. Once again, though, the themes of the houses had already been evident in the Petite Maison de Weekend, and Le Corbusier had already written rhapsodically of the lessons to be learned from the French vernacular tradition in the early forties. The machine-age polemic had gone, but it had been replaced by new attitudes concerning the primal relationship between man and nature. Stirling himself seems to have sensed the cogency of the vision, for his Ham Common houses of the following year adopted the rough brick and concrete. Indeed, the Jaoul houses became one of the canonical works of the so-called 'New Brutalists' in England and elsewhere – a younger generation sensing the devaluation of the heroic vision of the earlier modern movement into something smooth and ersatz, and seeking a visual language to give body to their own rough awakening to the social realities of the post-war years.

The Maisons Jaoul were on the drawing boards at the same time as two dwellings for India – the Sarabhai House and the Villa Shodan in Ahmadabad – where effects of precision were out of the question, even had the architect wanted them, and where handmade sun-baked brick and rough concrete were right for the labour conditions, for the climate and for the ethos Le Corbusier was trying to express in a country which had not yet undergone the traumas of the industrial revolution. It seems that India entered his mythology as a place destined to bystep the chaos of the 'first machine age' and to enter directly the phase of natural harmony of the *deuxième ère machiniste* ('the second machine age'). These houses of Ahmadabad's well-do-do could, of course, be only partial vehicles for such a new strain of nature worship. The Sarabhai House (fig. 20.5) was built for Mrs. Manorama Sarabhai, sister-in-law of Gautam Sarabhai (who was director of the National Institute of Design in the town), and the site stood on a tree-filled estate. Mrs. Sarabhai belonged to the Jain sect, which stressed the inviolability of nature. Le Corbusier's design was a variant on his Monol type of 1919 (of which the Petite Maison de Weekend had also been a cousin) with low vaults and an earth-hugging character. He oriented the house to the prevailing winds and designed the façade with deep-cut piers which acted as *brise-soleil* and porticoes simultaneously. The Catalan vault system was again employed on the shaded interiors, while the roof had a thick mat of turf traversed by water channels (to cope with the monsoons) laid over it. There was even a dramatic scoop/slide sluicing the rain water down into a pool.

The Shodhan Villa, on the other hand, belonged to Le Corbusier's box typology: in the long run it descended from the Citrohan. Originally it was designed for Surrotam Hutheesing, the President of the Mill-owners Association (for which Le Corbusier also designed a building), but the house was then sold at the planning stage and transferred to another site. The building's cubic form was carved out with dramatic concrete crates and overhangs to create a textured, dynamic composition, and a habitation traversed by breezes. The whole was capped by a hovering slab on piers – recalling the image of the Dom-ino – but referring as well to the concept of a parasol against rain and sun. Le Corbusier had decided that this should be one of the central elements of any new Indian architecture; variants on a similar theme had recurred in the Indian architecture of the past.

These Ahmadabad commissions were relatively marginal to Le Corbusier's main Indian commitment: the design of the new city of Chandigarh (fig. 20.6) which occupied him from 1951 up to his death in 1965. In 1948 Western Punjab and the traditional state capital of Lahore were ceded to the newly created Pakistan, leaving the Indian Punjab and a large number of Hindu refugees in need of a capital. A scheme was drawn up by Albert Mayer and Matthew Nowicki, but in 1951 the latter was killed in a crash. The chief engineer, P. L. Varma, and the state administrator of public works, P. N. Thapar, toured Europe in search of an architect/planner, and on the re-

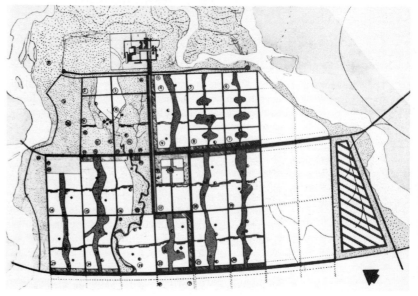

commendation of Jane Drew and Maxwell Fry (who eventually played a major role in the design of the housing sectors) turned to Le Corbusier. In February, 1951, in a little rest-house on the road to Simla, close to the small village of Chandigarh, the blueprint for the new capital was born. After all, Le Corbusier had been ruminating on the history and meaning of cities for over forty years, and came supplied with his own pre-existing vision of a modern urban ideal ready to be modified by particular conditions.

The main body of the city was planned on a grid of circulation (in fact, there were seven different 'hierarchies' of movement in the design), dividing up a variety

20.5 (*top*) Le Corbusier, Sarabhai House, Ahmadabad, 1955, interior view.

20.6 Le Corbusier, Chandigarh, plan of city, *c.* 1951.

20.7 (*top*) Le Corbusier,
Governor's Palace,
Chandigarh, *c.* 1954,
perspective showing
intended water gardens.

20.8 Fathepur Sikri,
India, late 16th century,
view towards Diwan-i-
Khas, the Private
Audience Hall.

distinction of urban functions, his notion of the essential joys of 'light, space, and greenery', his conception of social order and rationalization, his dream of a *polis* inhabited by forward-looking technicians and bureaucrats of high cultural aspiration. The form was a variant on the basic layout of the Radiant City, but without *à redent* housing blocks, and with free-standing sculptural monuments symbolizing government at the head, instead of the glass towers. However, Chandigarh also incorporated ideas from Paris – the grand boulevards and focal points; from ancient Peking – in the overall geometrical form; and from Lutyen's New Delhi, with its own extraordinary blend of garden city principles and Baroque vista planning. Le Corbusier fully appreciated another aspect of New Delhi, evident in the Viceroy's house and other monumental buildings: the way they fused the European and the Indian traditions in an iconography of state magnificence.

Much of Le Corbusier's attention over the subsequent years would be devoted to the capital complex, in which he allowed his ideas on monumental expression free rein. Like Lutyens, he learned his lessons from the Mogul tradition, in the provision of deep loggias, romantic roofscapes, and water. The 'parasol' upturned against water and sun incorporated a traditional image of authority, and became a sort of shared leitmotif at Chandigarh, recurring on top of the Governor's Palace (fig. 20.7) and the Secretariat, transformed into the colossal scoop of the Parliament building portico, becoming the very form of the Justice basilica itself. Indeed, the genesis of his monumental vocabulary seems to have involved a prodigious feat of abstraction in which devices from the Classical tradition – the grand order, the portico – were fused with Le Corbusier's generic system of forms in concrete (the 'five points', the *brise-soleil*, etc.) and in turn cross-bred with Indian devices like the 'chattri', the trabeated terraces, balconies, and loggias of Fathepur Sikri (fig. 20.8). In turn, this architectural language, rich in references and associations of a public institutional kind, was suffused with the artist's private cosmological themes – the fantasy of water dowsing and splashing over giant concrete roofs and surfaces, the image of the sun's path at the solstice and the equinox attached to the colossal lighting tower of the Parliament, and the curious 'Valley of Contemplation', emblazoned with signs representing different aspects of the architect's philosophy.

The apotheosis of this new state imagery drenched in Corbusian references was perhaps the 'Open Hand', a monument designed to stand close to the Governor's house (and eventually on its own when the latter function was dropped because Nehru found it undemocratic). Had it been realized, this would have been

of rectangular sectors, containing neighbourhoods of relatively low-rise dwellings in a sort of garden city arrangement. At the 'heart' of this body was the commercial centre off the main artery running up to the 'head', containing the main state buildings: the Governor's House, the Parliament, the Judiciary, and the Secretariat. The University, the Museum, the Stadium, and other 'leisure' activities were disposed on a cross-axis extending to the north, while out to the south-east, separate from the main body, was the railway station with its depots.

The rationale for this overall plan embodied Le Corbusier's major principles: his belief in the ordered

a bizarre compound of a Picasso peace dove and a giant gesturing hand. Some of the meaning of the symbol was spelled out by the architect:

> It was not a political emblem, a politician's creation ... [but] an architect's creation ... a symbol of peace and reconciliation. ...
>
> Open to receive the wealth that the world has created, to distribute it to the peoples of the world ... It ought to be the symbol of our age.

He then went on to say: 'The Open Hand will affirm that the second era of machinist civilization has begun; the era of harmony.'

The Parliament building itself (fig. 20.9) was loaded with symbolism and enriched with ancient references. Basically, it was designed as a large box with a grid of columns inside it, approached through a portico along one side supported on flange-like piers, with the large 'objects' of the main Assembly and Senate set down into it. These were made visible on the exterior through

20.9 Le Corbusier, Parliament Building, Chandigarh, 1953–62.

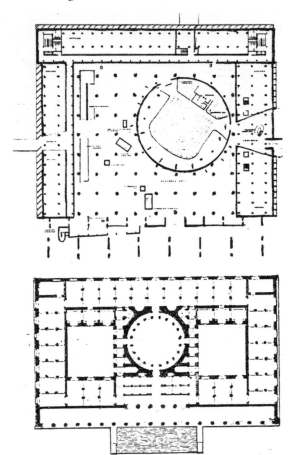

20.10 Parliament Building, Chandigarh, interior.

20.11 (*right*) Parliament Building, Chandigarh; plan compared to plan of Altes Museum, Berlin, 1825, by Schinkel.

the sculptural roofscape forms, a tilted pyramid for the Senate and a dynamic funnel-like shape for the main Assembly (fig. 20.14). Rugged concrete, with all the signs and enrichment of rough handicraft, was used throughout; the searing climate soon added its own patina. If the result has the appearance of a colossal, grave, and dignified ruin, this was probably intended: one has the sensation that these buildings must have stood on this plateau for centuries. The sides of the box were perforated by the deep-cut, repeated shadows of *brise-soleil*, while the main façade (on the cross-axis of the Capital plateau facing the Justice building in the distance) provided a gesture of considerable formality. The rhetoric was continued on the interior where one left behind the blazing heat and the jagged shadows to enter a cool, serene world of limpid cylinders rising to a black soffit (fig. 20.10). The light filtered in from the sides of this hovering element to reveal a space the ancient Egyptians might have revered. Indeed, the mushroom supports looked as if they had been inspired by hypostyle prototypes. Concrete was here endowed with the density and *gravitas* of hewn and polished stone. With the awe-inspiring volume of the great funnel containing the Assembly descending into it, with the rising sequences of ramps and the vast floors, this was a sure demonstration that monumentality had not died in the modern era.

The Assembly room itself was top-lit. It lacked the charismatic atmosphere of the hypostyle around it,

and its round floor plan was somewhat at odds with the function of accommodating a democratic, political debate. Nevertheless, it is interesting to probe the genesis of the 'funnel' concept as this gives clues concerning the way Le Corbusier translated images and ideas into forms.

In the earliest stages, the Parliament building was a close relative of the Hall of Justice opposite: a large box under a massive parasol in concrete. By degrees the theme of the portico emerged naturally from the expression of the rectangular trabeation within. At this stage the main chambers were submerged in the box as two gland-shaped rooms enclosed by free-form curved partitions set into the grid of supports. A key breakthrough was made in mid-1953 when the architect began to envision the dramatic possibility of sun and moonlight penetrating the roof; there were even vague hints of 'nocturnal festivals' and 'solar celebrations'. It was then that the idea of the light-tower – an object within the bigger object of the box – began to emerge, its form partly inspired by the hyperboloid shape of power station cooling towers

(indeed ventilation concerns may have triggered the analogy). In the placement of a stack-like form in the centre of a box, one recognizes a basic Corbusian habit of mind extending back at least as far as the villas of the 1920s. The suggestion has been made that the architect may have been inspired by the plan of Schinkel's Altes Museum in Berlin, where the theme of portico, grid, and circular form had been stated with great clarity and force (fig. 20.11). The choice of these forms far transcended utilitarian concerns (in fact, the solution was never entirely practical): they arose as much from the artist's aim of creating a sort of modern equivalent to the dome – an emblem of state authority and rule. Among the early doodles, there were some showing the Chandigarh stack alongside a section of the dome of the imperial church of Hagia Sophia in Istanbul, and others showing the sun streaming down through the top in a manner inevitably recalling the Pantheon (fig. 20.12). Whatever the precise 'sources', one is struck, once again, by the depth of the transformation into the stuff of the artist's own expression.

A funnel, a dome, a roofscape, a sculpture beckoning to the foothills of the Himalayas, the Chandigarh roof element partook of all of these things. From the earliest, too, Le Corbusier sought to incorporate some of his universalizing iconography. At one stage a spiral ramp was made to run around it (useful for cleaning, but equally a symbol of the Modulor); later a strange collage of upturned curves was attached, referring to the gesturing leitmotif of the whole scheme, as well as to the path of the sun. It is possible that these solar implications were prompted by a group of sculptural abstractions Le Corbusier enormously admired: the astronomical devices of the Jantar Mantar in Delhi, and at Jaipur. The architect spoke of his invention as 'a true physics laboratory, equipped to ensure the play of lights. . . .' The solar symbolism was linked in turn to the very notion of state authority, and to the architect's own conception of an all-embracing order of nature: the lighting system (fig. 20.12) was designed so that a beam would fall on the speaker's chair on the day of the opening of Parliament. On that occasion a procession would proceed from the civic space outside, through the great enamel door adorned with cosmic signs, 'reminding man once every year that he is a son of the sun'. The Parliament building exemplifies the extraordinary depth and texture of Le Corbusier's symbolic thinking in his late years (Plate 10).

At the inauguration of the Parliament in 1963, Nehru spoke of Chandigarh as 'a temple of the new India':

> . . . the first expression of our creative genius, flowering on our newly earned freedom . . .

20.12 (*above left*) Le Corbusier, sketch of lighting system for Parliament Building, Chandigarh, *c.* 1956.

20.13 (*left*) Le Corbusier jotting in his sketchbook during one of his trips to India, 1950s.

20.14 Parliament Building, Chandigarh, 1953–62, roofscape with attached cosmic signs.

unfettered by traditions of the past – reaching beyond the encumbrances of old towns and old traditions. . . .

There can be little doubt that it was these 'progressive' qualities of the new city and its buildings which were first to make their mark. But Chandigarh, even though it was not 'fettered' by tradition, was still steeped in it; and while in the Indian context it was an emblem of the new, in Le Corbusier's mind it was equally a symbol of values which transcended the Western progressive mythology altogether.

By 1960 Le Corbusier was 73 and generally acknowledged as the world leader in architecture. His small atelier at 35 Rue de Sèvres had become a sort of breeding-ground for a new international tradition. His own commissions involved him in constant travel. The publications of the *Oeuvre complète* ensured a wide following. The late works soon fostered a series of transformations in various countries. The 'New Brutalists' (to be discussed more fully later) learned from the direct use of materials, which they gave their own moral meaning. Architects as diverse as Kenzo Tange in Japan, Paul Rudolph in the USA, and

Balkrishna Doshi in India drew lessons from the monumental and rugged concrete expression. And just as the seminal works of the 1920s were frequently devalued and turned into clichés, so the late works were often imitated for their surface effects without due attention to underlying principles: *brise-soleil* and rough concrete finishes could become a sort of façade cosmeticism just as easily as strip windows and thin *pilotis*.

Le Corbusier must have been aware of the dual pressure to consolidate principles and to continue experimenting. This seems to show in two of his latest works, the Carpenter Center for the Visual Arts, in Cambridge, Mass., and the Venice Hospital (fig. 20.15), which remained only a project when the architect died. The latter scheme was envisaged for a site half on the land, half in the water, not far from Venice railway station. The architect decided on a low project so as not to interfere with the historic skyline of the city. But the most striking aspect of his strategy is revealed by a plan or the model. For the hospital was a sort of modern analogue to the urban structure around it: an extension of the neighbouring order, yet an intensification of it into a new form. This was not just a

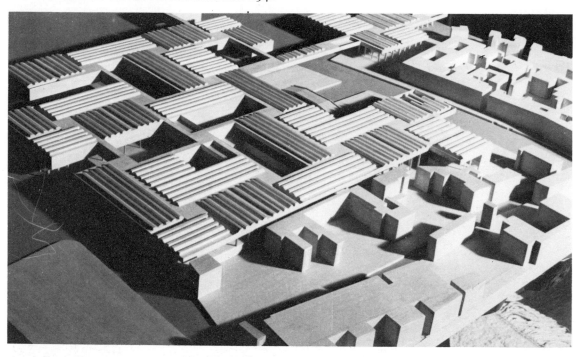

20.15 (*left*) Le Corbusier, Venice Hospital proposal, 1962.

20.16 (*right*) Le Corbusier, Carpenter Center for the Visual Arts, Cambridge, Massachusetts, 1960–63.

matter of imitating local house types, but of penetrating intellectually to the typical pattern of Venetian urban spaces and reinterpreting them in the shape of the building. It was the opposite of what might be called 'object planning' and indicated that Le Corbusier was sensitive when necessary to the historic tissue of a city. Perhaps, too, in setting the guidelines for the scheme he reflected awareness of the renewed debates of the Team X generation of architects, who identified a typical weakness of earlier CIAM planning as being its crass disregard for the sense of place, and for the unique qualities of context (see chapter 21). Unfortunately the hospital was not built, but the project exerted considerable influence on numerous 'mat' buildings of the early sixties, in which circulation became a major generator of form.

The Carpenter Center (fig. 20.16) was built, however, and seems to have issued from a retrospective state of mind. The function was to house a new department of Visual Studies at Harvard University. The site was jammed in between neo-Georgian neighbours close to the arcadian setting of 'Harvard Yard'. Le Corbusier's solution was a free-plan 'loft' building amply lit from the edges by a variety of fenestration devices, including *brise-soleil* and *ondulatoires*. The heart of the idea was an S-shaped ramp linking the new function to the nearby streets, and implying a continuity of the diagonal paths of Harvard Yard opposite. The main studios were formed as freehand curves, extending from a cubic volume to the

centre, the entire arrangement being twisted from the prevalent orthogonal geometry. The power of the scheme arose from the dramatic interpenetration of curved and rectangular volumes, of transparent and massive elements, whose dynamism was further varied by the fact of changing position. For the ramp supplied not only a show-case of the inner workings of the department (a response to a request in the programme), but an orchestrated sequence of architectural events.

Even considering its formal elements, Carpenter Center was a rich amalgam of various earlier phases of Le Corbusier's evolution. It was as if the 'acoustic' forms of Ronchamp had been cross-bred with the elemental attitude to structure manifest in the early works; the extremely pure skeleton inevitably recalls the primary statement of the Dom-ino. The evidence is abundant that the architect conceived Carpenter Center as a demonstration of his vocabulary in concrete and as a sort of *summa* of structural principles. In line with this intention, the Quincy Street façade was fitted with a barrage of different fenestration devices which far outstripped practical justification. Once again Le Corbusier was involving himself in demonstrations, in this case in a true 'teaching building'. The *Oeuvre complète* was right to claim that 'many of Le Corbusier's guiding ideas' found their place in Carpenter Center.

But this was also Le Corbusier's only building in the United States and thereby achieved further sig-

nificance. It was not industrially advanced America – spiritually poor in Le Corbusier's eyes – which gave him the opportunity to build a city, but the culturally rich, materially poor India. He had always hoped to persuade the American authorities to adopt his Ville Radieuse ideals, but without success. It seems possible that his didactic statement in Carpenter Center did include urbanistic ideas, however: the S-shape of the ramp appears to refer to the ideogram for the rise and fall of the sun ('which regulates all our urban enterprises'), while the ramp itself may well be a metaphor for the American freeways Le Corbusier had so admired as potential tools for the realization of his urban ideal. It seems, in other words, that Carpenter Center, despite its relatively humble size, was an emblem of Le Corbusier's philosophy – a building fusing his lifelong concerns as painter, sculptor, architect, and urbanist.

In 1965, a little over two years after the completion of Carpenter Center, Le Corbusier died in a swimming accident in his beloved Mediterranean, at Roquebrune, where he always spent his summers. Since then his ideas have continued to exert a great influence, but it is still too early to assess them in a balanced way in the light of history. Some of the standard reactions against a great man who left a major imprint on his time have already occurred, and this only serves further to blur the picture. It seems likely, though, when the mists clear, that Le Corbusier will deserve to be considered as an artist of the highest calibre. Whether one agrees with this assessment or not, it must surely be clear that the architect realized his ambition of creating for the modern era an architecture which extended principles from the past.

21. The Unité d'Habitation at Marseilles as a Collective Housing Prototype

Every important work of art can be regarded both as a historical event and as a hard-won solution to some problem ... other solutions to this same problem will most likely be invented to follow the one now in view. As the solutions accumulate the problem alters. The chain of solutions nonetheless discloses the problem.

G. Kubler, 1962

A tradition is composed of features other than the sequence of personal styles within broadly shared themes. Some of its lines of continuity may also be defined in terms of the 'evolution' of building types. These may cut across a variety of individuals' vocabularies yet still respond to certain kernel problems. It may even happen that a single building stands at the head of a sequence and takes on the role of a prototype. The Unité d'Habitation at Marseilles (1947–53) had something of this function in the field of collective housing. It was a difficult building to ignore for any later architect facing analogous tasks. To chart the lessons learned from it, and the various reactions against it, is to provide an extraordinarily clear summary of Western architectural attitudes over a period of nearly a quarter of a century.

The Unité stands off the Boulevard Michelet on the outskirts of Marseilles. The first impression is of a textured cliff towering above a dry landscape dotted with scrub and trees (fig. 21.1). In the summer, the deep crates of the *brise-soleil* are gashed with shadow and the concrete takes on the tawny colour of the stonecrop nearby. The slab rises to twelve storeys excluding the undercroft and the roof terrace, and has an ingenious interlocking section. Each apartment possesses a double-height living-room with a terrace and a lower portion passing through to the smaller balconies on the opposite side. There are twenty-three different apartment types catering for the entire range from the single individual to the family with four children. The elements of each are standardized, their combination varied. The factory-produced units are slotted into the overall lattice of the building's structural frame as wine bottles might be in a rack. But the aesthetic result is neither repetitious nor busy: banality is avoided, unity maintained, through judicious attention to proportion, rhythm, human scale, and sculptural control of the mass (fig. 21.2).

The hierarchy of individual cells to overall form, of private spaces to public whole, has been handled deftly throughout. The colossal *pilotis* (tapered descendants of the ones at Pavillon Suisse) define a public undercroft to the slab, and create a zone of shadow on which the fully lit volumes appear to rest. Major verticals are created by the lift, service and stair towers and by the flange walls at the end of the block. An interior street containing shops, a restaurant, even a hotel, is expressed half-way up the block as a glazed gap of increased transparency. The roof terrace on top is acknowledged by a series of sculptural objects – the gymnasium building, the crèche, and the bizarre form of the ventilator stack (fig. 21.3), a hollow version of the *pilotis* down below, reminiscent in its surreal mood of a chimney-scape by Gaudí. This terrace, with its running track, its pool, and its odd concrete sculptures rhyming with the Provençal hills in the distance is surely yet another celebration of Le Corbusier's Mediterranean myth. When the sun streams down on the bold concrete forms and flashes off the pool, when the trees rustle below and the bay is glimpsed in the distance, one is forcibly affected by the Corbusian dream of the good life – his antidote to the squalor of the industrial city. The memories of Greece are strong: this little acropolis of resounding silent objects in light

21.1 (*above*) Le
Corbusier, Unité
d'Habitation, Marseilles,
1947–53, view with
setting.

21.2 (*right*) Le
Corbusier, Unité
d'Habitation, Marseilles,
façade.

seems set up to celebrate a healthy balance between the mental and the physical. The Unité as a whole is a synthesis of social and formal imagination, of abstract and material qualities. It is far more dense and robust in its materials than the pre-war works, yet the whole is regulated by the numerical abstraction of the Modulor.

If the Unité stands at the beginning of a typological tradition in the post-war years, it also represents the culmination of a long quest for a collective order in Le Corbusier's philosophy. The pedigree stretches back through the Algiers viaduct, to the *à redent* houses of the Ville Radieuse, to the Pavillon Suisse, and, even further, to the *immeubles villas* and the Maison Citrohan. Each of these schemes considered different ways in which the modern building might anticipate the Utopian city. The Unité explored some of the same themes and may be interpreted as yet another demonstration of urbanistic principles, which also acted as a laboratory for experimentation. Central to the endeavour was the idea that mass production should be co-opted to deal with housing shortage, and it was probably this that ensured the support of Eugène Claudius-Petit, Minister of Reconstruction. Le Corbusier's analysis began with the individual family. He sought to reconcile high-density urban living with the provision of the essential joys of light, space, and greenery. This was reflected in the 2:1 ratio of each apartment section. The living-rooms were ample and spacious and had good views to the outside over balconies which (in Marseilles at least) could be used as living space. The kitchen, bathroom and bedrooms were half the height and tucked into the remaining part of each dwelling. It was the Citrohan section rethought: the Unité apartment even included a gallery, slung at the middle level of the double volume.

The communal aspects of the Unité were quite crucial to Le Corbusier's theorem. The individual apartments were ingeniously stacked so that the double-height part of one dwelling stood below or above the single-height part of another: the result was a jigsawed entity equal to three normal floor heights, with a corridor running through it. At the middle level of the building the corridor was amplified to become the *rue intérieure* or interior street, an element which recalled the walkways halfway up the Algiers viaduct fifteen years earlier. The other major public domain was the roof terrace. It was hoped that this would be a safe place for people to sit and unwind in the sun while their children played. As in Le Corbusier's 'five points of a new architecture', the roof was thought of as a new level of ground in the air. The actual ground beneath the *pilotis* was reserved for circulation and had little of the intimacy of the analogous area in the Pavillon Suisse. The society of the Unité was lifted bodily into space.

· The next scale of consideration was the relationship between the Unité and its physical setting. The theory behind the high-density vertical slab was the usual Corbusian one: modern techniques of construction and production were to be used to create high concentrations of population so as to liberate the ground for traffic and nature; in the process the old distinctions between country and city were to dissolve away. Le Corbusier had hoped to construct a number of Unités alongside one another in support of this idea. If he had done so some of the drawbacks of his concept might well have been dramatized. For while each block expressed the notion of a unified community, it is likely that a gulf would have existed between blocks. Mumford hinted at this problem when he criticized the interior street as an inadequate social equivalent to the traditional street at ground level in a dense urban setting. The individual Unité was just right for Marseilles and the Midi; but the *concept* of the Unité was liable to raise problems if applied indiscriminately to all situations. This was ironical: there can be no doubt that Le Corbusier thought his solution was normative and universal.

21.3 Le Corbusier, Unité d'Habitation, Marseilles, view of roof terrace and ventilating stack.

21.4 (*right*) Le Corbusier, sketch section of monastery at Ema, c. 1907.

21.5 (*far right*) Section through ocean liner illustrated in Le Corbusier's book *La Ville Radieuse*, 1933.

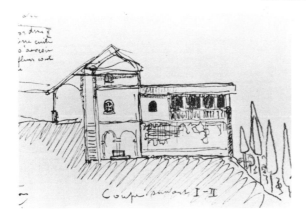

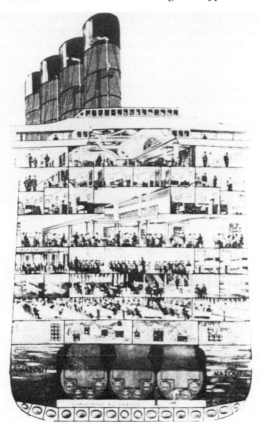

While the Unité stemmed from Le Corbusier's reflections on the sort of life possible for the majority in an industrial system, it drew on many earlier influences. It was no coincidence that 1,800 was the number posited as the ideal population for the mini-society, as the same figure had been suggested by Charles Fourier for his 'phalanstère' over a century before. There was another respect in which the Unité echoed its Utopian-Socialist prototype: the idea of an interior street linking the building from one end to the other and expressing the notion of a unified community. The double-height private dwellings looking out over nature recalled, once again, the monastery at Ema (fig. 21.4), while the disposition of decks, stacks, public and private areas was surely influenced by the image of the ocean liner. In his book *La Ville Radieuse* (1933) Le Corbusier had published a section of a Cunard transatlantic steamer and had called attention to its many admirable features as a model for collective living (fig. 21.5). The analogy between ship and Unité is, of course, an abstract one, but the image of a collective city 'floating' above the sea of verdure is nonetheless strongly felt at Marseilles.

In the twenties Le Corbusier might have played up the mechanistic aspects of this metaphor, but at Marseilles the overtones were archaic and the concrete was rugged, as in the other late works. In retrospect, it seems that the solution for a highly textured concrete showing the imprints of the form-work planks was forced upon the architect by immediate post-war building conditions and by the fact that so many different contractors worked together on the project that it became impossible to hope for smooth transitions. Even so, the architect turned these difficulties to good aesthetic use which accorded with changes in style and intention. At the opening of the building in 1953 he was happy to refer to concrete as a *natural* material and to compare it to stone. The *béton brut* (bare concrete) of Marseilles was the finish appropriate to the ethos of the 'second machine age', the era of

harmony in which a new contract would be formed between man and nature. The metaphor of mechanism was in retreat.

The opening of the Unité coincided with the 1954 meeting of the Congrès Internationaux de l'Architecture Moderne at Aix-en-Provence – the home of Cézanne, a founding father of the modern art faith. One wonders if the older members recalled the meeting twenty years previously on board the SS Patras, when they had sailed along the Mediterranean coastline and discussed the shape and politics of a new urban order. As they gathered together for the opening party on the roof terrace perhaps they realized that this robust concrete ship was the physical embodiment of the doctrines they had put together on that occasion as the Charter of Athens. But dry theories are one thing, life-enhancing forms another, and the younger generation at Aix were very clear about the difference. They saw a pallid version of the pre-war urban dream rising about them in the post-war reconstruction of Europe. They felt tricked, torn between disbelief in the tired doctrines of modern planning, and faith in the evocative power of the most poetic realizations of earlier modern architecture. This reaction, with its underlying dependence on the masters, led to the organization of the Dubrovnik meeting of CIAM in 1956 by 'Team X', an international affiliation of architects, mostly in their thirties, who wished to recapture the heroic moral drive, yet channel it in ways relevant to an utterly transformed world. For them the Unité at Marseilles was charismatic: its philosophy was rooted in the Utopianism of the pre-war modern movement but its forms embodied a new sensibility which suited their mood. Essentially their attitude was ambivalent. The same absolutism which gave the building its compelling power was also repellent to their pluralism. But as a prototype the Unité was unavoidable. The problem was to transform its fundamental lessons into a terminology more flexibly attuned to particular social, physical, and regional conditions.

The Unité idea had been published long before the building was completed, so the theorem had already influenced numerous housing schemes of the late 1940s. The critical attitudes later embodied in Team X had also been fermenting for some time. One of the most cogent statements of a new attitude had been conceived before the Aix meetings: the 'ATBAT' housing proposal for Morocco by Vladimir Bodiansky and Shadrach Woods (fig. 21.6). The idea had been to produce a collective habitat in tune with local climate, culture, and context. The architects therefore attempted to abstract some of the spatial features of the traditional North African city and to cross-breed the resulting order with such useful devices of the Unité idea as the street-in-the-air, the *brise-soleil*/balcony and the roof terrace. Evidently, the two sources blended together well; indeed, it is arguable that the tight aggregation of North African cities which Le Corbusier saw in the 1930s inspired some features of the Unité in the first place.

The Charter of Athens had separated urban functions into broad divisions of living, working, leisure, and circulation. The new sensibility required something less simplistic and mechanical. A new formal pattern was needed to express a more complex image of the city and of social behaviour. In the mid-fifties words like 'association', 'neighbourhood', and 'cluster' began to replace the earlier abstract terminology, while organic analogies for growth and change began to supersede the rigid, Cartesian geometries of the Ville Radieuse. The younger generation was troubled by the grand-slam aspect of *tabula rasa* Utopian planning and sought a more complex and sympathetic relationship between old urban tissue and new functions. Even so, it has to be emphasized that the inherited schemata of earlier modern architecture were not completely rejected; quite the contrary, they were accepted as valuable and then modified.

The English situation in the decade after the war offered every opportunity for experiment due to the

21.6 Shadrach Woods and J. Bodiansky, ATBAT housing Morocco, 1951–6.

combined impact of the blitz and a socialist government committed to public housing. Bland blocks of flats soon rose up, although London boroughs like Richmond, Pimlico, Finsbury, and Paddington were fortunate in acquiring creditable reworkings of Unité ideas. The other major paradigm was the Garden City which was reinterpreted in the New Towns; again little architecture of lasting value was achieved. Alison and Peter Smithson, two young architects who delighted in the role of *enfants terribles*, felt that none of these approaches captured the essence of English post-war life. With a little help from the critic Reyner Banham they indulged in the sensibility of 'the New Brutalism', a term which suggested their fascination with the toughness of English working-class existence and the 'art brut' of Dubuffet, and their rejection of the saccharine version of modern architecture they saw being built. It is tribute to the power of the Unité image that it should have intervened in what was a somewhat routine English exercise in sentimental populism of the 'kitchen sink' variety. But in their scheme for workers' housing at Golden Lane in the East End of London (1952) the hold of the prototype can be sensed in the use of slabs with access streets in the air (fig. 21.7). Like the ATBAT scheme for Morocco, Golden Lane also implied a critique of the free-standing block. The slabs were linked together in a linear way and disposed to respond to the surrounding street patterns, while the interior street was brought to the edge of the façade where it was repeated at every third

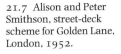

21.7 Alison and Peter Smithson, street-deck scheme for Golden Lane, London, 1952.

level. The 'street-deck' was intended to encourage chance encounters, and was a rather abstract attempt at restating traditional working-class doorstep life in the air. In the same period the Smithsons evolved designs with zigzags of linear housing based on patterns of movement, and designed a scheme for Sheffield University in which the street-deck was the unifying element. They pointed gleefully to the drip paintings of Jackson Pollock and the grainy photographs of Nigel Henderson as evidence of a new aesthetic blending change, coarseness, and the primitive. They insisted that they were seeking a new language for urban design, and rejected the Garden City and thirties' Rational models as equally irrelevant. Of the latter they wrote:

> The social driving force of this movement was slum clearance, the provision of sun, light, air, and green space in the over-populated cities.
> This social content was perfectly matched by the form of functionalist architecture, the architecture of the academic period which followed the great period of Cubism and Dada and De Stijl, of the Esprit Nouveau. This was the period of the minimum kitchen and the four functions, the mechanical concept of architecture.

Today in every city in Europe we can see Rational Architecture being built. Multi-storey flats running north–south in parallel blocks just that distance apart that permits winter sun to enter bottom storeys, and just high enough to get fully economic density occupation of the ground area – where the extent of development is sufficient we can see the working out of the theoretical isolates, dwelling, working, recreation (of body and spirit), circulation; and we wonder how anyone can possibly believe that in this lay the secret of town building.

Instead the Smithsons claimed that they were seeking an environment which would give 'form to our generation's idea of order', and that Golden Lane was a partial realization of this idea. Their polemics were heavily laced with illustrations of Greek islands, Bath, working-class backyards, kasbahs, and other dwelling arrangements of the past which seemed to be 'a direct expression of a way of life', but it was obvious that the dominant image was still the Unité d'Habitation; the vein of 'peasantism' that they detected in Le Corbusier clearly allied his post-war works in their minds with some of the traditional, pre-industrial qualities they sought to reinterpret. However, they remained committed to the definition of images which would be 'counterforms' to a post-war, mobile automobile world. At later Team X meetings in which they played a major role, the Smithsons were to discover that many of their enthusiasms and dilemmas were shared by the other members despite their varied backgrounds.

Among the housing schemes actually built in this period in England, Denys Lasdun's 'cluster blocks' in Bethnal Green, London, embodied a new position most clearly (fig. 21.8). These were also an attempt at forming a new image of community, appropriate to the problems of post-war urban reconstruction, in which it became increasingly clear that the new and the old must have a more complex symbiotic relationship than that proposed by 'diagrammatic' slab planning. Lasdun was older than the Smithsons, but younger than the generation of Lubetkin, and so straddled the pre- and post-war worlds. He remained aloof from the polemics of the 'Brutalists', and his own style was partly formed in the 1930s. A superficial inspection of the Uskdale and Claredale Street clusters (1952 and 1954 in design, respectively) reveals clear debts to Lubetkin's vocabulary, to the image of the modern tower and to the ideal of well-lit, well-ventilated flats open to the view and the sun. However, such themes were overlaid with others which amounted to a critique of the monolithic slab. The circulation and noisy service chutes were placed in a central core, while the 'maisonettes in the air' were located in four separate volumes linked to the core by bridges. Part of the rationale for this form was that it allowed maximum exposure of the living rooms to the sun; but it also involved the idea of turning the traditional Bethnal Green Street on its end, re-creating some of the indigenous features (backyards for washing, etc.) in the air, and avoiding the bleakness of a tunnel-like corridor in the usual 'block' of flats. The actual dwellings were made two storeys high and were thus based on the typical local house-type, while the sills and proportions restated the scale and rhythms of the neighbouring nineteenth-century façades. Thus the sanitary and sculptural qualities of the Unité were employed but in a way which incorporated the local social and physical context. The plan shape, with its splayed angles and its suggestions of stems and arteries, relied on biological analogies at odds with the Cartesian geometries of the Ville Radieuse slab idea.

Among the eventual members of the loose Team X affiliation were two Dutch architects, Joseph Bakema and Aldo Van Eyck. Despite the tenor of his theoretical remarks, the former seemed to do little in his actual works to modify pre-war housing tactics; but the latter was preoccupied with the contrast between the vapid post-war rebuilding of cities like Rotterdam and the

21.8 Denys Lasdun, 'Cluster', Bethnal Green, London, 1954.

close-knit traditional Dutch cities. Van Eyck realized that the way forward lay in the re-creation of basic psychological qualities of shelter, yet in a language attuned to modern realities. He spelt out the position clearly at the 1959 CIAM congress at Otterlo where Team X ideas began to dominate:

Each period requires a constituent language – an instrument with which to tackle the human problems posed by the period, as well as those which, from period to period, remain the same, i.e., those posed by man – by all of us as primordial beings. The time has come to gather the old into the new; to rediscover the archaic qualities of human nature, I mean the timeless ones . . .

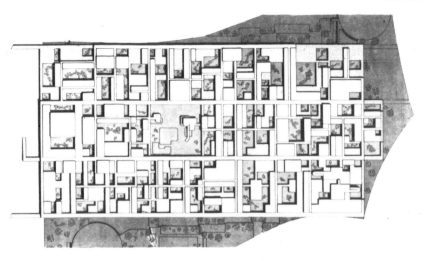

21.9 Shadrach Woods, Alexis Josic and Georges Candilis, Free University, Berlin, 1962–70, plan.

Van Eyck's quest for these timeless qualities eventually took him far afield to Dogon mud communities in the pre-Sahara and to the field of linguistic anthropology. His approach to vernacular forms was mystical; he saw them as expressions of coherent spiritual mythologies which he felt were sorely missing from most industrial building. His analysis focused on the cosmic meaning of symbolic elements like gates and entrances and on the hierarchies of spaces. He was also fascinated by the way buildings and streets were woven together. The problem came in translating these qualities to deal with the realities of an increasingly affluent Northern Europe. Van Eyck's orphanage near Amsterdam bore witness to his attempt at forming equivalent architectural systems using modern means of construction (see Chapter 26). But the process by which an authentic vernacular was conceived and constructed was necessarily far away from the activities of even a sensitive mind seeking basic values in an industrial society which seemed increasingly committed to a trashy and insubstantial consumerism.

The preoccupation with primary qualities of shelter, enclosure, procession, etc., grasped in part from the study of traditional urban structures, went hand-in-hand with an obsession with the notion of 'place' in numerous projects of the early 1960s. The Utopian ideas of the pre-war period had seemed to imply the imposition of a new, more 'rational' order on the texture of the metropolis. The problem was how to handle the demands of an automobile society, employing the means of industrialization, in ways which still maintained the sense of urban – or rural – identity. Forms had therefore to be found which allowed a gradual transition between the old tissue and the new object. Urban spaces and architectural objects needed to be coalesced in a more complex overlapping

order than was usual in modern planning. It is no surprise to discover that the urban theories of Camillo Sitte were avidly restudied in this period. Moreover, the social meaning of the street (which Le Corbusier had overlooked in his destruction of the *rue corridor*) was given new emphasis. Even the 'street-deck' concepts of the Smithsons seemed to lack a rich enough connection with pre-existing urban routes.

Something of this new urban consensus emerged in Alexis Josic, Georges Candilis and Shadrach Woods's project for Frankfurt-Romerberg of 1963. Like their later scheme for Berlin University (fig. 21.9), this was based on a system of upper decks and streets linking the buildings together as a sort of pedestrian net above the services and automobiles beneath. One might perhaps see this order as an abstraction of the form of ancient Classical towns like Priene (in Asia Minor), or as a relative (in procedure as well as form) of Le Corbusier's low-level Venice Hospital scheme. The buildings and the spaces between were locked together as a single system which attempted to restate the patterns of the neighbouring traditional city. The theme of the upper walkway – a place preserving the social character of the street against modern vehicular functions – was virtually a leitmotif of the period. The 'mat' concept of architecture was the antithesis, obviously, of the free-standing slab; even so it was still essentially part of the Unité tradition as a fusion was still sought between concepts of city and individual building. Indeed, a number of models antithetical to the free-standing slab with a vacuum at its base were reactivated in this period: the perimeter courtyard block creating an interior precinct and reinforcing the shape of the street; the village, with its hierarchy of buildings and spaces; the hill town (or its conceptual relative the kasbah) with its apparent unity of topography, social hierarchy, built form, and open space.

This last prototype may have influenced the planning of the Siedlung Halen outside Berne (1960, by the Atelier 5 group), a 'squashed Unité', packed down to conform to the patterns of the landscape (fig. 21.11). The social relations of the scheme were directly expressed in the gradual transition in scales from the main piazza and street in the middle, to the secondary routes, to the gardens, and then to the individual quarters. Giancarlo de Carlo's college at Urbino was another variant (fig. 21.10): indeed, universities were frequently employed as microcosms of urbanistic ideals, just as they had been in the inter-war years. In this case the buildings were laid out on the crest of a low hill and were splayed in a fan shape to maximize views and to harmonize with the contours. While the form probably reflected the influence of Aalto's 'organic' ideas, it was also a modern restatement of some of the typical elements and spaces of the medieval

Italian city. A semi-enclosed space, rather than a free-standing object, became the main social focus, and everything possible was done to express the hierarchy of individual cells and social functions. A far less coherent version of this hill town imagery was later pursued by Moshe Safdie in his 'Habitat' at Expo '67 in Montreal, while the most successful 'university-city' of the period was probably Denys Lasdun's 'urban landscape' University of East Anglia of 1963–8 (see Chapter 24).

The combination of high-rise towers, perimeter blocks, and courtyards was pursued in another variant of the 'unité', also for university housing, but this time in the United States. This was José Luis Sert's design for married-student housing at Harvard. Sert had been a friend and previous collaborator of Le Corbusier, one-time president of CIAM, and the author of the book *Can Our Cities Survive?* (1942) which spread CIAM pre-war urban doctrines in the English-speaking world. The Harvard scheme, known as Peabody Terraces, was disposed as three main towers in a cluster around the traditional communal device of a courtyard (fig. 21.12). The usual vacuum at the base of the tall building was avoided by gradations of scale between the main towers where lower perimeter dwellings stepped down to lawns, pathways, and sheltered pedestrian routes. Delicate frame-like balconies with

21.10 (*above*) Giancarlo de Carlo, University of Urbino, student residences, 1962–69.

21.11 (*left*) Atelier 5 Group, Siedlung Halen, Berne, 1960.

movable slats acted as sunshades and articulated the façades at a human scale. Variation was achieved on the basis of a few standardized apartment types, ingeniously arranged in section, and linked by upper gallery streets and bridges to the increasingly public spaces outside. One may see the scheme as an extension of the principles of the Unité, where such inherited ideas as the street-in-the-air, the sun-break, and the roof terrace have been fused with the local courtyard tradition for student residences, and with the light wooden balcony qualities of the nearby new England triple deckers. Thus a Utopian vision of an alternative city in which an ideal harmony of man, nature, and urban existence had been implied was modulated, rendered less absolute, and wedded with a pre-existing context. The strategy was loosely similar to the one adopted a decade before in Lasdun's cluster conception, but it was expressed in a different personal style and with different regional responses in mind.

Sert's scheme was remarkable for the attention it gave to the quality of spaces between, to the disguise of parking, to its townscape detail, as well as to the expression of the actual buildings. He was fortunate in having a client who intended the best, and was perhaps better able to achieve it than the usual public housing agencies in the USA, and indeed most countries. The story of inventive reinterpretation of the Unité ideal has, alas, the dreary and brutal backdrop of endless egg-crate high-rises built around the world in the fifties and sixties, in which minimum functional definitions were allowed to prevail over the rich elaboration of new communal images in touch with basic human needs. The problem must be traced to the oversimplification of a theorem: the Unité ideal needed all of its constituent parts to have a chance of succeeding. To reduce the matter to high density when no due attention was given to communal facilities was to court disaster; to create open space without greenery was to devalue the idea of the community living in nature. The imitations of the Unité usually involved such drastic omissions. Does this mean that the prototype should be blamed for the later disastrous variations? Or is the blame to be laid on housing agencies and their architects for cutting corners in an over-simple response to the urban crises of the post-war era? However one answers these questions, the fact remains that the slang appellation 'vertical slum' fits only too well many of the post-war experiments. It

21.12 José Luis Sert, Peabody Terraces, Cambridge, Massachusetts, 1964.

is scarcely surprising that the now notorious arson (and eventual dynamiting by officials) of Minoru Yamasaki's low-cost housing scheme for St. Louis – the Pruitt-Igoe scheme (fig. 21.13) – should have taken on the dimensions of a symbolic event: as the ultimate revenge of the populace for some supposed professional planning trick foisted upon them.

But it is hard to generalize about the 'high-rise' in the abstract. What may be good for Chicago's well-to-do may be bad, in its cheaper version, for the proletariat of Paris; what may be right for the outskirts of Copenhagen may be wrong for Willamaloo. Neither the proponents nor the opponents of high-rise ideas were very subtle in their arguments. Where the former, especially in the fifties, had succeeded in constructing a vulgate of 'virtues' (cleanliness, density, greenery, order, replacement of slums, etc.), the latter, in the sixties, assembled a standard set of complaints. It was argued that 'tall buildings' (all tall buildings, anywhere) caused social 'isolation', destroyed decent urban scale, were a strain for the very young and the very old, were lacking in domestic feeling, and represented the imposition of one social class on another. Whether or not these complaints were really traceable to architectural shortcomings, or to other forms of a malaise, it was evident that the charisma of the Unité, and of large-scale town planning, was beginning to fade.

The 1960s also witnessed further architectural critiques of the Unité concept that were not so nihilistic, but which reflected societal reaction against the free-standing slab. These embodied further attempts at blending new and old. One particularly successful version of this softer attitude was the Lillington Street estate in Pimlico, London, by Darbourne and Darke, built between 1967 and 1973 (fig. 21.14). Here the housing was wrapped around courtyards and precincts with sensitive level changes and vistas (recalling the townscape ideas of Gordon Cullen). The focus of the entire scheme was a pre-existing Gothic revival church by G. E. Street. The new housing paid respect to its neighbour's coloured bricks and stone lintels with red-brick balconies and slender concrete beams. The street-deck principle was employed but modified by planting and finely detailed brick surfaces. High density was achieved, but even the tallest parts of the estate had the feeling of connection with the surroundings and with the tree-filled courts. Traffic was excluded from the precinct by perimeter blocks so that the idea of the traditional London square was restated in a new form suitable to the automobile. Courtyard type, hill town and Unité were thus crossbred and blended with well-scaled responses to the Pimlico context. Standardization was still employed, but in support of the maximum visual variety, any sense of the free-standing monolith being avoided. The social make-up and ages of the scheme were also varied, and such communal functions as a welfare centre, a pub, a clinic, and an old people's home were included. A case could probably be made for the influence on Darbourne and Darke of Dutch housing schemes of the late 1910s such as the Eigen Haard

21.13 (*above left*) Minoru Yamasaki, Pruitt-Igoe housing, St. Louis, Missouri, 1958, being dynamited in 1972.

21.14 Darbourne and Darke, Lillington Street, housing, London, 1966–73.

by de Klerk, or of the red-brick vocabulary of Le Corbusier's Maisons Jaoul. Equally one might see Lillington Street as a fully domesticated and thoroughly Anglicized version of the Unité: a fitting image for the well-meaning impulses and compromised Fabianism of the Welfare State. It may have lacked the visual unity and polemical challenge of its parent building, but it was decent, socially responsible design nonetheless.

The history of the transformation of the Unité summarizes the process through which a major symbolic work, driven by an alternative Utopian dream, could be gradually sweetened and absorbed by the status quo. The Unité theorem was dragged from its remote position on the fringe of a Mediterranean myth

and forced to come to terms with the complexities of individual cities. In this process much fine housing was produced, and much that was disastrous, but in either case the contradictions of the avant-garde, visionary approach to planning were brought to the fore. Le Corbusier genuinely believed his was the right universal formula for the regeneration of the community. But the societies in which the debased versions of his dream were built grew increasingly sceptical of both environmental determinism and social engineering; in the process they became less and less able to project or define a sense of the possible social order in architecture. The single chapter of the Unité encapsulates the transition from the hopes of one era to the doubts, caution, and cynicism of another.

22. Alvar Aalto and the Scandinavian Tradition

> Only imagination can detect what is basic and what is not. The values with
> which architecture is concerned (should be concerned) are elementary
> values. . . .
>
> A. Van Eyck, 1967

The process described in the last chapter whereby the ideas of a powerful prototype were transformed to meet various conditions was repeated many times throughout the 1950s and 1960s. Linked to this pattern of dissemination were self-conscious attempts at blending modern architecture with national and regional traditions. Uninventive modern building was dull and seemed to represent technological brashness and social anomie. It was a long way from the poetic power of the finest inter-war works to the dreary housing schemes, offices and schools that constituted the debased international manner prevalent in the early fifties. Some sort of regeneration was evidently necessary.

In the search for new inspirations and primal signposts, peasant vernaculars once again came into vogue. They evoked a reassuring, pre-industrial world in which men, things, and natural forces seemed to work in unison. They also suggested keys for adapting to local environments, climates, and traditions, and were a good antidote to the diluted International Style. Vague yearnings for archetypes were sensed in many of the arts in this period. Pan-cultural aspirations towards a psychologically based theory of 'Man' kept uneasy company with a quest for regional identity which steered carefully around nationalist overtones. In this way a war-torn Europe sought internal equilibrium. The undercurrents were felt by artists as diverse as Le Corbusier and Aalto; they emerged in the debates around the conference tables and in the musings of Team X.

Giedion baptized the mood the 'New Regionalism' and hastened to point out that it had nothing in common with its inter-war blood-and-soil ideological cousins. The idea was to cross-breed principles of indigenous building with languages of modern design. A procured naïvety was evidently to be valued and modern architecture was to show both greater respect for differences of climate and a more sensitive appreciation of 'place'. At its worst this could end up in tepid imitations of vernacular forms; at its best it led to Le Corbusier's Maisons Jaoul, or to Utzon's houses at Kingo, in Denmark.

In Scandinavia the process of 'naturalization' of modern architecture had already occurred by the thirties, particularly in the work of Alvar Aalto. Indeed, the International Style had been a brief interlude and its lessons had soon been grafted to a substructure of national (or else National Romantic) building traditions. One is almost tempted to declare some Nordic genius for the sensitive handling of locale and of natural materials. But then conditions were different from elsewhere in Europe: industrialization and the Second World War had less of a drastic impact.

Although 'Scandinavian Modern Design' enjoyed a vogue in the 1950s and was associated with ovoid wooden salad bowls and organic bannisters, this was not the whole story. In his design for the SAS Hotel in Copenhagen (fig. 22.1), Arne Jacobsen demonstrated how Miesian ideas could be refashioned in a steel and glass vocabulary blending elegance of detail with lightness of touch; he also designed furniture, glassware, and other fittings. The manufacture of mass-produced models was aided by the strength of Scandinavian craft traditions which perhaps took to industrialization with less fuss than had been the case in Germany and England.

There was never quite an Aalto school, but he hovered as a sort of father-figure over Scandinavian architecture nonetheless. The fact was that his prototypes were well adapted to unique regional conditions and to such features as the scale of landscape and the stringencies of the Nordic climate. He was also inimitable, and the pasticheurs in this case evolved jagged ground-plans and clumsy sprawls of steps and brick surfaces. On the other hand, there were talents like Jørn Utzon and Ralph Erskine who were able to translate the basic lessons and emerge with their own creative identities. Aside from his influence on others, Aalto's late works contained a drama of their own: they need to be considered alongside the works of the other 'modern masters' in their maturity; as with them, new territories of expression were extended, while certain older themes continued to grow.

When the war came to an end, Aalto was 47 years old. He had managed to survive stagnant economic conditions in Finland by precarious trips across the Atlantic to teach in Cambridge, Massachusetts, at MIT, only a mile away from Gropius at Harvard (but very far removed in spirit). Aalto's first notable post-war commission stemmed from this institutional connection: it was to design 'Baker House', a student dormitory on a site to one side of the campus, with views over a busy road towards the broad basin of the River Charles (fig. 22.2). Aalto broke the programme down into its private and communal elements and disposed the former – the students' rooms – in a serpentine spine. This form was no mere whimsy, but

22.1 (*above*) Arne Jacobsen, SAS Hotel, Copenhagen, 1958.

22.2 (*right*) Alvar Aalto, Baker House, Cambridge, Massachusetts, 1947–51.

had a variety of practical, aesthetic, and symbolic justifications. It created considerable variety in the rooms and allowed diagonal views up and down the river; it made for an unmonolithic form of great sculptural vitality; and it marked out a small enclave to one side of the campus. The communal parts of the programme were enclosed in rectangular forms at ground level, laid out on a diagonal axis. This contrast in geometry was reinforced by contrasts in material between the horizontal, hovering concrete and stone-clad roofs of the lounge/dining-room area, and the rough red-brick textures of the serpentine wall punctured by windows of the private rooms. Overall, the organization seemed to suggest that Aalto had taken the formula of the Pavillon Suisse – a hovering rectangular slab for the student rooms, curved rubble areas for the public functions – and turned it on its head. Indeed, the Baker House design started as a parallel-piped block that was only gradually modulated into a curved form.

Although Aalto was probably inspired by the local Boston tradition of red-brick houses with sinuous, curved sequences of bays, the thinking behind the building and its forms was rooted in his pre-war explorations. The curves were related to Aalto's continuous search for anthropomorphic forms in everything from furniture design to the layout of large schemes on the Finnish landscape. Among the drawings for Baker House is one showing the building covered with trellises of thick greenery, like some vast natural formation. The rough brick surfaces gave the impression that the building was already old, and the effects of weathering were anticipated and invited. The contrast with the mechanical slickness then in vogue in America was extreme, and seemed to suggest a rejection of industrialism in favour of more lasting human themes. It is scarcely surprising that Baker House should have been perceived in America at the time as a challenge to the straitjacket of the International Style stemming from Gropius; it is equally notable that the building had little influence in the United States.

Aalto's concern for buildings as intermediaries between human life and the natural landscape was explored continuously in the post-war years. This was an architect who felt that there were almost archetypal building configurations to express the basic forms of human society. These he was able to intuit in both vernacular forms and the most ancient monumental buildings; indeed, there was no false opposition between 'high' and 'low' traditions in his search for fundamentals. One such archetype was the courtyard, or to be more precise, the 'harbour', formed by an inward-looking perimeter building on three sides, and linked to the surroundings by overflows of steps and

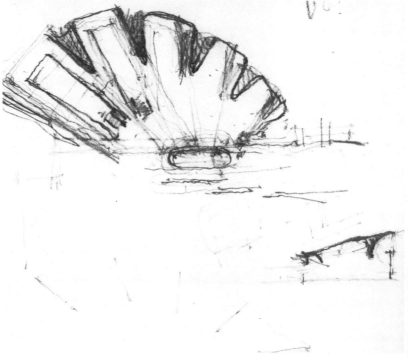

levels. The Villa Mairea had been a variant on this scheme before the war and it was to recur time and again in public and quasi-public schemes in the fifties and sixties when a focus was needed which nonetheless had to be linked to a larger context. Aalto's sensitivity to vernacular precedent emerges in his description of the 'Karelian House':

> A dilapidated Karelian village is somehow similar in appearance to a Greek ruin, where, also, the materials' uniformity is a dominant feature, though marble replaces wood. . . . Another significant special feature is the manner in which the Karelian house has come about, both its historical development and its building methods. . . . The Karelian house is in a way a building that begins with a single modest cell or with an imperfect embryo building, shelter for man and animals, and which then figuratively speaking grows year by year. 'The expanded Karelian house' can in a way be compared to a biological cell formation. . . .
>
> This remarkable ability to grow and adapt is best reflected in the Karelian building's main architectural principle, the fact that the roof angle isn't constant.

It is interesting to carry this image in mind when one approaches Aalto's town centre at Säynätsalo of 1949–52 (fig. 22.3). This was placed at the heart of an island community – the space to the centre becoming in a sense, the focal point of the entire local society. The complex included a council chamber together with a public library. At ground level there were shops which could be transformed into government offices once the need arose. The council chamber was contained in an almost cubic volume with a slanted roof and acted as the pivot of the scheme as one approached over the rising levels of land by means of a forest path, up the stairs, and across the court. Some variation of fenestration and texture was employed to articulate the different sides of the building; wooden slatted windows and balconies were set off against predominant rough brick surfaces. With its steps, overgrown with grass and weeds, its variations of silhouette, and its weathered materials, Säynätsalo had almost the air of an ancient complex of buildings which had grown gradually, bit by bit. The buildings blended with their forest setting and with the varying levels of the site. Any lapse into the merely picturesque was held in check by an underlying formal discipline (Plate 11).

Between 1950 and his death in 1973, Aalto produced an extraordinary number of buildings and projects. He received commissions in places as far apart as Oregon and Persia. Still, the majority of his buildings were for Finland and other Scandinavian countries.

The range of tasks handled was also very wide and included schools, libraries, churches, housing schemes, and university plans and entire urban layouts. Each building was marked by a unique response to the aspirations of the client, to the anticipated character of human behaviour, and to the configuration of the particular site, but there were still transcending themes suggesting a corpus of general principles. In other words – like Le Corbusier, Wright, Mies van der Rohe, and any other architects in the period who achieved a genuine style – Aalto was able to rely on certain type forms which had proved their worth time and again in a variety of contexts. Moreover, his architectural language, like theirs, was drenched in personal mythologies and reminiscences, as well as being a crystallization of values he felt central to the social fabric of his time.

An example of such a recurrent Aalto theme was the juxtaposition of the fan shape with an orthogonal, rigid form. Perhaps at a most basic psychic level, this contrast of motifs reflected his sense of polarities in the human condition. Certainly it was a pattern which signaled his interest in the contrast and dissolution of man-made and natural orders. Time and again the formal contrast was employed to soften and modulate edges, or to blend with landscape formations, nearby buildings of variable geometry, or clumps of trees.

On another level, the formal pattern was related to programmatic distinctions. Often the fan was made to contain a community of scholars (e.g., in libraries), an amphitheatre (e.g., in opera houses and university auditoria), or an outdoor public link (e.g., in the curved steps outside his own studio in Helsinki of 1955). By contrast the oblong flanges were often employed to contain more 'private' areas, such as offices or individual studies. Sometimes the fan shape would become a sort of extended ear or organ, creating a free-standing wedge like a detached piece of landscape; or again the shape might be embedded in a courtyard or grasped by a precinct wall.

Here, then, was one of those basic patterns intrinsic to a true style. But each time the type-form was re-used, it had to be rethought in its new context: it was not sufficient simply to re-use the form in a mechanical way. Thus in the Rovaniemi Library (1963–8) (fig. 22.4) and the Mount Angel College Library in Oregon, USA (1967), the fan was functionally related to the common-sense requirement of a single central point for the librarian (which led naturally to a variant of the radial plan) and to the need to maximize light around the edges. Moreover, the splayed treatment of the outer extremities allowed a variation of relationships to a setting and a variety of interior psychological moods and views for the readers. In these cases too the entrance to the buildings was through a 'hard' façade

22.3 (*above left*) Alvar Aalto, Town Hall and centre, Säynätsalo, Finland, 1949–52.

22.4 (*left*) Alvar Aalto, Rovaniemi, Finland, 1961, sketch plan of library.

22.5 (*left*) Alvar Aalto, Otaniemi Institute of Technology, Finland, 1955–64, the main lecture theatre.

22.6 (*below*) Alvar Aalto, sketch of the amphitheatre at Delphi, Greece, 1953.

of strong rectangular character, to which the fan shape supplied a softened opposite face, and a receptacle to receive the circulation across the building.

In a design for an art gallery for Shiraz, Iran (1970), the fan recurred once again, as a suitable way of creating flexible, parallel bays of varying height related to the viewpoint of someone entering (who could survey all at a single glance) and to the contour lines of the hilltop on which the building was to stand. In Aalto's numerous theatre and music buildings the fan shape was naturally well suited to auditoria requiring a focus of radial lines on a stage.

In the Otaniemi Institute of Technology of 1955–64 (figs. 22.5, 22.7), the form appeared again in one of its most daring manifestations. The site was irregular, fringed on two sides by motorways, with a slight slope in the terrain. Aalto made the main auditorium the focus of the whole group of buildings and placed it in a prominent position, expressed as a wedge-shaped volume. But it also acted as a hinge between the prevalent geometries of rectangular strip buildings containing offices, classrooms, and laboratories and laid out around courts or else with direct access to the

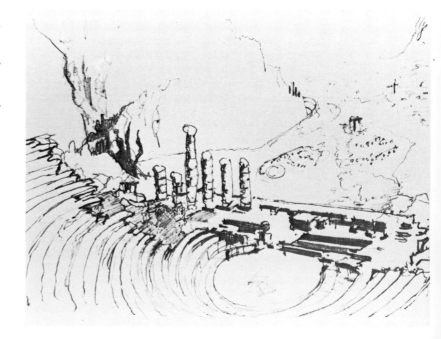

22.7 Alvar Aalto, Otaniemi Institute of Technology 1955–64, aerial view of ensemble.

main precinct. The main rectangle alongside the auditorium 'fan' was the administration block, while the smaller rectangles contained the teaching departments (geography, architecture, etc.). These were capable of future linear expansion, while the ceremonial theatre suggested a strong 'fix' in the composition. It was a plan which implied a hierarchy and separation of the parts, yet held all the bits in a close-knit order, which included the spaces between, the stepping landscape and the surrounding pathways. Similar sensitivity to the qualities of topography was to be seen in Aalto's larger urban design schemes, such as the one for Jyväskylä, where the council chamber and the theatre were expressed as free-form elements responding to the contours of the land, in contrast to the orthogonal geometry of the square. The result was an elusive order, flirting with the idea of irregularity, but unified through space tensions and vital interactions across the surrounding urban rectangularity.

One scarcely needs to point out some affinity of values between Aalto's 'landmass-sculpture' approach to architecture, and the late works of Le Corbusier, particularly Ronchamp. There can be little doubt that Aalto, like Le Corbusier in his late works, was preoccupied with the idea of an architecture close to 'Nature'. This conception implied not just an insistence on natural materials and a strong feeling for *genius loci* and regional setting, but also the treatment of nature as a source of 'Laws'. It was central to both architects' outlooks that an order should be unearthed in which man and nature should once again live in unison. In both Le Corbusier and Aalto there was therefore an almost totemic respect for natural forms.

Moreover, Aalto, like Le Corbusier, received stimuli from Classical sources, and was also intrigued by the forceful interaction of the intellectual with the sensual in the architecture of ancient Greece. But whereas for the Frenchman the Parthenon was the prime exemplar (a 'pure creation of the mind'), for the Finn the chief inspiration lay in the way the Greeks arranged their urban sites with amphitheatres, stadia, and ceremonial platforms linked by paths and routes. It was an 'irregular' order of this kind – in which there was, nonetheless, a harmony of buildings, landscape, and the spirit of place – that Aalto managed to evoke in his wonderful drawings of Delphi (fig. 22.6). Something of this landscape magic he attempted to translate into his own architecture and urban designs. It seems possible that the ultimate roots of the fan shape which so obsessed him lay in the amphitheatres of Greece.

22.8 Jørgen Bo,
Museum of Modern Art
at Louisiana, near
Copenhagen, 1958.

It is tempting at this point to stand back and make some generalizations about certain trends in the modern movement around 1960. In the late works of Le Corbusier and Aalto, in the aspirations of Team X, and perhaps even in the art of men like Robert Rauschenberg in painting, one senses a new sort of complexity and ambiguity concerning the relation of the art object and its surrounding spatial and cultural field. No doubt in time it may be possible to divine the underlying meaning of this tendency, which was certainly a continuation of some of the fundamental changes implied by Cubism at the turn of the century. Another prevalent trend seems to have been a more overtly traditionalist position. This was not a case of returning to nineteenth-century eclecticism, but of blending together, as it were, some of the primary devices of modern architecture with an ancient sensibility. Hand-in-hand with this development came a renewed interest in the unique qualities of materials and a sense of handicraft, which often had to be specially procured. Finally one notes a shift from pre-war mechanistic analogies to ones concerning complex geological or biological orders. Aalto seems to have grasped and incorporated all these tendencies within one huge imaginative structure; but far lesser talents seem to have paid increasing attention to values of this sort around the same time.

So far as Aalto's imitators are concerned, they tended, like Corbusier's or Wright's or Mies van der Rohe's, to acquire some of the external mannerisms without grasping the underlying meaning or structure of thought. This was usual and to be expected. Nor was it always a bad thing: Aaltoesque pastiches did at least have a complexity and texture which would have been lacking without his influence. However, there were some artists capable of extending Aalto's principles, and using them to feed their own.

Among these was Jørgen Bo, who designed the Art Museum at Louisiana, a few miles north of Copenhagen, in 1958 (fig. 22.8). The site was both demanding and rich in opportunity, in that a collection of modern paintings and sculptures needed displaying along a walkway between a fine eighteenth-century house and the sea. Bo planned the building to take maximum advantage of this sequence without disrupting the landscape. Essentially it was a linear building defined by white planar walls and low wooden roofs; the result was a quiet but elegant structure from which the garden was grasped as a series of vignettes, and these, in turn, enhanced the works of art. One of the most stunning effects was achieved by placing the stick-like Giacometti sculptures in a double volume against a backdrop of marshland and reeds; this particular space was entered at an upper level. The museum then gradually changed direction, to meander to the water's edge where the path continued (without the building over it) along a coastal way. The splay of the plan and the sensitivity to topography are reminiscent of Aalto. But the Louisiana design was also 'regionalism' of the best sort, since it seemed to fuse Miesian planar walls and spatial effects with the whitewashed enclosures and fine wooden structures of the Danish vernacular. The whole was permeated with a fine sense of proportion and a delicate scale which made it a comfortable neighbour for architecture of any age.

Another Danish architect to transform Aaltoesque lessons to good purpose was Jørn Utzon, who was born in 1918 and studied at the Academy of Art in Copenhagen under Steen Eiler Rasmussen. The period between the end of the war and 1957, when he won the Sydney Opera House competition, was one of constant travel, few commissions, and a vast absorption of impressions. He worked for a time with Asplund, then with Aalto, and visited Wright at Taliesin; he was also drawn to the sculpture of Henri Laurens, which provided basic lessons in abstraction and anthropomorphism. He travelled extensively in Mexico, the Far East, and North Africa, filling his sketchbooks with ideas and impressions. Among the strongest influences on him were the mud buildings he saw in Morocco and the cubic aggregate forms of Berber villages clustered around platforms and terraces in the High Atlas.

It is therefore insufficient to see Utzon as a mere follower of Aalto, though he did draw on Aaltoesque qualities of subtle ordering and spatial complexity. In the Kingo Houses near Elsinore in Zeeland of 1956–60, he designed an L-shaped type into the elbow of which a small garden was inserted. He disposed this standard in a variety of different ways over the topography to create a hierarchy between the individual home and the community and to maximize a variety of site responses on a gently sloping terrain. The terrace houses at Fredensborg (1962–3) continued something of this theme, but created an even greater variety of rhythms through a more complex form including towers. The materials were humble brick and pantiles, and the effect was akin to the 'anonymous' vernacular buildings so much discussed at the time. The overall plan layout of the Birkehoj at Elsinore (1963) introduced yet another pattern using standardized elements, by grouping them around a loosely defined 'harbour' in which the sculpting of land-mass platforms helped to link the parts and give meaning to the spaces between (fig. 22.9). In this case it is possible to perceive the lingering debts to Aalto and to vernacular expressions of community, but the style was Utzon's own. Moreover, the arrangement also suggests loose parallels with some of the ideas being pursued by Van Eyck, de Carlo (and other architects discussed in the last chapter) at about the same time.

Of course, the major building for which Utzon is internationally known is the extraordinary Sydney Opera House designed between 1957 and 1965 (fig. 22.10), and then brought to completion in a modified form after his resignation. Here is not the place to untangle the only half-known personal and political complexities which led to this sad state of affairs. The

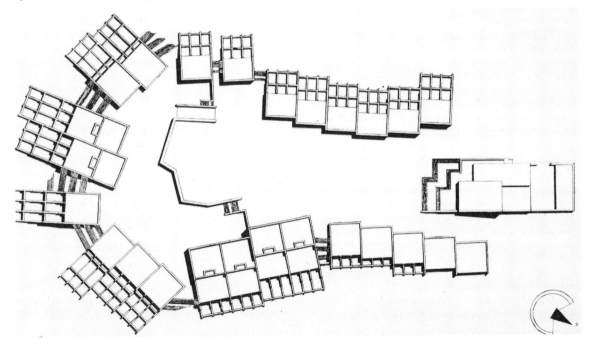

22.9 Jørn Utzon, houses at Birkehøj, Elsinore, 1963, plan.

22.10 Jørn Utson, Sydney Opera House, 1957–65.

result, so far as the architecture was concerned, was that the interior was quite different from Utzon's probable vision; that many of the details (of which he seems to have had an imprecise idea himself) were also gradually evolved by other minds than his own; and that the shells have a more vertical thrust than that envisaged in the earliest drawings.

But the image of these soaring white curves at the end of Bennelong Point, jutting out into the harbour and echoing the curves of the bridge and the sharp curves of the sails nearby, still has great power to move. They soar upwards from low platforms which themselves step up to their highest points at the water's edge. Into the platforms are laid the two main auditoria on a slightly converging geometry, while a small space to the landward side contains a restaurant. The sails, butting into and slicing one another, rising and pitching against the sky, seem to transmit visual force felt equally in the tense profiles, or their smooth but slightly textured surfaces. The original idea for the interiors is best grasped from a section which shows a sort of counterwave motion of curved ceilings flowing beneath the vast roofs above (fig. 22.11). The flytowers, finally, were buried under the highest of the shells, thus disturbing some hard-line puritans who were unable to enjoy the contrasts and complexities between the interior and the exterior.

As is true of most works of art of originality, it serves only a limited purpose to list possible sources or analogies. The platform theme was on Utzon's mind anyway, as is clear from his housing designs, but in a monumental context it may have been specifically inspired by the artificial hills with ceremonial steps of Monte Alban or some other Central American site. The shells were a staggering invention, perhaps partly influenced by knowledge of Taut's curved crustacean abstractions of the twenties, and perhaps partly prompted by the love of complex interlacing curvature which Utzon had seen in Aalto. But whatever the prototypes, the synthesis is quite new and seems to involve subtle abstractions of the sails in the harbour, as well as expressions analogous to the rhythm and flow of music. The same may possibly be said of the interior wave-ceilings; certainly they stemmed from the Aalto example of the Maison Carrée, but here they had as much to do with the flow of the nearby waves and the visualization of the flow of sound. It is curious that this *symbolic* visualization of musical rhythms should in fact have posed considerable acoustic problems. Then Utzon envisaged certain details like the window struts (immensely complex, as they had to reconcile the structural problems of vast openings with the difficulties of complex curvatures), which were perhaps traceable to an interest in the wing structures of birds.

But there was another level to the symbolism of the building. It was in a sense a modern cathedral consecrated to a supremely important national art.

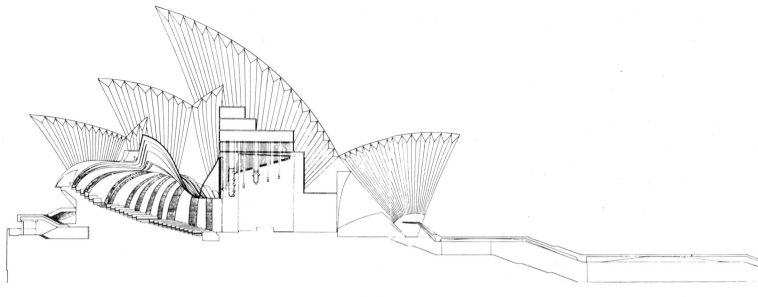

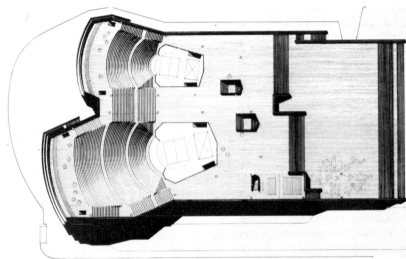

22.11 Jørn Utzon, Sydney Opera House, 1957–65, section of original scheme and plan.

One historian wrote of the concept that it:

> ... concentrates the unconscious meanings of its urban context in the same way as Notre-Dame, situated on the Île de la Cité, does for Paris. It manifests the spirit of the city ...

Utzon himself referred to the Opera House as a sort of church:

> ... if you think of a Gothic church you are closer to what I have been aiming at ... looking at a Gothic church, you never get tired, you will never be finished with it ... this interplay of light and movement ... makes it a living thing.

Indeed, Utzon attempted to design a standardized system of parts which could eventually be assembled into his free-form design, in much the same way that Gothic architects had used repeated systems to achieve their sublime and complex spatial effects. At Sydney this eventually necessitated a change in the geometry of the shells so that they conformed to a spheroid profile, and considerable experimentation with pre-cast concrete, in which the engineer Ove Arup played a major part. Many of the details remained to be worked out at the time of Utzon's resignation, and the Opera House looked for a time as if it might be a white elephant. At last it opened in 1973, having already become an Australian national icon.

Long before this, the Sydney Opera House had become part of the folklore of modern architecture. Sigfried Giedion published the design in the late editions of *Space, Time and Architecture*, and conferred upon Utzon the mantle of the great tradition. The Opera House was presented alongside Le Corbusier's late works and Kenzo Tange's monumental buildings in Japan as evidence of a new elemental tendency in which the fusion of buildings with their context was held to be crucial to the emergent spatial conception. In a sense the choice was premature, as it was not clear how buildable the Utzon design would be. Even so this was judicious appreciation of a great architectural idea. Moreover, it was an idea which, in its combination of the abstract and the naturalistic, in its fusion of the complex and the simple, in its enrichment of the structural and spatial ideas of earlier modern architecture, and in its transformation of ancient monumentality, encapsulated some of the aims of a new generation.

23. Louis I. Kahn and the Challenge of Monumentality

One should not be surprised to find, in fact one would *expect* to find an archaic quality in architecture today. This is because real architecture is just beginning to come to grips with a whole new order of artistic expression, growing in turn from the new set of tasks which society has set for the architect.

L. I. Kahn, 1960

Between the wars it was rare for modern architects to receive large commissions requiring monumental treatment. Certainly there were projects, like Tatlin's Tower and Le Corbusier's League of Nations, which suggested some ways in which the new architecture could be adapted to deal with the problems of size and symbolic expression posed by large institutions. But the hold of tradition over official taste remained strong into the 1930s in the USA and most of Western Europe, especially when civic ideals were concerned. Perhaps this was understandable given that these were situations in which the need to *preserve* values and to suggest continuities with the past was pressing. This was particularly the case under the totalitarian regimes, where ancient models enjoyed a skin-deep revival in the search for imperial symbols.

In the circumstances it was understandable that monumentality should have been temporarily regarded with suspicion, as if it was, in and of itself, an inherently anti-democratic characteristic. By 1943, however, Sigfried Giedion and José Luis Sert were already discussing a new monumentality to emerge in the post-war period. In a pronouncement entitled 'Nine Points on Monumentality' they referred to monuments as 'human landmarks ... intended to outlive the period which originated them', and as 'the expression of man's highest cultural needs'. They also discussed the role of collective symbols and the need for an urbanism giving 'more than functional fulfilment'. A decade later Giedion pleaded for the creation of symbolic centres to cities. CIAM meetings shifted gear from the 'four functions' towards a more nebulous and 'emblematic' characterization of urban form. Perhaps this change of mood was linked to the more 'permissive' view of tradition and precedent expressed by Giedion in the same period.

Between 1950 and 1965, the dissemination of the modern movement around the world meant that it became, by degrees, the rule of the established order rather than a fringe product of the avant-garde. Although it was often co-opted to express 'progressive' ideals (e.g., the UN), it had to come to terms with some of the traditional rhetorical functions of architecture such as the embodiment of the state. Architecture was itself changing in ways which allowed a greater grandiosity of expression. Le Corbusier, Mies van der Rohe, and Aalto gave indications in their works of the late 1940s and early 1950s of ways in which civic problems could be handled (e.g., Chandigarh, St. Dié, Crown Hall, Säynätsalo). External social conditions and the internal evolution of modern architecture were not out of step when it came to questions of monumental expression.

There was still the problem bequeathed by the nineteenth century, that no clear language existed to distinguish one civic function from another, or from lesser functions in a hierarchy. The increase in the number of building types fostered by industrialization conspired with confusions over 'style' to create a babbling urban order which no longer legibly portrayed the relationships of society in the cityscape. Ideal cities of the early modern movement certainly brought their own version of clarity, but tended to concentrate on living and working, leaving monu-

23.1 Oscar Niemeyer,
Brasilia, Brazil,
1957–60, the Senate,
Secretariat and
Congress.

mental expression for skyscrapers and freeways; in the Ville Contemporaine management and circulation had been those elements handled most forcefully.

After the Second World War Le Corbusier's architecture began to possess a new visual weight and heroic force, which was not unconnected with his own need to solve problems of monumental expression. At both St. Dié and Chandigarh he seems to have been preoccupied with some new vision of an Acropolis. Rough effects of *béton brut* and the strong articulation of shadow allowed him to create an allusive symbolic language in the service of an institutional pattern. In Chandigarh, particularly (as we have seen), he transformed various ancient types and formulations (e.g., the basilica into the Palace of Justice, the dome/portico combination into the Parliament) in an attempt at promoting images of a suitably honorific character. Pastiche of the prototypes was avoided by integrating them into a well-tried architectural vocabulary itself based on principle. The 'five points' were amplified and given a new sense of scale and dignity; *brise-soleil* in vast repeating rows proved suitable to the *gravitas* of the artist's intentions; and his impeccable sense of sculptural order ensured that unity and diversity were held in balance.

Oscar Niemeyer's State buildings at Brasilia (fig. 23.1), built in the late 1950s, drew more on the example of the pre-war Le Corbusier, or on the model of Harrison's and Abramovitz's version of the UN, than on the style of the late works. As at Chandigarh a new urban form had to be conceived on a virgin site.

Lucio Costa, the architect of the overall town plan, designed wings spreading out in a slight arc from the focal point. The president's palace and main congress buildings were laid out in front of vast piazzas with water and sky becoming essential elements of the composition. But Niemeyer's buildings lacked the force of those at Chandigarh. The president's palace, for example, had a mannered façade of smoothly finished inverted arches. The main chambers of the congress were expressed by saucer-shaped elements – one face down, the other face up – alongside the dominating element of the secretariat slab. It is possible that this imagery satisfied the technocratic aspirations and a thirst for grandeur on the part of the Brazilian élite: but the forms were inflated, diagrammatic and lacking in symbolic or sculptural substance.

This is not to suggest that a rugged sculptural treatment of the kind used at Chandigarh was an automatic recipe for good monumentality: the proposition is adequately disproved by the all too numerous examples around the world of concert halls, state houses, etc., in ungainly elephantine concrete forms surrounded by wildernesses of piazzas, conceived between about 1960 and 1970. But Le Corbusier's forceful late style could prove useful as a starting-point for more sensitive talents who took over not only the external effects, but also the intellectual strategies for the transformation of precedent.

The Boston City Hall by Kallmann, McKinnell, and Knowles of 1962–7 (fig. 23.2) is an example of such a valid extension of earlier discoveries. Here the problem was to give a suitable civic character to an institution whose identity seemed to imply both authority and openness. The architects produced a design in which massive visual weight and perforation from the surrounding urban spaces were held in balance. The main forms of the building expressed the hierarchical distinction of functions quite clearly, and allowed the large red-brick piazza to invade the structure at the lower levels by means of steps and ramps. The offices of the bureaucracy were on the top floors and were legible in the repeated pre-cast system of window elements, while the ceremonial functions (e.g., the mayor's office) were slung in amplified volumes at the middle level; the most public functions were at the ground level where most easily accessible. The programme seemed to suggest a rectangular plan around a court, but this basic *parti* in section and plan was articulated by dramatic interpenetrations of spaces and heavy concrete forms. The whole was composed into an overall form of considerable simplicity; at the top levels there was a marked horizontal emphasis which gave something of the character of a Classical cornice, and supplied a strong contrast to the nearby skyscrapers.

The rugged concrete and the variations in visual texture were clearly relying on the model of Le Corbusier's monastery of La Tourette; the overhanging section and broad concrete piers were also adopted from this prototype. But the historical references went further than this into the past. The architects were intrigued by those public palaces in Italy of the Middle Ages and Renaissance in which piazzas penetrated a lower storey of arcades. Such precedents were in tune with Kallmann's notion of an 'action' architecture in which interior spaces and exterior spaces were brought into vital juxtaposition, a concept like Lasdun's 'urban landscape' idea of making each building 'a piece of the city' (see Chapter 24), but expressed differently and perhaps less coherently. In the Boston City Hall the idea was encapsulated by the way the piazza ran in under the entrance to become a sort of interior forum, whose steps made a convenient bank of seats for meetings, exhibitions, and other public events. It has been suggested in an earlier chapter that the blend between the individual object and its setting was a major concern of the arts in this period.

Then again the City Hall attempted to pull together modern methods of component standardization with a restatement of Classical elements. The piers were a sort of 'grand order' in concrete, while the structural ceiling grid was reminiscent of coffering. These devices were firm reminders of the fact that the thin skins and slender *pilotis* of the International Style had proved themselves inadequate to handling a building of such

scale. Boston City Hall grappled with a wide range of issues central to the problem of monumentality, and presented solutions which, if not always totally resolved, were nonetheless propelled by serious thought.

Rough concrete was not the only medium through which schematic devices derived from Classicism could be restated. In his design for the New National Gallery in Berlin of 1962. Mies van der Rohe envisaged a glass and steel temple on a podium – a sort of shrine to German art (fig. 23.3). The main effect arose from the way the steel supports were carefully proportioned and spaced to recall Classical columns; while the vast overhanging steel roof was intended to evoke the *idea* of the entablature. On the interior the earlier Miesian notion of an abstract, 'universal' space was restated. In this case it was subdivided by supports and flexible planar partitions to bear pictures. Sculptures were left standing in the voids between. It was as if the trabeation, the overhangs, and the thin planes of the Barcelona Pavilion had been cross-bred with the symmetry and spatial ideas of Crown Hall at IIT. The Berlin Art Gallery also bore witness to Mies van der Rohe's consummate sense of detail and craftsmanship in steel. Like Le Corbusier at Chandigarh, he was able to achieve monumentality by expanding a pre-existing architectural system based on rigorous intellectual and expressive rules. What stopped the Classicism from being a game of mere quotation was the forceful expression of ideas in an abstract form. Classicism was once again rethought in a new material and in a new social context.

In the United States the expansive, optimistic, and, indeed, imperial undercurrents of the 1950s were

23.2 G. Kallmann, M. McKinnell and E. Knowles, Boston City Hall, 1962–7.

23.3 (*above right*) Ludwig Mies van der Rohe, New National Gallery of Art, Berlin, 1963, model.

23.4 (*right*) Eero Saarinen, TWA terminal, Kennedy Airport, New York, 1960.

expressed in many commissions for large-scale monuments. The influence of Beaux-Arts Classicism certainly did not die with the introduction of modern architectural ideas. At its deepest this tradition culminated in an architect like Louis I. Kahn; but a more obvious, less expressive, and often banal attempt at neo-classicism also emerged in the late 1950s. This was no doubt part of a general mood of dissatisfaction with the restrictive minimalism of the American version of the International Style (a reaction expressed in other ways as well, e.g., in the 'modern baroque' of Eero Saarinen's TWA terminal at New York Airport, fig. 23.4). Thus architects like E. Durrel Stone (the US Embassy in Delhi), Philip Johnson (the Art Gallery in Lincoln, Nebraska), and Harrison and Abramovitz (with Johnson, the Lincoln Center in New York, fig. 23.5) all indulged in grand axes, symmetry, expensive materials and tell-tale arches, to disguise an essentially bogus and skin-deep understanding of the nature of monumentality. Of course, their buildings employed modern techniques of construction in a Classicizing way just as Mies van der Rohe had hinted in his prototypes; moreover, these well-travelled architects were well aware of the high moments in the Classical tradition: but they were still unable to transcend a tendency towards 'camp'. Classical allusions were there in abundance; Classical principles were almost entirely lacking.

Abstractions of Classicism were not the only viable ways for creating a new monumentality, as was well demonstrated by Utzon's Sydney Opera House, or by Hans Scharoun's later Philharmonie in Berlin which was in the 'Expressionist' free-form tradition. At Coventry Cathedral, Basil Spence even attempted to design in an abstracted Gothic manner, but his spindly supports and fussy details were expressive failures. What was lacking was not so much conviction, as an ability to translate conviction into form. Nor were monumental tendencies in the late 1950s and early 1960s restricted to civic and religious programmes: especially in the United States there seems to have been a sort of inner will to grandeur affecting many architects and building tasks. The taut steel-frame skyscrapers gave way bit by bit to heavier looking boxes clad in marble and adorned with massive slivers of stone not unlike pilasters. Even housing was overwhelmed by a wave of megastructural thinking. Thus the myth of 'total design' came together with elephantine forms in yet another attempt at giving a clear shape to the American city.

The master of monumentality in the United States in this period was, without a doubt, Louis I. Kahn. Monumentality was not, of course, his only pre-occupation, but it was certainly a major one, and he evolved a philosophy and system of forms extraordinarily well suited to the expression of honorific themes and moods. Kahn was apparently able to avoid some of the pitfalls mentioned in earlier examples: he was well able to handle problems of large size without degenerating into either an 'additive' approach or an overdone grandiosity; he knew how to fuse together modern constructional means with traditional methods; he was steeped in history but rarely produced pastiche; and his architecture was infused with a deep feeling for the meaning of human situations, which enabled him to avoid the mere shape-making of the formalists.

Kahn's formation took place before modern architecture had established a firm foothold in the United States. He was trained in the Beaux-Arts system at Philadelphia and was therefore fully acquainted with the Classical grammar, with devices of axial organization and composition, and with an attitude to design which took it for granted that one should consult tradition for support. Certainly he sensed the decadence of most American architecture of the twenties and thirties, and realized the need for a change which better accommodated the needs and the means of the times. He seems to have learned primary lessons from Sullivan and Wright, and later from Mies van der Rohe, but he was a slow developer, and his house designs of the forties were unexceptional extensions of the International Style. The crystallization seems to have occurred in the early fifties, and to have been prompted in part by Kahn's stay at the American Academy in Rome, and his travels through Greece and Egypt. His sketchbooks of this period suggest he was trying to get back to basics – to probe the central meanings of architecture.

A key transitional work was the Yale Art Gallery of 1951–3, in which Kahn responded to the many levels and textures of an eclectic urban environment with a subtle, inward-looking design. The interior spaces (fig. 23.6) seemed to evoke an entirely different world from the brash mass-produced environment of standardized panels and suspended ceilings then prevalent in the USA, by subtle effects of light falling over the weave of a diagrid ceiling and the elegant, but bare, concrete supports. The stair was contained in a cylindrical volume, and rose through a series of triangular changes of direction, thus hinting at the architect's later tendency to make strong formal distinctions between circulation and 'areas served'. The exterior took over the Miesian glass and steel façade, but gave it a new irregularity and softness; the side walls and qualities of interior space, meanwhile, were loosely evocative of Wright.

The Yale Art Gallery was not a totally resolved work, and the sources were still not absorbed sufficiently for one to be able to speak of a coherent personal style. But

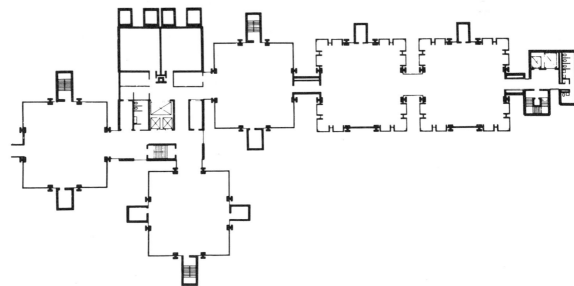

23.5 (*above left*) Philip Johnson, New York State Theater, Lincoln Center, New York, 1965.

23.6 (*left*) Louis I. Kahn, Yale Art Gallery, New Haven, Connecticut, 1951–3, exterior at night.

23.7 (*above right*) Louis I. Kahn, Richards Medical Laboratories, Philadelphia, Pennsylvania, 1957–62.

23.8 (*right*) Louis I. Kahn, Richards Medical Laboratories, Philadelphia, Pennsylvania, 1957–62. plan.

the building still suggested a new archaic direction for modern architecture in America. In the Richards Medical Laboratories at the University of Pennsylvania of 1957–62 (fig. 23.7), on the other hand, Kahn articulated a variety of ideas in a totally convincing statement. The laboratories required vast extract flues and flexible interiors, and the architect decided to express the distinction between the fixed and the variable, the serving and the served, by monumentalizing the service and stair towers and treating the laboratories as attached cellular elements. The site was to one side of a main walkway through the campus, not far from a number of neo-Tudor buildings with rich tower silhouettes and infill panels of windows, and it may be that Kahn was responding to this setting in making these moves. The plan was itself a subtle combination of the linear and the particulate, which also created external harbours of space around the exterior, so that there was a gradual shift in scale from the context to the individual details (fig. 23.8). The geometry of the plan, and the use of service and stair towers as monumental devices intermediary in scale between small and large parts of a design, suggest that Kahn may have been influenced by Wright's Larkin building.

But any influences there may have been were now absorbed into the internal logic of a personal style, and the formal and functional logic of a particular design. The structural system of the laboratory spaces was precast concrete, and Kahn attempted to show how the building was put together by the expression of joints and connections. This was no mere structural exhibitionism, as the aim was to give a suitable scale and character to the social organization of laboratory work. The approach was the opposite of the one which clothes everything in a single envelope; indeed one may almost go so far as to suggest that revulsion against the 'neutral box' was a world-wide phenomenon of the period. Kahn was here supplying a variety of formal devices, just as Le Corbusier had done in the Unité and at La Tourette, for the articulation of complex social programmes. Moreover, the Richards Laboratories had a direct, tactile character in the use of brick panels and concrete beams, which evidently also appealed to a generation of followers.

It has to be said that the Richards Medical Laboratories were more cogent as an 'idea building' than as successful laboratories. The principal difficulties arose from lack of sun protection in the façades, and despite all the effort of the design process, a certain lack of functional flexibility. Still, one has to accept that a work which does not function properly may be architecture of a high order. On the basis of a clear *parti* and logical system of servicing and structure, Kahn was able to create a building evocative of the antique

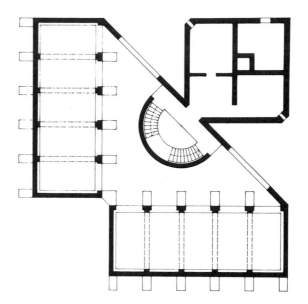

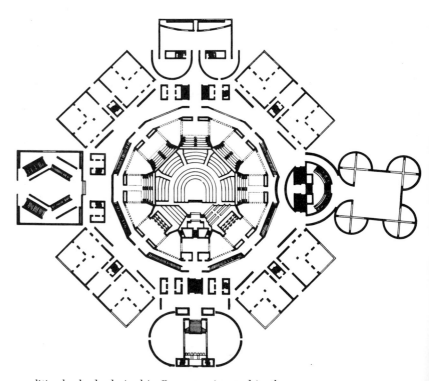

23.9 Louis I. Kahn. A consistent architectural strategy manifest in four plans: (*left*) Institute of Management, Ahmadabad, 1963, dormitory; (*below left*) Parliament Building, Dacca, 1963; (*right*) Bryn Mawr dormitories, 1964; (*below right*) Library, Phillips Exeter Academy, New Hampshire, 1969.

qualities he had admired in Roman ruins and in the towers and townscapes of medieval Italy. In the early 1960s in America, when the first stage was completed, the laboratories had almost the quality of a beacon towards timeless architectural values in an era otherwise beset with the extremes of meaningless formal gymnastics or arid functionalism. Kahn

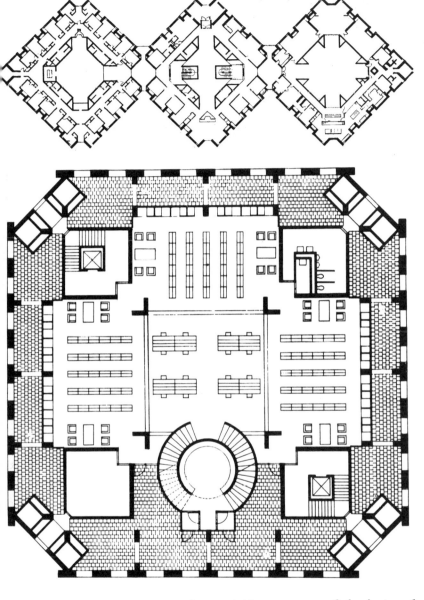

attempted to put his own sense of the basics of architecture into words:

> If I were to define architecture in a word, I would say that architecture is a thoughtful making of spaces. It is not filling prescriptions as clients want them filled. It is not fitting uses into dimensioned areas ... It is a creating of spaces that evoke a feeling of use. Spaces which form themselves into a harmony good for the use to which the building is to be put ...
>
> I believe that the architect's first act is to take the

program that comes to him and change it. Not to satisfy it but to put it into the realm of architecture, which is to put it into the realm of spaces.

Kahn's architecture was based in part on a social vision: this was a challenge to the status quo not through some Utopian expectation in the future, but through a mystical conservatism. For Kahn believed there to be archetypal patterns of social relationship that it was the business of architecture to uncover and celebrate. A good plan would be one which found the central meaning, as it were, of the institution housed. Related to this notion of a higher meaning in social forms was the distinction between 'form' and 'design'. Basically, Kahn believed that any architectural problem had an 'essential' meaning which far transcended a mere functional diagram. This organization would be found through a probing and detailed analysis of requirements followed by an intuitive leap which would uncover the 'type' of the institution. Only when this was discovered and embodied in a suitable symbolic form could the architect proceed to the stage of design – of giving the central, felt concept a material shape. A good design would be one where the 'form', the underlying meaning, was coherently expressed through all the parts.

This idealistic position with regard to the spiritual roots of both the social and the aesthetic realms motivated Kahn's major designs of the early 1960s and led him to clarify a simple set of 'type forms' based on primary geometries – the square, the circle, the triangle, etc. – capable of a vast variety of inter-relationships over certain kernel patterns of form and meaning. When one examines the plans of such diverse schemes as the Bryn Mawr dormitories, the Ahmadabad Institute of Management, and the Parliament building at Dacca, one is struck by the consistency of the approach (fig. 23.9). Time and again the architect reverts to a basic *parti* in which the primary meaning of an institution is expressed in a central space of a concentrated social character based on square, circle, or diamond, and related hierarchically to the surroundings by axes. Secondary spaces tend to be set out as a fringe around the primary generator, and to mark out variations on the theme; they tend too to contain smaller and more private functions. But these patterns of geometry – so like ornamental designs – are far from being arbitrary. They suggest mandalas or some other symbolic geometry. They remind one that Kahn, like Wright, had a pantheistic vision of nature which he attempted to contain in universalizing abstractions. Moreover, the strategy behind these plans recalls Kahn's Beaux-Arts training in which ceremonial routes of circulation

tended to be laid out along the primary axis of the most important symbolic space of a scheme.

Of course a plan did not exist independently of the volumes to be projected into space above it. Kahn never lost a feeling for the solidity of the wall as a major part of architecture, even when he employed reinforced concrete which might have allowed an open façade. Openings tended to be reduced to the most simple voids cut deep through the outer skin, and to be variants on the fundamental geometrical themes of a design – circles, squares, and so on. At Ahmadabad, in the Institute of Management, the architect created a deep zone of transition between the outer edge and the interiors, to allow for shaded porticoes and walkways. The colossal cylinders of baked brick and concrete had something of the quality of the Roman ruins that Kahn had so admired. But it was a poetry of shapes which seemed to transcend the merely European tradition:

Kahn, like Le Corbusier, was intrigued by the cosmological geometries of the Jaipur observatories, and these may have played a part in the distillation of his vocabulary (fig. 27.5).

In the project for the Jonas Salk Institute for Biological Studies (1959–65), close to La Jolla, San Diego, California (fig. 23.11), Kahn had to design for a community of scientists involved in concentrated research. Another architect might have attempted to embody the forward-looking aspirations of such a programme. But to Kahn the suitable references seemed to lie in such prototypes as monasteries or other forms of intellectual retreat. Three main clusters were planned apart from one another in the virgin landscape with views towards the Pacific: the community meeting and conference areas (the 'Meeting House'), the living-quarters (the 'Village'), and the laboratories themselves (the only part built), contained

23.10 Louis I. Kahn, Jonas Salk Institute for Biological Studies, La Jolla, California, 1959–65, view towards sea between study rooms.

23.11 Louis I. Kahn, Jonas Salk Institute. La Jolla, California, 1959–65, model showing ensemble.

in parallel blocks with a water garden between them. The laboratories themselves were large free-plan spaces capable of considerable variation in the design of experiments. They were linked by bridges to small studies with views into the garden or out towards the sea (fig. 23.10). Once again the distinction was made between the society of shared endeavour and the private world of thought. These studies were substantially furnished cells – or perhaps cabins – spaces for contemplation. On the exterior they were expressed by wooden panel apertures set into an otherwise bare-concrete wall vocabulary which clearly owed debts to Le Corbusier, except that the concrete finishes were deliberately refined and elegant. Vincent Scully has noted similarities between the Salk plan and such Roman schemes as Diocletian's palace or some of the buildings dotted about the landscape at Hadrian's villa: we sense that this might be the home of some ancient, hermetic cult.

Kahn's capacity for effective monumental expression was revealed to the full in his design for the Parliament building at Dacca in what is now Bangladesh (fig. 23.12). For this architect, government was one of the deepest and oldest forms of social order. The 'form' (using his meaning of the term) had to reflect the nature of such an institutional contract. One is scarcely surprised to find that variations on a circular theme were among the first to appear on paper (fig. 23.13), as this was the shape the architect used to express a coherent social grouping, a sense of unitary purpose, and a notion of 'centre'. Part of the meaning of the form, though, arose from its relationship to other institutions, and in the early diagrams exploring the

city layout the parliament was placed at the central point of converging smaller institutional relatives based on similar geometry. The full panoply of Beaux-Arts planning rhetorical devices – primary and secondary axes, a sense of climax, variations in size and shape – was employed to reinforce this sense of the building as the 'head' of the social order. It is interesting to recall that at Chandigarh, Le Corbusier had also used grand axes and hints from a variety of precedents in disposing the main elements of the capital complex, as well as in the design of the parliament building itself.

Rather as Le Corbusier had also done at Chandigarh, Kahn amplified his earlier architectural system to achieve effects of massive grandeur. The great chamber was circled by a family of other spaces – press galleries, members' rooms, etc. – expressed as smaller variations on the central formal themes. To one side was a mosque linked to the main body by steps; this was skewed slightly off the main axis to face Mecca, a deviation which served to reinforce the power of the prevalent geometrical order by contrast. The effect of these surrounding functions when projected into space was of a jostling series of cylinders and vast oblongs grouped around the central mass. With the deep cuts of shadow, the glaring force of the sun and the rudeness of the materials, the effect was entirely as if the buildings had been standing there for centuries. As Le Corbusier had done in India, Kahn made the most of local craftsmen in the creation of the surfaces and textures. The result was the obverse of mechanical slickness – something suggestive of age and weathering.

Without the underlying armature of Kahn's philosophy, his ruminations on the nature of man and architecture, and his ability to give these feelings a suitable and communicable symbolic form, such external textures would have been mere superficialities of patina, as skin-deep as the glossy intellectual packaging being employed by the devaluers of Mies van der Rohe at the same time. Kahn was able to make a convincing monumentality because his architectural system tended in that direction already and because his sensibility was open to the most ancient lessons of the great monuments of the past. Like Wright, Kahn believed in a 'Cause Conservative', invoking 'the elemental law and order inherent in all great architecture'. And again like Wright, Kahn was able to achieve this spirit, not by copying the externals of past styles, but by probing to the underlying principles and attempting to universalize them in the service of modern aspirations. For Kahn, the aims of architecture did not change; only the means.

23.12 Louis I. Kahn, Parliament building, Dacca, Bangladesh, 1963.

23.13 (*left*) Louis I. Kahn, Parliament building, Dacca, Bangladesh, 1963, sketch.

24. Architecture and Anti-Architecture in England

Whichever technique he chooses, the architect's function is to propose a way of life. . . .

P. Smithson, 1963

For a few years after the war the most pressing problems in England were urban reconstruction and the provision of housing. It is scarcely surprising that the relationship between architecture, urbanism, and a new way of life should have become a dominant obsession in the search for forms. The Welfare State provided more than a chance to build schools, hospitals, and flats: it also suggested an ethos, a social ideal, to which architects were not blind. The well-meaning housing experiments of the thirties, with their vaguely socialist underpinnings, were at last able to come to fruition under a Labour government facing the post-war housing crisis. However, the limitations of those paradigms soon began to show; besides, new ideas needed to be given a form.

Among the projects of the immediate post-war years were the 'New Towns'. Here the intellectual imperatives of Fabianism and the fading dreams of the Garden City movement were brought together in an adequate but uninspiring setting for the 'New Britain'. In the inner cities numerous repetitive blocks of flats rose from the rubble above the nineteenth-century slums. More often than not they were erected according to minimum standards. They seemed to embody a particularly modern and hygienic form of alienation. Certainly there were exceptions (one thinks of Powell and Moya's Churchill Gardens in Pimlico, of Lubetkin and Tecton's plans for Finsbury, of the LCC's 'Mini-unités' close to Richmond Park), but the norm was completely lacking in richness. It is scarcely surprising that those sectors of the avant-garde who sought to crystallize the inner meanings of working-class existence should have turned for inspiration to the dense street life of the old slums which either bombs or else bulldozers had done much to destroy.

In the Hertfordshire schools' programme of the early fifties standardization and clear planning came together in that 'quiet' and rational version of modern architecture which Pevsner so admired. Meanwhile at the Festival of Britain in 1951 the 'white forms of the thirties' went out with one last mannered fanfare. The Royal Festival Hall, designed by a team headed by Leslie Martin (fig. 24.1), was a fitting monument to the show as a whole, with its tidy elegance, its hooded roof so reminiscent of Lubetkin's High Point II, its attached coloured tiles and Scandinavian touches of detail. Here was public evidence of the way that the movement which had begun twenty years earlier under a polemical banner could become acceptable, sweetened, even a little academic.

A younger generation would have nothing of it. Among them were the Smithsons, whose ideas of 'urban re-identification' have been referred to earlier. Before the Unité at Marseilles catalysed them, they relied on the example of Mies van der Rohe (whose buildings they knew only through photographs). In the Hunstanton School in Norfolk of 1949–53 (fig. 24.2) they transformed the steel-frame vocabulary of IIT into an asymmetrical plan and left fixtures and materials deliberately crude. Without addressing the question of appropriateness to a junior school design, the critic Reyner Banham pointed to 'the memorable quality of image' of Hunstanton, suggested that its materials were expressed 'as found', and implied that a

24.1 Leslie Martin and others, Royal Festival Hall, Festival of Britain, London, 1951.

24.2 Alison and Peter Smithson, Hunstanton School, Norfolk, 1949–53.

Running through the Smithsons' thinking in the fifties was also a strain of socialist realism which led them to pinpoint icons of contemporary life in such varied things as machine design, advertisements, and the bric-a-brac of street life (which they called the 'stuff of the urban scene'). The strategy was a replay of the process Le Corbusier had gone through in his formative years, when he had battened on ships and silos in his search for images expressing the nature of the times. But where Le Corbusier had attempted to invest the images of the machine age with a Platonic idealism, the Smithsons rejected any intimations of a closed aesthetic in favour of an aesthetic of change. This was manifest in their sprawling and incomplete plans for the Golden Lane housing project (see Chapter 21) and in their refusal to indulge in an interest in Renaissance symbolic proportions (many of their English contemporaries were influenced by Rudolf Wittkower's book *Architectural Principles in the Age of Humanism*).

Apart from a scheme for a sort of science-fiction 'House of the Future' in 1956, the Smithsons had little chance to carry out their ideas until the early 1960s when the *Economist* newspaper asked them to design new offices on a site next to the eighteenth-century gentleman's club Boodles, off St. James's Street (fig. 24.3). The context and the institution seemed to require a sedate solution somewhat at odds with the wilful brashness the architects had been cultivating. They broke the programme down into three separate towers of varying height, placing the largest one, containing the *Economist*'s offices, to the rear of the site where it would not challenge the scale of the main street front. This strategy also created a small piazza, through which a meandering route over the site was possible. The middle-sized block was placed on the main street to the corner, and made to contain some elegant shops and a bank, which was inserted on a *piano nobile* of amplified scale and was reached up a moving staircase on the forty-five degree angle. A third, much smaller block, containing apartments, was set back on the site to Boodles' side.

The main office block was organized around a core of circulation with fairly intimate work spaces at the edges. The form was chamfered at the corners to give a distinctive image and to soften the relationship to neighbours. The architects claimed that the interior layout was influenced by monastic arrangements, and it may be that they were deliberately trying to introduce qualities of domesticity into work spaces. Travertine slivers attached to the steel frame lent the building an honorific character; the honey-coloured stone also allowed it to blend with the numerous warm colours of the setting.

The ideas behind the plan as a whole reflected the Smithsons' earlier urban polemics: in their minds, the

24.3 Alison and Peter Smithson, the *Economist* 'cluster', London, 1963–7.

moral stance (which he christened 'the New Brutalism') was on the point of emerging. Like the Smithsons, Banham was part of the '20th Century Group' in London, who admired the 'Art Brut' of Dubuffet, who were interested in the *béton brut* of Le Corbusier and who were involved – along with the sculptor Paolozzi and the photographer Nigel Henderson – in trying to convey the rough grain of modern urban life in a new art. The group were united in their distaste for the suavity of the English cultural élite and in their interest in continental ideas stemming from, for example, Existentialist writers like Camus and Sartre.

Economist group was a 'cluster', an image, a sign of the shape the future city might take. The asymmetry was a critique of the vapid axial prism/plaza formula, and was felt to be one of the keys to a subtle relationship between old and new. The processional character of the walkway was evidently inspired by a visit to Greece, while the piazza had obvious Italian overtones. The bay widths of each slab were subtly differentiated to create something like a tableau of the kind seen in the background of some Renaissance pictures. The placement of the bank on an upper level recalled the PSFS solution of 1931, while the idea was also related to the Smithsons' own Haupstadt scheme for Berlin (1957), in which raised pedestrian streets had been much in evidence. In turn, these ideas recalled Team X urban theories.

The Smithsons had to wait almost another decade to test their housing theories in the working-class context towards which they were originally directed. Admittedly there was their girls' dormitory for St. Hilda's, Oxford, but this was for a far softer and less demanding visual and social environment. By contrast 'Robin Hood Gardens' (1969–75) was to stand in Poplar (fig. 24.4), not far from the docklands of the East End, a traditional Smithson stamping ground. They arranged the housing in what amounted to yet another critique of the free-standing point block: two serpentine spines marking off a green precinct sheltered from the traffic and complete with an artificial hillock. The dwellings were made legible in the façades through attached concrete struts, while the triple-level access system was articulated by a larger set of fins. In theory these devices were probably supposed to be modern equivalents to the standardized yet variable usages of Classical orders in such eighteenth-century prototypes as Bath; in fact they seemed to be thin descendants of the texturing devices employed in the Unité d'Habitation. The street decks themselves seemed to fall short of their symbolic intention of expressing and embodying the ideal community. Indeed, Robin Hood Gardens as a whole seemed propelled by a stark vision of working-class life more in tune with realities of the early fifties than with the consumerism of later years.

Another architect to feel dissatisfaction with the diluted modern architecture of the fifties in England was James Stirling. Born in 1926, he was educated at Liverpool University from 1945 to 1950 where he came into contact with the ideas of Colin Rowe, a historian acutely conscious of the Utopian and symbolic values in the architecture of the twenties. From an early stage Stirling seems to have been conscious of his position in a modern tradition, and to have enjoyed employing references and quotations; even his student thesis was a clumsy but forceful reinterpretation of Pavillon Suisse, replete with nautical analogies. Like Lasdun and the Smithsons, Stirling felt the need to recharge English modern architecture and, in a sense, to enrich it through contact with earlier national traditions. In his case the tough industrial vernacular of Northern towns like Liverpool was a particularly compelling inspiration. He also visited and reviewed Le Corbusier's Chapel at Ronchamp and the Jaoul houses. He was ambivalent towards the primitivism, and what he called the deliberate and 'mannered imperfectionism' of Le Corbusier's late works. Yet his own Ham Common houses of 1956 (designed with Gowan) were clearly influenced by them. Stirling was fully aware of Brutalist polemics, but kept a certain distance from the main group; even so, repeated attempts were later

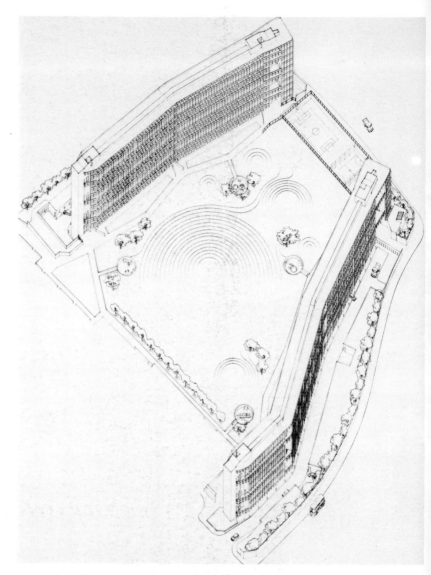

24.4 Alison and Peter Smithson, Robin Hood Gardens, Poplar, London, c. 1969–75, axonometric drawing of whole.

24.5 (*right*) James Stirling and J. Gowan, Engineering building, Leicester University, 1959–63.

made to claim that his rough and ready machine poetics were 'Brutalist'.

Stirling's strong personal style emerged in the extraordinary Leicester Engineering building of 1959–63 (fig. 24.5). This was formed from a slender tower on splayed legs, rising above the overhanging forms of the auditoria and linked to a lower block of engineering workshops with saw-tooth factory glazing laid out on a forty-five degree angle. As the programme called for a one-hundred-foot hydraulic supply and the site was confined, a tower seemed reasonable. However, programmatic logic was only the starting-point in a deliberate display of sculptural dynamics, in which individualized elements were played off against one another. Formal and functional considerations were in turn transcended by a preoccupation with mechanistic images and quotations from the 'heroic period' of modern architecture. Reminiscences of Hannes Meyer's 'factory' scheme for the League of Nations seemed to be blended with memories of Melnikov's constructivism; battleship details were rammed together with Corbusian ramps and elements not unlike those employed by Wright in the Johnson Wax laboratory tower. There was about all this something almost too knowing, as if the architect were deliberately mannerizing the machine-age polemics of thirty years before. It was understandable that the term 'Futurist revival' was invoked (Plate 12).

Stirling attempted to apply some of the discoveries made at Leicester in the very different functional context of the History Faculty building at Cambridge University of 1965–7 (fig. 24.6). This commission came from a limited competition and his design was the only one to attempt a complete integration of the library and the teaching spaces. This was done by placing the reading-room in a quadrant under a glass tent roof leaning back against an L-shaped block containing seminar rooms, lounges, etc. Stirling put the largest and most public accommodations at the lowest levels, and this led naturally to a gradually stepping shape. The radial plan of the main reading-room was also a response to a central demand of the programme: that there should be a single point of control from which the reading-room and the stacks could be surveyed. It was perhaps a combination of logic and erudition which led Stirling to readapt the 'Panopticon' principle from the Utilitarian philosopher Bentham, with its 'controlling eye' at the centre of a circle; this had frequently been employed in library designs throughout the nineteenth century.

24.6 James Stirling, History Faculty building, Cambridge University, 1965–7.

24.7 James Stirling, Florey building, Oxford University, 1967-71.

The polygonal stair towers, industrial glazing, red quarry tiles, raised podia, irregular silhouettes and engineering romanticism all recalled features discovered at Leicester. However, the glass tent over the reading-room was a staggering invention vaguely reminiscent of the Palm Houses at Kew Gardens or of the rocket-assembly building at Cape Canaveral. The roof was formed as a double layer to incorporate an environmental cushion against extremes of heat and cold, and was supported on an elegant steel-truss system with adjustable louvers and other mechanistic attachments. At the peak, above the point of command, an array of brightly coloured extractor fans was inserted above the smoked-glass inner layer of the roof. With its canted interior windows and its glazed galleries, the whole space was a bizarre evocation which seemed to oscillate between twentieth-century science fiction, the actualities of aircraft design, and nostalgia for the era of the *grands constructeurs* in steel

and glass of the nineteenth century. As before, the imagery seemed suffused with Futurist poetry: but there was a once-removed quality about this heroic stance – as if Stirling wanted to employ the icons of the machine-age polemic without embracing the moral and Utopian commitments.

In presenting his own buildings Stirling tended to insist on their functional rationale rather than indulging in speculation about the meaning or sources of his forms. Factory patent glazing – so obviously evocative of the crystalline fantasies of the twenties – was discussed in entirely pragmatic terms:

> Glass buildings are, I think, appropriate to the English climate. We are perhaps the only country where it is seldom too hot or too cold, and on a normal cloudy day, there is a high quality of diffused light in the sky. A glass covering keeps the rain out and lets the light through.

Even so, it was clear from the results that the architect was quite deliberate in his manipulation of precedents and that associational and compositional criteria were sometimes uppermost; sloped glass was not ideal to keep rain out and could let in too much light, cold, and heat. This may have been the case with the Florey building, a student residence designed for Queen's College, Oxford, between 1967 and 1971 (fig. 24.7) in which the student rooms, wrapped around a semi-open court looking towards fields and trees, were fully glazed from floor to ceiling, and ventilated by louvers. The outer sides of the building, where the access corridors and circulation towers were positioned, were largely clad in the usual red tiles, while the building as a whole sat back on a splay-legged A-frame in concrete and looked a bit like a grandstand. The main communal function – a breakfast-room – was situated at the focal point, embedded in the court, while the porter's lodge was contained in curved, free-plan shapes tucked in under the box.

Inevitably the image of the glass box lifted up on concrete supports and looking out over nature recalls the Pavillon Suisse; equally the stepping of the attached stair volumes and the placement of the breakfast-room alongside a slab calls to mind Aalto's Baker House; finally the 'cloister' under the A-frame at ground level and the vaguely courtyard-like plan are reminiscent of the Oxbridge collegiate tradition. Thus the form of the Florey building resulted not from a 'functionalist' position but from a deliberate cross-breeding of relevant types in tradition. Moreover, the solution adopted was beset with practical and acoustic problems and amounted to an imposition of machine-age constraints on the gentility of Oxford life. Possibly this was Stirling's version of the challenging social character he had sensed in the architecture of the twenties; however, the result smacked of an archaeological exercise into the sources of modernism. In his slightly later design for dormitories at St. Andrews in Scotland, he recalled another fetish of the twenties, the collective image of the ship.

Stirling's mechanistic rhetoric seems to have come fully into its own in a number of prestige schemes for industrial concerns designed in the 1960s and early 1970s. For Dorman Long, the steel corporation, he envisaged a linear, sealed-glass container of stepped form, bridging a motorway; for Olivetti, he conjured up collages of architectural syntax and business machine quotations; and for Siemens AEG, he projected a computer centre outside Munich (never built) of a distinctly mechanomorphic character (fig. 24.8). The huge cylindrical shapes of the main office spaces were laid out as a grand axial composition with moving conveyors running along the spine, while rows of poplar trees gave the image a curiously eighteenth-century feeling. The whole thing seemed to be some cybernetic equivalent to Ledoux's Utopian Saltworks at Chaux, put together to celebrate the values of a new European technocratic class.

It is possible that Stirling's picturesque manipulation of machine-age images may have received stimulus from another branch of the English architectural avant-garde of the sixties: the group known as 'Archigram'. This was founded around a nucleus consisting of Peter Cook, Warren Chalk, Ron Herron, Dennis Crompton, Michael Webb, and David Greene. The founding pamphlet, 'Archigram 1', was put together in 1961 and spelled out many of the group's later fascinations with such things as 'clip-on' technology, the throwaway environment, space capsules and mass-consumer imagery. As early as 1959, Mike Webb had designed a project for a 'Furniture Manufacturers Association Building' in the form of pods and capsules plugged flexibly into a frame; and in 1961 his 'Sin Centre' for Leicester Square envisaged a giant cybernetic pleasure machine aping computer reels and comic-book space ships. Robot fascination reached a peak in Ron Herron's 'Walking Cities' project of 1964, in which colossal spider-shaped cities on legs were shown clambering over the water towards Manhattan. Then in 1964 Peter Cook drew together most of the group's themes in a huge but ever-changing megastructure: the 'Plug-in-City' (fig. 24.9).

24.8 James Stirling, project for Siemens Computer Centre, near Munich, 1973.

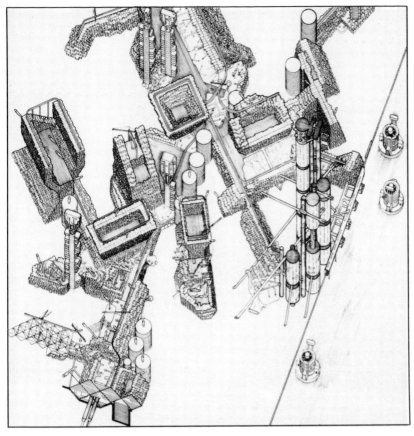

This contained no buildings in the traditional sense, but 'frameworks' into which standardized components could be slotted. Functions were not fulfilled by forms any longer, but by mechanical and electronic 'services'.

There was a deliberately anti-heroic stance in Archigram which rejected the high-mindedness and nature worship of the Team X generation. Archigram welcomed wholeheartedly, without moral stricture, the hedonistic possibilities of modern consumerism. There was certainly a rough parallel here to the Pop paintings of the early sixties produced by Hamilton, Warhol, Rosenquist, and Johns. The Archigram architects learned their lessons from the earlier '20th Century Group' (which had revelled in American advertisements) and from the engineer R. Buckminster Fuller, whose anti-monumentalism appealed to them. Broadly speaking, their aim was to portray and symbolize a new reality; as Warren Chalk stated:

> We are in pursuit of an idea, a new vernacular, something to stand *alongside* the space capsules, computers and throwaway packages of an atomic electronic age . . .
>
> We are not trying to make houses like cars, cities like oil refineries . . . this analogous imagery will eventually be digested into a creative system . . . it has become necessary to extend ourselves into such disciplines in order to discover our appropriate language to the present day situation.

24.9 (*above*) Peter Cook, 'Plug-in-City', 1964.

24.10 (*right*) Cedric Price, 'Potteries Thinkbelt', 1967.

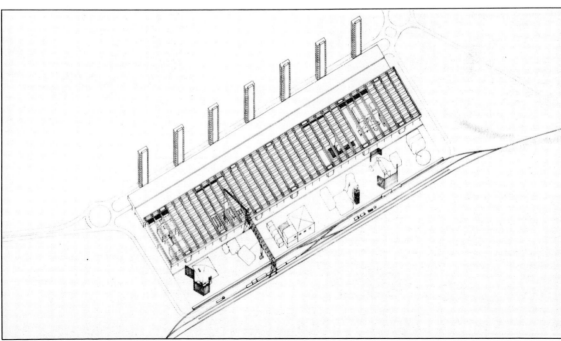

Archigram pronouncements and images had a notably Futurist quality about them, and the group was certainly interested in Sant' Elia's descriptions of the city of the future as a dynamic machine. Their commentary on reality was mostly undertaken in the paper world of collages and drawings, which was probably just as well, for Archigram developed an anti-architectural philosophy towards the end of the sixties. Thus the 'instant city' proposal of 1969 involved the sudden arrival of blimps which would drop the minimal hardware necessary to create the 'true' urbanism – a software dream world of electronic stimulation for the eye and the ear. The mythology of a non-oppressive environment rid of the tiresome weight of history, culture and architectural form was loosely entertained; it was an idea which blended well with the 'drop-out' consciousness of the decade.

The search for an anti-heroic imagery suitable to modern pluralism was given a considerable boost by the laconic ideas of the inventor Cedric Price in the same period. He maintained that society would, on the whole, be better off without the obsessions of form-makers. A typical Price project was the 'Potteries Thinkbelt' – a design for a university in which he envisaged the re-use of an existing railway system in the Midlands as a new 'non-architectural' source of knowledge (fig. 24.10). Standardized modules containing books, recorded lectures, etc. were to be moved up and down the region to service different parts of it with 'information', but without buildings. Despite the anti-style pose, the position did crystallize a style of quiet ordinariness. A similar functionalist mood had been articulated by Reyner Banham at the end of his book *Theory and Design in the First Machine Age*,

24.11 Denys Lasdun, Royal College of Physicians, London, 1960, view across Regents Park.

> The architect who proposes to run with technology knows that he is in fast company and that in order to keep up, he may have to emulate the Futurists and discard his whole cultural load . . .

However, by the sixties even the Futurist position and imagery had become part of a tradition. The paradox of the anti-architects was that, in attempting to overthrow the bonds of the past and the constraints of formal expression, they drew on tradition and employed forms to get their message across. Moreover, in the 1970s their 'anti-architectural' images became absorbed by architects: Renzo Piano and Richard Rogers's Pompidou Centre in Paris (1974) for example, would have been inconceivable without the legacy of Archigram.

One English architect whose work during the 1960s stood out in firm contrast to the obsessive play with technological imagery was Denys Lasdun. In his case technology was regarded as a means (rather than an end) towards the creation of what he called an 'architecture of urban landscape'. Lasdun was born in 1914 and experienced the seminal buildings of the modern movement without the historical and ironical distance of the generation whose formation took place after the war. He learned much from working with Lubetkin and Coates, but most of all from his study of Le Corbusier's buildings and ideas. Lasdun also knew Wright's architecture through drawings and photographs, and was deeply impressed by the English Baroque architect Nicholas Hawksmoor.

Lasdun's experimental cluster blocks of the fifties

have been mentioned earlier in connection with urbanistic reactions against the 'unité' in that period. In 1958 he designed some luxury flats in St. James's in which he employed a 3/2 section to provide ample living-room views and still make the most of expensive building land. The organization was expressed directly in the façades and handled adeptly through careful proportioning and fine detailing. The horizontal stratification also related to the buildings' neighbours and to a neo-Palladian building two doors away. The sensitive relationship of new and old buildings had been a matter of relatively small importance to the majority of early modern movement masters, the more so as they were often keen to heighten the 'modernity' of their solutions through contrast; but in the fifties and sixties the matter of context became increasingly important.

Indeed the relationship of the individual building to its historical setting was a major motive force in Lasdun's next design, for the headquarters of the Royal College of Physicians – an august academic medical body – to stand close to Nash's neo-classical terraces in Regent's Park. The main ceremonial part of the building was a white rectangular shell poised delicately on piers above its shadowy lower areas: this contained a grand hallway, the historical library and the focal 'Censor's room'. The transition in scale between these sharp, crisp forms and the setting was handled by a curved hump in blue brick containing the auditorium (fig. 24.11). Free in form, organic in association, this was intended to imply an ability to grow and to change. Behind the hump was a precinct. appropriate to an inward-looking community of scholars, while the main hallway contained a square spiral stair which rose in ever-wider turns to join stepped levels, which then opened out on one side towards Nash's terraces. Thus the heart of the institution was defined by a well-scaled space that was sensed as being, at the same time, a part of its surroundings.

Part of the subtlety of the Royal College of Physicians lay in the way the neo-classical setting was abstracted in its forms and finishes, without any recourse to a weak historical sentimentalism. Thus the main shell in white terrazzo was detailed in a manner recalling Nash's thin stucco surfaces, and the piers at the entrance were restatements of Classical orders. The blue brick hump echoed the neighbouring slate roofs and the sequence of spaces in the hall was analogous to the alleyways around the Park. Lasdun expressed his intention clearly: it was to 'rhyme' with Nash and to make the new building a 'microcosm' of the surrounding city (Plate 13).

The Classicism of the Royal College ran deeper than these witty references. At the Architectural Associ-

ation in the thirties Lasdun had been trained to deal with ceremonial sequences of space using Beaux-Arts devices like the axis, the vestibule and the grand stair. Moreover, he had studied the writings of Geoffrey Scott, who had stressed the anthropomorphic qualities of Classical design and the vital sculptural character of good architecture. These were features which Lasdun had sensed in the architecture of Hawksmoor. The dynamic contrast of light and shade, and the dramatic use of space were probably inspired by this early eighteenth-century precedent.

Thus the Royal College of Physicians was a turning point for its creator in which disparate strands in his background were brought together; his admiration for Le Corbusier and the English Baroque, his interest in biologically inspired patterns of growth, his fascination with the meaning of institutions. One of the main ideas to crystallize in the building was the concept of an 'urban landscape' of stepped levels linking spaces inside and outside an individual building so that it became part of its setting. This contextual obsession was carried through in Lasdun's next major design, for the University of East Anglia (1962–8) near Norwich (fig. 24.12).

The University was one of a number commissioned in the early sixties in England to stand in rural settings near Cathedral towns. The site was on open meadow land stepping down slowly to the River Yare. The client required a nucleus capable of later extension and eventually decided that traditional divisions between disciplines should be minimized. The architect therefore decided on a linear pattern based on circulation and adjusted to fit the contours. The main elements became the flexible, pre-cast concrete 'teaching wall' (running along the back), the upper walkway (conceptual spine of the scheme) and the stepped residences (attuned to the landscape setting), which were grouped around a space at the centre called simply 'the harbour'. Clearly there were loose parallels between this organization and ideas being pursued by Utzon, de Carlo, and Woods at the same time, but the UEA plan and its underlying strategies were equally an outgrowth of ideas which stretched back to Lasdun's cluster blocks, and even to the biologically inspired plan-form of Hallfield School in 1951.

The dominant architectural element of UEA was the platform or raised level. The section was worked out ingeniously to minimize the use of lifts and to allow splendid views from upper walkways over the landscape. Variation was achieved on the basis of a few standardized parts linked together by a strong overall idea and by a dominant geometry of ninety-degree and forty-five-degree axes. The architect hinted at the underlying landscape romanticism when he referred to the platforms as 'strata'. Indeed, UEA was nothing less

24.12 Denys Lasdun, University of East Anglia, near Norwich, 1962–8.

than a demonstration of his 'urban landscape' philosophy:

> Activities take place on platforms, floors, paths, terraces, etc. See Le Corbusier's pronouncement of 1915 – 'The actual ground of the town is a sort of raised floor, the paths and pavement as it were bridges . . .' A building can be looked at in the same way as a matter of platforms or connections and interlocking spaces. Sensitive gradations of levels and heights can be made to respond to site and function creating an endless variety of rhythms, satisfactory in themselves, and adaptable to any existing urban situation including the architecture of the past.

The system of strata (with accompanying vertical towers) was found to be relevant to Lasdun's next major commission, the National Theatre of 1964–75 (fig. 24.13). In the earliest scheme a National Opera House was also to be included and the two were to stand together next to the River Thames in front of the monolithic shaft of the Shell tower. Platforms were this time used to create a series of interpenetrating spaces along the riverside with fine views towards the historical city, to blend the building with its setting, and to express the openness and public nature of the new institution. These themes were taken up in the final scheme for a theatre on its own next to Waterloo Bridge (1967) in which the 'strata' supplied vantage-points towards St. Paul's and over the river, linked up with the bridge, and passed to the heart of the building where they supported the lobbies and auditoria (fig. 24.14). They thus created a series of 'stages' and 'auditoria' with the cityscape itself as backdrop. Lasdun put the matter succinctly when he stated 'the whole building could become theatre'. At the same time the strata suggested an interest in the ceremonial

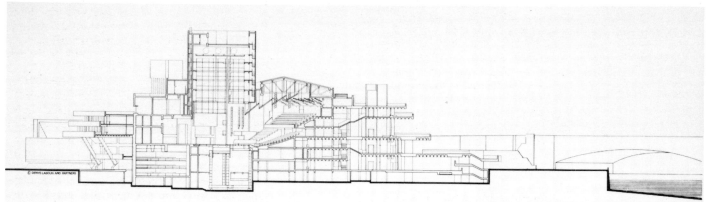

meanings of platforms in ancient architecture, and the artist's private myth concerning the roots of architecture in land-mass formations or strata of rock.

These themes were given added force through the powerful expressive character of the building's form. The composition was dynamic, asymmetrical and ever variable in mood according to the spectator's changing position. Space and light were handled as positive features to lend drama to the sequences. The rugged silhouettes of the fly-towers gave the whole an effect of grandeur; at the same time the strata stopped the building from becoming an overbearing monolith and maintained the human scale. Lasdun referred to the building as a 'monument-non-monument', perhaps

implying something of this ambiguity. He took the concrete cantilever from Le Corbusier's Dom-ino system and gave it a new meaning in the service of his own 'urban landscape' ideas.

The English situation in the quarter-century after the war was a pluralist one; nonetheless, there were shared preoccupations. One of these had to do with the expression of new social values; another with the cross-breeding of the international modern movement with national traditions; yet another with the relative human and architectural value of technology. The National Theatre took a strong stand on all these issues; it is a good place to stop and to consider how analogous issues were handled elsewhere.

24.13 (*top*) Denys Lasdun, National Theatre, London, 1967–73.

24.14 Denys Lasdun, National Theatre, London, 1967–73, section through main auditorium showing 'strata'.

25. The Problem of Regional Identity

Steel and reinforced concrete, in the form of columns and beams, provide framed structures and are, in this respect akin to traditional timber constructions.

N. Kawazoe, 1958

The modern movement, in its formative years between the world wars, was scarcely a worldwide phenomenon; it was the intellectual property of certain countries in Western Europe, of the United States and of some parts of the Soviet Union. In retrospect this is scarcely surprising since the very conception of modern architecture was linked to the existence of 'avant-gardes' seeking authenticity within (so-called) 'advanced' industrial societies. But by around 1960, transformations, deviations and devaluations of modern architecture had found their way to many other areas in the world. The pattern of post-war economic development, including rapid industrialization and the dissemination of 'progressive' Western ideas, certainly played an important role here. So did the reproducible media: architectural fashions were transmitted at a greater speed than before.

Many earlier inventions in architecture – the Gothic of the Île de France, the Renaissance of Florence – had gradually radiated their influences across frontiers. Although the speed of emigration was far more dramatic with modern architecture, some of the usual problems obtained. The first of these was not, strictly speaking, geographical by definition, since it had to do with the broader issue of prototypes being transformed into clichéd imitations. A second problem concerned the relevance of forms in the new context: if an architecture had been right for Manhattan could it be right for Malaya? If a form had emerged in Boulogne-sur-Seine what would make it fit the conditions of Buenos Aires? In other words: what should be kept of the prototypes and what transformed to match new climates, cultures, beliefs, technologies, and architectural traditions. A third problem was the complement of the second: if new ideas from abroad were accepted, which old or indigenous ones should be thrown out? Should one accept the avowed universality of modern design and bow down before it: or should one perhaps seek some fusion between the best of old and new, of native and of foreign?

One must beware of treating the 'modern invader' as some monolithic entity. The stage reached by ideas in the influencing countries conditioned, in some degree, the point of departure in influenced ones. Brazil, South Africa, England, and Japan all received modern architecture when it was still young in the twenties and thirties, and produced their own variants in the inter-war period. To compare, say, Martienssen's house designs in Cape Town with Lucio Costa's Ministry of Education in Rio de Janeiro (both of the mid-thirties) and to place the two alongside Sakakura's nearly contemporary design for the Japanese Pavilion in Paris is to be made aware of the extraordinary hold of the 'Internationalist Vision'. In this case too, all three designs were of an obviously Corbusian pedigree. By contrast the late forties, fifties and sixties were characterized by a far greater diversity within the modern movement in its originating centres, and by a higher valuation of the indigenous, the variable, and the regional. This greater pluralism was duly reflected in many parts of the world.

Some of the most vital immediate post-war experiments were undertaken in Mexico and South America. The International Style penetrated Mexico in the early

thirties and so formed a sort of platform from which post-war experiments could continue. In a sense, modern architecture was but another cultivated, colonizing influence, which replaced the models of the Belle Époque and the Beaux-Arts. The University of Mexico City, partly designed by Carlos Lazo and his associates in the late forties and early fifties reflected the influence of Le Corbusier's pre-war works in its disposition of broad, open spaces and free-standing slabs, and in its use of *pilotis*, curved entrance ways and roof terraces. Juan O'Gorman's University Library was dramatically decorated in highly coloured murals incorporating strong nationalist sentiments, but the anatomy of the architecture was little affected. In this case images of international modernity were no doubt intended to reflect a progressive intellectual outlook.

By contrast, the architecture of Luis Barragán employed modern devices of abstraction to condense images from many eras in Mexican history, especially

in his designs for gardens, private houses and luxury ranches, Barragán was born in 1902 and trained as an engineer. In 1924 he visited the Alhambra in southern Spain where he was captivated by the water-gardens with their dreamlike vistas, shifting axes and surreal atmosphere. He early absorbed the bold shapes and stark walls of Mexico's convents and peasant dwellings with their introspective patios and gardens. In the thirties he was influenced by the simple forms of the International Style, but he attempted to see beyond the machine age imagery to a deeper level of synthesis. In the same period he developed a taste for the metaphysical strain in European Surrealism (e.g., de Chirico, Magritte). Barragán's native style began to emerge in garden and landscape designs of the late 1940s such as El Pedregal, in which austere platforms of lava and abstract wall planes seemed to channel the flow of outdoor spaces and to link together cascades and pools. In the residential sub-division known as Las Arboledas (1958–61), close to Mexico City, the practical needs of riding stables and the elegant rituals of equestrianism were organized as a sequence of outdoor rooms delineated by boldly coloured stucco walls and held together by a network of water tanks, pools and troughs. Illusions of compression and depth, of size and perspective, were enhanced by contrasts of colour, controlled glimpses of distant landscapes seen through horizontal openings, and the dappled play of light off water (fig. 25.1). Here the Islamic water garden and the discoveries of the Barcelona Pavilion or the Villa Savoye came together in a labyrinth of curiously nostalgic character. To speak merely of the fusion of regionalism and the International Style, of the vernacular and of Le Corbusier, is to trivialize Barragán: his style expressed a genuinely archetypical mood in touch with the tragic vein in Mexican cultural history (Plate 14).

In Brazil, Lucio Costa and Oscar Niemeyer also took Le Corbusier as their starting-point, especially as they had his collaboration in the design of the Ministry of Education in Rio in the mid-thirties. In this case the slab was elegantly modified by sun louvers for shade – but these slender and moveable relatives of the *brise-soleil* hardly constituted an all-out attempt at designing a tropical regionalist architecture. In the Pampulha Casino of the early forties, Niemeyer reinterpreted the 'five points of a new architecture' in an imagery evocative of the 'high-life' function the building was to serve. Travertine and Juparana stone were used on the exterior, while the mood of the interior was enhanced by luxurious areas of pink glass and satin. The architect was not content with the limited role that the economic system of Brazil gave him and wrote later that he would like to have presented 'a more realistic achievement' reflecting 'not only refinements and comfort but also a positive collaboration between the architect and the whole society'. Of course, this was but one example of a dilemma which would face many architects who were to work in 'developing countries': their architecture, to be built at all, had frequently to become the chic plaything of the tiny and wealthy minority (fig. 25.2).

The majority of developing countries did not receive modern influences until the post-war period and therefore adapted not the pure examples of the International Style, but the much modified, later variants of modern architecture. India, for example, was heavily influenced by the late works of Le Corbusier rather than his early ones, the more so as Chandigarh did show obvious signs of a 'regionalist' adaptation. Louis Kahn's designs for Dacca had a similar parental role for Indian and Pakistani architects, while Wright's architecture tended to be more influential in temperate areas like southeast Australia. Mies van der Rohe's skyscraper designs of the fifties were of course absorbed as part of the standard imagery of international businesses and hotels, often with disastrous results of heat loss and heat gain in extreme climates. However, there was no obvious pattern of correspondences between prototypes and imitations – indeed, one wonders if the entire picture of world architectural development might not have been utterly different if, say, Wright rather than Le Corbusier had designed a major Indian city in his late years, and if Le Corbusier's vision of the *brise-soleil* skyscraper had been widely adopted by businesses and bureaucracies in the West, instead of Mies van der Rohe's steel and glass prisms. Moreover, as was suggested in earlier chapters, the post-war period in Europe was itself marked by pockets of resistance against sterile aspects of internationalism. The attitudes towards the vernacular intrinsic to the late works of Aalto, Le Corbusier and Team X, for example, suggested a more accommodating and flexible strategy with regard to local traditions; this attitude would bear fruit in many other parts of the world as well.

Something of this 'modern regionalist' position also emerged on the West Coast of the United States immediately after the war, where an attempt was made to cross-breed (as it were) certain devices of modern design (e.g., the free plan, the steel frame, the cantilevered flat roof) with the lessons of local vernaculars and turn of the century Arts and Crafts designs, both of which seemed to incorporate a special sensitivity to Californian climate, site conditions and style of life. In the 'Bay Region School' around San Francisco, William Wurster employed local materials like redwood in an affirmative way, and attempted to blend houses with their natural setting. Balconies, trellises, and Stick Style extensions were rehandled in a

manner which still bore the imprint of the intervening years of modern architectural experimentation. In Los Angeles, architects like Craig Ellwood and Charles Eames used industrial components and a steel-frame vocabulary, in a deliberately informal interpretation specially attuned to the luxurious hillside sites of Beverly Hills and Hollywood. There can be little doubt that these architects followed certain of the leads of Schindler and Neutra, who had already discovered ways of bringing together the sorts of spaces encouraged by the free-plan, open façades of glass, deep cantilevered overhangs and terraces with the rich vegetation of the area. Neutra's Kaufmann Desert House of 1947 at Palm Springs set the tone of the luxury health house of 1950s American suburbia while Schindler's late works took on a 'shed-like' character, in which cheap materials were assembled on site in a deliberately humble imagery.

Some insight into the tensions engendered by the arrival of international influences in a particular locale is revealed by the Australian situation immediately after the war, the more so as white Australian culture had a short architectural tradition of its own, and the indigenous population had not expressed its ideas in permanent buildings. As in the early United States, the architecture of the settlers had emerged from the gradual adaptation to local conditions of imported models. To be sure, there had been fragmentary modern influences between the wars, stemming especially from Walter Burley Griffin's introduction of Wrightian forms in the 1910s and 1920s, but a consolidated modern movement did not really get under way in Australia until the late forties with such designers as Sydney Ancher and Harry Seidler. Before this the problem of Australian cultural identity had influenced debates over the visual arts; this problem did not disappear with the increasingly international cultural atmosphere of the years immediately after the Second World War. Indeed nationalism and regionalist architectural tendencies were frequently allied, especially in countries asserting themselves after colonialism.

Seidler's formation was cosmopolitan: he was born in Vienna and educated in England and Canada before entering the Graduate School of Design at Harvard in the mid-forties under Gropius and Breuer. He worked with the latter and with Niemeyer before following his parents to Australia in 1947, partly lured by the promise of commissions. He appears to have thought of Gropius, Breuer and Albers (the colour theorist) as fountain-heads of modernist principles. His earliest houses in the Sydney suburbs (e.g., the Seidler House of 1948, fig. 25.3; or the Rose House of 1950) were clearly imitations of an architectural language which he had absorbed in the eastern United States and

25.3 (*above*) Harry
Seidler, Seidler House,
near Sydney, 1948.

25.4 Peter Muller,
Muller House, Whale
Beach, near Sydney,
1955.

which (as we have seen) was already watered down by comparison with the seminal works of the twenties. Seidler evidently believed in the universalizing ideas which had underlain his Harvard education and made only the slightest adjustments to International Style formulae to wed them with the strong sunlight, uneven sites and vegetation of Australia. In the new context this uncompromising stance was appreciated as a strong 'modernist position', though as Seidler himself admitted:

> The pioneering days of modern architecture are over. We are now in a period of consolidation and development.

In a broader perspective it appeared that Seidler was merely following the leaders in an all too obvious way. The American architect Paul Rudolph, who had also passed through the GSD at Harvard, but who reacted more strongly against the puritanism of his mentors, singled out Seidler's house for his parents and described it as 'the Harvard house incarnate' transferred to Sydney 'without any modifications whatsoever'. He made a plea for an enriching 'regionalism' if modern architecture were to avoid an ersatz blandness.

In Australia itself it did not take long for a similar mood to surface, and for a certain 'foreignness' to be sensed about Seidler's taut white boxes poised on slender stilts among the boulders and the eucalyptus trees. Instead a blend was sought between the principles of modern design and indigenous features. An example of this 'modern regionalism' was the Muller House at Whale Beach of 1955 (designed by Peter Muller), which was formed from low wooden overhangs nestling among the trees (fig. 25.4). The rocks of the site were incorporated in the living-room and an attempt was made to consult the special 'genius of the place'. Large areas of glass were employed, but carefully hooded from the glare. The vocabulary clearly had a Wrightian character and the strategy was not so very far from that pursued a little earlier in California. Muller also studied Japanese wooden architecture and was interested in Zen philosophy. His nature worship came through in a design which tried deliberately to respect the existing order of the hillside. The image of the International Style box was replaced by one which attempted to abstract features of the context. Other architects in Australia to work from Wright's philosophy were Neville Gruzman and William Lucas, each of whom was preoccupied with the casualness of a new suburban way of life, and with ways of linking the building to nature.

However, Wright was not the only example to be used in pursuit of regionalist tendencies. In the

Johnson House at Chatsworth of 1964 (fig. 25.5), Peter Johnson reflected his interest in 'Brutalist ideology' and in the Maisons Jaoul, in the use of rough and ready clinker bricks and overhanging pitched roofs of a type found in the area. The rooms became so many platforms following the natural slope and open to a variety of views. Slender wooden balconies attached to the brick piers blended with the dense vegetation on all sides. Johnson sought to combine the image of some indigenous shack with sophisticated conceptions derived from Europe. Thus a variety of influences and ideas were brought together, all within a few miles of one another, in an attempt at producing, among other things, 'a new Australian architecture'.

For such cases as these the process of finding appropriate architectural forms had the benefit of minds intent on crystallizing a new cultural situation. But by the early sixties the far more usual mode of influence was through straightforward exportation of

25.5 Peter Johnson, Johnson House, Chatsworth, Sydney, 1963.

25.6 The imagery of international development: Hong Kong in the late 1960s.

forms to provincial centres. Moreover, it was usually a devalued style of industrial building, rather than an architecture of any formal value. Thus the commercial offices of New York and London soon reproduced their imagery in cities as far apart as Hong Kong (fig. 25.6) and Lagos. It was as if the steel or concrete rectangular frame, the air-conditioner and the property developer conspired to reject national traditions overnight. This was not the true International Style – with its moral and aesthetic imperatives – so much as an 'international corporation style' – indeed big business and tourism played a major part in the proliferation of the clichéd forms. It will be suggested later that this development was linked to rapid mechanization and the confusion that was bound to ensue when countries proceeded in a single generation from peasant to industrial economies; the technocratic and Western style of education of new élites also played a part. The bland results around the world in the sixties soon engendered a strong reaction in favour of regionalism of various kinds in the seventies. The sophisticated 'peasantism' of the European avant-garde would be only partially relevant to this critique.

One country to offer a virtual case-study in the absorption of modern architectural ideas from the West was Japan. The history of Japanese ambivalence to Western cultural influence actually stretched back long before the advent of the modern move-

ment in Europe and America. Katayama Toyu's Hyokekan Museum in Tokyo of 1908 was an eclectic exercise combining the French seventeenth century with English Palladianism. It was a reminder that European revivalist tendencies of the nineteenth century played a role in ideological colonialism as well as in the political and economic varieties. This structure stood out in all its agonized and foreign self-consciousness against a setting in which religious and vernacular structures continued to be built in traditional styles, according to methods of craftsmanship which stretched back uninterruptedly for hundreds of years. Imported styles and methods of construction (particularly those which substituted brick for the usual wood) were not always welcome. In 1909 the architect Chinto Itoh, who had immersed himself in the old styles of Japan and Eastern Asia, argued that the country should rid itself of European influences and revive its own traditions; he claimed that a new formal language would arise automatically when these forms were cross-bred with imported building methods. A year later Yashukura Ohtsuka put the opposite argument: that Japan should whole-heartedly accept Western models but modify them to local conditions and means of construction. Both men had essentially the same aim: the creation of a specifically Japanese modern style. Different versions of their debate would recur many times around the world in the ensuing seventy years, especially in countries preoccupied with modernization and national identity.

In 1916 Frank Lloyd Wright designed the Imperial Hotel in Tokyo. Wright had, of course, been fascinated with the disciplines of Japanese design in the formation of his own architectural language,·but his hotel was highly ornate and mannered. Although its imagery was infused with respect for Japanese prototypes, the building had a limited local influence. During the years of its completion 'progressive' Japanese architects were eagerly taking up Art Nouveau, a full two decades after it had dropped out of favour with the European avant-garde. Mamoru Yamada's Central Telegraph Office in Tokyo of 1926 had a vaguely Secessionist air. It was through publications like Gropius's *International Architecture* and through detailed reports on De Stijl and Esprit Nouveau, that modern architecture gradually became known in Japan. Foreigners such as Bruno Taut (who wrote on Japanese traditional architecture) pointed out an affinity between the subtle simplicity and geometrical discipline of traditional design and the stripping to essentials involved in the modern movement of the West. A correspondence between wooden-frame constructions and reinforced-concrete skeletons was also suggested. This may have done something to remove suspicions of foreign construction techniques, as these had been directed at materials like brick and

stone: concrete could be moulded to national traditions in ways that these materials could not.

Antonin Raymond, a Czech who supervised the construction of the Imperial Hotel, opened his own office in Japan in 1921, and attempted to blend Western and indigenous forms. His own house of 1924 recalled the simple volumes of Wright's Unity Temple, while its interior spaces and details seemed to blend machine-age imagery with Japanese finesse. Kunio Mayekawa and Junzo Sakakura went to work in Le Corbusier's atelier in the late twenties and brought back an understanding of the inner principles of the new architecture rather than just surface effects. By the thirties a Japanese modern movement existed that was not just a pastiche of earlier European developments. In his design for the Okada House and gardens of 1933, for example, Sutemi Horiguchi blended the thin planes of the new architecture with traditional effects of lightness and airiness (fig. 25.7). The garden, with its slight level changes and rectangular pools continuing the patterns and dimensions of the straw mats on the interior, had as much to do with prototypes like the moon-viewing platform of the Katsura Imperial Villa as with abstract modern art. Sakakura's Japanese pavilion at the 1937 Paris Exhibition likewise restated the slender steel frame in a way which recalled the proportions and delicate joints

25.7 (*above*) Sutemi Horiguchi, Okada house, Tokyo, 1933, view of terrace.

25.8 (*left*) Shokintei, Katsura Imperial Villa, 17th century, detail of refined timber construction.

of traditional Japanese wooden construction.

But the flowering of the early modern movement in Japan was interrupted by a resurgence of nationalism and then by the war. In 1945, at the time of the surrender, 4.2 million new dwellings were needed. The architectural profession attempted to handle the problem by designing standardized, mass-producible low-cost units based on the module of the Tatami mat, and buildable in less than a week. The late forties was characterized by a gradual democratization of Japanese life. In architectural circles there were constant debates about the viability of reviving pre-war modernist tendencies and about the possibility of some form of 'Social Realism' in architecture. In 1950, with the outbreak of the Korean War, an inflationary period came to an end with a boom. At last paper projects could be set aside in favour of actual construction. Discussion turned once again to the question of a Japanese modern style. It was clear that this would have to be appropriate to a rapidly industrializing society in which Western technocratic values were more and more in evidence; indeed, Japanese life was being forcibly Americanized. Mayekawa's Nippon Sogo Bank or Raymond's more delicate Readers' Digest publishing house (both designed in Tokyo in 1951) reflected an attempt at continuing pre-war 'modernist' experimentation. The Peace Treaty of San Francisco in the same year, which gave Japan her independence from the USA, strengthened the consciousness of national traditions which had, nonetheless, to be disentangled from earlier imperialism. Once again the idea emerged that

internationalism should be purged, but here the problem lay in knowing quite how to *transform* earlier Japanese prototypes. The way forward seemed to lie in a sort of abstraction of indigenous spatial and structural concepts, and a mating of these principles with similar essential ideas of modern design. Noboru Kawazoe spelt out this 'modern regionalist' position clearly, in a manner which bolstered national self-esteem, by suggesting that Japan had, in a sense, anticipated modern architecture (fig. 25.8).

A frame structure allows a room to be more open and flexible and obviates the need for solid walls as a structural element. In the continuity of interior and exterior, in the flexibility of a room design using movable partitions, traditional Japanese architecture has pioneered many solutions, such as the integration of the garden and the interior, the protection of the interior by oversailing roofs, the use of the verandah as a link between interior and garden, the connection of different parts of a building by corridors, the introduction of the sliding wall (Fusama) by means of which a room can be enlarged or reduced in size, the use of screens (Byobu) for visual protection, and the Tatami mat serving as a module of floor area. Not only for the sake of industrialization, but also for the sake of flexibility, it is necessary to resort to standardization – something that the builders of the past have done. In traditional architecture 'Kiwari' signified a modular order and a 'grammatical' determination of components for the layout and design of rooms.

25.9 Kenzo Tange, Peace Memorial and Museum, Hiroshima, 1955.

Among the post-war Japanese architects to share similar sentiments to these was Kenzo Tange (1913–) who had been a pupil of Mayekawa and Le Corbusier, and so was able to handle the inheritance of the West with less nervousness than his predecessors. His Peace Memorial and Museum at Hiroshima of 1955 (fig. 25.9) employed an updated version of the 'five points of a new architecture', replete with delicate screens which were Japanese relatives of Le Corbusier's *brise-soleil*. Similar devices were employed in the Kagawa Prefecture of 1954, where concrete struts and trellises revealed the hierarchy of structure in a way recalling traditional timber. Tange was among the first in Japan to grasp the implications of the rugged blend of Asian and European traditions at Chandigarh for a language of monumentality in his own country. Indeed, in the late fifties and early sixties numerous town halls and civic centres were planned as genuine attempts at expressing both the notion of citizens' forums in the recently created democracy, and a new feeling of national self-confidence. The screen-like effects of earlier 'modern regionalism' gave way to denser and heavier visual effects produced by rough concrete. Here again national precedents could be identified as relevant – especially the giant logs and brackets of the Imperial treasure houses – but care had to be taken to avoid authoritarian overtones.

One of the breakthrough buildings in the new genre was Mayekawa's Kyoto Town Hall of 1958–60 (fig. 25.10) in which rough wooden patterns in the concrete and pre-cast beams were used in a manner analogous to the 'kit-of-parts' approach of traditional timber. Joints were freely expressed and an attempt was made to demonstrate and dramatize the process of construction. In the Metropolitan Festival Hall in Tokyo of 1961, the same style was extended further. Here the problem was to combine auditoria and approach spaces in a suitably impressive visual framework, and there can be little doubt that the architect modelled his design on the Parliament building at Chandigarh. The scooped overhangs and deep porticoes, the sculptural roofscape elements expressing the auditoria, and the bare concrete were all drawn from this source. However, the effect was subtly different: the silhouettes, shapes and proportions spoke a language evocative of monumental traditions in Japan.

Kenzo Tange took this tendency towards monumental expressionism still further in the Tokyo Olympic Stadium of 1964 (fig. 25.11), in which he employed tensile steel roofs to create interwoven curves with an architectural effectiveness matched only by Utzon, Nervi, Otto and Saarinen at the time. By the mid-sixties it was clear to the rest of the world that a distinctive Japanese modern architecture had emerged which was based on an almost aggressive use of modern technology. Japan's 'economic miracle' was proceeding so quickly that a glossy, uprooted urban culture was rapidly coming into being which seemed increasingly to threaten any sober assessment of the past and its meaning. In architecture this mood began to surface in schemes which celebrated industrial technique at the expense of all else.

Such a tendency emerged even in housing proposals made to deal with the uncontrollable urban sprawl of Tokyo. The rapid post-war increases in population, combined with the finite habitable land of the country, forced issues of town planning to the fore. Tange

25.10 Kunio Mayekawa, Kyoto Town Hall, 1958–60.

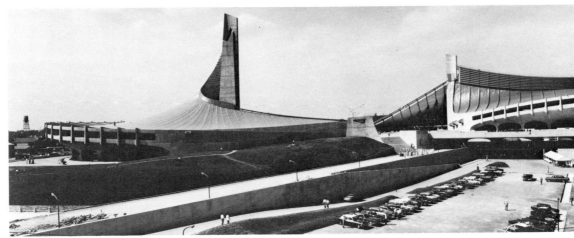

25.11 Kenzo Tange, Olympic Stadium, Tokyo, 1963.

25.12 'Metabolist' Group, scheme for a modern city, 1963, designer Arata Isozaki.

turned his mind to Tokyo's urban problems around 1960 with a scheme which envisaged an extension of the urban network into the bay, with giant stanchions rising out of the water (containing services and lifts) and huge attached structural beams and bridges (supporting housing and other urban facilities). While the idea was loosely similar to some of the raised-deck proposals being made in Europe at the same time, Tange's scheme had a far more forceful and mega-structural character. Critics who were still keen to emphasize the 'Japaneseness' of this daunting technological wizardry pointed lamely to similarities between the huge lattice of circulation and posts and brackets in wood. Tange's desperate attempt at simplifying and giving form to the chaos of a new industrial pluralism seemed to be emblematic of a larger question: how to find the deeper social meaning of an increasingly consumer culture?

Grandiose Utopian schemes based on a fantastic deployment of technology became increasingly frequent in the early sixties in Japan. The 'Metabolist Group' were not unlike the English 'Archigram' group in their obsession with mechanism, change and a vaguely spaceship imagery (fig. 25.12). The pivotal members were Kiyonori Kikutake, Noria Kurokawa, and the critic Noboru Kawazoe; the architects Asade Oe and Maki were also loosely affiliated. Kikutake spelt out the Metabolists' fascination with change:

Unlike the architecture of the past, contemporary architecture must be changeable, moveable and comprehensible architecture, capable of meeting the changing requirements of the contemporary age. In order to reflect dynamic reality, what is needed is not a fixed, static function, but rather one which is capable of undergoing metabolic changes ... We must stop thinking in terms of function and form, and think instead in terms of space and changeable function.

There was much in the Metabolist position that recalled the Futurists' suggestion that the modern city be made into a dynamic machine of moving and variable parts, and the Japanese architects, like their 'Futurist revival' counterparts in England, indulged in an imagery which made much of the way pods and cells could be plugged into or clipped on to lattice frames. The Metabolists also attempted to enforce the distinction between the fixed and changeable elements of a design, often resorting to giant towers of a monumental character to which less substantial-looking 'variable' standardized elements might be attached. As early as 1958 Kikutake had anticipated some of Tange's ideas by suggesting marine cities in

the form of vast discs on towers, and while the rhetoric was mechanistic, there was also a hint of an interest in organic structures like cells and beehives. Kurokawa outlined the typical Metabolist design strategy:

1. Divide the spaces into basic units.
2. Divide the units into equipment units and living units.
3. Clarify the difference in metabolic rhythms among the unit spaces.
4. Clarify the connectors and joints among spaces with different metabolic rhythms.

Although none of the grand visions of the Metabolists were realized, their ideas were sometimes carried out on a smaller scale and occasionally influenced other architects' schemes. Kurokawa's own bizarre Yamagata Hawaii Dreamland (fig. 25.13) was arranged as a curved belt of buildings around a pool with giant vertical cylinders containing the circulation, in a manner similar to his earlier 'Marine City' studies. Arata Isozaki's numerous buildings in the town of Oita, particularly the bank (1966–8) and the Girls' High School (1963–4), employed equally dramatic contrasts of structure and mechanical servicing. Yokoyama's Taisekiji Temple of 1966 was a clumsy pastiche of traditional religious forms, but the nearby lodging-house was a virtual manifesto of pre-cast concrete construction. Everything possible was done to express changes of function and the 'kit-of-parts' of the structural system, including the curious cylindrical volumes of the individual shower-rooms. The architect also endeavoured to give the impression that these elements were plugged into a larger infrastructure.

In the aforementioned designs there was the ever present danger that architecture might simply degenerate into an arid technological fetishism. Tange seems to have sensed this danger, while still realizing that the new Japan was releasing energies that the architect must try to express. In the Yamanashi Press and Radio Centre at Kofu (fig. 25.14), close to Mount Fuji (designed between 1964 and 1967) he managed to give images of a Metabolist character a dignified and monumental form. A variety of functions had to be accommodated – offices, shops, printing-works, broadcasting studios and distribution points – so that the programme itself seemed to imply the notion of a building as a small city. The main elements of Tange's design were a grid of cylindrical service shafts containing air-conditioning, stairs and lifts, and acting as a primary structural system; and large horizontal beams containing studios, offices, etc. set down in a secondary system of movable partitions. In plan the building gave the distinct impression of total flexibility within a fixed framework, and the division between 'serving' towers, and 'served' spaces inevitably recalled Kahn's Richards Medical Laboratories; indeed, the use of grand service towers and horizontal floors became a virtual leitmotif of the mid-sixties in many parts of the world. Something of the same idea of open-endedness was hinted at in the elevations of the building as well, as some of the beams were 'left out', thus implying that they might be clipped on at some other time. The Yamanashi building flirted with the idea of total change, while still retaining the elemental dignity of a finite composition; it suggested the character of a modern technological mechanism, while still recalling traditional post and beam construction. It held the forces of traditionalism and futurism so basic to post-war Japan in an anxious equilibrium.

25.13 Noria Kurokawa, Yamagata Hawaii Dreamland, 1968.

25.14 (*right*) Kenzo Tange, Yamanashi Press and Radio Centre, Kofu, 1964–7.

26. Crises and Critiques in the 1960s

I like complexity and contradiction in architecture . . . based on the richness and ambiguity of modern experience, including that experience which is inherent in art. . . .

Architects can no longer afford to be intimidated by the puritanically moral language of orthodox modern architecture. . . .

R. Venturi, 1966

However diverse their approaches, however varied their personal styles, the architects who came to maturity in the early 1960s had certain broad features in common. Their birth-dates tended to fall between 1910 and 1930, so their early years were strongly impressed by the Second World War. Their vocabularies were established against the background of the declining International Style, and they turned to the late works of the masters in their own search for an architecture of greater robustness and complexity. But while they respected some of the guiding tenets of modern architecture, they did not advocate a slavish orthodoxy. Their position was characterized by tension between allegiance to the founding fathers and the need for self-expression. Faith and scepticism were held in balance; dogma and schism were equally avoided.

Looking back at the early 1960s from a distance of twenty years, one is struck by the genuine optimism surrounding the production, criticism and even the public reception of modern architecture. The crises and introversions of the 1970s were far away indeed. Singling out the work of men like Utzon and Tange, and pointing to the emergence of new civic monuments like the Japanese town halls or the Sydney Opera House, Sigfried Giedion even saw fit to announce the presence of a 'third generation', as if his Grand Tradition was now safely on its way. The idea was a typical Giedionism in that it assumed the continuing movement of an inner spirit of modern design with the torch of inspiration being handed on from father to son. But the post-war development lacked linear simplicity, and the individual architects within it did

not stagger their birth-dates at convenient twenty-year intervals. Men like Sert, Lasdun, the young Stirling, Tange, Utzon and Kahn may have shared a certain consciousness, and even have exhibited some stylistic similarities in their search for sculptural enrichment, but they stopped far short of constituting any unified movement. Even the architects who rallied behind the banner of Team X had widely different ways of interpreting the rough concensus of ideas when it came to making forms. Leitmotifs of the period, such as the raised platform, the directly expressed service tower, the sprawling, organic plan, the rough concrete surface, never amounted to a coherent latterday version of the International Style.

But in the field of general construction a banal international formula did triumph. The resultant dull reductivism was a mockery of the passionate simplicity of the seminal works of modern architecture. Functional discipline became confused with the instrumental purposes of real estate; planning bureaucracies took over *tabula rasa* images of the modern city and applied them with a confident, moralizing and stupid sense of certainty; what had started as an alternative dream was absorbed by an all too dreary status quo. The pioneer modern masters had had no difficulty identifying their enemy: it had been the 'corrupt revivalism' of the nineteenth century. But by the early 1960s good and evil were harder to label and eclecticism was no longer a major issue. Now the enemy was cheapened modern architecture, and the critical exercise of distinguishing the genuine from the fake required greater subtlety: good and bad might even share the same features (simple geometrical forms, concrete frames, flat roofs). Thus the young architect committed to quality was confronted with a series of dilemmas: should he pretend that there was a core of modern architectural principles which he ought to uphold to get modern architecture back on its true path? Should he maintain that the modern spirit required a constant quest for innovation in relationship to changing technologies and values? Or should he perhaps abandon the operation of modern architecture as one which was failing, and turn to other traditions in his formulation of a language?

The full force of these doubts would not be felt until the early 1970s. In the two decades after the war they were entertained by few. European modern architecture still held out the promise of a hygienic brave new world, rising out of the ruins, and proclaiming a new esperanto which would gloss over the nationalist evils of the 1930s. Each country had its own preoccupations. In Germany, for example, the main tasks continued to be related to urban and economic reconstruction. Cultural questions concerning the meaning of architecture in contemporary society, which plagued avant-gardes in Holland, England and Japan, were notably lacking; so were regionalist explorations, as they recalled Nazi obsessions with national identity. American influences supplied a safe middle way – a bland and rather uniform technocracy.

As before the war, some of the best buildings were constructed for the large industrial combines. Hentrich and Petschnigg's Phönix Rheinrohr skyscraper in Düsseldorf was an elegant affair, even compared with the best of its cousins in the USA, with its three slabs, each a structural bay deep, linked by transparent corridor sleeves. The Interbau exhibition in Berlin of 1957 had something of the function of the pre-war Weissenhofsiedlung; Aalto, Niemeyer and Le Corbusier making their contributions alongside Germans like Luckhardt and Schwippert. Berlin acquired a museum of modern architecture, and its own version of the Unité d'Habitation. The New National Gallery by Mies van der Rohe (1963) unapologetically asserted the German Classical spirit, while the Berlin Philharmonie by Hans Scharoun (1965), brought to fruition some of the Expressionist fantasies of forty years before. But such poetic creations were rare; the strength of German modern architecture lay in a second-rate design of a consistently high order, rather than in works of philosophical intensity. An exception to this sweeping generalization was the Free University of Berlin by Josic, Candilis and Woods (1963–74), a virtual manifesto of their urban ideas. Like most of the architects linked to Team X in the fifties, this partnership had to wait until the sixties to carry out its theories.

Italy after the war also had problems disentangling its architecture from the totalitarian taint of the thirties, but the production was far richer and more diverse than in Germany. 'Neo-realists' such as M. Ridolfi and L. Quaroni attempted to produce an imagery rooted in proletarian consciousness and 'everyday urban reality'. In the I.N.A. Casa planning for the Tiburtino district of Rome, blocks of flats were laid out on an irregular plan and crowned with tiled

26.1 Pier Luigi Nervi, Exhibition Hall, Turin, 1962.

sloping 'Mediterranean' roofs. Calini and Montuori's Termini Station in Rome (1948–50) extended the lessons of pre-war Rationalism in an honorific mode, while Bruno Zevi, the historian, baptized an 'organic' architecture, to steer between arid technology and the confectionery of historicism.

Italian diversity was well represented by two skyscrapers that rose above Milan in the late fifties: the Pirelli building by Gio Ponti (fig. 26.2) and the Torre Velasca by Ernesto Rogers and Enrico Peressutti (fig. 26.3). The first was thirty-three storeys high and stood alongside the railway station. The plan was shaped to accommodate lifts at the core, and the structure was designed by Nervi on a double vertebrate system rather than a steel cage. These considerations led to a finely tapered form which was clad in an elegant, if slightly stylized, metallic cladding. The result was a unique prestige office building which mirrored the high technical standards of the company, and showed that not all high-rise designs in Europe had to ape the American models. By contrast the Torre Velasca stood close to Milan's Gothic cathedral and contained both office space and apartments. It rose to twenty-six storeys, but the top six (containing the domestic accommodation) were expressed as a deep overhang supported on splayed buttresses. Considerable variety was created in the façades by the straightforward revelation of different interior needs. The verticality of the concrete structural frame was stressed on the outside of the building to rhyme with the vertical shafts of the cathedral, and a stone cladding ensured that the tower did not depart too dramatically from its lower neighbours. The overall image was vaguely reminiscent of the tower of a medieval Palazzo Pubblico – indeed, the Torre Velasca caused something of a furore in the international press because of its 'historicism'.

As the pre-war Rationalists had asserted in the 1930s, tradition was unavoidable for the Italian architect, who did not necessarily have to strain for references to the past to incorporate its lessons. Even an engineer like Pier Luigi Nervi, who took pride in the purity of his intuitive and inductive methods of design, achieved buildings which seemed happy descendants of the grand constructions of antiquity. His numerous stadia, exhibition halls, factories and even autoroutes demonstrated how engineering discipline and rigorous sculptural expression might achieve a high synthesis of an almost natural character (fig. 26.1). Working at a

26.2 (*far left*) Gio Ponti, Pirelli building, Milan, 1957.

26.3 (*left*) Ernesto Rogers and Enrico Peressutti, Torre Velasca, Milan, 1958.

26.4 (*above right*) Aldo Van Eyck, orphanage at Ysbaanpad, near Amsterdam, 1961, plan.

26.5 (*right*) Aldo Van Eyck, Arnhem Pavilion, 1964, view of interior.

tiny and intricate scale, Carlo Scarpa was another designer whose work implied that tradition and modernity were capable of fruitful interaction. His finesse in abstract patterns of detail recalled Wright, but also fitted into traditions of Italian masonry and craftsmanship. Again, Giancarlo de Carlo, in his design for the University of Urbino (1963–, see Chapter 21),

demonstrated how mass production and a sense of place, a modern programme and ancient images of community might be brought together.

Of course de Carlo was yet another affiliate of Team X, and Team X had been preoccupied with issues of identity, scale and meaning which required a reconsideration of modern architectural principles in the light of regional traditions. Team X was never the source of a unified or rigid dogma, and each individual in the group had his own private concerns and background. The Dutchman Aldo Van Eyck, for example, was acutely conscious of the high social and spiritual aims, and outstanding formal qualities, of the Dutch modern movement between the wars. He attempted to inject into his work a humanism which was a respectable (though less extreme) descendant of the Utopianism of the pre-war period. Van Eyck was preoccupied with the degradation brought about by technology ('mile upon mile of nowhere') and sought to counter this with an architecture founded on spiritual values and (what he took to be) archetypal meanings (see Chapter 21). His design for an orphanage at Ysbaanpad, Amsterdam (1961), avoided the usual oppressive institutional image by making the building into a web of small pavilions looking into private courts, expressed as a repetitive but variable pattern (fig. 26.4). It was an order loosely reminiscent of an early Mondrian (rather than the hard-line images which had influenced De Stijl), or of the layout of a North African village: the intention was clearly to create a sort of field of spaces of different human pitch and intensity. Van Eyck detailed the orphanage so that the elements flowed ambiguously into one another: the regimentation of a systems building was avoided in a building which nonetheless employed standardization. The orphanage design was not so far in spirit from Lasdun's slightly later University of East Anglia, which also generated richness from repetition. Van Eyck wrote:

Whatever space and time mean, place and occasion mean more. For space in the image of man is place, and time in the image of man is occasion . . .
Provide that place, articulate the in between . . .
make a welcome of each door and a countenance of each window . . . get closer to the shifting centre of human reality and build its counterform – for each man and all men . . .

Similar preoccupations inspired the Arnhem Pavilion design of 1964 (fig. 26.5). Simple straight and semicircular partitions were set into an overall circular plan in such a way that the observer was forced into a sequence of events and encounters which were nonetheless held together by a firm geometrical

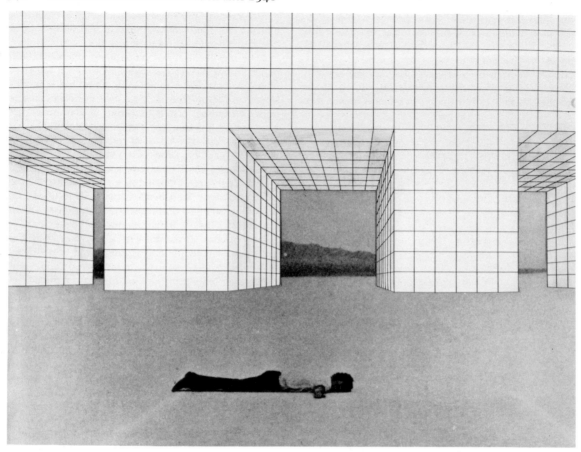

26.6 'Superstudio',
*Continuous Monument,
Arizona Desert*, 1969.

discipline. Van Eyck's mysticism emerged in the intense feeling for the psychological variation of space and in the imagery of the plan – a sort of talisman or emblem portraying a sequence of worlds within worlds. The building was like a small labyrinth and its shape recalled, once again, Van Eyck's interest in the cosmic symbolism of Dogon architecture.

Although English developments in the 1960s were discussed in Chapter 24, it is of some use to place them in the larger European context. Lasdun's 'urban landscape' ideas were never directly linked to Team X (to which he never belonged), but there were parallels between his preoccupations with growth and change, a sense of place and the articulation of social relationships, and theirs. The Smithsons, of course, were major figures in the group and with the other members eventually published the *Team 10 Primer* (1968) as a joint pronouncement of philosophy. The technological romanticism of James Stirling had no direct parallels in Europe, but Archigram and the anti-architecture lobby were not a unique phenomenon. In Italy 'Archizoom' and 'Superstudio' articulated similar ideas, usually in glossy collages based on Pop imagery

and surrealist aspects of advertising. The moral struggle for 'deeper values' of the modern movement was put aside, and culture was reduced to a sort of consumer pluralism delighting in technology as a plaything. The imagery of 'Superstudio', the Florentine group, was also taken up with sophisticated glass and steel packaging. The *Continuous Monument, Arizona Desert* of 1969 (fig. 26.6) was a photomontage of a patch of wilderness traversed by a thin glass viaduct of total monotony. The style of the structure recalled the stripped, Classical buildings of the Fascist period. However, the image was intended as a critique of the cluttered world of modern materialism:

Beyond the convulsions of production a state can be born of calm in which a world takes shape without products or refuse, a zone in which mind is energy and raw material and is also the final product, the only intangible object for consumption.

Another collage, *A Journey from A to B*, showed groovy kids in bare feet walking through an ethereal perspective grid into another hazy desert landscape.

The caption stated that 'There will be no further reason for roads or squares'. The forms and spaces of earlier architecture were to be rejected as so many pretensions towards an absolute order, which really masked oppressive social systems of power. Thus a curiously sensual attitude to technology was combined with the badinage of radical chic.

In the United States between 1955 and the late 1960s, architecture pursued some parallel courses with Europe, though patronage conditions required different reactions. Skidmore, Owings and Merrill evolved a standardized big business heraldry incorporating a somewhat glib version of Miesian purity, the steel frame, tinted glass and refined finishes of chrome and marble. The engineer R. Buckminster Fuller succeeded in popularizing the geodesic dome and stimulated a school of technological wizardry which even came up with the fantastic notion of covering Manhattan with a giant environmental bubble. American confidence in high technology was also reflected in a megastructure compulsion which hit the profession in the mid-sixties (influenced in part by Archigram and the Metabolists). This prompted Paul Rudolph to envisage a linear city of stepped section running for miles across the edge of New York. A scientific approach to the design process was argued forcibly by Christopher Alexander (*Notes on the Synthesis of Form*, 1963), who restated some of the traditional functionalist arguments but with the help of mathematical models. And a certain admiration for social science was reflected in the foundation of numerous university departments with such titles as 'School of Environmental Studies'. The danger in all this was obvious: the role of intuition, imagination, and tradition in the genesis of forms could become severely demoted. The later self-conscious and strenuous assertion of the primacy of aesthetic values which would bedevil the American avant-garde in the 1970s probably needs to be understood against the background of this quasi-scientific methodology.

But the emulation of the processes and images of technology was only one strand of the complex American development. At another extreme was the wilderness romanticism of Bruce Goff, who delighted in *ad hoc* combinations of natural materials and found objects from industrial waste. The Bavanger House of 1957, near Norman, Oklahoma, was organized around a central mast with a swirling wooden roof, and an idiosyncratic cable structure; the whole was fashioned from bits and pieces found close to the site. It is not surprising that Goff should have been adopted as a sort of hero of the counter-culture of the late 1960s, for his buildings implied a critique of total design and a rejection of the corporate values that were associated with it in the American context.

Although there was no direct equivalent to Team X in America, the ideas of the group did filter in by a number of routes. J. Bakema, S. Woods and J. Soltan taught in American architecture schools, while J. L. Sert (who was not a member, but whose ideas were not dissimilar) preached a new unity of architecture and town planning at Harvard Graduate School of Design (of which he was Dean) in the late fifties. In his design for Peabody Terraces (see Chapter 21) he gave form to his theories. Holyoke Center and Boston University (1964) dealt with similar ideas: the subtle linkage of townscaped spaces, tall towers, interior streets, intermediary buildings of transitional scale, the articulation of different uses through highly textured façades of louvers and balconies, the delicate composition of concrete frames and bright colours. As in Europe, these urban demonstrations remained the property of well-to-do universities, having little effect on the increasingly brutal development of the capitalist city. The sixties witnessed the wholesale destruction of vast areas of historical fabric in the interests of 'economic development'. Earlier modern movement platitudes concerning the value of space and light (though rarely greenery) were co-opted to rationalize financial motives, to justify the construction of freeways, or else to support grotesque civic monuments with compulsory piazzas. The American architect was constantly demoted to a sort of exterior decorator for business interests. Those housing agencies which existed encouraged simplistic, grand-slam solutions of an insensitive kind, and American architects had little tradition of radical criticism. The artist architect was thus forced into the gilded cage of upper-crust patronage: museums, prestigious university buildings, villas on Long Island. The aspirations towards an integrated society implicit in Team X thinking seemed foreign indeed.

If Mies van der Rohe dominated the early fifties in America, late Le Corbusier dominated the early sixties. Curiously enough his one American building the Carpenter Center at Harvard, was little understood, but replicas of La Tourette popped up all over the place as city halls or even department stores. Rough concrete piers, heavy crates of *brise-soleil* and rugged overhangs were the order of the day. An elephantine tendency seems to have gripped America in the early sixties in any case: veneers of *brise-soleil* or coatings of marble were laid over massive steel frames and trusses. Scully coined the phrase 'paramilitary dandyism' to describe it: one thinks of the grand monumentality of Roche and Dinkeloo's Knights of Columbus Headquarters at New Haven (1968) or of the huge piers coated in expensive stone of their Ford Foundation in New York (1967), or again of the eerie surrealism of their sliced glass pyramids for College Life Insurance in Indiana

(1969), where 'high tech' and the pristine visions of Boullée seemed to come together (fig. 26.7). As always in American luxury commissions, the craftsmanship and detailing were of the highest level: I. M. Pei's Hancock Tower in Boston (designed by Henry Cobb) used reflecting glass and a slender steel mullion system of a precision unthinkable in Europe (fig. 26.8). American corporations needed to express their power, their efficiency, their belief in advanced technology, their preoccupation with styling: the sharp-edged minimalist creations of the aforementioned firms were able to supply them with just the right imagery.

The rugged concrete tradition in monument building was best represented by Kallmann and McKinnell's Boston City Hall (see Chapter 23) or by Paul Rudolph's works of the mid-sixties. These buildings were surely part of a robust reaction against the spindly International Style of the fifties. Rudolph had been trained under Gropius at Harvard, and had soon rejected the reductivism of his mentor. The Jewett Arts Center at Wellesley (1953) was coated with references to its neo-Gothic setting, and highly mannered in its use of ornamental sunscreens, but it still represented a quest for formal richness. The late works of Le Corbusier, the spatial dramas of the Italian Baroque, and the complexities in section of Wright's works helped Rudolph to find his way. By the time he designed the Art and Architecture building at Yale (1964), his personal style was assured: violent contrasts of scale and colossal piers in rough corduroy concrete gave the whole building a vaguely primitive air (fig. 26.9). Silhouettes and sequences were expressed in an exaggeratedly irregular external volume. The same vigorous style was taken still further in the buildings for Boston's Government Center (1964), where curved stairs and cascades of platforms were linked to spiralling towers. But Rudolph's expressionism seemed overdone, giving the feeling that all these displays of virtuosity perhaps contained no social content. Once again, an American artist resorted to formalist gestures, albeit of considerable aesthetic interest.

Against this setting of the mechanistic at one end, and of dandyism at the other, the sober figure of Kahn stood out like a sentinel of ancient sense and principle. As well as being the major talent of the post-war years in America, he was also an inspiring teacher. In the 1950s he taught regularly at the University of Pennsylvania School of Architecture in Philadelphia, where he was a living link to the enlightened aspects of Beaux-Arts discipline. He encouraged a respect for the past and an understanding for the role of *ideas* in architectural expression. His pupils were presented with a very different diet from their Harvard contemporaries, who still laboured under the inheritance of Gropius. Most notable of the younger men to be taught

26.7 (*above*) Kevin Roche and John Dinkeloo, College Life Insurance building, Indiana, 1969.

26.8 (*left*) I. M. Pei and Associates (designer H. Cobb), Hancock Tower, Boston, 1969.

26.9 Paul Rudolph, Art and Architecture building, Yale University, New Haven, Connecticut, 1966.

by Kahn was Robert Venturi, who won a scholarship to the American Academy in Rome, and then went into private practice in the late fifties. He received few commissions and devoted much time to teaching and writing. His book *Complexity and Contradiction in Architecture* (1966) pulled together the reflections of a decade, and functioned as both a personal 'Towards an architecture' and a handbook of sensibility for a generation bored by the blandness of what they called 'orthodox modern architecture'.

'Orthodox modern architecture' turned out to mean not so much the entire architectural production of the previous half century (Venturi singled out both Le Corbusier and Aalto for special praise) as the simplistic and skin-deep version of modern design that had been prevalent in America for the previous twenty years. Venturi took the well-known Miesian jingle 'Less is more' and parodied it with the retort 'Less is a bore'; however, he was quick to point out that the complexity he sought could not be found by simply sticking on more ornamental details. Rather he was in favour of a tension bred by perceptual ambiguity – a richness of both form and meaning – which should affect the overall form of a design:

The tradition 'either–or' has characterized orthodox modern architecture – a sun screen is probably nothing else; a support is seldom an enclosure; a wall is not violated by window penetrations but is totally interrupted by glass; program functions are exaggeratedly articulated into wings or segregated pavilions ... Such manifestations of articulation and clarity are foreign to an architecture of complexity and contradiction, which tends to include 'both–and' rather than exclude 'either–or'.

If the source of the both–and phenomemon is contradiction, its basis is hierarchy, which yields several levels of meanings among elements with varying values. It can include elements that are both good and awkward, big and little, closed and open, continuous and articulated, round and square, structural and spatial. An architecture which includes varying levels of meaning breeds ambiguity and tension.

Venturi supported his case with numerous illustrations of buildings and plans from past periods in history. Lutyens, Hawksmoor, Le Corbusier or a humble stone building might all be used to illustrate a certain quality of complexity. The method was thus loosely similar to that pursued in *Vers une architecture*, but where the lesson of this earlier work had been the integration of certain underlying essentials of Classicism with an imagery for the machine age, Venturi's approach seemed to imply a less profound synthesis and a more fragmented aesthetic. He claimed that his 'both–and' approach to architectural elements and meanings was more in tune with the complexity of modern experience than the sterilities of the preceding generation, but gave little evidence of an underlying social vision or ideal. Clearly his sensibility had some loose links with contemporary painters like Jasper Johns or Robert Rauschenberg, who deliberately confronted the spiritual heroics of the abstract expressionists with banalities drawn from everyday life; but there was no automatic step from such a sensibility to a set of architectural forms. Positive reviewers of Venturi claimed that he was all for enriching the language of modern design: detractors suggested that his forms were arbitrary and that he was simply opening the doors to eclecticism again. Whichever way you looked at it, it was obvious that he was avoiding the arid sociological and technical definitions of architecture then prevalent, in favour of a discussion in which issues of form (and even meaning) did at least play a part.

Towards the end of the book Venturi applied some of his arguments to the American urban scene, claiming that 'Main Street is nearly all right' and that official planning (he might have called it 'orthodox modern urbanism') in the USA had done much to destroy street life and to subdue the vitality of the flashing signs and advertisements. This mood of reaction against over-discrete and over-simple categories was in tune with the age: sociologists like Richard Sennett would soon write in favour of 'disorder' and Jane Jacobs (in *Death*

26.10 Robert Venturi, house in Chestnut Hill, Philadelphia, Pennsylvania, 1963.

and Life of Great American Cities) would praise the complex weave of meanings of the most 'ordinary' urban places. Venturi and his partners Denise Scott-Brown and Steven Izenour expanded on this point of view in *Learning from Las Vegas* (1973), in which they claimed that the coloured street signs in front of the casinos were some native, indigenous form of expression of 'ordinary American people'. Thus populism and Pop Art sensibility came together in the curious illusion that products of Madison Avenue should be seen as a grass-roots, public, 'low art'.

There was a regionalist flavour to Venturi's ideas which was related to his feeling that a truly American architecture should be created. The 'vernacular' to which he turned to find appropriately popular and reassuring images was artificial and mass-produced: it was provided by the commercial strip and the suburban crackerbox house, both areas traditionally despised by élitist planners with European pretensions. In his design for a house for his mother in Chestnut Hill, Philadelphia (1963), Venturi had evaded the fifties 'orthodox modern' cliché of the glass box pavilion, in favour of an elusive image of the home replete with gable, sloped roof, attached mouldings, façade, back porch, etc. (fig. 26.10). However, this was no mere replica of the standard suburban image, since the allusions to the humble American home were combined with witty and ambiguous quotations from Le Corbusier and Palladio. The façade had a deliberately dead-pan character which disguised the welter of internal complexities and contradictions of the plan: Venturi praised the billboard character of

American urban streets and coined the term 'decorated shed' to describe the type; this he contrasted to the concrete sculptural buildings of the early sixties, which he referred to contemptuously as 'ducks'.

Despite Venturi's populist stance, his architectural jokes were obviously directed at the initiated. His buildings were even provided with the artist's own elaborate explanatory texts. Of the small house just described he wrote:

This building recognizes complexities and contradictions: it is both complex and simple, open and closed, big and little: some of its elements are good on one level and bad on another; its order accommodates the generic elements of the house in general, and the circumstantial elements of a house in particular. It achieves the difficult unity of a medium number of diverse parts rather than the easy unity of few or many motival parts.

In the Guild House, an old people's home in Philadelphia of 1962–66 (fig. 26.11), Venturi extended the same approach on a larger scale and for a function where his interest in 'commonly understood imagery' might be tested. The building had to include ninety-one apartments of varying types with a common recreation room; it was to house elderly folk from the neighbouring area. Venturi disposed the rooms in a symmetrical plan with a façade that came up to the street line. This elevation was also symmetrical, with the entrance doors placed tantalizingly either side of the axis at the base. A large arch

26.11 (*right*) Robert Venturi, Guild House, Philadelphia, 1962–66.

26.12 (*below*) Charles Moore, Faculty Club, University of California at Santa Barbara, 1968, interior.

was cut through the top of the façade perhaps to try to give the building an image of openness and shelter. Finally, on the very top was placed an anodized gold television aerial, which (according to the artist) could be interpreted 'as a symbol of the aged, who spend so much time looking at TV'.

The Guild House was constructed from cheap bricks and simple standardized windows, and detailed so that a planar character was emphasized. The windows were chosen to rhyme with those in the area and were commonplace, standardized sashes of the kind found in the cheapest housing schemes. In the context of such a self-conscious architectural composition they recalled Venturi's observations on Pop artists who employed 'old clichés in new settings' and so gave 'uncommon meaning to common elements by changing their context or increasing their scale ...' One scarcely needs to emphasize at this point the contrast between Venturi's approach and vocabulary, and those of Rudolph, Kallmann, Roche and Dinkeloo, and Pei at the same time. However, his ideas were usually more convincing in writing than when built. The agonized self-consciousness betrayed the lack of an instinctive feeling for form, space or even proportion. Venturi set the tone for a literary conception of architecture in which more emphasis was put on imagery and quotation than on formal integration.

Another American architect to react against the blandness of clichéd modern architecture of the fifties was Charles Moore, who was based in California, where the weight of imported European modernism of the Gropius variety was far less. Moore and Lyndon's

'Sea Ranch' on the Pacific coastline north of San Francisco was a somewhat routine essay in redwood cabin regionalism. But by the late sixties Moore had gone beyond this folksiness and absorbed some of the lessons of Pop Art. The interior of his Faculty Club for the University of California of 1968 (fig. 26.12) was designed as a sort of stage set of thin planes and screens (planarity was once again in fashion), evoking simultaneously modern architectural icons (e.g., van Doesburg's forms of the twenties), the image of a baronial hall (replete with electric neon 'banners'), the standard effects of the American faculty club (portraits, stuffed animal heads, etc.) and Spanish Colonial touches (a sort of tongue-in-cheek regionalism). In this case it has to be said that too much complexity and contradiction ended up being simply a witty hotch-potch without underlying order or tension. But Moore's design, despite its lack of formal resolution, was still symptomatic of an increasingly eclectic mood in which all periods of the past (including the modern movement) were regarded as 'game' for quotations.

Venturi's and Moore's positions suggested that at least some of the guiding principles of modern architecture were losing hold, although, of course, their attitudes, styles and strategies would have been inconceivable without the numerous intellectual and formal inventions of the previous fifty years. Nonetheless they could be portrayed as iconoclasts who were deliberately playing mannerist games, and who were undermining some of the hard-won battles of the pioneers. In the circumstances, it was not surprising to find shrieks against their heresy, related to attempts at returning to 'the fundamentals of the faith'. This led to the curious situation of theorists arguing for a return to some mythical and crystalline principles of 'modernism', and of practitioners reviving some of the white forms of the 1920s.

Most of the architects involved in this exercise were linked to East Coast architecture schools like Princeton and Cornell. Chief among them were five (briefly called the 'New York 5'): Peter Eisenman, Richard Meier, Charles Gwathmey, John Hejduk, and Michael Graves. In the late sixties most of these men were in their mid-thirties, and therefore grew up with modern art and architecture as entirely established facts. They were loosely united by a strong feeling for the seminal works of the inter-war years, like the Schroeder House, the Villa Stein or the Casa del Fascio; by an obsession with formal issues at the expense of content and function (their formalist definitions of 'modernism' parroted those used by defenders of the American 'hard-edged' abstraction of the late sixties); and by their allegiance to the opinions of Colin Rowe, who taught in America from the sixties onwards, and who seems to have conveyed the twenties to his acolytes as some lost

Golden Age. But reviving the forms of the early International Style in the late sixties, forty years afterwards, was by no means a simple exercise: it was every bit as dangerous as reviving any other set of forms of the past. The problem of pastiche hovered over the endeavour; and there was little evidence that the 'New York 5' were in any position to supply a cogent new content in their renaissance of earlier forms.

Despite the insubstantiality of their philosophical positions, some of the New York 5 architects achieved buildings of a dainty elegance. The Benacerraf addition by Graves (1969) may stand as an example (fig. 26.13). This was a sort of pavilion attached to a house in Princeton. Its architectural language was compounded from a variety of modern architectural sources, but elements were put in unexpected juxtapositions which challenged expectations concerning their usual role. Thus the knowledgeable observer might note that cylindrical *pilotis* turned up as horizontal handrails; or he might sense that coloured struts and exploding spatial effects derived from the Schroeder House were being deliberately collided with free-plan curves recalling Le Corbusier's villas. Giulio Romano had relied, in the Palazzo del Tè (1534), on the knowledge of his audience, so that they might react with a frisson of shocked delight when they noticed his dropped keystones, and other breaks with the Classical rules of the High Renaissance; in the same way Graves relied on a historical perspective which made of the twenties a classic age, and on an audience, who, knowing this, would admire his virtuosity in breaking the rules. This was complexity and contradiction, but applied to revered prototypes of the modern movement, rather than to American domestic sources as with Venturi. It was an architect's architecture aimed at a profession thoroughly acquainted through coffee-table books and college art-history courses with the monuments of modernism. Philip Johnson characterized the Benacerraf rather aptly as 'a wonderfully sporty piece of lawn sculpture'. Indeed, it is arguable that the Graves style, with its interest in delicate coloured struts and a sort of backyard pastoralism, may have owed something to the abstract sculptures of Anthony Caro.

In the broad context of the 1960s in the United States it is possible to see the New York 5's self-conscious interest in formal issues as a reaction against the technological school on the one hand, and the preoccupation with social scientific methodologies on the other. In turn their stylistic emphasis on thinness, planarity and transparency may perhaps be seen as a formal reaction against the brutalist antics in heavy concrete of some of their predecessors. It is interesting, in retrospect, how little attention they devoted to late Le Corbusier, and how much they concentrated on the

26.13 Michael Graves, Benacerraf addition, Princeton, New Jersey, 1969.

any cultural significance in this choice of prototype or in the resultant analogies between his work and Italian Rationalism of the 1930s. Instead he argued that such buildings as 'House II' (1969) were explorations of basic formal syntax and the logical structure of space. It seemed to matter little to the New York 5 architects that the forms they imitated had been the outward expression of utopian philosophies and social visions. Discussions of moral content were displaced by concentration on issues of a purely formal kind. In their revulsion against sociology they perhaps neglected the different question of the idealization of a way of life in symbolic form. In that respect they followed in the Greenbergian critical tradition, or even the formalist version of the International Style set by Hitchcock and Johnson forty years before.

Indeed, the International Style revival was cloaked in smoke-screens of verbal rhetoric implying that it was throwing aside false doctrines of functionalism in favour, once again, of the 'art of architecture'. Venturi and Moore tended to be rejected for their slumming in Americana, and it became customary by the early seventies to contrast the 'whites' (the New York 5) and the 'greys' (Venturi et al.) in rather the same way that critics had contrasted pure geometrical abstraction with Pop Art, namely as a contest between modernism and realism, or as a battle between exclusiveness and inclusiveness. In fact the architectural movements had a good deal in common: both placed a high value on complex formal manipulations of screens and planes; both were involved with quotations and overt revival; both were conceived (in part) as reactions against debased modern design; and neither had much to say about the general state of American society. Both were precious flower architectures, conceived and concocted in the hothouses of the élite American universities; and both were prone to a bloodless and over-intellectualized academicism.

Broadly speaking the path between 1955 and 1975 in Western Europe and the United States was one from a loosely felt consensus (which nonetheless took many forms) to a position of greater scepticism in which various spectral versions of mythical orthodoxy came under attack. The quest for deeper meanings in the fifties avant-garde gave way to a brittle formalism proud to announce that it had no social polemic, and dubiously supported by intellectualizations derived from linguistics and formalist criticism. The age of conviction gave way to an era of broken faiths, where no strong, new generating ideas seemed to emerge, leaving the architect in a sort of suspension, free to stick together fragments, but uncertain of the meaning of their combination. It was symptomatic of the change that, by the late seventies, one could find the word 'revolutionary' applied to revivals of earlier styles.

villas of the 1920s as sources. However, where the exemplars were often made of stuccoed concrete, and indulged in machine quotations, the replications were often made of wood, were related to the American timber frame tradition, and were even more spindly in appearance. But it is not appropriate to treat the group's work monolithically. Gwathmey, for example, relied on bold contrasts of volume and dumpy proportions for his aesthetic effects. Meier was preoccupied with the contrast and resolution of vertical and horizontal layering in his house designs (a concern which he claimed derived from the inherent properties of Le Corbusier's Dom-ino skeleton and Maison Citrohan respectively). Hejduk built rarely and expressed his ideas through crisp geometrical exercises based on a somewhat academic view of Purism. Eisenman, a theorist as well as a practitioner, modelled his style extensively on that of Terragni, but disclaimed

27. Modern Architecture and Developing Countries since 1960

Every people that has produced architecture has evolved its own favourite forms, as peculiar to that people as its language, its dress, or its folklore. Until the collapse of cultural frontiers in the last century, there were all over the world distinctive local shapes and details in architecture, and the buildings of any locality were the beautiful children of a happy marriage between the imagination of the people and the demands of the countryside.

H. Fathy, 1973

Modern architecture was created in industrialized countries where a progressivist world view flourished temporarily, and where avant-garde cliques attempted to produce an authentic modern style appropriate to rapidly changing social conditions. This curious pattern was not repeated elsewhere, but its results were copied all around the world, and were often misapplied. Moreover, as has been emphasized, it was not until the 1940s and 1950s that modern forms had any appreciable impact on the 'less developed countries', and these forms were usually lacking in the poetry and depth of meaning of the master-works of the International Style. The dissemination of this degraded version of modern design occurred in a number of ways: through rapid economic development of a kind which fostered functions, technologies and urban circumstances in which some sort of modern architecture seemed either relevant or unavoidable; through continuing colonization, in which case images of modernity functioned as emblems of foreign economic or political control; and through the brainwashing of post-colonial élites (native-born but foreign-educated) with Western images and ideas which were upheld as 'progressive' counter-agents to an earlier era of 'backwardness and stagnation'.

Some sense of the problems following from rapid modernization has been given already with the example of Japanese architecture in the twentieth century (see Chapter 25). In the 1960s and 1970s many other parts of the world, especially in Africa, the Far and Middle East, were afflicted by similar difficulties of cultural identity. The arrival of modern architecture was usually linked to foreign businesses, and while the multi-storey, air-conditioned offices and the expensively clad airports may have served as instant status symbols for those intent on attracting international capital, the results were usually crude and lacking in sensitivity to local traditions, values, and climate. Even had there been architects keen on reinterpreting national traditions, they would have had difficulty finding relevant local precedents for such functions. As it was, cultural introspection was not high on the list of priorities of the typical patron.

This collision of old and new was another version of the crisis of industrialization which Western European countries and the United States had themselves begun to experience in the nineteenth century. But there were at least two major differences: the 'advanced' nations had themselves invented the Industrial Revolution; and they had had over a century to adjust to the far-reaching social and cultural changes it brought with it. The rapidly developing Third World country of the 1960s or 1970s (e.g., Iran or Nigeria) could find itself passing from a rural and agricultural economy to an urban and industrial one in the course of a single generation. Moreover, the tools (including buildings) with which this rapid change was achieved were imported ones: little wonder that a form of cultural schizophrenia should have emerged at the same time.

Pleas on the part of 'sensitive' Western observers that national and rural traditions be preserved or used as the basis of a new regionalism were liable to fall on deaf ears in these circumstances, since peasant vernaculars could easily be identified with backwardness and the exploitation of rural labour. The case in favour of preserving fine nineteenth-century colonial buildings (which might also possess subtle adjustments to local traditions and climates) was even harder to make. The new *arriviste* classes seemed to wish to disassociate themselves from the weight of their recent history and to experience nothing less than the consumer 'freedoms' of the West. They grew greedy for glossy images with technological and international overtones which could affirm their own position. Skin-deep modern building (rather than any substantial form of modern architecture) was waiting in the West, all too ready to overwhelm yet another area of the international market. The irony was that so many countries, at last liberated from overt colonial rule, should so quickly have been persuaded to adapt vulgar versions of Western architectural dress.

By the early 1960s city centres were springing up around the world which seemed closer in spirit to Manhattan or modern London than to local, national, or colonial precedents. The new ersatz international modern design with its standard clichés – the glass-slab hotel with balconies and kidney-shaped pool, the air conditioned lobby with tinted plate-glass windows, the whitewashed concrete frame, etc. – was not *just* the face of 'Western economic imperialism', for parallel developments occurred in countries under Soviet influence at the same time. Perhaps Le Corbusier had been right when he had suggested that the machine caused a revolution of its own transcending political ideologies. Some of the same distressing features which had crept up on the cities of the West during the nineteenth century, and to which modern architecture had been an attempted answer, now impinged on places where there was the added problem of a split between adapted Western models and native values. The safety valve of an avant-garde, or at least an élite intent on visual quality and symbolic depth, was usually missing or else a pale shadow of its Western relatives.

One way out of the impasse was to try and put together some combination of the indigenous and the imported. Here fake regionalism – with a few gingerbread 'historical' attachments over an ill-conceived modern structural box – was a constant danger. A sounder approach lay in the sort of modern regionalism mentioned in Chapters 21 and 25, in which an attempt was made to unearth fundamental lessons in local tradition and to blend them with an already evolved modern language. The problem came in translating these basic features expressing regional adaptation and meanings of the past into a form appropriate to changing social conditions: no set recipes existed which could guarantee success, and

lesser talents ran the risk of producing buildings which were pastiches of both modern *and* traditional forms.

In the transactions between industrialized and industrializing nations there were also collisions in the ways buildings were designed and put up. Modern architecture presupposed a division of labour between architects, manufacturers, engineers and construction workers, but in many 'underdeveloped' countries there were fewer steps in the process between conception and construction. Thus a building conceived on a Parisian drawing-board might require imported and expensive mass-produced components which entirely ignored local patterns of construction and labour when built in the Persian Gulf. The resultant forms were immediately at odds with centuries-old traditions of craftsmanship in which methods had been evolved to handle local materials. The practical logic behind regional style was undermined, and the delicate details and intuitions of handicraft were replaced by tatty industrial building components.

The problems attached to importing foreign technologies were compounded by others related to the imposition of alien social theories, especially in the field of housing. What were conceived in Europe as low-cost models might be inappropriate when built elsewhere. In Egypt, for example, the philosopher/architect Hassan Fathy discovered that concrete-frame housing schemes were liable to be far more expensive in terms of money, transport costs, and salaries, than local, traditional, self-build methods, and that they were at odds with non-Western ways of life. In his book, *Architecture for the Poor, an Experiment in Rural Egypt* (1973), he suggested that labour-intensive construction methods using local materials were the obvious answer. He conducted an experiment at New Gourna, close to Luxor in the Nile valley, in which he schooled the local peasantry in Nubian techniques using mud-brick vaults and simple domes (fig. 27.1). These elements had stood the test of time and were well attuned to the resources and climate of the region; by contrast 'modern' solutions were often unfunctional and ill-fitted to the particular environment. Fathy expressed his scepticism of modern architecture succinctly:

Modernity does not necessarily mean liveliness, and change is not always for the better ... Tradition is not necessarily old fashioned and is not synonymous with stagnation ... Tradition is the social analogy of personal habit, and in art has the same effect of releasing the artist from distracting and inessential decisions so that he can give his whole attention to the vital ones.

Fathy's critique of industrialization and its accom-

would be disrupted by a new spirit of rationality. The uprooted urban proletariat would be cut off from its countryside origins, but at the same time hard put to adjust to the chaos of industrial urban life.

A crisis of this kind was felt acutely in places as far apart as India and Brazil by the early 1960s. Architects were powerless in the face of it. Neither bland low-cost housing slabs, nor agrarian romanticism of the type espoused by Fathy were much use in dealing with this urban poverty and overcrowding. Vast new self-built slums made of tin cans, cardboard and industrial wastes grew around the urban fringe. In these circumstances, 'Architecture' – whether glass-boxed or regionally sensitive – was a luxury. It is scarcely surprising that urban theories should have reflected a feeling of hopelessness in the face of such chaos. Indeed the argument was put forth that the squatter and satellite forms did at least provide shelter for the poor, which the official housing agencies were unable to do. Around Cairo the illegal settlements even hinted at the shape of a new, half-industrialized vernacular, employing a rough-shod concrete frame with a flat roof, a courtyard, and infill walls of pot-tile and brick (fig. 27.3).

By the early 1970s in any case, concepts of total planning were under attack. This anti-absolutist attitude was well reflected in an experiment conducted in Peru for 'Barriada' housing in 1970, in which a variety of well-intentioned international architects supplied a rational plan based on the patterns of life which had emerged in the slums themselves, and left each family free to alter the individual house at will. In Papua New Guinea, in towns like Port Moresby, native inhabitants who had recently arrived from the country were encouraged to transform rural vernacular patterns which coped well with

27.1 (*left*) Hassan Fathy and the citizens of Gourna, New Gourna, near Luxor, Egypt, 1947–70; the mosque.

27.2 (*above*) Hassan Fathy, house near Luxor, Egypt.

panying forms was thus quite basic. He simply refused to accept the myths of progress and claimed that in most Third World circumstances the peasant could build better for himself than any architect. He argued that each individual family should build to suit its own needs, employing the wisdom of tradition rather than the expensive whims of professionals. There can be little doubt that romanticization of the peasant was part of a larger ideological quest for national roots; his philosophy would have particular appeal wherever the rural past was idealized and treated as a source of cultural mythology.

Fathy's experiments were conducted in a country whose vernacular had, in fact, suffered severe disruption under Ottoman rule, and his programme involved something of a self-conscious revival of indigenous craft (fig. 27.2). In many Third World rural areas no such revival was necessary, as local traditions endured on their own. But even in these cases mechanization of materials and of the means of production might eventually affect the remotest countryside by drawing peasants to the city in search of jobs and by introducing labour-saving tools which interfered with the continuity of rural craft traditions. The intricate fabric of myths behind genuine vernacular forms

a tropical climate (fig. 27.4), rather than following the earlier way of dreary, ill-adapted, imported house-types. One theorist, Z. Plocki, even went so far as to propose a 'New Guinea' architectural style, advocating a sort of 'modern regionalist' approach and arguing in favour of a new vernacular applicable to the broad range of building tasks, large and small:

Most architectural styles were the products of their own societies. Its religious values, climate, technology, social and political structures dictated the need and style of buildings. Shapes, proportions and decorations were symbolic and had meaning, often ending up with strict architectural orders. This 'internal stimulus' created cultures and architectural expressions that differed greatly from each other . . . Many of the better examples are being preserved, but rarely copied, and when they are it's apparent they have no meaning . . . Today, with jet travel, intercontinental news media. cinema, political structures and cultural exchanges, the world is smaller and the bulk of the influences which dictate a style are international, based on technology and economics . . . But, even accepting the International Style, technology and the stimulus from the outside, and not copying the

27.3 (*above*) Cairo, Egypt, the 'industrialized vernacular' of the outskirts, 1970s.

27.4 (*right*) Urban village, Hahuabada, Port Moresby, Papua New Guinea, mid 1970s.

traditional, rules can be formulated within which architects can create architecture and a character that can become the Niuginian style.

Here it was admitted that new urban patterns required a new architecture aping neither traditional tribal nor imported forms. The pretensions of the modern movement towards 'universality' showed up with embarrassing clarity, as did the limitations of a superficial and nostalgic regionalism. Moreover, Plocki extended his arguments to simple and self-built structures, not just to the creations of the well-to-do. The few touches of local colour required by the tourist industry were scarcely adequate to the problem of defining a new post-colonial style. This would have to come partly from 'within' and be a direct expression of new life patterns.

Where basic shelter was the concern, regionalist sensitivities may have seemed a luxury, but it was still possible to treat middle-class commissions as a laboratory for general formulations. As always, architectural value would reside in the convincing synthesis of the practical, the aesthetic and the symbolic, and in the creation of a unity in harmony with the setting. Vernacular structures provided many basic clues in achieving such ends by revealing age-old patterns of adaptation. In India both Kahn and Le Corbusier had turned to this source in originating elements for handling the extremes of climate; the former's Ahmadabad Institute of Management (1964) was built in a rugged, handmade brick vocabulary with ingenious shading and ventilating apertures (fig. 27.5), while the latter's buildings in the same city and in Chandigarh revealed the relevance of the concrete frame, the parasol and the *brise-soleil* to Indian needs. Among the Indians to take these hints were Charles Correa and Balkrishna Doshi. Doshi's housing and university schemes of the 1960s extended the imported language and blended it still further with indigenous realities. He established simple standardized systems of construction and patterns of plan arrangement adapted to climate and use, and laid these out in variations which enlivened the spaces between. His housing at Hyderabad of the 1970s employed terraces and overhangs derived from the vernacular of the region; careful thought was given to orientation, shading, and natural cross-ventilation, as well as to gradations between public and private space (fig. 27.6). Doshi tried to avoid the gaping spaces between buildings that had been made at Chandigarh, and to create something closer to the tight-knit and dense street patterns of traditional Indian towns. He was acutely aware of the irrelevance of indulging in a merely romantic peasantism, especially in a country where the peasant's lot was anything but romantic.

27.5 (*left*) Louis I. Kahn, Ahmadabad Institute of Management, India, 1964.

27.6 (*below*) Balkrishna Doshi, mixed income housing at Hyderabad, India, 1976.

27.7 (*right*) J. F. Zevaco, holiday housing, Agadir, Morocco, 1965: an attempt at cross-breeding traditional and modern forms.

His buildings were usually constructed for an emergent bourgeoisie and were rigorously designed to meet
the demands and habits of a new India where values
reflected Western mores. Forms were needed which
crystallized this situation. After all, much of the finest
architecture in Indian history had emerged from the
cross-breeding of foreign and local influences. Even the
hardest-boiled nationalist might have to admit that not
all the best things were entirely home-grown.

A satisfactory blend of old and new was also
achieved by J.F. Zevaco in his design for courtyard
houses in Agadir, Morocco (1965). Here the social
context was positively luxurious compared with that
which had confronted Fathy in Egypt as these were
holiday dwellings (fig. 27.7). Nonetheless, the architectural strategy was one which was transposible to
somewhat less expensive situations. Zevaco's solution
drew together the concrete technology, planning logic,
and simple volumes of a modern architectural
vocabulary, with the traditional, inward-looking,

North African courtyard dwelling. The approach was similar to that which Bodiansky and Woods had suggested in their ATBAT scheme of the early 1950s (see Chapter 21). Like its predecessors, the Zevaco design was valuable for its straightforwardness and the way in which it abstracted underlying social and climatic features from a local tradition and rephrased them in a new context. A certain formal elegance was assured by the fine handling of proportions and details, the play of light and the control of scale and greenery.

Agadir was a city already undergoing drastic modernization: it was a resort which had been largely rebuilt after a major earthquake. Mopti in Mali was a traditional sub-Saharan city with one of the most splendid mud mosques in North Africa. The Medical Centre, by André Ravereau (completed in 1976), had to be inserted between this major symbolic monument and the river Niger (fig. 27.8). The solution was to distribute the functions in low, well-protected volumes, linked one to another by shaded walkways, and disposed to maximize cross-ventilation. The style was simple and unadorned, and in tune with the abstraction of the local Saharan vernacular; the typical rectangular geometries and flat roofs of the region, gashed by deep shadows and enlivened by repetitions and variations of simple themes, might have been designed with a Cubist sensibility in mind. The technique of construction was also a happy blend of the regional and the imported, since concrete and mud were both materials cast in a wooden form-work. In the Medical Centre, the traditional mud walls were strengthened (and given a longer life than usual) by

27.8 (*above*) André Ravereau, Medical Centre, Mopti, Mali, 1976, with the traditional mosque in the background.

27.9 (*above right*) Minoru Yamasaki, Dharan airport, 1961.

27.10 (*right*) Alison and Peter Smithson, project for Royal National Pahlavi Library, Tehran, 1977.

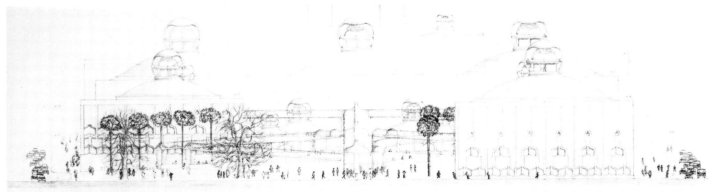

the addition of cement. The contextual sensitivity of the scheme extended from its colour, materials, and shape (which blended with the neighbouring mosque), to the overall arrangement, which restated traditional urban alleyways and pedestrian links in the building itself. Arguably these were strategies of a kind which had originated in the West (e.g., with Team X) but in Ravereau's design, the ideas were carried through to create a subtle blend of the old and the new, of the African and the European. Part of of the richness of the building came from the use of local handicraft methods, which gave the forms a sensitive touch lacking in most industrialized buildings. To have achieved similar effects in the West would have been extremely expensive, as such craftsmanship was altogether rare. Ravereau attempted to incorporate the best qualities of both worlds.

Evidently the Mopti Medical Centre was a context which demanded a quiet, almost anonymous, solution. But Western architects might also be called upon to design prestige buildings. Among the competitions held in the 1970s for grand new buildings in the wealthier developing countries were numerous ones for 'cultural centres', museums and state palaces, where issues of 'representation' were paramount. One of these was held in 1977 for the Royal National Pahlavi Library to stand in Tehran and embody (presumably) the munificence of the Shah's imperial court. Architects from all parts of the world made entries and indulged in confused efforts at 'cultural

SOUTH ELEVATION

364 · Transformation and Dissemination after 1940

expression'. Alison and Peter Smithson, for example, departed drastically from the safe path of their usual vocabulary (no doubt sensing that it lacked sufficient 'rhetoric' to deal with the symbolic requirements of a state building which should be identifiable by the populace), and embarked on a perilous road involving an imagery based on the 'Peacock Feather' (a motif from the Shah's heraldry) and the dome (a traditional Persian symbol of authority). The result was a fussy orientalism which failed entirely to capture the spirit of traditional monumentality (fig. 27.10). The mannered attempt at aping Islamic ornamental patterns recalled the Baghdad University scheme of over a decade before by Gropius and TAC, in which a bogus historicism had come very close to the spirit of a Hollywood production of the Arabian Nights. Minoru Yamasaki's Dharan airport for Saudi Arabia, of the early 1960s, also came dangerously near kitsch in its pre-cast supports emulating palm trees, and its tracery screens supposedly modelled on traditional fenestration (fig. 27.9). However, the Western architect intent on even a genuine regionalism might find himself faced by a client or an advisory body keen to have the latest from New York or London. In this scenario the theorist armed with his arguments about 'locale' and 'genius of place' might be rejected as an agent of the West intent on holding the developing world back from 'progress'.

There were some situations in which the Western architect might be called upon to design for religious or state institutions with highly defined traditional types of building such as mosques. In these cases the conflict between new and old, imported and indigenous, was at its most extreme. If the designer simply followed the formula of the traditional type he ran the risk of producing a sham, for his vocabulary and structural systems were not, in fact, traditional, and his forms lacked symbolic conviction. If he stuck to his own, modern vocabulary, he might fail to adhere sufficiently to the traditional elements and conventional meanings, and end up with a design that failed to communicate its purpose. The problem was not so very different in kind from that facing an architect in the West when presented with a cathedral: what was needed was an imaginative transformation of prototypes. However, it was rare that a Western architect grasped the spirit of the culture for which he was designing, and the employment of a native architect was no sure guarantee of authenticity either. At one extreme one might have a mosque that was indistinguishable from an office building; at the other, a bogus version of dome and minaret clumsily coated in industrial tiles and related uneasily to an entirely foreign constructional system in concrete.

Thus a major element of the architectural crisis of developing nations arose from a failure to establish an architectural language suitable to both modern and traditional tasks. It was no good pretending that modernization was not occurring, and hoping that the clock would stand still or even go backwards to some (entirely illusory) 'pure period', when foreign influences and chaotic changes were held not to have occurred. Nonetheless, these sentimental traditionalist emotions were often rehearsed in the confused search for 'cultural identity', whether this was defined in nationalist or pan-cultural terms. The architectural tradition in question might involve Islamic monuments or Melanesian wooden huts, but the traditionalist still shared all the predicaments of his revivalist counterpart in nineteenth-century Europe: even once a 'cultural essence' had been divined and linked to some 'golden age' or another in the past, there was still the problem of representing this core identity architecturally. One could not simply imitate the earlier forms: precedents needed transforming into meaningful images in the present.

1973 was a crucial year for the economies of the West because it was then that the 'oil crisis' came to a head. The revenue which flowed into the oil-producing countries was exchanged for Western expertise, including the talents of the architectural profession. A lull in Western production (often filled with paper projects and theoretical researches) corresponded with a boom in construction in previously undeveloped parts of the world which had usually been ignored by the West. It was not a happy contract of forces: get-rich-quick clients had little time to spend on niceties of architectural culture, and Western architects intent on financial gain were abysmally ignorant of local customs and traditions. An epidemic of technological brashness hit the shores of the Persian Gulf and the fringes of the desert. The matter was further complicated by the relative lack of monumental and urban examples in a primarily nomadic region. Relevant models were few. What was needed was a thorough assessment from first principles, of the formal suggestions inherent in climate, materials, social patterns and the like. Unfortunately, such rigour was not usually applied, and the new buildings of Saudi Arabia or Kuwait looked as if they could have stood anywhere.

A possible exception was the Intercontinental Hotel designed for Mecca by Frei Otto, the West German architect/engineer. In his Olympic Games structures for Munich, Otto had employed delicate high-tension nets and webs of irregular geometry to cover huge spaces. His forms were derived from a careful assessment of function and materials, but were also partly inspired by natural structures and by nomadic tents. His hotel design incoporated the basic principles of a Bedouin tent but at a much larger scale and using steel cables and wooden slats instead of rope and cloth.

27.11 Ministry of Building, Peking, 1950s.

The building was laid out as a sequence of small pavilions in a lush garden and the tent was drawn over the whole thing as a minimal shading device, open at the edges for the flow of air. A similar concept of the 'high-tech' tent was employed by Skidmore, Owings, and Merrill in their design for the airport at Mecca, a building of some symbolic importance as the modern arrival point for Muslims from all over the world making their pilgrimage to the Holy City.

The international resurgence in the cultural power and confidence of Islam was another major force to influence relationships between industrialized and less industrialized nations in the mid-1970s. This coincided with a period of soul-searching in the West, well reflected in a sort of architectural introversion and mannerism which replaced any serious attempt at expressing human values. 'Islamic revival' took many forms and was fuelled by many fires, among them a revulsion against the materialism which (it was held) could be traced to 'Western modernizing influences'. Architecture could not remain immune for long: the images of the debased International Style were soon condemned as emblems of demonic secularism.

The backlash against 'modern values' implied nothing distinct beyond a greater reverence for traditional moral and aesthetic forms. Once again, the issue of identity was at stake, but Pan-Islamic sentiments could even be manipulated to imply a community of culture between Morocco and Manila; with the wave of a wand they conveniently overlooked schisms, national boundaries and centuries of change. It was a mood which was hard to translate into an architectural philosophy, let alone architectural forms. The traditionalist designer who pretended that 'modern' and 'Western' models should be expunged

courted a number of teasing difficulties. He had to decide on the common denominators of 'Islamic architectural identity' (a tall order when one included the whole Muslim world, and when one admitted that many other factors than religion influenced forms). He felt compelled to believe that 'the nature of Islam' was some fixed and unchanging entity, which it clearly had not been. And, like any other revivalist, he had to decide which period of the arts was closest to the 'essential Islam', then to restate these forms without debasing them. There were other tricky issues arising from real changes in functions and needs: what, for example, was an 'Islamic railway station' supposed to look like? The fundamentalist architect had the further theoretical difficulty of deciding whether or not architectural quality might transcend religious dogmatism.

Such dilemmas were not, of course, uniquely Muslim property, but were shared by most countries confronting rapid change. After its revolution in 1949, China embarked upon a tricky path of cultural self-definition which had to steer its way between Soviet influence and its own quest for modernization. Grand State buildings such as the Great Hall of the People and the Museum of Chinese History and the Revolution built in the 1950s in Peking reflected a Classicizing line from Moscow, with mild touches here and there of bland ornament abstracted from the Imperial tradition. The Building Ministry, erected in the 1950s (fig. 27.11), had more overtly nationalist overtones, but its oriental touches were still skin-deep. Most matters of visual culture in China have been highly controlled by the Ministry of Culture and by the propaganda arm of the Chinese Communist Party. A dogmatic framework of this sort has done little to encourage visual excellence. Indeed, it is an ideological premiss of the system that social function should always be considered before formal quality. Evidently the idea that life-enhancing formal arrangements might have an elevating role to play in the formulation of a new society has not yet penetrated the official platitudes which stress realism and obvious propaganda devices.

It is interesting to conclude an all too brief survey of emergent world architecture with a monument which seems as if it may succeed on the social, symbolic, and formal levels simultaneously, and which has been conceived within a complex weave of cultural influences. This is the Hurva Synagogue, designed by Denys Lasdun between 1978 and 1981 (fig. 27.12) for the old city of Jerusalem on the site of a synagogue shelled in the 1967 war. The rebuilding (including part of the ruin) obviously has a significance of renewal for international Jewry as well as ardent local Zionists. Originally Louis Kahn was employed to prepare a design, but this was left incomplete at his death. His

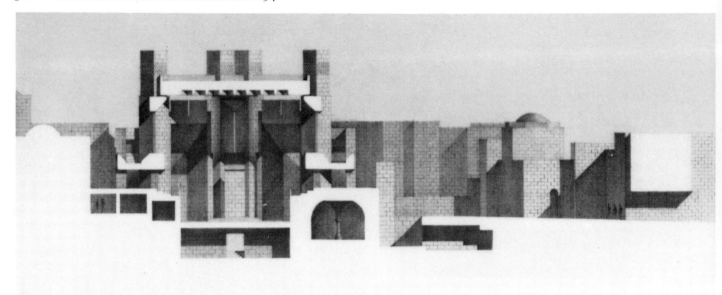

27.12 Denys Lasdun, Hurva Synagogue, Jerusalem. 1978–81, project.

sketches suggested a large symmetrical building of almost fortified appearance towering above the neighbouring flat roofs of the old city.

Lasdun sought a less forbidding but no less monumental solution. In accord with his urban landscape philosophy he thought of the main chamber of the synagogue as a piece of the city, and of the building as a whole as a more intensified form of the surrounding urban patterns of streets, squares, and flat roofs. A synagogue is not a building type of fixed form, although Middle-Eastern variants have often used domes. But even if there had been a firm convention, the architect would still have had the problem of injecting the standard image with a new meaning and vitality. Lasdun envisaged a central room of great formality on a clearly defined main axis running from the small access street to a square at the rear of the site. Galleries were placed at the middle levels for the women, and were focused towards the arc and the bema. This main space was surmounted by a grand parasol roof – a much enlarged version of his usual strata – supported on polygonal towers containing stairs and providing natural ventilating chimneys. The deep overhangs sheltered the interior from the glare and gave a feeling of enclosure to the room. The light, filtering in from the edges, added to the mysterious character of the space. The lowest portion of the synagogue was enclosed by the walls of the ruin. No attempt was made at employing domes or other elements of local usage, because they were not specific to synagogues as a type, and because they were not part of the Lasdunian conviction and language. Nonetheless, the lighting system under the parasol gave a hooded character to the interior, while the roof itself restated the meaning of a sacral umbrella and gave an almost primeval feeling of shelter. The rhetoric of the Hurva scheme arose, not from the spurious attachment of devalued symbols, but from an imagery and a mood associated with the basic meaning of a place of dignified assembly in a city-space. Lasdun 'rethought' the significance of the synagogue in terms of an authentic language (the strata and towers) already attuned to the idea of congregation. This he managed to do without any frantic search for 'Jewish essences'.

The obsession with cultural representation which came into focus in the mid-1970s was ever in danger of ignoring issues of architectural quality and authenticity. A building that fitted some passing prescription or dogma, that illustrated values that were noisily proclaimed as 'Islamic', 'Jewish', 'Melanesian', 'Communist' (or whatever), was not necessarily architecture of lasting quality. Indeed, too facile an acceptance of conventional iconography could lead quickly to kitsch. The post-Second World War era began with the emancipation of various architectural cultures from a debased international formula; this was desirable and inevitable. But regionalism could easily become the facile tool of religious and nationalist dogmatism of a sort which left no room for the universal aspects of both the human condition and the language of art. What was needed was a blend of the local and the universal which avoided the limitations of each and led to forms of lasting symbolic resonance. Skin-deep modernism and glib traditionalism were evils to be avoided in every part of the world.

28. The Traditions of Modern Architecture in the Recent Past

> I dislike a sentimental antiquarian attitude towards the past as much as I dislike a sentimental technocratic one toward the future. Both are founded on a . . . clockwork notion of time.
>
> A. Van Eyck, 1967

It is a standard part of art historical folklore that one should never attempt to write the history of the recent past. The reason given is that one is liable to be biased. Why this should not be true of studies of the more distant past too is not explained. It tends to be taken for granted that the true shape of recent history will emerge on its own.

Caution is obviously required in describing contemporary developments, but it is misleading to imagine that an acceptable consensus will come about naturally. If the historian steps back, the propagandist with an axe to grind steps in, usually with his own polemical version of what is 'salient'. This danger seems greater than ever in the past ten years when so much emphasis has been placed on the printed word and the photograph: movements and 'isms' have been fervently discussed on the basis of a few drawings in glossy magazines without so much as a brick being laid or a concrete slab poured. Factions of the avant-garde have grappled for control over the media and over university departments to assert that their own ideas (rather than someone else's) are the 'right' ones for the times. Architects have even developed the habit of writing their own histories (sources and all), thus leaving the impression that the most significant features of the period must be the ones that are most published and discussed.

The problem of examining the recent past dispassionately is compounded by the repeated refrain that 'modern architecture is dead'. This emotive slogan has encouraged the view that one period is in its decadence and that another one may be dawning, though its character remains unclear to all concerned. Those who contribute to this view will obviously play down continuities with the modern tradition and do all they can to inflate the originality of architects selected to fit a 'post-modern' label. Those who find the idea unsavoury will hang on tenaciously to the habits of their upbringing and claim that they stem from some core identity of 'modernism'. Neither position is based on a subtle view of the genesis of forms within traditions, and each tends to posit a simplistic and monolithic version of modern architecture. Neither is willing to admit that the most profound innovations tend to blend together old and new, and that the seminal works of the modern movement have value for the future precisely because their principles transcend period limitations. In fact, both views seem too concerned with changes of architectural dress. The 'newest' (and rarest) thing that one can hope for is a building that is simply very good, whatever its relationship to traditions near and far, however it fits the prescriptions of the fashion-mongers or the yearnings of the old guard.

There are probably two extremes which should be avoided when dealing with the recent past. The first is identification with the values of one school or clique; the second is a lofty pretence at knowing what is 'essential' about recent development. Both positions are too exclusive and amount to forecasting in disguise rather than to history. Perhaps one should adopt a different strategy and pretend that one is looking back at the 1970s at a distance of a few decades. From such a vantage-point movements that claim opposition to one another reveal underlying similarities. Events, ideas and personalities blend into longer temporal perspectives, including the developments described earlier in this book. Claims to originality made by younger architects appear excessive, and the weight of the modern tradition may seem more insistent than some would like. Even styles of criticism and rejection may be seen to have a pedigree. Such a description is bound to be lopsided and incomplete, but I can at least claim that I have set out to portray the complexities – and contradictions – of recent pluralism. If I have, on occasion, adopted a critical position with regard to an idea or a building, I have attempted to lay bare the basis of the judgement. In case there is any doubt, I have reserved the next chapter – the conclusion – for a statement of critical principle.

It is as well to begin by bearing in mind that the 1970s was not a self-sealed episode exactly ten years long. Its preoccupations and problems, its crises and its critiques, were rooted in previous decades. Underlying the period as a whole was an increasingly vocal scepticism about the tenets of modern architecture, or, to be precise, what were *thought* to have been the tenets. In fact wholesale rejections of one aspect of modern architecture were often accompanied by unconscious continuations of another. One of the striking features of the styles of the 1970s is the way in which they were mostly continuations of the earlier modern movement tradition. In some cases (e.g., the designs of the New York 5 or those of Aldo Rossi), a revival of inter-war forms was even involved. It could be argued that those happy to be called 'post-modernists' themselves drew on devices such as fragmentation, planarity and collage with an obvious modern pedigree. We should be on the look-out, then, for a certain divergence between rhetoric and actual production, between words and forms. Strong protestations are only to be expected when a younger generation emerges in the shadow of the likes of Le Corbusier, Aalto or Kahn. Nor is it surprising to come across the oedipal scenario in which the repressive father-figures of 'modernism' are cast aside to allow young minds to engage with the luxuries of more distant traditions. After all, the previous generation also crusaded for greater richness, also turned to the past, also portrayed *its* predecessors through a demonology.

Having said this, it must be admitted that the atmosphere of the early 1970s was altogether different from that surrounding the rallying of Team X in the early 1960s. There was little of the optimism of a decade earlier. The well-meaning frameworks supplied by Europe's welfare states or by wealthy patronage in the United States for modern architecture had exposed too many of their contradictions for their adopted architecture to go unscathed. Too many oppressive housing schemes, too many clumsy skyscrapers, too many acres of windswept concrete, too many alienating and gaunt arrangements of form had been insinuated into the programme of urban and social renewal, and in the late 1960s there was a backlash which took many shapes. One recurrent theme was that modern architecture should blend more apologetically with its historical context; another demanded a greater participation of users; another required obvious signs of identity and association. An extreme critique claimed, of course, that modern architecture was merely the face of a decaying and contradictory capitalism, but this did little to help the designer make his necessarily piece-meal improvements more effective. The counter-culture of the late 1960s perhaps did its bit to undermine modern movement pretensions towards universality, while a concurrent populism implied the extent to which architects' palliatives were class-bound. Ideas derived from the theory of signs were drawn in to reveal the supposed 'arbitrariness' and 'conventionality' of architectural forms, while relativism mounted its attacks on the sociological and functional determinism which so mattered to one wing of the modern movement. Perhaps the death of the modern masters had a further corrosive effect within the fold, by removing charismatic leaders. Even tame scholarship may have had a role by undermining the notion of a simple grand tradition of modernism. With progressive fervour dowsed and a profession increasingly uncertain of its aims, it is scarcely surprising that the word 'crisis' should have occurred in numerous book titles and articles. For some it was a 'crisis' of consumer society, for others a 'crisis' of identity for architects, for others again a 'crisis' of 'modernism'. Increasingly one encountered the suggestion that the way forward lay in going back: whether it was to the golden days of radiant modern architectural faith or to some earlier phase of supposed certainties.

But this is to speak of only one revisionist mood among many in the seventies. As in most periods, the myths, preoccupations, and problems of a number of generations and individuals existed side by side. Men like Utzon, Kahn, and Lasdun produced mature works of a high order which evaded changing fashion; obviously this did not mean that they should be regarded as 'out of date'. Philip Johnson changed like a chameleon in an effort to keep his architecture adjusted to the latest hem-lines; evidently this did nothing to give his work a depth it perhaps needed. James Stirling's style altered drastically as he attempted to incorporate overt references to urban contexts and to historical precedent, and a new, younger generation, devoted to a self-conscious manipulation of formal language (e.g., Graves, Isozaki) began to receive major commissions. Whatever else one may say about the seventies, it entirely lacked uniformity. It would be futile to suggest a main-line; preposterous to attempt an equation between style and quality; parochial to fix one movement as the key one. I have decided to avoid 'isms' as much as possible, and to describe broader tendencies on the basis of a few individual case studies. To make this easier, I have grouped together buildings of analogous function, as this provides some basis for comparison.

One may begin with housing. An earlier chapter traced reactions to the Unité and various critiques of it, unfolding around the need to give dwellings a greater sense of identity. Following the point of view that a major problem of post-war housing had been a failure

28.1 Ralph Erskine, Byker Wall, Newcastle, 1969–75.

of communication between architects and users, it was understandable that various forms of advocacy planning, in which the future inhabitants of public housing schemes were involved in the design process, should have been attempted in the sixties. Indeed, the radical critiques of that period even went so far as to discount the role of formal planning altogether, as if good moral intentions were on their own sufficient for the creation of a decent home.

One architect who attempted to bridge these difficult currents was the Scandinavian Ralph Erskine (yet another member of Team X). With the Byker Wall housing scheme for Newcastle (1969–75), Erskine and his team immersed themselves in the needs and hopes of the eventual users before proposing design hypotheses, which were in turn open to criticism by the inhabitants (fig. 28.1). The task was made easier by the fact that most of the population were already living in the neighbouring area. But it has to be admitted that even the most democratic design process could not decide on an overall form, whatever it might do to make interiors and thresholds more accommodating. The architects' job, as ever, was to translate social aspirations into a suitable three-dimensional organization.

The resultant Byker Wall thus bore the imprint of the Erskinian architectural style. The site was close to the path of an intended motorway and sloped down gently to rows of nineteenth-century houses; the solution was to make a long serpentine wall of varying height as a barrier against noise, and to place smaller terrace houses with gardens in the resultant enclosure. The idea of a protective wall of housing had occurred already in Erskine's college design for Clare Hall, Cambridge, but stretched back much further to his schemes of the sixties for settlements north of the Arctic circle, where barriers against cold winds and a rugged, hostile landscape had been essential; the strategy was even reminiscent of Aalto's perimeter walls and serpentine slabs (one thinks particularly of Baker House). At Byker, the collective wall was mated with other typical Erskinian images: the shed roof (to suggest domesticity and to protect against rain), sprawling stick balconies in bright colours (to add human touch and variety), interwoven bricks of different colours (to break down the mass), and delicate entrance structures (to ensure a gradual transition from public to private worlds). Erskine's interest in defining territory and responding to local patterns of life obviously reflected Team X ideas; but of the various 'anti-heroic' housing schemes of the seventies, Byker Wall was perhaps the most successful socially and architecturally.

Despite the attempts of champions of Byker to argue that the good folk of Newcastle had virtually generated the architecture on their own, it was obvious that the imagery had resulted from the interpretation of an architect intent on form and symbol-making. The most extreme left-wing critiques rejected the strategy for precisely this reason, claiming that housing should be left to individuals, and not 'monumentalized' by architects with 'imposing concepts'. One brand of this anti-élitist opinion suggested that it would be better to imitate the types of existing 'vernaculars' than to allow any further housing schemes on the Unité model, but remained unclear about *which* vernaculars should be used as examples. As a result of this passive mood, it became morally respectable in the mid-seventies (especially in housing agencies in Western Europe) to ape hip-roofs and mouldings in the belief that this was an automatic guarantee of a 'humane image' of the home.

The linear apartment block for the Gallaretese district of Milan (1969–76) by Aldo Rossi was in strong contrast to both the Byker Wall and to the vernacular revival (fig. 28.2). The contrived complexities of Byker were replaced by a gaunt and repetitive simplicity; its serpentine and picturesque accents were superseded by an obsessive linearity; the nooks and crannies were replaced by a monotonous street gallery running from one end to the other. It seems that Rossi's design strategy was situated between what he called 'inventory and memory' and involved the deliberate fusion of earlier types. In the Modena Cemetery (1971) the ancient mausoleum had been cross-bred with the abstract visions of Boullée or Ledoux from the late eighteenth century; in the Gallaretese, Rossi seemed to pull together the organization of the Unité, the street-deck, melancholy reminiscences of Northern Italian arcades (with some help from Giorgio de Chirico's metaphysical cityscapes) and images of modern engineering:

> . . . . . there is an analogical relationship with certain engineering works that mix freely with both the corridor typology and a related feeling I have always experienced in the architecture of the traditional Milanese tenement where the corridors signify a life style bathed in everyday occurrences, domestic intimacy and varied personal relationships.

In 1966 Rossi had published a book entitled *L'Architettura della Città*, which had tried to establish the case for a set of urban archetypes, founded on 'basic' institutions, which were held to have existed before the chaos of industrialization. His idea was that one should transcend functionalism by an analogical mode of design, blending the earlier types with present-day needs in a language of simple geometries. Rossi's

28.2 Aldo Rossi, Gallaretese housing, near Milan, 1969–76.

theory of urban types recalled Terragni's earlier reflections on the ancient beginnings of architecture, and there can be little doubt that Rossi's style, with its dead-pan rows of windows punched through simple white surfaces, owed a good deal to the prototypes of the Italian International Style. It was not entirely misleading then that the term 'neo-Rationalist' should have been coined to describe the work of Rossi and his movement named 'Tendenza'. The stripped forms of the thirties were purged of their Fascist associations and given an almost nostalgic character. Neo-Rationalist sensibility delighted in axial composition and in reduction to the most primary geometries. Rossi's numerous evocative sketches of beach cabins, light-houses, barns and vernacular structures in the Po valley suggested a wistful involvement with northern Italy's past, and even a latent classicism. His influence was considerable, especially in the Ticino in southern Switzerland (e.g., Mario Botta), where a mood of revulsion against the technological aridity of so much modern design set in during the early 1970s. Rossi's ideas were also popularized in the United States where their classical undertones were rather wilfully linked to Italophile obsessions with Terragni and Palladio.

Ricardo Bofill's Walden Seven housing in Barcelona (1975) supplies another example of an architectural philosophy concerned with the allusive transform-ation of images from the past. In this case the formal emphasis is primarily vertical, the building being formed from tall cliffs of walls clad in red tile, with variations on cylinders being attached as balconies. A front entrance to the complex is formed by a vertical slit over forty feet high, and the general theme of

28.3 Norman Foster,
Willis, Faber and Dumas
building, Ipswich, 1974.

faceted interpenetrations is carried through where gaping openings twelve stories high are cut into the blocks. The result is not unlike a fortress which has been turned over to habitation, and Walden Seven even has mildly Surrealist overtones in its bizarre jumps in scale. Perhaps the influence of Gaudí's curious chimney designs can be sensed in the anthropomorphic character of the balconies. In any event, Walden Seven, and Bofill's other designs of the period, stemmed from an interest in the transformation of simple geometries into complex arrangements and metaphors with a power to evoke castellated images from the past.

The three aforementioned examples suggest different ways in which the inheritance of modern architecture has recently been extended into new expressive territories. A similarly broad range of ideological commitments and vocabularies emerges if one analyses architectural solutions to the work-place in the 1970s, particularly office buildings. By the late sixties, of course, the standard modern types were the glass-box skyscraper and its suburban relative, the glass-box on its side. It is scarcely surprising that attempts should have been made to enrich these bald formulae by incorporating atria, gardens, balconies, etc.; the luxurious Ford Foundation by Roche and Dinkeloo in New York of 1967 was one example which in-

corporated all these devices and also tried to open the building to the street visually. Another strategy was represented by the Willis, Faber and Dumas building in Ipswich, England (1974), by Norman Foster Associates (fig. 28.3). In this case no critique of modern technology was implied; quite the contrary, the imagery of the building rejoiced in the appearance of a precision mechanism. However, the partitioning and rigid grid of the usual type were broken open on the interior to create an entirely continuous work space (the free plan taken to its logical, and not completely practical, conclusion); the floors were also linked by a large central space with moving staircases passing through it. The finishes of chrome and stainless steel were matched by the highly polished glazed cladding, which embodied a similar ethos. The reflecting glass was clipped on without any intervening struts or mullions and the resultant taut curtain-wall skin mirrored the setting. The building was curved in plan to fit the shape of the site, and this maximized the play of reflections. Obviously the plan strategy was a descendant of Mies van der Rohe's 'universal space'; the imagery also drew on both the minimalist skyscrapers of the American sixties and the original crystalline fantasies of the twenties. The Willis, Faber and Dumas building, and Foster's other designs of the period (e.g., the Sainsbury Art Centre at the University of East Anglia) thus represented an extension of the technological wing of the modern movement. However, with their elegant and crisp styling, they had an entirely different character from their 'first machine age' ancestors like the Van Nelle factory. The utopian driving force was not recoverable; perhaps inevitably, there was a loss of intensity and resonance in the later version of mechanistic imagery.

The Centraal Beheer office building at Apeldoorn in Holland (1974) by Herman Hertzberger (fig. 28.4) represented quite a different human position, which embodied scepticism about the values of a technocracy. Where the Willis, Faber building celebrated the continuous, open work space, the Centraal Beheer concentrated on the private domain of the individual worker; where the former worked inwards from a uniform envelope, the latter was assembled inside to out on the basis of small standardized units related to activity and human scale. The Hertzberger design was like a higgledy-piggledy kasbah of alleyways, tortuous streets, and level changes, but it was still based on a module. Where the high-tech position implied a total control of image and finish by designers and management, the rough concrete blocks, pre-cast beams and irregular trays of the 'workers' village' embodied an ideal of participation and implied that the structure would be incomplete until dressed in each individual's knick-knacks, plants and place-making symbols. The Centraal Beheer was a worthy descendant of Van Eyck's orphanage of ten years earlier, and, like its prototype, sought to create a variety of ambiguous spaces on the basis of a small-scaled standardized kit of parts. The idea of interior galleries and trays was perhaps a long-range descendant of Wright's Larkin building or Johnson Wax; However, the Centraal Beheer lacked the coherence of its great prototypes, especially on the exterior, where the forms were somewhat mute and confused (fig. 28.5).

By contrast, Lasdun's European Investment Bank outside Luxembourg (1974) presented a clear and dominant *gestalt* without destroying a sense of human scale (fig. 28.6). The building had to be a ceremonial headquarters as well as an office space, and the site, close to the ravines of the Val des Bons Malades, virtually demanded a scheme attuned to landscape. Lasdun modified the typology of strata and towers to create a sort of pin-wheel plan with four low wings of horizontal emphasis cascading to meet the land masses at various levels. Where the four wings came together, the ceremonial zones were situated, traversed by a diagonal axis from the *porte-cochère* at the entrance to the document-signing room at the other end under a low soffit on piers standing in a pool. The entrance way was clearly signalled by directional piers and towers which set up a strong forty-five degree axis; the

28.4 (*left*) Herman Hertzberger, Centraal Beheer office building, Apeldoorn, 1974, interior.

28.5 (*above*) Herman Hertzberger, Centraal Beheer office building, Apeldoorn, 1974, aerial view.

sequence as a whole recalled the College of Physicians or the National Theatre, if not Lasdun's fascination with compressed and expanding spaces in Baroque architecture. The office wings were designed on the same system of horizontal floors and soffits but their treatment was less intense sculpturally. The slabs were designed to incorporate natural cooling and heating, and each office was given an opening window protected from glare with a view over nearby trees. The result was a building which countered the anomie of the glass box with both humanity and dignity. The European Investment Bank was a palace among office buildings, but its forms were closely related to human purposes and to the richness of a natural setting. Here the work-place was given a monumental character with devices which descended in the long run from the horizontality and stratification of both Wrightian and Corbusian prototypes.

Skyscraper design in the 1970s also reveals a search for varied solutions on the basis of the discoveries of the previous decades. Yamasaki's two enormous slabs for the World Trade Center at the base of Manhattan were an extreme statement of the elegant, minimalist notion of the parallel-piped box standing in a plaza. In the early 1970s two areas of skyscraper design seem to have come in for particular scrutiny: the top (either for practical reasons to do with servicing or solar energy, or else for symbolic purposes), and the bottom (which was more frequently opened out as an atrium connected to the street). The Citicorp headquarters in Manhattan (1978) by Hugh Stubbins was one variant on this scheme. Stylistically it was a sort of 'high tech' revival of the International Style, replete with strip windows and taut volumes clad in a reflecting metallic skin. Another approach to the dull glass box formula was, of course, to adorn it but without severely challenging its interior limitations. This dubious form of 'enrichment' was pursued in the context of the Manhattan skyscraper by Philip Johnson, in his design

28.6 Denys Lasdun, European Investment Bank, Luxembourg, 1974–9, view past document signing room towards landscape.

for the American Telephone and Telegraph building on
Madison Ave., 1978 (fig. 28.7). Johnson rejected the
glass-box formula and revived the tripartite division of
the tall building so often used in the American
twenties. He emphasized the entrance way with an
arch (intended to be reminiscent of Brunelleschi's Pazzi
Chapel), the lobby with grand columns (supposedly
based on a hypostyle), and the top with a broken
pediment (which journalists compared to Chippendale
furniture). When the design was published it was
proclaimed as a wholesale rejection of modernism and
linked to so-called 'Post-Modernist' tendencies. In fact
Johnson had done little more than stick some historical
quotations on to a standard office space; most of what
was called 'Post-Modern' tended to be cosmetic.

A comparison of museums in the seventies also
offers a rich variety of architectural approaches. The
Pompidou Centre, in the Place Beaubourg, Paris, by
Renzo Piano and Richard Rogers (1974) took the
image of the flexible *machine à cultiver* to the extreme
(fig. 28.8). The programme required a mixed use
'cultural centre' incorporating the old Musée de l'Art
Moderne, a public library, an audio-visual centre, and
a vast amount of exhibition space. The site was to one
side of the Marais, facing on a square not far from the
old Market sheds (demolished just previously) of Les
Halles. Evidently the aim was to make a 'popular'
institution rather than a 'palace of culture', and it was
this aspect of the brief which clearly appealed to Piano
and Rogers (who were chosen by competition). They
designed the building as a vast, serviceable hangar
supported by a megastructural steel-tubed frame. The
floor slabs were made to span adjustable interior
spaces, and the elevations were entirely glazed. An
appropriate ornament was provided by festoons of
mechanical tubes, including a long glass canister
enclosing a moving staircase up the main façade. The
imagery was obviously prompted by Archigram
fantasies of half a decade earlier, and was supposed to
imply 'openness' and 'social pluralism'. The stylized
play with technological effects, and the honest
expression of tubes and ducts placed the Pompidou
Centre in yet another tradition: the Futurist revival of
the 1960s in England, with Reyner Banham, apostle of
the architecture of mechanical services, at its head.

The contrast with the Roman severity, *gravitas* and
restraint of Louis Kahn's Kimbell museum at Fort
Worth, Texas (1972) could scarcely have been more
complete (fig. 28.9). Kahn's design was arranged as a
series of parallel bays surmounted by curved concrete
vaults with light filtering through the top. The
repetitive system was overlaid by a symmetrical
armature of circulation implying a hierarchy. The
interiors were finely scaled to complement the
individual works of art but not overwhelm them.

28.7 (*left*) Philip Johnson, American Telephone and Telegraph building, New York, 1978, model.

28.8 (*above*) Richard Rogers and Renzo Piano, Pompidou Centre, Paris, 1974–6.

Architectural effects arose from the dignified rhythm of spaces and the refined treatment of materials: the silver-grey concrete, the panels of travertine, the stainless steel reflectors at the peak of each vault. Technology was here employed in the service of a controlling idea, and not as some extravagance in its own right. Once again Kahn succeeded in producing a design of a timeless character.

The third museum example houses the Getty collection on the coast of California and was designed in 1973 by Langdon, Wilson and others (fig. 28.10). The building was modelled on the example of an antique Roman villa of a type Paul Getty had admired in ruins at Herculaneum as a young man. The museum spaces were arranged en suite around a sequence of pools containing antique statuary. Classical orders, pilasters and pediments were used throughout, but in a way which suggested more some Disneyland scenario than a serious attempt at transforming Classicism: indeed, Kahn's gaunt concrete vaults had more of antiquity about them.

One might have thought that the Getty Museum would have received an automatic rejection by critics

28.9 Louis I. Kahn, Kimbell Museum, Fort Worth, Texas, 1972, interior.

as an obvious example of kitsch. But in the changing intellectual atmosphere of the mid-seventies the opposite was as likely to, and did occur. For it was about then that revulsion against the supposed lack of recognizable imagery in modern architecture came under attack. The argument was put forth that the architect must make it a prime responsibility to communicate to his public through popularly established conventions. This resembled the usual 'realist' complaint against abstraction, but in this instance the position was bolstered by a smattering of ideas from semiology and by a Pop sensibility perhaps derived from Venturi. From this standpoint the Getty Museum was evidently acceptable because its garish imagery was 'evocative' of a wealthy collector's museum. Architects and critics were invited to climb down from the abstruse plane of formal concerns and to occupy themselves instead with easily legible images.

It was in the late seventies too that the curious phrase 'Post-Modern' began to be used, especially by the architectural critic Charles Jencks. Once again earlier modern architecture was rammed together in a simplified demonology. The target of the post-modernist animus emerged as a composite caricature combining 'functionalism', simple forms, truth to structure, mute imagery and a belief in the *Zeitgeist*. Even at the theoretical level it was hard to be sure just what 'Post-Modernism' proposed instead. One gathered that multivalence of meaning had some part to play and that buildings ought to be regarded as communications devices employing well-known and easily understood 'codes'. Historical quotations were also, apparently, to be encouraged on the grounds that these would enrich architectural vocabulary. Eclecticism was no longer to be sneered at, indeed mannerized commentaries on earlier architecture were to be considered valuable as a source of meaning.

But like its predecessor 'the New Brutalism', Post-Modernism was more a vague cluster of aspirations (or, at any rate, rejections) than a blueprint for a clear-cut style. In a book on the subject of Post-Modern architecture, Jencks pulled together an odd assortment of buildings to illustrate the new tendencies. Kitsch neo-classical hotel lobbies appeared close to the buildings of men like Moore and Kurokawa; Gaudí was brought in as historical support because of the 'multivalence' of his imagery, and Mies van der Rohe was castigated for designing buildings which did not 'signify' their uses clearly; garish images were gleaned from the commercial strip, and the illustrations were mostly in colour to reinforce the contrasts employed in

28.10 Landgon,
Wilson and others,
Getty Museum,
California, 1974.

the buildings. Most of the visual terminologies illustrated were simply extensions of movements which had started in the sixties, many of them of quite divergent appearance and ideology, and many of the ideas had been rehearsed by Venturi a few years before. However, one thing was entirely clear: neither the author nor his examples showed much concern for questions of expressive authenticity – the buildings illustrated shared a tendency towards superficiality which took earlier architectural precedents as a sounding-board for references and quotations, but for little more.

The Post-Modern mood (perhaps it is best to call it that) was one of a number of revisionist tendencies which came to the fore from the mid-seventies onwards; ostensibly, these too were in favour of aesthetic and symbolic enrichment. The increase in historical self-consciousness was undoubtedly related to an erosion in faith concerning the validity and relevance of an abstract and unadorned aesthetic, and the clichés of the critique made no distinction between bland simplicity and the intense formal purification of the best modern architecture. However, this wholesale rejection fitted a public mood of dissatisfaction with the debased modern movement, and it served the polemic *not* to attempt fine distinctions. In a similar manner, an

immense literature flowed forth in the late 1970s of which the avowed aim was the undermining of 'modern movement assumptions'. Many of these 'assumptions' turned out to be illusory. One found anti-functionalist arguments rehearsed *ad nauseam* when modern architecture had been anything but functionalist. One found history being proudly reinstated when the best modern architects had remained rooted in tradition. One found the idea of a single monolithic style for the twentieth century being rejected when the notion had long before been abandoned. Utopianism also came under attack despite the fact that it too had been gradually undermined in the previous three decades. Very little of this intellectual noise penetrated anywhere near the sources of inventive power which had led to Le Corbusier, Wright, Aalto, Kahn, and the rest; and most of it was shooting at intellectual bodies which were already dead.

Theories and the productions of artists are interwoven in complex ways. Sometimes a theory emerges which is then taken up and translated in a personal terminology of form; sometimes it is the other way round, and a theory is invoked as a post-rationalization. The free-wheeling eclecticism of Charles Moore may have encouraged Jencks's formu-

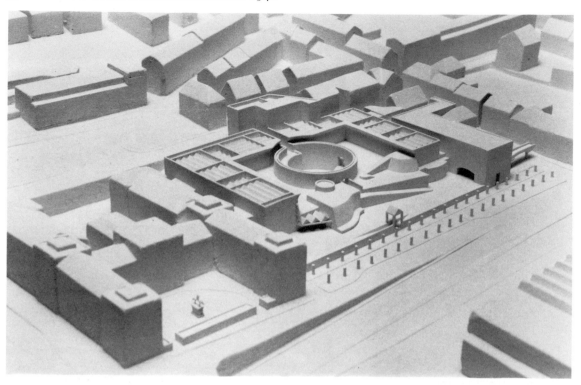

28.11 James Stirling, Museum for Stuttgart, 1977, model.

lation of post-modernism; equally the critical writing may have prompted further architectural licence. In the Piazza d'Italia, New Orleans, 1979, Moore erected a fountain from a series of brightly coloured curved screens of classical columns, entablatures and arches, including capitals made from reflecting materials and insets bearing the self-portrait of the architect. The result was scarcely a serious transformation of classical order, having more the atmosphere of a piece of fairground equipment or a stage-set assembled out of literal quotations. Moore's building was greeted by the criticism that it was a shallow joke, and a self-indulgent one at that. The riposte was that it was a suitable piece of festivalia to celebrate the 'Italianness' of one of the city's ethnic neighbourhoods. This was not very convincing since it seemed, in this instance, that little of sustaining power was left once the shock or amusement had worn off. However, self-consciousness in the use of precedent was not automatically doomed to glibness: all depended on the imaginative synthesis of sources into a new unity bearing conviction and expressing a new meaning. It is interesting in this connection to refer to yet another museum design, this time by James Stirling for Stuttgart (1977), as this seems to incorporate elements of the positions just outlined in a building of some formal power (fig. 28.11). In the early seventies, Stirling had employed increasingly overt metaphors and historical references in his designs, and a sort of 'collage' method of composition involving the collision and articulation of separate fragments. In the plan for Derby Civic Centre (1971) he had already demonstrated a fascination with 'figure/ground' relationships between urban spaces and solids. The juxtaposition of outdoor rooms and free-standing objects was continued in the scheme for Cologne Museum, and in this case the ground plan of the neighbouring cathedral was restated as a sunken piazza along a sequence of vaguely surreal incidents. Evidently, Stirling was also seeking inspiration from such things as ancient Roman plans with their sequences of curved rooms flowing into one another (the assumed collage character of Hadrian's 'fragmented' villa plan was much discussed at the time), and in the Stuttgart Museum design all these features seem to have converged.

The plan, with a large circular well cut out of it, was perhaps modelled on the type of the Altes Museum by Schinkel, while the subtleties of the cross-axis relationship between this cylindrical form and the auditorium suggested a possible Piranesian model. The inflections of the main façade, with serpentine curves indicating the presence of the entrance and ramps pointing the way along the ensuing sequence, recalled earlier Stirling devices for handling analogous conditions, just as the giant cylindrical space was as much a relative of the piston shapes of the Siemens scheme as it was a derivative from Classical planning. Thus 'modern' and ancient were deliberately confronted but without being fused, in a technique of 'bricolage'. Curiously enough, Stirling still insisted on speaking of his designs in terms of their programmatic logic.

Another museum will serve to complete the sequence, and perhaps to illustrate the changing aspirations of young architects in the late seventies. In this case the designer was once again Michael Graves (mentioned in Chapter 26 in connection with the New York 5), and the design was the Fargo–Moorhead Cultural Center between North Dakota and Minnesota of 1978 (fig. 28.12). During the 1970s the other members of the New York 5 had continued to extend their pure geometrical vocabularies without drastic breaks. But Graves's development in the same period illustrated an increasing preoccupation with naturalistic metaphors and with quotations from history, but transformed into his own elusive and fragmented terminology. In the Crooks House (1976), pieces of Corbusian vocabulary confronted elements of some Renaissance villa garden dream, replete with wedge-shaped topiary hedges. By the late seventies, Graves was revealing an increasing preoccupation with late eighteenth-century sources, especially the metaphorical language of Ledoux. These influences were evident in his Fargo–Moorhead project. The building had to stand on each side of a river which was also the State line, and the bridge between was obviously pregnant with symbolic possibilities. Graves took his cue from Ledoux's *architecture parlante*, particularly from the protect for a sluice-house over the River Loue: a shape

which blended a semi-circular abstraction, an arch, and the image of a sluice. This motif was adapted for the Fargo bridge, and Graves then assembled the rest of the building in geometrical overlays and fragments on each side. In other schemes in the same period, he organized entire plans around the 'reference' of the Classical keystone. It must remain for history to decide whether this was simply a facile game of quotation and private day-dreaming, or some deeper replay of Classical values. One thing was certain, Graves's designs placed a personal lyricism high in the scale of values, and cocked a snook at 'functional appropriateness'.

Indeed, the new traditionalist mood was not much troubled by a search for rigour, and for that reason often degenerated into eclectic candyfloss. Imagery was high in its priorities; functional resolution was low. Formal sophistication was praised; social concern was denigrated. Conceptual exploration was prized; structural necessity was sneered at. In the circumstances, it was not surprising that some critics attempted to link the more facile aspects of revivalism to the values of consumerism. Although the new trends were not restricted to the United States, they were strongest there and seemed to mirror a preoccupation with colourful packaging and bright imagery. A less far-fetched connection could be made with American nineteenth-century eclecticism of the type which had treated historical elements as a kit-of-parts to be stuck together in a new 'instant tradition'.

Despite the populist arguments that were used to launch 'radical eclecticism' (to use Jencks's term)

28.12 Michael Graves, Fargo–Moorhead Cultural Centre, North Dakota and Minnesota, 1978, project.

against the haughtiness of earlier modern architecture, the evidence was slight that buildings employing historical references were any less obscure to the public than their 'modern' predecessors. It could even be argued that the manipulation of quotations required an in-crowd of *savants* for its full communicative effect. It was in architecture schools that the devices of commentary and allusion were most entertained, since these were places where the ground-rules for communication could be learned or even enforced. A further area of difficulty was that of craft: columns and entablatures of plywood scarcely possessed the presence of the originals, and traditional links between historical vocabularies and the building industries were long since dissolved. Robert Stern, a New York architect interested in historical quotation as a means of expression, had to resort to thin appliqués of mouldings and coloured paint in his domestic designs of the mid-1970s (fig. 28.13). However photogenic they may have been, the results had a certain thinness. Kahn, Wright, Aalto or Le Corbusier had attempted to translate core principles of the Classical tradition into modern terminologies rigorously disciplined by constructional and structural capabilities. But the 'radical eclectics' ran the risk of producing work of symbolic and material insubstantiality. Not even the craft of their nineteenth-century forebears was available to them in their attempts at a new ornamentation. It was no accident

in this milieu that the architectural drawing should, on occasion, have been praised more highly than actual realized buildings, since historical commentary was much more easily done in graphics than in three dimensions using real building materials. By the late 1970s it was even possible to enter prestigious architecture schools in the United States and to come across drawings showing white cubes perforated by plane rectangular openings, and preceded by axes of topiary hedges, being discussed earnestly as abstractions of Palladio. The social science jargon of the architectural conferences of the late sixties gave way to a gossipy acquaintance with Renaissance villas and French *hôtels particuliers*.

However, eclecticism was by no means uniquely American property, as was well demonstrated by two events in the Western architectural world of 1980. The first was an exhibition held at the Venice Biennale in the summer of that year and entitled 'The Presence of the Past'. The centre-piece of the show was an interior street lined with variations on Classical façades in the form of large painted wooden models, designed by a selection of architects from various European centres, as well as the United States. The other public gesture of the new eclecticism was a re-run of the 1922 Chicago Tribune Competition. The entrants had a field-day of revivalism alongside which the original event seemed relatively restrained. As in the 1960s the well-organized publishing industry saw to it that the new

28.13 Robert Stern, 'House for an Academical Couple', Connecticut, 1974–6.

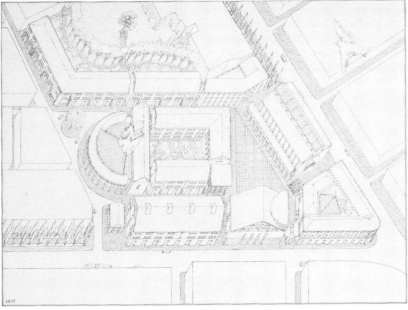

28.14 (*top*) Romaldo Giurgola, Mitchell and Thorp. Parliament building, Canberra, Australia, 1980, competition winner, view of model.

28.15 Leon Krier, project for revitalization of Kingston-upon-Hull, 1977.

with others from the International Style, and others from Japanese tradition. This reflected a shift in approach from the era of Tange's and Mayekawa's monumental works. They had sought a more disciplined abstraction in their assimilation of prototype. Isozaki, on the other hand, was interested in achieving meaning through collision and collage. Once again Venturi's influence is sensed, and, like some of his American contemporaries, Isozaki also drew on popularized semiology to support his self-conscious manipulation of architectural language.

As the trends of the late 1970s were so varied, there was no single architect who encompassed them all. But there were some projects which combined a number of approaches. Among these was the entry to the competition for a new Australian Parliament building (1980) by Romaldo Giurgola and his associates Mitchell and Thorp (fig. 28.14). The programme required two main chambers, a residence for the prime minister, and the usual array of pressrooms, conference areas, offices, etc. The site was the one left for the Parliament in Walter Burley Griffin's original plan for the city of Canberra, made over a half-a-century before: it was the low hill at the apex of the triangular main streets. Giurgola's scheme made the greatest effort to preserve the character of this hill as seen from the direction of the War Memorial and the lake. He buried some of the functions in the ground and placed the two main chambers equidistant from the centre point on a cross axis, and inserted them into curved residual spaces carved out of the sides of the hill. These spaces – which were shared by the building and its context – were backed by screen walls whose curvature attempted to draw together and resolve the main geometries of the setting with the idea of a quasi-centralized monument. Journalists who saw the plan inevitably compared the concave shapes to boomerangs laid back to back, while more erudite critics suggested the image of a human figure with its arms and legs outstretched. The architect's attempt at interpreting the democratic ideal was probably most clearly reflected in his placement of the public forum at the heart of the building, between the main chambers. Above this point, the Australian flag, which had traditionally always flapped above the hill, was maintained on a somewhat awkward mast supported on four splayed legs. The legs traced out a pyramidical form – a sort of monument of thin air – and this shape was probably intended to recall Griffin's original proposal that the Parliament should be surmounted by a transparent pyramid to reflect its openness to the people. The vocabulary of the lower part of the scheme used the device of parallel screens of slender profile. The main façade was low in key and designed to be seen from a distance behind the old Parliament,

vogues and buzz phrases were transported quickly. In the mid-1970s the Japanese architect Arata Isozaki (mentioned briefly in Chapter 25) caught the mannerist mood and expressed it in designs which played deliberate games of contrast between 'traditional' and 'modern' elements. Rather ingeniously he argued that Japanese architecture had always borrowed from the outside and that eclecticism therefore lay near the heart of the national genius: he felt justified in combining elements from the Western Renaissance

standing close to the lake. Indeed, the shapes of the old (undistinguished) building were reflected in those of the new structure.

Regarding the Giurgola proposal in terms of its relationship to the trends of the preceding years, it can be argued that it was a virtual inventory of contemporary preoccupations. The interest in blending the building with its context was typical of a reaction against the heavy-handed and often free-standing monuments of a decade before. The mawkish attempt at populism implied by the flag and its supporting armature had a Venturiesque flavour. The vocabulary of screens suggested possible neo-Rationalist sources, while the Beaux-Arts order of the plan was certainly sanctioned by eclectic fashion, though it might be traceable to Giurgola's Beaux-Arts training. Modern prototypes were also represented, especially (one guesses) in the recall of the concave geometries of Le Corbusier's Palace of the Soviets scheme. To commentators convinced that a new richness was in the making, the building had an appealing collagist aspect; but to cooler critics the sources seemed not to be adequately blended, while the forms seemed loosely resolved and lacking in expressive conviction. It was as though complexity and contradiction had become recipes of an all-too-simple sort, without the tension and ambiguity to which Venturi had referred in his book fifteen years before.

A mood of increasing respect for historical context, and even of nostalgia, was not restricted to architecture: it extended to town-planning theories as well. By the late sixties, the destruction of city centres around the world by motorways, skyscrapers, and financial greed had reached the dimensions of a major crisis. While the causes were complex, it became common to lump such destruction together as the result of 'modern architecture', and to point the finger at such Utopian schemes of the 1920s as the Ville Contemporaine because they happened to contain skyscrapers and because they seemed to imply clean-sweep methods. The Team X attempts at humanizing modern architecture also came under attack on the grounds that they too were oppressive and too abstract to be understood by the general public. One learned that salvation must now lie in a sentimental revivalism.

One result of the reaction against modernization was preservationism, and by 1975 there were quarters where anything old was valued over anything new. Another result was an obsession with street-scapes at the expense of individual buildings. This emerged in, for example, the writings and proposals of Leon and Robert Krier (e.g., *Stadtraum in Theorie und Praxis*, 1975) in which a morphological index of street and square types (e.g., boulevards, circuses, piazzas) was assembled as an antidote to the CIAM version of the city as a park filled with objects. Where Le Corbusier had posited the health of the city on the death of the old, choking 'corridor street', the opposite now happened. The Kriers returned to the street with a nostalgic revenge (any street type would do) and treated it as a virtual fetish, as if the refined design of open spaces and outdoor rooms would on its own guarantee life to the badly mauled urban body. They inveighed against zoning and praised the mixed living and working arrangements of traditional European cities. Their images had a vaguely eighteenth-century air (fig. 28.15), while their utterances suggested a somewhat impractical nostalgia for an era of handicraft.

Another statement of urban philosophy to emerge in the late seventies was the book *Collage City* by Colin Rowe and his follower F. Koetter. Here the arguments were more sophisticated. The authors attacked the determinism basic to Utopianism (with some help from *The Open Society and its Enemies* by Karl Popper), by exposing the totalitarianism implicit in holistic urban schemes. Against such large-scale social engineering they proposed a piecemeal and democratic metaphor which relied a great deal on the principles of 'collage' and 'bricolage' in its implementation and visual style. As a sort of allegory of this position they used such examples as Hadrian's villa at Tivoli with its informality, its sprawling picturesque character, and its quotations from numerous places and times. They too emphasized the importance of 'spaces between' and criticized the object fixation of early modern urbanism – indeed, a 'figure/ground conception of the city, which treated urban spaces with the same weight as buildings, was proposed as a more textured and complex antidote. The modern building was to blend in with the patterns of the historical city.

In retrospect it is possible to see that *Collage City* relied for its full impact on the acceptance of a caricature of modernist sensibility as something holistic, teleological and essentially forward-looking. It did not do justice to the ideological and formal complexities of earlier twentieth-century utopianism in urban design, let alone to the variegated role of tradition in the formation of utopian images of the city; even the 'Ville Contemporaine', after all, had been a 'collage' of sorts, drawing together bits of Paris, New York, monasteries, ships, and boulevards. Nonetheless, *Collage City* was a symptom of a state of scepticism in which irony was a basic requirement and any too positive or gushing a prosposal was treated with dismay. As to its possible intentions in influencing the formulation of an urbanistic or architectural language, the book was circumspect. The plates and drawings encouraged admiration for complex urban tissues, a figure/ground view of spaces and forms in the city, and reverence for certain key Renaissance squares. The fragmentation and ambiguity of Cubism were somehow linked to Camillo Sitte's love of outdoor rooms. 'Object buildings' (i.e., some of those within the modern tradition) were severely castigated. However, even those who agreed with the rhetoric still had the problem of translating the book's insights into a three-dimensional vocabulary, and it was noticeable that some of Rowe's acolytes took the allegory all too literally by spicing their plans with Uffizi corridors, Piazza Navonas and antique theatres. At his most facile the collagist could be as vapid as the simple-minded adherent of radical eclecticism in architecture. But sticking little bits of history here and there into the modern urban fabric was scarcely a guarantee of environmental quality or even of spatial enrichment. Rowe's intentions were obviously more serious than those of his facile imitators, but even his own text positively encouraged flippancy:

> ... a collage technique, by accommodating a whole range of *axes mundi* (all of them vest pocket utopias – Swiss canton, New England village, Dome of the Rock, Place Vendôme, Campidoglio, etc) might be a means of permitting us the enjoyment of utopian poetics without our being obliged to suffer the embarrassment of utopian politics.... collage is a method deriving its virtue from its irony ... it seems to be a technique for using things and simultaneously disbelieving in them ...

The tone is knowledgeable, acutely self-conscious, and aware of both the dissolution of a past system of beliefs and the lack of any alternative which rings true; the result seems to be an elegant parlour despair that makes the most of erudition by manipulating the outer shells of past kernels of meaning; the assumption is that greater conviction is not for the moment possible. A similar mood of chic cynicism, and a suggestion (unwarranted but assumed) that this is the only possible viable one for the moment, is to be found in an essay by Jorge Silvetti written in 1977:

> ... we find ourselves looking back on the Modern Movement itself from a real historical perspective. Its 'classicism' has now been experienced, its effects sensed, and its postulates questioned; yet with all this nothing seems to have appeared to replace it. Like the Mannerist architect, we can only manipulate the known. Such is, in my view, all that can be said in general terms about the state of architecture today.

It can be seen from this survey of the past decade that a variety of beliefs have, in fact, been operative, and that the traditions of modern architecture have continued to be effective and influential. As Silvetti points out, nothing has yet emerged to replace the modern movement as the most relevant source of paradigms. Even the convinced revivalist nowadays finds that he cannot see the past in the same way as his nineteenth-century predecessors, for modern architecture itself has become a filter through which history is perceived. But a great deal of the rhetoric surrounding recent attempts at 're-invoking the past' has relied on a grotesquely simple view of modern architecture as something essentially anti-historical. In the process useful allies in the quest for architectural essentials have been unfairly overlooked: those outstanding buildings within the modern tradition itself which re-tapped some of architecture's fundamental roots.

That is why it may be relevant to draw this book to a close with a recent building conceived outside the realms of fashionable doubt, yet which has managed to blend in a single entity qualities of ancient and modern traditions: the Church at Bagsvaerd outside Copenhagen, designed by Jørn Utzon between 1969 and 1975 (fig. 28.16). The Church is formed from three main spaces, an atrium at the entrance; a main meeting-hall with an altar; and an ancillary garden space surrounded by small offices. These are contained by parallel cloisters running the entire length of the building and expressed as slender walls surmounted by triangular skylights. On the exterior the dominant church space is clearly visible towards the centre, and all parts of the building step up gradually towards it. However, unity is assured by a uniform structural treatment: a concrete frame with pre-cast infill slabs of silver-grey colour. The interior ceiling of the building makes a strong contrast with this stratified system, as it is formed from a curved concrete surface which protrudes over the entrance, then flows gradually upwards in a wave motion which reaches its peak over the main church space, to descend out of sight to the rear. This extraordinary organic shape modulates the light and contains the community within (figs. 28.17–19).

The aesthetic effects of the church are thus based on the simplest of means: fine proportions, contrast between similar elements, finesse in joints and craftsmanship, the play of light over plain materials. There is an elusive and quiet imagery which is at one with the idea of a religious 'meeting-house'. This is suggested by the small glass gables atop the parallel walls and by the stepping silhouette of the whole, which recalls the typical Zeeland country church with its characteristic stepped gables. The corrugated aluminium attached to the tower introduces a bizarre

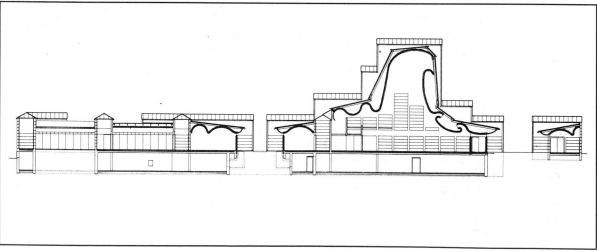

28.16 (*above*) Jørn Utzon, church at Bagsvaerd, near Copenhagen, 1969–75

28.17 (*left*) Jørn Utzon, church at Bagsvaerd, 1969–75, section.

28.18 (*above*) Jørn Utzon, church at Bagsvaerd, 1969–75, interior.

28.19 (*above right*) Jørn Utzon, church at Bagsvaerd, 1969–75, detail.

but enriching note, and associations that perhaps evoke the simplicity and sharpness of the modern agricultural vernacular. It is a house, a hall, a church, all in one, and its shapes recall one aspect more than the other in different parts.

However, imagery is not overplayed and is supported by form. Form in turn arises directly from a simple structural means attuned to serve ideas. The driving concepts of the design are rooted in Utzon's own earlier solutions, and in a style rich in metaphors and abstract images. The theme of the curved interior ceiling recalls the wave motion of the intended ceiling for the Sydney Opera House (which in turn relied on Aaltoesque precedent); the preoccupation with precast, modular discipline also takes one back to experiments like the Kingo Houses. As before, the opposition and coalescence of the stratified and the curved imply two primary kinds of order and other layers of polarity – the rational and the organic, the

supporting and the supported, the stable and the dynamic. The frame seems to be a descendant of both the concrete trabeated tradition stretching back to Perret, and of the wooden-frame tradition of the Scandinavian vernacular. However, all such allusions are tightly held in check in a design characterized by intellectual crispness and clarity.

Whatever the sources of Utzon's building, they have been transmuted into a new terminology, a genuine style, based on private, intuitive rules. A guiding image informs all the parts and brings them into a tense unity. Without pretension or show, the lessons of the modern tradition, of the vernacular, and of old ecclesiastical types have been fused. Surely this was what Van Eyck had in mind when he rejected 'the sentimental technocracy of the future' and 'the sentimental antiquarianism of the past' and suggested that 'past, present, and future must be active in the mind's interior as a continuum'.

Conclusion: Modernity, Tradition and Authenticity

> Every artist finds certain visual possibilities before him, to which he is bound. Not everything is possible at all times.
>
> H. Wölfflin, 1915

The early propagandists of modern architecture were convinced that a century-old problem had been solved in their own times, that a genuine modern style rather than a revival of past forms had at last been achieved. They may have been wrong in treating this style as monolithically as they did, and they certainly over-simplified its relationship to tradition, but they were probably right in stressing its epic significance. The present-day pundit with his feeble post-modernist construct denies this and treats the past eighty years as a passing phase, about to be replaced by another. The historian with a longer view tries to argue the opposite: that the revolution in sensibility, which affected all of the arts soon after the turn of this century, constituted a break as drastic as the Renaissance, and that we are closer to the beginning of a tradition than the end of it. Thus the present is defined by sweeping assertions, none of which are provable and none of which ring entirely true.

That the creation of modern architecture constituted a major development must be beyond doubt. Periods with the creative intensity of the 1920s are altogether rare in the history of architecture. They rely on uncommon coincidences of talent, patronage, and luck, and on phases of cultural transition in which new world-views strive for expression. The generation which came to maturity after the First World War happened to contain individuals of the calibre of Le Corbusier, Walter Gropius and Mies van der Rohe, each of them obsessed with the problem of defining an architectural language appropriate to industrialized society. They inherited this problem, and some of the means for solving it, from an earlier generation containing artists of the order of Frank Lloyd Wright,

Charles Rennie Mackintosh, Peter Behrens and Auguste Perret. But the protagonists of the modern movement of the 1920s had other ideas in common. They shared a commitment to social improvement through design and a feeling for the progressive potential of modern technology. They were fascinated by the spatial possibilities inherent in Cubism and in steel and concrete construction. They were united in their belief in a universal and international language of form, and in their hope that lessons might be abstracted from the past without facile imitation. Despite a degree of alienation intrinsic to their avant-garde position, they thought of themselves as the prophets of a new society and as preservers of higher values: their Utopias combined apocalyptic expectation with a vein of nostalgia. The bringing of art to life, of form to industrialism, seemed a worthwhile and meaningful cultural programme in the service of human betterment. And while each artist chose to express these euphoric sentiments in his own way, the results had certain broad features in common.

This happy coincidence of historical circumstance and aesthetic intentions was brief, but it still changed many of the formal, spatial, structural, and symbolic bases of architecture. Since the early years of this century conditions and intentions have continued to change and the conventions of modern architecture have been stretched and agitated into new combinations, but they have not been fundamentally revised. The architects who first inherited the modern tradition in the 1930s, Aalto, Terragni, Martienssen, Niemeyer, Lubetkin and the rest, absorbed the principles of the seminal buildings and extended their lessons. Even the reformulations necessitated by the cataclysmic event of the Second World War did not dislodge the majority of the premises laid out in the heroic period. The modern masters themselves extended their vocabularies on some levels, while maintaining core qualities from their earlier works. Lesser figures built the skyscrapers and housing schemes envisaged on paper in the twenties in a much debased form three decades later. Probing inheritors of the tradition took over some concepts and rejected others: the ideas of Team X or of artists as individual as Kahn, Van Eyck, Tange, Lasdun and Utzon were characterized by a tense recognition of the continuing relevance of modern architectural schemata, combined with a feeling that new expressive territories should be discovered. This is not to denigrate such figures for a lack of originality: it is rather to emphasize that an inventor's task may vary according to the point at which he enters a tradition, and to stress that creative individuals and traditions need one another if they are to stay alive.

Despite the noisy proclamations of 'post-modernists' about the end of an era, their actual vocabularies have involved little more than the sticking-together of pre-existing pieces of modern architecture, with appliqués here and there, of skin-deep historicism. This scarcely amounts to a basic critique; it is rather a change of clothes. By contrast, the inventions of the masters, of Le Corbusier and Wright in particular, altered the very spatial anatomy of design and constituted a fundamental reorganization of the deep structures (so to say) of the medium itself. As Picasso, Braque, Matisse, and Kandinsky had for painting, they made available new expressive languages of vast range and applicability on which others, whether faint-hearted or intensely intelligent, could build. The worldwide production of the past half century tends to confirm this. There are airport buildings in remote parts of Africa which would not have their present appearance without the prototypes of Mies van der Rohe, and recent buildings of high poetic intensity, such as Lasdun's European Investment Bank, which rely on the formulations inherent in the Dom-ino skeleton of sixty-six years ago. For better or for worse, the modern movement has become the dominant tradition of our time.

But this tradition is neither monolithic nor static. It is composed from the creations of individual artists of varying belief and from buildings which each have a unique life; it encompasses considerable regional variety and a very broad spectrum of quality. The architect of the present inherits this tradition whether he likes it or not, but the way in which he sees it will depend on the obsessions dominant in his time and even on the filters created by historians. What he chooses to do with his inheritance will in turn vary according to his temperament, the possibilities made available by patronage, and the relevance of prototypes to new situations. The average talent will take over a little piece and trot out an imitation of it: that is what average artists have always done throughout history whether they built with pointed arches, columns or steel frames. But the original mind is bound to grapple with his version of his tradition, rejecting some of it, welcoming part of it, and taking a good deal of it for granted. Gradually he will move from imitation of his forefathers to the crystallization of a personal style, blending his own preoccupations with solutions appropriate to the new problems which face him. The quality of his results will depend in some degree on his ability to avoid repeating the mere surface effects of his predecessors, and on his capacity to inject new meaning into the basic formulations of his tradition.

If the available style is beginning to show signs of fatigue, to become irrelevant, or to stand in the way of a valid or vital interpretation of reality, then it may have to be cast away. Surely this is the combination of reasons which led to the formulation of modern architecture in the first place: the existing forms were inadequate to the task of containing the new functions, materials, aspirations, and ideologies fostered by the Industrial Revolution. There are those who claim that modern architecture is also in a period of profound *malaise*. The introverted mannerism and symbolic devaluation portrayed in the last third of this book are scarcely signs of health. But alongside these jaded versions of modern design (really no worse than the decadent versions of earlier styles) are buildings of high quality; as ever they are in a minority and their excellence transcends mere period concerns. It seems that the schemata of modern architecture are firmly in control and that they will continue to support inventions of considerable richness.

The architect who is convinced otherwise still has the problem of formulating an architectural language. Perhaps he will attempt (as some have attempted) to turn back to earlier phases in history for support. If so he will have the problem of reviving an earlier style without pastiche. He must rethink the past in terms of present-day tasks, techniques and meanings. Along the way he may discover that superficial mimicry of past forms is really no better than skin-deep modernity and that past forms had their own reasons for being, most of which no longer apply. If the resolution to this problem is found in an intuition of past principles, then the artist will still need a language in the present through which he can abstract precedent. He will then be face to face with the problem of modern architecture again and, perhaps, with the realization that its formal and spatial conceptions are closer to present functions and meanings than he had hoped. There is a solid core of wisdom to Malraux's observation that 'no man builds on a void, and a civilization that breaks with the style at its disposal soon finds itself empty-handed.'

The problems that the inventors of modern architecture set out to solve are still very much with us. As the whole world gradually industrializes it confronts difficulties similar to the ones which first faced the West a century ago, some of which remain. New building problems emerge to which pre-existing traditions have no adequate solution; changing techniques undermine the reason for traditional forms and the craft systems in which they were made; new patterns of life lead to new needs and values which cry out for an adequate architectural home. Neither regressive sentimentalism nor slick technocracy hold out adequate answers ideologically or architecturally. Evidently forms have to be found which are equal to the new problems but which embody lasting values as well. Muthesius's observation made just after the turn of the century continues to ring true:

> Far higher than the material is the spiritual; far higher than function, material and technique stands Form. These three material aspects might be impeccably handled but – if Form were not – we would still be living in a merely brutish world.

Since the loss of authority of Classical norms in the eighteenth century, architects have lacked a vocabulary which appeared to have a universal sanction. This remains the position today. But where the architect at the turn of the century had to battle to formulate a new style, the architect of the present has the intervening chain of discoveries of the modern tradition to rely on. It seems sensible to build on the wisdom embodied in works of quality in this tradition and to avoid the mistakes of the lesser creations. This does not imply the imitation or mannerization of earlier architectural forms, but the rigorous redefinition of the principles behind them in the context of new problems. Modern architecture is intrinsically neither better nor worse than past architectures: all depends on how it is used in any one case. There is no short cut in the creation of quality; no recipes will do; and a preoccupation with passing fads will only result in work of transient value. Indeed, 'modernity' can become a distraction since what really counts is authenticity.

Authenticity suggests genuineness and probity – the opposite of the fake. It implies forms based on principle, forms which avoid arbitrariness, and which are appropriate on a number of levels. Whether it uses *pilotis* or piers, rectangles or curves, the authentic building transcends the convention in which it was conceived. It possesses a sublime unity subsuming part and whole, revealing different aspects of a dominating image, and suggesting a character of almost natural inevitability. Through a marvellous abstraction, its materials, details, spaces, and forms reveal the hierarchy of intentions. It is never merely a rational structural solution, nor merely an elegant play with shapes, but an embodiment of a social vision, an intuitive interpretation of a human institution. Its forms may conform to the regulations of a period, a style, or a building type, but the authentic work will cut through the customary to reveal new levels of significance.

Such authenticity is inconceivable without the basis of a genuine personal style. In the vocabularies of Wright, Le Corbusier, Mies van der Rohe, Aalto, Kahn (and a few others) one recognizes some of the necessary features: a limited family of forms capable of rich variation on the foundation of consistent patterns of thought; a system of type-forms blending the practical, the aesthetic, and the symbolic; shapes pregnant with meaning embodying a mythical interpretation of the world. The genuine style is the opposite of a cliché: it is a vital formula and a source of discipline, and it functions as a filter through which the artist draws experience and translates it into form; it places limits on any new problem and provides the shape of hypotheses while reflecting the artist's most obsessive themes.

When a style possesses this prodigious power of abstraction, it becomes a tool for transforming precedent. Its external physiognomy may relate to contemporary relatives, but its inner life will rely on nourishment from tradition. A single abstract shape may derive simultaneously from a dome, a funnel, a cooling-tower, an Indian observatory, a syntax for concrete, a favourite form in painting and a particular institutional interpretation, as happened with the curved volume at the heart of Le Corbusier's Parliament at Chandigarh. A modern solution to the roof may blend the wisdom of the Classical cornice with an intuition about a basic order in nature, and even with the shape of a Froebel block, as happened in the architectural system of Wright. And as each new task is faced, the range of a style is extended a little, but without a loss of consistency: the chemistry of a genuine poetic language continues to fuse new unities out of well-tried parts.

The Robie House, the Villa Savoye, the Barcelona Pavilion, the town centre at Säynätsalo, the Kimbell Art Museum, the church at Bagsvaerd – these are among the buildings in the modern tradition to possess such extraordinary depth. To slot them into the modern movement is to miss much of their value, for they are also relatives of past works of excellence. It was this timeless character to which Le Corbusier referred in 1923 when he wrote: 'Architecture has nothing to do with the various styles.'

The Search for Substance: Recent World Architecture (1987)

> We must return to the source, to the principle and to the type.
>
> Ribard de Chamoust

It is six years now since the final chapters of this book were written, and an addendum on recent world architecture seems justified. A review made at such short range cannot hope to be exhaustive but it can single out some buildings that are likely to live on when contemporary fashions have long since died away. A description of the recent past that relied too heavily on 'isms' would run the risk of blurring together seminal buildings with weaker relatives that simply wore the approved period dress. An approach that left out developing countries like Mexico or India could make no claim to historical or critical balance. Some of the best work now being produced is remote from the Western centres that happen to dominate the published discourse.

As predicted half a decade ago, the debate between 'Modernism' and 'Post-Modernism' has contributed little to an understanding of the contemporary situation. The caricature of modern architecture as something rootless, functionalist and without meaning has warped the historical perspective. The seminal works of the modern masters touched deep levels in tradition even as they innovated; their lessons continue to be extended, criticized, transformed, regionalized in places as varied as Ahmadabad, Tokyo and Ticino. A more forceful body of prototypes has yet to emerge and recent revivalisms have produced only a shadow of the past. This is not an argument in favour of an academy enforcing stylistic norms, it is rather a reminder that this is a period of evolution rather than revolution. The 'modern tradition' (with its various tributaries) seems to be alive, for it continues to support unexpected combinations of new and old, regional and universal. The issue then is not so much

Modern versus Post-Modern as principle versus pastiche: the notion of authenticity outlined in the conclusion continues to hold good.

There is no agreement over style in the world of architecture today but there are certain communities of concern. Precedent remains an obsession, responsible for trite façadism in some cases, for profound enrichments of meaning in others. Context is another, usually resulting in a passive imitation of whatever stands there already, occasionally leading to the intensification of the spirit and memories of a place. Polychromy and ornament are further concerns that may end up in wilful pattern-making or else in a true grammar of detail rooted in a building's fabric of ideas. Symbolism continues to worry theorists, though the distinction is not often made between arbitrary references and those transformations which bring form, space, light and sequence to life. The most convincing buildings continue to be those that give shape to human meaning in forms of a timeless character.

During the early 1980s there have been various attempts at reviving classical forms. Some have been literal and scholastic and the results have often been hackneyed. Neo-Rationalists like Aldo Rossi or Mario Botta have tried to abstract principles of organization and to blend these with the elemental geometries of modern architecture. 'Post-modern classicists' have indulged in games of quotation and irony. Even for supporters of this inherently superficial approach the lapse between drawings and realized buildings has been disturbing; witness the critical disillusionment which surrounded Michael Graves's Portland building or Ricardo Bofill's housing at Marne La Vallée near Paris. One of the more sophisticated attempts at

dealing with classical precedents has been James Stirling's and Michael Wilford's Neue Staatsgalerie in Stuttgart, for which the model was discussed in Chapter 28. The Staatsgalerie splices together a neo-classical type derived from the Altes Museum by Schinkel with spatial devices derived from Cubism, Le Corbusier and Aalto. Some inherited elements, such as the serpentine glass flanges, are handled with knowing virtuosity and in the process are invested with new twists of meaning (fig. A1). In that respect Stirling takes a Mannerist stance towards his mentors. The building is also gratuitously clad in historicizing gimmickry which outdoes the pop classicists on their own territory. Now that the building is finished it is possible to guess what will last and what will fade with fashion. The gaudy masonry veneers, the High Tech pediments and fat pink and blue railings are adjusted to magazine fads, whereas the spatial sequence through the drum and the clever way in which a collage of forms is adjusted to multiple pressures in the setting carry lessons of longer-range value. Later commentators may see the Staatsgalerie as more jocular than profound.

The utopian drive behind the early modern movement has long since dissipated but there are those who still return to the forms of the 1920s, less for the visionary force behind them than for the formal devices that they reveal. Richard Meyer uses Le Corbusier's Purist syntax as his starting point, reinterpreting it in a vocabulary of rotated grids, superimposed planes, reverse curves and ramps. In the Museum for Handicrafts in Frankfurt (1981–3) he has picked up the proportions of the existing neo-classical pavilion and used slight shifts in geometry to respond to accents in the setting. The southern Californian architect Frank Gehry also uses fragmentation, combining commonplace materials such as wooden studs, chain-link fencing and corrugated metal sheet, in designs that are collages of different geometries. Sometimes the result is chaotic but the Spiller House in Venice, California, maintains tension and hierarchy (fig. A2). The primary volumes are orthogonal to the street grid, while diagonal inflections respond to the angle of a solar collector on top and to the zigzag route that passes through a small central court between the two units, before rising as a *promenade architecturale*

A2 Frank Gehry, Spiller
House, Venice,
California, 1980.

through the interiors to the roof terrace. The Spiller House reworks ideas from Le Corbusier's studio houses of the 1920s (elevated boxes, strip windows etc.) but in an aesthetic that is attuned to the bric-a-brac of the modern American urban scene. It comes as no surprise to learn that Gehry may have been inspired by those *papiers collés* of Robert Rauschenberg which splice waste products of industrialism – rags, rubber tyres, labels, bits of newspaper – into compositions of abstract planes.

During the past decade there has been a boom in skyscraper construction, not only in the United States but also in the Middle and Far East. The type presents a fairly consistent set of formal and technical problems but this does not mean that the solutions have to be standardized or repetitive. The reaction against the glass box which began in the early 1970s has continued to take a number of routes: ornamental dressing; tripartite composition; structural experimentation; contextual, regional and climatic adaptation. The machinations of American capitalism are disguised behind a high-sounding discourse which pretends to reintroduce 'tradition' into the city centre, but which in reality is creating a species of built advertising loaded with glib and flashy references. Playboy eclecticism has fitted the bill temporarily, especially as a way for developers to publicize rentable space. By now the evidence is abundant that a decorated box is really no more interesting than a plain one if it lacks architectural control; at last Mies van der Rohe is being appreciated again for his elegance, scale and latent classicism.

Beyond the pantomime of publicity-seeking there have been some worthy attempts at making skyscrapers more sensitive to their context. The office building at 333 Wacker Drive (1982) by Kohn, Pedersen and Fox (chief designer Bill Pedersen) is curved to respond to a bend in the river which cuts off the corner of the city grid, while at the back it is rectangular to deal with the orthogonal street pattern (fig. A3). The two geometries coalesce towards the top where sharp tucks are cut into the taut curtain wall. The glass is green, and this vast aqueous surface is as sensitive to changing light as the river which is its foreground. The building really works at three different scales; that of the overall silhouette and edge of the city; that of the immediate setting of river, walkways, roads and bridges; and that of the pedestrian who walks by or enters the building. Thus there is a species of tripartite composition but the different pieces are not just stuck on top of one another, rather they are overlayed and unified in a pattern of coherent rhythms and sharp profiles. Pedersen admits to being interested in the shining metal sculptures of Brancusi; in 333 Wacker Drive he has reconciled a simple sculptural form with the multiple forces in a context.

The Hong Kong and Shanghai Bank (1979–84) by Norman Foster and Associates expresses the giant piers and lateral megatrusses on the outside (fig. A4). The curtain wall is recessed and treated to a delicate grille of metal *brises-soleil*. In this case the tower becomes a glistening, transparent machine penetrated by light; there is even a reflector attached to the outside which directs rays into the huge atrium at the heart of the structure. The usual idea of a skyscraper as a stack of even floors around a core is exploded open to accommodate a new vision of the work space in an era of electronic communications. The piers are pushed out to the corners to maximize stability in typhoons, but this also allows the building to be thought of as a ladder, from which the floors are suspended, rather than a frame. A major public space is inserted between the legs at ground level and atria are tucked in at upper levels. Lifts are pushed out to the edges of the building while internal moving staircases link some of the floors. The Hong Kong and Shanghai Bank belongs to a Rationalist tradition but Foster goes well beyond the utilitarian in his poetic celebration of glass, steel moving components and machine metaphors. There are echoes of Constructivist fantasies, of aviation technology, even of the work of Jean Prouvé, whose project for the National Ministry of Education (1970) in Paris must be counted a direct model. But the building possesses Oriental overtones too, especially in its subtle lattices and its modular order. The bank looks back to Kowloon over the water proclaiming high technology and capitalist ingenuity, as the future of Hong Kong comes into doubt. It speaks of the new financial status of South East Asia: 'a building for the Pacific century'.

The National Commercial Bank in Jeddah, Saudi Arabia, designed by Gordon Bunshaft and the firm of Skidmore, Owings and Merrill between 1979 and 1983, cross-breeds an international type with regional principles for dealing with a hot damp climate (fig. A5). The building stands between a lagoon and what remains of the old Medinah; its plan is triangular and a sharp edge faces out to sea like a prow. It rises out of the flat landscape declaring wealth, self-assurance and restraint. The monolith is gashed by huge rectangles of shadow behind which oases in the air protect internal trays of offices from direct glare, heat and sandstorms. At the core is a shaft which

syphons the warm air upwards and draws in cool air from below. Thus the design uses local climatic principles – courtyard houses, wind towers etc. – but in a way that informs the very anatomy of the structure. The imposing mass evokes ancient seaside forts but without resorting to a bogus orientalism of attached horseshoe arches. The National Commercial Bank is a building of today that manages to make

A3 Kohn, Pedersen and Fox (design partner Bill Pedersen), 333 Wacker Drive, Chicago, 1982–3.

A4 Norman Foster and Associates, Hong Kong and Shanghai Bank, Hong Kong, 1979–84.

tectural press: in the Fujimi Country Club (1977) he even resorted to classical references such as a Serliana motif on the entrance. Recently he seems torn between a subtle use of primary volumes, light and texture, and a chic but obvious appeal to fashion. Kazuo Shinohara and Tadeo Ando have taken a more critical stance towards the 'ad mass' world of instant imagery. The Koshino House (1981) by Ando uses taut modernist planes subtly bathed in light to define an inner sanctum, an 'abode of vacancy' recalling the tranquillity of the traditional teahouse. Abstraction is the means through which the architect tries to reinvigorate metaphysical qualities in the architecture of the past.

Fumihiko Maki has spoken of the need to expand modernism rather than reject it. The Spiral Building in Minato, Tokyo (1986) combines a free-flowing movement on the inside with a fragmented collage of different-sized openings on the outside, the latter helping to reconcile multiple scales in the setting. Maki exploits the high-quality industrial craft available in Japan to make refined steel joints, pristine patterns of glass blocks and sharp reveals in plastic. His buildings are disciplined by structure and thus avoid the caprice of those facile revivalists who conceive images on paper with little sense of how they may actually be built. Maki's version of expanded modernism includes: 'a search for a more subtle relationship between structure and expression, a search for the power that details within abstract figures seem to possess, a study of the dynamic equilibrium between part and whole, the expression of the present that comes about from the simultaneous awareness of past and future'.

The internal space and external form of Maki's Fujisawa Municipal Gymnasium (1984) are generated by two giant curved roofs whose outside surface is coated in stainless steel (fig. A6). The building owes obvious debts to Tange, to Saarinen and even to Utzon's Sydney Opera House, but there is nothing hackneyed about Maki's reinterpretation of this type. The building is a social centre and a focal point in an increasingly industrialized landscape. The lunging silhouettes suggest temple roofs, Japanese armour, even space technology (to mention some of the architect's own associations), but the imagery is held in check by a coherent sculptural form. Maki's architecture addresses the complex mentalities of a society which combines frantic industrial activity with a continuing reverence for tradition.

During the past decade there has been a resurgence of interest in 'regionalism', though there is no general agreement about the exact meaning of the term. For some it implies a direct recall of indigenous forms in reaction against the homogenization that industrialization seems to bring with it. For others it means

serious architecture out of the unlikely combination of green micro-processor screens and palm trees, international finance and national prestige, the mores of a new technocratic class and desert traditions of building.

The tension between international and regional informs much recent work in Japan. Arata Isozaki seems to design with one eye on the western archi-

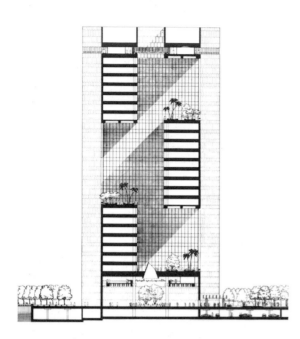

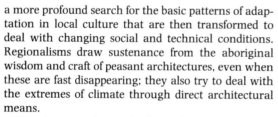

a more profound search for the basic patterns of adaptation in local culture that are then transformed to deal with changing social and technical conditions. Regionalisms draw sustenance from the aboriginal wisdom and craft of peasant architectures, even when these are fast disappearing; they also try to deal with the extremes of climate through direct architectural means.

Even in some advanced industrial nations there are pockets of regionalist consciousness which hold out against cosmopolitan fashion. These tend to occur at the fringes where native habitats are still visible even if native culture has been undermined. In these circumstances the best work eschews direct imitation and uses abstraction to go deeper. An example of this approach is the Ramada House in southern Arizona designed by Judith Chafee (fig. A7). The building stands on the edge of the desert and is formed from a protective parasol of mesquite logs and saguaro fronds that hovers above an adobe structure half buried in the ground. Seen in drawings this is an uncompromisingly modern design which descends from Le Corbusier's hot climate principle of the shading slab (e.g. the Shodhan House in India of 1951–4), but this idea has been fused with two local archetypes: the simple log and twig shelters of the nomads (reinterpreted by the Spanish colonial ranchers as the shading 'ramada') and the pit dwellings in mud of the more sedentary

communities. The result is a building of haunting poetry, its mood changing from minute to minute as light and shade dapple the walls, the roof a stable horizontal in a turbulent landscape of cacti, sand and crags.

The revival of past traditions takes on a special meaning in developing countries that are recovering from colonial occupation because it becomes associated with the search for identity. Here the danger is a superficial imitation of national stereotypes such as onion domes or Chinese roofs, which leads to kitsch. Even the earnest adherents of vernacular revivals find that they can only deal with a limited range of programmes using traditional village forms. Since imported solutions often prove to be inadequate to local climates and social habits, as well as being ideologically suspect, it is necessary to find some other way. The ideal is an authentic blend of new and old, regional and universal.

The stock of buildings attempting this difficult synthesis is growing. One thinks of the work of the Turkish architect Sedad Hakki Eldem, in particular of his Social Security Complex (1970) in Istanbul which adjusts the concrete frame to the cadences of the wooden house vernacular; or of the Iraqi architect Rifat Chadirji who has cross-bred the elemental lessons of Louis Kahn with the primary geometries in brick of his native country. Foreign architects working in the

A5 Skidmore, Owings and Merrill (main designer Gordon Bunshaft), National Commercial Bank, Jeddah, Saudi Arabia, section, 1979–83.

A6 Fumihiko Maki, Fujisawa Municipal Gymnasium, 1984.

A7 Judith Chafee,
Ramada House,
Arizona, 1980.

Middle East can no longer always be accused of just dumping irrelevant imports: the Haj Terminal in Jeddah, Saudi Arabia – gateway to the Holy Places for airborne pilgrims – was designed by Skidmore, Owings and Merrill in the early 1980s in the form of repeating series of Teflon tents on steel poles. Beyond its pragmatic success this building captures exactly the paradoxes and nuances of twentieth-century air travel in search of the essentials of Islam. The Kuwait National Assembly (1971–85) by Jørn Utzon also resorts to the solution of a broad protective roof, but in this case it is made of concrete and stands over a rectangular plan with a central street giving on to the different departments around courtyards – an arrangement that recalls the traditional souk (fig. A8). The roofs over the Assembly and the entrance hall (which beckons towards the sea) stand on monumental, tapered piers whose precast joints call to mind the bindings on rush huts or the tackle of a dhow. The debts to Le Corbusier's monuments at Chandigarh are evident but Utzon has also referred to 'the purity of Islamic structure' and even, in the case of his curved and billowing roofs, to the princely tent of the elders: 'the hall which provides shade for the public meetings could perhaps be considered symbolic of the protection a ruler extends to his people'.

The Ministry of Foreign Affairs (1979–83) in Riyadh, Saudi Arabia, by the Danish architect Henning Larsen, combines modern simplicity, regional innuendo and Pan-Islamic references in its interpretation of the enclosed institution (figs. A9, 10). The Saudis wanted a building that would combine offices and ceremonial spaces, that would reflect the stern moral values of the heartlands and the central position of the country in the Islamic world. Larsen made an inward-turning building with a large triangular hall in the middle and offices looking down into courtyard gardens around the perimeter. The exteriors are of brown stone and have small windows that let light in through a baffle so that glare is avoided (a device from the vernacular of Bahrain). The low towers at the corners and bastions flanking the main entrance hint at the mud fortresses of the Nejd, thus alluding to the home region of the Saud family. The interiors are chaste, white and luminous, filled with the sound of fountains. Allusions to the Alhambra or Morocco mingle with abstract surfaces that have a Corbusian pedigree: the hovering ceiling plane with light creeping around its edges recalls Ronchamp. The plan itself is an ingenious fusion of spaces in masses, and masses in spaces, that has surely drawn something from Louis Kahn if not from more ancient models such as the Mogul tomb of Hummayum in India. Stairs lead from the central hall into the tall interior streets that ring the building and give access to the offices. Rays of sunlight stream through small holes in the vaulted ceilings in a way that recalls the souks of Tunisia.

Larsen could very easily have lost control of all these references and sources, but apart from a slight tendency to theatricality he did not. He has tried to understand tradition at the level of types, not just images, and even to seek out analogies between the substructures of different periods and styles. At the core is the archetype of the Arab house with its blank exteriors and its rich interior life around a courtyard. Around this kernel he has worked with other themes such as the fabric of streets and squares in desert towns, or geometrical water gardens. Larsen has tried to invoke the symbolic value of squares, triangles and other abstract shapes and to endow these with new meanings. Beneath the more obvious allusions there is an inventive reinterpretation of the spatial layering and visual ambiguity of Islamic architecture.

Mexico has a lineage of modern architects who have attempted to combine the regional and the international and who have also been concerned with drawing lessons from the numerous layers of the architectural heritage. During the 1950s and 1960s Luis Barragán worked with coloured wall planes, platforms and pools in a way that extended the reductivism of the International Style while echoing memories of convent walls, village vernaculars and ancient precincts. More recently, Ricardo Leggorretta has continued the style but without the same mystery and depth. Teodoro Gonzalez de Leon had his starting point in the late works of Le Corbusier (with whom he worked during the 1940s) and has tried to use a vocabulary of rough concrete planes and bold forms gashed by shadows to make the most of the sunlight, vegetation and materials of Mexico. In his work too there are many ancient echoes. He returns again and again to the idea of a central space served by galleries, especially in large public buildings needing an institutional heart. The Collegio de Mexico (1979–82) combines stratified concrete terraces (reminiscent of the platforms and contours of pre-Columbian architecture) with an ample atrium that follows the slope of the land and is covered by a trellis of plants. Gonzalez de Leon has spoken of the need to touch on the 'constants' in tradition: in his case those spatial archetypes which are found in the vernacular and which recur in both pre-Hispanic and Hispanic examples. In particular he is obsessed with the protected court: 'In the present day the patio continues to offer the most natural way of articulating space in complex programme buildings. The task of integrating the patio into our work involved translating it into personal and contemporary terms.'

During the past ten years Indian architects have become increasingly concerned with national archi-

A8 Jørn Utzon, National Assembly Building, Kuwait, 1971–85.

tectural traditions and with ways in which these may be translated into a modern expression. The seminal lessons of Le Corbusier and Louis Kahn have been adjusted to deal better with the demands of the climate and with the needs of a traditional society undergoing rapid change yet seeking roots. The recent work of Balkrishna Doshi offers an example of this tendency. His own studio 'Sangath' (1981) on the outskirts of Ahmadabad is formed from low protective vaults rising from grassy platforms (fig. A11). The interiors are half buried in the ground: a transversal section suggests a primordial earth shelter. To one side there is a shallow cascade of grass steps making an outdoor theatre for informal gatherings, not unlike the communal place in a village. In the rainy season water swills off the broken white china surfaces of the roofs into gurgling troughs. The vaults are constructed of ceramic tubes covered in concrete; combined with a natural cooling system this insulation helps to reduce temperatures in the summer months. Sangath is approached on axis, but after an alluring glimpse of the shaded underside of the vaults one is forced on to a diagonal line of approach past giant clay pots and earth mounds that rhyme with the curved silhouettes. This is the prelude to a meandering path through interiors that combine single, double, and even triple-height volumes. Doshi admires the temple cities of southern India with their labyrinths of halls, galleries and courts, and it is possible that these have influenced the warren-like interiors of Sangath. There are also rhythmic contrasts between top-lit and shaded areas, ambiguous transitions over ledges and steps, shifting axes and vistas – devices that the architect associates with the flux of Indian life. Sangath is certainly a long-

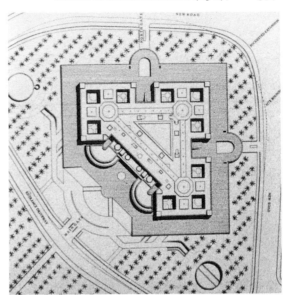

A9 Henning Larsen, Ministry of Foreign Affairs, Riyadh, Saudi Arabia, 1979–83.

A10 Ministry of Foreign Affairs, Riyadh, site plan.

range descendant of Le Corbusier's earth-hugging Sarabhai House (1953) in Ahmadabad, but the type has been transformed to serve a different social vision. In larger institutional schemes such as the Indian Institute of Management in Bangalore, Doshi has explored similar themes, resorting to the analogy of the traditional Indian town with its lattice of streets, squares and courts.

Charles Correa has also explored the overlaps between new and old, monumental and folk. His Gandhi Ashram Museum in Ahmadabad of 1961 took certain propositions from Le Corbusier and Kahn and rendered these in a different sensibility of humble but airy pavilions linked by an ambling route. Since then

he has continued to explore a kit of parts for Indian conditions which includes platforms, sunken terraces, sections which encourage natural ventilation and shaded overhangs. Correa adjusts these typical elements to the programme and the place, whether it is low-cost housing in a hot dry area or a tourist hotel in the tropics. In the case of the Kanchanjunga Apartments in Bombay (1973) a section derived from village architecture has even been reinterpreted in the context of a high-rise building (the strategy anticipates that used in Bunshaft's Jeddah tower although the particular form is different). The Bharat Bavan in Bhopal (1982) combines an arts centre and a museum, and in this case the solution has been to make a sequence of courts sunken below the terraces which flow gently down to a lake. The hooded skylights are descendants of the funnel in the Chandigarh Parliament but adjusted to a distant skyline of white domes. The project for the Madhya Pradesh State Assembly in Bhopal (now under construction) resorts to a circular geometry crossed at the centre by axes, presumably drawing upon the forms of the nearby stupas at Sanchi.

Most of Raj Rewal's buildings are in or around New Delhi, and he has been particularly concerned with urban problems. The Asian Games Housing (1982) to the south of the city rejects the free-standing block of flats in favour of aggregations of courts and precincts separated by gates (fig. A12). This way of handling public space recalls Rewal's deep fascination with the structure of desert towns like Jaisalmer in which houses and streets are formed from variations on a few basic elements. His individual units are reinterpretations of *havelis* – courtyard houses with tall

A11 Balkrishna V. Doshi, 'Sangath' Studio, Ahmadabad, India, 1979–81.

A12 Raj Rewal, Asian Games housing, New Delhi, India, 1982.

rooms, small openings and interlocking terraces. But Rewal does not resort to a merely picturesque town-scape; vistas are controlled by axes, and combinations of types are as logical as they are visually effective. The structure is a concrete frame with an infill of brick, covered with a washed terrazzo finish. This is amber in colour and is incised with grooves that indicate the actual structure while evoking the honey-coloured stone of old desert towns. In the nearly completed National Institute of Immunology Rewal has defined a community of scientists as a series of courtyard clusters linked to one another by shaded walkways, terraces and steps. The rhythm of horizontals echoes the rise and fall of the land. The pink and brown bands of the façades intensify the primary themes and recall the polychrome marble stripes of Mogul architecture. Rewal explores the parallels between concrete trabeation and the stone frame vocabulary of complexes like Fathepur Sikri: the scholars' court in the institute has horizontal galleries around it on various levels and these look down upon an open-air theatre. The view towards nature – the scientist's province – is dramatically framed. Rewal penetrates beyond the particular historical example to the geo-metrical and spatial principles that underlly past vocabulary, and tries to make an equivalent for the present day. Again we notice the quest for the *type* (Plate 16).

The Sir Lankan architect Geoffrey Bawa attempts to build in harmony with the tropical climate, lush vegetation, handicrafts and architectural traditions of the island. The local vernacular is a hybrid of Portuguese, Dutch and indigenous influences that combines whitewashed walls, tiled roofs and deep wooden verandas. Bawa has transformed this vocabulary to his own purposes and blended it with many other influences that he has absorbed over the years. His own studio in the Colombo suburbs (1981) celebrates the poetics of the bungalow in a controlled sequence of indoor and outdoor spaces in which use is made of alluring vistas and shifting axes (fig. A13). The moment that one enters the forecourt one is drawn along the main route by a rectangle of greenery to the rear and by a reflecting pool at the heart of the building. But distances are hard to judge and this engenders a sense of mystery. When one reaches the pool one is forced left onto a parallel path which has an old wooden column as its focal point. So the promenade proceeds through airy spaces of varying intensity that are linked directly to the outside but protected from the sun and rain by deep eaves. Immediately above the pool the tiled roofs part, leaving a gap through which air circulates and monsoons pour. The device probably comes from the southern Indian palace of Padmanabhapuram though the principle is that of the ancient Roman *impluvium*. Bawa works closely with local craftsmen and the wooden columns have a delicate entasis, carved stone capitals and bases. In larger

A13 Geoffrey Bawa, own studio, Colombo, Sri Lanka, 1981.

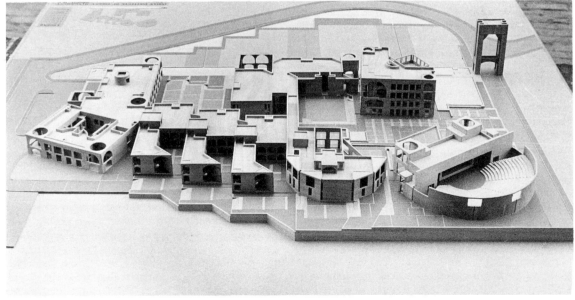

A14 Anant Raje, Indian Institute of Forest Management (model), 1985–.

projects such as the recently completed Parliament on an island outside Colombo, the architect has amplified the same system. Hut, house, palace, temple – in traditional timber architectures of South East Asia these types are all cousins of each other: Bawa explores an analogous gradation for contemporary functions of different sizes.

It has been a guiding theme of this book that a tradition is formed from a chain of inventions. The young architect extends the forms of his predecessors and gradually creates a vocabulary of his own around a new cluster of concerns. This was true of earlier periods like the Renaissance and it is still true today. The most convincing contemporary transformations of Louis Kahn's ideas are found in the Ticino of southern Switzerland (Mario Botta) and in the parched North West of India, particularly in the work of the Ahmedabad architect Anant Raje. Raje's starting point was Kahn's Indian Institute of Management in that city, on which he actually worked, so he saw the principles operating from within. In recent years he has gradually pulled away into expressive territories of his own which probe monumental qualities in the architecture of the Indian past. One can sense this in his recent scheme for the Indian Institute of Forest Management (in construction) near Bhopal, which stands on a slope looking over lakes and city (fig. A14). The programme has been broken down into separate pieces such as curved auditoria and rectangular teaching blocks. These have then been reunited on the sloping contours so that axes are inflected to respond to wind, views and topography. Raje's vocabulary is intricately connected to the means of construction: concrete piers, arches and beams, walls in textured stone or brick. He creates complex interpenetrations in plan and section using parallel slots of structure, and these extend across the site as galleries, courtyards and pavilions. One of Raje's chief inspirations is the palace and garden complex at Mandu near Indore – a dream world of ruined halls, terraces and water tanks overrun by greenery – but he has also sketched and analysed Hadrian's Villa at Tivoli, concentrating upon the way in which fragments are scattered across the landscape. Raje tries to reinvigorate a sense of order that is shared by ancient complexes whether they be Roman or Islamic.

Mario Botta has also profited from the elemental lessons of Kahn and Le Corbusier. In his formative period he was influenced by the northern Italian architect Carlo Scarpa as well. Botta explores the common ground between the primary geometries of modern architecture and certain schemata from the Classical tradition. He has also been inspired by regional prototypes such as the simple Alpine barns of his native

Ticino. In his case abstraction serves to blend and to compound historical precedents, not to exclude them. But Botta makes no bones about his commitment to the needs and methods of construction of today. He tries to infuse forms that have a basis in structure, use and geometry with a poetic mood arising from proportion, hierarchy, light and a sense of appropriate detail. The Casa Rotonda at Stabio (1980–1) turns a two-car-family home constructed from concrete blocks into a solid monument that defies the recent suburban sprawl (fig. A15). The cylinder is cut in two

A15 Mario Botta, Casa Rotonda, Stabio, Ticino, Switzerland, 1980–1.

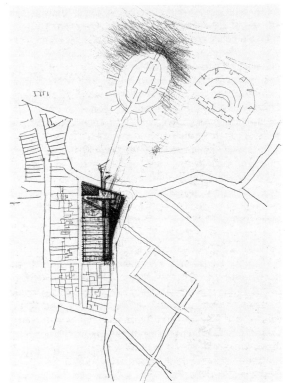

A16 Rafael Moneo, Museo de Arte Romano, Merida, Spain, 1981–5.

A17 Museo de Arte Romano, Merida: sketch showing urban context and ancient theatres.

form is now completely embedded in a new expression. The jointing to the larger cylinder is handled adeptly by corbelled bricks, so that the form evokes a column, but one generated from within, functionally and in terms of ideas, not just a 'sign' or quotation. This column possesses resonance with Romanesque as well as Roman: it touches on the idea of the column in general.

Rafael Moneo the Spanish architect is also concerned with the notion of type. His recently completed Museo de Arte Romano in Merida cuts back to the anatomy of Antiquity, reinterpreting the brick arches and repetitive systems of Roman engineering (figs. A16, A17, Plate 15). Merida was at the junction of two major roads and under the early Empire was expanded to include theatres, aqueducts and a long bridge. The museum was constructed to house sculptural and architectural fragments from the ruins of the city, most of them in white marble. It stands at a transitional point between the rather sleepy Spanish town and an open space containing the amphitheatre and theatre. Moneo seems to have picked up both the grain of the nearby houses and the flanges of structure supporting the theatres, for he has organized the building as a series of parallel brick walls penetrated by different sized arches. The largest of these align to create a noble and airy hall, a cross between an industrial structure and a Roman bath. The view down the

by a slot that contains the stairs, covered by a delicate steel and glass skylight. The circular plan with an axis on the compass points suggests a solar calendar, as if slits had been aligned to catch the sun's rays at specific times of the day or the year. It is an observatory, a bastion, a tower for spiritual retreat that hints at a return to archaic, rural values. On the street side the walls step down and away to create room for cars at either side but also to reveal the curved end of the stairs. Kahn's massive circulation towers or Le Corbusier's silo-shaped stairways come to mind, but the main axis past rows of receding piers towards the statues at the other end is made even more dramatic when a beam of light falls across the fragments from an unseen source. Other pieces are displayed at the end of each lateral bay and these too are top-lit against the biscuit coloured Roman bricks. The route is then channelled to the upper levels supported on thin concrete slabs that slice through the walls and thread the visitor back and forth through arches that are made smaller to go with pottery, jewellery, and mozaics. The lateral walls are brought through to the street side where they are expressed as a row of vertical buttresses. Only in the entrance wing does the building lose coherence, especially where the architect has been tempted to mimic the domestic scale of neighbours in his windows.

The museum stands over remnants of the street pattern of the Roman city, and Moneo has made the bold move of shifting his geometry a few degrees to accentuate the contrast between new and old. Underneath there is a subterranean area where the walls become thicker and the arches smaller and more numerous. The forced theatricality of post-modern classicism finds no place among these grave and sober forms in dim light. It is like wondering through a Roman cistern, though Piranesi and Kahn also come to mind. Moneo's reading of a place and its strata of memories has involved him in an imaginative excavation of the ages to unearth the informing types of a past civilization. There are echoes too of later transformations such as the eighth-century mosque at Cordoba with its parallel rows of arches and its massive buttresses. But the Museo de Arte Romano does not linger on any single source; it tries to subsume its influences in a haunting abstract order that is enlivened by the rhythm of construction and the play of light over forms.

Certain works of architecture seem to touch a timeless core. To do this they have to emerge from the depths of the mind, giving shape to myths that have a universal dimension. Some of Carlo Scarpa's late buildings, designed since the early 1960s, possess this otherworldly character. A superficial inspection of his stratified forms and details reveals debts to Wright, but he was an eclectic in the best sense of the word, who drew sustenance from abstract painting and from numerous places and times. He contained his impressions and ideas in a private language of hieroglyphs – squares, diamonds, circles – which emerged like a stream of consciousness in his studies for buildings. His dream was nourished by the aqueous landscapes of the Veneto, by that poetic sense that penetrates to the spirit of a place. One feels this with his conversion into a museum of the Querini-Stampalia Palace in Venice. The route is guided through the old

structure by a raised pathway above the level of the *aqua alta* – the winter high tide that periodically floods the ground-floor rooms and piazzas of the city. It continues through the exhibition room into a garden at the back where the theme of matter crossing water is reversed: a slow channel is raised above the ground on top of a wall. Papyrus poking out of a square hole surrounded by a rim of water hints at some subterranean level. A source dribbles into a white marble basin in the form of a labyrinth; it repeats the themes of the building in miniature but is also like a hermetic map of Venice, its waterways, streets and squares. For Scarpa ornament was a microcosm of larger worlds (fig. A18).

A18 Carlo Scarpa, Querini-Stampalia Museum, Venice: water trough in garden, 1961–3.

A19 Carlo Scarpa, Brion Cemetery, San Vito d'Altivole (near Bassano), Italy, 1969–78: the final precinct.

The Brion Cemetery near Bassano uses some of the same themes to evoke a field of the dead and the passage to the world beyond (fig. A19). It is a family burial ground that wraps around the back of the village cemetery in the form of an 'L'. The flat land is sculpted into trenches, paths, mounds, platforms and is populated with curious tombs in abstract shapes like large amulets. Concrete walls and steps are eroded, faceted, weathered to give the impression of an abandoned archaeological site swamped with pools. There is a poignant mood of time past, but rectangular areas of sky glimpsed through slots in walls hint at infinity. Close to the gate is the family chapel, a block rotated off the axis, standing in a sombre pond of green lily pads, and flanked by a bank of cypresses. Marble and brass underline the archaic patina of the concrete. The path goes on into a maze of half sunken passages allowing glimpses here and there of funerary caskets. It then turns 90 degrees along the back of the old cemetery wall into a shaped tunnel lit through two intersecting circles – an emblem perhaps of the duration of the Brion marriage after death. A door on pulleys thuds shut as one emerges in the final precinct, a *campo santo* with a perimeter wall enclosing a still rectangle of water. On an island a tomb-like form is lifted on legs like a medieval funerary monument. A cruciform plaque appears to float on the surface, a void at its centre: 'the still point of the turning world'.

Bibliographical Note

It would be quite impossible to include even a fair representation of the vast and ever-growing bibliography on architecture this century without writing another, separate volume. The reader who seeks a more detailed coverage is referred to Dennis Sharp (ed.), *Sources of Modern Architecture* (Architectural Association, London, Paper no. 2; New York, Wittenborn, 1967), and to Muriel Emanuel (ed.), *Contemporary Architects* (New York, St. Martins Press, 1980).

Like architecture, scholarship has its traditions. Monographs and articles are referred to (where relevant) in the notes. The present note is reserved for general works which have helped me form a picture of the overall development, even when I have disagreed with the point of view or have felt that crucial material was missing.

The picture is necessarily less complete the earlier one goes. One might begin with the modern movement's first attempts at understanding itself, such as Walter Gropius's *Internationale Architektur* (Munich, 1925) or Ludwig Hilbersheimer's *Internationale neue Baukunst* (Stuttgart, 1927). Perhaps these influenced the formulations and title of Henry-Russell Hitchcock and Philip Johnson's *The International Style, Architecture Since 1922* (New York, 1932). This book attempted to explain the visual principles behind a selection of modern architectural works, and to relate these to structural effects of concrete and steel. As the title suggests, the emphasis was stylistic; ideological aspects of the new architecture were ignored, as were buildings which did not conform visually.

In 1932 P. Morton Shand published a series of articles in the *Architectural Review* (London) dealing with the evolution of modern architecture in the late nineteenth and early twentieth centuries. These may have influenced the picture given by Nikolaus Pevsner in his better-known *Pioneers of Modern Design from William Morris to Walter Gropius* (London, 1936). Pevsner traced the impact of Morris's moral ideas and of nineteenth-century engineering on the formulations around the turn of the century. He examined Art Nouveau, the work of Perret, Behrens, Hoffmann and Wright, and brought his story to a close in 1914, with buildings like Gropius's Werkbund Pavilion at Cologne of that year. The implication seemed to be that these individual buildings were part of a saga, resulting in what Pevsner felt was the true, rational style of the twentieth century.

Sigfried Giedion's *Space, Time and Architecture* (Cambridge, Mass., 1941) had something of this character too. Perhaps influenced by historicists like Heinrich Wölfflin, he believed it was the historian's task to characterize the 'constituent' facts of a period which truly represented the 'spirit of the age' and to ignore the rest. As he wrote, his new Grand Tradition of modern architecture was under threat of extinction in Europe: his tone was lofty and apostolic. His view of the origins of modern architecture did much to emphasize the role of new materials like iron, glass, steel and concrete in the nineteenth century, and of a new 'space conception' stemming from Cubism and culminating in the rich spatial ambiguities of modern architecture. His treatment went further than Pevsner's in that it covered urbanism and architecture in the 1920s and 1930s. Expressionist tendencies were played down; rationalist ones emphasized; extensions of nineteenth-century revivalism ignored. Even the later editions of the book, which included buildings of the 1940s and 1950s, were selective tracts in favour of a cause with which Giedion was directly involved.

The perspective altered drastically after the war as a new, younger generation of historians looked back at the 'heroic' years as a separate period of history, and became more conscious of the symbolic and ideological flavour of modern architecture. The most notable products were the fragmentary essays of Colin Rowe written in the late 1940s (e.g., 'The Mathematics of the Ideal Villa: Palladio and Le Corbusier Compared', *Architectural Review*, 1947) and the remarkable *Theory and Design in the First Machine Age* (London, 1960) by Reyner Banham. This was on a sounder documentary foundation than its predecessors, as it was based on theoretical texts of the first three decades of this century. It is probably pointless to blame Banham's work for its cursory treatment of Wright, its Europocentrism and its near-avoidance of politics, as these were not close to its central aims. However, the book did draw to a close around 1930, and analysed texts more than it did forms.

Banham's book was conceived in parallel with Henry-Russell Hitchcock's magisterial *Architecture, Nineteenth and Twentieth Centuries*, which appeared in the Pelican History of Art series in 1958. This was sound scholarship of an undaring kind belonging to that tradition of art history which concentrates on the description of stylistic movements. Only the last third of the book was devoted to the twentieth century and it closed in the early 1950s. There was little sense of the social role of architecture and even individual artistic personalities were blended into 'phases' and 'developments'. However, the treatment of Art Nouveau was extensive, and the book retains its function as a weighty reference work with a good bibliography and useful notes.

Leonardo Benevolo's *History of Modern Architecture* (2 vols., Cambridge, Mass., 1971; original Italian edition, 1960) amplified Giedion's treatment of the nineteenth century. It stressed the reformist roots of modern architecture and urbanism, and the crises following from industrialization. Volume 2, dealing with the twentieth century, took a broad view and included political debates surrounding the modern movement, and the impact of Nazi and Fascist critiques. As he was writing in the late 1950s, his treatment of the years after the Second World War was cursory; he also abstained from a close analysis of individual works.

Peter Collins's *Changing Ideals in Modern Architecture* (London, 1965) must be counted among the seminal works of modern architectural scholarship. In this case the emphasis was on the intellectual history of the nineteenth century and on the emergence of the *idea*, rather than the forms, of modern architecture. This was seen against the background of the various philosophical debates underlying nineteenth-century styles. Collins provided the most succinct treatment of Rationalism, an attitude to design which would be rethought in the modern movement of the twentieth century.

For coverage of the period since 1960, one has to resort to lesser works than those mentioned so far. Charles Jencks's *Modern Movements in Architecture* (Doubleday Anchor, 1973) was written by a critic who has made no bones about the propaganda value of 'history' writing. The book reflects the agonies and hesitations of the convinced pluralist. Jencks was determined to avoid the 'single strand' method of Giedion and Pevsner, and implied instead (with the aid of charts and diagrams) a series of 'discontinuous movements', six in all. These had names like 'The Idealist', 'The Intuitive' and 'The Activist'. Architecture covering half a century or more was thus parcelled rather uncomfortably into arbitrary categories. The result of all the straining after relativism was a confused picture which clearly acknowledged the difficulty of *selection* and the need to avoid presenting modern architecture as a monolithic entity.

In the mid-1970s the publications on 'Modern Architecture and Design' of the BBC Open University course A-305, run by Tim and Charlotte Benton, began to appear. The eighteen 'units' on architecture from 1890 to 1939 presented some previously unpublished facts, sources, images and opinions. Most useful too were the two anthologies of source material: *Architecture and Design, 1890–1939, An International Anthology of Original Articles* (New York, 1975), (eds. Benton and Benton, with D. Sharp) and *Documents* (ed. C. Benton). A curious habit seems to have developed in the architectural history confraternity, of not acknowledging the 'units' as publications; I have avoided this in my own references.

More recently Manfredo Tafuri and Francesco Dal Co published *Modern Architecture* (New York, 1979) – translated from the Italian edition of 1976. The emphasis of this lavish book was on the evolution of the modern industrial city more than on individual buildings or artists. The authors were proud to announce their Marxist affiliations and to mar any pretence at objectivity in a social polemic. Even so their treatment of American and Soviet city planning was most useful. However, the years after 1950 were given little coverage and next to nothing was said about architecture outside Europe and the United States. Another book which emphasized ideology at the expense of other matters appeared in 1980, too late to influence the present work one way or another. This was Kenneth Frampton's *Modern Architecture, a Critical History* (New York, 1980), nearly half of which was devoted to architecture before 1914. I have recorded my reactions to the strengths and weaknesses of these two most recent studies in a review in the *Journal of the Society of Architectural Historians*, 40, no. 2, May 1981, pp. 168–170.

The 1987 edition of this book contains a new chapter entitled 'The Search for Substance: Recent World Architecture (1987)'. This section has been worked out against the drift of much recent critical opinion and has studiously avoided some of the usual, but misleading, intellectual postures concerning 'Modernism' and 'Post-Modernism'. The main sources have been: unpublished documents; interviews with architects; a handful of worthwhile critical articles; and – of course – the evidence of the buildings themselves.

Books referred to in shortened form in notes

Banham, Reyner, *The New Brutalism – Ethic or Aesthetic?*, New York, Reinhold, 1966.

Banham, Reyner, *Theory and Design in the First Machine Age*, London, Architectural Press, 1960.

Benevolo, Leonardo, *A History of Modern Architecture*, Cambridge, Mass., MIT Press, 1971, 2 vols., translated from *Storia dell' architettura moderna*, 1960.

Benton, Charlotte (ed.), *Documents, a Collection of Source Material on the Modern Movement*, Milton Keynes, Open University, 1975.

Benton, Tim and Charlotte (eds.), with Dennis Sharp, *Architecture and Design, 1890–1939: An International Anthology of Original Articles*, New York, Whitney, 1975;

also published as *Form and Function: A Source Book on the History of Architecture and Design 1890–1939*, Milton Keynes, Open University, 1975. I have followed the Benton's translations unless otherwise stated.

Collins, Peter, *Changing Ideals in Modern Architecture*, London, Faber and Faber, 1965.

Curtis, William J. R., *Le Corbusier: Ideas and Forms*, Oxford, Phaidon, 1986; New York, Rizzoli, 1986.

Curtis, William J. R., and Sekler, Eduard (ed.), *Le Corbusier at Work, the Genesis of the Carpenter Center for the Visual Arts*. Cambridge, Mass., Harvard University Press, 1978.

Drew, Philip, *The Third Generation: Changing Meaning in Architecture*, London, Praeger, 1972.

Egbert, Donald Drew, *Social Radicalism and the Arts*, New York, Knopf, 1970.

Giedion, Sigfried, *Space, Time and Architecture*, Cambridge, Mass., Harvard University Press, 1941; 5th edn., 1967.

Hitchcock, Henry-Russell, *Architecture, Nineteenth and Twentieth Centuries*, Harmondsworth, Penguin, 1958.

Hitchcock, H. R., and Johnson, Philip, *The International Style: Architecture Since 1922*, New York, Museum of Modern Art, 1932.

Jencks, Charles, *Modern Movements in Architecture*, New York, Doubleday Anchor, 1973.

Jencks, Charles, *The Language of Post-Modern Architecture*, New York, Rizzoli, 1977.

Jordy, William H., *American Buildings and their Architects*, volume 3, *Progressive and Academic Ideals at the Turn of the Twentieth Century*, New York, Doubleday Anchor, 1972.

Jordy, William H., *American Buildings and Their Architects*, volume 4, *The Impact of European Modernism in the Mid Twentieth Century*, New York, Anchor Doubleday, 1972.

Le Corbusier (Jeanneret, Charles Edouard), *Vers une architecture*, Paris, 1923. Translated by Frederick Etchells as *Towards a New Architecture*, London, 1927, and frequently republished thereafter.

Le Corbusier and Pierre Jeanneret, *Oeuvre complète* in 8 volumes: 1910–1929; 1929–1934; 1934–1938; 1938–1946; 1946–1952; 1952–1957; 1957–1965; volume 8; editors, W. Boesiger, M. Bill, O. Stonorov, Zurich, Éditions Girsberger or Éditions d'Architecture, 1929–70. These have been translated as the *Complete Works*, and into numerous other languages than English.

Pevsner, Nikolaus, *Pioneers of Modern Design from William Morris to Walter Gropius*, London, Faber and Faber, 1936.

Smith, Norris Kelly, *Frank Lloyd Wright, a Study in Architectural Content*, Englewood Cliffs, N.J., Prentice Hall, 1966.

Smithson, Alison (ed.), *Team 10 Primer*, Cambridge, Mass., MIT Press, 1968.

Tafuri, Manfredo, and Dal Co, Francesco, *Modern Architecture*, New York, Abrams, 1979; translated from *Architettura contemporanea*, Milan, Electa Editrice, 1976.

Viollet-le-Duc, Eugène, *Dictionnaire raisonné de l'architecture*, Paris, 1854–68.

Viollet-le-Duc, Eugène, *Entretiens sur l'architecture*, Paris, 1863–72. Translated as *Discourses on Architecture*, Boston, 1876.

Von Moos, Stanislaus, *Le Corbusier: Elemente einer Synthese*, Frauenfeld and Stuttgart, 1968; translated as *Le Corbusier, l'architecte et son mythe* (1974) and as *Le Corbusier, Elements of a Synthesis*, Cambridge, Mass., MIT, 1979.

Walden, Russell (ed.), *The Open Hand, Essays on Le Corbusier*, Cambridge, Mass., MIT Press, 1977.

Notes

Introduction

p. 8 Motto: Ernst Kris, *Psychoanalytic Explorations in Art*, New York and London, 1952, p. 21.

Modern Age: the conception of history as a sequence of ages, each with a dominating spirit, owes a good deal to the theories of Hegel. See Norris Kelly Smith, *On Art and Architecture in the Modern World*, Victoria, B.C., 1971. Also, Chapter I below.

Forms, Meanings, Moralities: for new aspirations in the nineteenth century, see Collins, *Changing Ideals*.

Propagandists: particularly Henry-Russell Hitchcock, Sigfried Giedion and Nikolaus Pevsner. See Bibliographical Note. Also David Watkin, *Morality and Architecture*, Oxford, 1977 for an attempted refutation of the determinist underpinnings of these historians.

p. 9 Pioneers: Pevsner's title of 1936, *Pioneers of Modern Design from William Morris to Walter Gropius*.

Earlier Histories: see Bibliographical Note.

p. 11 Origins: a distinction is deliberately drawn between ideas of modern architecture, and forms. As I suggest in Chapter I, the notion of modern architecture is traceable in the long run to progressive theories of history with their roots in the late eighteenth century. But the emphasis of the present work is on architecture as a visual and symbolic art and it is not reasonable to speak of a new style, distinct from overt revivalism, until the 1890s. (See Chapter I below.) It only confuses matters to give the title *The First Moderns* to a work on 17th- and 18th-century architecture, as Joseph Rykwert has recently done (1980). This conforms to the present fashion of nostalgia for the 18th century and no doubt extends all too crudely some of the subtle parallelisms suggested by Emil Kaufmann, *Von Ledoux bis Le Corbusier*, Vienna, 1933.

If one wished to take the 'sources' further back and confuse the matter still more, one could show that Le Corbusier drew crucial lessons from the Parthenon, and that the 'first moderns' therefore existed in the 5th century B.C.! Like any complex imaginative phenomenon, modern architecture drew on a number of past eras simultaneously.

Tradition: the avant-garde mythos tends to imply a constant rejection of the past, but modern architecture, like any other gradual development in time, has relied on exemplars and gradual transformations, as well as on the restrictive bonds of slowly changing stylistic conventions. The view of tradition presented in this book undoubtedly owes something to Ernst Gombrich, *Art and Illusion*, London, 1960, and to George Kubler, *The Shape of Time*, Yale, 1962. However, in describing a tradition it is also crucial to be aware of the unique character of individual works within it, and of the interplay between private artistic fantasy and the shared 'rules' of period or regional styles.

Chapter 1. The Idea of a Modern Architecture in the Nineteenth Century

p. 14 Motto: Viollet-Le-Duc, *Dictionnaire raisonné*, vol. 1, p. ix.

Modern: Collins, *Changing Ideals*, see particularly chapter 13, 'The Demand for a New Architecture', pp. 128 ff. This chapter is heavily indebted to Collins's treatment. For an extremely subtle analysis of the significance of 'modernity'

culturally and psychologically in a particular milieu, see Karl E. Schorske, *Fin de Siècle Vienna, Politics and Culture*, New York, 1981.

Spiritual Core: for a discussion of determinist theories in historiography, see Karl Popper, *The Open Society and Its Enemies*, London, 1945, also R. G. Collingwood, *The Idea of History*, Oxford, 1946, and M. Bury, *The Idea of Progress*, London, 1920. For the concept of the *Zeitgeist* ('spirit of the times') in art historiography, see Ernst Gombrich, *Art History and the Social Sciences*, Oxford, 1975. For the relationship of determinism to modern architecture, see N. K. Smith, *On Art and Architecture in the Modern World*, Victoria, B.C., 1971 and D. Watkin, *Morality and Architecture*, Oxford, 1977. It needs to be stressed that a *belief* in determinism does not determine history.

Absolute Authority: see John Summerson, 'The Case for a Theory of Modern Architecture', *RIBA Journal*, 64 (June 1957), pp. 307–13. See also Rudolf Wittkower, *Architectural Principles in the Age of Humanism*, London, 1949 for an attempt at explaining the idealist world-view underlying Renaissance forms.

New Methods: Collins, *Changing Ideals*, Ch. 20, 'New Planning Problems'; also Giedion, *Space, Time and Architecture*, and Benevolo, *History of Modern Architecture*, Vol. 1, for the impact of industrialism on architecture and engineering in the 19th century. Also, Francis D. Klingender, *Art and the Industrial Revolution*, London, 1947.

p. 15 Nineteenth-century Moralists: see Paul Thompson, *The Work of William Morris*, London, 1960 and Edward P. Thompson, *William Morris: Romantic to Revolutionary*, London, 1955. Also: John Ruskin, *The Stones of Venice*, London, 1851–3. For Morris's role in the evolution of modern architectural ideas: Pevsner, *Pioneers*, and Watkin, *Morality and Architecture*.

p. 16 Alternative Social and Urban Structures: see Egbert, *Social Radicalism*, especially pp. 117 ff. for Saint-Simon, pp. 133 ff. for Fourier, and pp. 87 ff. for Karl Marx. The Utopian character of modern architecture is discussed more fully in Chapters 12 and 15 below. The ideological roots of any single modern architect vary considerably.

Theorists of modern Architecture: For a fuller discussion, see Collins, *Changing Ideals*, pp. 128 ff.

Greek, Gothic, Egyptian: for a detailed account of the various style phases of nineteenth-century European architecture see Hitchcock, *Architecture*, and Stefan Muthesius and Roger Dixon, *Victorian Architecture*, New York, 1979.

Gothic: see, for example, the polemics employed by A. W. Pugin in *An Apology for the Revival of Christian Architecture in England*, London, 1843.

p. 17 Primitive Hut: M. A. Laugier, *Essai sur l'architecture*, Paris, 1753; W. Herrmann, *Laugier and Eighteenth-Century French Theory*, London, 1962; J. Rykwert, *On Adam's House in Paradise; the Idea of the Primitive Hut in Architectural History*, New York, 1972.

Rationalism: see chapter 19 of that title, in Collins, *Changing Ideals*. For a critique of functional determinism see Alan Colquhoun, 'Typology and Design Method', *Perspecta*, 12 (1969), pp. 71–4.

p. 18 Truth to Programme and Structure: the most succinct discussion of Viollet-le-Duc's rationalism is to be found in John Summerson, *Heavenly Mansions*, London, 1949, pp. 135 ff. For Viollet's own arguments see particularly, *Entretiens sur l'architecture*, Chapter 10.

p. 19 Beaux-Arts: for a somewhat fragmented treatment see

Arthur Drexler (ed.), *The Architecture of the Ecole des Beaux-Arts*, New York, 1977. Modern architects like Le Corbusier and Walter Gropius lumped the École together unfairly and monolithically. Their principal objections were against a formulaic use of precedent, axial plans of a decorative sort, the extensive use of ornament, and an ignorance of modern technologies. In short they took the Beaux-Arts to exemplify traditionalism in the worst sense of the word. However, as Banham (*Theory and Design*, Chapter 1) has shown, ideas of Academic extraction influenced the pioneers of modern architecture much more than they would have admitted.
Abstraction of Tradition: it is instructive that the original French title of Le Corbusier's *Towards a New Architecture* of 1923 was *Vers une architecture* (without the 'New'). While he was concerned to produce a vocabulary appropriate to the industrial age, he was equally concerned to purge architecture of fakery and bogus historicism so as to *recapture* essentials which underlay past styles. Viollet-le-Duc had also made the distinction between 'styles' (as passing conventions of a superficial sort) and the character of 'style' which implied a far deeper quality of genuineness. Walter Gropius concluded *The New Architecture and the Bauhaus*, 1926 with the following thoughts: '... my conception of the role of the New Architecture is nowhere and in no sense in opposition to "Tradition" properly so called. "Respect for Tradition" does not mean the complacent toleration of elements which have been a matter of fortuitous chance or of individual eccentricity; nor does it mean the acceptance of domination by bygone aesthetic forms. It means and always has meant, the preservation of essentials in the process of striving to get at what lies at back of all materials and every technique, by giving semblance to the one with the intelligent aid of the other.'
Universal Formal Values: see Adolf von Hildebrand, *Das Problem der Form in der bildenden Kunst*, Strasbourg, 1893 and Heinrich Wölfflin, *Die klassische Kunst*, Munich, 1899.
Analogies: Collins, *Changing Ideals*. If, one day, a subtle psychology of style is written, it may demonstrate that all architectural vocabularies may be thought of as abstract symbolic forms which incorporate analogical references to the artificial and natural worlds.

Chapter 2. The Search for New Forms and the Problem of Ornament

p. 21 Motto: Otto Wagner, *Moderne Architektur*, Vienna, 1895, from the preface. The expanded version of this book, entitled *Die Baukunst unserer Zeit. Dem Baukunstjünger ein Führer auf diesem Kunstgebeit*, 4th edn., Vienna, 1914, contains the quotation, on p. 76.
Hitchcock: *Architecture*, p. 416. Hitchcock's Chapters 16 and 17 offer a concise history of the spread of Art Nouveau.
Pevsner: *Pioneers*, p. 90.
p. 22 Ornament: Owen Jones, *The Grammar of Ornament*, London, 1856. The special appeal of this book to artists of the 1890s probably lay in its abstraction of vegetal and plant motifs into simple geometrical forms.
p. 24 Maison du Peuple: Victor Horta, 'Reminiscences of the Maison du Peuple' (undated), Benton and Benton, *Architecture and Design*, p. 65.
p. 25 Horta: 'Reminiscences of the Maison du Peuple'.
Van de Velde: for a concise assessment see P. Morton-Shand, 'Van de Velde to Wagner', *Architectural Review*, October, 1934, pp. 143–5.

Van de Velde: 'A Chapter on the Design and Construction of Modern Furniture', 1897; Benton and Benton, *Architecture and Design*, pp. 17–18.
p. 26 Turin Art Nouveau: Silvius Paoletti, 'For the Workers', *L'Arte Decorativa Moderna*, year 1, no. 2, February 1902.
Gaudi: for neo-Gothic antecedents see T. G. Beddall, 'Gaudi and the Catalan Gothic', *Journal of Society of Architectural Historians*, 34, no. 1, March 1975, p. 48. Also George Collins, *Antoni Gaudi*, New York and London, 1960 for an interpretation of the architect's guiding principles.
Dragons: see Jencks, *Language*, p. 99–100 for an idiosyncratic interpretation of the roof shape.
p. 30 Mackintosh: see T. Howarth, *Charles Rennie Mackintosh and the Modern Movement*, London, 1952.
p. 33 Spatial Effects of Library: Pevsner, *Pioneers*, p. 167.
August Endell: 'The Beauty of Form and Decorative Art', 1897–8; cited by Benton and Benton, *Architecture and Design*, p. 21.
Wagner: for *Moderne Architektur* see note to Motto of this chapter.
p. 34 Stoclet: Eduard F. Sekler, 'The Stoclet House by Josef Hoffmann', *Essays in the History of Architecture Presented to Rudolf Wittkower*, London, 1967.
p. 36 Ornament: Adolf Loos, 'Ornament und Verbrechen', may be found in the original in A. Loos, *Trotzdem*, Innsbruck, 1930. I have followed Banham's translation in *Theory and Design*, p. 93.

Chapter 3. Rationalism, The Engineering Tradition, and Reinforced Concrete

p. 37 Motto: from the preface of the first issue of the periodical *L'Architecture vivante*, Paris, 1923, ed. Morancé.
Viollet-le-Duc: *Entretiens*, vol. i, p. 186.
Auguste Choisy: See Banham, *Theory and Design*, pp. 23 ff., for a concise discussion of Choisy's ideas. The role of nineteenth-century engineering in the formation of modern archtecture is discussed most obsessively by Giedion, *Space, Time and Architecture*, but he has insufficient to say about the symbolic transformation of these sources into architecture in the modern movement. See also, P. Morton-Shand, 'Architecture and Engineering', *Architectural Review*, November 1932.
p. 38 Louis Sullivan: 'The Tall Office Building Artistically Considered', 1896; cited by Benton and Benton, *Architecture and Design*, p. 11. Arguably the 'Chicago School', to which Sullivan belonged, played a considerable role in the creation of forms deemed appropriate to modern techniques. I have not meant to diminish this contribution by singling out Sullivan as a representative. Were there more space I would have discussed Burnham, Root, Jenney as well. For a lengthy analysis of Sullivan's philosophy, see Jordy, *American Buildings and their Architects*, vol. 3, especially Chapter 2, 'Functionalism as Fact and Symbol: Louis Sullivan's Commercial Buildings, Tombs and Banks'.
p. 39 Concrete: see Peter Collins, *Concrete, the Vision of a New Architecture, A Study of Auguste Perret and His Precursors*, London, 1959.
p. 40 Reinforced Cement: Collins, *Concrete, the Vision of a New Architecture*, pp. 113 ff.
Julien Guadet: *Éléments et théories de l'architecture*, Paris, 1904.
p. 43 Auguste Perret on Ornament: Collins, *Concrete, the Vision of a New Architecture*, p. 199.

Kahn: see Grant Hildebrand, *Designing for Industry: the Architecture of Albert Kahn*, Cambridge, Mass., MIT, 1974.

p. 45 Tony Garnier: *Une Cité Industrielle: Étude pour la construction des villes*, Paris, 1917; see also Dora Wiebenson, *Tony Garnier: The Cité Industrielle*, New York, 1969.

p. 46 Dom-ino: see Paul Turner, 'Romanticism, Rationalism and the Domino System', in Walden (ed.), *The Open Hand*; also Eleanor Gregh, 'The Dom-ino Idea', *Oppositions 15–16*, Cambridge, Mass., MIT, 1979, pp. 61 ff.

p. 47 Le Corbusier's copy of Viollet-le-Duc: *Dictionnaire raisonné*, Vol. i, p. 66, is covered with notes. The page illustrates the principle of the flying buttress in Gothic architecture, a 'skeleton' of sorts.

Chapter 4. Arts and Crafts Ideals in England and the USA

p. 48 Motto: Hermann Muthesius, 'The Meaning of the Arts and Crafts', 1907, from his speech given at the Berlin commercial academy in spring of that year.

Pevsner: *Pioneers*; see also 'William Morris and Architecture', *RIBA Journal*, 64, 1957, by same author.

p. 49 Pevsner: *Pioneers*, p. 150. See also David Gebhard, 'The Vernacular Transformed', *RIBA Journal*, 78, March 1971, pp. 98 ff.

p. 52 Lutyens: The best treatments of Lutyens are to be found in A. S. G. Butler and Christopher Hussey, *The Architecture of Sir Edwin Lutyens*, London, 1950, and L. Weaver, *Houses and Gardens by E. Lutyens*, London, 1913.

p. 54 Hermann Muthesius: *Das englische Haus*, Berlin, 1902–5; quotation from the conclusion of vol. II, 'The Development of the English House'.

p. 55 W. R. Lethaby: 'Modern German Architecture and What we may Learn from it', a talk given at the Architectural Association, London, 1915; cited by Benton and Benton, *Architecture and Design*, p. 55.

Vincent Scully: *The Shingle Style and the Stick Style*, Yale, New Haven, Conn., 1971.

p. 55 American Architecture: The most probing study of late 19th-century American architecture is still Lewis Mumford's, *The Brown Decades: A Study of the Arts in America 1865–1895*, New York, 1931.

p. 56 Frank Lloyd Wright: 'The Art and Craft of the Machine', a talk given to the Chicago Arts and Crafts Society, at Hull House, on 6 March 1901; cited by Edgar Kaufmann, *Frank Lloyd Wright: Writings and Buildings*, New York, 1960, p. 55.

The Craftsman: ran from 1901 to 1916 and bore the sub-title 'an illustrated monthly magazine for the simplification of life'.

Greene Brothers: see Jordy, *American Buildings and their Architects*, vol. 3, Chapter 4, p. 217 ff., for detailed analysis of the Gamble House.

p. 58 Maybeck: Jordy, *American Buildings and their Architects*, vol. 3, Chapter 5.

Irving Gill: *The Craftsman*, vol. 30, May 1916, pp. 142 ff. for both quotations. For further treatment of Gill's ideas see Esther McCoy, *Five California Architects*, New York, 1960; Jordy, *American Buildings and their Architects*, vol. 3, pp. 246 ff.

Chapter 5. Responses to Mechanization: The Deutscher Werkbund and Futurism

p. 60 Motto: Antonio Sant' Elia, 'Messagio', 1914; see

Banham, *Theory and Design*, p. 128. Banham is to be praised for having given Futurism its due role in the evolution of modern architecture.

p. 61 Hermann Muthesius: 'Wo stehen wir?', a speech given at the Werkbund congress, 1911; cited and translated by Banham, *Theory and Design*, p. 73. For further discussion of Werkbund ideology see J. Campbell, *The German Werkbund: The Politics of Reform in the Applied Arts*, Princeton, 1978; Tilmann Buddensieg, *Industriekultur: Peter Behrens u.d. A.E.G. 1907–1914*, Berlin, 1979; Stanford Anderson, 'Modern Architecture and Industry: Peter Behrens and the Cultural Policy of Historical Determinism', *Oppositions 11*, Winter 1977. These three works were unknown to me when this chapter was formulated but seem to square with my interpretation.

p. 64 Walter Gropius: 'Die Entwicklung moderner Industriebaukunst', *Deutscher Werkbund Jahrbuch*, Jena, 1913, pp. 19–20, translated by Benton and Benton, *Architecture and Design*, p. 53, as 'The Development of Modern Industrial Architecture'.

p. 65 Werkbund Debate 1914: excerpts are published in English translation in Benton, *Documents*, pp. 5 ff.

p. 66 Fagus Factory: for a detailed discussion of the design process see Tim Benton, Stefan Muthesius and Bridget Wilkins, *Europe 1900–1914*, Open University, Units 5–6, 1975.

p. 70 Paul Scheerbart, *Glasarchitektur*, Berlin, 1914. See also Dennis Sharp (ed.), *Glass Architecture by Paul Scheerbart and Alpine Architecture by Bruno Taut*, London, 1972.

p. 71 Futurism: see Banham, *Theory and Design*, pp. 99 ff. for the most incisive treatment of Futurism; I have followed Banham's translations of the various manifestoes. The Manifesto of Futurist architecture is reproduced in full in Ulrich Conrads, *Programmes and Manifestoes on 20th-Century Architecture*, Lund Humphries, 1970. See also M. Martin, *Futurist Art and Theory 1909–1915*, Oxford, 1968 and U. Apollonio, *Futurist Manifestoes*, London, 1973 for further analysis of texts.

Chapter 6. The Architectural System of Frank Lloyd Wright

p. 75 Motto: Frank Lloyd Wright, 'In the Cause of Architecture', *Architectural Record*, 23, March 1908, p. 158.

Historical Views of Wright: Pevsner, 1936 was content to treat Wright as a pioneer of modern design. Hitchcock (*In the Nature of Materials: The Buildings of Frank Lloyd Wright 1887–1941*, New York, 1942), simply described the externals of Wright's style; in *Architecture Nineteenth and Twentieth Centuries*, he slotted early Wright into a chapter entitled 'The Detached House in England and America', and abstained from generalizing about his historical significance. Norris Kelly Smith, *Frank Lloyd Wright: A Study in Architectural Content*, 1966, forcibly removed Wright from any simplistic evolutionary scheme by concentrating on the institutional metaphors of his buildings and their suburban cultural context. Banham, in *Theory and Design*, treated Wright only in so far as he was relevant to the European modern movement. More recently David Handlin, *The American Home, Architecture and Society, 1815–1915*, Boston, 1979, has placed Wright's domestic architecture in a long American tradition of home-building and has emphasized some of the Classical influences on his architectural grammar. Mention should also be made of

Grant Manson, *Frank Lloyd Wright to 1910: the First Golden Age*, New York, 1958, for its precise and evocative analyses of Wright's houses, and of Jordy, *American Buildings and Their Architects*, vol. 3, for its detailed account of the Robie House. This by no means exhausts the Wright literature, but it serves to demonstrate the range of views about him.
Wright's Biography: see R. Twombley, *Frank Lloyd Wright, An Interpretive Biography*, New York, 1973; also the inaccurate but gripping *Autobiography*, New York, 1932 by Wright himself.

p. 77 William Channing Gannett, *The House Beautiful*, River Forest, Ill., 1897.
Institutional Metaphor: Smith, *Frank Lloyd Wright*.
Winslow House: quotation from R. Spencer, 'Work of Frank Lloyd Wright', *Architectural Review*, 7, Boston, June 1900, p. 65.
p. 78 Tripartite Division: Handlin, *The American Home*, discusses the relationship to Classical base, shaft and cornice, pp. 305 ff.
Clients: Leonard K. Eaton, *Two Chicago Architects and their clients*, Cambridge, Mass., MIT, 1969, p. 62.
Abstraction: see Frank Lloyd Wright, *The Japanese Print: An Interpretation*, Chicago, 1912.
p. 79 Home in Prairie Town: *Ladies' Home Journal*, February 1901.
p. 80 Frank Lloyd Wright: 'The Cardboard House', 1931; cited by Benton and Benton, *Architecture and Design*, p. 60.
p. 83 Robie: for reminiscences by the client of his intentions see Eaton, *Two Chicago Architects and Their Clients*; for the climatic functions of the roof see R. Banham, 'Frank Lloyd Wright as Environmentalist', *Architectural Design*, April 1967; for detailed analysis of house, Jordy, *American Buildings and Their Architects*, vol. 3, p. 180.
p. 88 Unity Temple: Wright, *Autobiography*, pp. 138 ff.; O. Kakuzo, *The Book of Tea*, Rutland, Vt. and Tokyo, 1906.
p. 89 Schinkel: see Handlin, *The American Home*, pp. 317 ff.
Wasmuth Volumes: *Ausgeführte Bauten und Entwürfe von Frank Lloyd Wright*, Berlin, Ernst Wasmuth, 1910, with introduction by Frank Lloyd Wright; *Frank Lloyd Wright Ausgeführte Bauten*, Berlin: Ernst Wasmuth, 1911, introduction by W. R. Ashbee.
p. 90 Prairie School: see H. A. Brooks, *The Prairie School*, Toronto, 1972.

Chapter 7. Cubism and New Conceptions of Space

p. 91 Motto: T. van Doesburg, G. Rietveld, C. van Eesteren, 'Vers une construction collective', *de Stijl*, VI (1924), columns 91, 92.
p. 92 Avant-Garde: see Renato Poggioli, *The Theory of Avant-Garde*, Cambridge, Mass., 1968.
p. 92 W. Kandinsky: *Über das Geistige in der Kunst*, Munich, 1912.
Spirit of Times: see notes on 'modern age' and 'propagandists' in Introduction and on 'spiritual core' in Chapter I. It is evident that Le Corbusier, for example, saw himself as a revealer of the 'true nature' of his own 'epoch'. See Chapters 8 and 15 below.
p. 93 Geoffrey Scott: *The Architecture of Humanism*, London, 1914, p. 210.
Cubism, Abstract Art, Architecture: Banham, *Theory and Design*, pp. 106–213 contains a subtle analysis of the interrelations between painting, sculpture and architecture,

and theories about all three. See also Giedion, *Space, Time and Architecture* for a different emphasis which makes much of the so-called 'space–time' conception intrinsic to Cubism and modern architecture.
p. 94 H. P. Berlage: lecture given in Zurich, March 1912, cited in H. de Fries, *Frank Lloyd Wright*, Berlin, 1926, and by Banham, *Theory and Design*, p. 145–6. See note on 'Wasmuth volumes' at end of last chapter.
p. 97 De Stijl: see H. L. C. Jaffé, *de Stijl 1917–1927*, Amsterdam, 1956.
p. 97 The Machine: see Banham, *Theory and Design*, pp. 151 ff.
p. 98 Number and Measure: J. P. Oud, 'Der Einfluss von Frank Lloyd Wright auf die Architektur Europas', in *Holländische Architektur* (Bauhausbuch 10) Munich, 1926.
p. 99 Schroeder House: T. Brown, *The Work of Gerrit Rietveld, Architect*, Utrecht and Cambridge, Mass., 1958, contains a useful discussion of the design process of the house.
p. 101 Barren Rationalism: J. P. Oud, 'Über die zukünftige Baukunst und ihre architektonischen Möglichkeiten', 1921, eventually published in Oud, *Holländische Architektur*, 1926.

Chapter 8. Le Corbusier's Quest for Ideal Form

p. 104 Motto: Le Corbusier, *Towards a New Architecture*, p. 31. I have altered Etchell's translation of the French 'volumes' to 'volumes', rather than 'masses', as this seems more precise.
International Style: see below, Chapter 13, for a more intricate discussion of 'this shared language of expression'. While internationalist cultural tendencies were influential in the 1920s, the term 'International Style' did not gain general currency until the 1930s, particularly after Alfred Barr used it in connection with the Museum of Modern Art show on modern architecture in 1932: see Chapter 13.
Le Corbusier Formative Years: the number of books and articles on Le Corbusier is vast. Von Moos, *Le Corbusier: Elemente einer Synthese*, provides a useful overall introduction. Peter Serenyi, *Le Corbusier in Perspective*, Englewood Cliffs, N.J., 1975, supplies an anthology of writings on him, and an extensive bibliography. For the architect's formation see: M. Gauthier, *Le Corbusier – ou l'architecture au service de l'homme*, Paris, 1934; Paul Turner, 'The Beginnings of Le Corbusier's Education, 1902–7', *Art Bulletin*, 53, June 1971, pp. 214–24. For the gradual emergence of Le Corbusier's architectural system see William Curtis, 'Le Corbusier: the Evolution of his Architectural Language and its Crystallization in the Villa Savoye at Poissy', *Le Corbusier/English Architecture 1930s*, Open University, 1975. Throughout this chapter it is useful to consult the *Oeuvre complète 1910–1929*.
p. 105 Travels: Charles Edouard Jeanneret, *Le Voyage d'Orient*, Paris, 1966.
p. 106 Own Antiquity: James Ackerman is the historian in question.
p. 107 Amédée Ozenfant: *Foundations of Modern Art*, New York, 1952.
Amédée Ozenfant and Charles E. Jeanneret, *Après le Cubisme*, Paris, 1919. See also Christopher Green and John Golding, *Léger and Purist Paris*, London, 1970.
Platonism: see Banham, *Theory and Design*, p. 211.
p. 108 L'Esprit Nouveau, Paris, 1919–25. The quotation is

from no. 1, October 1920. Reproduced, *Towards a New Architecture*, p. 83.

p. 108 Le Corbusier: *Towards a New Architecture*, pp. 16, 31.

p. 109 Le Corbusier: *Towards a New Architecture*, pp. 124–5.

p. 110 Wyndham Lewis: *Time and Western Man*, New York, 1929, for 'upper middle class bohemia'.

Le Corbusier: *Towards a New Architecture*, p. 92. For details of Maison La Roche, see R. Walden's article in Walden (ed.), *The Open Hand*.

Type: see A. Ozenfant and C. E. Jeanneret, *La Peinture moderne*, Paris, 1926, passage cited by Banham, *Theory and Design*, p. 211.

Plan: Le Corbusier, *Towards a New Architecture*, p. 166.

p. 113 Le Corbusier: *Oeuvre complète*, *1910–1929*, p. 130.

p. 116 Le Corbusier: *Oeuvre complète*, *1910–1929*, p. 140; *Towards a New Architecture*, p. 89.

p. 117 Palladio: Colin Rowe, 'The Mathematics of the Ideal Villa: Palladio and Le Corbusier Compared', *Architectural Review*, 101, March 1947, pp. 101–4.

Chapter 9. Walter Gropius, German Expressionism, and the Bauhaus

p. 118 Motto: Gropius, 'The Development of Modern Industrial Architecture', 1913; the same sentiments were expressed in almost exactly the same words by Gropius in *Idee und Aufbau des Staatlichen Bauhausses Weimar*, Weimar, 1923.

Walter Gropius: essay in *Ja Stimmen des Arbeitsrates für Kunst in Berlin*, Berlin, 1919, p. 32.

Bruno Taut: *Alpine Architektur*, 1919; for translation see D. Sharp (ed.), *Glass Architecture by Paul Scheerbart and Alpine Architecture by Bruno Taut*, London, 1972; *Die Stadtkrone*, Jena, 1919.

p. 119 Bauhaus Proclamation: Walter Gropius, 'Idee und Aufbau ...' ('Programme of the Staatliche bauhaus in Weimar'), April 1919; cited by Banham, *Theory and Design*, p. 277. The best analysis of the ideas and events leading to the Bauhaus is to be found in Marcel Franciscono, *Walter Gropius and the Creation of the Bauhaus in Weimar: The Ideals and Artistic Theories of its Founding Years*, Urbana, Ill., 1971.

p. 120 Adolf Behne: review of Scheerbart's *Glasarchitektur*, 1918–19; see Benton and Benton, *Architecture and Design*, p. 77.

p. 121 Expressionism: for a simple introduction. Dennis Sharp, *Modern Architecture and Expressionism*, London, 1966; see also W. Pehnt, *Expressionist Architecture*, London, 1973; J. M. Richards and N. Pevsner (ed.), *The Anti-Rationalists*, London, 1973. While 'Expressionism' is not a happy historical label, it should be mentioned that architects of an 'expressionist' tendency were played down by Giedion and Hitchcock particularly, in their major books on 20th-century architecture. The answer to this neglect is not to overplay the importance of an 'ism' but to delve deeper into the ideas and inspirations of each architect.

p. 122 Mendelsohn: see Arnold Whittick, *Eric Mendelsohn*, Leonard Hill, 1964; O. Beyer (ed.), *Erich Mendelsohn: Letters of An Architect*, New York, 1967; E. Mendelsohn, *Das Gesamtschaffen des Architekten—Skizzen, Entwürfe, Bauten*, Berlin, 1930.

Einstein Tower: Erich Mendelsohn, lecture given to Architectura et Amicitia, 1923, cited by Banham, *Theory and Design*, p. 182, and reproduced in original in Mendelsohn, *Das Gesamtschaffen des Architekten*.

p. 123 Mies: Philip Johnson, *Mies van der Rohe*, New York, 1947; P. Westheim, 'Mies van der Rohe: Entwicklung eines Architekten', *Das Kunstblatt*, 2, February 1927, pp. 52 ff.

Utopian Content in Glass Skyscrapers: William Curtis, 'Der Wolkenkratzer—Realität und Utopie', in *Die Zwanziger Jahre Kontraste eines Jahrzehnts*, Zurich, 1973, pp. 44–7.

p. 124 Mies, Skyscrapers: see Mies van der Rohe, 'Hochhaus—projekt für Bahnhof Friedrichstrasse in Berlin', in *Frühlicht*, ed. B. Taut, 1922; translated in Johnson, *Mies van der Rohe*, p. 182, as 'Two Glass Skyscrapers of 1922'.

Le Corbusier: *Towards a New Architecture*, p. 28.

Mies van der Rohe: 'Working Theses 1923', G, vol. 1, 1923; translated in Uhlrich Conrads, *Programs and Manifestoes of 20th Century Architecture*, London, 1970, p. 74.

p. 126 Walter Gropius: *Idee und Aufbau des Staatlichen Bauhausses Weimar*, 1923; I have followed Banham's translation, *Theory and Design*, pp. 279 ff.

p. 127 Bauhaus Criticisms: K. Nonn, 'The State Garbage Supplies (The Staatliche Bauhaus in Weimar)', 1924; cited by Benton and Benton, *Architecture and Design*, p. 129. For further discussion of the Bauhaus see Hans Wingler, *Das Bauhaus, 1919–1933*, Cologne, 1962; for political debates see Barbara Miller-Lane, *Architecture and Politics in Germany, 1918–1945*, Cambridge, Mass., 1968.

p. 129 Golden Age: see particularly L. Moholy-Nagy, *Von Material zu Architektur*, Munich, 1928; O. Schlemmer, L. Moholy-Nagy and F. Molnar, *The Theatre of the Bauhaus*, Middletown, Conn., 1964; G. Adams, 'Memories of a Bauhaus Student', *Architectural Review*, September 1968, pp. 192 ff.; W. Kandinsky, *Punkt und Linie zu Fläche*, Munich, 1925; P. Klee, *Pädagogisches Skizzenbuch*, Munich, 1926; W. Gropius, I. Gropius and H. Bayer, *Bauhaus 1919–1928*, New York, 1938; W. Gropius, *Internationale Architektur*, Munich, 1925; W. Gropius, *The New Architecture and the Bauhaus*, London, 1935.

p. 131 Mies van der Rohe, Objectivity: see Banham, *Theory and Design*, p. 271; see also F. Schmalenbach, 'The Term Neue Sachlichkeit', *Art Bulletin*, 22, September 1940.

Weissenhofsiedlung as Kasbah: postcard reproduced in Benton and Benton, *Architecture and Design*, ill. 23.

Hannes Meyer: C. Schnaidt, Hannes Meyer, *Buildings, Projects and Writings*, London, 1965.

Chapter 10. Architecture and Revolution in Russia

p. 132 Motto: A. and V. Vesnin, from *Sovremennaya Architektura* (Contemporary Architecture), 1926. This chapter is indebted to Anatole Kopp, *Town and Revolution, Soviet Architecture and City Planning 1917–1935*, New York, 1970, originally published as *Ville et Revolution*, Paris, 1967.

Prolecult: see El Lissitzky, *Russia: An Architecture for World Revolution*, London, 1970 (originally published as *Russland: Die Reconstruktion der Architektur in der Sowjetunion*, Vienna, 1930), pp. 14 ff., 'Translator's Introduction', by Eric Dluhosch; see also Camilla Gray, *The Great Experiment: Russian Art, 1863–1922*, London, 1962.

p. 135 Tatlin's Monument: N. Punin, 'Tatlin's Monument', 1922; cited by Benton and Benton, *Architecture and Design*, p. 86; for further discussion of the symbolic implications of spirals see Berthold Lubetkin, 'Architectural Thought since the Revolution', *Architectural Review*, May 1932, pp. 201–14.

p. 138 F. Yalovkin: 'OSA [Association of Contemporary Architects] Vopra and OSA', 1929, cited by Benton, *Documents*, p. 30. For an incisive discussion of different ideological positions in the 1920s in the Soviet Union, see Lubetkin, 'Architectural Thought since the Revolution'; also, Tafuri and Dal Co, *Modern Architecture*, pp. 204 ff.

p. 143 Palace of Soviets: for a discussion of the change in official policy see Hans Schmidt, 'The Soviet Union and Modern Architecture', 1932; in English edition of Lissitzky, *Russia: Architecture for a World Revolution*, p. 218.

Chapter 11. Skyscraper and Suburb: America between the Wars

p. 144 Motto: Sullivan, 'The Tall Office Building Artistically Considered', *Lippincotts Magazine*, March 1896.
'291': this was the name of the gallery opened by Alfred Stieglitz in 1908, in which he showed the avant-garde work of the 'Photo Secessionist' movement.
Marsden Hartley: 'Art – and the Personal Life', *Creative Art*, 2, June 1928.
Lewis Mumford: *The Brown Decades: A Study of the Arts in America, 1865–1895*, New York, 1931.
p. 146 Le Corbusier: *Towards a New Architecture*, p. 42.
Skyscrapers: see Carl Condit, *The Chicago School of Architecture*, Chicago, 1964, specially for the early stages of the type; Vincent Scully, *American Architecture and Urbanism*, London, 1969 is a useful overview, as is J. Burchard and Bush Brown, *American Architecture: a Social and Cultural History*, Boston, 1961; see also W. Weisman, 'A New View of Skyscraper History', in *The Rise of an American Architecture*, ed. Edgar Kaufmann, Jr., New York, 1970.
Tribune: *Chicago Tribune Competition*, Chicago Tribune, 1922, contains illustrations of the entries and the programme sent to competitors.
p. 147 Glass Skyscrapers: for the contrast in ideology between Europe and USA, see Curtis, 'Der Wolkenkratzer— Realität und Utopie' (see note to p. 123), and Manfredo Tafuri, 'La Dialectique de l'absurde Europe–USA: les avatars de l'idéologie du gratte-ciel 1918–1974', *L'Architecture d'Aujourd'hui*, 178, March/April 1975. pp. 1–16.
p. 149 Reliance Building: see Giedion, *Space, Time and Architecture*, p. 386.
New York Skyscrapers: see Rosemary Bletter and Cervin Robinson, *Skyscraper Style – Art Deco New York*, New York, 1975; also Jordy, *American Buildings and Their Architects*, vol. 4, and W. A. Starrett, *Skyscrapers and the Men who Built Them*, New York, 1928.
p. 151 Louis Sullivan: *Kindergarten Chats and Other Writings*, New York, 1947, p. 77; written in 1918.
Skyscraper as Tool: Le Corbusier, *Quand les cathédrales étaient blanches: voyage aux pays des timides*, Paris, 1937, p. 62, author's translation.
p. 153 Hugh Ferris: *The Metropolis of Tomorrow*, New York, 1929.
Rockefeller Center: see Jordy, *American Buildings and Their Architects*, vol. 4, and C. Krinsky, *Rockefeller Center*, London and New York, 1978.
p. 154 Frank Lloyd Wright: *A Testament*, New York, 1972, p. 111.
p. 155 Schindler: see E. McCoy, *Five California Architects*, New York, 1960; David Gebhard, *Schindler*, London, 1971; Reyner Banham, *Los Angeles, The Architecture of Four Ecologies*, Harmondsworth, 1971.

p. 157 Richard Neutra: *Wie Baut Amerika?* Stuttgart, 1927.
p. 158 PSFS: George Howe, cited by Jordy in *American Buildings and Their Architects*, vol. 4, pp. 47–83.
Hitchcock and Johnson: *The International Style*, p. 20.

Chapter 12. The Ideal Community: Alternatives to the Industrial City

p. 159 Motto: Karel Teige, 'Contemporary International Architecture', 1928, in Benton and Benton, *Architecture and Design*, p. 200.
Industrial City: see L. Benevolo, *Le Origini dell'Urbanistica Moderna*, Bari, 1963, translated into English as *The Origins of Modern Town-Planning*, Cambridge, Mass., 1967. Françoise Choay, *The Modern City, Planning in the 19th Century*, New York, 1969.
Friedrich Engels: *The Condition of the Working Classes in England in 1844* (tr. Wischnewetzky), London, 1952, p. 49.
Critiques of Industrial City: see Benevolo, *History of Modern Architecture*, pp. 127 ff., and Egbert, *Social Radicalism*, pp. 133–43 for Fourier, pp. 67–77 for Marx, p. 104 for Engels, also pp. 117–19. For Fourier's phalanstère see Benevolo, *The Origins of Modern Town-Planning*, p. 56, and Charles Fourier, *Traité de l'association domestique-agricole* in *Oeuvre complètes*, Paris, 1841, vol. 4, pp. 500–2.
p. 160 Camillo Sitte: *Der Städtebau nach seinem künstlerischen Grundsätzen*, Vienna, 1889, translated as *City Planning According to Artistic Principles*, London, 1965. See G. and C. Collins, *Camillo Sitte and the Birth of Modern City Planning*, London, 1965. For Soria y Mata and the linear city see G. Collins, 'Linear Planning Throughout the World', *Journal of Society of Architectural Historians*, 18, October 1959, pp. 74–93.
Ebenezer Howard: *Tomorrow: a Peaceful Path to Real Reform*, London, 1898, re-issued with slight changes as *Garden Cities of Tomorrow* in 1902.
p. 161 John Ruskin: *Sesame and Lilies*, London, 1865.
Garnier: *Une Cité Industrielle*, Paris, 1917; see also D. Wiebenson, *Tony Garnier: the Cité Industrielle*, New York, 1969.
p. 162 Tafuri and Dal Co: *Modern Architecture*, p. 110.
P. 164 Le Corbusier City Planning: see Le Corbusier, *Urbanisme*, Paris, 1925, translated as *The City of Tomorrow*, Cambridge, Mass., 1971; Norma Evanson, *The Machine and the Grand Design*, New York, 1969; Robert Fishman, *Urban Utopias in the twentieth Century*, New York, 1977; P. Boudon, *Lived-In Architecture*, Cambridge, Mass., 1972; Brian Taylor, *Le Corbusier at Pessac*, Cambridge, Mass., 1972.
p. 166 Monastery: see Peter Serenyi, 'Le Corbusier, Fourier, and the Monastery of Ema', *Art Bulletin*, 49, 1967, pp. 277–86.
Frankfurt: see B. Miller-Lane, *Architecture and Politics in Germany, 1919–1945*, Cambridge, Mass., 1968, Tafuri and Dal Co, *Modern Architecture*, and G. Uhlig, 'Town Planning in the Weimar Republic', *Architectural Association Quarterly*, 11, no. 1, 1979, pp. 24 ff.
p. 170 Oud: Hitchcock, *J.J.P. Oud*, Paris, 1931.
Soviet Urbanism: see Berthold Lubetkin, 'Recent Developments of Town-Planning in the USSR', *Architectural Review*, May 1932, pp. 215 ff.; K. Frampton, 'Notes on Soviet Urbanism 1917–32', *Architects' Year Book*, 12, 1968, pp. 238–52.
El Lissitzky: *Russia: an Architecture for World Revolution*, London, 1970, p. 59.

p. 171 N. A. Milyutin: *Sotsgorod: The Problem of Building Socialist Cities*, Cambridge, Mass., 1974.

Karl Marx Hof: Tafuri and Dal Co, *Modern Architecture*, p. 193.

C.I.A.M.: 'Declaration of Aims', La Sarraz, Switzerland, 1928; see Benton and Benton, *Architecture and Design*, for excerpts; also Benevelo, *History of Modern Architecture*, vol. 2, p. 497.

p. 173 Charter of Athens: see Benevelo, *History of Modern Architecture*, vol. 2, p. 539; for Gropius on high-rise dwellings see 'Flach, Mittel- oder Hochbau?', *Rationelle Bebauungsweisen*, Stuttgart, 1931, p. 26. the doctrines of the Athens Charter later appeared as José Luis Sert, *Can Our Cities Survive?*, Cambridge, Mass., 1942

Chapter 13. The International Style, The Individual Talent, and The Myth of Functionalism

p. 174 Motto: Gombrich, *Art and Illusion*, London, 1960, p. 78.

Hitchcock and Johnson, *The International Style*, p. 19

p. 177 El Lissitzky, *Russia: An Architecture for a World Revolution*, London, 1970, p. 32.

Van Nelle: for Le Corbusier's panegyric see *Plans*, 12, February 1932, p. 40.

p. 180 Kenneth Frampton: 'The Humanist versus the Utilitarian Ideal', *Architectural Design*, 38, 1968, pp. 134–6.

Hannes Meyer and Wittwer: Report on League of Nations Entry, cited by Frampton, 'The Humanist versus the Utilitarian Ideal'.

R. Buckminster Fuller: passage cited by Banham, *Theory and Design*, p. 325. See also R. W. Marks, *The Dymaxion World of Buckminster Fuller*, New York, 1960. Evidently Banham shared Fuller's sentiments, since he concluded his book (pp. 329–30): 'It may well be that what we have hitherto understood as architecture, and what we are beginning to understand of technology are incompatible disciplines. The architect who proposes to run with technology knows that he will be in fast company, and that in order to keep up, he may have to emulate the Futurists and dump his whole cultural load.' This seems to be a classic case of the confusion of means and ends: by what law should art keep abreast of technical change? Moreover, Fuller's own Dymaxion House was scarcely without symbolic overtones, however functional it may have appeared. As an aesthetic arrangement, admittedly, the building was scarcely inspiring.

p. 182 William Jordy: on 'objectivity' in *American Buildings and Their Architects*, vol. 4, p. 182; by the same author, see 'The Symbolic Essence of Modern European Architecture of the Twenties and its Continuing Influence', *Journal of the Society of Architectural Historians*, 22, October 1963, pp. 177–87. While 'pure functionalism' may be an impossibility, it would be wrong to suggest that the leading architects of the modern movement were in favour of aesthetic wilfulness or arbitrariness. A rigorous functional and structural rationale was used as a starting-point for aesthetic and symbolic expression. See Le Corbusier, *Towards a New Architecture*, p. 187: 'By the use of inert materials and *starting from* conditions more or less utilitarian, you have established certain relationships which have aroused my emotions. This is Architecture.'

p. 183 Henri Focillon, *The Life of Forms in Art*, trans. G. Kubler, C. Hogan, New York, 1958, p. 74.

p. 185 Mies van der Rohe: The passage was written in 1928, but is clearly relevant to the Barcelona Pavilion. See also J. Bier, 'Mies van der Rohes Reichspavillon in Barcelona', *Die Form*, August 1929, pp. 23–30. For detailed analysis of critical and historical reactions to the Barcelona Pavillon see J. Bonta, *Anatomia de la interpretacion in arquitectura: resegne semiotica de la critica de la Pabellon de Barcelona de Mies van der Rohe*, Barcelona, 1975.

Chapter 14. The Image and Idea of Le Corbusier's Villa Savoye at Poissy

p. 186 Motto: Le Corbusier, *Towards a New Architecture*, p. 165. For detailed discussion of the Villa, see Curtis, 'Le Corbusier: the Evolution of his Architectural Language and its Crystallization in the Villa Savoye at Poissy', in *Le Corbusier/English Architecture 1930s*, Open University 1975.

p. 191 Fresh Air: for Le Corbusier's own description of the Villa Savoye, see *Précisions sur un état présent de l'architecture et de l'urbanisme*, Paris, 1930, pp. 136 ff. 'Air circulates freely, light abounds and penetrates everywhere.'

p. 192 Standards: Le Corbusier, *Towards a New Architecture*, p. 123.

Design Process: see Tim Benton, 'Radiovision, Villa Savoye: Preliminary Drawings', Open University 1975, and Max Risselada, 'Le Corbusier and Pierre Jeanneret, Ontwerpen voor de woning 1919–1929', exhibition catalogue, School of Architecture, Delft, 1980.

p. 194 Le Corbusier: *Towards a New Architecture*, p. 189.

p. 195 Idealism, Rationalism: see P. Turner, 'The Beginnings of Le Corbusier's Education', *Art Bulletin*, June 1971, and Curtis, 'Le Corbusier: the Evolution of his Language and its Crystallization in the Villa Savoye at Poissy'.

Chapter 15. Wright and Le Corbusier in the 1930s

p. 196 Motto: Frank Lloyd Wright, 'Broadacre City, A New Community Plan', *Architectural Record*, 77, no. 4, April 1935, pp. 243–4.

p. 199 Edgar Kaufmann Jr.: 'introduction', to D. Hoffmann, *Frank Lloyd Wright's Fallingwater, the House and its History*, New York, 1978.

p. 200 Frank Lloyd Wright, 'The Cardboard House', 1931; Benton and Benton, *Architecture and Design*, p. 61.

Frank Lloyd Wright: cited by Olgivanna Lloyd Wright, *Frank Lloyd Wright: his Life, his Work, his Words*, New York, 1966, p. 159.

Frank Lloyd Wright, on rock ledges, 'The Meaning of Materials – Stone', *Architectural Record*, 63, April 1928, pp. 350, 356.

Falling Water and Johnson Wax: for ingenious interpretations of these buildings see Smith, *Frank Lloyd Wright*.

p.202 Usonian Houses: see J. Sergeant, *Frank Lloyd Wright's Usonian Houses*, New York, 1976.

p.203 Heat Gain: see Reyner Banham, *The Architecture of the Well Tempered Environment*, London, 1969, for discussion of Le Corbusier's glazing.

p. 204   Formal Changes: see Peter Serenyi, 'Le Corbusier's Changing Attitude toward Form', *Journal of Society of Architectural Historians*, 24, March 1965, pp. 15–23.

p.205   Pavillon Suisse: for extensive discussion of design process and meaning see W. Curtis, 'Ideas of Structure and the Structure of Ideas: Le Corbusier's Pavillon Suisse, 1930–1931', *Journal of Society of Architectural Historians*, 40, December 1981.

p.206   Maurin: in *Oeuvre complète 1929–34*, p. 84, caption to illustration of *pilotis*. For 'à redent' housing, see Le Corbusier, *Ville radieuse*, Paris 1933, p. 158.

Le Corbusier: in *Oeuvre complète 1929–34*, p. 19.

p. 207   Syndicalism and the Ville Radieuse: see Kenneth Frampton, 'The City of Dialectic', *Architectural Design*, 39, October 1969, pp. 515–46; also R. Fishman, *Urban Utopias in the Twentieth Century*, New York, 1977, for a discussion of Le Corbusier's politics in the thirties; and Serenyi, 'Le Corbusier, Fourier and the Monastery of Ema', *Art Bulletin*, 1967.

p. 208   Reyner Banham: for extensive discussion of CIAM doctrines and reactions against them see *The New Brutalism*, especially pp. 70ff.

Algiers: Stanislaus Von Moos, 'Von den Femmes d'Alger zum Plan Obus', *Archithèse*, 1, 1971, pp. 25–37; see also unpublished essay by Catherine J. Dean on the various Algiers schemes, their political context, and Le Corbusier's sensitivity to the pre-existing site and culture, MIT, School of Architecture, 1978; for a syndicalist reading of Algiers, see M. Macleod, 'Le Corbusier's Plans for Algiers 1930–1936', *Oppositions 16/17*, 1980.

p. 209   Manhattan: see W. Curtis, 'Le Corbusier, Manhattan et le rêve de la ville radieuse', *Archithèse*, 17, 1976, pp. 23–8.

Le Corbusier: *When the Cathedrals Were White*, New York, 1947, the English translation of *Quand les cathédrals étaient blanches: voyage aux pays des timides*, Paris, 1937.

p. 210   Broadacre City: for a flavour of Wright's urban thinking, see Frank Lloyd Wright, *The Disappearing City*, New York, 1932; also Fishman, *Urban Utopias in the Twentieth Century*.

Frank Lloyd Wright: *When Democracy Builds*, Chicago, 1945, p. 67.

Chapter 16. Totalitarian Critiques of the Modern Movement

p. 211   Motto: Adolf Hitler, 'Speech on Art', 11 September 1935; cited by R. Taylor, *The Word in Stone, the Role of Architecture in National Socialist Ideology*, Berkeley, Calif., 1974, p. 31.

p. 212   Bauhaus Criticisms: see B. Miller-Lane, *Architecture and Politics in Germany 1919–1945*, Cambridge, Mass., 1968, pp. 69 ff.

Anti-Semitism: see, for example, P. Schultze-Naumburg, *Kunst und Rasse*, Munich, 1929; for Bolshevist innuendoes see Alexander von Senger, *Krisis der Architektur*, Zurich, 1928.

p. 214   Half-Baked Art History: see Taylor, *The Word in Stone*, pp. 83 ff.

Speer: for his own version of events see Albert Speer, *Inside the Third Reich*, New York, 1970.

p. 215   Regionalism: the intention was to mimic directly local styles and patterns of building. The hip roof took on a strong nationalist overtone in contrast to the 'internationalist' flat roof, which was seen as a foreign, rootless import. This overt revival of a vernacular must be contrasted visually and ideologically with the 'modern regionalism' of the 1950s which sought to blend the best of modern architecture and local traditions.

p. 217   Soviet Union in Thirties: see Anatole Kopp, *L'Architecture de la période stalinienne*, Grenoble, 1978. For the reaction against the avant-garde and the re-use of Classicism see the retrospective analysis of the Palace of the Soviets Competition by M. P. Tsapenko, *O Realisticheskykh Osnovakh Sovietskoi Arkhitektury*, Moscow 1952, pp. 73 ff. The Committee in charge announced on 28 February 1932 that 'both new techniques and the best methods of Classical "architecture" should be employed henceforth'.

Official Criticism of Avant-Garde: registered by Vzik, the Central Executive Committee of the Communist Party, 1930, cited by Lubetkin, 'Recent Developments of Town-planning in the USSR', *Architectural Review*, May 1932.

p. 218   Mussolini and Town-Planning: see Spiro Kostoff, *The Third Rome*, Berkeley, Calif., 1977. The best general discussion of Italian architecture in the Fascist period is to be found in Benevelo, *History of Modern Architecture*, vol. 2, pp. 561 ff.

Gruppo 7: see 'Architettura' in *Rassegna italiana*, December 1926. One of the Group's pronouncements was: 'That the new architecture could be compared with that of the distant past.' See also S. Danesi and L. Patetta, *Rationalisme et architecture en Italie 1919–1943*, Venice, 1976, and A. Sartoris, *Gli elementi dell'architettura funzionale*, Milan, 1941.

p. 219   Terragni: see P. Koulermos, 'The Work of Terragni, Lingeri and Italian Rationalism', *Architectural Design*, March 1963; also E. Mantero, *Giuseppe Terragni e la città del razionalismo italiano*, Bari, 1969.

p. 221   Danteum: Thomas Schumacher, 'From Gruppo 7 to the Danteum: a Critical Introduction to Terragni's Relazione Sul Danteum', *Oppositions 9*, 1977, pp. 92–105; for Terragni quotation, see p. 92.

Chapter 17. The Spread of Modern Architecture to England and Scandinavia

p. 223   Motto: Hitchcock, *The International Style*, Preface to 1966 edition, p. xiii.

England in the Thirties: H. R. Hitchcock and L. K. Bauer, *Modern Architecture in England*, New York, 1937, catalogue of an exhibition at the Museum of Modern Art; J. M. Richards, *An Introduction to Modern Architecture*, Harmondsworth, 1940; Anthony Jackson, *The Politics of Architecture, a History of Modern Architecture in Britain*, London, 1970; W. Curtis, 'The Modern Movement in England 1930–9; thoughts on the political content and associations of the International Style', in *Le Corbusier/English Architecture 1930s*, Open University, 1975.

p. 225   Lubetkin: see W. Curtis, 'Berthold Lubetkin or "Socialist" Architecture in the Diaspora', *Archithèse*, 12, 1974, pp. 42–8; also R. Furneaux Jordan, 'Lubetkin', *Architectural Review*, July 1955, pp. 36–44.

p. 226   Le Corbusier: 'The Vertical Garden City', *Architectural Review*, 79, January 1936, pp. 9–10.

p. 227   Lucas, Connell, Ward: see *Architectural Association Journal*, November 1956, special issue.

p. 228 J. M. Richards: 'The Condition of Modern Architecture and the Principle of Anonymity', *Circle*, eds. N. Gabo, J. L. Martin, B. Nicholson, London 1937.
High Point II: *Architectural Review*, 83, October 1938, pp. 161–4; also, Anthony Cox, 'High Point Two, North Hill, Highgate', *Focus*, 2, 1938, pp. 76–9.
p.229 Aalto's Absorption of Modern Architecture: see P. D. Pearson, *Alvar Aalto and the International Style*, New York, 1978; for a general treatment, see Giedion, *Space, Time and Architecture*, 4th edn., also Benevelo, *A History of Modern Architecture*, vol. 2, pp. 607 ff. For Paimio, see P. Morton Shand, 'Tuberculosis Sanatorium, Paimio, Finland', *Architectural Review*, September 1933, pp. 85–90.
p. 230 Aalto and Duiker: see Pearson, *Alvar Aalto and the International Style*, p. 87.
p. 232 Alvar Aalto: see essay entitled 'National Planning and Cultural Goals', 1949, for his reflections on nature, excerpt in G. Schildt (ed.), *Alvar Aalto, Sketches*, Cambridge, Mass., 1978.

Chapter 18. The Continuity of Older Traditions

p. 234 Motto: Reginald Blomfield, 'Is Modern Architecture on the Right Track?', *The Listener*, 10, 1933, p. 124.
Survivals: it is to Hitchcock's credit that he included a chapter entitled 'Architecture Called Traditional in the Twentieth Century' in *Architecture 19th and 20th Centuries*.
p. 236 Art Deco: see G. Veronesi, *Style and Design 1909–29*, New York, 1968; D. Gebhard, *The Richfield Building 1926–1928*, Los Angeles, 1970; Bevis Hillier, *Art Deco in the 1920s and 1930s*, London, 1968.
p. 237 American Eclecticism between the Wars: W. Kidney, *The Architecture of Choice, Eclecticism in America, 1880–1930*, New York, 1974.
p. 238 Lincoln Memorial: for details of the commission see U.S. Office of Public Buildings and Public Parks of the National Capital, *The Lincoln Memorial, Washington, D.C.*, Washington, 1927.
p. 239 New Delhi: the most interesting assessment of Lutyens' designs is still Robert Byron's, in *Architectural Review*, 69, January 1931.
p. 241 Asplund, Imagery: for an intriguing attempt at explaining metaphors within Asplund's work, see S. Wrede, *The Architecture of Eric Gunnar Asplund*, Cambridge, Mass., 1979.
p. 242 Classicism: at the time of writing (1980), it is fashionable to insist that modern architects cut themselves off from all precedent and even to ignore the differences between profound and superficial classical usages. For the cheap stylism at present fashionable in America, particularly, see Chapter 28 below.
Blomfield: 'Is Modern Architecture on the Right Track?'
p. 243 Blomfield: 'Is Modern Architecture on the Right Track?'; the fact that Blomfield identified modern architecture with 'functionalism' is not entirely his own fault. In England in the thirties the functional and moral aspects of modern architecture were stressed by its supporters at the expense of formal and symbolic qualities. See, for example, the critical writings of N. Pevsner and J. M. Richards in this period, or F. R. S. Yorke, *The Modern House*, London, 1934.

Chapter 19, Modern Architecture in America: Immigration and Consolidation

p. 258 Motto: for Giedion on tradition see *Architecture You and Me*, Cambridge, Mass., 1958.
p. 259 Gropius and Breuer in America: see particularly Giedion, *Space, Time and Architecture*, vol. 4; also W. Curtis, *Boston: Forty Years of Modern Architecture*, Boston, Institute of Contemporary Arts, 1980, for discussion of diaspora; and Jordy, *American Buildings and Their Architects*, volume 4, for Breuer's problems of transplanting modern architectural ideas from Europe to America.
p. 260 Harvard: among those to study under Gropius in his early years as a teacher were Barnes, Rudolph, Johnson, and Pei. The version of modern architecture they absorbed was somewhat puritanical and ever in danger of lapsing into a glib, abstract formalism or else into a skin-deep utilitarianism. What Robert Venturi was later (in *Complexity and Contradiction in Architecture*, 1966) to pillory as 'orthodox modern architecture' suffered from just such ills. Modern architecture was bound to go awry when divorced from the emotional and utopian *Weltanschauung* which produced it. It is testimony to the power of the architectural historian as a myth-maker that Giedion managed to convey Gropius as if he represented the core positions of the modern movement, whereas, by the late thirties, his direction seemed a debased and prettified version of the 'International Style' of the twenties, especially by contrast with his earlier works or with the inventiveness of Le Corbusier and Aalto in the same period.
p. 261 Mies: for a simple introduction to Mies van der Rohe's entire career see Peter Blake, *Mies van der Rohe: Architecture and Structure*, New York, 1960, also P. Carter, *Mies van der Rohe at Work*, New York, 1974.
p. 262 Mies and Classicism: Colin Rowe, 'Neoclassicism and Modern Architecture', *Oppositions 1*, 1973, pp. 1–26.
p. 263 Colin Rowe: 'Introduction', *Five Architects*, New York, 1975.
p. 264 Lake Shore: for a most subtle analysis of this building and of Mies van der Rohe's use of the steel frame, see Jordy, *American Buildings and Their Architects*, vol. 4, pp. 221 ff.
Mies van der Rohe, in Prologue to W. Blaser, *Mies Van Der Rohe*, New York, 1965.
p. 266 Imitations of Mies: it is surely a fundamental characteristic of all traditions that seminal works are imitated for superficialities of language until a sort of slang results. In case this argument sounds too haughty let me say that Mies van der Rohe in particular learned many lessons from the existing industrial vernaculars of commercial frame buildings. One suspects that the relationship between 'high' and 'low' architectural traditions always works both ways.
Mechanical Ventilation: see Banham, *The Architecture of the Well Tempered Environment*, London, 1969, pp. 226 ff., for a discussion of the interrelationship between air-conditioning and the curtain wall.
p. 267 UN: see Le Corbusier, *UN Headquarters*, New York, 1947.
p. 268 Modulor: Le Corbusier, *The Modulor, a Harmonious Measure to the Human Scale, Universally Applied to Architecture and Mechanics*, Cambridge, Mass., 1954.
Guggenheim: for a detailed analysis see Jordy, *American Buildings and their Architects*, vol. 4, p. 279.
Frank Lloyd Wright, in *Solomon R. Guggenheim Museum* (brochure put out by museum, New York, 1960).
p. 270 Wright: in *Solomon R. Guggenheim Museum*.

Wright: on Unity Temple, *Autobiography*, New York, 1932, pp. 138 ff.

Chapter 20. Form and Meaning in the Late Works of Le Corbusier

p. 271 Motto: Focillon, *The Life of Forms in Art*, p. 74.
Surrealism: arguably the totemic fascinations of the Surrealists influenced the primitivism already visible in Le Corbusier's paintings and buildings of the 1930s. One suspects that his interests in multiple meanings and hermetic erotic references may be related too. For the invention of the bizarre 'Ubu' sculptures, see Le Corbusier, *New World of Space*, New York, 1948, p. 23.
p. 273 James Stirling: 'Ronchamp: Le Corbusier's Chapel and the Crisis of Rationalism', *Architectural Review*, 119, March 1956, pp. 155–61. For the patronage of Ronchamp, see Martin Purdy, 'Le Corbusier and the Theological Program', in Walden (ed.), *The Open Hand*, p. 286.
Le Corbusier: *Oeuvre complète 1946–52*, p. 88.
Le Corbusier: *The Modulor*, Cambridge, Mass., 1954, p. 32. For influences on Ronchamp, see Von Moos, *Le Corbusier, Elemente einer Synthese*, p. 323.
p. 274 La Tourette: see Serenyi, 'Le Corbusier, Fourier, and the Monastery of Ema', *Art Bulletin*, 1967; also Purdy, 'Le Corbusier and the Theological Program', and also Colin Rowe, 'Dominican Monastery of La Tourette, Eveux-sur-Arbresle, Lyons', *Architectural Review*, 129, 1961, pp. 400–1.
Le Corbusier: *Oeuvre complète 1957–1965*, p. 49.
p. 275 A. and P. Smithson: *Ordinariness and Light*, London, 1970, p. 169.
James Stirling: 'Garches to Jaoul: Le Corbusier as Domestic Architect in 1927 and 1953', *Architectual Review*, 118, 1955, pp. 145–51.
p. 276 Second Machine Age: once again one senses the epochal style of Le Corbusier's historical and social thinking. For a lengthy discussion of the philosophy underlying Le Corbusier's late works see W. Curtis in Curtis and Sekler (ed.), *Le Corbusier at Work*.
Sarabhai: for brief observations on Ahmadabad patronage conditions see Peter Serenyi, 'Le Corbusier in India', exhibition catalogue, Northeastern University, Boston 1980.
Chandigarh: for the broad principles of the urban layout see Norma Evenson, *Chandigarh*, Berkeley, Calif., 1966; for a sceptical analysis, Sten Nilsson, *The New Capitals of India, Pakistan and Bangladesh*, Lund, 1973.
p. 277 Open Hand: see Patricia Sekler, 'Le Corbusier, Ruskin, the Tree and the Open Hand' and S. Von Moos, 'The Politics of the Open Hand: Notes on Le Corbusier and Nehru at Chandigarh', in Walden (ed.), *The Open Hand*, pp. 42 ff. and 412 ff. The Le Corbusier quotation is from a letter cited by Von Moos, note 65.
p. 279 Parliament, Sources and Meaning: see Von Moos, 'The Politics of the Open Hand', also W. Curtis, *Fragments of Invention: The Sketchbooks of Le Corbusier*, Cambridge, Mass., 1981. The latter discusses the portico/dome theme, the origins and multiple meanings of the lighting funnel, and the way in which Le Corbusier's sketchbooks reveal his reactions to, and transformation of, such Indian phenomena as oxcarts and bull horns.
p. 280 Observatory, Sun, etc.: see Le Corbusier, *Oeuvre complète, 1952–57*, p. 94.

P. Nehru: from the inauguration speech, 1963, see Von Moos, 'The Politics of the Open Hand'.
p. 281 Carpenter Center: see Curtis in *Le Corbusier at Work*, for a detailed analysis of the building's form, meaning and genesis, especially Chapters 3 and 11.
p. 282 Le Corbusier: *Oeuvre complète 1957–65*, p. 54.

Chapter 21, The Unité D'Habitation at Marseilles as a Collective Housing Prototype

p. 284 Motto: Kubler, *The Shape of Time*, Yale 1962, p. 33.
Unité: see Le Corbusier, *L'Unité d'Habitation de Marseille*, Souillac, 1950.
p. 286 Lewis Mumford: 'The Sky Line: the Marseille "Folly"', *New Yorker*, 5 October 1957, pp. 76 ff.
p. 287 Ships: see Von Moos, 'Wohnkollektiv, Hospiz und Dampfer', *Archithèse*, 12, 1971, pp. 30–41.
Béton Brut: see Curtis and Sekler (ed.), *Le Corbusier at Work*, p. 166, for explanation of the architect's intentions at Marseille.
Aix: for the importance of this meeting to the new, younger generation see Banham, *The New Brutalism*, p. 70.
p. 288 Team X or 'Team Ten': see Smithson (ed.), *Team 10 Primer*, for a collection of maxims and theories.
ATBAT: 'Atelier de Batisseurs'. The Moroccan housing envisaged courtyards in the air. The architects were aware that many of the future users would come from the south of the Atlas and therefore studied vernaculars from that region when preparing their design.
New Brutalism: evidently the term was invented before there were buildings to constitute a movement: See A. and P. Smithson, 'The New Brutalism', *Architectural Review*, April 1954, pp. 274–5; also Banham, *The New Brutalism*.
p. 289 Alison and Peter Smithson: 'The Built World, Urban Re-Identification', first published *Architectural Design*, June 1955, then in *Ordinariness and Light*, pp. 105–6.
p. 290 Clusters: see William Curtis, 'A Language and a Theme', in Denys Lasdun (ed.), *A Language and a Theme, the Architecture of Denys Lasdun and Partners*, London, 1976, pp. 9 ff.; the Smithsons published an article entitled 'Cluster City – a New Shape for the Community', in *Architectural Design*, 1957, some three years after Lasdun's first clusters.
Van Eyck: see J. Joedicke (ed.), *CIAM '59 in Otterlo*, London 1961; for a full flavour of his ideas, Smithson, *Team 10 Primer*; for the interest in 'place' see Jencks, *Modern Movements*, pp. 301 ff.
p. 291 Atelier 5: The architects were Erwin Fritz, Samuel Gerber, Rolf Hesterberg, Hans Hostettler, Niklaus Morgenthaler, Alfredo Pini.
p. 292 Sert, Peabody Terraces: see Catherine J. Dean, 'The Design Process and Meaning of J. L. Sert's Peabody Terraces at Harvard', unpublished senior thesis, Harvard, Fine Arts, 1976.
p. 294 Pruitt-Igoe: designed by Minoru Yamasaki, 1952–5, was dynamited on 15 July 1972. Until more is known about the reasons this scheme failed, it can only be misleading to claim that the event represents 'the death of modern architecture', as does Jencks, *The Language of Post Modern Architecture*, p. 9.
Lillington Street: see W. Curtis, 'A Century Spanned: Lillington Street Housing, Pimlico by Darbourne and Darke', *Connoisseur*, May 1970, p. 45; for Gordon Cullen's ideas, see *Townscape*, London, 1966.

Chapter 22. Alvar Aalto and the Scandinavian Tradition

p. 296 Motto: Aldo Van Eyck, in Smithson (ed.), *Team 10 Primer*, p. 9.

New Regionalism: see, for example, Sigfried Giedion, 'The New Regionalism', 1954, an essay published in *Architecture You and Me, Diary of a Development*, Cambridge, Mass., 1958, p. 138.

p. 299 Karelian House: see Alvar Aalto, 'Karjalan rakennustaide', *Uusi Suomi*, 1941, translated in Alvar Aalto, *Sketches*, ed. G. Schildt, tr. S. Wrede, Cambridge, Mass., 1968, p. 82. This small volume gives considerable insight into Aalto's preoccupations with landscape formations, ruins and vernacular forms, and into a world view in which the harmony of man and nature was paramount. The most useful introduction to Aalto is otherwise still G. Baird's *Alvar Aalto*, London, 1970. See also R. Glanville, 'Finnish Vernacular Farmhouses', *Architectural Association Quarterly*, 9, no. 1, 1977, pp. 36–52 for analysis of precinct forms in the Nordic vernacular.

p. 301 Delphi: see Aalto, *Sketches*, particularly ills. 9 and 11, drawn in 1953. Aalto seems to have been preoccupied with earth-forms, platforms, steps and public places in Delphi. Analogous elements were used in many of his own civic schemes. Once again one finds a 'modern' architect returning to some of the most archaic roots of architecture.

p. 303 Utzon: little has been written on the architect. For an introduction see Giedion, 'Jorn Utzon and the Third Generation', in the 1967 edition of *Space, Time and Architecture*.

p. 304 Platforms: see 'Platforms and Plateaux: Ideas of a Danish Architect', *Zodiac 10*, Milan, 1962.

p. 305 Philip Drew: *Third Generation*, pp. 15–16.

Jørn Utzon: 'The Sydney Opera House', *Zodiac 14*, Milan, 1965, p. 49.

Chapter 23. Louis I. Kahn and the Challenge of Monumentality

p. 306 Motto: Louis I. Kahn, cited by Jordy, *American Buildings and Their Architects*, vol. 4, p. 361.

Monumentality: see Giedion, *Architecture You and Me*, Cambridge, Mass. 1958, p. 25, for 'The Need for a New Monumentality', formulated in 1943–4. The 'Core of the City' was taken as the theme for CIAM 8 at Hoddesdon, England, July 1951. Giedion recorded his reactions to the proceedings in an essay 'The Humanization of Urban Life', 1951, in *Architecture You and Me*, p. 125. For other views on civic monumentality in this period see Henry Hope Reed, 'The Need for Monumentality?', *Perspecta*, 1, 1950.

p. 307 Niemeyer: see S. Papadaki, *Oscar Niemeyer: Works in Progress*, New York, 1956. In a lecture at São Paulo, Max Bill stated that: 'Architecture in your country stands in danger of falling into a parlous state of anti-social academicism. I intend to speak of architecture as a social art; an art which cannot simply be set aside ...' See Report on Brazil, *Architectural Review*, 116, 1957, p. 234.

p. 308 Action Architecture: see G. Kallmann, 'The "Action Architecture" of a New Generation', *Architectural Forum*, 3, October 1959, pp. 132–7. For discussion of Boston City Hall and a sketch of the scheme, see W. Curtis, *Boston: Forty Years of Modern Architecture*, Boston, 1980, p. 10.

p. 309 Kahn: the best general introduction is still Vincent Scully, *Louis I. Kahn*, New York, 1962; also Jordy, *American*

Buildings and Their Architects, vol. 4, pp. 361 ff., for the architect's philosophy of design and a detailed analysis of Richards Medical Laboratories'.

p. 313 Kahn: for quotation and other statements of intention see J. Rowan, 'Wanting To Be', *Progressive Architecture*, April 1961, pp. 130–49.

p. 315 Scully, *Louis I. Kahn*, p. 37.

Dacca: for further analysis of the symbolism and drawings of the scheme, see William Curtis, 'Modern Architecture, Monumentality and the Meaning of Institutions: Reflections on Authenticity', forthcoming in *Harvard Architectural Review*, 1983. For extensive illustrations of Kahn's drawings, see R. Giurgola and J. Mehta, *Louis I. Kahn*, Boulder, Col., 1975.

Chapter 24. Architecture and Anti-Architecture in England

p. 317 Motto: Peter Smithson, in Smithson (ed.), *Team 10 Primer*, p. 42.

English Architecture in Fifties: the most useful analyses of this period are supplied by Jackson, *The Politics of Architecture*, Banham, *The New Brutalism*, and Jencks, *Modern Movements*. The pages of the *Architectural Review* supply a fairly precise synopsis of the debates and concerns of the decade.

Reyner Banham published an article entitled 'The New Brutalism' in *Architectural Review*, December 1955, pp. 355–62. It was an era in England which delighted in 'isms' (e.g., the 'New Empiricism'). For further analysis of Hunstanton, see Philip Johnson, 'Comment on School at Hunstanton Norfolk', *Architectural Review*, September 1954, pp. 148–62; also A. and P. Smithson, 'The New Brutalism', *Architectural Review*, April 1954, pp. 274–5.

Smithsons: for their relfections on 'Urban Re-identification' throughout the 1950s, see series of articles in Architectural design, republished in *Ordinariness and Light*.

p. 319 Rudolf Wittkower, the architectural historian, was teaching at the Warburg Institute in the 1940s and seems to have influenced the theory, practice and historiography of modern architecture. For example, Colin Rowe, his pupil, applied similar methods and insights to Le Corbusier ('The Mathematics of the Ideal Villa', 1947) as his mentor was applying to Palladio at the same time: both were concerned with the role of symbolic geometries in the expression of an idealistic world view. Wittkower's book, *Architectural Principles in the Age of Humanism*, London, 1949, seems to have excited a Neo-Palladian obsession in some English architectural circles. Architects were also quick to note parallels between the harmonic proportions supposedly used by Palladio and the mathematics employed in Le Corbusier's Modulor, which became known in the early fifties. See H. Millon, 'Rudolf Wittkower, *Architectural Principles in the Age of Humanism*: its Influence on the Development and Interpretation of Modern Architecture', *Journal of the Society of Architectural Historians*, 31, no. 2, May 1972, pp. 83–91.

Economist: for the role of the Smithsons' earlier urban theories in this design, see Kenneth Frampton, 'The Economist and the Hauptstadt', *Architectural Design*, 1965, pp. 61–2. For the impact of picturesque aesthetic theories on the arrangement, see Reyner Banham, 'Revenge of the Picturesque: English Architectural Polemics 1945–65', in J. Summerson (ed.), *Concerning Architecture*, Baltimore, 1968, p. 265.

p. 320 **Robin Hood:** for the architect's intentions see article on scheme by Peter Smithson in *Architecture d'aujourdhui*, January 1979.

p. 322 **Futurist Revival:** This tag was in gossip circulation in the London of the late 1960s but the source is not certain. However, it suggests the impact of Banham's 'rediscovery' of Futurism in *Theory and Design in the First Machine Age*, and his own 'Neo-Futurist' arguments concerning the progressive role of technology. Stirling's steel and glass buildings in bold colours of the 1960s might almost be illustrations of Sant' Elia's tract of 1914, the 'Messaggio'. In presentations Stirling continued to argue the primacy of programmatic logic in the genesis of his designs; in fact he seems to have been involved in an eclectic commentary on the imagery of earlier modern architecture. The overt 'mannerism' of his buildings of the 1970s was operative in a more subtle way many years earlier. For further discussion of his sources see J. Jacobus, *James Stirling, Buildings and Projects, 1950–1974*, New York, 1975, introduction.

p. 323 **James Stirling,** 'Architect's Approach to Architecture', *Zodiac 16*, Milan, 1966, p. 161.

Typology: for the influence of Pavillon Suisse on later university dormitories see W. Curtis, 'L'Université, la ville et l'habitat collectif, reflections sur un thème de l'architecture moderne', *Archithèse*, 14, 1975, p. 29. In the same article I argued that university residences in the modern tradition have frequently been employed to demonstrate ideal collective and urban proposals.

p. 325 **Warren Chalk:** 'Architecture as Consumer Product', *The Japan Architect*, 165, 1970, p. 37. For further taste of Archigram polemics, see *Archigram I-IX* (published from 1961 to 1970, London) and Peter Cook, *Experimental Architecture*, London, 1970.

p. 326 **Thinkbelt:** see C. Price, 'Potteries Thinkbelt', *Architectural Design*, Nov. 1967, pp. 507 ff.

p. 327 **Denys Lasdun:** for a summary of his work and philosophy of urban landscape see W. Curtis, 'A Language and a Theme', in D. Lasdun (ed.), *A Language and a Theme, The Architecture of Denys Lasdun and partners*, London, 1976. My sense of Lasdun's intentions is based on numerous discussions with the architect from 1969 onwards.

p. 329 **Denys Lasdun,** 'The Evolution of a Style', *Architectural Review*, May 1969. It is hard to say exactly when the term 'strata' was first used by the architect to convey his ideas about platforms. In the mid-1960s Lasdun was much preoccupied with geological fissures and rock formations. Raised urban levels were being discussed at the time, particularly in Team X circles, with which Lasdun had relatively slight contact. In any case, stratification was a device basic to his own designs from the early 1950s onwards, and the horizontal terraces allowed by concrete cantilevering had caught his attention by the early 1930s when he read Le Corbusier's *Vers une architecture*. The word 'strata' should probably be taken as short-hand for an entire philosophy, concerned with the reintegration of man, nature and the city.

National Theatre: For Lasdun's intentions see 'Building Vistas/1', a conversation between Lasdun and Peter Hall, in *The Complete Guide to Britain's National Theatre*, ed. J. Goodwin, London, 1977, p. 25; also W. Curtis, 'Description', 'Past Perspective', 'Criticism', in *Architectural Review*, January 1977, National Theatre Special Issue.

Chapter 25. The Problem of Regional Identity

p. 331 **Motto:** Noboru Kawazoe, 'Modern Architecture Confronts Functionalism, New Buildings of Japan', *Zodiac 3*, Milan, 1958, pp. 117 ff.

p. 333 **Oscar Niemeyer:** statement made in introduction to S. Papadaki, *The Work of Oscar Niemeyer*, New York, 1950; see also P. L. Goodwin, *Brazil Builds*, New York, 1943; Oscar Niemeyer, *Work in Progress*, New York, 1956; H. R. Hitchcock, *Latin American Architecture*, New York, 1955. Also, for a general overview, Benevolo, *History of Modern Architecture*, vol. 2, Ch. 20, 'The New International Field', pp. 748 ff.

p. 336 **Harry Seidler,** *Houses, Interiors and Projects*, Sydney, 1954, p. ix. For Paul Rudolph's criticisms of Seidler, see 'Regionalism in Architecture', *Perspecta*, 4, 1957, p. 13. For general treatment of arrival of modern architecture in Australia, see D. L. Johnson, *Australian Architecture 1901–51, Sources of Modernism*, Sydney 1980, also the numerous writings of Robin Boyd on the Australian environment.

Regionalism: for ideas behind houses in the Sydney area reflecting a concern with 'place' and 'identity', see Jennifer Taylor, *An Australian Identity, Houses for Sydney 1953–63*, Sydney, 1972.

p. 337 **Japanese Modern Architecture:** for the first half of the 20th century see A. Drexler, *The Architecture of Japan*, New York, 1955, and for a modern architect's view of Japanese tradition see Bruno Taut, *Grundlinien japanischer Architektur*, Tokyo, 1935; translated as *Fundamentals of Japanese Architecture* in the same year. For more recent developments, see M. Tafuri, *L'Architettura moderna in Giappone*, Bologna, 1965, and R. Boyd, *New Directions in Japanese Architecture*, New York, 1968.

p. 339 **N. Kawazoe:** for reflections on the analogies between modern architecture and Japanese tradition see 'Metabolism 1', *The Japan Architect*, 44, Dec. 1969, pp. 191–8; 'Metabolism 2: The Progress of Modern Architecture: Architectural Values and Pragmatic Values', ibid., Jan. 1970, pp. 97–101; also 'Modern Architecture Confronts Functionalism', in which the author hinted at the difficulties of creating an authentic architecture under a regime of neo-colonialist American influence: 'It is a fact that in capitalist society, concrete products are treated as abstract values. This is the reason why modern architecture is inhuman and denationized . . .'

p. 341 **Metabolism:** Kikutake's statement is quoted in J. Donat (ed.), *World Architecture 2*, London, 1965, p. 13. See also, K. N. Kurokawa, and K. Kikutake, *Metabolism, Proposals for a New Urbanism*, Tokyo, 1960, and Kurokawa, 'Metabolism: the Pursuit of Open Form', in Donat (ed.), *World Architecture 1*, London 1964.

p. 342 **K. N. Kurokawa:** 'Two Systems of Metabolism', *The Japan Architect*, Dec. 1967, p. 80.

Chapter 26. Crises and Critiques in the 1960s

p. 344 **Motto:** Robert Venturi, *Complexity and Contradiction in Architecture*, New York, 1966, p. 16.

Third Generation: Throughout the 1950s Giedion attempted to define the essence of a new post-war sensibility as exemplified in the inheritors of the modern movement. Since he thought of men like Perret and Behrens as pioneers, and men like Le Corbusier and Gropius as the next stage, those who came to maturity around 1950–60 were regarded as a

'third generation'. In an essay entitled 'Spatial Imagination',
1957, Giedion referred to the concrete vaulting techniques
of Catalano and Utzon as evidence of a new dimension to the
'space–time' conception at the heart of modern architecture:
this he compared to the vaulting and grand interior spaces of
Roman antiquity. He expanded his reflections on recent
world architecture in the introduction to the 1962 edition of
Space, Time and Architecture, where he included Tange, and
spoke of a new consciousness binding the traditions of East
and West. He also pointed to an emergent civic
monumentality and a synthesis of the rational and the
organic. Jorn Utzon became the hero of the third phase in an
article written in 1962–3, entitled 'Jørn Utzon and the Third
Generation', eventually published in the 1967 edition of
Space, Time and Architecture. Presumably Drew took his book
title from this source.

p. 345 Two Decades After War: Giedion's and Benevelo's
fragmentary accounts are filled out somewhat by J. Jacobus,
Twentieth Century Architecture: The Middle Years 1940–65,
New York, 1966, and J. Joedicke, *Architecture Since 1945*,
London and Stuttgart, 1969. Drew's *Third Generation* is
useful for some aspects of the 1960s. Otherwise the series,
New Directions in Architecture, published by Braziller in the
late 1960s (e.g., *New Directions in Swiss Architecture . . . in
British Architecture . . . in Italian Architecture*, etc.), is most
useful. See also G. E. Kidder Smith, *The New Architecture of
Europe*, New York, 1961.

p. 346 Historicism in Italy: for an incisive critique see R.
Banham, 'Neoliberty, the Italian Retreat from Modern
Architecture', *Architectural Review*, 125, April 1959,
pp. 230–5.

p. 347 Aldo Van Eyck: in Smithson (ed.), *Team 10 Primer*,
p. 43. For further clues concerning this artist's remarkable
insights see: 'Labyrinthine Clarity', in J. Donat (ed.), *World
Architecture 3*, London, 1966, pp. 121–22; and 'Interior
Time/A Miracle in Moderation', *Meaning in Architecture* (ed.
Jencks, Baird), London, 1969, pp. 171 ff.

p. 348 Superstudio: see A. Natalini, 'Description of the
Micro-Event . . .', E. Ambasz (ed.), *Italy: The New Domestic
Landscape*, New York, 1972, p. 242.

p. 349 American Architecture 1960s: for a useful if
polemical survey, see R. M. Stern, *New Directions in American
Architecture*, New York, 1969. Stern's outlook seems to show
the influence of Venturi's theories.
Paramilitary Dandyism: see V. Scully, *American Architecture
and Urbanism*, New York, 1969, p. 200.

p. 351 Venturi: *Complexity and Contradiction*, pp. 23, 104;
see also R. Venturi, D. Scott-Brown, S. Izenour, *Learning from
Las Vegas*, Cambridge, Mass., 1972.

p. 352 Venturi, *Complexity and Contradiction*, p. 118; p. 116;
pp. 43–44.

p. 354 New York 5: see Eisenman (ed.), *Five Architects*.
Twenties as Classic Age: once again one senses the influence
of a historian on practioners: Graves's 'mannerist' exercises
on the elements of an earlier tradition illustrate, in some
degree, the insights of Colin Rowe in 'Mannerism and
Modern Architecture', *Architectural Review*, 107, May 1950,
pp. 289 ff. Rowe hinted at parallelisms between the shapes of
the modern and the Renaissance traditions. Perhaps the
New York 5 imagined themselves as so many latterday
Vasaris and Giulio Romanos twisting the 'normative'
statements of an earlier Classic age into new and perverse
patterns?

Chapter 27. Modern Architecture and Developing Countries since 1960

p. 356 Motto: Hassan Fathy, *Architecture for the Poor, an
Experiment in Rural Egypt*, Chicago, 1973, p. 19. Most of the
reflections made in this chapter grow from first-hand
observation. An entire world history needs to be written
which examines the impact, region by region, of colonialism,
industrialization and rapid change on architecture. The
existing historiography of 19th- and 20th-century
architecture and building continues to reflect a Western bias.
p. 357 Modern Regionalism: Some valuable strategies were
suggested in the 1950s by, for example, J. L. Sert in housing
for South America, and Maxwell Fry and Jane Drew for West
Africa: see *Tropical Architecture*, New York, 1956 and *Village
Housing in the Tropics*, London, 1953 by Fry and Drew.
Fathy, *Architecture for the Poor*, p. 24.
p. 358 Romanticization of peasants: for further discussion of
peasantism and nationalism see W. Curtis, 'Type and
Variation: Berber Collective Dwellings of the Northwestern
Sahara', to appear in *Muqarnas*, 1, New Haven, in 1982. The
same article examines the gradual modification of
vernacular types over a century of rapid change.
Self-build Housing: see J. F. Turner, *Housing By People,
Towards Autonomy in Building Environments*, London, 1976,
for a critique of housing concepts imposed from above, and
for an evaluation of self-built structures.
Barriadas: In 1967 the Peruvian government approached
the United Nations Development Programme for support of
'PREVI' (Proyecta Experimental de Vivienda). Notable
international architects were invited to submit low-cost
proposals for infrastructures which could be completed by
the users. Among those involved were Maki, Stirling and
Van Eyck. Typically, the last-named attempted to respond to
the life and form patterns of the pre-existing Barriadas. (The
government had tried previously to remove them.) See
Architectural Design, April 1970, pp. 187 ff.; also W. Mangin,
'Urbanisation Case History in Peru', *Architectural Design*,
August 1963, pp. 366–70. Possibly the 'PREVI' programme
was influenced by Turner's theories; he worked in Peru in
the late fifties and early sixties. For another housing theory
based on the idea of a fixed infrastructure and variable
components (in this instance for industrialized nations), see
N. J. Habraken, *Supports: An Alternative to Mass Housing*,
New York, 1972.
p. 359 Z. Plocki: *Towards a Melanesian Style of Architecture*,
Institute of Papua–New Guinea Studies, Boroko, 1975,
p. 22.
p. 360 B. V. Doshi and C. Correa: for something of Doshi's
philosophy see 'The Proliferating City and Communal Life:
India', *Ekistics*, 25, Feb. 1968, pp. 67–9; for Correa see, for
example, *Architecture in Hot Dry Climates*, 1973.
p. 361 Jean François Zevaco: for brief treatment of his early
works see Udo Kultermann, *New Directions in African
Architecture*, New York, 1969, p. 40. The Agadir housing
was given an Aga Khan award in 1980; see *Aga Khan Award
for Architecture* (brochure), Geneva and Philadelphia, 1980.
p. 364 Smithsons: see 'Pahlavi National Library',
Architectural Review, 164, Aug. 1978, pp. 79–85.
p. 365 Pan-Islamic Sentiments: see, for example, S. H. Nasr,
'The Contemporary Muslim and the Architectural
Transformation of the Urban Environment of the Islamic
World', *Proceedings of the Aga Khan Award for Architecture*, 1,
Philadelphia, 1978. The subtitle of the proceedings was:
'Toward An Architecture in the Spirit of Islam'. Some of the

intellectual and historical difficulties lurking in this formulation were raised by other participants. For an incisive study of problems of cultural identity in the Middle East, see Abdullah Laroui, *The Crisis of the Arab Intellectuals: Traditionalism or Historicism?*, trans. Cammell, Berkely, 1976.
China: see J. L. Cohen, 'Museums in the Service of Revolution', *Art News*, Summer 1980, pp. 80 ff.

Chapter 28. The Traditions of Modern Architecture in the Recent Past

p. 367 Motto: Aldo Van Eyck; 'The Interior of Time', Jencks and Baird (eds.), *Meaning in Architecture*, New York, 1969, p. 171.
Rejection of Absolutism: this seems to have worked on a number of levels. One thinks of the popularization of the ideas of Ivan Illich (e.g., *De-schooling Society*) and Karl Popper (e.g., *The Open Society and its Enemies*); of the increasing scepticism about the dominant values of Western industrial nations; of the increased respect for architectural vernaculars (Bernard Rudofsky's *Architecture Without Architects*, 1964, must be counted a cult book); of a pervasive distrust of cultural élites in the so-called 'counter-culture' of the late 1960s; and so on.
p. 368 Crisis: for example, M. MacEwen, *Crisis in Architecture*, London, 1974. For a more probing critique, this time of the avant-garde and from a somewhat confused Marxist standpoint, see M. Tafuri, *Architecture and Utopia: Design and Capitalist Development*, Cambridge, Mass., 1976. For the gradual erosion of closed frameworks of aesthetic reference see, for example, Leo Steinberg, *Other Criteria*, New York, 1972. From the early 1970s onwards the glossy art and architectural magazines are full of the 'crises of modernism'. The rejected 'modernism' usually turns out to be an amalgam of opinions about art from earlier magazines.
p. 369 Radical Critiques of Planning: see, for example, the ideas of John Turner cited in the notes to the last Chapter; also M. Pawley, *Architecture Versus Housing*, New York, 1971, and Jacobs, *The Death and Life of Great American Cities*.
Byker: for the design process and intentions of the scheme see *Architectural Design*, November–December 1974, special issue on Ralph Erskine.
p. 370 Vernacular Revival: for a sample of pop sociology combined with the myth of a grass-roots architectural expression, see Conrad Jameson, 'Modern Archirecture as An Ideology', *Architectural Association Quarterly*, October–December 1975. It is curious how the arguments in favour of a 'heimatstil' in opposition to an abstract, alienated form of dwelling (i.e., the one supposedly produced by modern architecture) recur in different ideological guises over the past sixty years.
Rossi: the passage may be found in 'An Analogical Architecture', *A + U*, May 1976, p. 74; for the architect's urban theories see *L'Architettura dell citta*, Padova, 1966. For a far from dispassionate treatment of Rossi see R. Moneo, 'Aldo Rossi: the Idea of Architecture and the Modena Cemetery', *Oppositions* 5, Summer 1976, pp. 1–30.
p. 371 Foster: see T. Nakamura, 'Foster and Associates', *A + U*, September 1975, particularly the essay by R. Banham.
p. 372 Centraal Beheer: see A. Colquhoun, 'Centraal

Beheer', *Architecture Plus*, September–October 1974, pp. 49–54. For a sample of Hertzberger's ideas, see 'Place, Choice and Identity', *World Architecture 4*, London, 1967, pp. 74 ff.
p. 373 European Investment bank: see Lasdun (ed.), *A Language and A Theme*, London, 1976, for an earlier stage of the design, and brief statement of intention.
p. 374 Post-Modern: see C. Jencks, 'The Rise of a Post-Modern Architecture', in *Architectural Association Quarterly*, October–December 1975, for a trial run of the ideas he later published as his book *The Language of Post-Modern Architecture*.
Beaubourg: for an exceptionally generous criticism of a problematic work see R. Banham, 'The Pompidolium – Criticism', *Architectural Review*, May 1977, pp. 277 ff.
p. 376 Getty Museum: in his book on Post-Modern architecture Jencks illustrates the building on p. 83 and gives 'Dr. Norman Neuerburg et al' credit for its design. Langdon and Wilson and Stephen Garrett also had a role. Jencks gives the building extensive coverage.
Post-Modernism and Linguistic Analogies: see, for example, Jencks's criticism of Hertzberger and Van Eyck: The architect still believes he is providing universal identity with his articulated forms when he is really just giving identity within his own *limited, historical code* and not one shared by the majority of his architectural clients....' Later, referring to Bakema's buildings with their 'traditional modern architect's code': 'Why, if he is really interested in identity, would he not use historical codes. Dutch gables, or even plastic Corinthian columns?' (Both statements from: 'The Rise of a Post-Modern Architecture'.) The argument recalls the traditional 'realist' criticism of 20th-century 'abstraction' in that it disallows general communication because of a break with traditional conventions, and echoes E. Gombrich in 'The Vogue of Abstract Art'. *Meditations on a Hobby Horse*, Oxford, 1963, p. 143. However, architecture communicates through many other means than imagery, and it remains to be seen whether the addition of plastic columns will make for a 'publicly understood' architecture, let along one possessing visual qualities of the sort that buildings must have if they are to transcend the conventions within which they are conceived.
p. 377 Revisionist Tendencies: attempts at ideological criticism have not been the exclusive property of left-wing critics. See, for example, Watkin, *Morality and Architecture*, Oxford, 1977, for right-wing, p. 115: 'Our conclusion is that an art-historical belief in the all-embracing *Zeitgeist*, combined with a historicist emphasis on progress and the necessary superiority of novelty, has come dangerously close to undermining, on the one hand, our appreciation of the imaginative genius of the individual and, on the other, the importance of artistic tradition.' For the severe limitations of Watkin's rather caricatured version of 'modern architecture', see my review of Watkin's book in *Journal of Society of Architectural Historians*, 38, October 1979, pp. 304 ff.
p. 378 Figure/Ground: this method of urban analysis seems traceable to Colin Rowe, Stirling's one-time mentor. See below, 'Collage City'. The concept of 'bricolage' (derived from Levi-Strauss on the 'savage mind') is also traceable to Rowe, and reflects an interest in composition from pre-existing stylistic, typological and urban 'fragments'.
p. 379 Graves: for his gradual transition from a mannerization of 1920s sources to a mannerization of

1920s and late 18th-century sources, see *Architectural Design*, Architectural Monographs, no. 5, 1979. For a stab at the increasing introversion of the American architectural world of the 1970s, see M. Tafuri, 'Architecture dans le boudoir: The Language of Criticism and the Crisis of Language', *Oppositions* 3, May 1974, pp. 37–62.
Consumerism: one critic to suggest links between facile stylism and the glibness of consumer packaging is Kenneth Frampton, an editor of *Oppositions* magazine, a forum of new tendencies.
p. 382 Kriers: see R. Krier, *Stadtraum in Theorie und Praxis*, Stuttgart, 1975, and L. Krier, *Reconstruction of the European City*, Brussels, 1978.
Collage City: Like Gombrich and Colquhoun ('Typology and Design Method'), Rowe was clearly influenced by the ideas of Popper on the role of pre-existing theories and of deduction on invention (viz. *The Logic of Scientific Discovery*), in this instance as a critique of the 'functionalist' proposition that form may 'follow' from function. However, in the wrong hands an obsession with 'schemata' may end up in a facile game played with inherited images and fragments. See also J. Silvetti, 'The Beauty of Shadows', *Oppositions* 9, Summer 1977, pp. 44 ff.
p. 385 A. Van Eyck: 'The Interior of Time'.

Conclusion
p. 386 Motto: Heinrich Wölfflin, *Principles of Art History, The Problem of the Development of Style in Later Art*, trans. M. Hottinger, New York, 1950, p. 11.
p. 388 André Malraux: *The Voices of Silence*, trans. S. Gilbert, New York, 1953, p. 281.
Muthesius: 'Wo stehen wir?', 1911.
Unity in the Accomplished Work: Frank Lloyd Wright had this to say in 1954 (*The Natural House*): 'Every house worth considering as a work of art must have a grammar of its own. "Grammar", in this sense, means the same thing in any construction – whether it be of words or of stone or wood. It is the shape-relationship between the various elements that enter into the constitution of the thing. The "grammar" of the house is its manifest articulation of all its parts. This will be the "speech" it uses....'
Le Corbusier: *Towards a New Architecture*, pp. 27 ff.

Addendum. The Search for Substance: Recent World Architecture (1987).
p. 389 Motto: Ribard de Chamoust, *L'Ordre françois trouvé dans la Nature*, Paris, 1783.
Principle, pastiche: William J. R. Curtis, 'Principle versus Pastiche: Perspectives on Some Recent Classicisms', *Architecural Review*, August 1984.
Post-Modern Classicism: the first appearance of this curious 'ism' is uncertain, but it was certainly popularized by the critic Charles Jencks, in *Post-Modern Classicism: The New Synthesis*, special issue of *Architectural Design*, 1980.
Critical disillusionment: see for example the review by Paul Gapp, 'Post-Modern Promise turns into a Hulking High-Rise Dud', *Chicago Tribune*, 31 October 1982, which rejected Portland as a 'dud'.
p. 390 Staatsgalerie: for discussion of strengths and

weaknesses see *Architectural Review*, December 1984, especially William J. R. Curtis, 'Virtuosity around a Void'.
p. 391 Mies: for critical reassessment see for example Franze Schulze, *Mies van der Rohe: a Critical Biography*, University of Chicago Press, 1985.
p. 392 Wacker: for intentions and analogy with Brancusi, lecture by Bill Pedersen, Graduate School of Design, Harvard, July 1984.
Pacific century: see review of HKS Bank by Chris Abel, 'A Building for the Pacific Century', *Architecural Review*, April 1986, p. 55.
Jeddah: for both NCB and HKS Bank, Hong Kong, see Arthur Drexler, *Three New Skyscrapers*, MOMA, New York, 1983. Also William J. R. Curtis, 'Towards an Authentic Regionalism', *Mimar* 19, Spring 1986.
p. 393 Maki: an 'expanded modernism', 'New Directions in Modernism', *Space Design*, no. 256, January 1986, pp. 6ff.
Regionalism: see for example Kenneth Frampton, 'Prospects for a Critical Regionalism', *Perspecta 20*, Yale Architectural Journal, 1983, pp. 147ff.
p. 394 Eldem: see publication *Aga Khan Awards 1986*, Aga Khan Awards for Architecture, Geneva, 1986; also Rifat Chadinji, *Concepts and Influences Towards a Regionalized International Architecture 1952–78*, KPL Press, London, New York, Sydney, 1986.
p. 395 Islamic structure protecting roof: Jørn Utzon, 'A House for Work and Decisions, Kuwait National Assembly Complex', in Denys Lasdun, *Architecture in an Age of Scepticism*, Heinemann, London, 1984, pp. 222ff. The dhow, incidentally, is the national symbol of Kuwait.
Ministry, Riyadh: for detailed analysis and assessment, William J. R. Curtis, 'Technical Review Report, Ministry of Foreign Affairs, Riiyadh' (1986), on file at Aga Khan Awards for Architecture, Geneva.
p. 396 Patio: see Teodoro Gonzalez de Leon, 'On Two Constants in Our Work', 1985 (unpublished).
Doshi: Curtis, 'Towards an Authentic Regionalism'; also William J. R. Curtis, *Modern Architecture in an Indian Tradition: Balkrishna Doshi*, Mapin, N.Y., Ahmadabad, 1987.
Correa: *Charles Correa*, Mimar, Singapore, 1984.
Rewal: William J. R. Curtis, 'Architecture Moderne, Racines Indiennes: Raj Rewal', in *Raj Rewal*, Moniteur, Paris, 1986.
p. 399 Bawa: see Curtis, 'Towards an Authentic Regionalism'; also Brian Brayce Taylor, *Geoffrey Bawa*, Mimar, Singapore, 1986.
p. 400 Anant Raje: Raje's remarkable work is very little published. The assessment made here is based on detailed study of his projects as well as interviews with the architect.
Rotonda: see Curtis, 'Principle versus Pastiche: Perspectives on Some Recent Classicisms'; also *Mario Botta*, MOMA, New York, 1986.
p. 401 Merida: for insightful reviews see Peter Buchanan, 'Rafael's Spanish Romans', *Architectural Review*, November 1985, p. 43.
p. 403 Scarpa: for discussion of architect's vocabulary, Giuseppe Zambonini, 'Process and Theme in the Work of Carlo Scarpa', *Perspecta 20*, Yale Architectural Journal, 1983, pp. 147ff. For sketches of Brion, Francesco Dal Co and Giuseppe Mazzariol, *Carlo Scarpa: The Complete Works*, Rizzoli, New York, 1985, pp. 284ff. The phrase 'still point of the turning world' is, of course, adapted from T. S. Eliot's *Four Quartets*.

Acknowledgements

Copyright A.C.L. Brussels, 2.3, 2.4, 2.5; © ADAGP 1987 9.2; Aeronautica Militaire-Doc. e A.P. 16.10: the Aga Khan Awards for Architecture, Geneva (photos P. Maréchaux) A8, A9, A10; Albertina. Vienna. Loos-archiv 2.19; Alekan. Paris 2.6; Glen Allison Photography A7; Wayne Andrews 4.11; The Architects Collaborative Inc. (photo Robert Damora) 19.1, 19.2; Ove Arup 22.10, 22.11; Architectenburo Herman Hertzberger 28.4, 28.5 (© Aerophoto Shiphol); The Architects' Journal 17.7; Courtesy of The Art Institute of Chicago 6.18; Atelier 5 21.11; Australian Information Service 28.4; Morley Baer 26.12; Daniel Bartush 27.9; Bauhaus-archiv 5.6, 5.7, 5.9, 9.2, 9.3, 9.4, 9.10, 9.12, 9.14, 9.15, 11.5, 13.9, 13.12; Tim Benton 2.13, 2.16, 3.7, 5.2, 5.4, 9.16, 9.17, 12.8, 13.2, 14.3, 16.8, 16.11, 17.4, 18.1, 24.7, 26.2, 28.1; Raccolta Bertarelli, Milan 5.13; Ted Bickford 28.12; Bildararchiv Foto Marburg 16.1; Bildarchiv Preussicher Kulturbesitz 23.3; D. Billington 3.12; Brecht-Einzig Ltd 24.5, 24.6; British Museum; by courtesy of the Trustees, 2.1; Richard Bryant/Arcaid A1, A13; Busch-Reisinger Museum, Cambridge, Mass. Harvard University, 9.11; Geremy Butler 1.4, 3.4, 3.6, 6.7, 6.15, 9.1. 11.12, 12.1, 12.11, 21.4; Caisse nationale des Monuments Historiques et des Sites 1.5, 28.2; G. Candilis 21.6; Giancarlo de Carlo 21.10; Chicago Tribune 11.2, 11.3, 11.4, 11.5, 11.6; Civico Museo Storico G. Garibaldi. Como 5.14, 5.15, 5.16; Peter Cook, Archigram (1964) 24.9; Country Life 18.7; Courtauld Institute of Art 13.10, 17.6, 17.8; J.A. Cox pp. 256–7; Dennis Crompton, 24.9; William Curtis 2.7, 3.5, 3.8, 4.6, 4.7, 4.8, 6.1, 6.2, 6.8, 6.12, 6.13, 6.16, 6.17, 11.8, 11.9, 11.16, 11.17, 13.4, 13.5, 14.4, 14.7, 16.13, 17.2, 17.5, 18.6, 19.4, 19.8, 20.8, 20.14, 21.14, 22.8, 23.2, 24.3, 24.12, 26.8, 28.16, 28.19, A11, A15, A16, A18, A19, Plates 2–7, 9.10, 12–15, frontispiece; © DACS 1987 7.1, 7.2, 7.10; Danske Arkitektens, Copenhagen, 18.8; Dienst Verspriede Rijkscollection Den Haag 17.11; Douglas Dickens 25.6; John Donat 28.3, 28.11; B.V. Doshi, 27.6; Ray Eames 19.6; Stephen Estock 26.10, 26.11; Mary Evans Picture Library 3.2; Foster Associates, Architects and Engineers 28.3, A4; Lionel Freedman, New York 23.6; Frank O. Gehry and Associates (photo Tim Street-Porter) A2; Joseph Giovannini 14.6; Glasgow School of Art 2.14, 2.15, Plate 1; Michael Graves, architect, 26.13, 28.12; courtesy of the Greater London Council, Department of Architecture and Civil Design 18.11; Guggenheim Museum 19.13, 19.14; Harvard University 18.5; Hedrich-Blessing 3.3, 9.7, 9.8, 9.9, 15.2, 28.7; Heinrich Helfenstein, Zürich 28.2; Keld Helmer-Petersen, Copenhagen 28.18; Lucien Hervé/Fondation Le Corbusier/© DACS 1987 14.8, 14.9, 15.8, 15.9, 15.10, 15.12, 15.14, 19.12, 20.1, 20.3–20.6, 20.10, 20.13. 20.15, 21.1–21.4, 21.9, 22.3, 23.1, 25.2; Japan Architect Co. Ltd. 25.10, 25.13, 28.5, A6; E.R. Jarrett 12.15; Sharad Jhaveri, Zürich 27.5; R.N. Johnson 25.5;

courtesy Johnson Wax 15.4–25.7; Albert Kahn Associates, Architects & Engineers, Detroit 3.11; Anthony Kersting 2.8, 4.1, 4.2, 4.3, 4.5, 16.2, 17.1; Kimbrell Museum, 28.9; KLM Aerocarto 12.4; Kohn Pedersen Fox Associates Pc. Photographer Barbara Karant A3; Leon Krier 28.15; Kröller-Müller Rijksmuseum, Otterlo 7.2; Kunstmuseum, Basel 7.1; Ladies Home Journal 6.3; Denys Lasdun 21.8, 24.11, 24.13, 24.14, 27.12, 28.6; M. Lindsay, 28.14; Christopher Little (Aga Khan Foundation) 27.2, 27.7, 27.8; Loewy International Ltd 18.4; MAS, Barcelona 2.9, 2.10, 2.11, 2.12, pp. 11–12; Laurin McCracken 26.13; Madan Mahata A12; Robert E. Mates 19.13, 19.14; Ricardo Moncalvo, Torino 26.1; Rafael Moneo A17; David Moore, Sydney 25.5; Museum of Finnish Architecture 17.9–17.15, 22.2–22.5, 22.7, Plate 11; Collection, the Museum of Modern Art, New York 5.12, 6.4, 6.6, 6.14, 8.4, 11.15, 11.18; National Monuments Record 18.3; Nederlands Documentatie-centrum voor de Bouwkunst, Amsterdam 7.6, 7.7. 7.8, 7.9, 12.10–12.13; New York Historical Society 11.7; Brenda Norris 1.2, 1.3, 1.6, 2.2, 3.3, 3.10, 3.13, 3.14, 6.11, 11.1, 16.5, 26.4; Novosti Press Agency 10.3–10.12, 10.14–10.18, 13.6; Paul Ockrassa 21.13; Open University 5.11, 7.4, 7.5, 7.14, 13.11, 14.5; Papua New Guinea University of Technology 27.4; Phokion Karas and Sert, Jackson and Gourley Associates 21.12; George Pohl, Philadelphia 23.11; Publifoto Notizie, Milano 26.3; R.I.B.A. 1.4, 3.3, 3.4, 3.6, 6.7, 6.15, 9.1, 11.12, 12.1, 12.11, 23.9, 23.13; Anant Raje A14; Retoria, Tokyo 25.12; Raj Rewal Plate 16; Gordon Robertson (A.C. Cooper) 14.2, 14.10; Kevin Roche, John Dinkeloo and Associates 26.7; Royal Academy, London 9.13; A. Salas Portugal 25.1; Sandak, Inc. 11.11; Scandinavian Airline System 22.1; Joseph E. Seagram & Sons, Inc. 19.9; Harry Seidler & Associates 25.3; Mona Serageldin 27.3; Julius Shulman 4.9; 4.12, 11.13, 11.14, 28.9, 28.10, pp. 102–3 (Carlos von Frankenberg); W.H. Sims 15.3; Skidmore, Owings and Merrill A5; Alison and Peter Smithson 21.7, 24.2, 24.4, 27.10; Stedelijk Museum, Amsterdam 7.10, 7.12, 7.15; James Stirling & Partners 24.8, 24.11; Ed Stoecklein 28.13; Franz Stoedtner, Düsseldorf, 5.1, 5.10; Erza Stoller 19.5, 23.5, 26.9; Todd Stuart 20.16; Swedish Museum of Architecture 18.9; Toshio Taira 25.10, 28.5; Kenzo Tange 15.9, 25.11, 25.14; Toledo Museum of Art 1.1; Ullstein Bilderdienst, Berlin 12.9, 16.3, 16.4, 16.6; United Nations 19.11; University of Glasgow 4.4; Venturi, Rauch and Scott Brown 26.10, 26.11; Victoria & Albert Museum Photographic Studio 1.2, 1.3, 1.6, 2.2, 3.1, 3.10, 3.13, 3.14, 4.10, 6.11, 16.5, 26.4; Jorgen Watz 18.8; Western Pennsylvania Conservancy 15.1 (Bill Hedrich), 15.2, 15.3 (W.H. Sims), Plate 8 (H. Corsini); Kurt Wyss 23.12; Xinhua News Agency 27.11; Minoru Yamasaki & associates 27.9; F.R. Yerbury 2.17, 2.18, 3.9, 8.8, 8.9, 8.13, 8.16, 9.6, 12.5, 13.1, 18.2

Index